STREET MAP OF SANDWICH
WITH MEDIEVAL AND MODERN PLACE NAMES

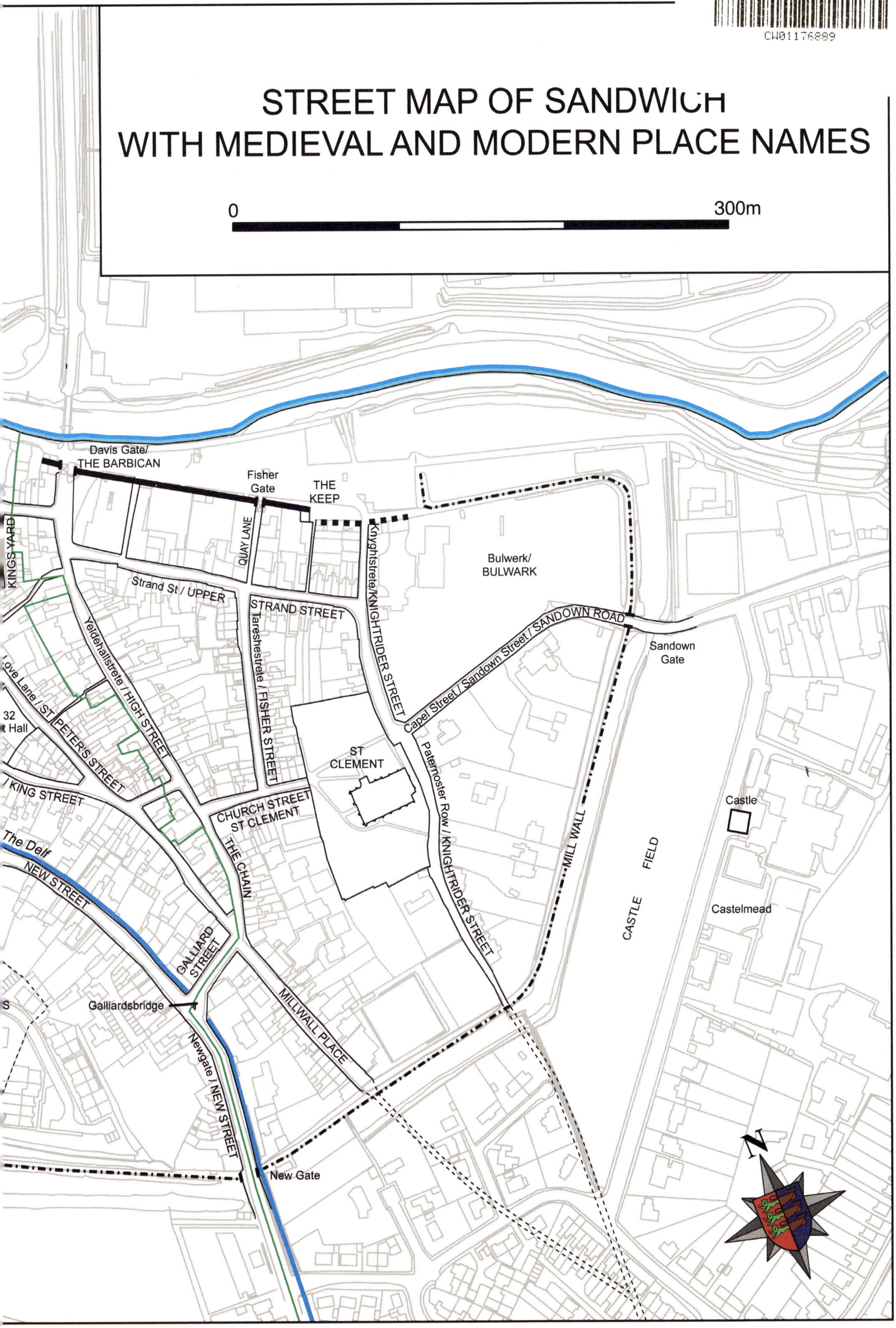

0 — 300m

SANDWICH
the 'completest medieval town in England'

Aerial view of Sandwich from the west (D. Grady © English Heritage 24064/04)

SANDWICH

the 'completest medieval town in England'

A study of the town and port from its origins to 1600

by
Helen Clarke, Sarah Pearson, Mavis Mate and Keith Parfitt

Documentary Research
Sheila Sweetinburgh, Bridgett Jones

Illustrations
Allan T. Adams, Barry Corke, John Hills, Howard A. Jones, Peter Williams

Oxbow Books
Oxford and Oakville

Published by
Oxbow Books, Oxford

© Oxbow Books and the authors 2010

ISBN 978-1-84217-400-5

This book is available direct from

Oxbow Books, Oxford, UK
(Phone: 01865-241249; Fax: 01865-794449)

and

The David Brown Book Company
PO Box 511, Oakville, CT 06779, USA
(Phone: 860-945-9329; Fax: 860-945-9468)

or from our website

www.oxbowbooks.com

A CIP record for this book is available from the British Library

Library of Congress Cataloging-in-Publication Data

Sandwich : the "completest medieval town in England" : a study of the town and port from its origins to 1600 / by Helen Clarke [et al.] ; documentary research, Sheila Sweetinburgh, Bridgett Jones ; illustrations Allan T. Adams [et al.].
      p. cm.
   Includes bibliographical references and index.
   ISBN 978-1-84217-400-5
 1. Sandwich (England)--History--To 1500. 2. Sandwich (England)--History--16th century. 3. Sandwich (England)--Antiquities. 4. Sandwich (England)--Social conditions. 5. Sandwich (England)--Buildings, structures, etc. 6. Historic buildings--England--Sandwich. 7. Middle Ages. I. Clarke, Helen. II. Sweetinburgh, Sheila. III. Jones, Bridgett E. A.
   DA690.S21S36 2010
   942.2'3--dc22
                                2010002775

Printed in Great Britain by
Cambrian Printers
Aberystwyth, Wales

Contents

Foreword ix
Acknowledgements x
Summary xii
Résumé xiii
Zusammenfassung xiv
List of Figures xv
List of Tables xviii

PART I: INTRODUCTION

Chapter 1: Background to the Sandwich project 1
1.1 The project and its aims 1
1.2 The research area 3
1.3 Methods 4
1.4 Previous research and publication 9

PART II: ORIGINS

Chapter 2: Environmental background and origins 11
2.1 The geology of the Sandwich area 11
2.2 Communications and the location of Sandwich 12
2.3 The site of earliest Sandwich 17
2.4 A hypothesis for earliest Sandwich 22

Chapter 3: Sandwich in the eleventh century: the establishment of the medieval town 23
3.1 Urban beginnings: Sandwich at the turn of the tenth and eleventh centuries 25
3.2 Evidence for urbanisation in the first half of the eleventh century 25
3.3 The second half of the eleventh century 30
3.4 The topographical development of Sandwich in the eleventh century 34
3.5 Conclusion 38

Chapter 4: Sandwich in the twelfth century: the growth of an urban society 40
4.1 The developing town 40
4.2 Sandwich Haven and Stonar 41

4.3	The churches	42
4.4	The Christ Church Priory site	49
4.5	The topographical development of Sandwich	49
4.6	Conclusion	52

PART III: 1200–1360

Introduction 55

Chapter 5: The port and town: consolidation and outside influences 58

5.1	The growth of independence	58
5.2	Sandwich and the Cinque Ports	61
5.3	Population	61
5.4	Sandwich people	62
5.5	The economic background	64
5.6	The defence of Sandwich	66
5.7	Sandwich Haven and the route through the Wantsum Channel	72

Chapter 6: Religious buildings 76

6.1	The parish churches	76
6.2	New religious foundations in the thirteenth century	88
6.3	Conclusion	92

Chapter 7: Secular buildings 93

7.1	Excavated buildings	93
7.2	Stone buildings	94
7.3	Timber-framed buildings	102
7.4	Building materials used in the construction of domestic buildings in Sandwich	108
7.5	The function of rooms and the size of plots	110
7.6	Conclusion	111

Chapter 8: The topography of the town by the mid-fourteenth century 112

8.1	From the priory headquarters to Harnet Street	112
8.2	The town centre	114
8.3	Strand Street and the waterfront	115
8.4	The town south of the Delf	118

PART IV: 1360–1560

Introduction 119

Chapter 9: Trade and the haven 121

9.1	Sandwich Haven and its ships to the end of the fifteenth century	121
9.2	Trade through Sandwich Haven in the fourteenth and fifteenth centuries	124
9.3	Sandwich Haven and its ships in the first half of the sixteenth century	127
9.4	Trade through Sandwich Haven in the first half of the sixteenth century	130

Chapter 10: The life of the town 131
10.1 The governance of the town 131
10.2 Population and property 136
10.3 People and occupations 138
10.4 Conclusion 144

Chapter 11: War, rebellion and defence 146
11.1 War and civil unrest 146
11.2 The defences 148
11.3 Conclusion 162

Chapter 12: Secular buildings 164
12.1 Large courtyard houses 165
12.2 Open halls 167
12.3 The town centre: open-hall houses 169
12.4 The outskirts of town: open-hall houses parallel to the street 176
12.5 The size of houses 178
12.6 Houses of the poor 179
12.7 Changes in the late fifteenth and early sixteenth centuries 180
12.8 Commercial and industrial buildings 186
12.9 The function and use of medieval houses 194
12.10 The proportion of surviving medieval houses 197
12.11 Conclusion 197

Chapter 13: Churches and hospitals 199
13.1 The churches 199
13.2 The religious life of the town 205
13.3 The hospitals 209
13.4 Conclusion 213

Chapter 14: The landscape of the town 214
14.1 The waterfront: access and facilities 214
14.2 Strand Street between Pillory Gate and Davis Gate 217
14.3 The Fishmarket 218
14.4 The Butchery 219
14.5 Love Lane 219
14.6 The Cornmarket 220
14.7 Luckboat 221
14.8 The streets and property in the west end of town 221
14.9 The streets and property in the east end of town 224
14.10 The ramparts, watercourses and land south of the Delf 225
14.11 Conclusion 226

PART V: 1560–1600

Chapter 15: The town 228
15.1 Trade and Sandwich Haven 228
15.2 The influx of religious refugees 231
15.3 The governance of the town 232
15.4 Sandwich society 235

Chapter 16: The buildings 240
16.1 The school 240
16.2 The new court hall and related buildings 242
16.3 Homes for the increasing population 244
16.4 Surviving houses 247
16.5 Probate inventories and the function of rooms 256
16.6 Probate inventories, houses and Sandwich society 262

PART VI: CONCLUSIONS

Chapter 17: Sandwich in the context of wider studies of historic towns: an assessment 265
17.1 Archaeology and topography 265
17.2 Surviving buildings 266
17.3 Heritage management and future research 267
17.4 Evaluation of the methods used in the project 270

APPENDIX 1: Sandwich archaeological sites, 1929–2007 273
APPENDIX 2: Sandwich houses that appear on the maps 277

Notes 281
References and abbreviations 303
Index 317

Foreword

It is difficult for the casual visitor to Sandwich today to understand the town's former status among English ports. It looks like a small inland market town on the bank of a modest river. But locals and historians have long known that in the Middle Ages it was a strategic and commercial seaport of great significance, trading with northern Europe and the Mediterranean and growing prosperous on this business. Decline, due to shifting patterns of trade and dramatic changes in the local topography, have helped to preserve Sandwich's medieval fabric to a remarkable extent, and this makes it an extremely rewarding subject of study.

The research that has produced this book does two things. First, it provides us with new theories on how, when and why the town developed its present form. Historians and archaeologists have never agreed on quite where the first settlement was located. Nor has there been close study of what the surviving medieval buildings can tell us about Sandwich's development. These, and many other issues, are examined in this new account: the result is that we now understand much more about this small Kent town.

This is of great value in itself, but the book has wider implications. Sandwich was undoubtedly influenced in its rise and fall by peculiar circumstances affecting its location and the nature of its trade. But it also shares much with other English medieval towns in terms of its physical growth and the role of its major institutions. The story of the town, therefore, is both particular and general, and this detailed study gives new insights into the influences affecting urban development, both in the formative period of growth and in later periods in which towns adapted to new circumstances.

An important aspect of the research into Sandwich lies in the range of disciplines that have been brought to bear on the story. Archaeology, the study of standing buildings, topographical analysis and extensive documentary investigation have all contributed in a complementary way to producing a rich picture of development. Not all the sources point to the same conclusions, but this divergence produces a healthy dialogue, testing one source against another and in the process leading to a better understanding of the reliance that can be placed on the evidence. This is especially important where material is uneven and fragmentary and where the picture has to be formed from a complex web of disparate bodies of evidence.

As far as possible, the different sources are interwoven to form a narrative account. Some aspects of the town's historic environment are singled out for individual treatment, for they contain material that is of great importance in their areas of study and they deserve extensive treatment. But throughout the book the primary subject is the development of the town. So, even though we learn a great deal in detail about the medieval houses, the churches and the defences, the knowledge is applied to produce a better understanding of the town's physical evolution. A picture of social zoning emerges from the study of the houses; the churches suggest differences in social make-up between the three parishes; and the town walls tell us something about how defence was combined with the facilitation of trade. Material evidence, therefore, is used to draw out important social, economic and cultural facets in Sandwich's development.

For English Heritage, the multidisciplinary approach to the study, as well as the intrinsic interest and importance of its subject matter, recommended the research project for funding support. Of course, English Heritage is delighted that we now know more about a highly significant town and that, on the basis of the sound research undertaken during the project, its historic environment can be managed more effectively and confidently in the future. But of wider importance are the methodological lessons that can be learned from the experience. These should have an impact throughout the community of urban historians and archaeologists, reaffirming what we aspire to – that is, a holistic view of the historic environment.

Dr Simon Thurley,
Chief Executive, English Heritage

Acknowledgements

This book owes considerable debts to a great many people. It was largely researched and written by Helen Clarke (archaeology), Mavis Mate (history) and Sarah Pearson (buildings), and edited by Helen Clarke and Sarah Pearson. But they were assisted by a much larger team of colleagues. Keith Parfitt of the Canterbury Archaeological Trust has unrivalled knowledge of the archaeology of east Kent, and his direction of the archaeological fieldwork and his contributions to the text were indispensable. The initial creation of a purpose-built database of local historical sources by Mark Merry was crucial to the success of the project, while it could not have been compiled without the hard work of Sheila Sweetinburgh, who, herself an experienced medieval historian of the region, provided advice on many historical matters and was far more than a mere data inputter. Further research into documentary sources, particularly from London repositories, was provided by Bridgett Jones. The fieldwork on the Sandowns was undertaken by volunteers from the Dover Archaeological Group under the direction of Keith Parfitt. They laboured for many weekends of an inclement autumn, and we are indebted to their dedication. Barry Corke of the Canterbury Archaeological Trust not only assisted in the field, but also produced the archaeological drawings and the basic material for many of the maps, in some of which he was assisted by Peter Atkinson. Funds for the close contour survey carried out by Keith Parfitt and Barry Corke were raised by James Graham-Campbell and Gustav Milne of the Institute of Archaeology, University College London. Many of the final maps were drawn on a GIS system by John Hills, and we are grateful to him and to Peter Vujakovic of the Department of Geographical and Life Sciences at Canterbury Christ Church University for giving us so much of their time, experience and expertise. The publication drawings of the surveyed buildings were produced by Allan T. Adams, who also came to Sandwich on two occasions to help with fieldwork, turned a number of surveys into excellent three-dimensional reconstructions to help the reader visualise the structures, and assisted in a number of other ways. The reconstruction drawings of St Clement's and St Mary's churches were the work of Howard A. Jones, who contributed considerable insights into the development of the churches. The photographs were largely taken by Peter Williams of English Heritage, who, with the help of Mike Hesketh-Roberts, also prepared for publication those taken by the team, while Damian Grady of English Heritage took a set of aerial photographs of the town. The authors are extremely appreciative of the hard work and support of all these colleagues over the past four years.

Without the support of English Heritage the project would not have taken place, nor would the publication have seen the light of day. Interest began when Colum Giles visited Sandwich and, faced with the quantity and quality of the surviving medieval houses, realised that this was a place of national importance for the understanding of medieval towns in England. We owe a great deal to his continuing support, encouragement and perceptive criticism, all of which have played a major part in bringing the project to a successful conclusion. As the team discovered, writing about a place over time, rather than in a single period or on a specific theme, has meant that the authors have sometimes had to move outside their areas of specialisation. To counteract this, a Steering Group of established scholars with expertise in a number of fields proved to be invaluable in supplementing the team's own particular skills. We are extremely grateful to Paul Everson, Jon Iveson, Susan Reynolds, Judith Roebuck and John Williams, who have all discussed various aspects of the project and commented with rigour on draft texts; as a result, the publication has been immeasurably improved, although the final text is the responsibility of the team alone. In addition, other scholars have read parts of the text, and we are very grateful to Paul Barnwell, Caroline Barron, Nicholas Brooks, Barbara Crawford, Mark Gardiner, the late Margaret

Gelling and David Martin for their most helpful comments.

During the course of fieldwork a number of scholars have visited Sandwich to view and discuss particular aspects of the archaeology or buildings in the town. Paul Barnwell, Howard Jones, Hugh Richmond and Tim Tatton-Brown all provided useful insights and advice on churches. Allan Adams, Peter Lambert and David and Barbara Martin helped solve puzzles in some of the more difficult domestic buildings. Pat Ryan discussed the intractable problems of dating brickwork. Nicholas Brooks spent a day roaming the course of the Wantsum Channel, discussing the extent of the grant to Cnut and the medieval Liberty of Sandwich. Linda Hall gave her opinion on the dating of many decorative details in buildings, and Peter Hoare and John Potter provided advice on the geology of the stones in the town walls. Very little dendrochronology has been undertaken in Sandwich because of the unsuitability of the timbers, but three buildings were sampled, two of which gave results, and we are grateful to Alex Bayliss of English Heritage for financing this, and to Alison Arnold and her colleagues of the Nottingham Tree-Ring Dating Laboratory for undertaking the work. Others whose help and advice has been sought and readily given on a wide variety of subjects are Clive Alexander, Jane Andrewes, Brian Ayers, Birte Brugmann, Nick Dermott, Gill Draper, Steve Fuller, Tarq Hoekstra, Peter Kidson, Jane Laughton, Gustav Milne, Derek Renn, Catherine Richardson, David Rollason, the late Andrew Saunders, Charles Tracy and Keith Wade. John Newman readily agreed to our using a phrase of his from his North-East and East Kent volume of the *Buildings of England* for our title, and Yale University Press kindly gave its consent.

Many archives and libraries were consulted during the course of research and we are grateful to the staff for their assistance on numerous occasions. In particular, we would like to thank Stuart Bligh and the staff of the Kent archives and libraries, especially Alison Cable at the East Kent Archives Centre and Mark Bateson at Canterbury Cathedral Archives and their staff. Denis Anstey provided us with copies of illustrations housed in the Kent Archaeological Society library at Maidstone and we are grateful to members of the Society for their help. We are also grateful to the staff of the National Monuments Record for assistance over supplying various maps and photographs.

Jon Iveson, curator of Dover Museum and Bronze Age Boat Gallery, managed the project for its last three years, and we are grateful to him and Linda Mewes, as well as to Dover District Council, for their administrative support. In Sandwich, the Sandwich Heritage Group, chaired by Jon Iveson, provided finance for the maps drawn by John Hills, and practical help and advice when required. In particular we are indebted to Ray Harlow, the archivist of the Sandwich Guildhall Archive, who has taken a great deal of trouble on our behalf, especially by making various categories of material available electronically. All the members of the Heritage Group have been welcoming and supportive, and information has readily been provided by Frank Andrews and Charles Wanostrocht. Results of archaeological fieldwork undertaken by the late Alf Southam, the late Joe Trussler and the late Dennis Harle, the last two former members of the Heritage Group, have been incorporated into the present texts, and their pioneering efforts in the 1960s and 1970s should not be overlooked. We have also appreciated the enthusiasm and keen interest in the history of the town shown by members of the Sandwich History Society over the course of the project. Working with Sandwich town council has been a pleasure, and we record our thanks to the successive town clerks at the Guildhall, Miriam Bull and Tracey Ward, and their colleagues, and the town sergeant, Kevin Cook, who have smoothed our paths in numerous ways. In the town itself we have made many friends and received many welcome cups of tea. The rector and present and past churchwardens of St Clement's church have always been willing to open up at awkward times, and, as anyone who surveys domestic buildings knows, without the cooperation of the owners and occupiers no surveys could take place – the people of Sandwich have been both welcoming and interested in what we were up to and we are grateful to them all. We hope that they will find the resulting book of interest.

We would also like to thanks all those who saw the book through the publication process: Delia Gaze for copy editing, Sarah Harrison for indexing, and Val Lamb, Clare Litt and Hilary Schan at Oxbow. Their skill and patience in handling all aspects of production are greatly appreciated.

Finally, Helen and Sarah thank Giles Clarke and Peter Kidson for their unfailing support throughout all the vicissitudes of the past five years, and Helen would like to record her personal thanks to Dr Alan King and the staff of University College Hospital who enabled her to see the project through to the end.

Summary

This publication is the outcome of research into the origins and development of the small town of Sandwich in east Kent, which has aptly been described as the 'completest medieval town in England': town walls surround three parish churches, a number of hospitals and streets lined with houses dating from the thirteenth to sixteenth centuries. In 2004, with the encouragement of English Heritage, an initial survey of domestic buildings was extended to incorporate archaeological and historical research with a study of all the surviving medieval structures in the town. The aim was threefold: to study the evolution of the town from its origins to *c.*1600; to test whether combining the three disciplines gave greater insights into its development than would the findings from one discipline alone; and to set the results in the broader framework of studies of similar English towns.

The book traces the history of medieval Sandwich, tackling subjects such as the question of its establishment and original location, the influence of the underlying topography on the growth of the settlement, and its role as an important trading port and military base. The development of the town's administration, the growth and decline of its prosperity and population, and the occupational and social structure of its inhabitants are all discussed. The sizes, forms, functions and distribution of domestic buildings have been combined with documentary evidence to reflect social and occupational zoning throughout the town and provide a chronological framework for its changing fortunes. Study of the architectural development and late-medieval usage of the churches and hospitals elucidates the fluctuating prosperity of the town, as well as the diverse nature of the parishes and the religious beliefs of the parishioners. Throughout the project, buildings, archaeology and documents have been used as equal partners in this exploration of the town's history.

The results have modified many long-held assumptions about Sandwich's urban growth and general development. What has been discovered has also been compared to other English towns, allowing Sandwich, often disregarded in architectural and historical literature, to take its rightful place alongside better-known English ports of the south and east coasts. In addition, the new information presented here should provide a basis for decisions about the future management of the town's archaeological potential and built heritage.

Résumé

Cette publication est le fruit de recherches sur les origines et le développement de la petite ville de Sandwich dans l'est du Kent; une ville décrite avec justesse comme l'exemple le mieux conservé d'une ville médiévale en Angleterre; des remparts entourent trois églises paroissiales, plusieurs hospices, ainsi que des rues bordées de maisons qui datent du 13ème au 16ème siècle. En 2004, avec l'appui de "English Heritage", une première étude des bâtiments familiaux a été poursuivie afin d'incorporer des recherches archéologiques et historiques à une étude de toutes les structures médiévales subsistantes de la ville. Le but en était triple: étudier l'évolution de la ville à partir de ses origines jusqu'aux environs de 1600; mettre à l'essai si une combinaison des trois disciplines donnait une meilleure compréhension de son développement que les résultats d'une seule discipline; insérer les résultats dans le cadre plus élargi des études faites sur d'autres villes anglaises semblables.

Le livre retrace l'histoire de la ville de Sandwich à l'époque médiévale, abordant des sujets tels que: la question de son établissement et de son emplacement initial; l'influence de la topographie sous-jacente sur la croissance de la colonie, et le rôle de la ville en tant que port commercial et base militaire. Les matières du développement de l'administration de la ville; de la croissance et du déclin de sa prospérité et de sa population, ainsi que sa structure sociale et le profil des métiers des habitants sont traitées. Les dimensions, les formes, les fonctions et la distribution des bâtiments familiaux sont alliées à l'évidence documentaire pour refléter la concentration sociale et des métiers à travers la ville et cette information fournit une chronologie à ses revirements de fortune. Une étude de l'évolution architecturale et de l'usage vers la fin du moyen âge des églises et des hospices a servi pour tracer la prospérité fluctuante de la ville, ainsi que la nature hétérogène des paroisses et des croyances religieuses des paroissiens. Tout au long du projet, bâtiments, archéologie et documents ont été traités comme partenaires égaux dans cette exploration de l'histoire de la ville.

Les résultats ont modifié de nombreuses hypothèses, émises depuis longtemps, concernant la croissance urbaine et le développement général de la ville de Sandwich. Ce qui en ressort a été comparé à d'autres villes anglaises, ce qui permet à Sandwich, qui figure rarement dans la littérature architecturale et historique, de prendre sa propre place à côté des ports anglais mieux connus des côtes sud et est. En plus, les nouvelles données ici présentées devraient fournir une base aux décisions concernant la gestion future du potentiel archéologique et du patrimoine construit.

Lesley Orson

Zusammenfassung

Die vorliegende Publikation ist das Ergebnis von Forschungen, die sich mit dem Ursprung und der Entwicklung Sandwichs im Osten Kents befassten, einer Kleinstadt, die treffend als die „vollständigste mittelalterliche Stadt Englands" beschrieben wurde: Stadtmauern umschließen drei Pfarrkirchen, eine Anzahl von Spitälern sowie Strassen, die in das dreizehnte bis sechzehnte Jahrhundert datieren. Unterstützt durch English Heritage wurde 2004 eine erste Aufnahme von Wohngebäuden durch archäologische und historische Forschungen erweitert, die eine Studie aller erhaltenen mittelalterlichen Strukturen beinhalteten. Es wurde ein dreifaches Ziel angestrebt: die Entwicklung der Stadt von ihrem Ursprung bis circa 1600 zu untersuchen; zu testen, ob die Kombination der drei Disziplinen bessere Einsichten in die Entwicklung Sandwichs geben würde, als die Ergebnisse einer einzelnen Disziplin; und diese Ergebnisse in den größeren Zusammenhang von Studien ähnlicher englischer Städte zu stellen.

Das vorliegende Buch zeichnet die Geschichte des mittelalterlichen Sandwich auf, befasst sich mit Themen wie der Gründung und ursprünglichen Lage der Stadt, dem Einfluss der Landschaftstopographie auf das Siedlungswachstum und der Rolle Sandwichs als wichtigem Handelshafen und Militärstandort. Die Entwicklung der Stadtverwaltung, der Aufstieg und Niedergang der Stadt gemessen an ihrem Wohlstand und ihrer Einwohnerzahl und die Einwohnerstruktur werden ausführlich behandelt. Die Untersuchung von Größen, Formen, Funktionen und der Verteilung von Wohngebäuden in Kombination mit schriftlichen Quellen ergibt ein Bild von der räumlichen Gliederung der Stadt nach Erwerbstätigkeiten und sozialen Kriterien und bietet einen chronologischen Rahmen für ihr wechselreiches Schicksal. Die bauliche Entwicklung und spätmittelalterliche Nutzung von Kirchen und Spitälern gibt Aufschluss über den fluktuierenden Wohlstand Sandwichs ebenso wie über unterschiedliche Charakteristiken der Pfarreien und religiöse Ausrichtungen der Mitglieder. Über das gesamte Forschungsprojekt hinweg wurden Baudenkmäler und archäologische und schriftliche Quellen gleichermaßen berücksichtigt.

Die Ergebnisse der Studie berichtigen viele über lange Zeit vertretene Vermutungen über das städtische Wachstum und die allgemeine Entwicklung Sandwichs. Sie wurden mit Forschungsergebnissen über andere englische Städte verglichen und verschaffen der Stadt Sandwich, die oftmals in der Fachliteratur vergessen wurde, ihren rechtmäßigen Platz unter den besser bekannten englischen Häfen an der Süd- und Ostküste. Zusätzlich bietet die Studie wichtige Erkenntnisse für die künftige Boden- und Baudenkmalpflege der Stadt.

Birte Brugmann

List of Figures

Frontispiece
Aerial view of Sandwich from the west

PART I: INTRODUCTION

Chapter 1. Background to the Sandwich project
1.1 Sandwich in east Kent showing land routes 2
1.2 Location map of archaeological interventions in Sandwich, 1929–2007 3
1.3 Interpretation of close-contour survey of Sandwich within the walls 4
1.4 The subsoil of archaeological sites in Sandwich 5
1.5 Interpretation of the contour survey of the hinterland 6

PART II: ORIGINS

Chapter 2: Environmental background and origins
2.1 Roman and early medieval land routes around Sandwich 13
2.2 The Wantsum Channel and its rivers 14
2.3 The geology of the Deal Spit 15
2.4 Aerial view of the Deal Spit from the north 16
2.5 Estate map of Sandown Manor, 1615 20

Chapter 3: Sandwich in the eleventh century
3.1 Plan of Sandwich by 1200 24
3.2 Map of area east of St Clement's church 25
3.3 St Clement's church, plan and elevation in the eleventh century 26
3.4 St Clement's church, detail of west wall 27
3.5 St Clement's church, cross section of nave 27
3.6 St Mary in Castro, Dover, plan 28
3.7 St Mary in Castro, Dover, external view 28
3.8 Plan showing evidence for porticus or transepts 31
3.9 St Peter's church, pier base at north-west corner of tower 32
3.10 Plan of Sandwich parishes 33
3.11 Aerial view showing route to St Mary's church 36
3.12 The North Stream and Delf through the Lydden Valley .. 37

Chapter 4: Sandwich in the twelfth century
4.1 St Mary's church, plan in the twelfth century 42
4.2 St Mary's church, reconstructed cross section at west end 43
4.3 St Mary's church, reconstructed elevation of north side of church 43
4.4 St Mary's church, capitals at west end of nave, south side 43
4.5 St Mary's church, capitals at west end of nave, north side 43
4.6 St Clement's church, reconstructions of twelfth-century plan and elevation 45
4.7 St Clement's church, the tower from the north-east 46
4.8 St Clement's church, capitals in the tower 46
4.9 St Clement's church, door head to stair turret 47
4.10 St Peter's church, plan showing twelfth-century evidence 47
4.11 Plan showing possible original alignment of the Fishmarket and plots on the east side 51
4.12 Excavation of clay-floored timber building behind 10 Market Street 52

PART III: SANDWICH, 1200–1360

Introduction
III.1 Plan of Sandwich in the mid-fourteenth century 56

Chapter 5: The port and town
5.1 The site of excavations in Castle Field 67
5.2 Sections through the earth ramparts 70
5.3 Aerial view of street pattern in south-east part of town 71
5.4 The south-eastern area of the Liberty 72
5.5 Reconstruction drawing of the Sandwich ship 73
5.6 The fourteenth-century seal of the port of Sandwich 74
5.7 Reconstruction drawing of the Bremen cog 74

Chapter 6: Religious buildings
6.1 Plan showing thirteenth-century details 77
6.2 St Clement's church, chancel, looking east 77
6.3 St Peter's church, plan in the thirteenth century 78
6.4 St Peter's church, looking south-east 78
6.5 St Clement's church, plan in the mid-thirteenth century 79
6.6 St Mary's church, west end 80
6.7 St Mary's church, plan in the fourteenth century 82
6.8 St Mary's church, window at west end of north aisle 82
6.9 St Mary's church, window on north side of north aisle .. 82
6.10 St Clement's church, plans in the fourteenth century ... 83
6.11 St Clement's church, drawing from the north-east 84
6.12 St Clement's church, piscina in south chancel aisle 84
6.13 St Peter's church, plan showing 14th-century work 85
6.14 St Peter's church, extension at the east end of the south aisle 85

xv

6.15 St Peter's church, probable charnel house at east end of south aisle 86
6.16 St Peter's church, north aisle 87
6.17 St Peter's church, tomb in north aisle 88
6.18 Carmelite friary site, plan of site..................................... 89
6.19 St Bartholomew's hospital chapel from the north-east ... 91
6.20 St Bartholomew's hospital chapel, plan........................ 91
6.21 St Bartholomew's hospital chapel, north aisle 92

Chapter 7: Secular buildings
7.1 Excavation behind 10 Market Place showing plan of stone building c.1300 93
7.2 Distribution of thirteenth- and early fourteenth-century buildings and wall fragments.......................... 94
7.3 18–22 High Street in the nineteenth century 95
7.4 20 High Street (36), reconstructed plan and cross section through open hall 95
7.5 Garden wall of 29 Harnet Street (27) 96
7.6 27 Strand Street (82), plan and section of undercroft... 96
7.7 27 Strand Street (82), view looking north 96
7.8 Map of buildings on south side of Strand Street in the early fourteenth century... 97
7.9 50 St Peter's Street (73), east wall 98
7.10 50 St Peter's Street (73), plan of cellar and elevation of east wall 98
7.11 Building in Three Kings Yard, behind 11 Strand Street (78), first floor plan 99
7.12 Building in Three Kings Yard behind 11 Strand Street (78), doorways 99
7.13 Building in Three Kings Yard (78), east face of first floor 99
7.14 Building in Three King's Yard (78), windows.............. 100
7.15 39 Strand Street (85), floor plans................................ 100
7.16 Reset doorway in Paradise Row (67)........................... 101
7.17 Reset doorway at 3 Vicarage Lane (99)....................... 101
7.18 33 Strand Street (83), floor plans................................ 103
7.19 33 Strand Street (83), reconstruction from south-east 103
7.20 39 and 41 Strand Street (85, 86), from the north 105
7.21 39 Strand Street (85), long section 106
7.22 39 Strand Street (85), reconstruction.......................... 106
7.23 41 Strand Street (86), plan and cross sections through open hall 107
7.24 33 Strand Street (83), brick filling to framing 109
7.25 33 Strand Street (83), brick filling to framing 109

Chapter 8: Topography of the town by the mid-fourteenth century
8.1 The original of the map of Sandwich printed in Boys 1792.. 113
8.2 Excavated wharf at King's Lynn, Norfolk................... 115
8.3 Aerial view of Strand Street... 116
8.4 Plans of King's Lynn and Hull in the Middle Ages..... 117

PART IV: 1360–1560

Introduction
IV.1 The built environment of Sandwich in the early sixteenth century.. 120

Chapter 9: Trade and the haven
9.1 Customs ports in the fifteenth century 125
9.2 Chart of Sandwich Haven, drawn c.1548 129

Chapter 11: War, rebellion and defence
11.1 The Rope Walk from west... 149
11.2 Mill Wall from south 149
11.3 Plan of Sandown Gate... 149
11.4 Exposed brickwork of Sandown Gate 150
11.5 Reconstructed plan of the excavated Sandown Gate... 150
11.6 Sandown Gate in the early eighteenth century 151
11.7 Sandown Gate in the 1780s.. 151
11.8 North roundel of Canterbury Gate observed in 1929 .. 151
11.9 Canterbury Gate, in 1792... 152
11.10 West Gate, Canterbury 152
11.11 Plans of Sandwich Canterbury Gate, Canterbury West Gate and Canterbury St George's Gate 153
11.12 Woodnesborough Gate in 1792.................................. 154
11.13 The east face of the Bulwark rampart.......................... 154
11.14 Recently exposed brick arch on east face of Bulwark rampart 154
11.15 Reinterpreted section through the town wall between 62 and 66 Strand Street.. 155
11.16 The town wall in the cellar of the Bell Hotel.............. 156
11.17 The town wall along the Quay.................................... 156
11.18 Fisher Gate from the north 157
11.19 Fisher Gate, plans.. 157
11.20 Davis Gate (now the Barbican) from the north 158
11.21 Plan and section of Davis Gate................................... 158
11.22 Detail from a map of Great Yarmouth, c.1580 159
11.23 Blackfriars Tower, Great Yarmouth............................. 160
11.24 The Round House (now the Keep) from north-east ... 160
11.25 Wall scars on north face of the Round House 160
11.26 The Round House and Fisher Gate, 1791 161
11.27 Boom tower at Lendal Bridge, York............................ 161
11.28 Detail from a mid sixteenth-century map of Kingston-upon-Hull 161

Chapter 12: Secular buildings in the late Middle Ages
12.1 29 Harnet Street (28), ground-floor plan and sketch of roof truss 165
12.2 29 Harnet Street (28), location plan 166
12.3 11–23 Strand Street, suggested layout of in the fifteenth and sixteenth centuries................................. 167
12.4 11–23 Strand Street (77–81) 167
12.5 Distribution map of the number of storeys in medieval timber buildings c.1330–c.1540 168
12.6 18, 20 St Peter's Street (70), first-floor plan, and cross section 169
12.7 Doorway to Holy Ghost Alley, formerly into the hall of 18 St Peter Street (70) 169
12.8 Distribution map of open halls with galleries 170
12.9 Schematic open hall with gallery and some Sandwich examples 171
12.10 34 High Street (38), plan and sections 172
12.11 17 Delf Street (16), plan and cross section 172
12.12 38 King Street (49), the open hall 172
12.13 4–10 Market Street (58, 57, 55, 53), from the south ... 173
12.14 7 Market Street (56), long section, reconstruction and window detail.. 173
12.15 3 Strand Street (74), window...................................... 174
12.16 8 Cattle Market (7), roof light.................................... 174
12.17 34 Harnet Street (30), doorway.................................. 174
12.18 8 Cattle Market (7), plan and long section................. 175
12.19 7 Potter Street (68), plan and sections 175
12.20 38 King Street (49), long section 176
12.21 22, 24 Upper Strand Street (96), reconstruction......... 177

xvi

12.22	19, 21, 23 Upper Strand Street (95), from the west	177
12.23	7 Fisher Street (20), plan and reconstruction	178
12.24	70, 72 New Street (64, 65), reconstruction	178
12.25	Distribution map of open halls by size	179
12.26	27, 29 King Street (48: St Peter's rectory), plan and sections	181
12.27	27, 29 King Street (48: St Peter's rectory), parlour fireplace	181
12.28	27, 29 King Street (48: St Peter's rectory), parlour ceiling	181
12.29	21 King Street (45), plan and sections	182
12.30	32, 34 Upper Strand Street (98), plan and section	182
12.31	32 Upper Strand Street (98), window in cross wing	183
12.32	32 Upper Strand Street (98), doorway in cross wing	183
12.33	Four late fifteenth- and early sixteenth-century fireplaces	184
12.34	3 Strand Street (74), reconstruction	185
12.35	11–15 Strand Street (77, 78, 79), ground-floor plan	187
12.36	13 Strand Street (79), cross section through east wing	187
12.37	23 Strand Street (81), reconstruction of shop at front	188
12.38	8 Cattle Market (7), reconstruction of shop front	188
12.39	1 The Butchery (3), plan and section of two semi-detached shops	188
12.40	No Name Shop, No Name Street (66), from the north-east	189
12.41	No Name Shop, No Name Street (66), reconstructions	189
12.42	13, 15 Strand Street (79), front range of four shops	190
12.43	13, 15 Strand Street (79), detail of archway to courtyard	190
12.44	13, 15 Strand Street, (79), reconstructed plan and elevation of shops	190
12.45	1, 3 King Street (41, 42), with St Peter's church behind	191
12.46	23 Strand Street (81), long section	192
12.47	3 Strand Street (74), possible evidence for a hoist at roof level	193
12.48	6 King Street (44), cross section	193
12.49	21 King Street (46), cross section of outbuilding	193
12.50	25 High Street (37), plan and cross section	194

Chapter 13: Churches and hospitals in the late Middle Ages

13.1	St Clement's church, chancel roof looking west	200
13.2	St Clement's church, nave roof looking east	200
13.3	St Clement's church, reconstructed plan	201
13.4	St Clement's church, squint from St Margaret's chapel to the high altar	201
13.5	St Clement's church, image niche and aumbries in St George's chapel	202
13.6	St Clement's church, choir stalls	202
13.7	St Thomas's hospital, plan of buildings	209
13.8	St Thomas's hospital, drawing of south-west side of the great hall	210
13.9	St Thomas's hospital, re-erected window	210
13.10	St Thomas's hospital, re-erected archway from the porch	210
13.11	St Bartholomew's hospital, photograph possibly of the hall being demolished	211
13.12	St Bartholomew's hospital, detail of plan (Boys 1792)	212
13.13	2 St Bartholomew's hospital, plan and long section	212

Chapter 14: The landscape of the town

14.1	Sandwich quay in 1833	215
14.2	North face of town wall, 62 Strand Street	216
14.3	North face of town wall, 68 Strand Street	216
14.4	South side of Strand Street from the east	217
14.5	Fishmarket and St Peter's church in 1792	218
14.6	The Cattle Market in 1906	220
14.7	Distribution of bequeathed properties, 1458–1508	223
14.8	Distribution of bequeathed properties, 1509–1558	223
14.9	The area around Canterbury Gate	226

PART V: 1560–1600

Chapter 15: The town in the late sixteenth century

15.1	Map of the Wantsum Channel drawn by William Lambarde, c. 1585	229

Chapter 16: Buildings in the late sixteenth century

16.1	Manwood School, 91, 93 Strand Street (93)	241
16.2	Manwood School, 91, 93 Strand Street (93), plans	241
16.3	The Guildhall, the mayor's chair of 1562, details of the armrests	242
16.4	The Guildhall, first-floor plan	243
16.5	The Guildhall, cross section	243
16.6	The Guildhall, decorated bracket	244
16.7	Distribution map showing of late sixteenth- or early seventeenth-century buildings	246
16.8	The Star Inn, Cattle Market (9)	247
16.9	Detail of Elizabethan house off Strand Street	247
16.10	The Long House, 62 Strand Street (90), from the south	248
16.11	The Long House, 62 Strand Street (90), plan and sections	249
16.12	The Long House, 62 Strand Street (90), wall painting	249
16.13	The Long House, 62 Strand Street (90), plasterwork	249
16.14	Richborough House, 7 Bowling Street (2), from the east	250
16.15	Richborough House, 7 Bowling Street (2), plan	250
16.16	The King's Arms PH, 63, 65 Strand Street (91), from the east	251
16.17	The King's Arms PH, 63, 65 Strand Street (91), caryatid	251
16.18	Fireplace in the King's Lodging (formerly the Old House, 46 Strand Street (88)	252
16.19	Fireplace in the King's Lodging (88)	252
16.20	8 Bowling Street (1), fireplace	252
16.21	6, 8 Bowling Street (1), plan, and cross section of No. 6	253
16.22	16, 18 New Street (63), view from north	253
16.23	16, 18 New Street (63), plans	253
16.24	19, 21 Church Street St Mary (13)	254
16.25	17, 19 High Street (34)	254
16.26	17, 19 High Street (34), plan	254
16.27	27 Church Street St Mary (15), plan	255
16.28	16 St Peter's Street (69), plan	255
16.29	16 St Peter's Street (69)	255

Endpapers

Map of modern Sandwich with medieval and modern place names

List of Tables

PART III: SANDWICH, 1200–1360

Chapter 5: The port and town
5.1 Occupations mentioned in the mid-thirteenth to early fourteenth-century court rolls 63

PART IV: 1360–1560

Chapter 10: The life of the town
10.1 The wards in 1478 133
10.2 Numbers and assessed wealth of Sandwich taxpayers, 1513 137

Chapter 13: Churches and hospitals in the late Middle Ages
13.1 Locations of burial in Sandwich wills 206
13.2 Sandwich wills, 1402–1558 207
13.3 Bequests to religious institutions in Sandwich wills, 1460–1538 207

PART V: 1560–1600

Chapter 15: The town in the late sixteenth century
15.1 Inventory values 237

Chapter 16: Buildings in the late sixteenth century
16.1 Numbers of rooms overall 257
16.2 Room numbers (168 examples, divided into four quartiles) 257
16.3 The incidence of commonest rooms 257
16.4 Location of cooking 258
16.5 Chronological table of chambers over the hall ... 259
16.6 Parlours, beds and heating 260
16.7 Heating in chambers 261

PART I: INTRODUCTION

1 Background to the Sandwich project

1.1 The project and its aims

Sandwich lies in north-east Kent, about 3km from the coast and approximately 15km east of Canterbury, to which it is connected by the modern A257. This is the successor of the Roman road from Canterbury to Richborough, a branch of which continued to be used in the Middle Ages (Fig. 1.1). But of more importance to the town in its early years were water communications with London, Canterbury, the south coast and the Continent, for which Sandwich, located at the foot of the dip slope of the North Downs on the south bank of the river Stour and the shores of the former Wantsum Channel, was ideally situated. Around the town, the varied topography is typical of a region where the land meets the sea and where there has been constant interaction between them for centuries. The location of Sandwich at the south-eastern mouth of the channel, where there was a large, calm anchorage, was fundamental to the growth and prosperity of the port in the Middle Ages. But the coastline changed, and while the inhabitants endeavoured to halt the silting of the Wantsum Channel, they were ultimately defeated by the forces of nature, with the result that one of the greatest ports of medieval England is no more, and now lies a considerable distance from the open sea. It can be reached today only by small pleasure craft navigating the river Stour. One of the consequences of this decline in the town's fortunes is that a remarkable number of its early buildings have survived within a recognisable medieval town plan. This survival offers great potential for study, and was the primary reason for the architectural research that was the genesis of this book. As will be shown in the following pages, the claim that Sandwich is probably the best-preserved medieval town in southern Britain is well founded.

The current study began in the late 1990s as an investigation by a building historian into the development of the medieval houses of Sandwich. In 2004, with the encouragement of English Heritage, the scope of the project was broadened to encompass the evolution of the town from its origins to 1600. This involved increasing the types of buildings to be studied to include all extant structures constructed before that date, and supplementing the architectural surveys with topographical and archaeological evidence (gained from analysis of previous investigations and some limited new work). To this essentially material evidence was added new research into the historical sources for the town. The project's aims evolved, therefore, into producing a detailed account of Sandwich's urban development as seen through this variety of source material, and of setting this development within the broader context provided by studies of similar English towns.

Although English Heritage has sponsored monographs on towns in recent years,[1] those publications have been primarily concerned with assessments of the archaeology, largely to the exclusion of standing structures, and have deliberately included no more than a most basic consideration of the historical documentation, since this was deemed to be a separate subject. The authors of this book believe that the separation of archaeology from other branches of history is not the most perceptive way of studying the past, and while the amount of archaeology undertaken in places such as Lincoln and St Albans may mean that an exclusive approach is feasible in these cities, it is not possible for what today is a small town like Sandwich, where little excavation has taken place and resources are considerably more limited. The project therefore adopted an approach different from those purely archaeological volumes. It built on the town's strong suits, specifically the extremely good survival of medieval buildings and the existence of extensive and informative documentation. Those two sources were studied independently, but then the information obtained was combined, along with what could be extracted from the archaeological resource, to obtain an

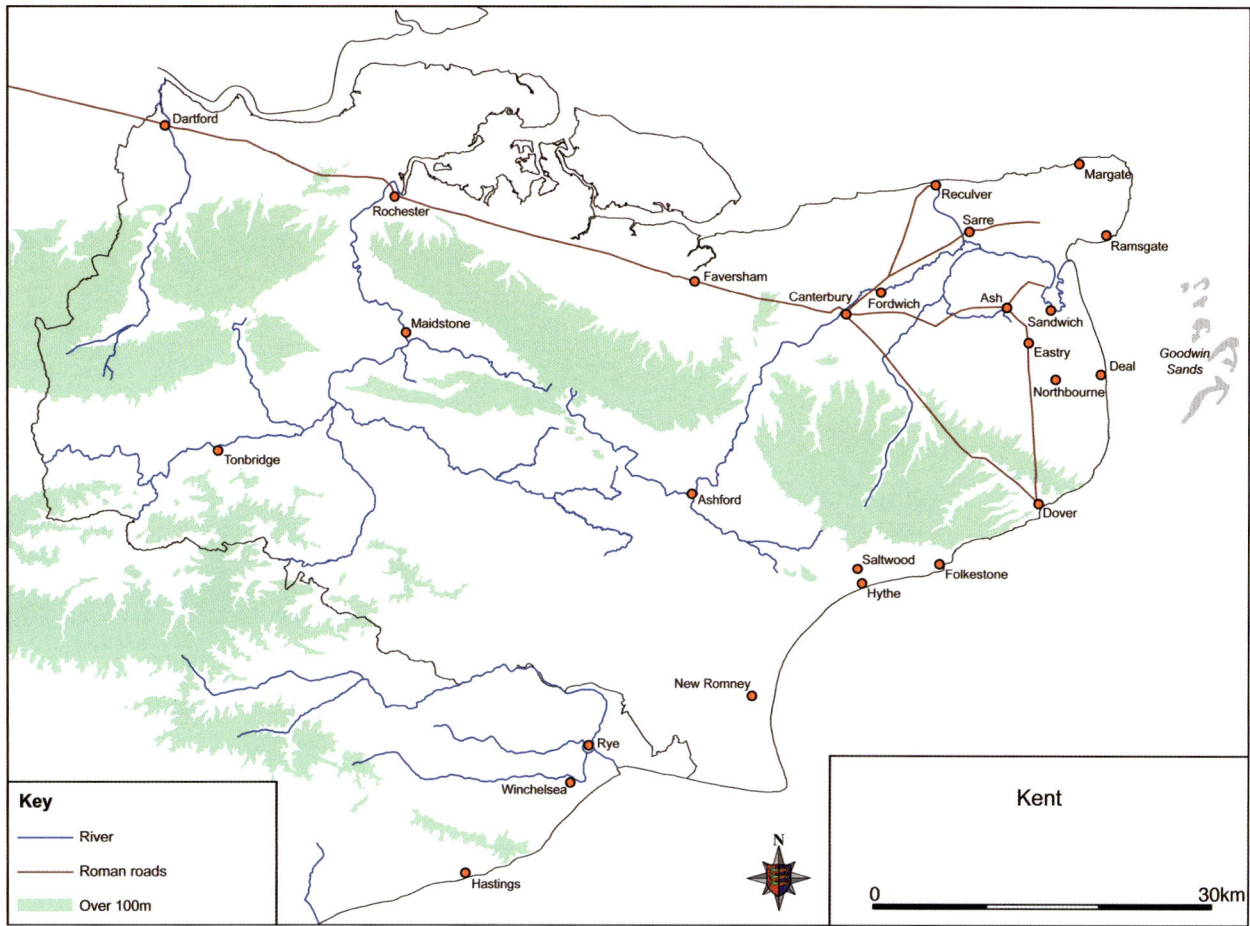

Fig. 1.1: Sandwich in east Kent, showing the main land route to London in both Roman and medieval times (B. C. & J. H.)

outline of the evolution of the town and an explanation for why Sandwich developed its particular character. Although the method involved separate treatment of subjects, such as trade and building types, which are sometimes given specific chapters, the aim of the project and its publication has been to show how the combination of such sources can lead to new ways of looking at medieval urban development. This work is perhaps the first truly multidisciplinary study of a medieval town in which archaeology, standing structures and documentary sources have been given equal weight.

The approach has proved highly effective in throwing new light on Sandwich's urban development through the formulation of hypotheses dependent on knowledge of the three disciplines. For example, archaeology has led to new theories on the siting of the original settlement and its subsequent growth; study of the surviving church architecture has provided crucial evidence for the early development of the present town; and investigation of the domestic buildings has revealed otherwise undocumented evidence of urban growth and decline, important not just for understanding Sandwich but also for the study of towns elsewhere. All this new information has been set against a new exploration of the archival sources, which has given insights into governance, trade, industry, society and fluctuations in the population – all evidence of the changing urban conditions, which have in large measure accounted for the patterns of survival on the ground.

At the outset it was decided to produce a single integrated text, not a series of parallel and mutually exclusive contributions by specialists in their own fields, and in the course of writing up the results it became clear that a multidisciplinary approach is not without its problems. Achieving a satisfactory fusion has proved extremely difficult and time-consuming, for different disciplines have their own ways of approaching and presenting information. The task of combining everything into a seamless whole has led to more rewriting than usual, and the publication presented here is the outcome of much cooperation and collaboration, as well as a test of the methodology involved.

1.2 The research area

The medieval town of Sandwich is well defined by its walls, and there is no evidence that the late medieval urban area ever spread beyond them. But before the fourteenth century the walls and ramparts did not exist, a fact that is sometimes forgotten, and the history of the wider area is critical to understanding the earlier period. Indeed, all three of the town's parishes extend at least a small way beyond the walls, probably occupying the same ground as the south-eastern part of the hundred and Liberty of Sandwich (Figs 3.10, 5.4). These are medieval creations with no meaning for the very early history of the place, but their boundaries were fixed for sound historical reasons, and the study area has in large measure respected this wider region. The town within the walls has seen the most concentrated work during the project, but there have also been investigations further afield, in a block of about 4km² as shown on Figure 1.5. Sandwich also had medieval and earlier connections with neighbouring settlements outside its immediate hinterland, as shown on Figure 2.1.

The urban area stands partly on an outcrop of Thanet Beds, creating a low ridge flanked by Alluvium on the north-west, north-east and south, and by Marine Sand on the east (Fig. 1.3). To the south and south-west, its hinterland is made up of gently undulating clay lands composed of Thanet Beds. The Sandowns lie to the east and the Lydden Valley to the south-east. The present landscape is the product of at least two millennia of change resulting from natural forces and human intervention, and its appearance is very different from that of the prehistoric and early historic periods.

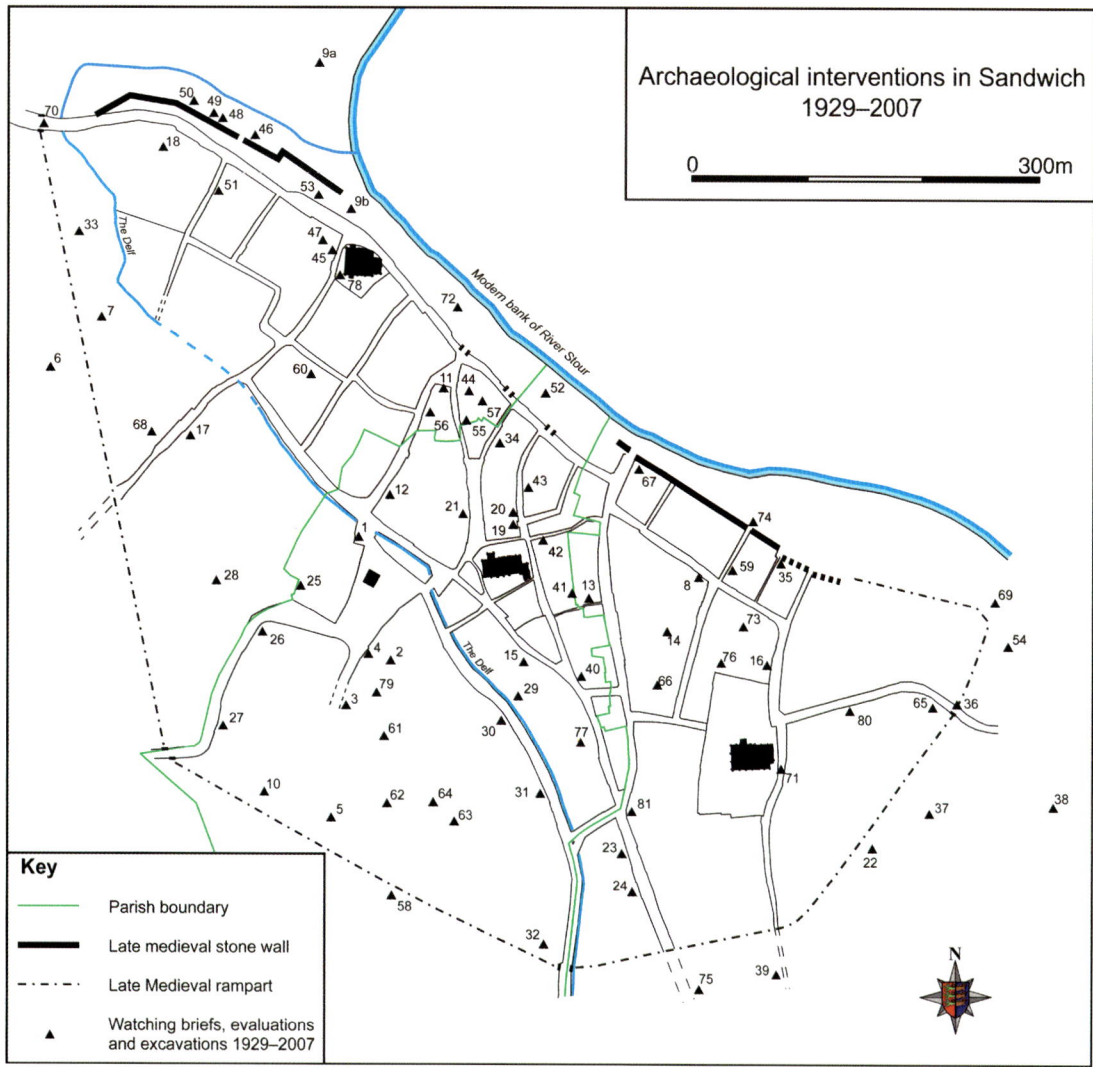

Fig. 1.2: Location map of archaeological interventions in Sandwich, 1929–2007. See Appendix 1 for explanation of numbers and details of sites (K. P., B. C. & J. H.). Reproduced by permission of Ordnance Survey on behalf of HMSO. © Crown copyright 2009. All rights reserved. Licence number 100046522

1.3 Methods

1.3.1 Archaeological methods

Sandwich's status as a Conservation Area and the survival of so many fine medieval and early post-medieval structures, plus the absence of substantial urban regeneration, have provided few opportunities for modern archaeological excavation within the heart of the walled town, although during the years of the project there were a few small interventions routinely undertaken as part of the planning process (PPG 16). The constraints were not so severe in the hinterland of the town, and an extensive programme of test-pitting was carried out across the Sandowns to the east, largely by volunteers from the Dover Archaeological Group who also undertook field-walking and geophysical survey on Mary-le-Bone Hill (Chaps 2.3.4, 2.3.5).[2]

Ground surveys of the town and its hinterland resulted in close-contour maps of both areas, the interpretations of which are shown on Figures 1.3 and 1.5. Even taking account of the potential problems in matching modern contours with ancient land surfaces, the two surveys have greatly assisted in defining the local topography and in detailing areas of high and low ground, which reflect the underlying geology of Thanet Beds and Alluvium. They have been vital tools for the current project's research into the topography and history of the town. In addition, a database of previous, often unpublished, archaeological interventions was compiled.

1.3.1.1 Database of archaeological sites (Fig. 1.2)[3]

The database consists of the details of seventy-four interventions known to have taken place within the walled town from 1929 to 2007 (Appendix 1). The

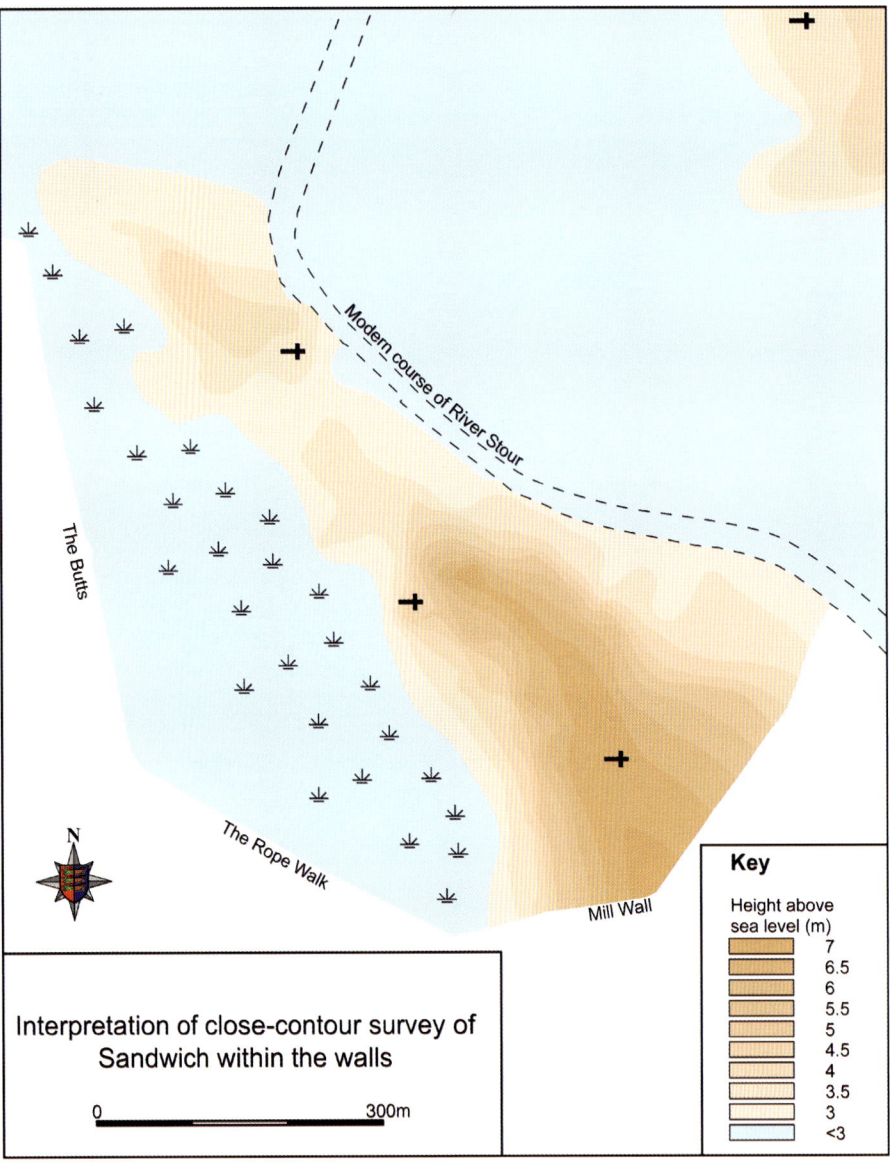

Fig. 1.3: Interpretation of the close-contour survey of Sandwich within the walls, contours at 0.50m intervals (K. P., B. C. & J. H.)

information that can be culled from the interventions is extremely variable, with very little of it being of the standard expected today. Nevertheless, it was useful in supplementing other sources in testing the results of the contour surveys, and modifying the British Geological Survey map of 1988.

1.3.1.2 The close-contour survey of the town (Fig. 1.3)[4]
The contour survey was conducted by a two-man team in 2003, just before the project officially began. The first task was to locate all the Ordnance Survey benchmarks on the modern 1:1250 OS map, some of which have been destroyed. For those that remained *in situ*, the distance to the adjacent ground surface was measured to give an initial set of precise levels around the town. Study revealed that OS spot heights shown along road lines were not always accurate, so they were generally ignored.

The survey was carried out using traditional means: a surveyor's level and 5m staff. About 375 spot heights were taken along roads and paths and on accessible open ground and within the walled town. All readings were taken in metric and recorded to two decimal places, related to the nearest OS benchmark. Check measurements were taken regularly; errors of between 1cm and 5cm were deemed acceptable for the purposes of the survey. Contours were drawn by interpolation between the recorded spot heights, with a vertical interval of 50cm between them. Figure 1.3 shows the interpretation of the close-contour survey, emphasising the difference between the higher and lower areas of the town within the walls. This is also borne out by the distribution of archaeological sites where the type of subsoil could be established (Fig. 1.4).

1.3.1.3 The survey in the hinterland (Fig. 1.5)[5]
During autumn and winter 2004 the same two-man team surveyed and mapped an area of 4km², recording

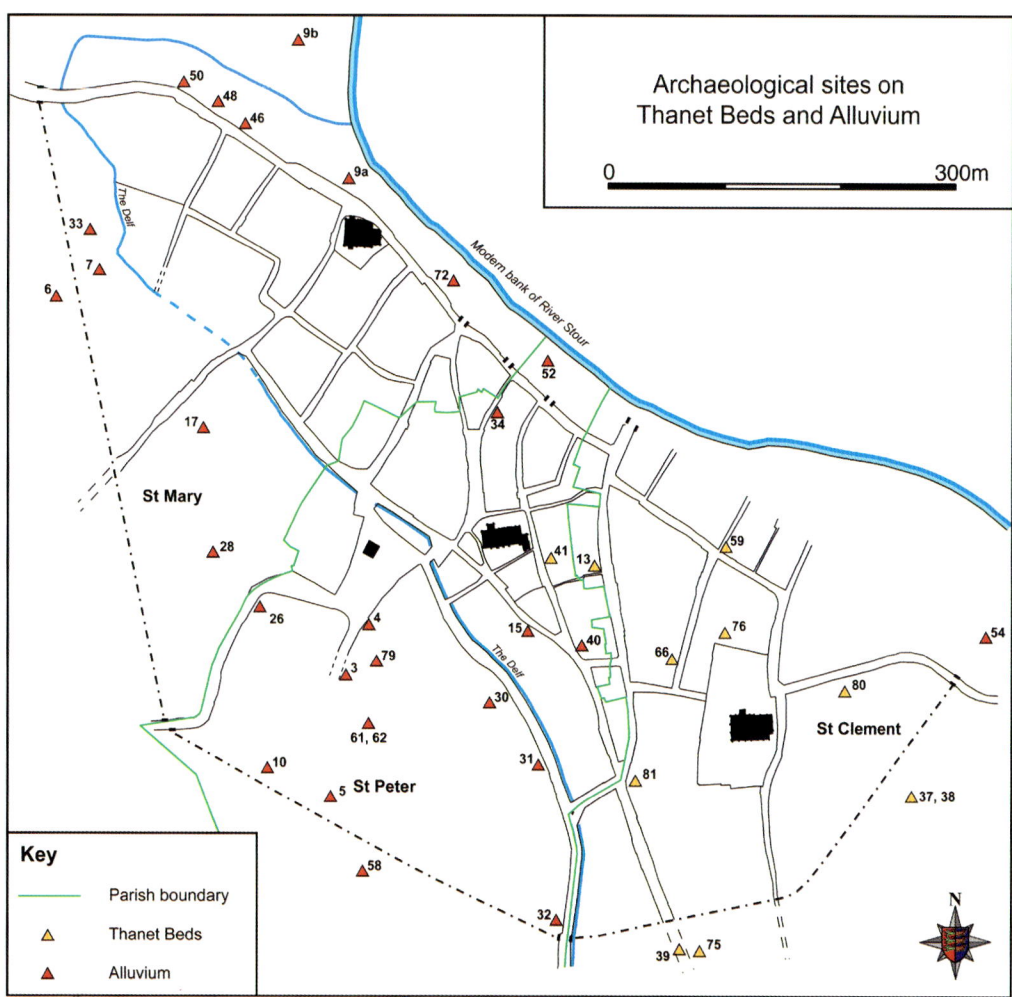

Fig. 1.4: The subsoil of archaeological sites in Sandwich (K. P., B. C. & J. H.). Reproduced by permission of Ordnance Survey on behalf of HMSO. © Crown copyright 2009. All rights reserved. Licence number 100046522

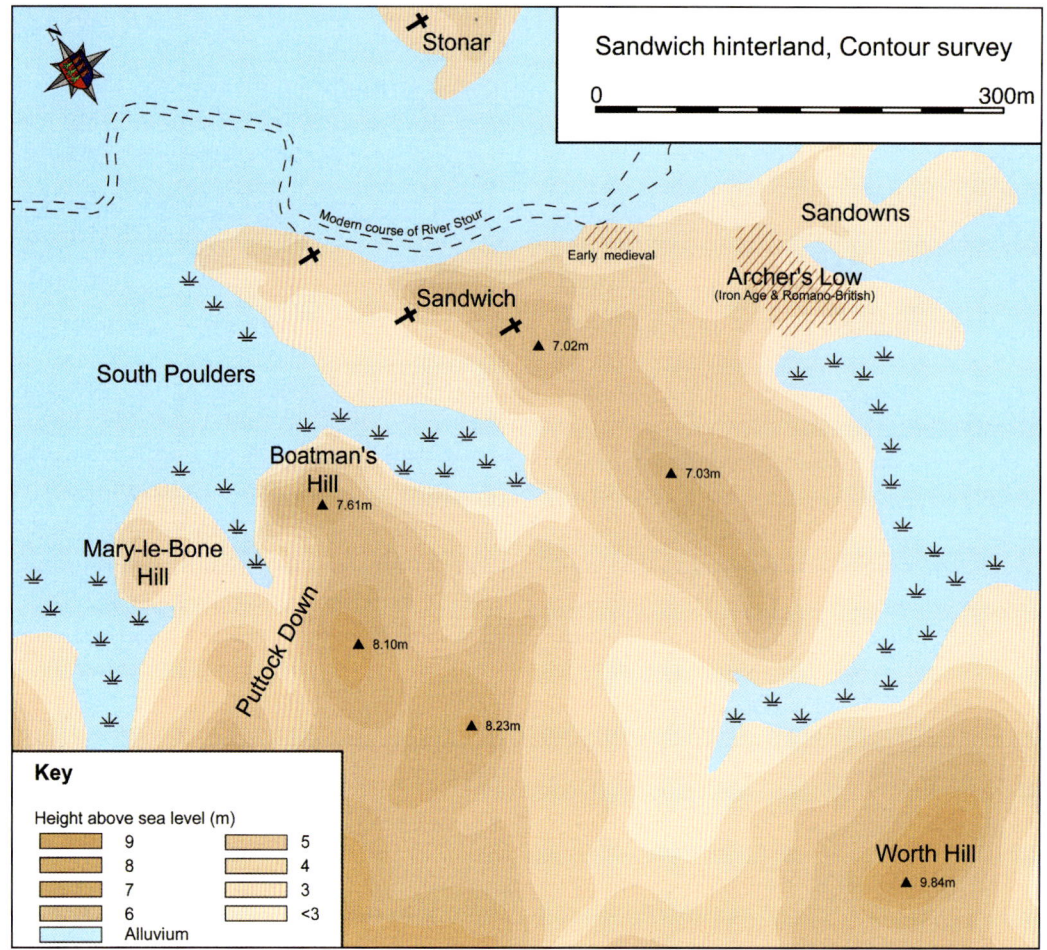

Fig. 1.5: Interpretation of the contour survey of Sandwich's hinterland, contours at 1m intervals (K. P., B. C. & J. H.)

the contours at 1m intervals to produce a generalised picture of the overall configuration of the landscape. Using the same methods as before, approximately 730 spot-height readings were taken over as wide an area as possible, although some private land was inaccessible.

The suburban and rural landscape around Sandwich town displays many anomalies in its contours, deriving from sunken ways, terracing into slopes to create level building platforms and positive lynchets along the margins of fields. Where possible, readings were taken at representative points, ignoring local anomalies.

1.3.2 Topography/urban morphology

In a project in which new archaeological interventions were never going to play a large part, the study of topography took on a critical role, and the intimate relationship between the urban nucleus and its rural hinterland was appreciated from the start. In order to elucidate the changing topography, nineteenth-century Ordnance Survey maps were used to supplement the few earlier maps of the town and its surroundings (most of which appear in the present volume), and they show fundamental topographical changes, such as in the courses of the rivers Stour and Wantsum and the development of Sandwich Haven, and less visible modifications to the landscape, such as the diversions of the Delf, the Guestling and the North Stream. Studying the network of overland routes led to a hypothesis about earliest Sandwich, which was tested by archaeological examination and close-contour surveying of the hinterland. Within the town, the close-contour survey showed the significance of slight changes in height for the development of the street pattern, and when supplemented by the results of previous archaeological interventions it became apparent that the earliest occupation in what was to become the historic core of the town was almost certainly confined to the slightly higher and drier areas of Thanet Beds, with the lower-lying Alluvial land not being occupied until later. This produced a basic framework for the town plan, which was then refined by using other methods. Analysis of plots and boundaries shown on the nineteenth-century maps, crucially supplemented by an appreciation of the later but surviving medieval buildings, enabled the early development of the town centre and the fluctuating sizes of plots at different periods in the Middle Ages to be proposed and the process of land reclamation along the waterfront to be suggested.

Reinterpreting the evidence for the royal castle, of which no vestiges remain, and its association with the town's earthen ramparts, notably Mill Wall, have shown how the street pattern and perhaps the whole emphasis of occupation in the eastern part of the town changed in the fourteenth century and later, and detailed examination of the surviving fabric of the three parish churches has given more insights into the growth of the town. The topographical element within the research project is perhaps not strictly urban morphology as often practised, and we have made no attempt to produce full-scale maps of plan components or plot boundaries throughout the town, as pioneered by Conzen in the 1960s and developed by Slater and others.[6] This is an approach that others may take forward in the future. Nevertheless, the multidisciplinary approach that this project has pursued throughout, drawing in evidence from archaeology, buildings and documents, has provided a new view of the topographical development of the medieval town.

1.3.3 Architectural investigation

Architectural survey in historic towns is always challenging. The practical difficulties are well known; for example, shops and the dwellings above them may be in different hands, and in almost all of today's commercial premises diagnostic features on the ground floors have either been disguised by later fittings or stripped out. In addition, medieval buildings always pose particular problems. Even though it has been possible in Sandwich to create reconstruction drawings of the original state of a few of them, most of the buildings have been altered significantly and some are little more than fragments. A comparison of Figures 12.13 and 14.5, both of which show the same row of houses, indicates that that in the late eighteenth and nineteenth centuries most jettied or overhanging frontages in Sandwich were replaced by flat façades. Sometimes this was achieved through under-building the lower storeys, advancing the street frontage by the width of one or two jetties, depending on the height of the building, and leaving the upper storey intact, but more usually, in order not to diminish the already narrow width of the streets in the town centre, the top part of the building was cut back and the front of the roof was rebuilt. Thus, few original medieval hips or gables survive. Since, as will be argued below, the roofs may have contained important clues to understanding the function of the upper parts of many buildings, such changes have made interpretation problematic. In addition, most of the multi-storeyed ranges at the backs of open-hall houses have been rebuilt on smaller footprints in order to allow light into the ground floors of formerly open halls. Once again, this makes it difficult to understand how the buildings were used. The suggestions about building form and function put forward in this book are based on a lengthy rehearsal of the evidence from the standing remains, although the format of the publication allows neither the minutiae of that evidence nor the detailed arguments always to appear in print. For these it is essential to read the original reports.

When single buildings are recorded in great detail, for example in the course of conservation work, it is often possible to see evidence not usually visible and to discover features that may not be comprehended fully until drawn and measured. Such in-depth recording can have significant advantages. But since so many buildings are incomplete, it is often impossible fully to understand a single building on its own, for its missing parts can be postulated only by analogy with similar surviving structures. The aim here has been to understand the medieval buildings of the town as a group, and to place them in an historical perspective and a wider geographical context. To do this it was deemed essential to survey a large number of buildings, for features surviving in one structure may no longer be present in another, and a general view of structural, functional and chronological development can be obtained only through the accumulation of knowledge from a number of examples. There has been no attempt to produce a complete inventory of all the surviving buildings erected before 1600; rather, each sector of the town was explored to see what had survived, to identify and record the different types of buildings present, and to establish a basic chronology. But not every post-medieval house was visited to discover whether it was hiding one more example of a type already well recorded. Some 150 buildings were visited during the course of the survey, resulting in around 100 surveys (Appendix 2).

For the buildings to play their part in tracing the history of the town, reasonably accurate dating was essential. The possibility of a large-scale dendrochronological or tree-ring dating programme was explored, but it turned out that the timbers in most Sandwich buildings were too fast grown to be susceptible to the technique. Three buildings were sampled, and important results were obtained for two of them,[7] but since further dendrochronology proved impossible, dating in all other cases had to be undertaken by conventional means. This meant assessing stylistic and structural components, using the framework provided by the features that had been dated reliably during the dendrochronological project undertaken in Kent by the RCHME in the late 1980s.[8] The topic is further discussed in Chapter 12.

As in most large-scale surveys, buildings were recorded to various levels. Where the complexity and importance of a building demanded it, survey and drawing were undertaken to English Heritage Level 3 in order to elucidate its main development and features.[9] Where a building proved to be one of a type already adequately covered, or where remains were fragmentary, recording might be at Levels 1 or 2. This means that some buildings have multiple measured plans, sections and details; others have a simple sketch plan to approximate dimensions. The church plans were also measured to Level 3, with some extra measurements to enable sections of St Clement's and St Mary's to be reconstructed.

All the recorded buildings were photographed, and a report, sometimes detailed, sometimes brief, was compiled for each. Reports were not intended as full descriptive records of every building, but to make the structure and history of each building comprehensible for the purposes of the project, for the owner or occupier, and for future building historians. Reports and drawings are deposited in the Sandwich Guildhall Archives. The completed field surveys, which were drawn by hand, were redrawn for publication, at which time some reconstructions and extra three-dimensional drawings were produced to assist the reader.

1.3.4 Historical sources

The documentary sources for medieval Sandwich used in this study come from ecclesiastical, royal and civic records, together with some miscellaneous sources, found in the Kentish archives at Canterbury, Maidstone and Dover, and in the National Archives and the British Library.

1.3.4.1 Ecclesiastical records
The records of Christ Church Priory are largely housed in Canterbury, and provide essential information on the management of its affairs before 1290, when the priory relinquished its rights in Sandwich to the crown. They begin with Cnut's charter of 1023, which was copied into the priory registers, and comprise copies of property transactions, financial records relating to the priory's holdings in Sandwich and a few, not very detailed, late thirteenth-century court rolls. In addition, deeds and a register belonging to two of the town's hospitals, and deeds, leases and an early bede roll and churchwardens' accounts for St Mary's parish illuminate other aspects of town life before the late fifteenth century. Considerable use has also been made of the probate records of the late fifteenth and sixteenth centuries.

1.3.4.2 Royal records
There are many useful records concerning trade and the impact of war in the printed calendars and rolls. After 1290 tolls formerly collected by the priory, and some court rolls (again lacking in detail), were recorded in the Exchequer records. As a member of the Cinque Ports, Sandwich was not subject to the royal courts, although people occasionally appear in Chancery records and those pertaining to the Court of Star Chamber. Sandwich freemen were also exempt from national taxation on property in Sandwich, although recorded on land outside the town, and aliens living in the town sometimes appear in royal taxation records.

1.3.4.3 Civic records
At the heart of the book are the records of the town itself. A few relate to the twelfth and thirteenth centuries, but most belong to the fourteenth century and later. The town's custumal was written in 1301, and survives in later copies, and the first deeds date from the early fourteenth century. The crucially important town year books survive only from 1432 onwards. They record the annual elections of the mayor and jurats and the names of all office-holders, as well as ordinances, copies of royal and Cinque Port documents, disputes relating to petty criminal or civic actions brought before the town court, and many property transactions, including an early sixteenth-century book concerning the property transactions of the daughters of freemen. A few treasurers' rolls also survive and provide invaluable information on leases and rents of town property, and expenditure on town buildings and the defences.

1.3.4.4 Miscellaneous
In addition to these sources, the archives in Kent and London have been trawled for the survival of early maps, so essential to elucidating the topographical development of the town and its hinterland.

1.3.4.5 Historical databases
Information extracted from the documents was entered on two relational databases, a small one for printed documents and a large one, containing more than 3,000 items, for the unpublished documents in Kentish archives. Both were tailored to the research questions and topics established at the beginning of the project;

in other words they were geared towards material evidence, and did not include all that could be extracted for other aspects of the town's history. The more complex primary sources database contained more than twenty-five tables, each with a number of fields, covering in broad terms 'document', 'agent', 'structure', and specialist structures such as 'ship' and 'cargo'. Record linkage was critical, so that members of the project could search the database easily to find relationships between individual people, places, structures or other items from different entries. It proved an invaluable research tool by giving all participants access to the unprinted material housed in the Kent archives.

1.4 Previous research and publication

1.4.1 Historical works

All modern researchers into the history of Sandwich must pay tribute to the eighteenth-century antiquary William Boys, whose *Collections for an History of Sandwich*, published in 1792, laid the foundations for all subsequent work. He was not the first antiquary to recognise the medieval significance of the port and town, but all his predecessors incorporated Sandwich in general histories of country or county.[10]

In the twentieth century a grand survey of the history of medieval Sandwich was planned by Mabel Mills and Edith Scrogg. This remains as an unfinished typescript and therefore unpublished, but it and the notes that informed it, now deposited in the East Kent Archives Centre in Dover, are testaments to dedicated research.[11] That project was completed by Dorothy Gardiner, whose *Historic Haven* (1954) is the most comprehensive published account of the town's history to date.[12] More recently, there have been a number of more specialised contributions to the origins and development of Sandwich. Best known to archaeologists will be Tim Tatton-Brown's publications on the early medieval settlement, where, in the absence of excavated evidence, the few known historical references to the port are used to outline one view of Sandwich's urban beginnings.[13] Other works have concentrated almost entirely on historical documentation, with Andrew Butcher writing about the finances of Christ Church Priory in Sandwich in the thirteenth century, and Justin Croft analysing the composition of the 1301 custumal and its successors, and discussing its place in late thirteenth-century Sandwich.[14] Sheila Sweetinburgh included detailed accounts of the Sandwich hospitals in her book on medieval hospitals; Catherine Richardson has written on the probate material of the fifteenth and sixteenth centuries; and Zoe Ollerenshaw worked on the civic elite of the sixteenth century.[15] The influx of the Flemish and Walloon communities in the late sixteenth century was extensively studied by Marcel Backhouse, and their effect on the population of the town has been charted by Jane Andrewes and Michael Zell.[16] The Sandwich Local History Society has a tradition of supporting books on various aspects of the town's history, including those by Elizabeth Martin on the Sandwich Guildhall and on occupations in the town, Charles Wanostrocht on St Bartholomew's hospital, and Tom Richardson on the trade of medieval Sandwich.[17]

1.4.2 Archaeological investigations[18]

There was little archaeological interest in Sandwich town until the twentieth century, and most urban archaeology has taken place since 1990, therefore being development-led. The following summary presents those few sites from which useful information can be extracted (see also Appendix 1).

1.4.2.1 To the early twentieth century

The Sandwich hinterland rather than the town was the focus of interest for early antiquaries such as Boys, who was the first to conduct scientific archaeological investigations in Richborough and a Roman site at Worth.[19] Henry Wood, another antiquary, unearthed the foundations of the medieval church of St Nicholas at Stonar in 1821,[20] and a little later William Henry Rolfe investigated Roman sites in the sand hills near Deal,[21] the 'Great Foundation' at Richborough,[22] and a probable Roman cremation cemetery near Sandwich railway station.[23] Boys also assembled a large collection of finds from around the town, including grave goods from the Guilton Anglo-Saxon cemetery near Ash.[24] His collection was purchased by Joseph Mayer in 1857[25] and formed part of the collections that were later brought together to form the Free Public Museum in Liverpool (now part of Liverpool Museums).[26]

1.4.2.2 Twentieth-century archaeological work in the town (Fig. 1.2)

Richborough continued to be the main focus of archaeological interest, being chosen as the site for a major research excavation in 1922.[27] Sandwich benefited indirectly from this, with some locals acquiring archaeological experience there. One such was W. P. D. Stebbing, who was the first to carry out a research-orientated excavation in the town, the Carmelite friary in Whitefriars meadow dug in 1936. He published no more than an interim report, and nothing more was done about the site until the 1960s and then in 1992–3 (Chap. 6.2.1). Members of the Sandwich History Society and the Sandwich

Archaeological Group carried out a few research excavations in the 1970s (Chap. 11.2.1.3), and the castle site was more thoroughly excavated in the 1980s and in 1996 (Chap. 5.6.1).

All other excavations in Sandwich have been development-led, and therefore restricted to very limited areas and depths by statutory constraints. Many remain unpublished and their results unavailable to the members of the present project, but all are included in the database of archaeological sites. When possible, information from them has been incorporated in the following chapters.

1.4.2.3 Twentieth-century archaeological work in the hinterland (Figs 1.5, 2.1)
What little is known about medieval Stonar is largely thanks to Stebbings's activities from 1935 to 1960, when he examined and recorded deposits and structures that were being destroyed by quarrying.[28] Although he recovered many interesting artefacts and groups of pottery, much that he found has been lost without record and few details of his work are now available.[29] Excavations carried out between 1969 and 1972 were briefly reported on in 1991.[30] The only other medieval site in the hinterland is on Mary-le-Bone Hill *c.* 1 km west of the town, where the foundations of a small masonry building, perhaps an isolated chapel, were unearthed in 1959 (Chap. 2.3.4).[31]

The building of Sandwich bypass in 1978–9 enabled a number of archaeological sites to be investigated. The most significant were a small late first- to second-century Roman villa on high ground overlooking what had been the course of the Wantsum Channel and close to the Roman road running north-east from Woodnesborough, and a site at Harp Field near Biller's Bush, which was occupied during prehistoric and Romano-British times. Between 1987 and 1991 trenches dug at Archer's Low Farm, south of Sandown Road, with the aim of discovering the context of coins found there earlier, unearthed an extensive site occupied from the late Iron Age to the end of the Roman-British period (Section 2.3.5).[32]

1.4.3 Architectural surveys
Apart from antiquarian drawings of buildings in Sandwich, such as those published in Boys's *History of Sandwich* or sketched a hundred years later by Rolfe,[33] the only previous extensive survey of buildings in the town was undertaken by E. W. Parkin, who published some results in 1984.[34] He was the first to identify the large number of open halls surviving in the town, and his work deserves to be better known than it is.[35] His article provided a preliminary assessment of the medieval buildings in Sandwich, but more remained to be discovered, especially through more detailed surveying, and by asking questions about construction, function and patterns of development that were not normally asked at the time when Parkin was working.

Of the three churches, only St Clement's, which is still in use as the town's parish church, had a report included in the Canterbury Diocese Historical and Archaeological Survey, compiled by Tim Tatton-Brown.[36] St Mary's has been the focus of several studies, notably when excavation took place in the late nineteenth century, and when the church was threatened in the mid-twentieth,[37] but there is only a guidebook to St Peter's.[38]

* * * * *

The published works of all the authors cited above, together with other unpublished manuscripts and many other references in more general literature, have been invaluable to the current study. The present publication, however, is the only one to have attempted to amalgamate evidence from different disciplines with the aim of enhancing knowledge about Sandwich's history and interpreting it. The authors hope that this approach will encourage others to look in more detail at topics only touched on, to put forward alternative interpretations to those suggested here, and to publish currently inaccessible archaeological evidence. Beyond the immediate concerns of Sandwich, the members of the project feel that future studies of historic towns in England would benefit from the multidisciplinary methodology used here.

PART II: ORIGINS

2 Environmental background and origins

This chapter will trace the history of Sandwich from its early medieval beginnings as a small settlement on the south bank of the river Stour to *c.*1000, by which time it was an incipient medieval town. It will be shown that Sandwich differed from some other early medieval sites in England by being established on previously unoccupied land, with no urban Romano-British predecessors. Many towns in north-west Europe grew from Roman roots, although the question of either continuous occupation or continuity of institutions remains unproven. Continuity in English towns has been much discussed. For example, many Romano-British towns such as London, Winchester and York became royal and ecclesiastical centres from the early sixth century, as did Canterbury, less than 20km west of Sandwich. Canterbury is an excellent example of an early medieval royal and ecclesiastical centre situated within a Romano-British town (Durovernum Cantiacorum), and there are some signs of continuous secular occupation within its Roman walls. The latter may also be true of Dover (Portus Dubris) on the coast south-east of Sandwich, and of Richborough (Rutupiae), which occupied a limited area of high ground in the Wantsum Channel. For Sandwich itself, there are signs of Romano-British occupation in the environs, but no urban centre, so it is likely that it began as a settlement on what today would be called a 'greenfield site'.

The growth and development of Sandwich were probably largely dependent on its location, where land and water routes met (Fig. 2.1). Prehistoric trackways and Roman roads ran along low ridges of Thanet Beds clay, the local 'high ground' rising to little more than 10m above OD to meet the south bank of the river Stour, which, with its tributary the river Wantsum, formed one of the most important water routes in south-east England in the Middle Ages and before. Their navigable waters enabled vessels to reach the outer Thames estuary from the English Channel, and the east mouth of the Stour formed a calm anchorage away from the rigours of the open sea. It was against this background that medieval Sandwich developed on the south bank of the Stour, first as one settlement, or perhaps two small settlements approximately 1km apart, later to be transformed into the medieval and modern town.

2.1 The geology of the Sandwich area

Sandwich's location was critical to its success as a town and port, and its precise position was very much influenced by geology. It lies at the junction of the low-lying Alluvium of the flood plain of the rivers Stour and Wantsum with higher, drier land. Natural silting of the sluggish rivers, accentuated by deliberate drainage over at least the past millennium, has given the alluvial landscape its characteristic flat appearance, varying between only 1.5m and 2.7m above OD. Intruding into the Alluvium in the south-east is the Sandown Spit, made up of Marine Sand that has been blown into low dunes in places, with a maximum height of +4.0m OD. The spit stretches eastwards for approximately 1km from the east side of the present town, and in the Middle Ages it was independent of Sandwich, forming part of the manor of Sandown.

The relatively high clay lands south and south-west of the present town are made up of Thanet Beds (olive-green silty to slightly sandy clays) overlain by a drift deposit of fertile Head Brickearth. Basal Upper Chalk outcrops about 1.5km to the south, but there is no useful building stone, other than beach flint, in the vicinity. The Thanet Beds give rise to a gently undulating landscape that tends to form peninsulas and promontories of slightly higher ground, projecting out into the Alluvium. The highest point to the south-west of the town is a small hill, its crest at 11m above OD, on which a Roman villa was built, and closer to Sandwich there are several lower hillocks, between 7m and 9m above OD (Fig. 1.5).

The medieval town of Sandwich occupies the

northerly end of one of the spurs of Thanet Beds as it descends into the Alluvium, with Marine Sand from the westernmost fringe of the Sandown Spit skirting its easternmost edge. Recent survey work in the area of the historic town (Chap. 1.3.1.2) has resulted in a few modifications to the surface geology as outlined by the Geological Survey.[1] For example, the outcrop of Thanet Beds beneath the present town is less extensive than previously mapped, and unlikely to have extended much further north-west than St Peter's church, beyond which the solid geology is overlain by Alluvium, below +3m OD. This suggests that more than half of the medieval town must have been constructed on Alluvial wetland.

The close-contour map in Figure 1.3 reveals a well-defined ridge running from south-east to north-west in the eastern part of the town. This is composed of Thanet Beds, with a maximum height at 7m above OD, now crowned by the church of St Clement. St Peter's church stands at one edge of the Thanet Beds ridge, virtually on its junction with the Alluvium. On the west side of the town, the third church, St Mary's, is on what passes as high land in Sandwich, with a maximum height of 4.4m above OD. Although first thought to be a localised outcrop of Thanet Beds, subsequent archaeological observations have not confirmed this and clayey subsoil has yet to be encountered there.

When the area of the present town was first occupied, the land below 3m OD would probably have been too wet for habitation,[2] so initial occupation must have been confined to the Thanet Beds ridge in the east, and perhaps to the slightly higher ground around St Mary's church. It is impossible to be certain when the low-lying land became habitable through drainage.

Drainage may have been piecemeal. For example, archaeological observations in the low-lying land off Loop Street and at Moat Sole suggest occupation along their street frontages during the thirteenth century (Sites 17 and 28). By *c.*1270 the Carmelite friary was founded on ground approximately 2m above OD (Chap. 6.2.1), which had presumably been drained earlier. Eventually, the land must have been consolidated enough for a substantial masonry church and other claustral buildings to be built (Sites 3, 61, 62 and 64). In contrast, an archaeological evaluation behind the New Inn (Site 12) at the corner of Harnet Street and Delf Street showed that the land there (present ground surface 3.6m above OD) was waterlogged and uninhabitable until *c.*1400.

2.2 Communications and the location of Sandwich

From a geological viewpoint, medieval Sandwich developed in an unpromising area, with its low-lying site at first only partially suitable for occupation and much of its surroundings consisting of the wetlands forming the flood plains of the rivers Wantsum and Stour (the area that has become known as the Wantsum Channel). There were, however, things in favour of the location, above all the navigability of the rivers and the anchorage at the mouth of the Stour. These features were enhanced by good overland communications, with roads and trackways taking advantage of the higher ground to the south of the Stour to connect the site with much of east Kent.

2.2.1 Land routes to the river Stour (Fig. 2.1)

Land routes seem to have converged at the waterside, near the site of the present town. They can be traced back to Roman or slightly later origins, and many remain in use for vehicular traffic to the present day. They include the Roman road from Canterbury to Richborough (Margary 10),[3] which forked at Ash, with one branch going south-eastwards towards Dover (Margary 100) and the other north-east to Richborough itself. A stretch of metalled roadway revealed through excavation at Each End, approximately 2km east of Ash, suggests that by the late first century AD the road from Canterbury had been extended eastwards, perhaps on the line of a prehistoric trackway.[4] Beyond Each End, the west–east line is continued by a causeway over the Poulder marshes, only a couple of metres above sea level, ending near where the present St Mary's church stands. It is possible, although far from certain, that the causeway is also of prehistoric or Romano-British date.

A Roman road (Margary 101) also headed north-eastwards from Woodnesborough, an early medieval and later settlement on the Dover road, to the south bank of the Stour. It was probably aligned on the 7.6m-high Boatman's Hill on the outskirts of Sandwich, although no Roman remains are known there, and passed a small villa near Poulders Gardens. One stretch of it survives as a metalled road, but the remainder of it is traceable only though footpaths and field boundaries. This road may have led to a Roman crossing over the water to the Stonar Bank.

Another route branched off the Richborough to Dover Roman road at Eastry, little more than 2km south of Woodnesborough. It headed north-east towards the east side of present-day Sandwich, its line still evident from the course of minor roads such as

2 Environmental background and origins

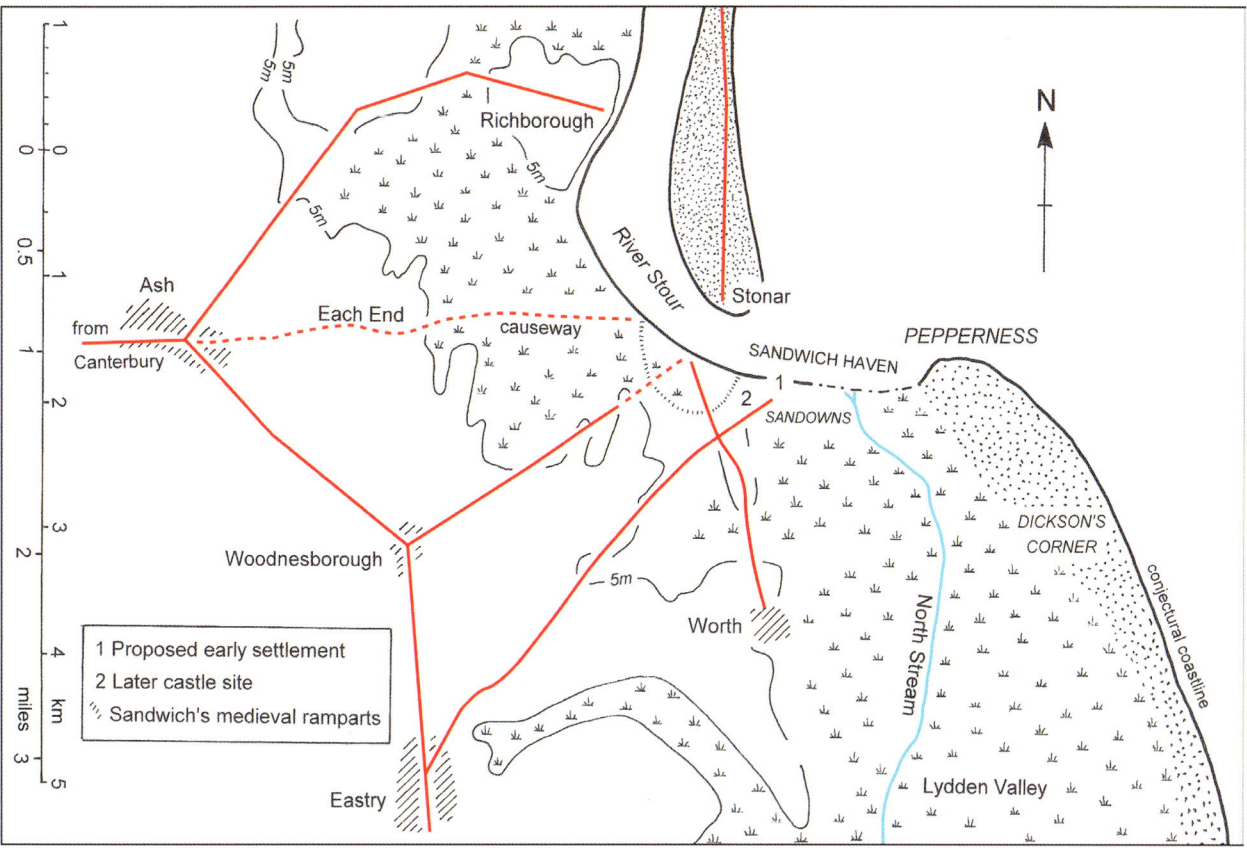

Fig. 2.1: Roman and early medieval land routes around Sandwich (B. C.)

the old Deal road and St George's Road (First Lane on the OS map of 1898) as far as the present (but not early medieval) Sandown Road, approximately 400m outside and east of the medieval town walls. Its original destination must have been the south bank of the Stour, now much changed through medieval and modern drainage and the construction of the road from Sandown. This route may date from as early as the sixth century, when Eastry may have become the administrative centre of east Kent (Section 2.3.2). There may have been another track leading towards the river from the Worth area, some 3km north-east of Eastry. It would have headed to the Stour from almost due south, crossing the road from Eastry, and it perhaps defined the western boundary of the land on which the later royal castle stood. Worth was a Romano-British settlement, with late Iron Age origins, and a temple was in use until the end of the fourth century AD.[5] The precise route of the track south of Worth is difficult to trace, but probably headed westwards to Eastry at some point.

The only route leading north on Figure 2.1 is the present Ramsgate road, which runs along the crest of the shingle ridge (Stonar Bank) to connect the north bank of the Stour with Ebbsfleet and Cliff's End, once on the southern shore of the Isle of Thanet. The modern bridge connecting the south end of the Ramsgate road to Sandwich may be on much the same site as the documented medieval ferry, or even the Roman crossing mentioned above. Thus, the route along the Stonar Bank is likely to have early origins, although of uncertain date.

So all the land routes ran towards the feature that dominated and influenced the development of Sandwich from earliest times: the Wantsum Channel and the rivers Stour and Wantsum flowing through it.

2.2.2 The Wantsum Channel

Today, what was the Wantsum Channel is an arc of flat, mainly agricultural, land with an average height above sea level of 2m. It is depicted in Figure 2.2 as being bounded by the +5m contour, which roughly conforms to the edge of the dry land shown on early maps, notably Lambarde's map of 1585 (Fig. 15.1). This defines the low ground as being approximately 5km wide and 20km long, from the outer Thames estuary to the English Channel, although the shores of the channel seem to have fluctuated throughout the ages.

The wide channel was probably first formed around 8,000 years ago when sea levels rose after the last Ice Age, causing marine flooding of the lower reaches of an eastward-flowing river (the Stour).[6] The subsequent formation of a long shingle spit at Stonar (the Stonar Bank), perhaps starting c.4,000 BC as an island of shingle at the bank's present southern extremity, may have impeded the flow of water along the Stour and caused further flooding of the adjacent lowlands. In response, the river created an additional, northerly exit to the sea near Reculver, so forming an important connection between the outer Thames estuary and the English Channel. The waters of the secondary (northern) arm then contracted to become the river Wantsum.

2.2.2.1 Terminology

The name 'river Wantsum (*fluminus Uantsumu*)' was first used by the Venerable Bede in the eighth century, although he must have been referring not just to the northern tributary but also to the whole length of the channel, which, he said, went from coast to coast and cut off the Isle of Thanet from mainland Kent.[7] He subsequently used Genlada or Genlade for the name of the river on which Reculver stood (*iuxta ostium aquilonale fluminis Genladae*) suggesting that this, and not Wantsum, may have been the true name of the short, north-flowing watercourse.[8]

The name Wantsum was not employed again for another thousand years, because in the Middle Ages it was referred to as 'the sea', as in the Sandwich custumal of 1301, or 'the king's river to Northmouth'.[9] In 1744 the river surrounding the south-west coast of the Isle of Thanet was called the 'Wantsume',[10] but only in 1840 did 'Wantsum channel' appear in print for the first time.[11] It was then taken up by nineteenth- and twentieth-century scholars to describe the drained flood plains of both the Stour and the Wantsum, from the Thames to the English Channel.[12]

The old northerly flowing river Wantsum is now reduced to a sluggish stream less than 8km long from its junction with the river Great Stour, at a sluice just north of Stourmouth, to the outer Thames estuary, where it is blocked by the Northern Sea Wall. It amounts to little more than a wide drainage ditch, with its direction of flow having been reversed by modern engineers so that it now drains Wade Marsh and Chislet Marsh, carrying the water southwards (away from the sea), to join the Great Stour shortly before its confluence with the Little Stour. Some clue to its former importance is recorded on the first edition OS map surveyed in 1872, where this now seemingly insignificant stream is the boundary between the parishes of Sarre and Chislet; it is still the dividing line between the modern administrative districts of Canterbury and Thanet.

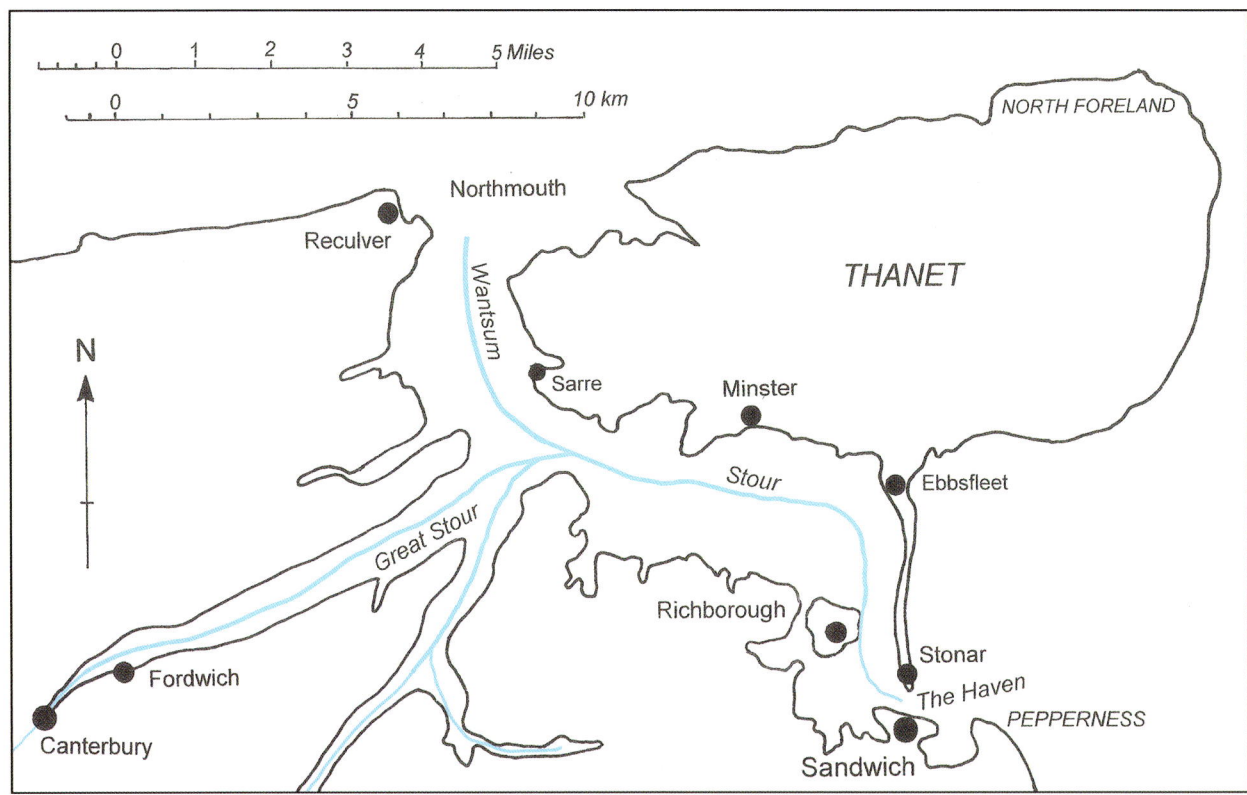

Fig. 2.2: The Wantsum Channel and its rivers (H. C. & B. C.)

The river Stour continues to be the main watercourse along the southern stretch of the Wantsum Channel. Modern Ordnance Survey maps show the name Stour from Plucks Gutter as far as the east side of Sandwich, whence it is shown as Sandwich Haven along its remaining length to Shell Ness and Pegwell Bay. In the town records 'le haven' was commonly used for that stretch of the Stour, but was also applied to the length flowing along the north side of the medieval town where there were harbour facilities. Medieval Sandwich Haven thus had two aspects. It was both an anchorage to the east of the town, in the lee of the spit culminating in Pepperness, and also the stretch of river that separated Sandwich from Stonar. The haven may also have included an indeterminate length of the navigable river Stour to the west, perhaps as far as the Stour was tidal (today that is as far as Fordwich) or until it met the river Wantsum.

2.2.2.2 Changes in the Wantsum Channel
Insufficient research has as yet been carried out for the development of the flood plain and waterways to be described with confidence, but it seems that the south-eastern mouth of the Stour began to be obstructed from *c*.4,000 BC, when the Stonar Bank and the Deal Spit started to accrete (see above). As a result, the river seems to have flooded the adjoining land in some areas and receded in others. The fluctuations are recorded by the presence of a submerged land surface to the south-east and west of present-day Sandwich. Objects of late Neolithic and early Bronze Age date have been recovered, demonstrating that in these areas what had been dry land during the third millennium BC was later inundated.[13] These natural changes were later exacerbated by human intervention in the form of large-scale drainage works, to produce the landscape as it appears today.

The Deal (or Sandwich Bay) Spit is the present name for the complex of sand and shingle deposits that extend across Sandwich Bay and which are still accreting, so that the spit's present northern extremity (medieval Pepperness, now known as Shell Ness) is 9km from Deal and only 1.5km south of the Isle of Thanet. The spit's origins are attributed to longshore drift from the south, and ridges of shingle outlining the progress of accretion are clearly visible on geological maps and aerial photographs (Figs 2.3, 2.4). The chronology of its development is difficult to establish with precision, but a combination of geological and archaeological work and cartographic evidence has enabled an approximately dated sequence to be proposed.[14] In the early eighth century, for example, when Bishop Wilfrid is said to have reached safety at Sandwich (*in portum Sandwicae salutis*),[15] Pepperness would have been perhaps 4km south of the present position of Shell Ness, with Wilfrid's 'port' thus lying much more open to the sea (Fig. 2.2).

The development of the Stonar Bank and the Deal Spit must have narrowed the connection with the English Channel and caused the river's course around Stonar to develop a long meander, forcing the mouth of the river northwards to the sea (now Pegwell Bay). Although there is no firm dating evidence for the growth of either the bank or the spit, both are likely to have been well developed by Roman times. Taken in conjunction with the evidence for late Iron Age and Roman occupation on the Sandowns east of Sandwich, it seems probable that the south-eastern entrance into the Stour was already significantly reduced by that time.

The establishment of Richborough (Rutupiae) in the first century AD as the Romans' port of entry to Britain adds to the confusion, for why would Richborough have been founded if the Stonar Bank had already taken shape as a peninsula running south from the Isle of Thanet? At that time, the width between the Stonar and Sandwich shores may not have been much greater than it is today, so presenting difficulties to navigation. Bearing this in mind, it is difficult to understand why the invading Romans would have chosen Richborough

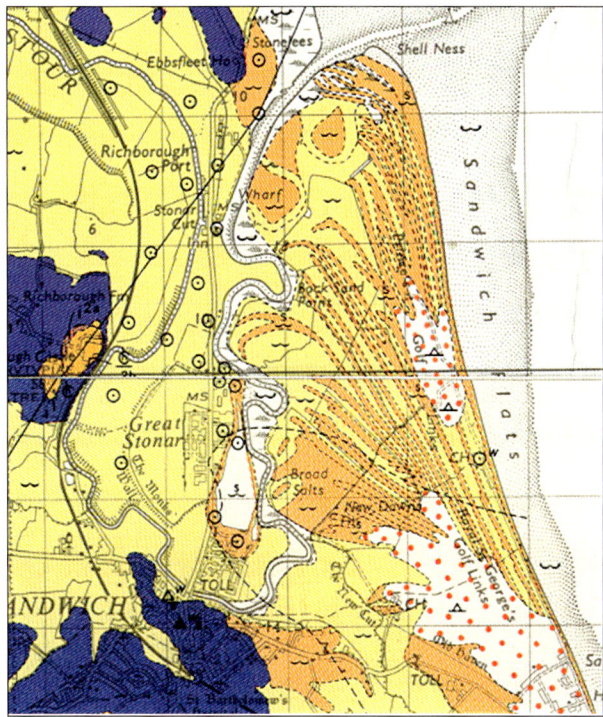

Fig. 2.3: The geology of the Deal Spit (Extracts from BGS maps 271 and 290). IPR/111–36CT British Geological Survey © NERC. All rights reserved

Fig. 2.4: Aerial view of Deal Spit from the north (CAT, F11844_6200)

as their port of entry to Britain. Perhaps the bank had not taken on its present form by then and there was no peninsula, but rather an island with open water between it and Thanet. That would have enabled Roman ships to reach Richborough from the English Channel by sailing north of the Stonar island, past Ebbsfleet, reputed to be St Augustine's landing place in AD 597.

The 1,500 years since that landing have seen even greater changes. In the early years of the eighth century Bede wrote of east Kent at the time of Augustine's mission:

> Over against the eastern districts of Kent there is a large island called Thanet which . . . is divided from the mainland by the river Wantsum (*fluminus Uantsumu*) which is about 3 furlongs (*circiter trium stadiorum [c.600m]*) wide, can be crossed (*est transmeabilis*) in two places only, and joins the sea at either end.[16]

As mentioned above, Bede's 'fluminus Uantsumu' must have been the whole Wantsum Channel, not just the river Wantsum. The width of 3 furlongs presumably refers to the watercourses and their adjacent mud flats, salt marshes and flood plain, even though that measurement bears no relation to the flat land between the 5m contours shown on Figure 2.3. It seems highly unlikely that the rivers themselves were 600m wide (which is the present width of the Thames between Gravesend and Tilbury). As a comparison, in the tenth century the river Medway cannot have been more than approximately 133m wide,[17] narrow enough to be bridged, whereas Bede's Wantsum was probably crossed by two fords or ferries.

Sarre, on the dry east bank of the river Wantsum, may have been one of the crossing points from the mainland to the Isle of Thanet. A charter of *c.*763 (only about thirty years after Bede was writing) mentions tolls exacted on ships at Sarre,[18] and it could have been associated with waterborne transport at an even earlier date, for clench nails from clinker-built boats have been found in some sixth- and seventh-century graves.[19] The second crossing mentioned by Bede could have been near the site of present-day Sandwich, on the south bank of the river Stour, as indicated by the early land routes in the area. Until the Thanet Way (A299) was upgraded in the 1990s, Sarre and Sandwich remained the two main entry points to the island, by then with bridges rather than ferries.

The navigability of the rivers Stour and Wantsum was of great importance for the development of their environs for many centuries, probably from the Iron Age until the end of the Middle Ages. But the Stour, in particular, had other useful features. That the calm water of the Haven provided a safe anchorage for fleets of ships is very well documented in the fourteenth and fifteenth centuries, when foreign merchantmen gathered there (Chap. 9.1), but its advantages were also recognised in earlier periods for more warlike activities. For example, in 851 King Æthelstan of Kent defeated a Danish Viking fleet in a sea battle at 'Sandwic',[20] and in 1009 King Æthelred II's warships were assembled there to defend the realm.[21]

2.3 The site of earliest Sandwich

The following sections will explore the evidence for the character and location of early medieval Sandwich. First, consideration will be given to the claim that Sandwich was the medieval replacement of Richborough, the Roman port that served as the entrance to Britain during the early centuries AD (Section 2.3.1). Evidence for the origins of Sandwich as an early trading settlement (Section 2.3.2) and a possible ecclesiastical site (Section 2.3.3) will then be examined, using place names and historical sources. These will be supplemented by results from the project's survey work on Mary-le-Bone Hill (Section 2.3.4) and the Sandowns (Section 2.3.5). A new hypothesis on the site of earliest Sandwich will then be proposed.

2.3.1 Richborough as Sandwich's precursor

The earliest accounts of the origins of Sandwich appear in the writings of the sixteenth-century antiquaries Leland, Lambarde and Camden, who agreed that Sandwich was founded after Richborough, whose ruined fortifications stand less than 2km to the north of Sandwich, had declined as both port and fort. Such an idea was taken up by Lewis in 1736 and 1744,[22] and by Battely in the next year.[23] About twenty years later Seymour elaborated on the relationship between the two places, saying that Sandwich was probably the place 'for landing and embarking' whereas Richborough was the garrison fort.[24]

The replacement of Roman Richborough by 'Saxon Sandwich' would have involved a shift in settlement approximately 2km southwards, bringing the site closer to the open sea. Such a shift could have been associated with changes that were already taking place in the Wantsum, and perhaps also with the need to maintain a serviceable landing place with access to the English Channel. The question is whether there was chronological continuity between the two sites. Was Richborough still occupied after the withdrawal of the Roman troops in the early fifth century? And when was Sandwich first inhabited?

Roman fleets and large bodies of troops were still frequenting Richborough during the second half of the fourth century. In AD 368 it was described as 'a safe and quiet station',[25] and the last known garrison was a detachment of the old Second Augusta legion, recorded in the *Notitia Dignitatum* of *c*.AD 400. This was the most senior regiment stationed in any of the late Roman forts of the Saxon Shore and the unit's posting here seems to imply that Richborough was regarded as the principal fort of the series. This no doubt reflects the fact that the site had long been one of the main ports of entry into the British province.

It is unknown how long this unit remained in post and the date of the total abandonment of the site by the Romans has yet to be precisely established.[26] An unusually large number of coins dating from the period between AD 388 and 402 found at the site suggests, however, that it remained important into the early fifth century. The consensus of opinion seems to be that Richborough was one of the last British military bases to have its garrison removed, although the site seems to have been deserted by the later fifth century. There are some archaeological finds indicating limited post-Roman activity on Richborough island, but there is little evidence to suggest that permanent Roman occupation continued here much after *c*.AD 425. The abandonment of Richborough sometime during the first half of the fifth century is comparable with nearby Roman Canterbury, where a phase of abandonment during the middle decades of the fifth century appears to separate the final Roman occupation from the earliest Anglo-Saxon habitation.[27] Situated some 3km inside the south-eastern mouth of the Wantsum, it may be that by the fifth century the Roman port of Richborough had become difficult, or even impossible, to reach by water. In addition, the ships of the time differed from Roman vessels in having no need of harbour facilities, which by then may even have presented a hazard rather than an aid to berthing.

There is as yet no physical evidence for the direct replacement of Richborough by Sandwich, or for chronological continuity of human presence at the two sites, although a single inhumation burial of Anglo-Saxon type was discovered some 220m north of the fort. Although it had suffered subsequent disturbance, it was apparently the grave of a late fourth- to early fifth-century warrior interred with his sword, shield and spear, together with a pewter bowl.[28] It appears to have been an isolated find and its exact interpretation remains unclear. The excavators thought that it was the grave of a Germanic warrior slain while attacking the fort, but it has recently been suggested that it was from the fort's cemetery, and that it was dug for an individual, perhaps an officer from a garrison made up of Germanic auxiliaries or mercenaries there to defend the fort.[29] A few other pieces of Anglo-Saxon metalwork from the Richborough area are listed in Richardson 2005. Some of these items could be from burials, but the details of most are not clear.

Although Richborough's early Christian associations are dubious,[30] it is reasonably well documented during the medieval period, with a chapel (Fleet Chapel) in regular use until at least the early seventeenth century.

By the nineteenth century, however, the building had been demolished and all surface traces of it were gone. Its foundations were excavated in the early twentieth century and although they were difficult to understand, the structure appeared to have gone through at least three phases of development.[31] The earliest foundations were provisionally assigned to the later Anglo-Saxon period, but the building seems to have been partially reconstructed during Norman times, when all trace of an even earlier chapel here, perhaps built of timber and dated on the basis of some seventh- to ninth-century coins, could have been obliterated.[32]

Other early medieval artefacts that may be associated with Richborough are two small gravestones, one with a runic inscription, discovered by a labourer digging in a field 'near Sandwich' during the 1830s. According to Parsons, the runic inscription, which may or may not have Scandinavian associations, could be of seventh- or eighth-century date,[33] whereas the other stone may have been carved as early as the fifth century.[34] It has recently been suggested that they may originally have come from nearer Richborough than Sandwich, although it is far from certain. A very weathered block of tooled sandstone built into St Mary's churchyard wall is even more enigmatic. It could carry diagonal tooling such as that on stones in Roman sites, or Anglo-Saxon herringbone carving and interlace; but its state of preservation makes it impossible to draw conclusions with confidence. Thus, there remain many unresolved questions about the end of Rutupiae and its possible reuse after its abandonment by the Romans.

Elsewhere in east Kent, there are few known early Anglo-Saxon settlement sites, and cemeteries containing firmly dated fifth-century graves are not common. Much of the evidence comes from old excavations, where the contexts are not always well recorded. Nevertheless, a recent study of the distribution of known fifth-century graves has shown some clustering in north-east Kent, around the shores of the Wantsum Channel, and extending inland up the valley of the river Little Stour.[35] Sites with good evidence for fifth-century burials include Sarre and Ozengell on the Isle of Thanet, and Westbere, Guilton, Ringlemere and Eastry on the mainland. Westbere and Ringlemere have yielded cremation burials, a rite that is generally thought to characterise the earliest Anglo-Saxon settlers in Kent. Overall, then, the evidence seems to suggest that Anglo-Saxon colonists were establishing settlements in the general area of Sandwich by AD 450–75, even though there seems to have been no occupation on the site of the future town at this early date.

2.3.2 Sandwich: an early trading settlement?[36]

Sandwich's place name has often been used as evidence that the present town within its medieval walls was the site of an early medieval trading place, or *wic*, active (and in some cases described as prosperous) from the early eighth century throughout the next three centuries, after which it was transformed into the town of Domesday Book. As will be shown below, there is both archaeological and topographical evidence to suggest that there was some form of settlement, perhaps a harbour, in the vicinity of the modern town, but not precisely where the town now stands. This section will review that evidence, and a hypothesis for the site of earliest Sandwich will be proposed in Section 2.4.

The name Sandwich is first mentioned in the *Life of Bishop Wilfrid*, a hagiography of the bishop of York (died 709 or 710), written in the early eighth century.[37] In *c*.665, when returning from France to take up his episcopal duties, Wilfrid's ship was blown off course so that he landed involuntarily in Sussex. The heathen South Saxons of Sussex attacked the ship and its crew and slew five of Wilfrid's companions before high tide, when the ship could float off the shore to the safety of the sea. He finally arrived *in portum Sandwicae*, but there is no indication that he landed there. If Sandwich then stood roughly where it does today, it would have been a welcome sight, for the Wantsum would have offered a respite from the open sea and the possibility of a calm passage to Northmouth and probably onwards along the east coast to the mouth of the Humber, and finally York.

The phrase *in portum Sandwicae* in the Latin text may lead to some confusion, because it is often translated simply as 'in the port of Sandwich'. Today, the word 'port' carries connotations of a coastal town with a man-made waterfront and harbour installations, but in the early Middle Ages it was ambiguous. It was sometimes applied to a settlement with some form of trading function, be it inland, riverine or coastal, but sometimes it had the sense of harbour or haven, although that would not have implied a place with waterside structures such as are associated with modern ports.[38] Bearing in mind that Wilfrid must have been travelling in a shallow-draught vessel (that was able to float away from the Sussex coast at full tide), no more than a gently shelving beach would have been needed.[39]

The modern name 'Sandwich' is made up of two Old English elements, *sand* and *wic*, both of which can be used to investigate Sandwich's early medieval role and location.[40] Its suffix *wik* or *wic* has been much discussed in a national and European context, by place-name specialists, historians and archaeologists, who have come to many different conclusions about its significance.[41] *Wik* or *wic*, considered by some scholars to derive from the Latin *vicus* (village, hamlet),[42] occasionally occurs in Old English as a separate common noun,[43] but is mainly known from its use as a place-name element. It has become widely accepted that early medieval settlements in north-west Europe that were either called *emporia*[44] or, more commonly, have *wik* or *wic* in their names were trading places, usually of international importance.[45] This interpretation is true in some instances, notably on the Continent, where, for example, Quentovic in France and Dorestad (modern Wijk bij Duurstede) in the Netherlands can stand as examples of truly international markets with maritime trading interests, active during the middle centuries of the first millennium AD.[46] In England, convincing cases have been argued for London (Lundenwic), York (Eorforwic), Saxon Southampton (Hamwic) and Ipswich (Gippeswic), where the place-name evidence has been supplemented by abundant archaeological finds, notably pottery imported from the Low Countries, the Rhineland and France, and coins. The equation of *wic* and *emporium* with 'early medieval trading centre' has become popular with archaeologists in recent years, with no less than thirteen other English sites being interpreted as such by various authors.[47] Other scholars are more cautious, with the suggestion that in England only a few places carrying the element *wik* or *wic* were *emporia*.[48]

Sandwich has been taken to fit the model of an early trading place,[49] but such archaeological investigation as has been done there raises doubts about this. In particular, the only finds of eighth- or ninth-century date are represented by six potsherds (mostly Ipswich ware) found as residual material in later layers on five separate sites, two of them (Site 38 and the unnumbered site in modern St George's Road) east of the medieval walls.[50] Site 20 is the only excavation within the walled area to yield some tenth- to eleventh-century sherds, also redeposited in later contexts. With fewer than fifty Anglo-Saxon potsherds, covering possibly four centuries, and only a handful of 'Middle Saxon' type, and no coins at all, Sandwich stands in stark contrast to the four sites in England that have been defined as *wics* on the basis of archaeological finds.[51] It may be that more archaeological evidence will be recovered at Sandwich, but until that is the case there is little to suggest the presence of anything more than a possible landing place, sporadically used at best.

The paucity of evidence for Sandwich's earliest medieval phase has been explained in various ways, one suggestion being that its remains lie far below the modern ground surface within the walled town, out of reach of the restricted archaeological work that can be undertaken in the currently densely built-up town centre. Recent evaluation of the close-contour survey and the subsoil of archaeological sites suggests that this is unlikely (Figs 1.3, 1.4). Much of the land within the town walls would have been uninhabitable before drainage, and in the heart of the medieval settlement and away from the riverbank the sequence of stratified archaeological deposits appears to be comparatively thin. From the available evidence it would seem that in most areas they amount to little more than one metre in overall thickness. No undisturbed Anglo-Saxon deposits have so far been located and, as mentioned above, only a very limited number of sherds of this date have been identified in later pottery assemblages.

In view of the scarcity of early finds from the town within the walls, it is difficult to propose that present-day Sandwich overlies an early medieval trading place. It is suggested here that if there were any sort of early medieval settlement in the vicinity, it must have stood not within the area of the present town, but outside the medieval walls, probably some hundreds of metres to the east (Section 2.4). This location would also agree with the suggestion that *wics* were trading places dependent in some way on elite settlements nearby. The royal centre of Eastry, approximately 4km to the south-west, may have been such a focus for early medieval Sandwich. Figure 2.1 shows the route from Eastry to the Stour, near the 'old haven' shown on William Boycote's map of 1615 (Fig. 2.5). It can be argued that this would have been a likely position for a landing place or trading settlement, and it is not far from two of the sites on which Ipswich ware sherds were found. The road may have linked the early medieval royal centre with the coast; it also skirts the site of the later medieval castle. Although no signs of activity earlier than the late eleventh century have been found on the castle site, the area could have been a royal site from a much earlier period.[52] This raises the question, discussed later, of royal continuity in this area from the early Middle Ages to the seventeenth century.

The interpretation of Eastry as a royal site derives from documentary and place-name evidence, with archaeological support being less helpful. Eastry's royal associations are attributed to a rather dubious source. It is a twelfth-century account, probably written in the north of England, of the seventh-century murder of two young princes, Æthelred and Æthelberht, nephews of King Ecgberht of Kent.[53] The story that they were killed in a 'palace' (*in villa regali quae vulgari dicitur Easterige pronunciatione*), their bodies being buried under the floor of its hall, has been used, alongside place-name evidence, to support a royal association,

Fig. 2.5: Estate map of Sandown Manor surveyed and drawn by William Boycote, 1615 (CKS: S/EK/Ch 10b/A10)

for Eastry is said to have derived from Old English *easterna *ge* (the easterly district)[54] or perhaps *Easter-ge* (the eastern district capital).[55] This has been taken as an indication that Eastry also had a minster or mother church, and thus was of ecclesiastical, as well as royal, importance for the area.[56] Thus it could have been the centre on which the early medieval trading place or *wic* of Sandwich depended.

No archaeological evidence for the 'palace' has been discovered,[57] although four fifth- and sixth-century cemeteries in the vicinity of the present village are indicative of a settlement there at that date.[58] Five surviving charters issued between 788 and 1042, however, indicate that the Eastry district, if not the centre itself, maintained its importance during the pre-Norman Conquest period.[59] For some of that time it was one of the possessions of the church of Canterbury, as Sandwich was to become in 1023 (Chap. 3.2.3). Whether this eleventh-century connection reflects an earlier association between the two sites must remain an open question.

The second piece of information to support the idea that the possible trading settlement may have lain outside and east of the present town is the first element of its name – *sand*. This seems perfectly straightforward, a word indicating that the settlement, of whatever type, was on sand. But the substrate of the present town is Thanet Beds clay and alluvial clay, with only a very localised deposit of sand inside the late medieval wall in the east. Unless the settlement were on precisely that rather small area, it is more likely to have been situated further east, where there is sand in abundance, in the area known as the Sandowns, which has recently been investigated with this in mind.

The probability that there was some sort of settlement in the vicinity of the later medieval town is enhanced by the brief mention in Wilfrid's *Life*, referred to above. When stating that Wilfrid arrived *in portum Sandwicae*, the author of the work implies that he considered that there was a place there worthy to be given a name, but neither its character nor its size can be confidently reconstructed from the phrase.

2.3.3 Sandwich: an early ecclesiastical site?

Some of the early antiquaries who were enthusiastic about Richborough being Sandwich's precursor also held the belief, apparently first put in print by Leland, that St Mary's church was originally part of a nunnery. Leland's fairly anodyne statement grew over the years, to incorporate the name of the founder (Domneva or Æbba, mother of St Mildred, first abbess of Minster-in-Thanet) and the date of its foundation (640).[60] Kilburne added more circumstantial detail, such as that it was destroyed by the Danes and subsequently rebuilt by Queen Emma, wife of Cnut (king of England and Denmark 1016–35), and that the present church was built in 1529 from monastic ruins.[61] It is now an often reiterated piece of popular folklore.

Despite exhaustive searches, no supporting evidence has yet been found for the above assertions. Although there is good documentary evidence for Domneva's foundation of Minster abbey, some kilometres away to the north-west, there is no mention of Sandwich in any of the sources.[62] Moreover, the date of 640 given by Seymour and his successors is more than twenty years earlier than the accepted date of Minster's foundation, and the modern authority on St Mildred and her abbey has confirmed that nowhere is there a hint of an association between Minster and Sandwich in the seventh century.[63] The attribution of St Mary's to Minster-in-Thanet may have been a simple misunderstanding on the part of the antiquarians. The church could have been dependent on a minster, but possibly that of Eastry,[64] not the nunnery of Minster-in-Thanet. The question remains unanswered.

Nevertheless, the possibility of an early date for settlement on the slightly higher ground at the west of the medieval town needs to be examined. The close-contour map of the town (Fig. 1.3) shows an isolated 'island' of ground above the 3m contour, and therefore possibly habitable before drainage, around the present St Mary's church. This area seems to be the destination of a causeway approaching the town from the west, and it was also the site that Canterbury Cathedral Priory chose for its Sandwich outpost in the early eleventh century.

Several recent archaeological interventions in the area near the church (Sites 45, 78) have, however, thrown some doubt on the 'island' theory, which in large part depends on a comparison between it and the high ridge in the east of the town. In the east, there is only a thin layer of topsoil and occupation debris above Thanet Beds. In the west, however, the disturbed upper layer is at least 2m thick, and no sign of Thanet Beds has been found. It may be, therefore, that the 'island' around St Mary's is illusory, and that the ground there is today higher than its surroundings not because of a natural feature but because of an artificial build-up of material at some unknown date. The priory itself may have contributed to this accumulation, but the only excavations in the priory grounds (Chap. 4.4; Site 18) produced no helpful information about this.

The dating of the causeway is also problematic. It could be of prehistoric or Romano-British origin, or it could have been laid out as a sea wall to drain the wetlands west of Sandwich in the twelfth or thirteenth centuries. Perhaps the Sandwich example is comparable with the ceremonial routes to religious sites that have been proposed for causeways across wetlands in the Witham Valley, Lincolnshire.[65] Unfortunately, the present state of knowledge does not allow such a conclusion.

Equally, the current state of evidence provides no positive support for the presence of an early medieval religious centre on the west side of the town. Nevertheless, the siting of the priory residence in the area suggests that the possibility should not be ruled out.

2.3.4 Fieldwork and the site of earliest Sandwich: Mary-le-Bone Hill (Fig. 1.5)

Despite the earlier excavated evidence for a chapel,[66] and the belief that aerial photographs of the hill show traces of a motte-and-bailey castle, the quantity of medieval and post-medieval material recovered from a survey in 2006 was insufficient to suggest intensive occupation on the site during the Middle Ages. All the finds can be explained as domestic rubbish spread as manure across fields outside the later medieval town. Moreover, the clay soils on the site were heavy and ill drained and not at all well suited to occupation, let alone to the *sand* of the Sandwich place name. There is, therefore, no evidence to support the suggestion that Mary-le-Bone Hill was the site of early Sandwich.

2.3.5 Fieldwork and the site of earliest Sandwich: the Sandowns

The survey undertaken in 2005 covered almost the whole area of the Sandowns, the earliest cartographic depiction of which dates from 1615 (Fig. 2.5).[67] Study of the geological sequences revealed in the test pits and results of the close-contour survey has enabled the nature of the Sandowns to be understood in more detail than before, although the broad outlines are recorded on modern Geological Survey and Soil Survey maps.[68] The new investigation has shown that the Sandowns comprise at least three separate, and probably successively formed sand ridges, each roughly aligned east to west and separated by slightly lower areas where sand is absent. Centuries of cultivation have smoothed out the sand ridges so that they are now not very distinct on the ground. By combining the most recent discoveries with previous finds around Archer's Low Farm (Section 1.4.2.3; Fig. 1.5) it has been demonstrated that the southernmost sand ridge was the site of an extensive settlement,[69] which extended for some 450m south-eastwards from modern St George's Road (the road from Eastry shown in Fig. 2.1), along what was probably then the shoreline of the Wantsum Channel. Pottery and coin evidence suggests that the peak of its activity was during the period *c*.50 BC to AD 80, but occupation continued into the late fourth century AD. The finds and the settlement's situation make it highly likely that the site was a late prehistoric landing place or port, which towards the end of the first century AD was eclipsed by the rapidly developing Roman port and supply base at Richborough, some 2.5 km to the north-west.

But there is good archaeological evidence for Archer's Low continuing into the late Roman period, perhaps meaning that we should look to this site rather than Richborough as a possible precursor of early medieval Sandwich. In addition, the north-west end of the Archer's Low occupation area included the site where one of the very few Ipswich ware sherds was discovered. Although no other early medieval artefacts were found during the survey of the Sandowns, there is sufficient archaeological and topographical evidence to suggest that earliest Sandwich may have stood on the sand east of the medieval town, at the end of the road from Eastry and in the region of the 'old haven' on the 1615 map, a possibility.

2.4 A hypothesis for earliest Sandwich[70] (Fig. 1.5)

The above discussions about the origins of medieval Sandwich have shown that, while some claims such as early medieval Sandwich being the direct successor to Roman Richborough or the site on Mary-le-Bone Hill being its forerunner are unlikely to be correct, there is sufficient evidence to make a more positive suggestion. On the basis of that, the following hypothesis is put forward for discussion and testing in the future.

The area in which Sandwich was later to grow was initially the focus of several prehistoric and Romano-British trackways that perhaps converged on a crossing point over the river Stour. They were later supplemented by an early medieval route from the royal site of Eastry, possibly linking it with one of its possessions in the form of land on which a royal castle was subsequently built. The track from Eastry seems to have run along the eastern boundary of that land and ended on the riverbank a little further north. This is where a small settlement, which perhaps had some form of trading function, may have grown up. Although six scattered sherds of eighth- or ninth-century pottery make up the only archaeological evidence, it can be argued that they derived from an early medieval equivalent to the late Iron Age and Romano-British settlements of which traces have been discovered on the Sandowns. At the same time there may have been an ecclesiastical centre approximately 1km west of the secular settlement, in the region of the present parish church of St Mary. As mentioned above, this is highly speculative, but the area became incorporated into the later town, remaining in occupation throughout the Middle Ages. In contrast, the postulated eastern settlement on the Sandowns was abandoned, probably by the tenth century, its focus perhaps shifting to a location some 600m to the west of it, where St Clement's church now stands. Some stonework in that church suggests building activity there *c*.1000, and, as discussed in Chapter 3, the neighbourhood around and just west of the church may have become the new commercial centre of Sandwich at that date.

Such a hypothesis for the first settlement implies that early medieval Sandwich was made up of three foci: an ecclesiastical centre, a royal site and a trading settlement. The ecclesiastical and royal sites continued their roles into the high Middle Ages, but the trading centre was abandoned, never to become part of the later town. If, as has been suggested, it were replaced by occupation near St Clement's church around the end of the tenth century, it may be regarded as an example of the 'shifting site' phenomenon, fairly common in England and on the Continent in the early Middle Ages, whereby a settlement's location, and probably function, changed over time. Archaeological research at Southampton, for instance, indicates that the seventh- to ninth-century site of Hamwic was supplanted in the tenth century by 'New Hampton', a site less than 1km south-west of Hamwic; there was then a final move to the position of medieval and modern Southampton.[71]

At Sandwich, the replacement of the eastern site by one further west may have marked the beginnings of the later medieval town, the history of which is the subject of the following chapters. This suggested sequence of events is the one that best brings together what few pieces of evidence we have for the origins of the town of Sandwich. It is a working hypothesis for the beginnings of the town and port and needs to be tested by future archaeological investigations, both within and, particularly, to the east of the walled town.

3 Sandwich in the eleventh century: the establishment of the medieval town

The most commonly accepted definition of a town was proposed in 1977 by Reynolds, as 'A permanent human settlement . . . [in which] a significant proportion of its population lives off trade, industry, administration and other non-agricultural occupations . . . It forms a social unit more or less distinct from the surrounding countryside.'[1] This will be used here when exploring the evidence for the emergence of Sandwich as a town, while still bearing in mind that more recent work has proposed that 'the impact of [early medieval] towns on the rural population' should be included in any discussion of the origins of urbanism.[2]

By the beginning of the eleventh century there were probably about fifty places in England that may be described as towns. The evidence for Sandwich is insufficient to prove whether or not it was urban before 1000, but as a settlement it probably developed rapidly during the next decades, so that by 1086 it was ranked among the twenty largest towns of England on the basis of the number of its inhabited houses. In Domesday Book it is called *burgum*, suggesting that by that time the settlement was a town in the eyes of the authorities, as it must already have been by the beginning of Edward the Confessor's reign, when a mint was established there. Further confirmation of its perceived urban status can be seen from other features such as the presence of what was essentially a toll station on the waterway through the Wantsum Channel, controlled by Christ Church, Canterbury, and a substantial stone church probably begun *c.*1000. In addition, there must have been a secular population of some size, its economy probably based on sea fishing and trade. The town's dependence on fishing is illustrated by its obligation, as recorded in Domesday Book, to provide Christ Church Priory with 40,000 herrings every year (Section 3.3.1), and implies that Sandwich had a considerable number of fishing boats by then. If this were so, the boats might have cooperated with those from other south-east ports on the annual expeditions to the deep-sea fishing grounds of the North Sea, with a collective action of this kind indicating organisation on the part of all the ports. This may have been the origin of the close contacts between the ports of the south-east coast that manifested itself in Edward the Confessor's decision to demand ship service,[3] and later in the formation of the confederation of the Cinque Ports (Chap. 4.1).

The geographical position of Sandwich continued to play a formative role in its development into a fully urban place. There is evidence for royal fleets using the haven as an assembly point and a refuge, and of the waterways through the Wantsum Channel being regarded as a route from the English Channel to the Thames estuary. Its south bank must have been growing in importance as a harbour for Sandwich's own fishing fleet and probably vessels from elsewhere, and the growth of trade would have been stimulated by the landward access to Sandwich's hinterland along routes that, in the town itself, merged with streets running along the ridge of Thanet Beds down to the waterfront, with its ferry and possibly wharfs. One of the streets (now the High Street) probably also served as a marketplace. All in all, there is no reason to doubt that by the middle of the eleventh century Sandwich was a flourishing urban centre, as suggested by the approximately 400 dwellings and 2,000 inhabitants of Domesday. Although much of the town plan probably derives from then, it is not until the end of the following century that a convincing map can be drawn (Fig. 3.1).

Perhaps the most momentous action in the transformation of early medieval Sandwich from an assemblage of ephemeral features east of the later town to a settlement in a permanent location was the building of St Clement's church in stone.[4] It is here suggested that this happened around the year 1000, before which time there is no sign that there were masonry structures anywhere nearby, other than the Roman villa near Poulders Gardens approximately 1.5km south-west of the later town, which had been abandoned some 600 years earlier. The stone-

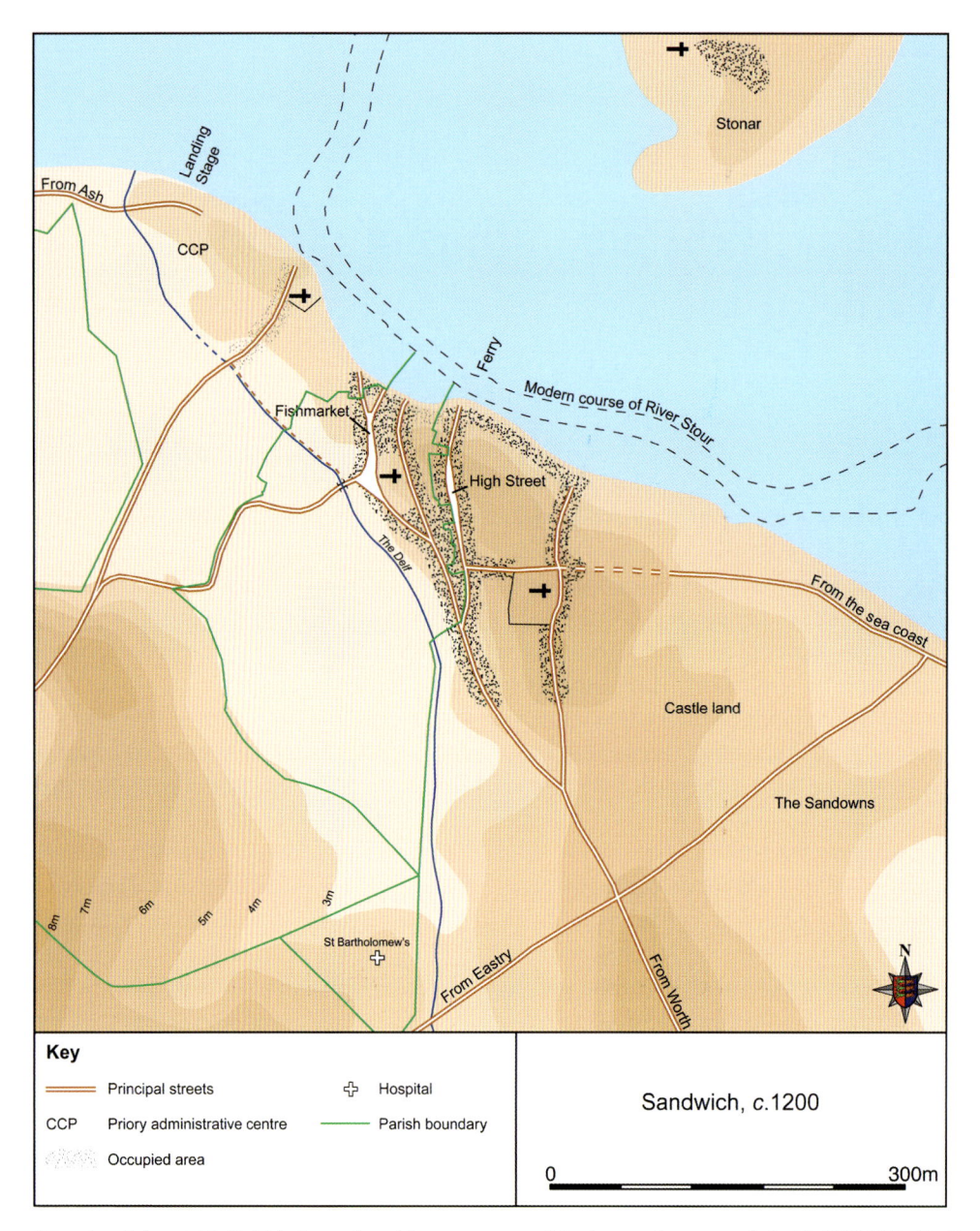

Fig. 3.1: Plan of Sandwich by 1200 (J. H.). Reproduced by permission of Ordnance Survey on behalf of HMSO. © Crown copyright 2009. All rights reserved. Licence number 100046522

built church may have had great significance for the location of Sandwich, for it possibly fixed the nucleus of the town in its formative period. The 'shifting site' phenomenon, common in England and on the Continent during the early Middle Ages, may have come to an end with the movement from the suggested site of the early trading settlement to the area around the new church (Chap. 2.4).

Once this had happened, an urban infrastructure probably had more chance of developing, and the physical layout that evolved became a template for subsequent growth. Streets on the high ground ran to the waterfront, soon probably incorporating two marketplaces along their line. At least two churches served a growing population. The watercourse known as the Delf was probably diverted during the eleventh century to provide a water supply for the whole town, its route defining the southern edge of the built-up area. At this time the inhabited area was largely confined to the dry land of the Thanet Beds. There is no evidence that the low-lying parts of the town were occupied, although some roads ran across them, perhaps on causeways. It seems that deliberate drainage of the lowest land came later (Chaps 5.6.2, 8.4), although the Delf may have had some part in drying out the ground immediately beside it.

3.1 Urban beginnings: Sandwich at the turn of the tenth and eleventh centuries

Apart from two potsherds attributable to the eighth or ninth century and a few more dated AD 950–1050 but found as residual and redeposited material,[5] all evidence for the existence of Sandwich in the early Middle Ages is based on its place name, its topography, and on documents relating to it (Chap. 2.3.2); the inferences drawn from these sources are inevitably speculative.

This is still true of the tenth and early eleventh centuries, although it will be argued here that the first surviving fabric in St Clement's church may date from around 1000. Nonetheless, documents continue to provide most information, although sometimes of a dubious nature. Two apparently tenth-century charters fall into this category. Until recently, scholars writing on the early history of Sandwich used them as evidence for the existence of a tenth-century settlement.[6] One purports to date from c.963, when King Edgar supposedly restored Sandwich to Christ Church, the monastery attached to Canterbury Cathedral; the other from 979, when King Æthelred II reputedly granted to it his lands at Sandwich and Eastry.[7] It seems, however, that the charters were forged by the monks of Christ Church in later centuries, so they should no longer be considered relevant to the growth of early Sandwich.[8]

Late tenth- and early eleventh-century entries in the *Anglo-Saxon Chronicle* suggest that Sandwich was an anchorage at the mouth of the river Stour, used by both English and Scandinavian fleets, as, for example, when King Æthelred II's ships assembled there in 1009.[9] It could also have referred to a landmark at the south-east end of the navigable waterway formed by the Stour and Wantsum through the Wantsum Channel, which was probably the route taken by the ninety-three ships of the fleet commanded in 991 by Olaf Tryggvason (king of Norway 995–9), when they sailed from Folkestone, past Sandwich to East Anglia, and finally into battle at Maldon, Essex.[10]

It is not until the entry for 1014 that there is a hint of a settlement on land; in that year, King Cnut put ashore at Sandwich the hostages whom his father Swein had previously taken.[11] The abandonment of hostages on land does not necessarily argue for the presence of anything other than a landing place where Cnut's shallow-draught vessels could have beached, but the next written reference provides a picture of Sandwich as something more than an anchorage.

In 1015 it is referred to as 'Sanduich . . . the most renowned of all the ports of the English (*qui est omnium Anglorum portuum famosissimus*)'.[12] This is from the *Encomium Emmae Reginae*, written between 1040 and 1042 in praise Queen Emma, wife of Cnut.[13] 'Sanduich' lay on or near the westerly sea route from Jutland, which closely followed the north-west coast of continental Europe until reaching the shortest English Channel crossing, near modern Calais or Dunkirk. On arriving in English waters, any ships sailing to London or further north would have sought out the Wantsum Channel with Sandwich at its south-eastern entrance.

3.2 Evidence for urbanisation in the first half of the eleventh century

During the reign of Edward the Confessor (1042–66) Sandwich Haven was apparently a much-used anchorage for the English fleet. The king was there in person in 1044, 1045, 1049 and possibly 1052, when forty English ships were assembled in the haven to watch for the approach of the rebellious Earl Godwin from his refuge in Bruges.[14] When Edward is said to have 'stayed' in Sandwich he was always there with a naval force, and so, by analogy with later custom, he may have lived on board ship rather than in accommodation on shore, though it is not impossible that the later castle area already contained a royal residence (Fig. 3.2).

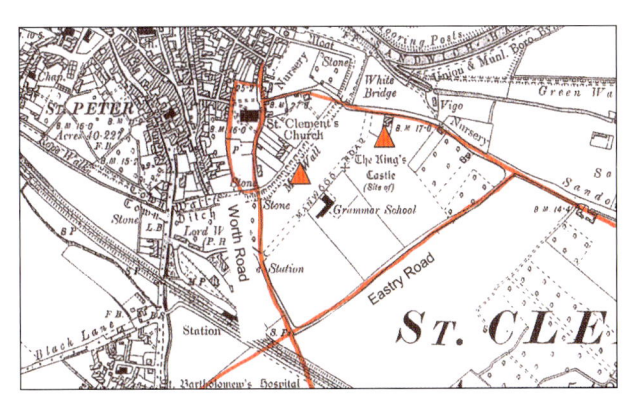

Fig. 3.2: The area east of St Clement's church, probably royal land from the early Middle Ages and later known as Castelmead. Red triangles show Sites 37 and 38 (H. C., based on OS 1:10,560 map of 1877)

None of the documentary sources includes any hint that a church overlooked Sandwich Haven and the Wantsum Channel. But it is likely that it did, and that from at least c.1000 St Clement's formed an important landmark for approaching shipping. By the time of Edward it was certainly an imposing stone-built church in which the king attended Mass.

3.2.1 St Clement's church

Recent work on the church of St Clement has shown that parts of the surviving building were in existence by the mid-eleventh century at the latest.[15] The remains

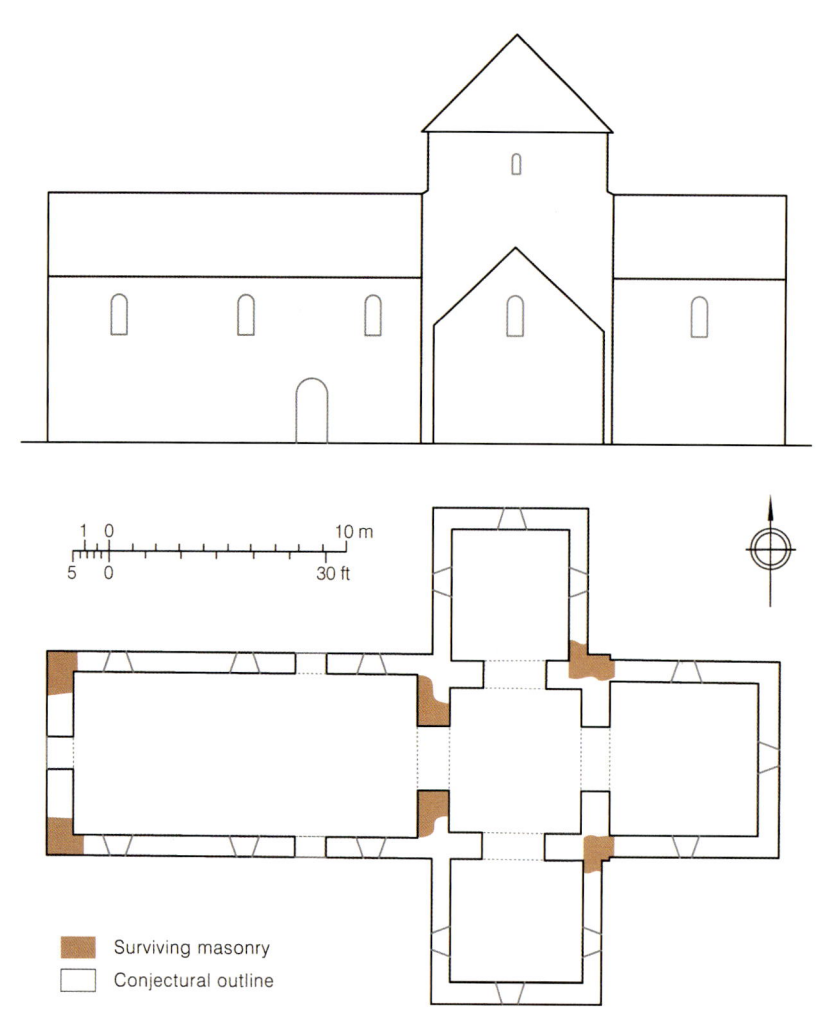

Fig. 3.3: St Clement's church, reconstructed plan and elevation in the eleventh century (H. A. J. & A. T. A.)

suggest a cruciform stone church, with transepts – or more likely porticus – to either side, and a nave as long as the present one.

Evidence of the east walls of former north and south transverse compartments can be seen attached to the crossing piers of the later tower. Although these walls are not quite aligned with each other, both their east faces are recessed from the east side of the twelfth-century tower. In addition, the surviving stubs of the walls of the original chancel before it was rebuilt in the thirteenth century show that the chancel was formerly narrower. These two features together indicate that salient angles protruded at the corners in a manner typical of Anglo-Saxon architecture (Fig. 3.3). The east wall of the southern compartment is visible only at pavement level, but on the north side a short stretch of wall projects to full height with a square string course or platt band of pre-Conquest form at 1.4m above floor level, which is about the right height for a string course below windows. It is probable that the side compartments were Anglo-Saxon porticus that would have been entered from the crossing through small doorways, rather than true transepts separated from the main space by full-height arches. The salient angles occur only on the east side, and were not repeated where the side projections joined the nave on the west; thus the nave must have been wider than the chancel.

The width of the early nave can be seen at the west end of the church, where straight joints at the corners of an originally unaisled nave are visible externally (Fig. 3.4). Each joint is marked by an extremely tall stone at its base (rising to 1.15m above present ground level), with the higher quoins of the early nave walls having been replaced. The two base stones have been identified as Marquise stone, an oolitic limestone quarried near Boulogne. It is found in some Roman and Anglo-Saxon buildings in Kent, and is also well documented as having been imported for use in early Norman buildings in Canterbury.[16]

Finally, the lower parts of the east and west external faces of the twelfth-century tower, which are now visible inside the church, show the creases of earlier

which was probably written down around 1057, soon after the earl's death, is said to have taken place while Leofric was attending Mass in St Clement's, before the party sailed with the fleet.[18] In it, he stood north of the altar, with the king on the south side. In the north-east corner, behind the altar, was a 'triple-threaded hanging', which mostly obscured a large rood behind it. While Mass was being celebrated, Leofric saw a hand above the rood blessing the congregation, and then he was able to see the whole rood and the blessing hand, as if there were no hanging in front.[19]

As Gatch points out, since the wall hanging obscured the cross, which was behind it in the north-east corner, it must have been wider than the altar, which had space behind it, and the fact that there was a north-east corner suggests that the altar lay in front of a square east end rather than an apse. A 'triple-threaded' textile would have been rare and expensive, and it can be inferred from its presence that the church was well endowed. Indeed, the fact that the king heard Mass in St Clement's could be taken to imply that this was the main, or even the only, church of the town.[20] When Gatch published his article, no one had suggested that St Clement's had an Anglo-Saxon core, but Leofric's vision complements the newly discovered evidence for an eleventh-century church.

The church, both as surviving and as described in Leofric's vision, closely resembled the plan of St Mary in Castro at Dover (Fig. 3.6), which is usually now

Fig. 3.4: St Clement's church, west wall, north side, straight joint of unaisled nave, with long Marquise stone at base to left of later buttress (S. P.)

roofs. They cut the outer edges of the Romanesque arches awkwardly (Fig. 3.5), almost certainly because the tower was inserted between the chancel and nave of an earlier church, the roofs of which had to be cut back and reset against the new tower walls.

That there was a sizeable church at St Clement's by the time of the Conquest is suggested by an account of a vision vouchsafed to Earl Leofric of Mercia, who attended Mass there with Edward the Confessor on one of the king's visits to Sandwich, possibly in 1049 or 1052.[17] This is the earliest documentary reference for any of the three churches in Sandwich. The vision,

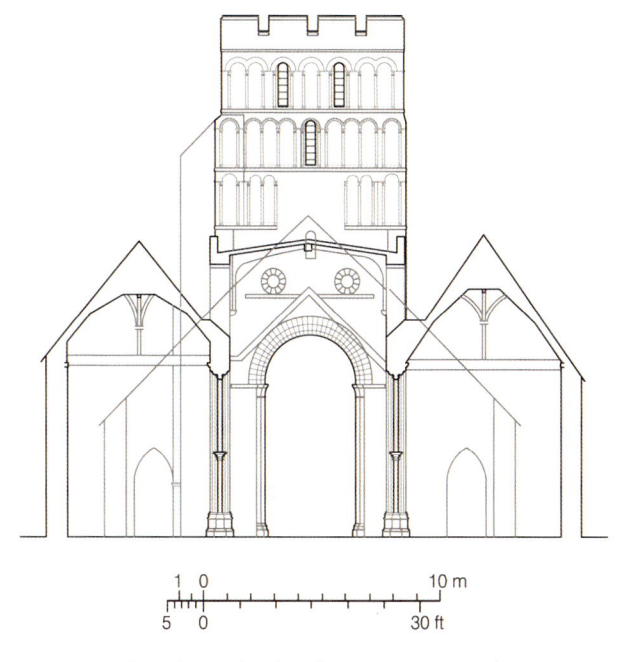

Fig. 3.5: St Clement's church, cross section showing scar of Anglo-Saxon roof line against west face of tower, below thirteenth-century roof line and fifteenth-century roof (H. A. J.)

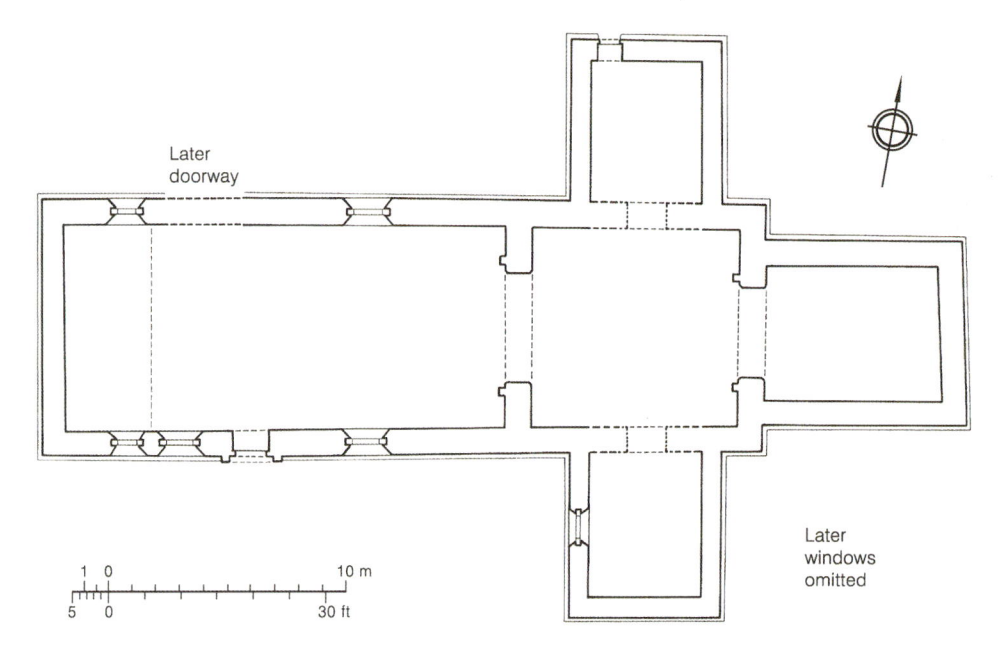

Fig. 3.6: St Mary in Castro, Dover, plan (A. T. A., based on Taylor and Taylor 1965, fig. 94)

Fig. 3.7: St Mary in Castro, Dover, view of nave, tower and porticus (A. Brodie)

dated to the late tenth or early eleventh century,[21] and has a tower over the crossing (Fig. 3.7). Although there is no surviving evidence for such a tower at St Clement's, the church's situation on the highest point of the town and close to the entrance to Sandwich Haven suggests that there may well have been one as an aid to navigation, especially as we know that the towers at Sandwich were used for such a purpose later in the Middle Ages.[22]

It seems likely that the site of the church was carefully chosen for this very purpose. St Clement was the patron saint of mariners, and dedications to him are associated with pre-Conquest churches around the south-east coast, as at Hastings, Old Romney and Rochester.[23] Many St Clement churches in eastern England and also Scandinavia overlook harbours or river crossings,[24] and at Sandwich the church is not only situated near the entrance to the haven, but was also close to the ferry to Stonar and the Isle of Thanet, for which there is early eleventh-century evidence. In addition, most St Clement churches in south-east England are found in places that were of strategic importance for coastal defence or were where Anglo-Saxon and Danish fleets assembled in the eleventh century, as occurred in Sandwich Haven. In Denmark they are also associated with high-status, usually royal, founders,[25] and it may be significant that St Clement's in Sandwich is situated at the apex of the triangular area surrounding the later royal castle (Fig. 3.2).

Although smaller, St Clement's is so similar in plan to St Mary in Castro that there must be a strong possibility that it was built at much the same time and perhaps, as has been suggested for the latter,[26] as a royal foundation during the reign of either Æthelred or Cnut. It has no known association with a royal patron at that date, but both kings had an interest in the highly strategic position of Sandwich. Cnut, however, is not known as a founder of churches other than in

East Anglia, and the 1020s and 1030s are said to have seen a recession in church building in England,[27] so an earlier date may be more likely.

3.2.2 The establishment of a mint

One of the signs of urban status in England in the tenth and eleventh centuries was the presence of a mint. Æthelstan's laws issued at Grateley *c.*926–*c.*930 stated that coins could only be struck in a town (*port, burgum*).[28] In general, larger towns had the most moneyers, with set numbers laid down by law.

Sandwich seems not to have had a mint until *c.*1042. This is indicated by Scandinavian Viking Age silver hoards that contain hundreds of coins from the reigns of Æthelred and Cnut, but no examples minted in Sandwich. Coins were, however, struck at Sandwich for some years during Edward's reign, although none has been discovered in the town itself. Leofwine and Godric were the moneyers there between 1042 and 1050, with most of the surviving coins dating between 1048 and 1050, when Edward was in Sandwich with his fleet.[29] The output was very small in the overall context of Edward's mints, and the Sandwich mint, operating at a very low level, was probably less important than others in south-east England.[30] In eleventh-century Kent, Canterbury had by far the largest mint, followed by Dover and Rochester. That of Dover was first recorded in 928 and remained active throughout the next 150 years. Even the mints at Romney, opened *c.*1000, and Lympne seem to have been more important than Sandwich.[31] Nonetheless, the fact that there was a mint at Sandwich in the 1040s suggests that it was by then distinctly urban in character.

3.2.3 Christ Church Priory and the importance of the waterways

In 1023, according to a charter possibly compiled later in the century but based on a grant by the king, Cnut granted rights in the *hæfene* of Sandwich to Christ Church, Canterbury, for the support of its monks.[32] The rights consisted of a monopoly on tolls charged on vessels travelling along the rivers Wantsum and Stour (the Wantsum Channel) and the income from the ferry across to Thanet, not the lordship of the town itself. Many authorities have published this charter over the years, and its authenticity has been discussed and disputed.[33] The most recent and exhaustive study is by Brooks and Kelly, who believe that the substance of the charter can be taken as genuine, although possibly a late eleventh-century copy of an early eleventh-century original.

Christ Church Priory probably needed a headquarters from which to administer its rights, and may have chosen the site that we know they used later; this lay to the west of the settlement, on the relatively high land to the west of where St Mary's church was established. It is possible that a church already existed, but there is no certain evidence of a stone structure at this date, and the documentary evidence for early occupation on the site is slight (Chap. 2.3.3). On the other hand, St Clement's and its associated secular occupation were almost certainly already present on the ridge approximately 500m to the east.

Cnut's charter is of no help in reconstructing the early town plan, for its only purpose was to specify the monastery's rights, which did not involve anything in the secular settlement. Thus, it mentions no features other than landing places (Latin *exitus*; OE *lændinge*) along both sides of the waterway that Christ Church was to control. It could exact tolls at all the landing places between Pipernæsse (Pepperness, the northern extremity of the Deal Spit in the eleventh century) and Mærcesfleot (Northmouth), where the river Wantsum flowed into the Thames estuary near Reculver.[34]

The area that came under Christ Church's control in 1023 was probably the same as that of the Liberty of Sandwich as described in the custumal of 1301 (Chap. 5.1.3).[35] If this is so, it included not only the rivers Stour and Wantsum and their banks 'as far inland as can be reached by a taper-axe thrown from a boat', but also land south and east of Sandwich that was already, or became, part of St Clement's parish. The same area may also have been the Sandwich Hundred of Domesday Book, the size and location of which suggest that it was carved out of the much larger and earlier lathe of Eastry.

The next significant date in the history of the town was 1037, when another charter records that on his deathbed King Harold Harefoot restored Sandwich to Christ Church after having unlawfully seized it from the hands of the monastery.[36] Although this may be a later forgery, devised by Christ Church to denigrate its great Canterbury rival, St Augustine's Abbey, which owned Stonar, it nevertheless provides us with some details that may relate to the early eleventh-century haven.[37] According to the charter, when Abbot Ælfstan of St Augustine's heard that Harold was to return to Christ Church the rights conferred by Cnut, he claimed that his abbey should retain a third ('the third penny') of the tolls. Failing in that plea, he asked that he should be allowed to built a wharf (OE *hwerf*) opposite Mildrith's field (or acre, OE *gen Mildryþe æker*) 'to protect against the raging [tide]'. This shows that by then wharfs were accepted features along the waterfront, and thus that the 'landing places' of 1023 could well have included man-made structures. In addition, we learn that a wharf could protect a riverbank and vessels from turbulent water, and by inference that the river Stour may have been subject to tidal surges. This implicitly confirms that Sandwich was then much closer to the open sea than it was later, and that the tide flooded in much more violently than it does today. The incoming tide from the English Channel would have had a scouring effect on the south bank of the haven, and thus, if the proposed wharf were intended as a protection against the tide, it is likely to have been against the Sandwich side, not on the other side, and Mildrith's field would have been in Stonar, contrary to previously published opinions, a suggestion that perhaps makes sense in the light of the fact that Mildred's foundation at Minster lay on that side of the river.

When Ælfstan was refused permission to build the wharf, he took a band of men to Ebbsfleet to dig a 'great trench' where ships could 'lie in a channel there, just as they did at Sandwich'. He may have been attempting to divert vessels from heading to Sandwich, where Christ Church would exact tolls, by providing a safe but artificial harbour on the south-east coast of the Isle of Thanet. The reference to a channel at Sandwich may mean that there was an artificial inlet, deliberately dug there to shelter vessels. This, however, may be reading too much into the obscure wording of this section of the charter. The opacity of the language has also led to Ælfstan's 'great trench' being interpreted as a proposed but unachieved precursor of the canal (the Stonar Cut) through the Stonar Bank in 1775.[38] It seems more likely, however, that the trench was intended to be the eleventh-century equivalent of a dock.

3.3 The second half of the eleventh century

3.3.1 Sandwich by the time of Domesday

From the death of Harold Harefoot in 1037 until the compilation of Domesday Book, the lordship of Sandwich was held by several hands, and in a complicated sequence. It reverted to Christ Church through Harold's will, but must soon have passed back to the crown, for Domesday records that Edward the Confessor subsequently returned it to Canterbury. But it may again have changed hands, for in 1072 Archbishop Lanfranc claimed Sandwich as one of the places that had been lost to his church, possibly having been seized by Odo, Bishop of Bayeux and Earl of Kent, very shortly after 1066. Whether Odo ever held the whole of Sandwich is unknown, but he held some houses there until sometime between 1070 and 1083, when he surrendered them to Lanfranc.[39] In 1086 Sandwich paid dues (£50) only to the archbishop, with the record also showing that by then it had developed in both size and economic strength. Its importance to the king is indicated by the fact that men from estates elsewhere in Kent had to be supplied for six days a year to guard the king when he was in Sandwich or Canterbury.[40]

Sandwich's size can be inferred from the main entry, which states that it had contained 307 inhabited dwellings (*mansurae hospitatae*) in the time of Edward the Confessor and that there were 383 by 1086, an increase of seventy-six in little more than twenty years. There may even have been more than the 383, for in a separate entry the archbishop is said to have had in the town thirty-two *mansurae*, which belonged to his manor of Woodnesborough (Gollesberge).[41] In addition, the late eleventh-century survey of St Augustine's lands adds thirty *mansurae* (and an acre of ground with a church) to the total as shown in Domesday Book.[42] It has been suggested that this does not describe the situation in 1086 but a later arrangement between Christ Church Priory and St Augustine's Abbey,[43] so the archbishop's thirty-two and St Augustine's thirty *mansurae* may be considered too questionable to be used in calculating the number of dwellings in Sandwich in 1086. But whether there were 383 or 445 in total, a substantial quantity of households that were too impoverished to pay royal dues should probably be added,[44] and a population in the region of 2,000 is unlikely to be an over-estimate.[45]

These numbers imply that Sandwich was second only to Canterbury in size among the towns of Kent, although it is likely to have been smaller than Dover. Dover's size cannot be estimated from its entries in Domesday Book, but since it had a flourishing mint from as early as 928 and a well-established harbour with a tide mill, it was probably an important town before Sandwich acquired an urban role. Nevertheless, Canterbury and Dover excepted, in 1086 Sandwich was bigger than other towns in Kent, with Hythe having about 1,000 inhabitants, Romney about 800, Rochester not many more than 500 and Fordwich about 400.[46] The size of the population means that Sandwich ranked among the top twenty towns in England.[47]

Domesday Book may also illustrate Sandwich's increase in prosperity in the decades before 1086. While it was in the hands of Edward the Confessor, Sandwich paid £15 a year to the king. There is no information for 1066 when its dues went to Canterbury, but by *c*.1080, after Lanfranc had regained control from Odo, the town's obligation to the monks of Christ Church had become as much as £40 and

40,000 herrings annually, and by 1086 the render to the church had risen to £50, although the number of herrings remained the same. The late eleventh-century Domesday Monachorum records a further increase to £70 (although still 40,000 herrings).[48] The figures may indicate the growing prosperity of the place, but they may also be evidence that the church was demanding more as time went on.[49] It is impossible to be sure how the town met the financial demands made upon it, but the herrings that it paid in kind suggest the primacy of fishing in the economy. Moreover, the imposition of ship service implies that seafaring was a common occupation among the townsmen.

Sandwich's ship service to the king was the same as that owed by Dover (*reddit simile servitium regi sicut Dovere*);[50] that is, twenty ships, each with twenty-one men for fifteen days annually.[51] At Dover the service was rendered in return for being able to keep the profits of justice in the town. If, as the text suggests, Sandwich also received this right, it implies that the town was important enough to negotiate with the royal officials and that its inhabitants were sufficiently organised to act collectively on their own behalf.[52]

Hythe and Romney, much smaller settlements than either Dover or Sandwich, were also expected to provide vessels and men, although fewer than was the case in the two larger ports.[53] These obligations have traditionally been taken as the first reference to a confederation that was later to become formalised under the name Cinque Ports, though there is no real evidence of it until the next century (Chap. 4.1).

3.3.2 *The churches of St Peter and St Mary*

Although Domesday Book does not refer to churches in Sandwich, Domesday Monachorum mentions an unnamed church. Both St Clement's and St Mary's would have been in the patronage of the archbishop at that time (being transferred to the archdeacon of Canterbury at a later but unknown date), and each of them has been suggested as that unnamed church.[54] St Clement's is the more likely since it was certainly in existence by that time. A second unnamed church, recorded in the late eleventh-century survey of the lands of St Augustine's Abbey,[55] must have been St Peter's since the abbey held the advowson later in the Middle Ages, and it was also mentioned by name in the eleventh-century list of churches attached to the abbey.[56] There is some uncertainty as to when St Augustine's acquired its Sandwich property.[57] It may have come into the possession of the abbey only after the Conquest, but since some features in St Peter's church suggest a pre-Conquest (or at least pre-Domesday) date, it is possible that it was in existence and belonged to St Augustine's

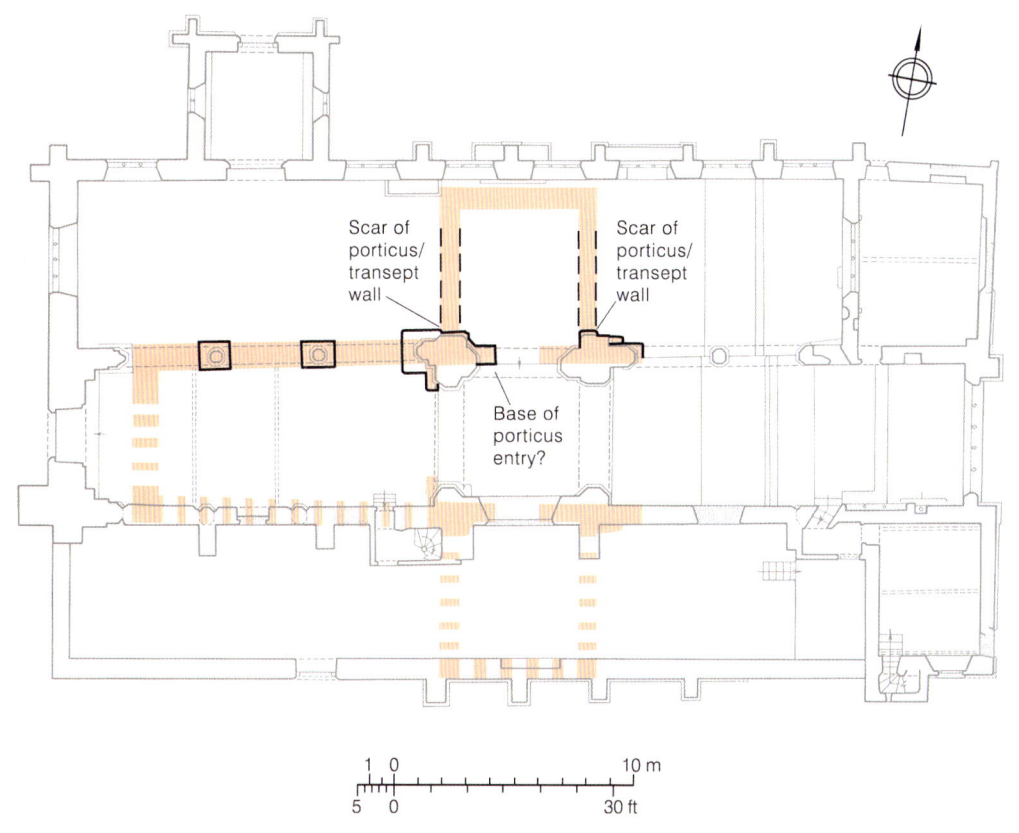

Fig. 3.8: St Peter's church, plan, as existing, showing evidence for porticus or transepts (S. P. & A. T. A.)

during the rivalry over the rights in the town in 1037. By the mid- to late eleventh century the church of St Peter was in existence.

As the plan shows (Fig. 3.8), the thirteenth-century tower piers at St Peter's are exceptionally large and asymmetrical, indicating that there was an earlier tower whose piers were reused and enveloped by the thirteenth-century masonry. It is also clear from stub walls to the north of the two north piers that there was once a transept. A projecting low slab visible below the base of the north-west pier, with a simple chamfered plinth round its north and east faces, may be the remnant of an east–west wall between the two piers with a narrow opening in the centre, implying a porticus rather than a transept proper at one time (Fig. 3.9), while further remains at the base of the north-east pier could indicate a salient angle between the transept or porticus and the chancel. Although very fragmentary, these traces suggest that St Peter's may have been an eleventh-century stone church with a crossing somewhat similar to that postulated for St Clement's.[58] No comparable evidence survives on the south side of the crossing, which was severely damaged and then rebuilt after the tower collapsed in 1661, nor is there anything as early as this elsewhere in the building. The form of the eastern and western arms is unknown, although the road layout discussed below suggests that the nave may originally have been shorter than it is now.

No evidence for early or mid-eleventh-century work has been discovered at St Mary's church, although the presence of Quarr stone reused in the walls at the east end in the later Middle Ages makes a late eleventh-century date possible. Quarr stone was employed in building churches in east Kent in the late eleventh and very early twelfth centuries,[59] so its occurrence in St Mary's could mean that a stone church was erected here before the surviving mid-twelfth-century building. The only other sign that there might have been an earlier church or chapel at this end of town is supplied by the direction of the road from Woodnesborough (Section 3.4.2; Fig. 3.1), which appears to lead to the church. Apart from this, the known evidence suggests that St Mary's may have been the latest of the three churches to be built in Sandwich.

3.3.3 The formation of the parishes and the presence of churchyards

None of the three Sandwich parishes is large, but they vary considerably in area (Fig. 3.10). By the late eighteenth century, when their boundaries were marked, and the nineteenth, when they were mapped, St Clement's, encompassing 535 acres (216.5ha),[60] was by far the largest of the three. It stretched out beyond the later town walls to take in a considerable spread of rural land, its southern boundary largely coterminous with the boundary of the hundred and of the Liberty as walked by Stephen de Pencestre in the 1290s (Chap. 5.1.3). St Mary's is the second largest parish (125 acres, 50.5ha), and also stretches beyond the town boundaries to take in marshland to the north and farmland to the south, both reclaimed sometime in the Middle Ages. Meanwhile, St Peter's, with only 40 acres (16.2ha), is almost confined within the later town ramparts, only a small portion stretching beyond them to the south, where it touches the north point of the 6 acres (2.4ha) of extra-parochial land forming the home estate of St Bartholomew's hospital (1190 and later), which was probably created in the south-east corner of St Mary's parish where it had previously stretched eastwards to a boundary line on the Delf.[61]

The origins of parishes in a number of towns have been studied, and different proposals put forward for their formation.[62] Among them is the suggestion, based on work at Nottingham, that urban parishes with large amounts of rural land were often created at an early date, whereas small and entirely urban ones are likely to be later, carved out of existing parishes.[63] This proposition seems to apply in the case of Sandwich. St Peter's parish, running south from a very narrow frontage on the water, cuts the other two parishes off from each other. The arrangement implies that it was a late insertion, probably resulting from the acquisition of land in the centre of town by St Augustine's Abbey, which, it has been suggested above, occurred in the mid- to late eleventh century. This accords with the currently accepted opinion that new urban parishes usually date

Fig. 3.9: St Peter's church, pier base at north-west corner of tower, seen from north, suggesting porticus entry (P. W. © English Heritage DP032236)

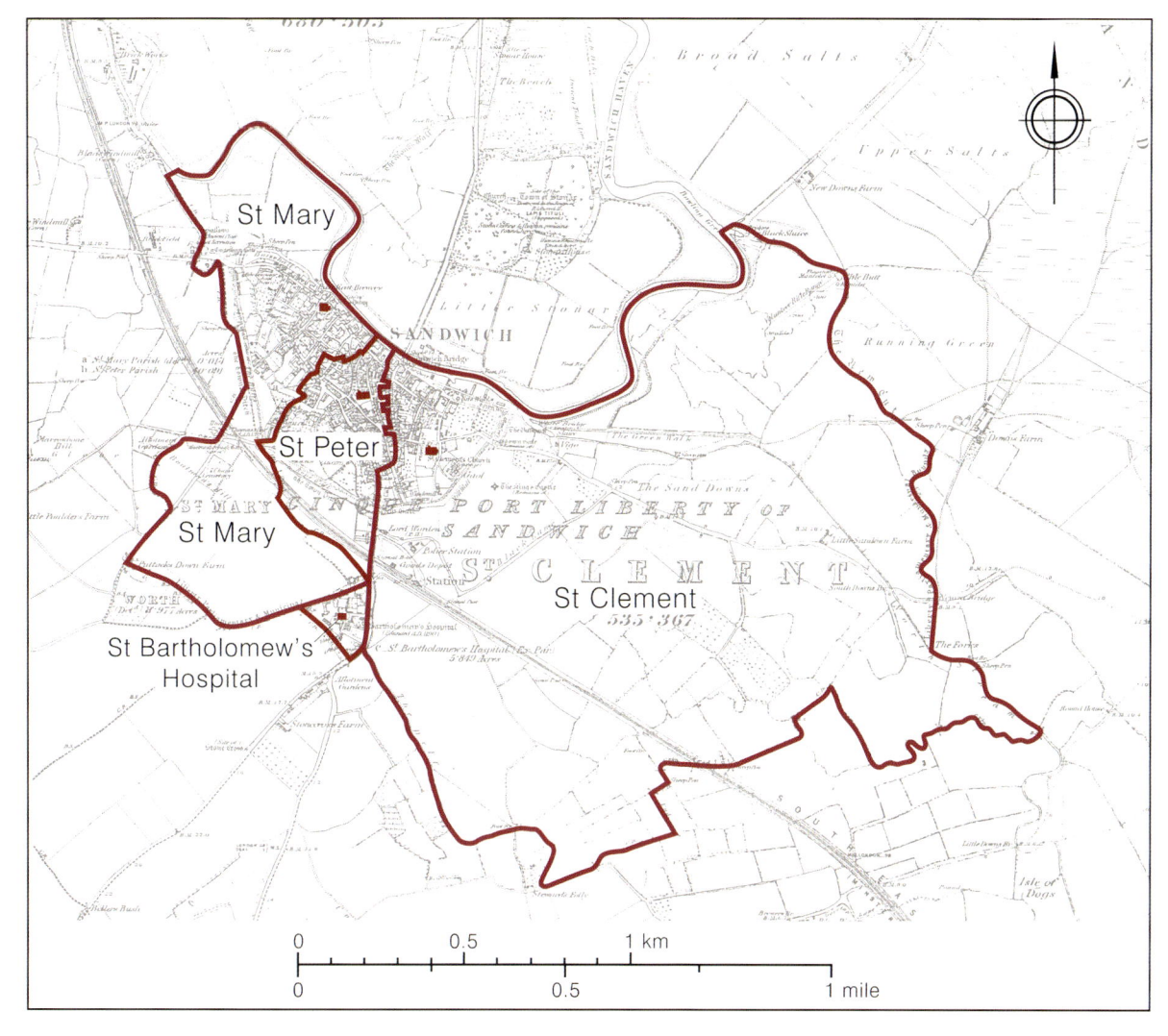

Fig. 3.10: Plan of Sandwich parishes (A. T. A., based on OS 1:10,560 map of 1877)

from the late eleventh century or the first half of the twelfth, their establishment becoming increasingly rare by the second half of the twelfth century.[64]

St Peter's parish may have been inserted between the two existing parishes of St Clement's and St Mary's, but the absence of definite evidence for a pre-Conquest church at St Mary's and the small size of that parish in comparison with St Clement's make another interpretation possible. There may initially have been a single church in the town (St Clement's) held by the archbishop and serving the whole community. When this arrangement was disrupted by the building of St Peter's on St Augustine's land and the creation of parishes, the west end of town would have been cut off from St Clement's, so that three parishes were required rather than two. This could have been the moment when a late eleventh-century church dedicated to St Mary was built using Quarr stone. If this is so, Sandwich might not have acquired three parishes until the end of the eleventh century. The details of the parish boundaries and further evidence for their date are discussed in the topographical section below.

There is no contemporary evidence for the cemeteries of the three churches. Today, St Clement's is by far the largest, measuring just over 1.5 acres (0.6ha), including the church, although since the churchyard was extended in 1349, 'the great plague having filled the old cemetery', it may now be larger than it originally was.[65] St Peter's, again including the church, measures just under three-quarters of an acre (0.3ha), although this was not its original size. It was deemed too small in 1776, when 12.75 perches (0.08 acres, 0.03ha) were acquired from the town.[66] During the later Middle Ages, when the parish was probably the most densely populated of the three, it is likely that heavy demands were made on a charnel house, for which there is late medieval evidence. St Mary's churchyard is the smallest of all, measuring under a quarter of an acre (1,000m²) including the church, although it has almost certainly lost ground for the construction, and later widening, of Strand Street.

It is by no means certain that all three churches had graveyards from the beginning, although it is likely that there would have been one in the town from the start. It is difficult to date when burial in designated cemeteries, usually attached to minsters or mother churches, was replaced by interment in parochial precincts. In Sandwich, the sheer size of St Clement's churchyard in comparison with the other two suggests that it may have been an early foundation intended for use by the entire community, with the other graveyards being established later when space was already limited.

3.4 The topographical development of Sandwich in the eleventh century (Figs 1.2, 3.1 and endpapers)

3.4.1 The waterfront

The haven was highly significant for the physical development of the town in the hundred years after 1000. Between the town and the Deal Spit, there was an area of usually calm water that could serve as an anchorage for the shallow draft vessels that were standard in north-western Europe for several hundred years before *c*.1200. They could assemble there as royal fleets, seek refuge from the English Channel and North Sea, approach Sandwich itself with trading goods, or enter the Wantsum Channel along the river Stour. The south bank of the Stour opposite Stonar was the waterfront and harbour area of the port. In medieval documents the stretch of river fronting on the inhabited area was usually called the haven, so it is often difficult to be certain whether the records are referring to the immediate harbour or the anchorage further east, which in this publication is referred to as Sandwich Haven (Chap. 2.2.2.1). In the absence of archaeological evidence, documents must be used as the sole source for the eleventh-century waterfront, and even so there is little evidence for its appearance or even its position before the fourteenth century. The line suggested on Figure 3.1 is largely based on the contour map.

There may have been some man-made features along the south bank of the Stour by the early eleventh century. The 'landing places' of the 1023 charter seem to have been present along the rivers Wantsum and Stour and not just on the Sandwich waterfront of the time. They may have been built as revetments such as have been found by excavation in London,[67] but it is equally, if not more, likely that they were hard standings, perhaps formed by wattle mats laid out along the foreshore; such features have been discovered under the tenth-century boat found in the Graveney Marshes between Faversham and Whitstable in north Kent, in eleventh-century London and, more recently, in a pre-Conquest context on the Ipswich waterfront.[68]

The first time that a wharf at Sandwich itself is specifically mentioned is in 1037, when Abbot Ælfstan applied for permission to build one on the south bank of the river, opposite Mildrith's field in Stonar. Another statement in the same document can be interpreted as referring to an artificial channel at Sandwich in which ships could anchor or tie up safely; this must have been describing a man-made feature, perhaps some sort of revetment against the bank designed to provide berthing facilities. Thus, even though Ælfstan's wharf was not built, by the early decades of the eleventh century the harbour at Sandwich seems already to have been provided with at least one waterside feature.

There may already have been a jetty or other installation further east along the riverbank where, by 1023, there was a ferry boat, controlled by Christ Church. It connected Sandwich and Stonar, serving the traffic between mainland Kent and the Isle of Thanet. It seems most likely that it was located at or near the end of the High Street, where there was a well-documented ferry later in the Middle Ages. By that time the ferry boat set off from the Town Quay beside Davis Gate, where the High Street met the riverbank at approximately +3.5m OD, and the topography implies that it was in the same place as its predecessor. The fact that the monastery site at the west end of town and the ferry were so far apart from each other, with no sign of direct land access between them before Strand Street came into being in the fourteenth century, suggests that until then there was probably a footpath or track along the bank, as is thought to have been the case for the stretch of waterfront north of present Upper Strand Street (see below).

3.4.2 The street pattern and marketplaces

Although it is very difficult to date the origin of Sandwich's street system, its main outlines probably became fixed by the middle of the eleventh century to accommodate the number of dwellings recorded in Domesday Book. The overall plan has every appearance of being dependent on the natural topography underlying the inhabited area (Chap. 2.1).

The streets on the Thanet Beds ridge suggest that the road from Worth was a dominant influence, probably losing its pre-eminence only when the town ramparts were built across it after the thirteenth century (Chap. 5.6.2; Fig. III.1). About 400m south-east of St

Clement's church, the Worth road crossed the early medieval route from Eastry (Fig. 2.1), which could still have been the route to the south-west, as it seems to have been in earlier centuries. A little north of that crossing the road from Worth probably forked, one branch running past the east end of St Clement's church (present Knightrider Street) to the river Stour. The second, western, branch probably followed the line of present Mill Wall Place and then forked again, one street heading towards the haven and the ferry through what is now the High Street, and the other, Love Lane, running past the east end of St Peter's church. For most of their length these three streets lie above the 4m contour but the final street on the Thanet Beds, leading to the Fishmarket west of St Peter's church, is on lower-lying land and is unlikely to have been laid out before St Peter's church was established sometime during the eleventh century. Figures 3.1 and 4.11 show that the route of this street is different from the layout today, as it then curved to follow the contours in a manner that is no longer the case. The change almost certainly occurred in the twelfth century when the west end of St Peter's church was extended (Chap. 4.5), diverting the southern end of the Fishmarket which eventually became a street in its own right, known in the Middle Ages as Luckboat. In due course, Luckboat and the High Street, became the two main streets out of town, merging to form the Worth road.

The suggested development of the street system is reinforced by archaeological evidence from an excavation on the west side of Love Lane, at the rear of 10 Market Street (Site 20, on Thanet Beds). There is no evidence for a building on the site before the twelfth century (Chap. 4.5; Figs 4.11, 4.12) but pottery attributed to AD 950–1050 was discovered as residual material in later medieval layers. The sherds suggest that the street may have been in position by the tenth or early eleventh century and when laid out it was a main street, only becoming a back lane once the Fishmarket had been established.[69]

Two of the streets on the Thanet Beds may have incorporated early marketplaces. Although there are no market charters for Sandwich and the first reference to a market dates only from 1127,[70] the size and importance of the town at the time of Domesday imply that there must have been at least one by then. This was probably in the High Street, the route connecting the hinterland with the ferry, where the slightly spindle shape is typical of a certain form of early marketplace (Chap. 4.5).[71] The second market may have come into being by the second half of the eleventh century, when the Fishmarket had been established. The above-average width of that street indicates that a marketplace was in existence by the time the plots to either side of it were laid out. Today, St Peter's church stands on the edge of, but slightly set back from, present Market Street with its west end somewhat awkwardly aligned to it (map on endpaper). If the Fishmarket originally curved into Luckboat (Fig. 4.11), the church in the eleventh century was not only shorter but also would have been sited at right angles to the marketplace, in a classic position for many town-centre churches.[72] There is no evidence at this time for The Butchery and Cok Lane, which run north from the Fishmarket, although by the next century they connected it with the riverbank. It is possible that the Fishmarket originally extended right to the water's edge, with the two streets developing only when it contracted slightly, to much its present size (Chap. 4.5).

An east–west street connecting St Clement's church to the High Street may originally have carried traffic from Knightrider Street to the High Street and then cut across to Luckboat, which led to the south end of the Fishmarket. In the easterly direction the present Church Street St Clement traverses the churchyard as a footpath before joining Sandown Road, which came into the town from the east, probably along the western edge of the Deal Spit and the south bank of the river Stour. It was a well-used track by the thirteenth century, and it may have defined the northern side of the royal land (Chap. 2.2.1). Where present Sandown Road runs through Mill Wall, the site of Sandown Gate, a distinct change in its alignment suggests that before the rampart and the gate were built the road ran directly towards the east end of St Clement's church. The modification presumably dates from sometime after the thirteenth century, before which time there was no barrier between the church and the castle (Chap. 5.6.1). There is no evidence until the thirteenth or fourteenth century for a waterside street where Upper Strand Street now runs. This suggests that until then the riverbank was reached by streets running from the slightly higher ground to its south, with a possible footpath or track along the bank, as suggested above for the western stretch of the waterfront between the Christ Church property and the ferry. No evidence of either has yet been discovered.

The map shows an absence of inhabited streets in the southern and western parts of the town, where, even as late as *c.*1200, the ground was too wet to be suitable for occupation until drained. Those areas were almost certainly crossed by roads leading into the town from outside. The proposed early medieval causeway from Ash (Chap. 2.2.1) probably reached as far as the land where Christ Church founded its headquarters, but there is no evidence that it continued eastwards from there. By the late eleventh century St Mary's church may have stood east of the Christ Church site in an apparently isolated position. Access to it and the riverbank immediately north of it was probably from the south, along the Woodnesborough road, which had led to the Sandwich area since the Romano-British period. The road divided south of the town, and the western branch can be traced through a field boundary that now ends at the medieval town wall but the line of which continues along present Loop Street. The hedge line also forms part of the boundary between St Mary and Woodnesborough parishes. Sherds of Andenne ware (1125–75) recovered from a watching brief give a *terminus ante quem* for Loop Street, which seems to have been permanently inhabited in part by the early twelfth century (Site 68).[73] The presence of approximately 8m of water-deposited silts overlying peat found at a site further south in the street (Site 17) reinforces the uninhabitable nature of the area until drained and underlines the likelihood of the route running on a causeway.[74] Present Loop Street and Church Street St Mary's perpetuate the line of a branch that headed northwards towards the water (Fig. 3.11).[75]

At the point where the northern route branched off, Woodnesborough Road now continues eastwards into town as Moat Sole. This branch has the appearance of an addition, created to provide access to the eastern settlement across boggy land. It probably led to a bridge across the Delf, first mentioned in the middle of the twelfth century.[76] The precise site of the bridge is unknown, but it is likely to have stood near the southern end of the Fishmarket, access to it forming the main reason for the awkward westward curve of the marketplace (Fig. 4.11). The route from Woodnesborough must always have been important as a connection between the river Stour and the hinterland. Its early medieval significance is supported by the statement in Domesday Book that thirty-two of Sandwich's 'inhabited dwellings' belonged to the manor of Woodnesborough (Section 3.3.1). Archaeological deposits of early thirteenth-century date are the earliest evidence for any form of occupation near Moat Sole, with little indication of occupation there at any time in the Middle Ages other than near the street frontage (Site 28).

3.4.3 The Delf

The Delf, a canalised watercourse that provided Sandwich with most of its fresh water until the late nineteenth century, is first mentioned a document dated 1152–67, by which time it was clearly an accepted landmark and boundary in the town and therefore may have been of much earlier origin.[77] It differs from most other known medieval water systems

Fig. 3.11: Aerial view showing line of route to St Mary's church (D. Grady © English Heritage 24064/05)

in that it was always an open stream, neither conducted through pipes nor concealed in a conduit.[78] In later centuries, documentary references to its maintenance and repair abound, but there is frustratingly little evidence for its earliest phase, apart from the single twelfth-century mention noted above.

The source of the Delf is a group of springs south of Sandwich, in the parishes of Northbourne and Eastry on the fringes of the Lydden Valley.[79] Sometime, probably in the early Middle Ages, the waters from these springs were diverted to flow towards the Lydden Valley along the South Stream and North Stream, which then merged to go through Roaring Gutter as a single watercourse – the North Stream (Fig. 3.12). On emerging from Roaring Gutter, the main stream flowed northwards to join the haven east of Sandwich, where its estuary was called the Guestling in the Middle Ages (Chap. 5.6.2), but a branch was diverted north-westwards towards Sandwich itself along the man-made Pinnock Wall (a canal rather than a wall).[80] The northerly flowing waterway is still called the North Stream and basically follows its medieval course, although it has undergone various modifications. The branch channelled off to the west was called the Delf by the twelfth century, as it still is today.[81]

The diversion of the North Stream to form the Delf may have been largely intended to drain the Lydden Valley in the early Middle Ages, as happened in Romney Marsh, another Kentish wetland, from possibly the ninth century.[82] No records survive to tell us who was responsible for the diversion, or when it took place, but the stretch that serves as the boundaries of St Clement's parish, the hundred and the medieval Liberty of Sandwich is likely to be of great antiquity, perhaps dating from the early eleventh century, when it may have formed the south-east extremity of the area that Cnut granted to Christ Church (Fig. 5.4).

The stretch through Sandwich to the Stour may have been dug at the same time as the initial diversion along the Pinnock Wall, and was certainly a named feature of the town by the middle of the twelfth century. It must have involved considerable engineering works, including the digging out of its bed to improve the flow through low-lying ground and to counteract the slight changes in contours (Fig. 1.3).[83] Its course is shown on Figure 1.4. The body responsible for this major project remains unknown.

The surviving documentary sources for medieval water systems in England suggest that before the thirteenth century they were enterprises carried out almost exclusively by religious houses or at the command of royalty.[84] This conclusion may well be skewed by the types of documents that have been preserved, for by the thirteenth century there is evidence that civic authorities in cities such as London were organising and financing water supplies for their inhabitants.[85] Civic bodies may have been responsible at a much earlier period; at Norwich, for instance, the Great Cockey stream was diverted to provide a source of drinking water, perhaps even as early as the tenth century. It also had another purpose in that it constituted the west boundary of Norwich before the Norman Conquest.[86]

Nevertheless, it may be that the urban stretch of the Delf at Sandwich and its diversion from its source were instigated by Christ Church Priory. The priory head-quarters were served by water from the Delf, which may have been diverted for that purpose, and it may be no coincidence that the first reference to the Delf is in a Canterbury Cathedral Priory document dating from the time of Prior Wibert. He was responsible for the highly elaborate water system in the Canterbury Cathedral claustral buildings, suggesting that Canterbury had sophisticated water engineers by that period.[87] The town clearly had an interest in the Delf, since the civic authorities were responsible for its maintenance by c.1300 and it probably formed the southern boundary of Sandwich's inhabited area until its ramparts were built in the later Middle Ages (Chap. 5.6.2). But if the Delf's origins date from the early eleventh century, it is doubtful whether the town would by then have been capable of organising such a project.

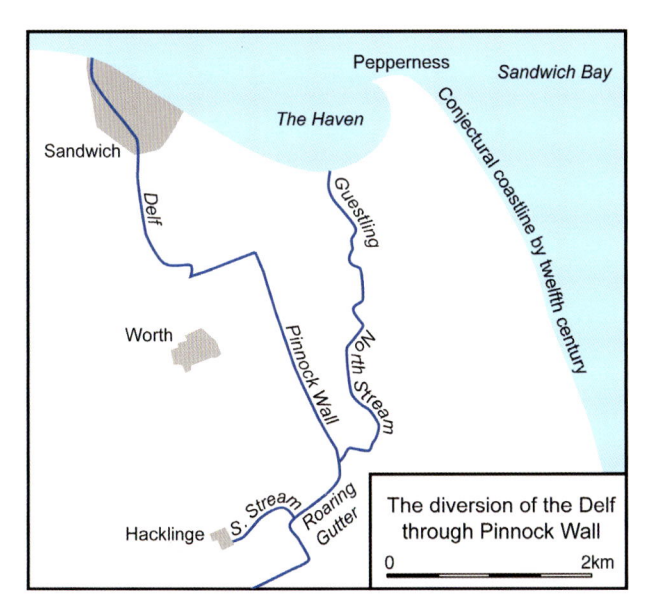

Fig. 3.12: The North Stream through the Lydden Valley, with the Delf flowing along the Pinnock Wall (J. H.)

3.4.4 The implications of the parish boundaries for urban development

It has already been argued that a single church, St Clement, was probably in existence before the Conquest, and that it may have served the whole town, possibly forming a single parish coterminous with the hundred. The division of this area into three parishes provides important evidence, in the form of their boundaries as marked on the first edition of the Ordnance Survey map, for the chronology and development of the urban area (Fig. 3.10 and endpapers). To the north, the east and west boundaries of St Peter's parish run in a straight north–south line from south of Strand Street to the haven, a good indication that the waterfront was moved northwards only after the parishes had been created. Further south, the division between St Peter's and St Clement's parishes lies, for much of its length, along the west side of the High Street. From Strand Street to Church Street St Clement the boundary defines the High Street properties, sometimes running behind them, sometimes along the street frontage in a complex line, suggesting that the boundary was negotiated after the tenements were established. But from Church Street St Clement southwards the character of the boundary changes to run in a single curve along the west side of the High Street to Galliard Street, where it occupies the middle of the thoroughfare. When it reaches New Street it turns south along the centre of the street, beside the western edge of the Delf, which continues to form the parish boundary outside the later gate (New Gate).

The boundary between St Peter's and St Mary's parishes is slightly less revealing. A complex and negotiated boundary can be identified from Strand Street westwards to modern Harnet Street. But once it turns south it runs in broad sweeps with only a few kinks, as if between fields or marshes with occasional obstacles such as a barn, rather than around tightly built-up tenements.[88] When it joins Moat Sole it runs down the west side of the street towards the boundary of Woodnesborough parish, before curving east towards St Bartholomew's hospital.

The pattern of the boundaries suggests that only the northern part of the town was densely settled when the parishes were formed. The complicated division between St Peter's and St Clement's implies that St Clement's was the dominant negotiator at the time since it obtained most of the property along the High Street. The south end of the High Street (now The Chain), Galliard Street and New Street are unlikely to have been built up by then, and Galliard Street and New Street, which were divided equally between the two parishes, may not have existed at all. In addition, a stretch of the parish boundary runs alongside the Delf, so the watercourse was already in existence when the parishes were being formalised.

From these details it seems likely that the town was divided into three parishes while the northern part of the town was still in the process of development and when the Delf formed its southern boundary. It has been proposed above that the Delf already formed a source of water and an urban boundary before its first documentary mention, and may have come into existence in the early eleventh century. But the division into three parishes is unlikely to have occurred until after St Augustine's gained a foothold in the town in the mid- or late eleventh century. The details of the parish boundaries in Sandwich, and the fact that the town already had approximately 400 dwellings by the end of the eleventh century, suggest that the present arrangement of the parishes came into being during the second half of the eleventh century, before the street patterns of the western and southern parts of the town were finalised and all the properties apportioned.

3.5 Conclusion

During the eleventh century Sandwich developed into a town with recognisable urban characteristics such as a street pattern and churches and churchyards, aspects of which can still be seen today. Less tangible features also began to take shape, including the urban administration and economy. Although both Christ Church and the king at different times collected the tolls charged on vessels visiting the port or travelling through the Wantsum Channel, the inhabitants of the town seem to have been able to exert some control over their own lives and their finances. There are implications in Domesday Book that the people of Sandwich felt confident enough to negotiate with royal officials and that they had a bargaining counter in the form of their deep-sea fishing fleet, which could combine with the others on the south-east coast to make up a formidable force, acknowledged by the king in his demand for ship service.

Sandwich's strategic position, which enabled it to control a huge natural harbour, was probably the main reason why it was favoured by the crown and the church. The former maintained land on the eastern side of the town, ideally situated to overlook Sandwich Haven and the vessels anchored there or approaching from the sea. St Clement's church, standing on its highest part, could have acted as a landmark, but also perhaps less prosaically as a status symbol, as its tower almost certainly was in the twelfth century. Christ Church held what seems to have been a less prominent position at the west side of the town. It must have looked predominantly westwards, not towards the anchorage and the sea but over the rivers Stour and Wantsum, along which vessels bound for Canterbury and London sailed. The town itself grew up between these two presences, its rapid growth to a settlement of about 2,000 people indicating its successful development in less than a hundred years.

4 Sandwich in the twelfth century: the growth of an urban society

The twelfth century is generally thought to have been a period of urban growth and consolidation across Europe, with old towns expanding and new towns founded. In some well-established places the central focus of the town shifted from its pre-Conquest position to a new one, perhaps because a new religious foundation attracted development, or because a new marketplace was created. During this century many English towns secured charters from the king giving them varying measures of self-government, and more evidence emerges about the ways they organised their collective affairs, and about economic activity in the form of markets.

Although there is no direct evidence for its size or importance, Sandwich may have remained in the third tier of towns in the country, as it had in the previous century (Chap. 3.3.1), which would still place it among the top twenty towns in England. It was perhaps also during this century that the area around St Peter's became fully established as the urban centre, marginalising the earlier developments to east and west. As before, the importance of Sandwich to the crown and the mercantile community was vested in its strategic location on the south bank of the river Stour and in its harbour facilities. While tantalisingly little is known about individuals and occupations at this time, documentary sources provide a few insights into the government of the town and its developing economic activity, including its role in the evolving confederation of ports round the south-east coast. Archaeological and topographical evidence for urban settlement and growth begins to increase our understanding of the street pattern (Fig. 3.1), and produces the first evidence for domestic buildings. But the most prominent surviving remains are the parish churches. These are examined in detail since they provide the best surviving evidence for the state of Sandwich during the twelfth century, and for the differences between the three parishes in their inhabitants and activities.

4.1 The developing town

Cnut's charter of 1023 enabled Christ Church Priory to exert economic influence over the port and town through exacting tolls on shipping passing through Sandwich Haven and controlling the ferry across the Stour to Stonar. This led to friction with St Augustine's Abbey, the other Canterbury religious house that had interests in Sandwich and Stonar, as exemplified by a lawsuit between the two houses in 1127, which was settled in favour of the priory by a jury consisting of men from Dover and the *provincia* of Sandwich, as well as men from the town.[1]

By the mid-1150s the men of Sandwich had petitioned Henry II for a charter confirming the customs and rights that they had had during the reign of Henry I: the right to pay no penalties over £10 and to plead only where they were accustomed. The wording of similar charters granted by Henry II to the other south-eastern ports, as well as to some towns elsewhere, implies that the rights were already in place, so that there was no need to reiterate the privileges and duties in detail. But, perhaps because of the intermediate control exercised by Christ Church Priory, Sandwich did not receive the coveted fee farm, the right to pay fixed annual dues directly to the Exchequer.[2] The financial importance of Sandwich to the king is underlined in the late twelfth century when the town and the Exchequer argued about lastage (a toll on trade). The Exchequer maintained that lastage should be regarded as additional to the annual tax paid by the town and that it should be paid to the royal house. The misunderstanding may have arisen because the lastage had previously been paid to Christ Church Priory. By 1165, however, the king was demanding £10 a year.[3] The Sandwich charter included nearby Sarre,[4] and the linking of the two names is significant, for by the thirteenth century Sarre was one of Sandwich's dependent ports, otherwise known as Cinque Port limbs. The term Cinque Ports, defining the loose confederation of ports on the south-east coast, is known from 1161, although the first charter granting them common liberties was issued only in 1260.[5] Each port acquired limbs in the thirteenth century, but the mid-twelfth-century grant to these two together suggests that they were already associated, with Sarre perhaps dependent on Sandwich as its head port. The privileges that the barons or freemen of the Cinque Ports enjoyed in 1189 (before which date there is no record) included the right to bear the canopy over the king at the time of his coronation.[6] The privilege may indicate the reliance of the king on the ports for naval service in the Channel during wars in France.

Sandwich had a guildhall by the middle of the twelfth century. It is first recorded in a document dating from between 1152 and 1167,[7] but, by analogy with Canterbury and Dover, the town may have supported one or more guilds well before that date.[8] It is not clear whether the Sandwich hall was the seat of the town authorities, or whether it was the property of a guild of merchants or of some other association of townspeople, but whichever was the case, its existence suggests an increasing awareness in the town of the rights and economic well-being of guild members, who may have been prominent townsmen and possibly leaders in the town assembly.[9]

Although the evidence is very slight, the few records that survive indicate that the townsmen were taking an increasingly independent hand in their own affairs, so that by the early thirteenth century there was a mayor who had presumably been elected by an assembly or council.[10] Sandwich was far from being alone in acquiring an elected mayor, for townspeople throughout England were becoming increasingly responsible for their own governance at that time. There was a mayor in London by 1191–3, and mayors of other towns such as Winchester, Exeter, Lincoln, York and King's Lynn are recorded shortly afterwards.[11]

Estimates of population in Sandwich before the fifteenth century are imprecise. While the number of taxable houses indicates a population in the region of 2,000 at the time of Domesday, it has been suggested that there may have been as many as 5,000 inhabitants by 1300 (Chap. 5.3). Whatever the precise numbers, it is certain that there was a considerable increase between the two dates, and some of this will have taken place during the twelfth century. Despite the lack of direct evidence for trade at this time, an increasing population indicates increased levels of economic activity, emphasising the suggestion made in Chapter 3.4.2 that the town already had two markets in the eleventh century. As will be discussed, the churches in particular reveal that the twelfth century was probably a high point in the fortunes of the town.

4.2 Sandwich Haven and Stonar

When the dispute between Christ Church Priory and St Augustine's Abbey was resolved in 1127, the adjudicators swore that 'all the issues and customs on each side of the water . . . from the place called Burgegate [or Edburgegate] as far as Merkesfliete [or Merkesfleot]' had belonged to Christ Church for as long as they could remember. Thus, Christ Church was confirmed in its claim and continued to control the area ostensibly granted to it by Cnut's charter of 1023. Merkesfliete or Merkesfleot must be the *Mærcesfleot* (that is, Northmouth) of Cnut, but the place name Burgegate or Edburgegate is less easily understood because it is not found elsewhere in documents relating to Sandwich. It could be the *Pipernæsse* (Pepperness) mentioned as a landmark in the charter of 1023, but may be a combination of two words: *burge* (town) and *gate* (street), that is 'town street'. This interpretation is difficult because *gate*, of Old Norse origin, is not otherwise used in south-east England (outside London) to denote a street.[12] If it did have this meaning in the document of 1127, however, it may have referred to a street in the town of Sandwich, perhaps the present High Street, which ran down to the waterfront and the ferry, which also featured in the dispute. This interpretation suggests that Christ Church had no control over the eastern part of the waterfront, that is, across St Clement's parish and the royal site to its east. There is currently neither documentary nor archaeological evidence to test this hypothesis.

Stonar was part of the abbey's possessions, acquired when St Augustine's was granted Minster Abbey and its property in the 1030s (see *Mildrype æker*, Chap. 3.2.3).[13] William II confirmed St Augustine's ownership in 1090,[14] but it seems that the area of Stonar beside Sandwich Haven may not have been built on until rather later, for it was the construction of 'little houses' there in the early twelfth century that brought the dispute to a head. They stood beside the water, opposite Sandwich, and therefore probably only approximately 400m north of Sandwich's own waterfront, and seem to have been built in response to the demands of ships calling at that shore ('*domunculas sibe propter naves advectantes ibidem fecerunt*'), which was said to have been 'a convenient place for ships to tie up in fair weather'. The qualification about the weather may indicate that there were no waterfront installations there, but that there may have been some on the Sandwich side.[15]

The usurpation of Christ Church's monopoly of ferry traffic was also a point at issue. The ferry was clearly an important means of transport for people and goods 'coming or going to the market (*mercatum*)', presumably in Sandwich, and the goods being brought to it were the produce of Thanet.

4.3 The churches

The only surviving twelfth-century buildings in Sandwich are its three churches, and it is these that provide the most cogent evidence for the prosperity of the town at this time. Later rebuilding, however, has left only partial remains, and it is necessary to examine and analyse the evidence before considering what the churches can tell us about Sandwich at this time.

4.3.1 St Mary's

Very little is known about St Mary's church before the mid-twelfth century, although a church may have occupied the site by the end of the previous century (Chap. 3.3.2). If there were a church there then, it was enlarged or replaced in the twelfth century by a new nave, crossing and the first bay of the chancel. All evidence for the termination of the east end went when it was entirely rebuilt in the thirteenth century, and later destroyed along with most of the church when the central tower fell in 1668.[16] However, part of the twelfth-century west end survives and the bases of nave piers on the north side were unearthed in the 1870s (Fig. 4.1). From this evidence and some other remains, the greater part of a fine twelfth-century church, built mainly of Caen stone, can be reconstructed. It seems to have consisted of a three-bay nave, a central tower and an east end. Both sides of the nave, the tower and the western bay of the chancel were flanked by relatively narrow aisles, which did not extend as far north and south as the present side walls. It is likely that the sanctuary was not aisled and it has been shown as square-ended in the reconstruction, but this is supposition for which there is no firm evidence.

The reconstructions shown in Figures 4.2 and 4.3 are based on the physical remains described below. To each side of a now blocked and undatable west doorway there is an engaged pier with central half-columns and flanking colonnettes, originally forming the west ends of the nave arcades. The south arcade is represented by part of a stilted arch, supported by double cushion capitals (Fig. 4.4). On the north, the cushions are augmented by a large central capital with leaves above stalks, the main elements emphasised by beading (Fig. 4.5). The original walls still rise to a considerable height above the arches, and remnants of string courses well above the arches probably lay below clerestory windows.[17] A corbel to carry the plate of the aisle roof is visible on the outer face of the south arcade wall.

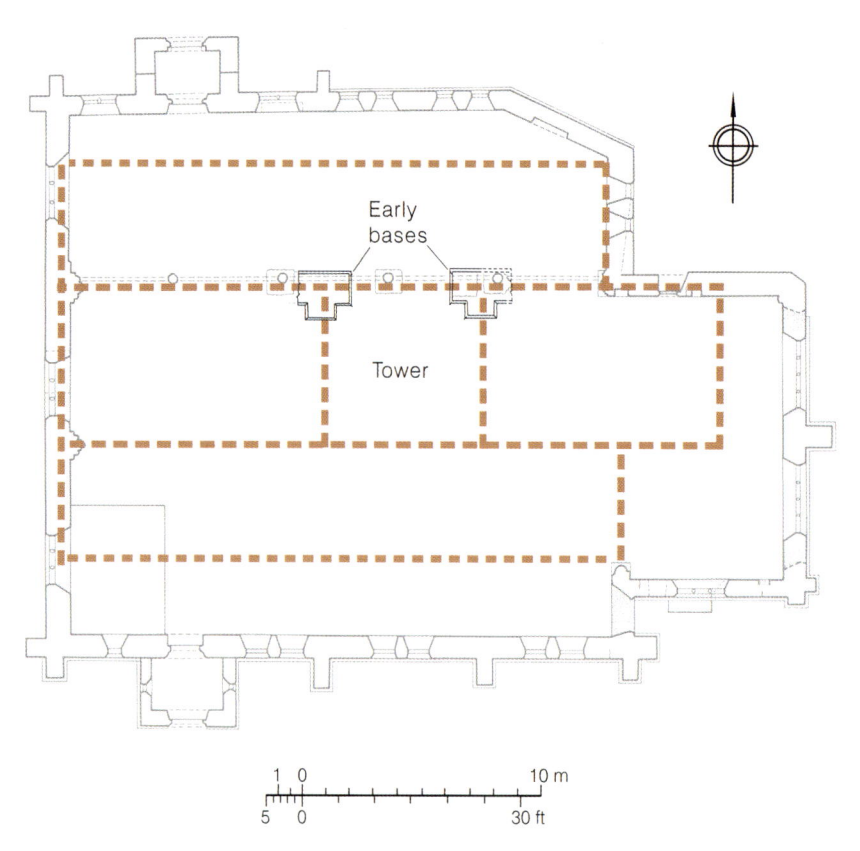

Fig. 4.1: St Mary's church, plan showing outline of twelfth-century church (in brown) (S. P. & A. T. A.).

4 *Sandwich in the twelfth century* 43

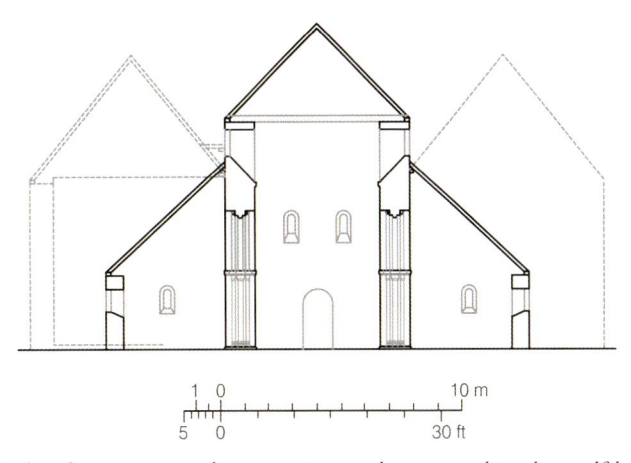

Fig. 4.2: St Mary's church, reconstructed cross section at the west end in the twelfth century (H. A. J.)

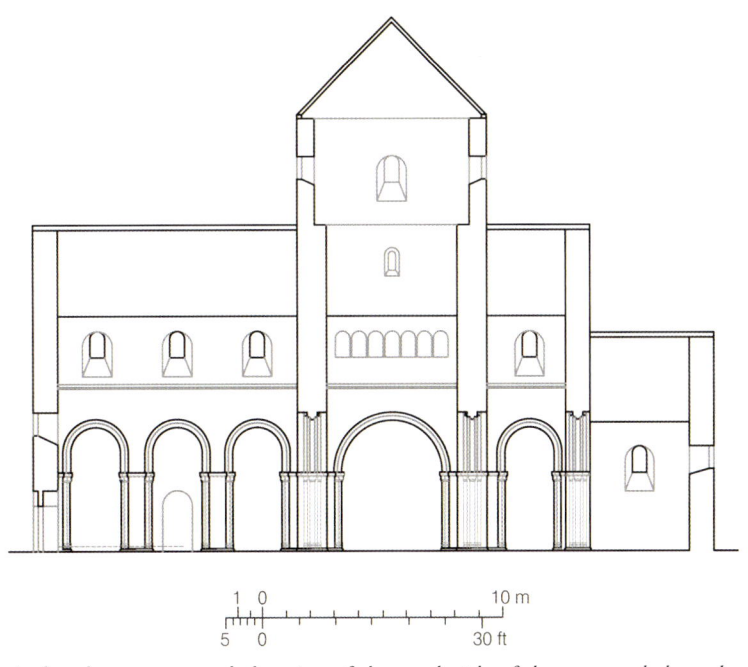

Fig. 4.3: St Mary's church, reconstructed elevation of the north side of the nave and chancel arcades (H. A. J.)

Fig. 4.4 St Mary's church, capitals at west end of nave, south side (P. W. © English Heritage DP68591)

Fig. 4.5: St Mary's church, arcade capitals at west end of nave, north side (P. W. © English Heritage DP68590)

The only other features *in situ* are the remains of two pier bases on the north side of the present nave, in line with the respond on the west wall (Fig. 4.1). Since their discovery in the nineteenth century, they have been left exposed under, but protected by, wooden shutters at current floor level. The western one was the plinth of a pier base, cut off on the west side but with chamfering around its north, south and east faces. The position of its original west edge can be gauged since the shape almost certainly mirrored its east side, the whole forming a T-shape. The eastern plinth is more fragmentary, but the surviving chamfers on the west and north sides provide the limits in these two directions. The plinth was formerly part of a pier of which the base proper can be seen above floor level further east,[18] where three simply moulded Romanesque half-column bases survive, the east and south ones probably being *in situ*, the layout suggesting that the eastern pier would have been T-shaped and identical to that further west. The column bases imply that there was at least one more bay to the east, as reconstructed in Figure 4.3. The purpose of these bases has been debated. When they were discovered their counterparts were apparently found on the south side of the nave, but were covered over. Although not very substantial, they appear to have been supports for a central tower. In addition, traces of the original north and south walls of the aisles were also found in the nineteenth century, and a surviving string course running round the wider thirteenth-century south aisle stops abruptly where it would have met the original aisle wall. These features indicate that the twelfth-century aisles were much narrower than at present. The nineteenth-century activities are said to have exposed pier bases on the north wall of the north aisle, which led to the suggestion that the aisles were vaulted.[19] More recently, it has been claimed that there are signs of groin vaulting in the north aisle, but no evidence for this was seen in the course of the present survey.[20]

The reconstructed cross section of the nave (Fig. 4.2) shows a clerestory, with deep splays to the windows above the arcade, and catslide roofs over the narrow aisles. The second reconstruction is a long section of the church (Fig. 4.3). At the west end, the curvature of the arcade arch surviving on the south side is compatible with three stilted arcade arches between the west end and the crossing piers. The T-shaped pier bases carrying the tower, together with the evidence for a further bay to the east, probably mean that the aisles ran past the tower without projecting transepts. The aisle bays to the east of the tower were almost certainly chapels. They probably contained altars and may or may not have had apsidal east ends. In the centre an unaisled chancel projected yet further east. At this time parts of the chancel might have survived from an earlier building, but details of the east end and the tower are unknown prior to the later Middle Ages.

Stilted arches are characteristic of Romanesque buildings where space was limited, as in the aisles of the chapel in the White Tower, London, and the entrance to the choir aisles at Tewkesbury Abbey, and this was probably the case at St Mary's. Its nave is far shorter than those of the other two Sandwich churches (9.5m as opposed to 14m) and gives the impression of a church in which the builders had no room to extend further west. This may have been because a street already lay on the line of Church Street St Mary, or because a powerful landowner had land to the west. Either way, this supports the view that there was not a large church on the site of St Mary's in the eleventh century, indicating that the space for building was severely restricted by the time the present one was erected in the mid-twelfth century. This perhaps explains why St Mary's received aisles earlier than the other two churches.

Early writers simply called the building 'Norman', but Bulmer-Thomas followed a local scholar in dating it 1100–10, comparing it to the late eleventh-century work at St Augustine's Abbey at Canterbury. Newman attributed it to the first quarter of the twelfth century.[21] The surviving capitals at the west end are, however, not true cushion capitals like those at St Augustine's, but have either double cushions or crude leaf carving with beading in a manner more reminiscent of the work carried out at Canterbury Cathedral under Prior Wibert, particularly the lower capitals of the Treasury, which was probably built *c*.1155–60.[22]

Fernie has suggested a date of *c*.1150 for St Mary's.[23] Even this may be a little early, both for the capitals and for the many pieces of carved Caen stone reused in the church, presumably from the twelfth-century building. These include a small tympanum filled with foliage surrounded by bead moulding (much rubbed away) set into the west front; part of a small arch with something that is not quite dog tooth; bits of simple billet moulding; fragments of decorative arcading; bases with simple spurs; and many small column blocks. The sculpture is not of high quality by the standards of Canterbury Cathedral, and so comparisons with such an important building are rather speculative, but a date in the late 1150s during the period when the Treasury was built at Canterbury seems possible.

The form, with aisles and a central tower, is both early and unusually sophisticated for Kent, where only a few parish churches of the mid-twelfth century have both aisles and a central tower. Most of those, like the Thanet churches, and churches with aisles but no central tower, such as St Margaret at Cliffe, St Mary's in the town of Dover and St Nicholas, New Romney, are generally accepted as having been built *c.*1160–80, therefore probably after St Mary's in Sandwich was begun. The closest analogies for earlier aisles, central tower and the relatively unusual feature in a parish church of an aisled bay east of the tower forming part of the east end are with the major Canterbury churches, or the church of the canons of St Martin-le-Grand at Dover. This was begun after 1070, with building halted in the early twelfth century before the nave was completed. It had aisles to both chancel and nave, a central tower over a crossing, unaisled transepts and two straight bays in the chancel with an ambulatory round the east end.[24] While there is nothing to suggest that St Mary's at Sandwich was as early as this or had an ambulatory, St Martin-le-Grand, like Canterbury Cathedral itself, would provide precedents for all the features found at St Mary's.

4.3.2 St Clement's

The overall plan of St Clement's church changed hardly at all in the twelfth century (Figs 3.3, 4.6), although A. M. Chichester, the vicar under whom the nineteenth-century renovations took place, reported that when new seating arrangements were put in 'Norman bases were found below the bases of the present Perpendicular nave columns, but in too rugged a state to be left in view'.[25] Despite this comment, the lack of any material evidence for the addition of aisles in the twelfth century, such as reused Caen stone, of which one would expect

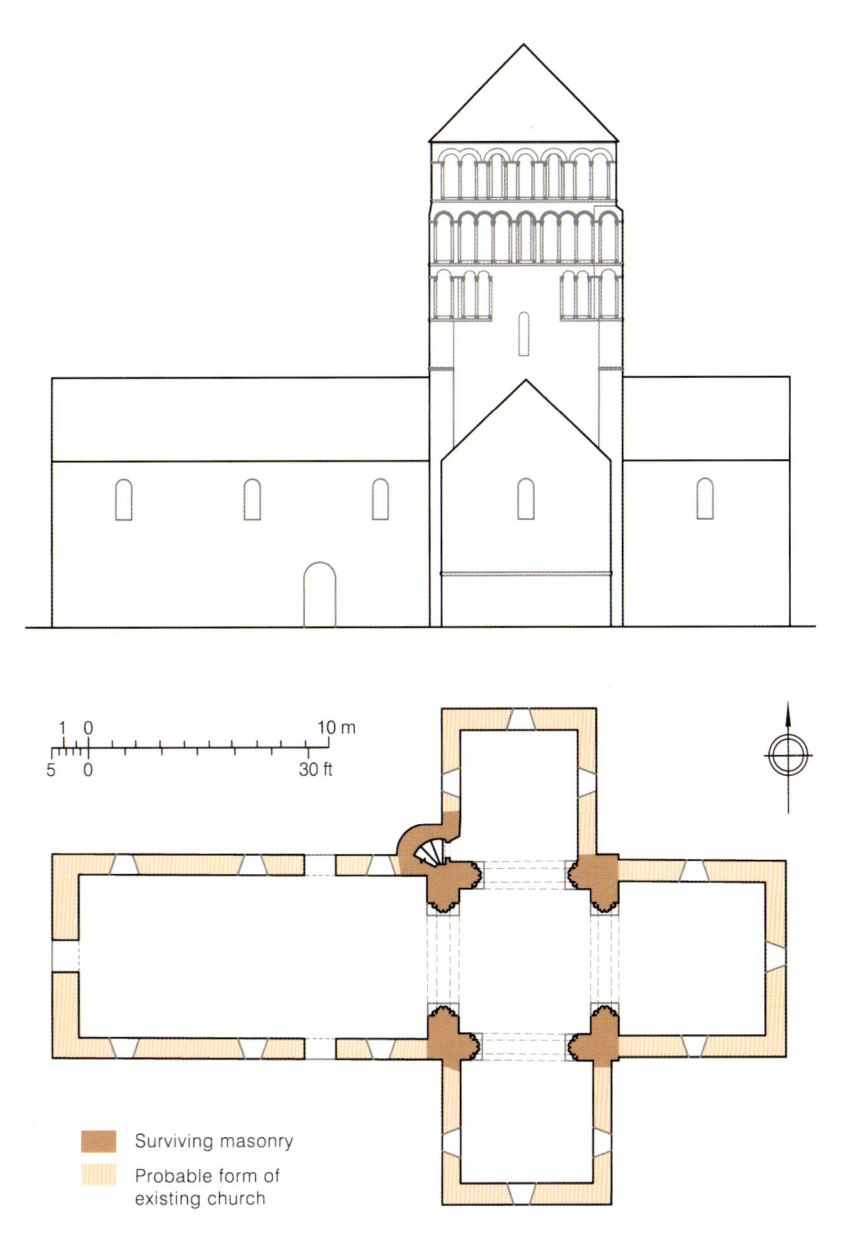

Fig. 4.6: St Clement's church, reconstructions of plan and elevation in the twelfth century (H. A. J. & A. T. A.)

Fig. 4.7: St Clement's church, the tower from the north-east (S. P.)

when the nave and chancel roofs were heightened in the later Middle Ages, and a floor subsequently inserted to turn this stage into a bell-ringing chamber. Above the ringing chamber are two stages for the bells, lit by windows and decorated externally with three rows of blind arcading.[27]

The decoration of the tower includes roundels, chevron moulding, scallop capitals and string courses formed by bands of beaded interlace. The piers of the tower arches have double half-columns in the centre with single ones to carry the outer arches to either side, and the main capitals are carved with scallops, volutes, leaves and grotesque animal heads, all with liberal use of beading (Fig. 4.8). The little doorway from the north transept to the stair turret is surmounted by a tympanum decorated with a deer and various patterns

such aisles to have been built at that date, suggests that the bases Chichester saw may have dated only to the thirteenth century.

St Clement's has one of the finest Romanesque towers in Kent. Inserted into the crossing between the earlier nave and chancel (Figs 4.7, 6.11), the new tower and its stair turret involved rebuilding this area, where there had originally been a crossing between the porticus and probably a low tower. It entailed cutting back short stretches of the nave and chancel roofs and then rebuilding them against the new tower; in so doing, the outer line of stones of the tower arches on the east and west faces were cut by the roof lines, perhaps inadvertently (Fig. 3.5).[26] At the same time, the porticus or low transepts of the Anglo-Saxon church were increased in height to form fully fledged transepts, with tower arches to north and south.

The tower has four stages decorated with five rows of arcading. It is entered by a stair turret attached to the north-west crossing pier, reached by a doorway in the transept. The lowest stage, marked by blind arcading on the interior only, has always been visible from inside. The second stage, with large blind arches on the interior, contained windows that formerly lit the crossing. These were blocked on the east and west faces

Fig. 4.8: St Clement's church, three capitals from inside the tower (P. W. © English Heritage DP044011, DP044023, DP044027)

Fig. 4.9: St Clement's church, door head to stair turret in north-west crossing pier (P. W. © English Heritage DP044053)

of beaded interlace set within an arch of fretwork (Fig. 4.9). The sculpture is more assured than anything that survives at St Mary's and may be a few years later, that is, dating from the 1160s.

The tower has been compared with the new towers erected over the east transepts of Canterbury Cathedral under Prior Wibert. They were decorated with blind arcading and roundels, and clearly influenced the west tower of Dover's parish church of St Mary and the tower of St Clement's.[28] The sculptural details are also found at St Margaret at Cliffe. The source of the decoration is acknowledged to be Normandy, and in particular the twelfth-century alterations to the abbey of La Trinité at Caen, where some details are close enough to suggest that masons actually accompanied the stone brought from Caen to build Canterbury Cathedral and the parish churches.[29]

The decoration of the tympanum of the doorway to the stair turret at St Clement's belongs to the same Canterbury milieu. The tympanum has sometimes been dated earlier, but the beaded arcading, geometrical interlace and fretwork around it are close in style to the decoration on the font of St Martin at Canterbury, thought to have originated as a wellhead at the cathedral dating from Prior Wibert's time, and to the lower storey of his Treasury.[30]

4.3.3 St Peter's

Very little of this church dates from the twelfth century, but, although virtually no twelfth-century masonry is identifiable today, the postulated stone-built church of eleventh-century date was altered to some extent at this time (Fig. 4.10). The transepts, for example, were probably made taller, since those that were destroyed in the fourteenth-century rebuild were full height. The

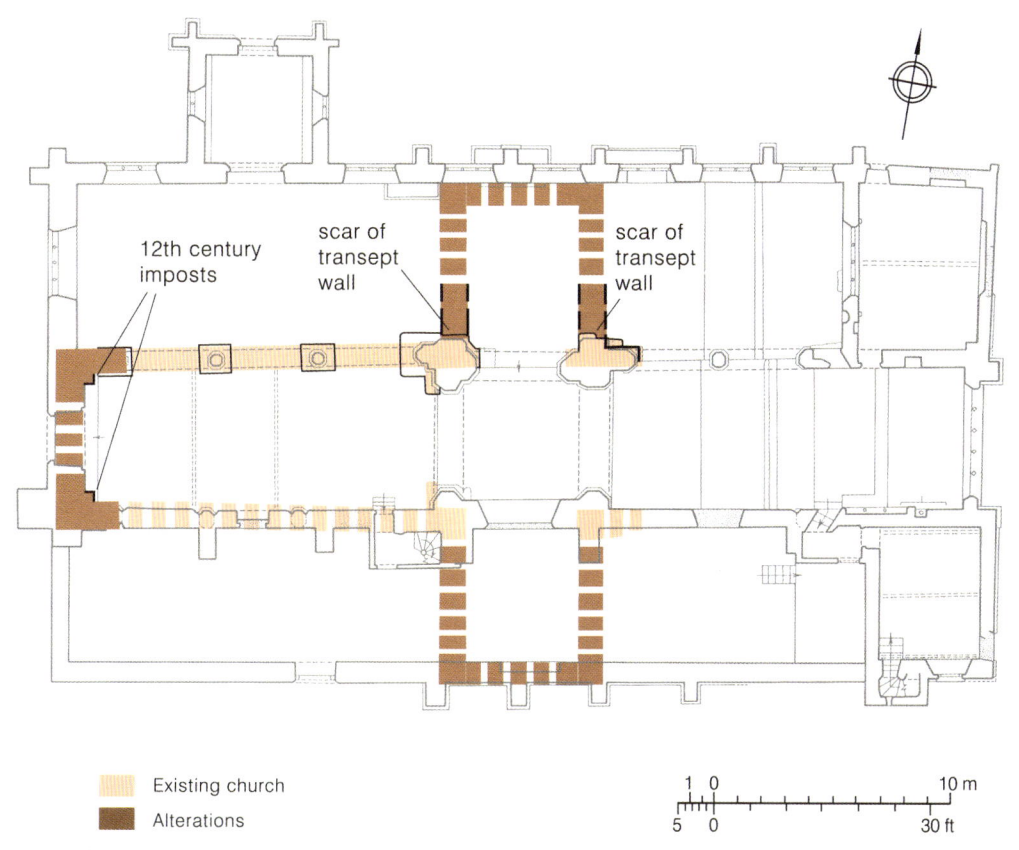

Fig. 4.10: St Peter's church, plan, as existing, showing evidence for twelfth-century transepts and imposts at the west end (S. P. & A. T. A.)

only twelfth-century remains are two short lengths of impost carved with Romanesque diaper work, set into plain responds on either side of the west doorway. They appear not to have been reset, but to have formed part of the west wall, which could mean either that the nave was reconstructed or, more likely, that it was originally shorter and lengthened in the twelfth century. Since the imposts are set inside the present arcades, the nave could have been narrower than it is today. Despite these signs of twelfth-century work, the tell-tale absence of reused Caen stone seems to indicate that St Peter's received nothing like the attention lavished on the two other Sandwich churches.

4.3.4 The implications of the evidence

The churches are the only physical remains in Sandwich from the second half of the twelfth century, and the only material evidence from which inferences can be made about the town. St Mary's and St Clement's were almost certainly unusual among Kentish parish churches of the time: St Mary's may have been ahead of other local churches in the county in adopting the aisled form; both churches were well decorated, with close ties to recent or contemporary work in Canterbury and Dover; and both were larger than average. Typical nave areas for churches of *c.*1150–1200 are said to have been between 60 and 80 square metres.[31] At St Mary's, despite its constricted length, the nave and aisles together occupied 150m², while the unaisled St Clement's had a nave area of 90m². Only St Peter's was nearer the norm, with an unaisled nave of 76m².

The size and elaboration of Sandwich's twelfth-century churches have important implications. It is probable that their form in large part reflects the fact that they were urban churches in a town that was growing rapidly at this time. That being so, it is strange that St Peter's, situated in what was later, and perhaps even then, the commercial heart of the town, was the smallest and least decorated of the three. Taken at face value there is a problem here, which touches on the larger question of how new building work was initiated and funded during the twelfth century.

It has been suggested that some of the earliest aisles added to the naves of parish churches were built as expressions of the prestige and status of the patrons, usually powerful men or institutions. In Yorkshire, for example, exceptionally fine twelfth-century decoration in rural churches has been associated with prominent ecclesiastical patrons, in particular the archbishop of York.[32] The same has been suggested for parish churches in Kent belonging to the archbishop of Canterbury or the great religious houses.[33] St Mary's and St Clement's, both of which have details reminiscent of Canterbury Cathedral, were owned by the archbishop, or possibly the archdeacon,[34] with vicars to look after the churches and their parishioners. Thus both churches certainly had a powerful patron, and it is possible that this is part of the explanation of why they were above average in size and quality of decoration. Another possibility, however, is that nave aisles, such as those in St Mary's, provided space for images, which would mean that they were associated with the needs of the laity and may have been built at their instigation.

The major legislation concerning the reform of the clergy and the way local churches were run and paid for dates only from the early thirteenth century. In particular, this means the enactments of the Fourth Lateran Council of 1215 regarding the discipline and organisation of churches, which in England resulted, from 1217 onwards, in episcopal statutes that effectively laid down responsibilities for different parts of the fabric. But much of this reflected a situation that had been developing for some time, with considerable changes in devotional practices and church management almost certainly taking place during the twelfth century.[35] It has been argued that during the second half of the twelfth century, if not before, the laity were actively involved in the building and extending of their churches.[36] Liturgical developments, when the altar moved further eastwards, led to sharper separation of clergy and laity,[37] and may in part explain the inclusion of side chapels at the east end of St Mary's (the only one of the three chancels for which we have any details at this time). It is not implausible that the twelfth-century work at St Clement's and St Mary's resulted from a combination of circumstances that included the patronage of the archbishop, the growing population, the increasing prosperity of the town and its inhabitants, and a new-found loyalty to the parishes that had probably been established not long before building work took place.[38]

The slighter changes to St Peter's in the twelfth century may also reflect the same combination of patronage, rising population and growing influence of the laity on church building, but with a different outcome. The church had a powerful enough patron in the form of St Augustine's Abbey, but the incumbent was a rector, not a vicar, and because he was less tied to the patron, may have had access to fewer resources. In addition, and perhaps crucially, the abbey's relations with the town were not easy in the late eleventh and twelfth centuries. In 1227, apparently after a considerable period of dispute between St Augustine's and the barons of Sandwich, it was agreed that they should take turns to appoint the rector to St Peter's.[39]

It is likely that the town's involvement in the affairs of that church began well back in the previous century. By the mid-thirteenth century St Mary's parish was undoubtedly where many of the wealthiest merchants who might have contributed to building their local church were living; on the other hand, St Peter's, which by that time probably contained the main market, has less evidence for wealthy merchants except along the waterfront. Instead, its inhabitants may have consisted largely of small retailers who were in no position to fund an ostentatious parish church. The situation was probably not very different seventy years or so before.

Despite the paucity of the remains, and the fact that nothing is known about either the contents of the churches or about the individuals who contributed to their construction, this is the only period when the Sandwich churches are above the county average in their size, form and decoration. This is crucial evidence for the growing prosperity of the town at this time.

4.4 The Christ Church Priory site

One of the dominating complexes in the town must have been the priory's headquarters, used as a base from which to administer its Sandwich estate and its rights in the town. Thirteenth-century documents reveal that it was at the west end, in St Mary's parish, not far south of the water, for by that date it had a quay to the north. By the mid-twelfth century the priory had a centralised system for managing its expenditure, with officials reporting to a treasurer.[40] Although no documents survive detailing the organisation in Sandwich, and no twelfth-century remains have been found in the town, it is likely that the priory already ran a highly efficient operation for its Sandwich affairs, and thirteenth-century documents suggest that the main residence was constructed during the mid- to late twelfth century.

The main house reputedly stood on the site that was later occupied by Sir Roger Manwood's School, and it was thought to have been demolished to make way for the school.[41] But references to a St Thomas's house in the 1580s suggest that while the school was built on part of the priory land in the 1560s, the main house probably survived until sometime later.[42] Three limited excavations outside the east end of the sixteenth-century schoolhouse (Site 18) revealed occupation debris, including thirteenth-century pottery, but no sign of a masonry structure, and since the priory acquired additional property to the west of its main site in the late thirteenth century, it is possible that Manwood School was built on that land. Meanwhile, it seems likely that the priory residence lay further east, in an area now occupied by gardens and later buildings.

Later documents reveal that the 'great house', the main residence of the priory, was built of stone. It is said to have been first mentioned in 1220, in a document now lost.[43] The earliest surviving reference is from 1252.[44] Accounts of repairs later in the thirteenth century indicate that it consisted of a stone hall with a chimney, a great chamber and a chapel, all elevated over a cellar. Both the hall and the cellar had windows onto the quay. A kitchen, probably detached from the main range by analogy with others of this date, is mentioned in 1299.[45] The only surviving piece of stonework associated with the priory site is a fine thirteenth-century doorway with ball-flower decoration, reset into a garden wall in what is now Paradise Row (House 67; Fig. 7.16), east of the sixteenth-century schoolhouse. It is an expensive piece of work and lies near the suggested location of the residence, but there is no evidence that it came from the great house itself as opposed to somewhere else on the site.

The fact that the cellar had windows to the quayside means that its floor cannot have been much below the ground level of the time. The high water table in Sandwich also suggests this. Thus, the main floor was elevated over a cellar or undercroft, a type of structure usually termed a 'first-floor hall'. Recent debate among architectural historians has led to the function of many such 'halls' being questioned, and many of the surviving structures have now been reclassified as two-storey chamber blocks that were once ancillary to ground-floor open halls that are now lost.[46] The few surviving halls that are still accepted as being truly of the first-floor or raised type tend to be of twelfth-century date, often having served specialised functions in castles, bishops' palaces, or wealthy merchant properties in towns. The Aula Nova of Christ Church Priory in Canterbury, built during Prior Wibert's time, is such a hall and there may have been others among the thirty stone houses that were recorded in Canterbury c.1200.[47] Few raised halls of thirteenth-century date are known, so the Sandwich example, which seems certainly to have been of that type, since it is documented as having a hall, chamber and chapel all raised above an undercroft, was probably built in the twelfth century.

4.5 The topographical development of Sandwich (Figs 1.2, 3.1 and endpapers)

The main outlines of Sandwich's urban plan had been achieved by the end of the eleventh century, and the next hundred years saw it supplemented by a few extra streets, the dates of some of which have been established by archaeological interventions. The three churches are the only standing structures from this century, but, as discussed above, there is documentary evidence for other major buildings in the town: the main stone residence of Christ Church Priory and a guildhall in the High Street, which might also have been built in stone.

The east side of the town seems still to have been defined by the area of probable royal land, stretching from St Clement's church to the road from Eastry, on which the castle was built in the following century (Fig. 3.2). Excavations (Sites 37, 38) have revealed little to indicate that the area was permanently occupied before the thirteenth century, and nothing to suggest that there was a building of high status there at this date. On the contrary, some post holes, stake holes, a hearth and a few potsherds from *c.*1150 are all that have been discovered. They might be the only remains of minor buildings within a royal enclosure, but there is nothing to indicate this and little can be said of them other than that they are signs of timber buildings of which nothing else is known.

The main streets were almost certainly still confined to the drier land of the Thanet Beds ridge, as they were in the previous century. Most led to the ferry and possibly to riverside quays, for which there is no positive evidence until the thirteenth century. It is likely that most of the waterfront remained without waterside revetments and that there was still no formal street alongside it. There is more supporting evidence for the High Street market in the twelfth century, where the spindle shape continued to define the street, still the main road from Worth and Eastry to the ferry over the river. The evidence includes the complex parish boundary along the street's western edge, the fact that an early guildhall was sited here ('yeldehallestrete' by the fourteenth century),[48] and the later association of the street with the fair of St Clement (Chap. 14.9).

Further west, the probably slightly later Fishmarket (Chap. 3.4.2) seems gradually to have supplanted the High Street market and to have become the main marketplace, perhaps as part of a general westward shift of the commercial heart of the town.[49] It was probably only in the twelfth century that St Peter's church reached its present length when the nave was extended to the west (Section 4.3.3), and this seems to have led to the realignment of the original curvature of the street into Luckboat (Chap. 3.4.2). The postulated repositioning is shown in Figure 4.11, where it is suggested that what had once been a single street became two, Fishmarket and Luckboat, joining at an angle from which a branch crossed the Delf at the bridge, to form the townward end of the eastern branch of the road from Woodnesborough, already described in Chapter 3.4.2. The bridge probably stood roughly where Fishmarket, Luckboat and Cornmarket now meet, and the changes in Fishmarket may have been the catalyst for the development of a third marketplace, Cornmarket, although there is no evidence for it until the next century (see Chap. 8.4). A further change to the area west of the church may then have taken place, with the infilling of the land on the east side in what may originally have been an open space.

At the north end of the Fishmarket, The Butchery and Cok Lane (now Potter Street) lead to Strand Street, but until the fourteenth century they would have ended on or near the south bank of the Stour. The earliest archaeological evidence from The Butchery dates from the twelfth century (Site 55), and from only the thirteenth century (possibly slightly earlier) for Cok Lane (Site 34). The site in Cok Lane also revealed waterlogged alluvial sand at +2.62 OD, so the street could have been a late development, laid out only after the edges of the dry land had been drained. The contour map suggests that at least the streets' southern ends may have been of a piece with the Fishmarket, and it could be that the market originally extended right down to the water, with the two streets being creations of the twelfth and thirteenth centuries. The change may be referred to in the custumal of 1301, where it states that if 'any [market] place be too much crowded or too narrow' the council may decide to move it to another place, 'as was the case with the fishmongers in the new street'.[50] This could mean that a newly created Cok Lane initially served as the fish market, but was deemed unsuitable, so that by 1300 the selling of fish had been moved into the truncated marketplace, where the retention of the name and the presence of shambles suggest that it remained throughout the later Middle Ages.

The best archaeological evidence in the town for twelfth-century buildings comes from an excavation in Love Lane (St Peter's Street) behind 10 Market Street where the remains of a mid- to late twelfth-century timber building were recovered (Site 20; Figs 4.11, 4.12). Owing to the constraints imposed by the proposed development on the site, the excavation could not go deep enough to reach the natural sub-soil of the Thanet Beds, although it did hit the current water table at a depth of 1.3m below present ground level (3.14m above OD). The earliest structure, dated by pottery to the late twelfth century, was a timber building with a clay floor and an oven, possibly domestic. This was replaced in the thirteenth century, and again around 1300 (Chap. 7.1), indicating the ephemeral nature of the construction at that time.[51]

This excavation is of particular importance because it provides the only evidence for timber buildings in

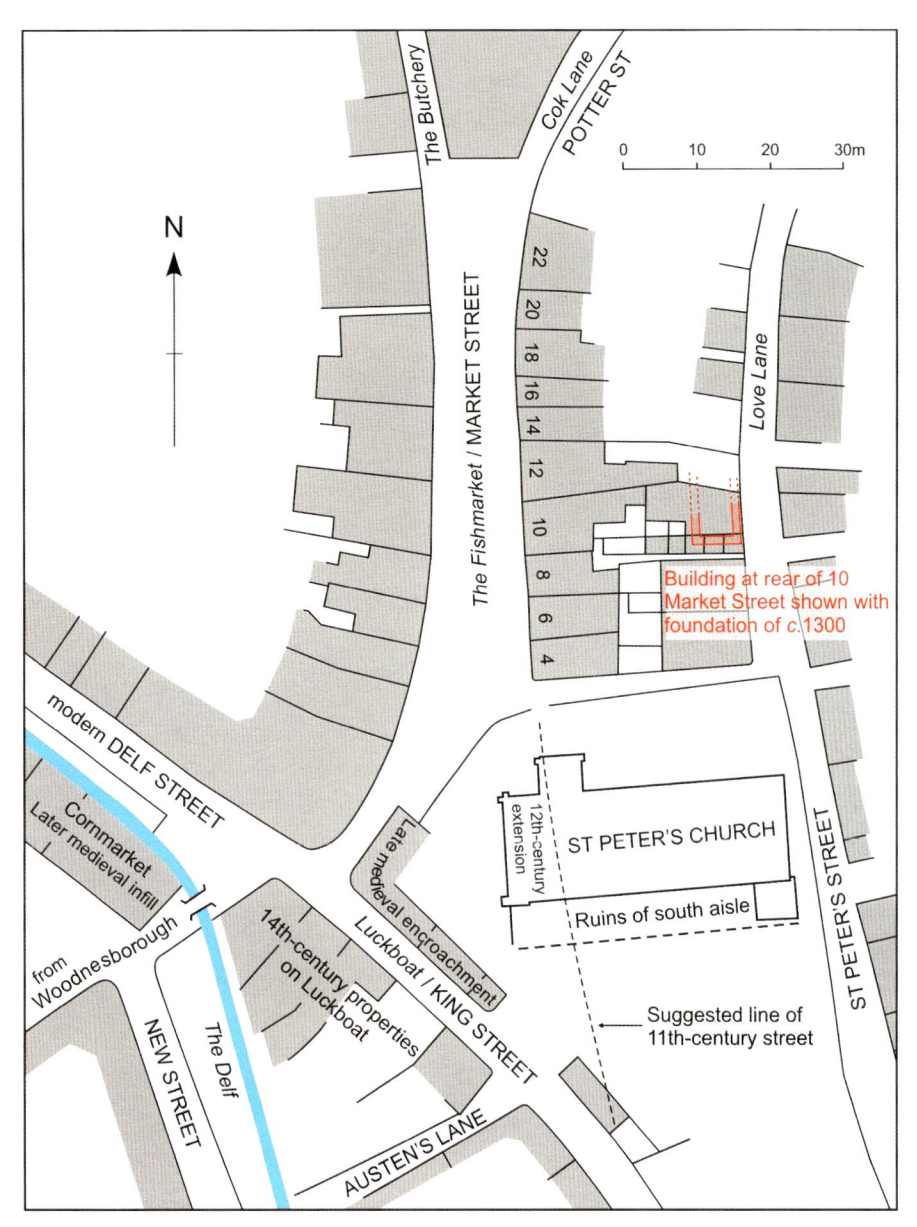

Fig. 4.11: Plan of the Fishmarket, showing the site of the building at the rear of 10 Market Street and the probable line of the Fishmarket before St Peter's church was extended (B. C. with Peter Atkinson, based on OS 1:500 map of 1873)

the town before the fourteenth century. The excavated remains extended 5.3m back from Love Lane and ran 5m along the street frontage, but its total width was irrecoverable because its north end had at some time become part of the plot to the north and was not included in the excavation. The building may originally have been rectangular, with its long side set parallel to Love Lane, but since there is no evidence of a doorway it is impossible to know through which wall it was entered. Nor can it be said for certain whether it was the front range of a building on its own plot or the back range of a tenement fronting on the Fishmarket. Because the distance between the two streets is only 30m (100ft), two plots back-to-back would have been very short, perhaps similar to the later property divisions shown on the OS map, in which the Fishmarket plots are approximately 18m deep and the Love Lane ones only about 12m. This would be remarkably short for a plot containing a building more than 5m in depth, allowing very little space for activity in a back yard. It is perhaps more likely that it was a rear building, perhaps a kitchen or a bakery, attached to the Fishmarket tenement onto which it backed.

That Fishmarket tenement, now 10 Market Street (House 58), is the northernmost in a row of four late medieval buildings measuring between 5.5m and 7m in width (Fig. 4.11). No. 10 is 7m wide, with room to accommodate the excavated building and a possible alleyway to the south of it. As mentioned above, the excavated building was once wider, extending beyond

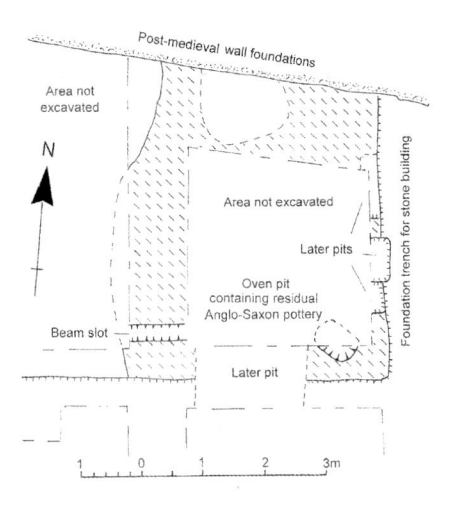

Fig. 4.12: Excavation of clay-floored timber buildings on Love Lane, behind 10 Market Street (K. P & B. C.)

the tenement's northern boundary, so had it originally been part of 10 Market Street, the whole plot would have been wider than it was when the fifteenth-century building was erected. This would mean that the Fishmarket plots were subdivided before the fifteenth century, a suggestion that is reinforced by the crooked line of the division between Nos. 10 and 12 Market Street, and the fact that although there is a straight line from the Fishmarket to Love Lane between Nos. 10 and 8, the plots to the south are irregular, with three properties of differing width on Market Street (Nos. 4, 6 and 8) and only two on Love Lane. The implication is that the original plots in the Fishmarket were 15m or more in width, subdivided into smaller units later in the Middle Ages. This would be in accord with early developments in towns elsewhere.[52]

Although some other writers have suggested that the western part of Sandwich was a planned Norman or earlier extension to what they argued had been an original core around St Peter's church,[53] there is no archaeological evidence for occupation between Harnet Street (west of The Butchery) and Church Street St Mary until the thirteenth or fourteenth century. It may be that at least part of this area, which is lower lying than the ground to west or east, was still not sufficiently drained for habitation before then. This is supported by the waterlogged nature of a site at the south-east corner of Harnet Street (Site 12), where occupation has been shown to have been impossible until *c.*1400. Luckboat now runs westwards into Delf Street, and this is the only street leading to the western part of town other than the way along the waterfront. While little alleys connect the main streets in the centre and east of town to each other, there are no such pathways further west,

and access is far more restricted, suggesting a rather different history of development. It may be that the changed alignment of the Fishmarket and Luckboat proposed above provides a *terminus post quem* for development in the landward side of the western part of the town.

Little is known today about the medieval street pattern on the slightly higher ground between Church Street St Mary and the Canterbury Gate, probably because much of the land was occupied by the Christ Church Priory estate and the chapel and cemetery of St James (foundation date unknown), both of which were dissolved at the Reformation. In addition to their enclaves, by the later Middle Ages there would appear to have been a number of lanes lined with small cottages (Chap. 14.8). The area, however, was severely depopulated and subsequently resettled, all during the sixteenth century, possibly leading to extensive reorganisation, for there were more medieval street names than can be accounted for today, suggesting that the street pattern may then have been simplified and some of the minor streets obliterated.

Despite our uncertainty about the occupation of parts of the west end of town, the quality of the twelfth-century church of St Mary's discussed in Section 4.3.1 implies a wealthy and possibly populous parish, and the unusual shortness of the church's nave suggests that Church Street St Mary was already in existence when the church was built. Although some of the landward part of the parish may still have been undeveloped, it is likely that properties filled the waterfront between St Mary's and the Christ Church Priory site. In the thirteenth century this was a prime location for wealthy merchants' tenements, and it may have been similarly occupied during the previous century.

There is little evidence that the land south of the Delf was occupied at this time, although there was late twelfth- or early thirteenth-century occupation on Moat Sole, the westerly branch of the Woodnesborough road mentioned in the previous chapter. This is confirmed by evidence from an archaeological evaluation (Site 28) where Scarborough ware (1200–50) was discovered along with later medieval building remains on the Moat Sole frontage.[54]

4.6 Conclusion

Twelfth-century evidence is sparse, but enough survives to indicate that the town grew in importance during this time. There was an assembly of townsmen who were in a position to negotiate with king and priory, and who may have been members of a guild. The Cinque Ports as a group first gained official recognition, and Sandwich was already associated with Sarre, which is later known to have been a dependent port. Although no figures are available, it is clear that the population was increasing, and likely that the prosperity of the town, manifested in its churches, was also rising. It is here suggested that it was during the twelfth century that Christ Church Priory spent a considerable sum on building a fine house on its property in the town, implying that the income gained from its rights in Sandwich was substantial.

Although the first dated and securely located archaeological finds (solely potsherds) found in Sandwich can be attributed to this century, they are not evidence for the town having originated in the twelfth century. On the contrary, the expansion of the street pattern on the Thanet Beds ridge, the extension of St Peter's church and the probable modification of the Fishmarket together strongly suggest that changes were being made to a layout that had been established in the previous century. Archaeology has contributed information about domestic buildings in twelfth-century Sandwich through a single excavation in Love Lane, in which the remains of a timber structure was uncovered. Its size and position, and the possible width of the plot in which it originally stood, imply a change in plot boundaries in the Fishmarket between the twelfth and fifteenth centuries, when also the timber building on that particular plot was replaced in stone (Chap. 7.1 and Fig. 7.1). The Love Lane site, although small in area, has been the most productive archaeological intervention in Sandwich during the lifetime of the project, and its results emphasise the importance of investigating every available site in the town, however small. This is true not only of the present town centre, but also of all other areas of the town, at whatever date they may have been occupied.

All the evidence that survives points to Sandwich having been a well-established urban unit by the end of the twelfth century. It grew in prosperity and consolidated its status during the following century and a half, when fine stone and timber buildings were erected, the churches flourished and the population reached its peak shortly before the Black Death of 1348.

PART III: 1200–1360

Introduction

These were years of consolidation, innovation and growth in Sandwich, both in terms of urban governance and contacts with the outside world and in its physical development. The steps towards urban governance outlined in previous chapters came to fruition with the establishment of a well-conducted council of the urban elite serving as jurats under an elected mayor. Until the end of the thirteenth century Christ Church Priory continued to play a significant role in the town's affairs, notably through its rights to charge customs and tolls, and its control of the hundred court. It had also extended its grip on the town through the acquisition of land and quays adjacent to its headquarters, as well as ownership of rental property elsewhere in the town. Its wealth and position were expressed in the stone buildings of its residence beside Monkenquay, and the storehouses and at least one crane that stood beside the water. Nothing of these survives, but all are recorded in the priory documents. In 1290, however, the priory exchanged its rights with the crown, this action apparently leading to an uneasy relationship between the town's inhabitants and the royal authorities. In this the town differed little from urban governments elsewhere, which were all pushing for greater self-determination at this time. This may have been the spur to the compilation, c.1300, of the Sandwich custumal, in which the customs and privileges claimed by the town were written down for the first time. The custumal is an invaluable source for the extent of self-governance and the aspirations of the community, and also provides more mundane information about the topography of the town and the measures taken to maintain its physical features.

During these years, too, Sandwich became more embroiled with events in the outside world. It was one of the most important ports in England, participating in foreign trade and also keeping close ties with London. Three or more fairs were granted, suggesting wide trading links, and many of the cargoes for the capital were transferred in Sandwich Haven from foreign merchantmen to smaller craft that could make their way through the waterways of the Wantsum Channel to the Thames estuary and beyond. As Figure III.1 shows, the riverbank fronting the town was at least partly revetted by wharfs, but had no defensive walls. Some of the wharfs belonged to Christ Church Priory; some were private; and there was a common quay for the townspeople. In the present work, the terms quay and wharf are used as synonyms, as they are in the medieval written records and in most modern publications. This terminology, currently used by maritime archaeologists and historians, is rather inadequate and there are many other words, such as 'groyne', 'groyne head' and 'dock', that occur in profusion in the Sandwich yearbooks but which cannot confidently be defined. A new study of such terms, along the lines pursued by Dyson several decades ago but with a wider remit, would be profitable.[1]

In the thirteenth century the parish churches were still growing and changing in response to changes in religious practice, to population pressure and to a greater involvement on the part of the laity. The needs of the increasing population were also addressed by the founding of a Carmelite friary and two hospitals. By the early fourteenth century benefactors to churches become known by name; they paid for chapels, chantries and fabric such as new windows. At the same time the north aisle of St Peter's church was enlarged, almost certainly to accommodate the town courts. The prosperity enjoyed by the wealthier townspeople is reflected in the earliest surviving stone and timber domestic buildings, all of high quality and of late thirteenth- and early fourteenth-century date. They include buildings of national significance, and are concentrated largely along the waterfront and in the central part of town around the marketplaces. Although no dwellings of the poor or even the middle sort are known, this is the first period in which we can begin to learn some of their names and trace their occupations.

Sandwich Haven and the Wantsum Channel were not only visited by peaceful traders; they were also the scenes of much activity during the wars with France that beset the country at the time. The royal castle was probably the mustering point for troops who gathered there before embarking for the Continent on the vessels that assembled in the haven. The castle seems to have had its own harbour, and shipbuilding and repair yards, to the east of the town. Nothing has been discovered of these, although remains of a fourteenth-century ship have been found in the vicinity. Closer to home, Sandwich also contributed its own ships for the wars as a leading member of the confederation of the Cinque

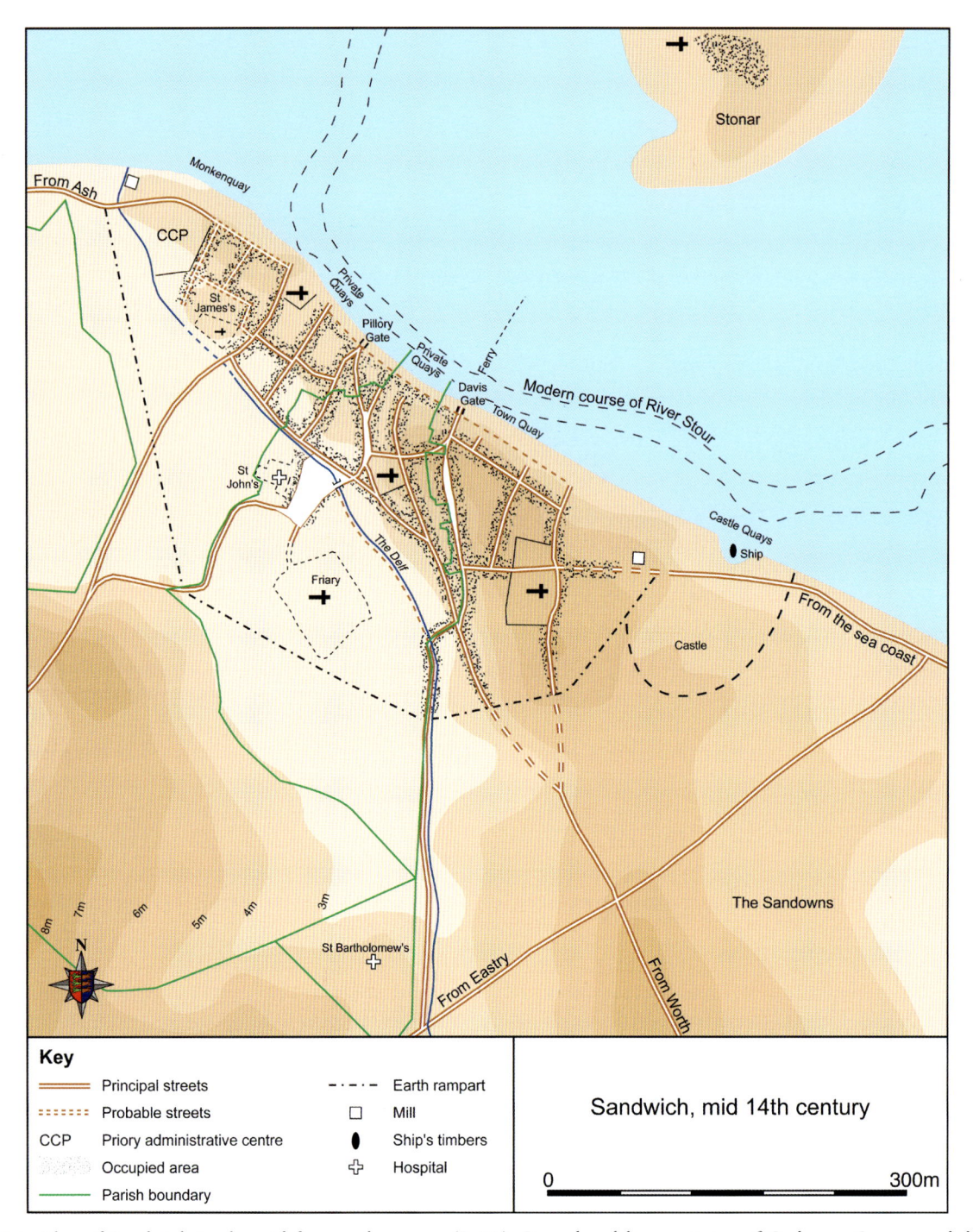

Fig. III.1: Plan of Sandwich in the mid fourteenth-century (J. H.). Reproduced by permission of Ordnance Survey on behalf of HMSO. © Crown copyright 2009. All rights reserved. Licence number 100046522

Ports, and it was during this period that it acquired its 'limbs', which lightened the obligation of the head ports for ship service.

As discussed in detail in Chapter 5, by 1300 the population of Sandwich may have been in the order of 5,000. This may be an overestimate, but that the town numbered among the fifty largest towns in England, all with populations of more than 2,000, cannot be in doubt. But, like other towns, it was badly hit by the problems of the mid-fourteenth century. Crop failure, war, taxation and finally disease, notably the Black Death, all took their toll. The scale of the disaster is unclear because of the lack of records. Different places suffered to varying extents, but towns are generally thought to have lost a third or even half of their populations, which would mean that by the end of this period the number of Sandwich inhabitants may have dropped to as few as 2,500. It is known that St Clement's churchyard was expanded to cater for the dead, and in the town centre an early fourteenth-century charnel house at St Peter's church was no doubt much in use. Not surprisingly, house building virtually ceased during the second half of the fourteenth century.

Figure III.1 shows that, by combining information provided by surviving domestic buildings, a few archaeological sites and documentary evidence, the physical appearance of the town by the middle of the fourteenth century can be mapped with more confidence than before. By then it seems to have achieved its greatest medieval extent, already bounded by earth ramparts and moats around its landward side. They surrounded an area of which roughly only half was inhabited. Apart from the Carmelite precinct, most of the land close to the ramparts was open ground, as it still was on the earliest reliable map of Sandwich in the eighteenth century. The ramparts to the south and west of the town were low, with shallow moats and laid out across alluvial ground, but the eastern stretch (Mill Wall) was much more substantial, built on the ridge of Thanet Beds along which most of the town's streets run. Its scale and position along the east side of the town, most open to waterborne attack, suggest that, possibly unlike the others, it had a seriously defensive role. Its construction had a profound effect on the town for it disrupted Sandwich's street pattern by blocking the main route into the town from the south-east. This increased the importance of the road from the south, thereby encouraging traffic to head towards the Fishmarket in the centre of the town rather than the market in the High Street. In addition, Mill Wall cut the urban settlement off from the royal castle and its grounds, one result being that they have never been included on town plans of Sandwich until this publication. Their inclusion on the maps changes the scale of the town in relation to its immediate surroundings.

5 The port and town: consolidation and outside influences

The 150 years preceding the Black Death were times of considerable importance in the history of Sandwich. On the one hand it is the first period for which records, both written and material, start to survive in some profusion, allowing us to see what was going on, and on the other its passing marked the end of the great period when the port and town were of national significance. This chapter charts the economic and political fortunes of the town during this period, and discusses its relationships with Christ Church Priory, the Cinque Ports and above all the king, for whom it had a crucial role during times of war.

By the late thirteenth century there is, for the first time, a little information about the people of the town and their occupations. Although the thirteenth and early fourteenth centuries were largely times of growth and prosperity, Sandwich, like other places, had its fair share of economic and social difficulties caused by poor harvests, sickness, war and high taxation. But nothing prepared the town for the devastating effects of the Black Death. Although we have few details, it is likely that the population of Sandwich was reduced by half. Things were never the same afterwards, not just because of the reduction in population and the time that economic recovery took, but because the growing predominance of London and the physical shrinking of the haven and the Wantsum Channel changed the dynamics of trade and prosperity for ever.

5.1 The growth of independence

5.1.1 Town governance in the thirteenth century

During the thirteenth century the governance of Sandwich became more firmly lodged in the hands of its mayor and council, the names of some of whom are known for the first time. Although references are few, from the very beginning of the century there may have been an increasing involvement in matters affecting the status and organisation of the town.

In 1205 rights previously granted by Henry II in the 1150s were confirmed by King John, the royal confirmation implying that the leading townsmen were capable of protecting their privileges, however limited they might have been.[1] Law and order was normally in the hands of the portreeve, Christ Church Priory's paid official who was usually a freeman of the town, but the mayor together with an assembly of leading citizens may gradually have taken over more responsibilities. From 1207 to 1213 the monks of Christ Church were in exile and Sandwich, along with the rest of the priory's estate, was in the king's hands, so it may be no coincidence that the term 'mayor' was first documented a year later.[2] In 1227 the mayor and freemen (*communitatus*) are referred to as owning land near St Bartholomew's hospital,[3] perhaps indicating that the municipal property portfolio, so much in evidence in the late medieval documents, was already being accumulated, and in 1248 the mayor and good men of Sandwich were asked by the king to help a royal official in connection with ship service.[4] By the end of the century, the mayor and jurats (*iurati*) had also taken on the normal urban collective responsibility of looking after orphans' property and appointing freemen to act as guardians.[5]

The inhabitants of Sandwich were also flexing their muscles by coming into conflict with the king during the civil war between Henry III and his barons (the Barons' War, 1259–67) when, together with the other Cinque Ports, the town supported Simon de Montfort. In 1266, however, after De Montfort's death, Sandwich was retaken by royal forces under Roger de Leyburn and briefly taken into royal hands.[6] Trouble arose again in 1275 when a dispute over a rabbit warren belonging to Dover Castle escalated, with access to the town being denied to the constable of the castle. Although the resultant court case was resolved in favour of the king,[7] the mutinous action indicates considerable self-assurance on the part of the town's administrative body.

Overall control of the town was a complicated and contentious issue, with the king and his officials undermining the authority and rights of Christ Church Priory, and the mayor and his council forced to submit to both. There were disagreements between the town and the priory over the latter's right to choose whom it wished to be its portreeve, and obstructions to his holding the hundred court. The disputes were settled in favour of the priory, but its jurisdiction in Sandwich and all its rights to the customs and tolls in the haven and the town did not last much longer, for in 1290 the priory exchanged its rights with the king, receiving in return payment and entitlement to land elsewhere in Kent.[8]

The replacement of the priory by the king may have simplified the situation, but it also raised fresh issues. A late thirteenth-century document, which may be a record of an early *quo warranto* inquiry of 1293, raises the possibility that civic officials had been usurping royal powers, such as the custody of weights and measures and distraints on the goods of foreign merchants.[9] Both these powers were claimed by the town but disputed by the royal justices. Nothing further happened at the time, but in August 1300 two itinerant justices on their way to Sandwich, perhaps to deal with this matter or coinage offences,[10] were intercepted at Ash by the mayor and a group of leading freemen, and disarmed. They were denied access to the town, and the bag containing the king's rolls was split open and the contents removed. These actions resulted in the men of Sandwich being summoned to appear before the Court of King's Bench at Westminster to answer for their actions.[11] Sometime earlier, in 1281, royal officials had attempted to execute a writ in Stonar, but they were attacked by men from Sandwich, who tore up the writ.[12] Probably this was all part of a struggle between the royal justices and the inhabitants of the Cinque Ports, concerning the latter's rights to trial only in their own town courts or the court of Shepway.

5.1.2 Town governance in the fourteenth century

The exchange with Christ Church Priory meant that the king not only assumed the rights to customs and tolls on merchandise in the Liberty and to lastage, a duty paid on the carriage of goods, but also gained control over the hundred court and the right to various fines and forfeiture of property imposed there (although see below).[13] The potential loss of perceived privileges, together with the dispute arising from the incident at Ash, may well have been the catalysts that led to the production, in 1301, of the first written custumal among the Cinque Ports. It was written by the town clerk, Adam Champneys, but certain sections that discuss the method of pleading and the type of pleas to be heard in both the borough and hundred courts seem to have been drafted by someone with legal training, probably Robert of Sturry, whom the town employed as a lawyer to help them in their current case in the Court of King's Bench.[14]

The custumal set out the claimed liberties, franchises, customs and usages of the town, and is the best evidence for all aspects of life in Sandwich from this period. It gives the impression of a place that was well organised and efficiently run by a number of elected or appointed officials who were dedicated to regulating the holding and transfer of property, to keeping the town clean and tidy, safe from fire, and protected from potential outside attack. Courts were held regularly and appropriate punishments were meted out to malefactors. The earliest extant version, dating from between *c*.1351 and *c*.1381, was in private hands until 1953 and has only recently been studied; it is thought to be a copy of the original custumal of 1301, with some later, mostly identifiable, additions.[15] The version printed in Boys's *Collections*, and used as the primary source since then, was written in the early fifteenth century, perhaps in late 1413 or early 1414, although it is probably an accurate copy of the late fourteenth-century text.[16]

Sandwich's mayor was elected by the freemen at a meeting of all the commonalty in St Clement's church, with the other officials, such as the town serjeant, the treasurer, the public broker and the warden for orphans being appointed the following week at another assembly in St Peter's. As soon as the officers were in place, the official weights and measures had to be checked, and a 'common weigher' appointed. The churches were also the venues for the courts: that for the hundred, presided over by the king's bailiff, was held in St Clement's, with the town court under the mayor taking place in St Peter's. Several thirteenth-century court rolls exist for the bailiff's court before the handover to the crown, and three more survive from the late thirteenth and early fourteenth centuries, although it is not made clear to which court these latter rolls refer (Section 5.4.2). They all dealt with minor cases of debt, *detinue* (withholding what is due), trespass and assaults resulting in bloodletting but not serious injury. In addition, they indicate that the assize of bread and the collection of fines from bakers were the responsibility of the king's bailiff, although at this time the proceeds were divided equally between the king and the town.[17]

The town serjeant seems to have been responsible for most of the upkeep and protection of the physical side of the town. He had to ensure that the streets were kept clean; that they were not overrun by stray pigs; and that their surfaces were protected from the passage of too many carts with iron-shod wheels. They had to be kept clear of obstacles, not just for pedestrians and travellers on horseback, but also to facilitate access to the haven for water in case of fire. To this end, each house had to have a tub of water at each door in dry weather. Butchers were not to kill animals in the streets; washerwomen could not rinse their clothes or their tubs in the Delf; and women generally were not allowed to scold or quarrel in the street or other public place. The serjeant was also in charge of the fifteen townsmen who made up the night watch, six men who patrolled the town and three others stationed at each of Monkenquay, Davis quay and the 'easternmost mill'.[18] There were other public officers with apparently slightly less onerous duties. These included the 'public broker' who bought and sold wine, weighed bulky commodities, freighted vessels in the haven and held the official measures for corn and cloth, and also four porters to whom the conveyance of wine to cellars and other stores was delegated.

The mayor and jurats seem to have had collective responsibility for what were considered to be public works. These included road mending, clearing out the Delf, repairing bridges and opening sluices to prevent flooding, all of which were paid for by the town's treasurer. In return, they seem to have had rather draconian powers, for the authorities could change the sites of or build upon marketplaces, which they clearly did on at least one occasion (Chap. 4.5), remove walls, buildings or quays if they thought fit, and change the line of watercourses. These actions may have arisen through the regular surveys, which were to be carried out at least every seven years and were to note encroachments onto the streets, passageways and drains.

5.1.3 *The Liberty of Sandwich*

As part of the exchange in 1290, the king acquired jurisdiction over the Liberty of Sandwich, the area throughout which his bailiff exercised the king's rights to various local customs and tolls. As mentioned in Chapter 3.2.3, the boundary defining the area may have been established as early as Cnut's charter of 1023, but the Liberty itself was not mentioned by name until a description of the perambulation of its boundaries, undertaken sometime in the 1290s by Stephen de Pencestre (warden of the Cinque Ports), was included in the custumal.[19] The perambulation took place shortly after the exchange with Christ Church Priory and was presumably intended to inform the king of the extent of his new acquisition

Stephen de Pencestre made his circuit of the Liberty in the company of the mayor, jurats and commonalty of Sandwich, following a route mostly still traceable today. Recent research published elsewhere has shown that in the Middle Ages the area was much greater than that defined by the Parliamentary, Municipal and Liberty boundary, first drawn out on the Ordnance Survey 6-inch map in 1877 and unquestioned since then.[20] The medieval Liberty stretched for more than 15km from Sandwich to Northmouth, following the course of the rivers Stour and Wantsum (Fig. 2.2). Its width is more debatable and probably not that of its nineteenth-century successor, for to contemporaries the important feature of the Liberty would have been not the land that it encompassed but predominantly the navigable waterways through the Wantsum Channel over which the priory, and now the king, could demand dues. To the west lay the Liberty of Fordwich, and on the north the Thanet lands of St Augustine's Abbey and Christ Church Priory. Maintaining and underlining rights over the rivers was an important issue for both the king and the community at the end of the thirteenth century.

5.1.4 *Economic regulation*

It was the king who appointed men to hold the pleas of the market and to view and examine the measures of bread, wine and beer throughout the Cinque Ports.[21] The custumal shows that the Sandwich administration, as in other towns at this time, was concerned to establish fair trading conditions. The market was controlled by the clerk, and also the town serjeant, one of whose many duties was to patrol the entrances to the town on market days to warn vendors about forestalling.[22] In addition, the quality of the products of the town's tailors, seamstresses and spinners of wool was strictly controlled, and the weights and measures on which all honest trade depended were checked annually.

It was not until the thirteenth century that all new fairs had to be authorised by the crown, so there is no record of when the first fair in Sandwich (St Clement's, held on his feast day 23 November[23]), came into being. It is very likely, though, that it was established at the same time as the market or markets, that is, in the eleventh century, and that it took its name from St Clement's church. Three other fairs are known from 1290 when, after the exchange between Christ Church Priory and the king, Edward granted to Queen Eleanor the rights relinquished by the monks, and also the revenues from three new fairs within the town, which her executors continued to hold until 1299.[24] The number of fairs suggests that a wide range of trading activities was taking place at the time,[25] and in 1303 a building for the use of the crown during the fairs was constructed.[26] A further fair was granted in 1317,[27] but it is not known whether this replaced one of those of 1290. The fairs probably diminished in importance during the course of the fourteenth century (Section 5.5.2), but new ones were granted in 1504 (Chap. 10.1.3), and St Clement's fair continued to be held throughout the Middle Ages (Chap. 14.9).

5.2 Sandwich and the Cinque Ports

The confederation of the Cinque Ports, which had previously been a loose association of south-eastern ports, became formalised in 1260 when Henry III granted them their first charter in common, confirming their freedom from all external courts of justice. This may have been an acknowledgement of the strength of the ports when acting in concert, as had been shown when they embraced the side of Simon de Montfort in the Barons' War. In 1278 Edward I granted a further charter, whereby the immunities and privileges previously enjoyed by individual ports were given to all. He also granted some new concessions to all the ports, including the right to land their catch and dry their nets on the shore at Great Yarmouth and to participate in the administration of justice at its annual herring fair. These may have been the most important concessions in the immediate term, but of more far-reaching consequence was the exemption granted from the royal prise of wine and other forms of national taxation. Although their liberties were confirmed again in 1290 and extended in 1298, Edward also sought to control the ports. To do this he appointed a new officer to be a permanent administrator; he was to be known as the warden of the Cinque Ports and was also the constable of Dover Castle.[28]

The main ports of the confederation each had limbs or minor ports that shared in the burden of ship service and enjoyed the same concessions as those gained by the head ports to which they were linked. By the end of the thirteenth century Sandwich had five limbs: Stonar, Sarre, Reculver, Fordwich and Deal.[29] The first three had been part of the Liberty of Sandwich perhaps since the early eleventh century, and Fordwich was on its westernmost boundary. Deal was the only limb on the coast and not in the Liberty.

In the mid-twelfth century a court of justice for all the ports had been set up. Known as the 'kynges high courte of Shepway',[30] it was presided over by the royal appointee, that is, the warden, although its jury was made up of portsmen.[31] It was a higher authority than the courts of the individual towns, acting as a court of appeal, and was felt by the inhabitants to be the only higher court to which they were bound, something that brought them into conflict with the king on several occasions.[32]

Although not mentioned in surviving documents until 1224, a second court, called the court of Brodhull, was probably as old as Shepway but independent of the warden of the Cinque Ports. Its main business was to regulate the herring fishery and fair at Great Yarmouth, for which each port had the right to elect its own wardens, with jurisdiction only over their own portsmen.[33] From 1357 the wardens had to account for their actions to the whole body meeting at the Brodhull,[34] so it came to be summoned regularly and became the general assembly both of the head ports and their limbs. After 1357 the Brodhull met in New Romney in July each year when the Great Yarmouth wardens were chosen and given their instructions. In December they met again to present their reports. Although these were the only regular and statutory sessions, extra business could be dealt with at other times if necessary.

5.3 Population

There are no direct figures from which to quote population numbers, and calculations are inevitably approximate. It has been suggested that by 1300 Sandwich was one of the towns that may have had about 5,000 people,[35] which would mean about 1,000 households. A piece of firm evidence that suggests these may be reasonably accurate figures are the entries in the lay subsidy rolls listing the men of the Cinque Ports who held land elsewhere in Kent and Sussex.[36] The listings, for there are several of them, appear to have taken place in 1346 and 1347, and some 600 people 'of Sandwich' are named, with not many occurring more than once. This number of people owning land, however tiny their parcels, suggests that approximately 5,000 inhabitants and approximately 1,000 households may not be much of an overestimate for the town on the eve of the Black Death.

The arrival of the Black Death in 1348 had a devastating effect overall, particularly on towns. In Rochester, at least 50 per cent of the tenants of the priory there are estimated to have died in the years 1348–50, and this figure probably also applied in Canterbury.[37] How many people died in Sandwich is not known, but in 1349 an extension was made to the churchyard of St Clement's because 'the great plague' had filled the old cemetery,[38] and the revised version of the custumal, dating from the mid-fourteenth century, incorporated new clauses dealing with the property of orphans because of the 'maxima mortalitatis' in the town in 1351.[39] Thus the 5,000 inhabitants of the early 1340s may have been reduced to somewhere around 2,500. Population and household estimates for the mid-fifteenth century suggest that this is a reasonable conclusion.

5.4 Sandwich people

5.4.1 The ruling elite and wealthy merchants

The town's administration was dominated by a small group of wealthy men. The early thirteenth-century people are shadowy figures, such as Henry de Sandwich, who was the priory's portreeve and one of the founders of St Bartholomew's hospital (Chap. 6.2.2), and Thorold de Kyvilly, a baron of Sandwich and the king's bailiff in the 1220s.[40] Only a few other names are recorded in land transactions before the middle of the century and whether the people mentioned held office is usually unknown. Among them, however, was John Condy, whose family became important in town administration in the fourteenth century (see below).

By the late thirteenth century, when there are more records, several of the wealthiest townsmen were merchants, and the richest among them seem to have been those who had received special trading licences in the 1270s, thus evading the restrictions imposed on commerce, particularly the export of wool and hides, during a period of conflict with Flanders.[41] Such men were willing to serve the crown as needed. For example, John Peny and Thomas de Shelving,[42] who both prospered through the licensing, became collectors of the Ancient and New Customs in the early 1300s.[43] The Shelving family had estates in Woodnesborough, and also property in Sandwich, which they used to benefit St John's hospital.[44] Other leading merchants were probably among the jurats, even though they are not known to have held particular offices. They include Thomas le Blak and Hamo de Snaxton, both of whom joined with Shelving in 1295 to export wool in a local vessel (*La Plentee* of Sandwich), and Stephen Bron, Adam de Cherche and Geoffrey de Arundel, who had had a joint venture with John Peny to trade in hides.[45] Wool and hide merchants, such as the Penys[46] and the Wynterlands (Winterlonds),[47] had messuages, almost certainly with quays, in St Mary's parish abutting the Christ Church Priory property,[48] while other merchants such as the Wyberds and Drapers had property in the other two parishes.[49]

The Condy family was prominent in Sandwich's administrative and mercantile life during the fourteenth century, with various members active as vintners, shipmasters and shipowners. William Condy was mayor in 1310 and 1311, and his son John was mayor in 1326 and 1338. After naval exploits at the Battle of Sluys, John was given the bailiwick of Sandwich in hereditary tenure, an office that he held until his death in 1345, when he established a chantry in St Mary's church (Chap. 6.1.4) with a grant of £4 from property in Sandwich. He was succeeded in the bailiwick by his son William, who resigned the post in 1355,[50] but was brought back into royal service in 1363, as controller of customs. By the end of the century the Condy family had property in all three parishes in the town, as well as in the hundreds of Wingham and Eastry.[51]

In the 1340s there are some indications of the landed wealth of some of the leading townspeople from the lists of men of the Cinque Ports, who, although exempt from taxation within the town, were assessed for property in the surrounding hundreds.[52] Among the seventy-seven people who paid more than £1 for their property were some of the town's richest merchants, such as Richard Loveryk and Peter Barde, who both held land in the hundred of Wingham; the latter was the king's bailiff and became an admiral of the fleet.[53] Another was Hugh Champneys, who had property in the hundreds of Cornilo, Eastry, Wingham and Bewsborough. He was mayor three times in the early fourteenth century and was probably from the same family as Adam Champneys, who wrote the custumal of 1301.[54]

5.4.2 Artisans and traders

The bulk of the population practised a wide variety of essential occupations of the kind found in all towns. Most of the information comes from the court rolls of the thirteenth and early fourteenth centuries.[55] Unfortunately, these are very short on detail, simply providing tantalising glimpses of the activities of some merchants and evidence of the occupations and commercial transactions of lesser folk. In some instances there is just a single reference, in others the cases are deferred from court to court with the same people appearing. This makes it impossible to establish the relative importance of the occupations or to learn much about peoples' lives. Moreover, many plaintiffs and defendants are referred to by their place of origin, rather than by their occupation. From this we can see that some people came from the Kent countryside, having travelled no more than 20 miles (32km) from the surrounding parishes and from towns such as Dover and Faversham. But others came from further afield, from Winchelsea and London, or even from

Ireland and Bayonne. Lack of specific details about the cases heard, however, makes it impossible to see how the town was relating to the hinterland: whether, for example, goods were being bought and sold between the two, and whether the people with place-name surnames were immigrants or had simply come into town on business.

More than fifty occupations are mentioned in the court rolls (Table 5.1). Among the better documented are practitioners of the victualling trade and the thirty bakers who were listed, seventeen to twenty of them being recorded in one year. Some of the latter may have had property (including their bakery) in the countryside, but some were very clearly town based, including Matilda de Davyesgate, who was later replaced by her husband (or son), William de Davysgate.[56] Almost certainly these families brewed as well, for at this time ale was frequently produced by women in their homes using domestic equipment.[57] Nonetheless, there were also two male brewers, although whether they appear as brewers themselves or simply as heads of households is not known.

Women clearly played an important role in the late thirteenth-century economy. In addition to Matilda de Davyesgate, Margaret Shepster, Isabel and Beatrice le Chandeler, Joan Sutor (shoemaker), Matilda Cowherd, Ionoria la Brower, Alice Applemonger and Basilia la Hore[58] all appeared before the court under their own names.[59] Five other women were involved in trespass cases, although it is not known what they had done. Matilda Long, on the other hand, was accused by Peter and Agnes Adrian of detaining malt.[60] Other female workers undoubtedly lived as servants in the inns, taverns and lodging houses that catered to the needs of the fluctuating population of mariners, fishermen and travellers.[61]

By the later fourteenth century a biannual list of taxes on produce and occupations, perhaps added to the custumal after it was first written, gives an indication of trades in the town. In addition to the occupations in the court rolls, there were dyers of different kinds of cloth, furriers and more trades relating to the sea, including pilots, ships' carpenters and boat builders, and there were house carpenters (linked to the last two) and thatchers.[62]

Although by no means clear from the court roll evidence, most of the working population were probably dependent on fishing and the sea, as had been the case from the eleventh century. In 1253 the herring house owned by Christ Church Priory was rented out.[63] This was a large building, perhaps originally constructed in masonry, to contain the annual render of 40,000 herrings due from the town's fishermen since the time of Domesday. From 1278, when the fishermen of the Cinque Ports acquired the right to dry their nets and land their herring and mackerel at Great Yarmouth during the North Sea fishing season, most of their catch would have been sold at the herring fair that in its thirteenth-century heyday attracted hundreds of ships and traders from all over England and the Continent. But after the fair declined in the middle of the fourteenth century, much of the Sandwich catch may have been salted and

Table 5.1: Occupations mentioned in the mid-thirteenth to early fourteenth-century court rolls

The numbers in brackets refer to the number of times the surname is used with a different Christian name.

Categories	Occupations deduced from court rolls
Shipping	Packer (2), porter (1), shipmaster (2), weyer (1)
Merchant	Draper (1), merchant (1), spicer (2), vintner (3)
Hide and leather	Cobbler (1), cordwainer (1), glover (2), shoemaker (1), skinner (1), tanner (2), tawyer (3)
Victualler: drink	Brewer (3), butler (1), cooper (2), maltster (1), taverner (4), victualler (1)
Victualler: food	Baker (30), butcher (5), chandler (1), cook (4), garlic seller (1)
Cloth	Shepster [dressmaker] (2), tailor (8), teynter (1)
Countryside	Applemonger (1), cheese maker (1), cowherd (2), falconer (2), warrener (?)
Service	Barber (2), miller (1)
Construction	Joiner (3), sawyer (1), tiler (2)
Metal trades	Cutler (3), goldsmith (2), ironmonger* (4), smith (4)
Ecclesiastical	Beadle (1), chaplain (3), cleric (14), deacon (1), palmer (5), usher (1)
Medical	Bloodletter (1), cupper (1)
Servant	Handyman (1), maid servant (1), man servant (1)
Various	Musician (*gygur*), (1) whore (1)
Categories not known	lobber (1), shuter (1)

brought back to the town for sale in the market and to local institutions such as Christ Church Priory and St Augustine's Abbey. Fresh fish, such as oysters harvested locally and plaice bought from Rye fishermen, were probably sold from fishmongers' shambles (stalls) or shops in the fish market.

The sheer number of names listed in the mid-fourteenth-century tax assessments on property outside Sandwich,[64] and the modest amounts some people were expected to pay, suggest that many ordinary Sandwich people owned small pieces of land in the surrounding countryside.[65] A total of 234 people paid less than 2s. in tax, with some paying as little as 2d. or 3d. While some of the smallest holdings may have been deliberately acquired, and perhaps used to grow a small crop or pasture an animal, others were likely to have resulted from partible inheritance, with heirs who received tiny, uneconomic, amounts of land moving into town to find work, no doubt leaving relatives or tenants to look after their property. This suggestion is perhaps supported by the occurrence of place-name surnames, such as Stephen de Hardres, who paid two amounts of 12d. in Eastry and Bewsborough, and Gilbert de Bircheholt, who paid 8d., also in Bewsborough. Curiously, the largest number of names occurs in the hundred of Bewsborough, separated from Sandwich by the hundreds of Eastry and Cornilo. The reasons for this are unclear.

5.5 The economic background

5.5.1 Trade in the thirteenth century

Trade had almost certainly always played a great part in the economic life of the town, but it is not until the later thirteenth and fourteenth centuries that the details are documented. During this period Sandwich was one of England's major ports, where cargoes from overseas were unloaded and vessels were freighted with commodities for export, and also where goods were transhipped, mainly for London. Some native merchants grew rich, but much of the Sandwich trade was not conducted by local inhabitants, but by outsiders, either Londoners or aliens.

The only evidence for trade in the earlier thirteenth century comes from the overall figures for the revenue gleaned from taxes and tolls. When the crown levied a tax of a fifteenth on merchants' goods in 1204, Sandwich's assessment of £16 was about half as much as at Dover (£32 6s. 1d.) and much less than Winchelsea (£62 2s. 4d.).[66] This may not, however, be a true comparison, for Sandwich's low assessment may reflect not the amount of trade, but the fact that so much of it passed through non-local hands. Another source of information about the amount of trade, which possibly excludes information about local merchants, is the accounts of Christ Church Priory, which contain a breakdown of the revenues received *de portu* from the 1220s onwards. They rose from between £50 and £60 in the 1220s to more than £100 in 1255–6, and remained well over £90 until the records temporarily cease in 1260–61.[67] What was comprised under this heading is not totally clear, but after the exchange with the crown in 1290 royal officials were collecting tolls on goods that were imported and exported by all merchants who were not freemen of Sandwich, together with charges on ships anchored in the haven, and on passengers, such as pilgrims, who used the port to cross to or come back from the Continent.[68] These tolls and charges were totally separate from the national customs duties that were later imposed and were probably the same as those levied earlier by the priory.

Before the survival of national customs accounts, little can be said about the volume of trade and the range of goods imported and exported. Although luxury goods, such as figs and almonds, were occasionally acquired by the king,[69] it is not known how common such products were or who else bought them. What is known is that in the early thirteenth century wine was purchased in Sandwich for the royal household, for use in provisioning Dover Castle or as gifts to allies such as Thomas, count of Flanders.[70] It is likely that, as later in the century, the export of wool and the import of wine lay at the heart of the Sandwich overseas trade. But precise figures for the number of wool sacks sent out are lacking before 1275, when the Ancient Custom began to tax aliens and denizens exporting wool, wool fells and hides. Further information becomes available in 1303 when the New Custom added a levy on aliens importing wine and exporting cloth, wax and other goods.[71] Arrangements for levying these taxes entailed each county designating 'the largest town where there is a port' as the collection centre (Fig. 9.1).[72] Thus, Sandwich became the customs port for Kent.

In the 1270s problems arose with the outbreak of the conflict between England and Flanders. The new countess of Flanders arrested all English goods in her domains and, in retaliation, by the end of the year all Flemish merchants and their goods were arrested in England, and trading with Flanders and Flemish merchants was banned. The effects of the embargo, however, were ameliorated by the grant of special licences to new groups of merchants – Germans from Lübeck and Cologne, Italians, northern French and English.[73] In 1279–80, 762 sacks of wool were exported through Sandwich. This figure is higher than that of other ports such as Ipswich, Chichester and Great Yarmouth, but pales in comparison with the 7,699 sacks shipped through Boston, and the very substantial amounts shipped through London, Southampton and Hull. Wool exports through Sandwich then dropped in the 1280s, to an average of only 277 sacks a year.[74] The figures show that Sandwich was not a major player in the export of wool.

Unfortunately, the detailed breakdown of Sandwich revenues that the local priory officials drew up have not survived for most of the 1270s and 1280s. The central accounts at Canterbury, however, recorded the money it received from its official who resided in the port. In addition to customs and tolls, this included all the rents from property, and probably also wages and expenditure on new buildings. In the 1280s the overall receipts ranged between £34 and £59 a year, compared with £80 to £90 annually in the 1250s. It is not known whether this was because a higher proportion of the receipts were being used in new building or other expenses, or whether returns from the collection of tolls had truly declined in adverse trading conditions. Butcher espouses the latter view, and believes that when the priory gave up its rights to the crown in 1290 this was an advantageous exchange, since the port was already beginning to decline.[75] That this may not have been so is suggested by the final receipt, for 1289–90, which was for £111 0s. 6½d. In addition, in the 1280s the priory was clearly still interested in building up its Sandwich estate, for it then acquired property from John Peny and the Packer family, and repaired Monkenquay and the so-called long house adjacent to it (Chap. 7.2; Fig. III.1).[76]

The war that Edward I waged on three fronts during the 1290s seriously disrupted trade in Sandwich as elsewhere, with merchantmen from the Cinque Ports being diverted from their function of carrying cargoes for civilians to performing ship service and acting as transports for the army. In 1296, for example, Sandwich provided twelve of the fifty Cinque Port vessels that gathered in the haven to carry Edmund Lancaster's troops to Gascony.[77] The supply of Gascon wine was interrupted, and a heavy increase in export duties followed by the seizure of wool by royal officials brought the wool trade to a virtual halt. Prices plummeted, and on the Christ Church estates coarse local wool accumulated unsold.[78] Further seizures of wool in 1297 exacerbated an already difficult situation. Five sacks belonging to Thomas de Shelving were confiscated at Great Yarmouth; others belonging to Sandwich merchants were seized in the port of London and yet more, owned by merchants of the Cinque Ports, were sequestrated at Sandwich.[79]

To finance the wars, Edward I laid an unprecedented burden of taxation on clergy and laity alike.[80] Purveyance – the compulsory purchase by royal agents of grain and other goods such as cheese – fell with particular severity on Kent, the effects being felt in both town and countryside. In 1295–6, for example, the sheriff collected 4,884 quarters of grain for provisioning the army in Gascony.[81] Although, in theory, the crown was supposed to pay for these provisions, in practice they were simply seized, or the suppliers were given credit notes rather than cash. The royal expedition to Flanders in 1297–8 again laid new burdens on the town as men and ships from the Cinque Ports gathered there in preparation for the royal departure,[82] and in 1298 more preparations had to be made in Sandwich for the king's speedy return from France to deal with the Scottish threat.[83]

5.5.2 Trade in the fourteenth century

After peace had been signed in 1303, Sandwich's overseas trade flourished once again,[84] although without a complete survey of the customs records for all the English ports, it is impossible to say how many 'ships of Sandwich' carried cargoes destined for abroad. The hinterland of Sandwich included the fertile fields of east Kent and plentiful pasture in the coastal marshes, providing the valuable export commodities of wheat, cheese and wool. In 1304–5 approximately 200 cargoes of grain left the port, 60 per cent of the total exports from the Cinque Ports in that twelve-month period, and in the years 1303–6 an annual average of 1,172 sacks of wool, together with large quantities of hides, were sent out from Sandwich.[85]

This contrasted markedly with Winchelsea, as shown by comparing the tolls paid on the roughly equal number of cargoes that passed through the two ports in 1307–8 (163 for Sandwich, 161 for Winchelsea), but the great discrepancy in the tolls paid. The value of Sandwich's imported goods was fifteen times greater than that of Winchelsea because the latter exported goods such as wood, timber and bark,[86] while Sandwich concentrated on the luxury market. That year, 122 cargoes valued at £2,961 and comprising a great variety of different products were brought into the port, with the largest and most valuable cargo being that of the Genoese merchant Anthony de Pesaigne, which included alum, almonds, cotton, pepper, dates, rice, leather and cheese.[87] Clearly, the high values recorded in the customs accounts for Sandwich were the result of the luxuries carried and not indicative of an increase in the volume of trade.

With the establishment of peace the wine trade also

recovered. Between 1322 and 1346, although only an average of four tuns a year was brought in by denizen merchants, 455 tuns were imported by aliens, meaning that in this respect Sandwich ranked just below London, Boston and Hull.[88] Some of these imports, both of wine and luxury goods, would have been transhipped to London in local ships under local masters. Some, however, would have been sold at Sandwich, most then being shipped on to Fordwich, whence they could have been taken by road to Canterbury and other Kent towns.[89]

Sandwich merchants not only imported wine but also supplied it to the royal household, as did Henry Wyberd and Robert de Snakeston in 1312.[90] As inhabitants of the Cinque Ports, they were exempt from payment of the New Custom. A few Gascon merchants, seeking similar privileges, established residence in Sandwich and paid local taxes (scot and lot) as denizens. This is the earliest known example of aliens (those born outside the jurisdiction of the English king) becoming domiciled in Sandwich – more than a hundred years before similar settlements by Italian merchants.[91] How much wine was imported by each of these merchants is not clear. The king, worried by his loss of revenue, accused them of bringing in 1,000 tuns of wine or more, but one merchant, Peter Garcies, when questioned by Exchequer officials, insisted that he had brought in no more than 10 tuns. He did, however, agree that he had acquired a tenement in Sandwich and was residing there.[92]

In the 1330s poor weather, especially drought, and outbreaks of animal disease seriously affected agriculture throughout much of Kent. Prices as a whole fell steadily throughout the decade, reaching their lowest level in the years 1337–9.[93] Although this made purchase easier, incomes were reduced so that both buying and selling were affected. In addition, as a result of the money required to finance the Hundred Years War, the demands of the tax collector bit more deeply than earlier. Maddicott has suggested that in the six years 1336–41 'the weight of taxation may have been greater than at any other time in the Middle Ages, greater even than in the years preceding the revolt of 1381'.[94] The resources of both peasants and townsmen might thus have been totally depleted. Those who had goods to sell could not always find a buyer; prospective customers, even though they might need the goods, no longer had the means to purchase them. In 1337 town officials at Sandwich were ordered to allow merchants to take away any unsold goods that had been brought to the fair held on 6 January.[95] In 1339–40 heavy expenses were incurred improving the town's defences (Section 5.6.2),[96] and in 1341 the bailiff, John Condy, petitioned the Exchequer for a reduction in the fee farm paid for the bailiwick from £70 to £40 on the grounds that, because of war, merchandise was prevented from coming to the town.[97] In 1355 the farm was further reduced to £30.[98]

But the situation in Sandwich may not have been as dire as the town authorities claimed. By the mid-1340s prices had begun to rise and the collection of local tolls by the royal bailiff was producing revenues of £60 a year, nearly the same level as in the 1280s, and in most months anchorage fees were collected from between fifty and eighty-two ships. As earlier, a wide variety of goods made their way in – figs, raisins, almonds (brought in by Spanish merchants), deal boards, salt fish, mercury, linen cloth and canvas. Meanwhile, going out were grain, cheese and butter.[99] Port revenues might have risen even higher if Sandwich had not become the major assembly and victualling point for warships, although some Sandwich inhabitants were able to take advantage of the unusual commercial opportunities that it presented. In 1340, for example, the receiver of victuals that had been gathered at Sandwich was forced to sell off goods such as flour and salt fish that were in danger of spoiling. The goods were bought at a good price by local men, including John Condy, and John, William and Richard Loveryk.[100] Subsequently, royal officials hired storage in Sandwich at the rate of 15d. a week. Richard Loveryk, for example, provided two granaries and one 'celer' in 1340, and Richard Spicer rented out a great warehouse (*hospitatum*) from 10 July 1340 to 23 May 1342.[101]

The arrival of the Black Death seriously affected trade. Instead of the 340 ships a year paying mooring tolls in the mid-1340s, just 133 merchant ships paid tolls in 1350.[102] Trade continued, but at a considerably lower level, and for the month of April 1351 the bailiff noted that no tolls had been received because no ship had arrived in port with goods on which customs could be levied. Overall, in 1351–2, the revenues collected by the royal bailiff dropped to about half – £30 – with fewer ships mooring and even fewer actually loading and unloading cargo.[103] What trade there was – wine and salt fish brought in and wheat, ale and malt sent out – was frequently in the hands of widows.[104]

5.6 The defence of Sandwich

The wars and civil unrest of the thirteenth and fourteenth centuries left their mark on Sandwich in several ways. Physical aspects of the town must have changed to accommodate its role as a port and town in the front line of defence, with the royal castle becoming the mustering point for troops on their way to France and the town itself acquiring defensible walls, probably first in the early fourteenth century. Sandwich Haven was a focal point in the military preparations, and it cannot have been unusual for fleets made up of scores of vessels to be anchored in its waters.

Sandwich's development as a defended town seems to have been piecemeal, with earth ramparts around the landward side of the town probably built in different phases, and with no stone walls until the fifteenth century, when they were erected along parts of the waterfront (Chap. 11.2.1.3). The stretches of rampart now known as The Rope Walk and The Butts were much slighter and probably rather earlier in date than Mill Wall on the east, which, when it was constructed, cut the castle off from the town and influenced the street pattern in its vicinity.

5.6.1 The royal castle

The area of royal land to the east of St Clement's church may have acquired its first castle in the thirteenth century, with the area subsequently becoming known as 'Castelmed' or 'Castelmead'.[105] Present Castle Field is only part of the original grounds around the castle, the probable size of which is shown on Figure 3.2. Small-scale archaeological excavations in Castle Field in the 1970s and 1980s (Fig. 5.1) revealed remains of a substantial ditch associated with an earthwork.[106] In 1996 excavations little more than 100m east of its centre uncovered another stretch of ditch and the base of a rampart, also attributed to the thirteenth century. It is unclear whether the two ditches originally formed part of the same feature, even though they are thought to be contemporary.[107] The foundations of two substantial stone walls, one at least 15m in length, were discovered along with traces of a timber building, but none could be dated any more closely than the thirteenth century or later (see Chap. 4.5 for the pre-thirteenth-century phases of the site).[108] One of the most interesting results of the excavation of the earthwork and ditch was its stratigraphic relationship with Mill Wall, the moat of which overlay the west edge of the ditch.[109]

The excavated remains suggest that the castle was a fairly simple structure in the thirteenth century, but it may have been the complex that Roger de Leyburn took when recapturing Sandwich in 1266. The account of Roger's success is the first documentary reference to the castle, and the only certain mention of it in the thirteenth century,[110] although several other documents may refer to it. In 1290, for example, the royal bailiff was paid £20 for 'works' at Sandwich, which could have been for work arising from the exchange with Christ Church Priory, when the king's bailiff became the most important external official in the town,[111] and in 1298 Edward I occupied the 'king's chamber' on his return from Flanders.[112] There is more convincing documentary evidence in the early fourteenth century, with the custumal noting the presence of the king's

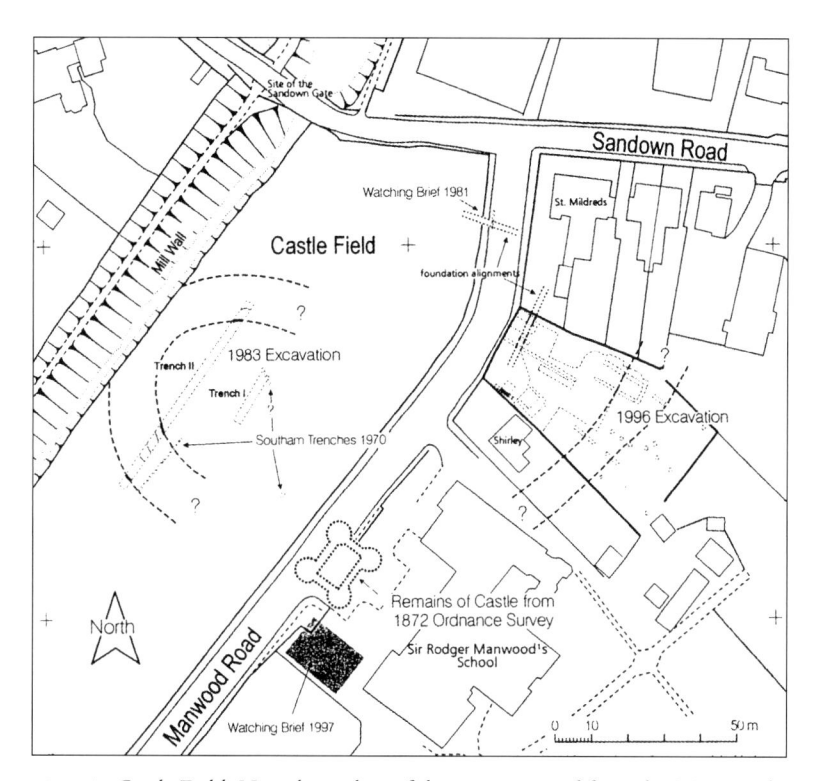

Fig. 5.1: The site of excavations in Castle Field. Note the outline of the tower inserted from the OS map of 1872 (Stewart 2000, fig. 2)

castle and its surrounding land.[113] Then, in 1303 the 'king's tower' was repaired,[114] and in the following year Ellis Scarlet was appointed bailiff with responsibility for 'the keeping of the king's tower in Sandwich'.[115] It may have been one of the castles in south-east England that the king's serjeants inspected in 1318 to 'survey the defects of arms and equipment', and if so that is the only time that its defensive capabilities are mentioned before the 1380s.[116] Although all the bailiffs after 1307 had their headquarters there,[117] and in 1345 King Edward III and Queen Philippa stayed in a chamber in the castle before the king set out for France,[118] its administrative characteristics were probably more important than its residential role or defensive capacity. Its primary purpose is likely to have been to administer the king's rights in Sandwich and to oversee the gathering of fleets and armies in the haven. It must, however, have had at least some features of a stronghold, for it housed a gaol in 1358,[119] perhaps the same building as, or a successor to, the 'prison in Sandwich' mentioned in 1293 and 1299.[120]

It is clear from both documentary sources and the small amount of archaeological work carried out that the castle at Sandwich was never one of the great fortifications of medieval England. It was not built until long after the first phase of Norman castle building, perhaps because at the time of the Conquest the port was overshadowed by Dover to the south and Canterbury to the west, both of which had late eleventh-century mottes. Dover castle remained pre-eminent throughout the Middle Ages, housing the warden of the Cinque Ports and acquiring the great stone keep and other structures that survive to this day. It may also have been considered sufficient to guard the entire stretch of the east Kent coast, but it is strange that Sandwich was so poorly served, particularly since its haven must have been well known throughout maritime Europe as an ideal naval base. This puzzle remains, perhaps only to be solved through much more thorough and targeted excavation in the future.

There are no surviving traces of the king's tower first mentioned in 1303, but the 25 inch Ordnance Survey map of 1872 may record its last days. The map shows an outline plan of a substantial structure, marked 'The King's Castle (remains of)', on the edge of what is today called Castle Field (Fig. 5.1). The plan is of a rectangular feature with a three-quarter-round turret at each corner, suggestive of a tower. Its remains were removed without investigation in 1881;[121] if any traces of the foundations survive they must be buried beneath Manwood Road and Sir Roger Manwood's School.[122] As measured from the map, its overall dimensions were approximately 12m × 15m (39 × 49ft). In the absence of archaeological investigations, the tower's date, appearance and even its building materials remain unknown, as does its purpose. It could have been the early fourteenth-century tower of the documents, but it is impossible to tell from the Ordnance Survey map, or from anything revealed by the excavations described above. There are some medieval parallels. Strand Gate in New Winchelsea is similar in plan but smaller (approx. 6m × 5m in area), and has been attributed to c.1300 on stylistic grounds. Ypres Tower, Rye, slightly larger in all dimensions and perhaps a hundred years later than Strand Gate, is also similar in plan.[123] If the tower at Sandwich were free-standing, as it appears from the plan, it could even be comparable with sixteenth-century brick-built lookout towers such as Freston Tower near Ipswich, Suffolk, and Clifton House tower in King's Lynn, Norfolk.[124] All interpretations must remain speculative until an opportunity for excavation arises.

The castle and surrounding royal land would have been dominant features on the east side of Sandwich, overlooking Sandwich Haven. It has earlier been suggested that the area was significant by the eleventh century, when royal fleets assembled in the haven, and perhaps much earlier because of its possible association with the royal estate centre of Eastry and the early medieval waterside settlement (Chap. 2.3.2). Its strategic potential must have been clear during the late Middle Ages, particularly during the Hundred Years War (1337–1453), when Sandwich was in the forefront of the national war effort. Troops destined for service overseas came to Sandwich on foot from all parts of England and would have needed to be accommodated there while awaiting the naval transports, possibly bivouacking on the land around the castle.[125] Fortunately for the town's inhabitants, the soldiers could have reached Castelmead without marching through the town itself, for the castle site was alongside the road from Eastry, which linked up with other routes from east Kent and further afield. There is very little evidence of how the men were provided for once they arrived at their camps, but there are some hints. For example, cattle were driven to Sandwich on the hoof;[126] corn and malt were brought by ship to be ground in local mills; and bakers and brewers were instructed to make bread and beer in preparation for the men at arms and archers who were expected to arrive in the port for embarkation 'for the defence of England'.[127]

Once arrived in Sandwich, the troops probably had weeks of idleness ahead of them. In 1359, for instance, they were ordered to assemble there by 30 August, but it was not until the beginning of October that the first of them set sail for France.[128] The main reason why the wait was so long was probably because ships needed to be brought from virtually all the east coast ports to assemble in Sandwich Haven and the Downs, where there was a sheltered anchorage. Then the ships had to be modified in various ways, depending on what was to be their cargoes. For example, many of them were destined to be horse transports, and needed extra fittings to secure the animals while on board. Vast numbers of horses accompanied the troops during the whole of the Hundred Years War, exemplified by the later (1431) account of 1,500 horses being embarked at Sandwich on a single occasion.[129] Gangways had to be specially made to take the horses on board. Once there, they were tethered in stalls partitioned from each other by hurdles.[130] In 1359 thirty bridges (gangways) and 1,000 hurdles were said to have been brought from Kent, Sussex and Essex to Sandwich while the army was gathering.[131]

The ships were also maintained and repaired in Sandwich Haven, and new vessels were probably built. Carpenters and shipwrights were brought to work on the king's ships,[132] and in 1358 a timber-lined 'dyke' (dock) was dug specifically to enable the royal vessel *Le George* to be repaired.[133] Slipways or boat houses of some kind would probably have been needed in the vicinity of the castle, perhaps 'penthouses' for sheltering royal vessels such as there were in Rye and Winchelsea in the thirteenth century.[134] Travellers on commissions for the king may well have set out from the castle to embark on the ships that were to take them across the sea. Thus, it is likely that there was a landing place of some sort on the shore to its north.

The structures involved in all the activities outlined above may have been ephemeral, as shown by the excavated medieval shipbuilding site of Small Hythe near Tenterden, Kent,[135] so it is not surprising that nothing has survived above ground at Sandwich. The changing course of the river Stour and the post-medieval reclamation of the riverbank compound the difficulties of discovering any signs of this work. Nevertheless, the timbers from a fourteenth-century ship were found nearby, and other features may have been preserved and await discovery (Section 5.7.1).

5.6.2 The development of urban defences

For a town so much exposed to external attack, Sandwich seems to have acquired urban defences relatively late. Elsewhere in England walls may have been under construction in the middle of the twelfth century, and certainly by the early decades of the thirteenth,[136] but in Sandwich the first documentary reference is 1266, and even then the urban defences seem to have been of only a temporary nature. This is in contrast to Dover, which had walls by 1231.[137] The walls around Sandwich also differ in other ways from the enceintes of medieval towns elsewhere. The landward approaches to the town are still guarded by earth ramparts approximately 1.25km in total length and of variable construction.[138] They were never replaced or supplemented by stone walls, although short stretches of masonry were erected along the eastern and western waterfront in the fifteenth century (Chap. 11.2.1.3).

The earliest reference to the defences is in 1266 when Roger de Leyburn recaptured the castle and town (Section 5.1.1). Town walls are not mentioned, but a siege engine (*ursus*) directed against a timber brattice or breastwork indicates a defensible structure of some kind, although probably impermanent.[139] The town seems to have been provided with more substantial boundaries by 1275, when the mayor and commonalty defied the king's authority by barring it with chains, ditches, 'barbicans' (*barbakani*, probably palisades) and 'other fortifications (*cetera aforciamenta*)', which held out for a month or more before the town capitulated.[140] After the dispute was resolved, the chains were removed, the ditches filled in and the other defences taken down and transported to Dover. Neither reference suggests anything other than temporary structures.

Other than these two late thirteenth-century references, the documents are silent on Sandwich's town defences until 1321, when the first murage grant was recorded.[141] This is not positive evidence for the town being undefended until that date, for it was not unusual for towns to have begun to erect walls before the documentation starts. At Dover, for example, the first grant was as late as 1324, although it had been at least partly walled a century earlier.

At Sandwich the custumal of 1301 makes no mention of town walls, although many other aspects of urban life are described in great detail, suggesting that it was not merely an omission but that the walls had not been built by the time the custumal was first composed.[142] Even though there was no wall around the town at that time, there were designated points of access, presumably where the highways entered the urban jurisdiction. These were described as exits or 'outlets of the town (*exitus villae*)' through which everyone had to pass, including the people coming in from the countryside to attend the market.[143] The 'outlets' may have been defined by barriers or bars across the highways (called 'turnpikes' at the end of the century),[144] probably the precursors of the masonry gates, for which there is much information in the fifteenth and sixteenth centuries. The only gates mentioned in the custumal stood alongside the haven, some perhaps protecting passages to the waterfront between properties, rather than gateways through walls.[145] Pillory Gate stood at the north end of Harnet Street and The Butchery. Davis Gate, after whom Matilda the baker was named,[146] probably stood near the ferry at the north end of the High Street.

The earth ramparts and ditches consist of three lengths of differing character, although The Rope Walk and The Butts are very similar in profile (Fig. 5.2). These two were both built on Alluvium at approximately 2m OD, with The Rope Walk probably overlying ditches that were dug to drain the land on which the Carmelite friary was to be built in the second half of the thirteenth century (Chap. 6.2.1). The Rope Walk rampart and ditch seem to have been constructed after the foundation of the friary and were designed to avoid its precinct, passing across open marshland to the south. The construction of this major new earthwork must have caused a significant amount of disruption to the existing drainage works, cutting through various ditches and interfering with their flow. Also, the wide but shallow moat in front of The Rope Walk rampart must have provided an important new element in the local land drainage scheme, taking water from pre-existing ditches. The eastern half of The Rope Walk rampart has a drainage ditch along its foot on the town side. This connects with a culvert and presumably was intended to take water from the ditches inside the town, under the rampart and out into the moat. What is less certain is whether the ditch leading to the sluice pre-dated the rampart and dictated its course, or whether it was constructed as part of the remodelling of the drainage works when the rampart was built. The Butts also runs across Alluvium at approximately 2m OD, and in other respects is similar to The Rope Walk, although there is no indication of intramural drainage ditches specifically associated with it. Its moat, however, must have had the same effect as that in front of The Rope Walk.

Mill Wall is totally different in scale from the other two ramparts. The evidence from the castle excavation suggests that it was constructed no earlier than the end of the thirteenth century, but no closer dating can be given. It may have been created as a result of the grant of 1321, but that is by no means certain. It could

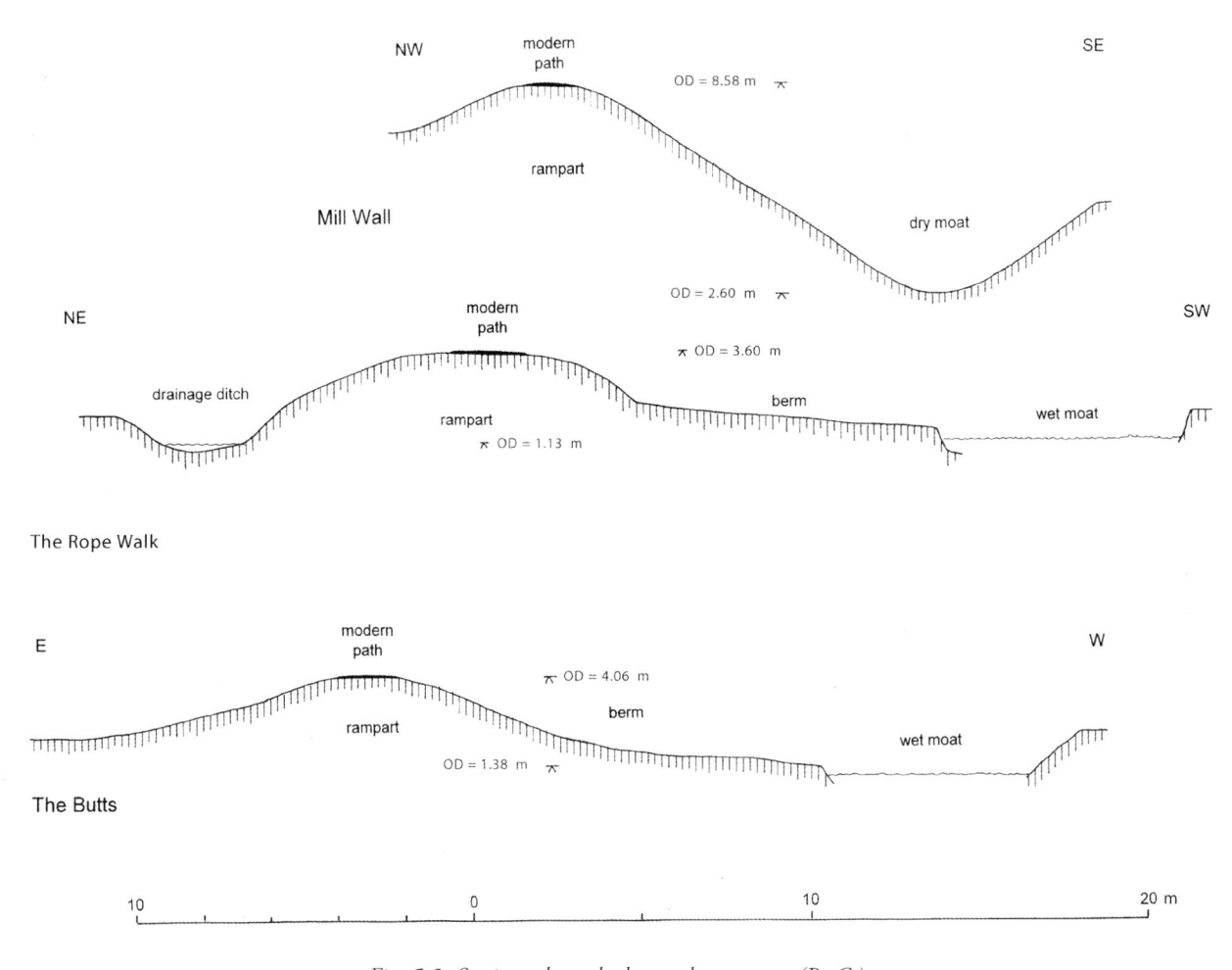

Fig. 5.2: Sections through the earth ramparts (B. C.)

also have been put up in 1338, when, in response to a general directive to all English ports to look to their defences, inhabitants who had left Sandwich in order to avoid 'the charges for the defence of the town against hostile invaders' were summoned back.[147] Mill Wall may have been built on such a massive scale as the town's prime defence against attack from the east, but it also cut the castle off from the town, separating St Clement's church from the royal land. It is impossible to say whether this was a deliberate outcome, for it goes against the usual practice of medieval town walls and castles being part of a defensive unit.[148] The king may have wished for some reason to isolate the castle from the town, or the town possibly needed to protect itself from the troops assembled in Castelmead while awaiting their transports to France. The amount of manpower that must have been needed for building Mill Wall suggests that its construction was the responsibility of the crown rather than the town, but no records survive to throw any light on the problem. A royal initiative may also be inferred from the fact that it fundamentally changed the topography and street pattern of the south-eastern quarter of the town by blocking what until then had been the main roads from the south and east (Fig. 5.3). The highways that had entered the town along Mill Wall Place and Knightrider Street were cut off and replaced by a single route from the south, which ran through a gap in the ramparts at the junction between The Rope Walk and Mill Wall, following the course of the Delf where New Gate was later built (Chap. 11.2.1.1). The change resulted in the east end of town becoming more isolated, an outcome

Fig. 5.3: Aerial view from south showing the changed street pattern following the building of Mill Wall (D. Grady © English Heritage 24064/07)

that could not be presumed to be in the interests of the civic authorities, but perhaps this was of little concern to the crown.

The ramparts were not the only manifestations of defence at Sandwich. As early as 1285 the authorities had enquired into the feasibility and expense of digging a trench to divert the North Stream,[149] which flowed through the Lydden Valley to the 'Guestlyng' where it met the south bank of Sandwich Haven (Fig. 3.12).[150] Nothing more is heard about the proposal until 5 September 1321, when the waterway was to be diverted for the 'better security' of the town.[151] On 8 September of the same year the first grant for the town walls was recorded. That the diversion was petitioned for immediately before murage was granted suggests that the town authorities were conscious of the importance of water defences, which had previously been provided by the Delf alone. Perhaps they had no prior knowledge of the murage grant that was to come three days later, and which may have made the whole exercise redundant after a few years. Nevertheless, the diversion must have been put into effect fairly rapidly, for the two watercourses ('le guestling' and 'waterdelf') are recorded as one, flowing in the same bed by 1335.[152] The course of the diversion is impossible to trace on the ground today, but a line approximately following the south-eastern boundary of the Liberty and hundred is likely (Fig. 5.4). If this were so, the Guestling would have connected the North Stream with the Delf south of the haven and north of Pinnock Wall. Since the second half of the eighteenth century the name Guestling has been applied solely to the stretch of the Delf that flows past the site of Canterbury Gate to join the river Stour near St Mary's church, at the west end of town.[153] The original location of the Guestling almost 2km east of the town has long been forgotten, causing much confusion in recent attempts to interpret the medieval topography of Sandwich.

5.7 Sandwich Haven and the route through the Wantsum Channel

Sandwich Haven was the defining feature of Sandwich, on which both the commercial and strategic importance of the port and town depended throughout the Middle Ages. It was used as an anchorage for both military and commercial fleets, as a harbour with an increasing number of facilities to serve visiting ships, and as the south-eastern entrance to a water route from the English Channel to the outer Thames estuary and eastern England. Its influence is underlined by the fact than once the silting of the Wantsum Channel, and therefore Sandwich Haven, became extreme, Sandwich fell from its previous international importance to a port of purely local character.

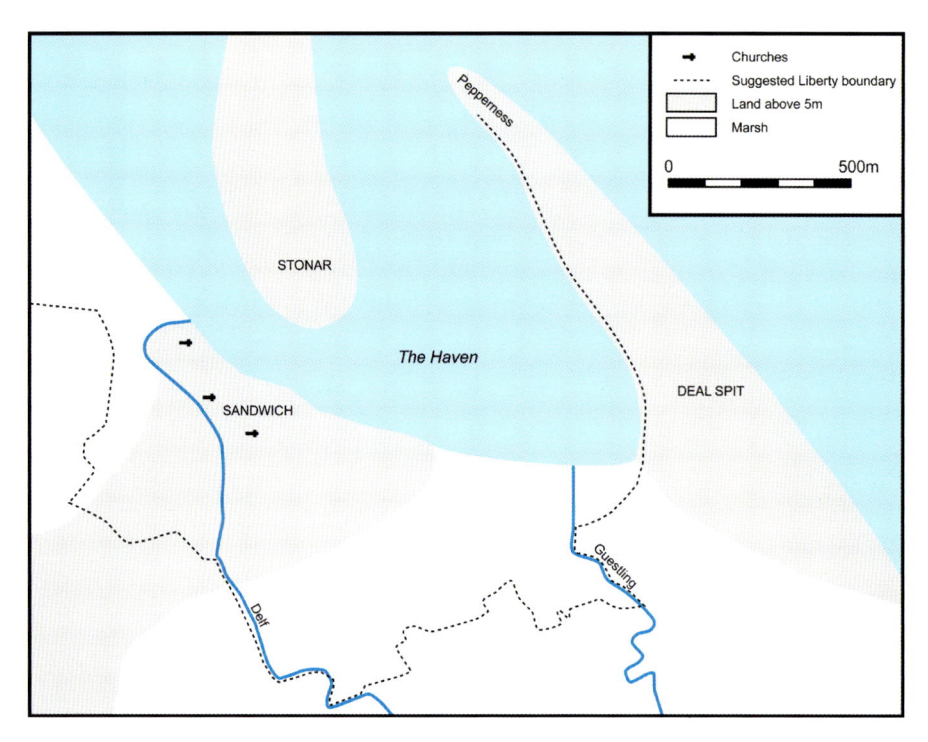

Fig. 5.4: The south-east area of the Liberty showing the Guestling before it was diverted to flow towards Sandwich, probably roughly following the Liberty boundary (J. H.)

5.7.1 The size of the haven

A rough idea of the size of the haven can be gained from one important documentary source in which, in 1324, anxiety was expressed about its openness to attack: 'on account of its ample size, a very large number of vessels can put in at the same time and this is a danger [from the French] to the town and adjacent parts'.[154] This can be supplemented by information about the size of the ships that frequented the haven (normally given in tuns, a measure of volume, so the dimensions of a vessel can be difficult to envisage) and sometimes the numbers of ships at anchor at any one time. The overall impression is of a great sheet of water sheltered from the English Channel and well known to English and foreign merchantmen as an anchorage, a destination for their cargoes or as a place where those cargoes could be transhipped for transport through the Wantsum Channel to the Thames and beyond. That it was also of military importance is indicated by the castle on its banks and the gathering of great fleets in readiness for war.

One such fleet assembled in 1337, when Edward III summoned ships from all the southern ports to meet at Sandwich in response to the French invasion of the English-held duchy of Aquitaine. About 169 ships, carrying almost 5,000 mariners and soldiers, gathered there, with Sandwich contributing eleven vessels. In contrast, Winchelsea provided twenty-five ships and 658 mariners,[155] and this pattern continued at least for the rest of the war; Sandwich's importance lay in its anchorage, not in the number of vessels it could provide.

The only physical evidence for the size of a ship that used the haven in the fourteenth century was obtained through the accidental discovery and fortunate survival of ship's timbers in a silted creek north of Sandown Road, just north of Sandwich castle.[156] Since 1973, when the timbers were found, they have been subjected to archaeological and scientific investigations that have shown them to have belonged to a fourteenth-century merchantman, built of oak grown in south-east England,[157] between 20m and 30m long, probably 7–8m wide amidships, and more than 4m high above the keel (Fig. 5.5). Statistics for fourteenth- and fifteenth-century cogs given below suggest that the Sandwich ship may have had a carrying capacity of about 150 tuns. To show how big that truly was, Milne suggests that its hull would have fitted snugly into the north aisle of St Peter's church (Fig. 6.16).

Bearing that analogy in mind, we might visualise the small fleet of merchantmen on its way to Gascony in 1326–7, which was arrested and brought back to

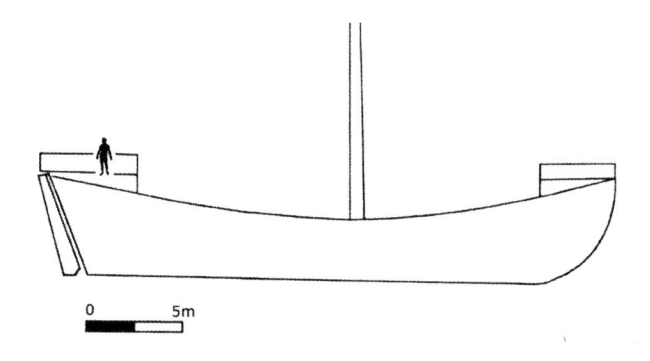

Fig. 5.5: Suggested reconstruction of the hull of the Sandwich ship (Milne 2004, fig. 14)

the port.[158] The ships varied in size from 180 tuns (*La Seyntmariecogge*) to 50 tuns (*La Laurence* and *La Petit James*). Ships trading to Gascony at this time are thought to have had one crew member for each three or four tuns carried, so the *Seyntmariecogge* may have had a crew of between forty-five and sixty men, the *Laurence* and *Petit James* between twelve and seventeen.[159] In similar circumstances, the Sandwich ship would have been manned by a crew of between thirty-eight and fifty mariners. These can only be extremely rough estimates.

5.7.2 The vessels that visited the haven

Most of the evidence for the vessels that used Sandwich Haven derives from fourteenth-century documentary sources, and relates to merchantmen and, more occasionally, royal warships. The sea-going cargo ships that visited Sandwich in the thirteenth and fourteenth centuries would have been mainly 'hulks' or 'cogs'. Hulks were constructed in the early medieval clinker-built tradition, with curved stem and stern posts, a side rudder, a single sail and oars. They are well known from manuscript illustrations and on town seals, such as that of Sandwich itself (Fig. 5.6), although no physical remains have survived, apart from two side rudders found on the Suffolk coast.[160] A side rudder could be pivoted to avoid damage when a ship was being beached and so was suitable for vessels that visited harbours with sloping foreshores and no waterside installations. By the mid-fourteenth century they seem to have been replaced by stern rudders, which were much more inflexible, meaning that by that time the hulks must have either anchored out in the fairway or been drawn up alongside a wharf.[161] Although many of the vessels either visiting the port or owned by Sandwich masters would have been hulks, it is unusual for them to be specified in documents at this date.

Fig. 5.6 The fourteenth-century seal of the port of Sandwich (Ray Harlow, Sandwich Guildhall Archives)

La Hulke Beatta Marie, owned by Jonah Burgeis and detained in Sandwich in 1263, is an exception.[162]

Cogs were in use in north-west continental Europe by the ninth century, but did not become common in English waters until *c.*1200, when one is depicted on the town seal of Ipswich.[163] In 1217 a cog formed part of the English fleet in the Battle of Sandwich; it must have been a tall vessel because it was said to tower over the heavily laden French ships.[164] Cogs differed from hulks in having straight stem and stern posts, a stern rudder and a flat plank bottom, a single square sail and no oars. Since they were dependent solely on the wind, they were slow and cumbersome to navigate, but with their rather 'tubby' shape and length to beam ratio of only 1:3, they were excellent carriers of bulky cargoes, and grew to dominate waterborne trade in the northern seas in the fourteenth and fifteenth centuries (Fig. 5.7). In addition, they may have had a mast that doubled as the centre post of a derrick, thereby enabling them to load and unload bulky goods without recourse to harbour-side cranes.[165]

Fourteenth-century evidence indicates that most non-local trading vessels visiting Sandwich came mainly from Gascony, Santander, San Sebastian and elsewhere in Spain, Portugal and the Mediterranean region. There is also evidence that the Genoese and Venetian trade, which was to become so important in the following century, was beginning in the early fourteenth.[166] Their cargoes were often destined for London, and this sometimes involved transhipment,[167] with the goods being transferred to small craft (*batellae*), the shallow-draught ships usually propelled by oars but also with a sail, not so very different from the ships of tenth- and eleventh-century fleets that assembled in Sandwich Haven (Chap. 3.1). *Batellae* were used to transport cargoes such as the building materials taken from Sandwich to Dover in 1221,[168] and would have been able to negotiate the shallow waters of the Wantsum Channel and the shoals of the Thames estuary. As cargo carriers grew larger, particularly in the fifteenth century, transhipment in Sandwich Haven became commonplace. Italian carracks, in particular, avoided the dangers of the North Foreland and the shoals of the Thames estuary by sailing no farther than the south-east mouth of the Wantsum Channel.

Italian merchants began to use cogs in the fourteenth century for transporting bulky and less valuable goods such as alum, which was in great demand in the cloth-making countries of the north, and raw wool on return journeys.[169] In contrast, most Italian luxury goods were carried in 'great galleys', first built in Venetian shipyards in the late thirteenth century. The great galleys were rowing boats with no sails and an average crew of 150 oarsmen; although originally designed as fighting ships, their speed and carrying capacity (one tun of goods for each man) soon made them the trading vessels par excellence between the Mediterranean and the northern seas. Their economic viability depended on carrying high-value merchandise – silks, spices and other luxury goods – to north-west Europe, generally in exchange for high-quality woollen cloth from Flanders and England, although they also carried fine raw wool.

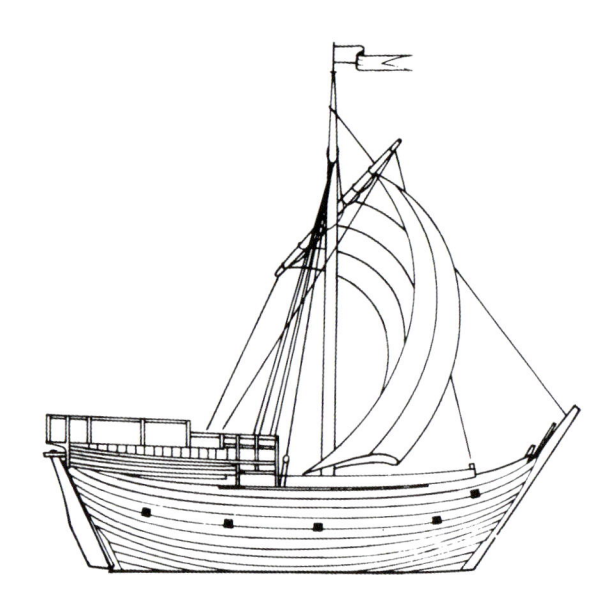

Fig. 5.7 Reconstruction drawing of the fourteenth-century Bremen cog (Unger 1980, fig. 15)

This is shown by the customs accounts for 1311, which record that Florentine merchants working in London sent five English ships laden with 112 sacks of wool to Sandwich, where they were transferred to a single galley for onward transport to Italy.[170] The value of the luxury items carried to England by the great galleys can be gained from a report of 1323 of the great ship *Dromundus*, whose cargo was said to have been worth the immense sum of £5,716 1s. 0d.[171] In the same year a galley from Majorca carrying silver, copper, tin and other merchandise was attacked by pirates and taken to Sandwich, its cargo obviously being an irresistible temptation to some portsmen.[172]

Sandwich Haven was also much used by royal vessels throughout the thirteenth and fourteenth centuries, it being an ideal place for the war fleet to gather before setting off for Flanders or northern France. If they were intended to carry troops to the scene of battle, they would have been warships, the royal 'galleys' that were shallow-draught, clinker-built ships with both oars and sail, which were fast and manoeuvrable, and suited to coastal or inland waters and also the open sea.[173] Other vessels were needed to transport victuals, horses and military machines as well as fighting men,[174] and they would have been converted merchant ships, as illustrated by the ship on the Sandwich seal of *c.*1300, where a merchantman has been provided with square fighting tops to transform it into a warship (Fig. 5.6).

6 Religious buildings

The thirteenth century was a time of significant building and rebuilding for churches in England. Changes in religious practice led to the extending of east ends and the rebuilding and enlargement of naves and aisles. Some expansion may have taken place to accommodate a growing population, something that was perhaps particularly significant in a prosperous town, but, as ecclesiastical historians have shown, there were other, equally important forces at work. These affected all three of Sandwich's parish churches, and the changes that took place and probable reasons behind them will be charted in this chapter. In addition, houses for mendicant orders, and hospitals to care for the sick and elderly, began to be established in major towns. They were mechanisms to cope with the problems of overcrowding and poverty that were among the penalties for successful towns everywhere. By 1300 Sandwich had a Carmelite friary and three hospitals.

6.1 The parish churches

Ecclesiastical buildings provide the earliest evidence for standing structures after 1200. Changing practices in religion meant that churches built in one century no longer fulfilled the requirements of the next. The trigger to change was the adoption of the doctrine of transubstantiation at the Fourth Lateran Council in 1215, when it was ruled that bishops must ensure that suitable priests were appointed to local churches and provided with all necessary resources for their ministration.[1] Communion was primarily restricted to the clergy, the laity being allowed to take it only once or twice a year. As a result, the clergy segregated themselves as much as possible in the church, although the laity had to be able to witness the elevation of the Host.[2] The positions of sedilias, piscinas and squints show that by the early thirteenth century the altar had reached its most easterly position in parish churches.[3] The small, dark, chancels of the twelfth century or earlier were swiftly replaced by larger, longer and far lighter east ends with the altar set near the east wall, thus removing the sacraments further from the congregation in the nave while still allowing them to see the ritual. Everywhere churches were rebuilt or extended, and Sandwich was no exception, with all three parish churches receiving new east ends and enlarged naves.

6.1.1 The east ends in the thirteenth century

St Clement's church was probably the first of the three parish churches to be rebuilt in the early thirteenth century. The chancel was extended eastwards (Fig. 6.1), and the roof of the east end was not only rebuilt, but raised to allow for large, plain, lancet windows to provide more light (Fig. 6.2). There were three stepped lancets in the straight east wall (the original outer jambs of the north and south lights survive), and parts of two lancets remain at the east end of the north wall. At the same time a two-bay north aisle was added, running eastwards from the transept. There is no evidence that a similar aisle was built to the south at this time. When one was erected in the mid- or late thirteenth century, it destroyed an early thirteenth-century sedilia in the south chancel wall just west of the piscina.[4] A fine early thirteenth-century door surround, with carved heads for label stops, now opens into an addition at the east end of this later south aisle. It was clearly reset there after the aisle was added, and may originally have been a priest's doorway from the churchyard directly into the chancel.

The original east end of St Peter's was rebuilt later in the thirteenth century, the new chancel probably being longer, and perhaps wider, than its predecessor. At the same time two aisled bays were added on each side, although that on the south side was largely destroyed when the tower collapsed in 1661 (Fig. 6.3). As at St Clement's, the end of the chancel extended east beyond the aisles. The octagonal piers, capitals and bases of the arcade, built of a mixture of Purbeck and Hythe stone,

6 Religious buildings

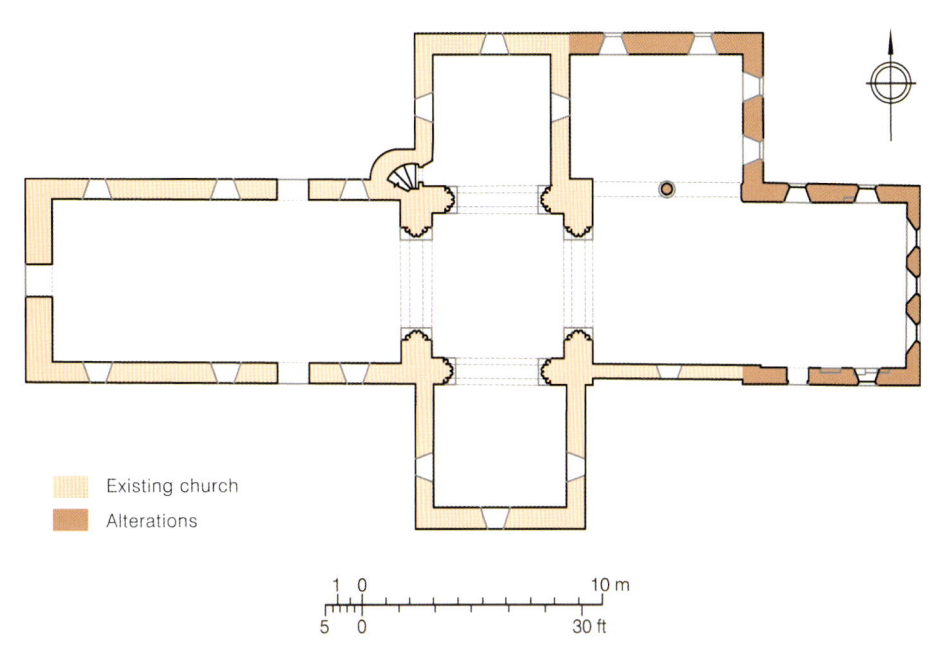

Fig. 6.1: St Clement's church, reconstructed plan showing additions and rebuilding in the early thirteenth century (H. A. J. & A. T. A.)

Fig. 6.2: St Clement's church, chancel, looking east to restored lancet windows and blocked lancet on north wall (S. P.)

appear to be contemporary with the south arcade of St Clement's, and are likely to date from the mid- or later thirteenth century. Above the arcade, the chancel was lit by double lancet windows; a straight joint in the east wall of the north aisle shows that the aisle was only 2.3m wide, much narrower than today, and a slope above the arcade arches suggests that it was covered by a catslide roof (Fig. 6.4). In addition to the main structure, a piscina and triple sedilia at the east end has trefoil heads to the arches and moulded surrounds, with the sedilias separated from each other by colonnettes with foliate capitals. All this has been

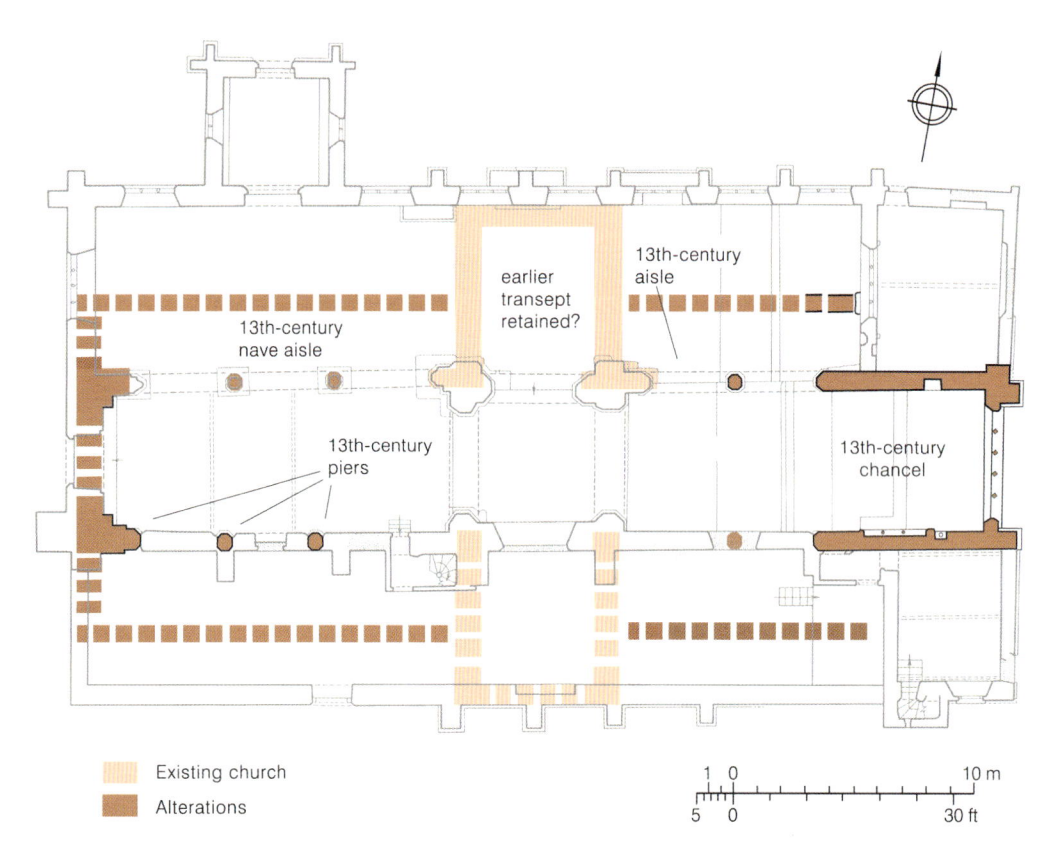

Fig. 6.3: St Peter's church, plan today showing thirteenth-century chancel and west end and possible outline of north aisles and transept, with suggested width of south aisle (S. P. & A. T. A.)

Fig. 6.4: St Peter's church, looking south-east, arcade and clerestory windows of chancel and nave, seen from north aisle (S. P.)

heavily restored but clearly belongs with the thirteenth-century rebuilding of the chancel.

St Mary's is particularly difficult to understand because most of the east end, including the roofs and the clerestory walls of the chancel proper, as well as any wall or arcade between the chancel and the south chapel, were destroyed when the tower fell in 1668. All that survives of a new thirteenth-century east end are the outer jambs of the north and south lancet windows in the east wall of what must have been a tall chancel with a clerestory, and a lower south chapel of the same length as the chancel. The remains are undatable, but a large engaged column at the entrance to the former south chapel has a turned capital and base, suggesting that rebuilding took place in the first half of the thirteenth century. The base of a free-standing double piscina, or a piscina paired with a credence or shelf, which must have served a thirteenth-century chapel, remains among the debris caused by the collapse of the tower.

6.1.2 Naves and aisles in the thirteenth century

By the end of the thirteenth century all three Sandwich churches had also been altered and enlarged at their west ends. The most obvious alterations can be seen in St Peter's. The north aisle of the nave was a slightly simpler version of the north chancel aisle, with three bays of octagonal piers with moulded capitals and bases, simple double-lancet windows above, and a sloping section between the two where the arcade wall was thinned back and a catslide roof supported over a narrow aisle (Figs 6.3, 6.4). All these features suggest a date in the second half of the thirteenth century. Similar arcade piers and clerestory windows on the south side of the nave indicate that, although now destroyed, a south aisle was added at the same time. Straight joints at clerestory level on the north side of the arcade, to the east and west of the tower, may indicate that the aisles stopped against the twelfth-century transept. The asymmetrical piers of the central tower, almost certainly the result of updating an earlier structure, have similar detailing to the arcades, and shorter nave bays on the south side show that the tower was always entered by a stair turret inserted at its south-west corner, although this was rebuilt after the tower collapsed.

Although the evidence is sparser, St Clement's seems also to have been enlarged by adding nave aisles and removing transepts. The clue is provided by the details of the low arches carrying thin walls that were inserted beneath the north and south arches of the Romanesque tower; their capitals and bases date them to the middle of the thirteenth century, and their relatively slender form shows that they were not added to strengthen the tower.[5] Instead, it appears that the twelfth-century transepts were taken down and aisles added, at least from the west end to the east side of the transepts (Fig. 6.5). The thirteenth-century north nave aisle was probably the same width as the thirteenth-century chancel aisle, but the wider nave aisles built in the fifteenth century have destroyed nearly all evidence of this phase. Nevertheless, a new nave must have been

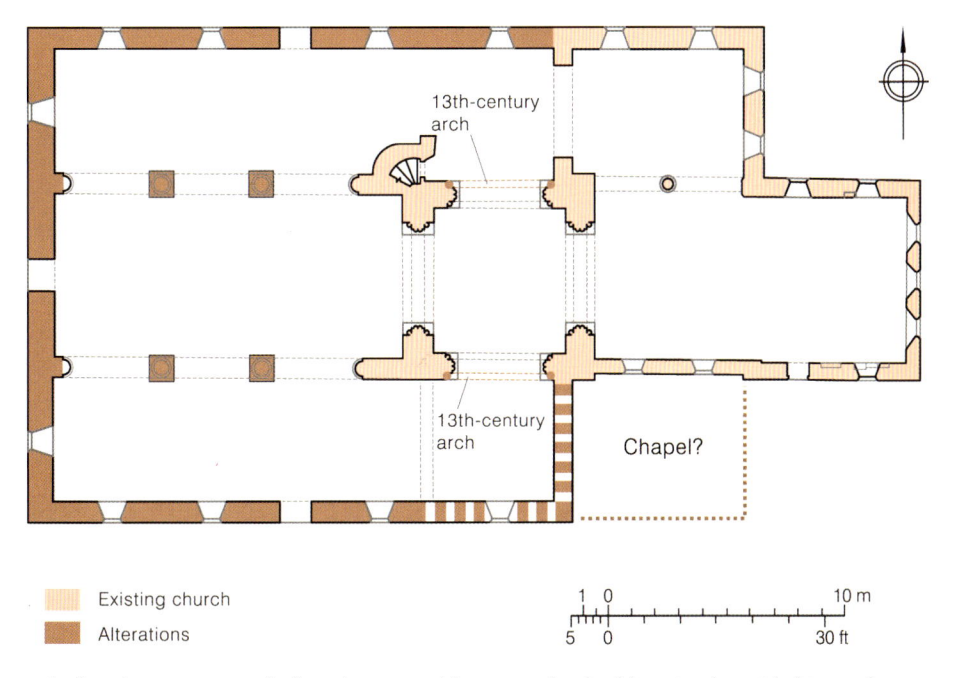

Fig. 6.5: St Clement's church, reconstructed plan showing additions and rebuilding in the mid-thirteenth century (H. A. J. & A. T. A.)

Fig. 6.6: St Mary's church, west end. The string course at the south end of the west wall and the lancet window in the north aisle indicate the widening of the south aisle in the thirteenth century (P. W. © English Heritage DP0322251)

built sometime between the twelfth century and the fifteenth, for the scar of its roof is plainly visible on the west face of the tower between the earlier and later roof lines (Fig. 3.5), while early pier bases were found in the nave in the nineteenth century (Chap. 4.3.2). On the south side, the low arch beneath the tower suggests that there was probably an aisle of similar date and width here, although it was largely rebuilt, first in the fourteenth century and again in the fifteenth.

The nave of St Mary's church, the only one to have had aisles in the twelfth century, was also remodelled during the thirteenth century, when the south aisle was enlarged to its present width (Figs 4.1, 4.2, 6.6). Parts of a string course and a lancet window at the west end of the south side survive, while a corbel with a simple crocket high up on the south side of the south-west pier shows the height at which the timber cornice of a new, gabled roof was carried. Most of this aisle was destroyed when the tower collapsed.

6.1.3 The implications of the thirteenth-century work in the parish churches

In rebuilding the chancels and adding nave aisles, the Sandwich churches were very much in line with church development elsewhere. There was more rebuilding in parish churches in Kent between *c.*1180 and *c.*1260 than at any other time in the Middle Ages.[6] The big questions, however, are why the churches were enlarged, and at whose expense. Population growth, while no doubt a contributory factor, is probably only part of the explanation. During the thirteenth century the laity were encouraged to take on more and more responsibility for church upkeep, and churchwardens were appointed to act as representatives of the parishioners and to oversee the parish funds.[7] What little written evidence there is suggests that during the century the laity became ever more involved with extending churches, particularly naves, maintaining the fabric in good repair, introducing images and altars, and enhancing the furnishings and decoration. Nave aisles became increasingly common, and earlier narrow ones, as at St Mary's, were widened. Aisles were not the best places from which to see the all-important elevation of the Host, but they may have contained fonts, were perhaps used for burial, and were where the growing numbers of images and altars came to be placed.[8]

After the doctrine of Purgatory was adopted in 1274, formalising beliefs that had long been held, there was a greater emphasis on the need for prayers and Masses for the dead, leading to a proliferation of late medieval chapels and altars. Religious guilds, which came to fund both Masses and altars, probably started to play an increasing part in the lives of parishioners from the thirteenth century.[9] The parishioners were also behind an increase in the number of images. In Essex, for example, episcopal visitations in the years 1249–52 and 1297 recorded the devotional images in a group of rural parish churches; in all of them there was an increase between the two sets of dates, in one case from two to twelve, and some of the images were specifically recorded as being in the nave.[10] Evidence everywhere is sparse, and none is to be had in Sandwich, but it is not unreasonable to assume that the laity became more involved in the development of their parish churches during this time.

Despite the amount of building that took place during the thirteenth century, the surviving details are simple and none of the churches has as much rich decoration as is found in the chapel of St Bartholomew's hospital (Section 6.2.2). Much, of course, may have been destroyed by later rebuilding, but what remains suggests that most of the thirteenth-century work was simple and unadorned. This is in contrast to the chancels and naves of many parish churches in Kent.[11]

At the end of the thirteenth century the Sandwich parish churches were not particularly wealthy. As mentioned in Chapter 4, the churches of St Clement's and St Mary's, which passed at some unknown date from the patronage of the archbishop of Canterbury to his archdeacon, were run by vicars. St Peter's was a rectory, and by 1227 the advowson, formerly in the hands of St Augustine's Abbey, was shared alternately with the mayor and barons of Sandwich.[12] In the *Taxatio Ecclesiastica* of Pope Nicholas IV of 1291, the valuations of £5 6s. 8d. for St Clement's (plus £5 for the vicarage), £8 for St Mary's (plus £4 for the vicarage), and £6 13s. 4d. for St Peter's contrast strongly with the valuations of major Kent parishes churches such as Eastry (a rectory, valued at £53 13s. 4d.), Faversham (£36 13s. 4d., plus £20 for the vicarage) and New Romney (£20, plus £4 for the vicarage).[13] This lack of affluence suggests that the amount of building that took place may have owed a good deal to the generosity of the parishioners rather than to the ecclesiastical authorities.

6.1.4 Chapels, chantries and donations to the fabric in the fourteenth century

By the end of the thirteenth century all three parish churches had been enlarged at least once. Although adaptation continued during the fourteenth century, most of it did not involve major rebuilding of the central space but was concerned with more personal efforts, such as adding a chapel, establishing a chantry, donating a window or erecting a private tomb. Furthermore, fuller documentation for the first time allows a few of the donors, at this time always members of the elite merchant families, to emerge from obscurity, and illustrates the consolidation of loyalty to the parish, a phenomenon that is more clearly documented in the fifteenth century.

The first documented evidence for lay involvement in the churches relates to St Mary's in 1312, when Walter Draper, a Sandwich wool merchant, gave 6s. 8d. annual rent from a messuage in 'yeldehallestrete' (High Street) to sustain a light before the image of the Holy Cross in St Mary's church.[14] The Condy family (Chap. 5.4.1) was also prominent, founding a chantry in 1345.[15] Another merchant family who benefited St Mary's were the Loveryks, one of whom built the chapel of St Mary at the 'Est hed of this chyrche'.[16] It has been suggested that this was the site of the Condy chantry, which was certainly in a chapel dedicated to St Mary.[17] Later wills make clear that the chapel of St Mary at the East Head was detached from the church, and although space outside is, and possibly always was, limited, it may have been located beyond the present east end.[18] The same Loveryk, Thomas, who was mayor in 1364,[19] gave three windows on the north side of the church. The twelfth-century north nave aisle was widened and heightened in the first half of the fourteenth century to match that on the south side (Figs 6.7–6.9). It is faced with fine, tabular flint work of the type found on the exterior of the church towers at Herne and St Nicholas at Wade in east Kent, and on a wall of an otherwise demolished house in Harnet Street in Sandwich (House 27). The aisle is entered by a well-detailed doorway, now inside a later porch, and lit by a large traceried window beneath the west gable and two other windows, one to either side of the doorway.

At St Clement's the chancel chapels were widened, and the north one lengthened eastwards, blocking one of the lancet windows of the choir. By the end of the fourteenth century the south nave aisle had

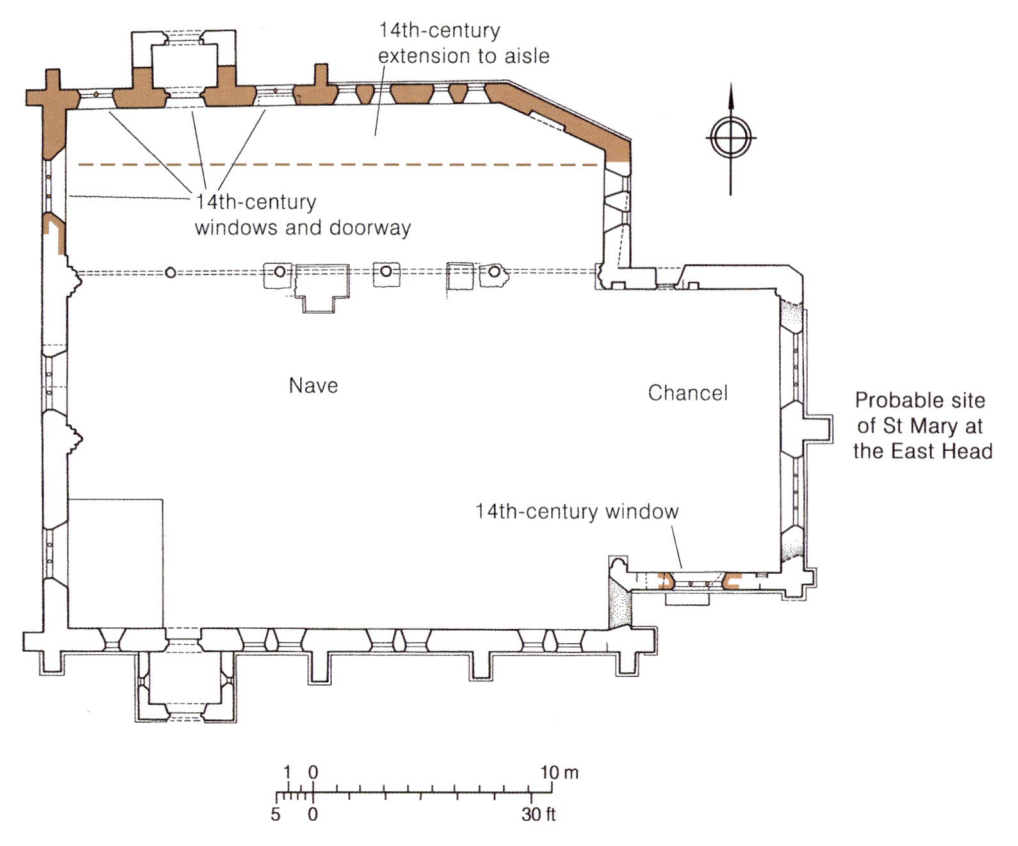

Fig. 6.7: St Mary's church, plan today indicating fourteenth-century work (S. P. & A. T. A.)

Fig. 6.8: St Mary's church, window at west end of north aisle (S. P.)

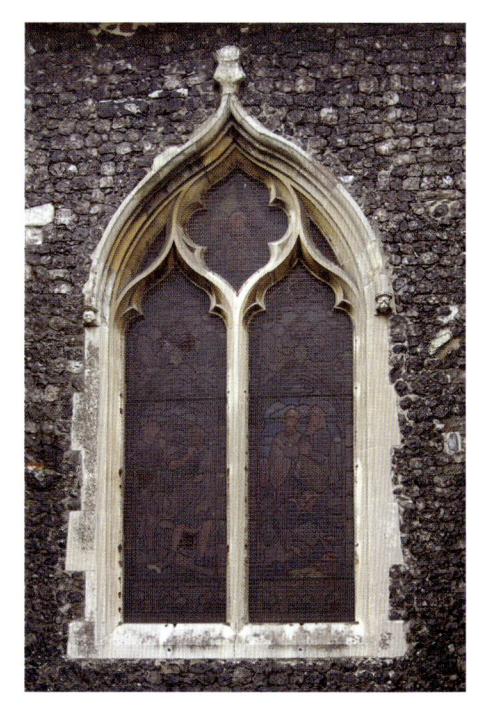

Fig. 6.9: St Mary's church, window on north side of north aisle (S. P.)

6 *Religious buildings*

Blocked chancel window

Existing church
Additions and alterations

Reconstructed plan: early fourteenth century

Existing church
Additions and alterations

Reconstructed plan: mid fourteenth century

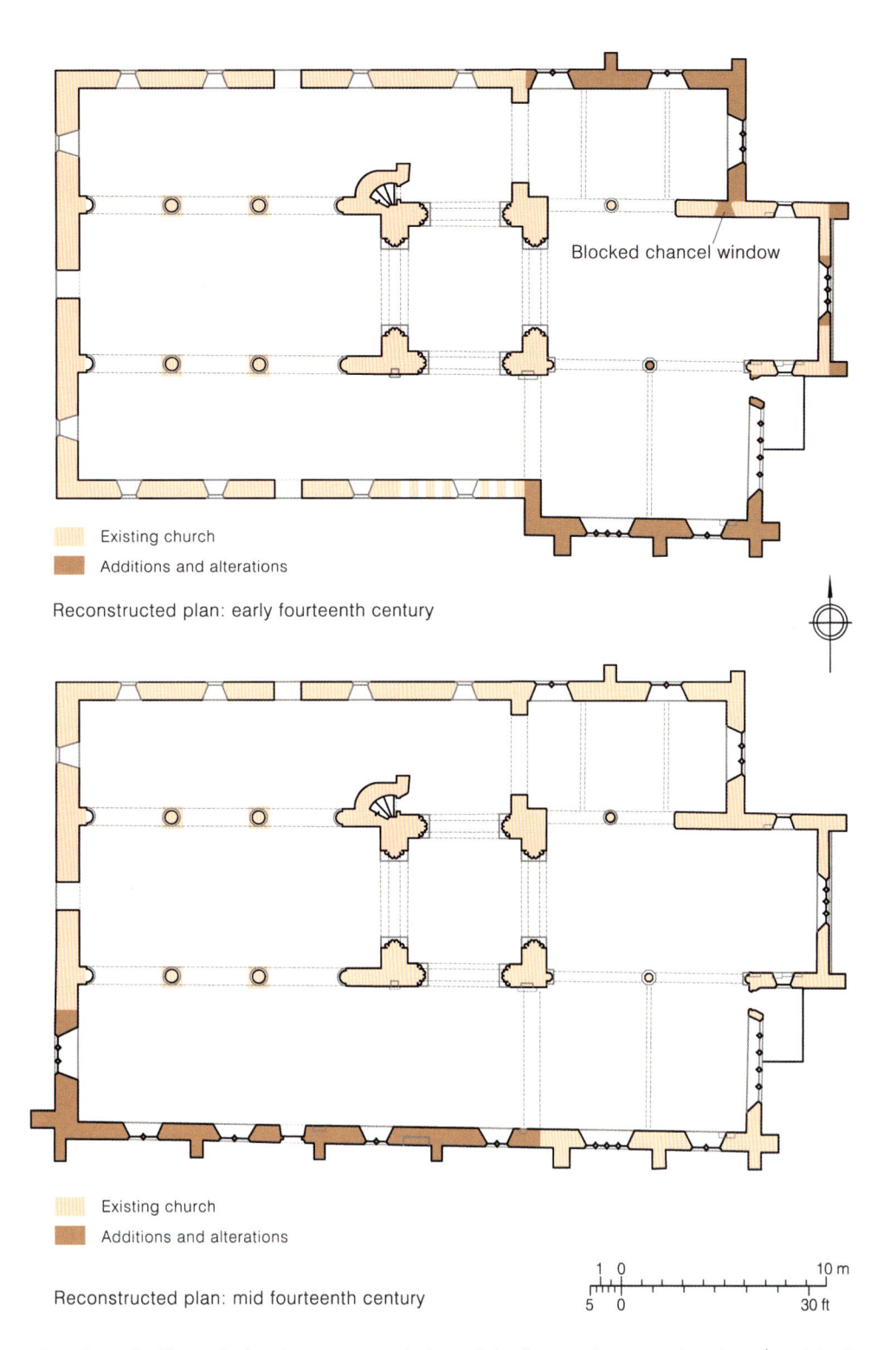

Fig. 6.10: St Clement's church, reconstructed plans of the fourteenth century (H. A. J. & A. T. A.)

Fig. 6.11: St Clement's church from the north-east. Drawn by J. or J. C. Buckler, 1824 (© British Library Board. All Rights Reserved Add. MS 36432, f. 1271)

Fig. 6.12: St Clement's church, remains of double piscina in south chancel aisle (P. W. © English Heritage DP044032)

been rebuilt to the same width as the new chancel chapel (Fig. 6.10). New windows, not all surviving, were made in the north and south chancel walls (Fig. 6.11), and a double piscina with decorative ogee heads was built into the south wall of the south chapel (Fig. 6.12). Although the donors' names at St Clement's are unknown, the purpose of the rebuilding was almost certainly to accommodate more chapels and altars, their positions indicated by at least one more piscina and two image niches. These will be discussed in Chapter 13.1.1 in connection with late medieval documentary evidence for the dedications and locations of chapels and altars.

6.1.5 The possible charnel house at St Peter's

In the first half of the fourteenth century, the thirteenth-century south aisle of St Peter's church, which probably contained the Lady chapel, was rebuilt and extended eastwards by a two-storey structure in which a raised upper room or chapel was set over a semi-sunken vaulted crypt or undercroft (Figs 6.13–6.15). The arrangement was complicated. The former narrow aisle with a catslide roof was replaced by a wider aisle with a gable roof, lit by a high east window that has a

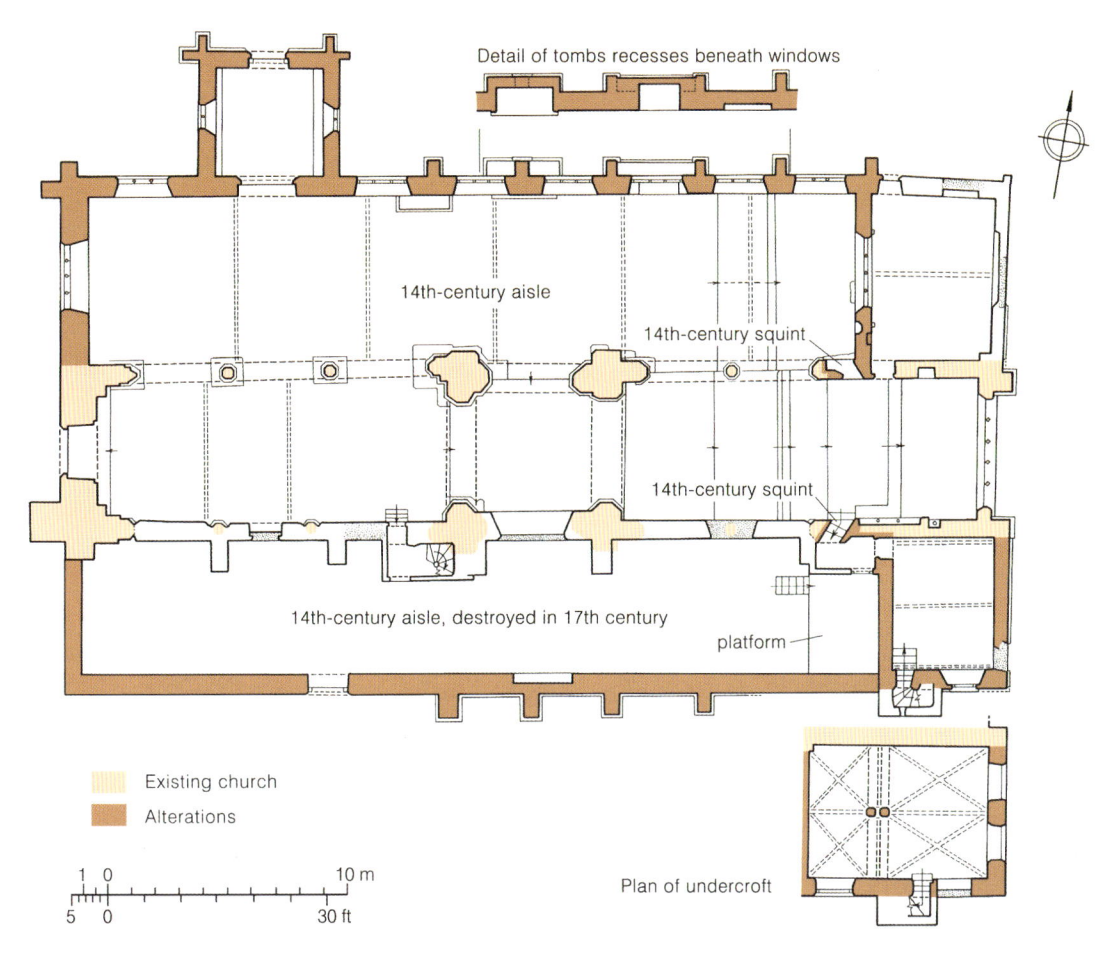

Fig. 6.13: St Peter's church in the fourteenth century, showing widened aisles and possible charnel house added at the east end of the south aisle (S. P. & A. T. A.)

fragment of window jamb still surviving. The east end of the aisle was raised over the western half of the crypt, and its main altar seems to have been situated west of the raised area, from which a squint (now turned into a doorway) had a direct view of the high altar. The eastern half of the crypt lies beneath the upper storey of the extension. This upper storey probably originally served as a chapel, but it was rebuilt as a room after the collapse of the tower in the seventeenth century. It is still entered internally from the west by an original small doorway, presumably once reached by steps from behind the aisle altar. Another internal fourteenth-century doorway, still surviving in the south wall of the seventeenth-century room, opened onto a circular stair turret leading to the vaulted crypt below. There may have been an external doorway into the crypt at the base of the stair, but if so, all trace disappeared when most of the stair turret was rebuilt in the seventeenth century.

The undercroft is of four bays, separated by a large central column (Fig. 6.15). The two west bays are smaller than the eastern ones and have plainer detailing, suggesting that the two halves may be different in date,

Fig. 6.14: St Peter's church, the extension at the east end of the south aisle: undercroft below and rebuilt first floor (P. W. © English Heritage DP068615)

Fig. 6.15: St Peter's church, probable charnel house in the undercroft at the east end of the south aisle (P. W. © English Heritage DP032242)

although not by many years. It has been suggested that the extension was the house given to Thomas Elys's chantry priests,[20] but since Elys's chantry was not established until 1392 (Chap. 13.1.3) and the form of the ribs, corbels and windows indicates that the extension dates from the first half of the fourteenth century, this could not have been its original purpose. Since St Peter's parish was probably the most densely populated of the three parishes yet had a very small churchyard (Chap. 3.3.3), it is more likely that the south-eastern extension was built as a charnel house with a chapel above. This suggestion is supported by late fifteenth- and early sixteenth-century wills, which make clear that there was a charnel house at St Peter's.[21]

Charnel houses, used when graveyard space was limited to store the bones of the dead after they had been interred for some time, first appear in the thirteenth century. Several have been identified and documented in great churches,[22] but less is known about those attached to urban parish churches. Most of the vaulted crypts that have been identified as charnels are of late thirteenth- or fourteenth-century date, with their use as such usually only being documented later.[23] No other charnels are known to comprise a two-storey structure set somewhat apart from the rest of the church, but the small size of the churchyard makes such a use likely at St Peter's. In addition, even if it were built with another purpose in mind, it probably soon became a charnel house given the problems of finding adequate burial space during the Black Death. In 1349 the cemetery of St Clement's was increased in size,[24] and the obvious response in a town-centre church such as St Peter's would have been to use a charnel house.

6.1.6 The secular role of the churches

The custumal of 1301 shows that St Clement's and St Peter's churches were used for the elections of civic officers, and that courts were also held in them. Every third Monday, the bailiff presided over the hundred court in St Clement's church, and each Thursday (or more frequently if the matter concerned strangers or non-freemen) the mayor held the town court in St Peter's.[25] Thus both churches had civic functions, with St Peter's used at least once a week.

Sandwich was not alone in holding courts in churches. It happened in several places,[26] but was particularly prevalent in the Cinque Ports. At New Romney, although the town paid rent for a 'chamber for the Jurats' in 1395, the court met in St Nicholas's church during the fourteenth and fifteenth centuries.[27] In Dover, the court may have been held in St Peter's church, but by the late fourteenth century may have transferred to a court hall;[28] regular meetings were also held in St Mary's, Fordwich. In addition, when the Cinque Ports abandoned the open-air meetings of the court of Shepway in the mid-fourteenth century, the warden usually held the court in St James's, Dover. After the Middle Ages the Cinque Ports' own court of Guestling convened in St Nicholas's, New Romney, since the hall built for the meetings of the fifteenth-century Brodhull had become too small for all the delegates.[29] The issue of why courts were held in churches in certain towns is one that is not fully understood, but probably relates to the authority that the use of a church bestowed.[30] Churches must also have been used when there was no court hall, or if it were too small. By 1432, when the first town books survive, the Sandwich courts had largely moved into a purpose-built hall, which seems to have been erected next to St Peter's churchyard.[31]

We do not know for certain where the town court met in St Peter's church, but it is possible that the north aisles of the chancel and nave were rebuilt specifically for this purpose, although the presence of an aumbry and a fourteenth-century squint directed towards the high altar means that services were also held in the aisle. This can be compared with St Nicholas's, New Romney, where the wide south chancel chapel, in which the court was held, was rebuilt, along with the rest of the east end of the church, in the early fourteenth century.[32] At St Peter's, the north transept and the narrow aisles of the chancel and nave were replaced in the first half of the fourteenth century by a single aisle wider than the main spans of the chancel and nave, the whole being surmounted by a continuous gabled roof.[33] This long space ran from end to end of the church, its generous proportions (31m × 6.6m, 103ft × 22ft) suggesting something rather out of the ordinary (Figs 6.13, 6.16). Since all the window tracery has been replaced, and the crown-post roofs could have been constructed at almost any time during the fourteenth century, there are no surviving details by which to assign a precise date to the rebuilding. But it is highly probable that it was carried out not long after the custumal was written, when the freemen of the town were clearly minded to make statements about their independence and corporate solidarity.

One reason for suggesting that a new space might have been created for holding the town courts soon after the production of the custumal is that Adam Champneys, the town clerk responsible for its composition in 1301, became the rector of St Peter's seven years later, and remained in that post until 1321, when he was appointed archdeacon of Worcester.[34] Supporting evidence for the hypothesis is perhaps provided by four fourteenth-century tombs situated in the north aisle. Unusually, all project through the north wall to allow clear space within the aisle, possibly indicating that the floor space was required for holding the courts. All the tombs are badly damaged. Two have surviving

Fig. 6.16: St Peter's church, north aisle (P. W. © English Heritage DP032232)

Fig. 6.17: St Peter's church, tomb in north aisle (P. W. © English Heritage DP032237)

wall canopies of ogee form and the remnants of richly carved surrounds with damaged armorials. In another, the tomb surround has gone but effigies of a man and a woman, their faces turned slightly to the south-east, as if to see the elevation of the Host, are preserved. The fourth is no more than a blocked arch in the wall.

It has been suggested that the tomb with the effigies was that of a John Elys or Ives (d. *c*.1360); and, on the basis of the armorials, that the most richly decorated one may be that of Thomas Elys (d. 1390; Fig. 6.17).[35] It is, however, unlikely that Thomas Elys was buried here since he requested interment next to his father, another Thomas, in the cemetery (Chap. 10.3.1). In addition, the decoration on the tomb is more in keeping with the style of 1340–70 than with that of later decades. Burial within a church, which had to compete with other demands on limited space, was a luxury granted only to a favoured few who could afford the higher costs involved.[36] Usually, these were men of power and authority, and often benefactors of the church in question.[37] Thus, the row of tombs in St Peter's may be those of parishioners who contributed to the rebuilding of the aisle and who, in addition to wishing to participate in the liturgy, may have wanted to be associated with the place where the court, in which they had played a prominent part in life, continued to be held after their death. While the most richly decorated tomb may not be that of the younger Thomas Elys, the inclusion of the Sandwich coat of arms may indicate that the interred had a close relationship with the governance of the town.[38]

6.2 New religious foundations in the thirteenth century

In line with other towns in England during the thirteenth century, a number of new religious institutions were established in Sandwich. By the end of the century there was a Carmelite friary and three hospitals. The hospital of St Bartholomew was founded in 1217, the friary in the late 1260s and the hospital of St John in the 1280s. All three will be discussed below. St Anthony's, a leper hospital, was built at Each End on the road from Ash, possibly in the mid- or late twelfth century, although it is not documented until the early fourteenth.[39] Although many late medieval testators left bequests to the lepers, little is known about the hospital and it has completely disappeared.[40] New foundations required charters, land and money. Since these establishments pre-date the documented donations to the parish churches, they provide the first glimpse of the kind of benefactors who were involved in giving to churches and charity. Most of those whose names we know were local merchants, although the elusive de Sandwich family figures in two cases, and one donor was possibly a foreigner.

6.2.1 The Carmelite friary

Sometime around 1268, a Carmelite friary, or Whitefriars, was established to the south of the built-up area and the Delf (Fig. III.1).[41] Like many friaries, this previously unoccupied site was low-lying and wet, requiring drainage before being developed.[42] It was one of only three Carmelite houses in Kent, and the only urban example.[43]

The founder was Henry Coufeld 'de Alemania', a German, who seems to have owned the land, and who might have had trading connections with the town.[44] The area on which the friary was founded was alluvial marshland and below 3m OD; thus, it would have had to be drained to make it suitable for occupation. In addition to the still extant drainage ditches in this area, traces of other, infilled ones have been discovered through excavation (Site 5). The date of the original

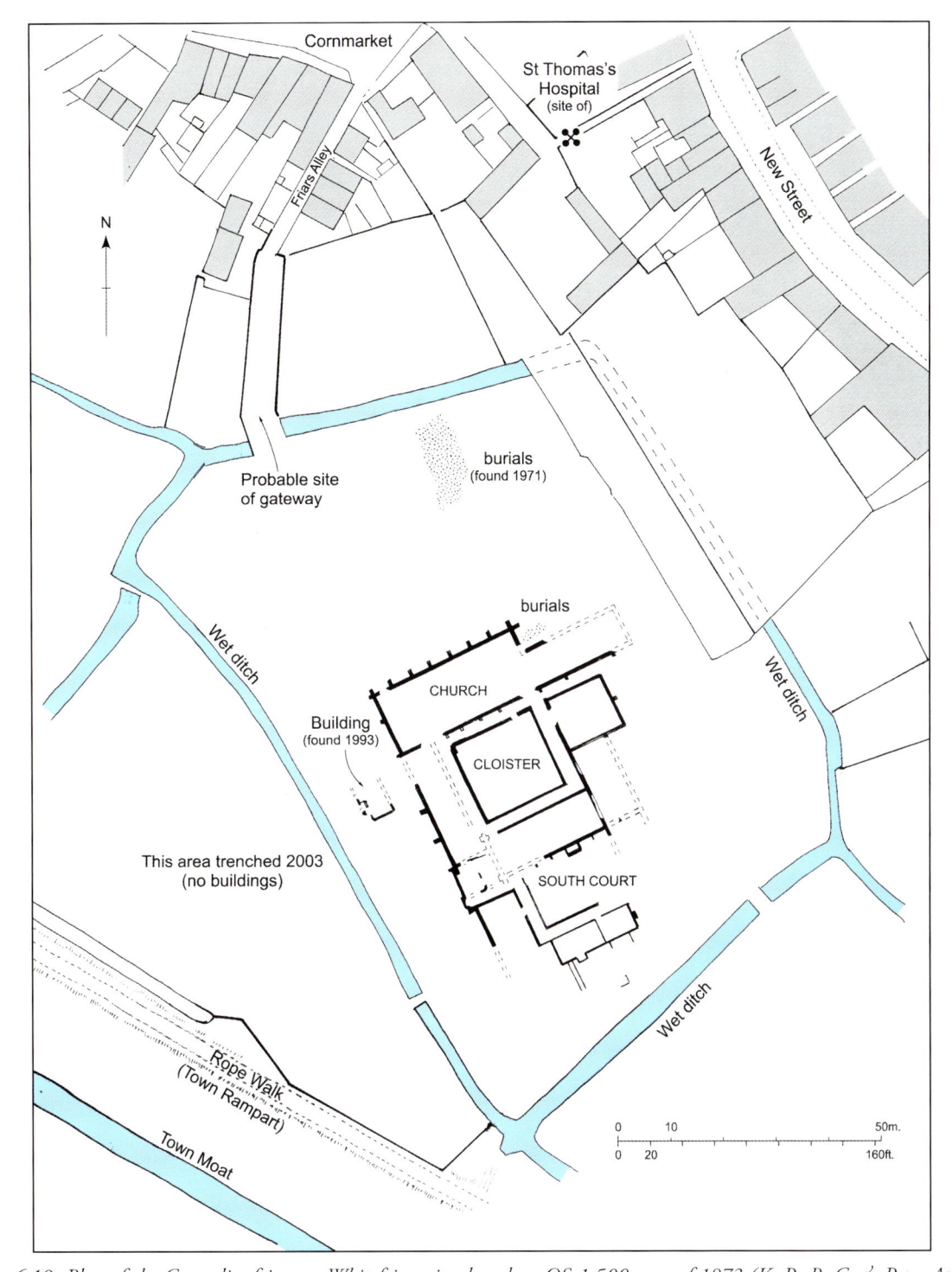

Fig. 6.18: Plan of the Carmelite friary or Whitefriars site, based on OS 1:500 map of 1873 (K. P., B. C. & Peter Atkinson)

cutting of these ditches is unknown, but it was probably carried out before Henry Coufeld donated the land, that is, before 1268. At a later date The Rope Walk rampart was constructed adjacent to the friary land (Chap. 5.6.2), although the friary did not make use of it as a precinct wall. The original foundation may have been small, but in 1280 Sir John de Sandwich was granted a licence to enlarge the site,[45] while Thomas Crawthorne, who was possibly a relation and some of whose family were Sandwich wool merchants in the later thirteenth century, is likewise mentioned as an early benefactor.[46] In 1300 there may have been fifteen friars; by 1331 there were twenty-four.[47]

The friary buildings have been completely destroyed, but the site has been excavated on four occasions (Sites 61, 62, 63 and 64).[48] The plan of the church was discovered in 1936, and published by Rigold in 1965. Unfortunately, his plan was based on a misinterpretation of measurements from the first excavation, and is incorrect in showing the choir and cloister angled to the north. This was rectified by Keith Parfitt in 1992, and is shown correctly on the plan published here (Fig. 6.18). The church was typical of friary churches, with a lengthy unaisled chancel, and a long seven-bay nave and north aisle used for preaching. It was smaller than the largest friary churches, such as those in London and Coventry, although comparable with, for example, the Carmelite church in Ipswich.[49] The choir almost certainly dates from the thirteenth century, and the nave and aisle were probably built soon after.[50] The bay at the east end of the nave has been interpreted as a passage bay in line with friary church developments in the last part of the thirteenth century, and there was evidence for rammed chalk footings at the east end of the aisle, which might have supported a bell-tower.[51]

Access to the precinct was from the Cornmarket, which lay to the north, allowing townsmen direct entry to the nave of the church.[52] All the claustral buildings stood on the south side, away from the public areas.[53] There seems to have been one large cloister directly south of the nave, separated from a second court by a range interpreted as a refectory.[54] Unfortunately, no archaeological phasing was undertaken in the earlier excavations, and the dating of the various ranges is uncertain. The only excavated dating evidence is a complete jug of Tyler Hill ware (1250–1350) found buried near the south wall of the choir, possibly suggesting an early date for that part of the church (Site 62).[55] Although Rigold thought the refectory could be dated by a chamfered ashlar plinth of late thirteenth-century type,[56] later excavations show that the cloister ranges were built on top of earlier foundations with a slightly different orientation. They consisted of low chalk walls that may have been footings to support timber-framed structures, probably from the first phase of friary building.[57] If so, the claustral buildings identified by Rigold would have been constructed some time after the original foundation. The precinct was surrounded by a wet moat, although, since the friars held 5 acres (2ha) of land by the end of the Middle Ages, their property outside the precinct boundary may have extended beyond it towards New Street in the north-east and the ramparts in the south-west (Chap. 13.1.4).

6.2.2 St Bartholomew's hospital

The hospital was founded as a direct result of the Battle of Sandwich, which took place on St Bartholomew's day (24 August) 1217. The battle is described in the poem, *L'Histoire de Guillaume le Maréchal*, which relates how, after the victory, William Marshall, the commander of the king's fleet, ordered that the booty should be shared out, with a part reserved for founding a hospital at Sandwich in honour of the saint who had given them victory. This was done, and the hospital is described in the poem as an establishment where 'are harboured and entertained God's poor'.[58] An unsubstantiated account states that St Bartholomew's had already been founded *c.*1190,[59] but it was refounded in 1217 by Bertine de Crawthorne and his wife, William Bucharde and his wife and Sir Henry de Sandwich. The last is the only one of the founders to have figured in a wider arena, acting as portreeve for the Christ Church Priory estate in Sandwich, and later serving as warden of the ports of Dover and Sandwich.[60] The foundation documents do not survive, but some of the details are set out in the Sandwich custumal.[61] An undated, but early thirteenth-century, grant relates to rents given to the hospital by William Bucharde for maintenance of a chaplain in the hospital chapel.[62]

The site lies about a third of a mile (approx. 500m) beyond the later town walls, on the road to Worth and Dover. It occupies 6 acres (2.4ha) of extra-parochial land and is bounded by Woodnesborough parish to the south and south-west, by St Mary's to the north-west, St Clement's and the Delf stream to the east, and touches the southern point of St Peter's parish to the north (Fig. 3.10). Despite the close associations that the hospital had with St Peter's church by the end of the thirteenth century,[63] its lands may have been carved out of St Mary's parish, which probably originally stretched as far as the Delf. Even though it was founded by named individuals, St Bartholomew's was managed by the town authorities soon after or perhaps even at its foundation, with the result that it was not dissolved at the Reformation.

By 1301 St Bartholomew's was an establishment for twelve men and four women, run by the mayor and jurats, with most expected to pay a £10 entry fee. The brothers and sisters had to work in the house or garden, or on the farm. By this date they each had a room of their own, although they cooked communally, and were expected to gather in the hall to dine on feast-days and to drink together each Sunday.[64] But an appraisal of the surviving chapel suggests that this may not have been the arrangement envisaged when the hospital was founded.[65]

The chapel must have been built shortly after the foundation. No major rebuilding took place until the nineteenth century, when the chancel and nave were heavily restored,[66] and it still contains the finest surviving early thirteenth-century architecture in the town. It consists of a chancel, a north aisle alongside the chancel and part of the nave, and a slightly wider nave (Figs 6.19, 6.20). The building is articulated by

Fig. 6.19: St Bartholomew's hospital chapel from the north-east (P. W. © English Heritage DP032259)

lancet windows with deeply moulded arches and free-standing Purbeck colonnettes with turned capitals and bases, the best details surviving in the north aisle (Fig. 6.21). On the north side, the hood moulding over the fifth window from the east drops for what may once have been an external doorway, and beyond this point a partly blocked window in the north wall of the nave indicates that the aisle was originally shorter, although extended not long after it was completed. Until the nineteenth century, the aisle was accessible only from the chancel, although it could probably also have been reached from outside by the postulated doorway in the north wall. The architectural details are of high quality, similar to those in some of Kent's best-decorated early thirteenth-century parish churches.[67]

At approximately 194m² the chapel is of more than average size for a relatively small hospital. Some larger hospitals, such as St John's, Canterbury, have chapels of this size, but those from hospitals comparable to St Bartholomew's are usually smaller. For example, the chapel at St Thomas, Eastbridge, in Canterbury was approximately 48m² at this date, and the chapel of St Bartholomew's hospital at Chatham is only 28m². Early hospital chapels usually occupied a single bay,[68] and often had halls directly attached, as at the monastic infirmary of Christ Church Priory, Canterbury, the Maison Dieu at Dover, and St Bartholomew's, Chatham, whose plan is not dissimilar to St Bartholomew's, Sandwich, although it is far smaller.[69] Given its size, Walter Godfrey suggested that the nave at Sandwich may originally have been an infirmary hall.[70] If so, it is possible that by c.1300 the room that each inmate is said to have occupied at that

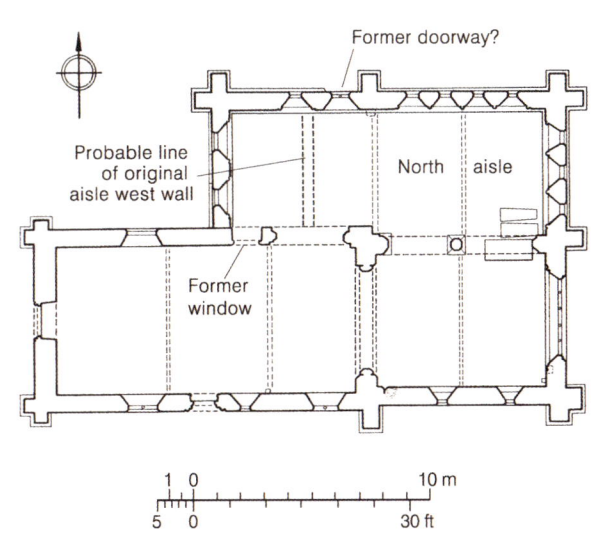

Fig. 6.20: St Bartholomew's hospital chapel, plan (S. P. & A. T. A.)

time was simply formed by screens within the existing nave and aisle, with the north aisle separated off for female accommodation. Even so, it is probable that the hospital had changed its function between its foundation and its description in the custumal of 1301.

Leland, writing in the 1530s, thought St Bartholomew's had been founded to care for 'maryners desesid and hurt', and according to Boys it was originally designed for the accommodation of pilgrims and travellers.[71] Early hospitals are known for their varied arrangements, and many were situated on main roads outside towns in order to cater for travellers, the infirm or the destitute. By the late thirteenth and fourteenth centuries some had disappeared from the records, and those that survived

Fig. 6.21: St Bartholomew's hospital chapel, north aisle looking north-east (P. W. © English Heritage DP032253)

had often changed their roles to provide long-term care for local people who were not wealthy but were capable of paying an entrance fee.[72] St Bartholomew's, Dover, for example, was established in the thirteenth century as a hospital for poor pilgrims, but soon became a leper hospital,[73] and the hospital of St Stephen and St Thomas at New Romney had become an almshouse for local townspeople by the mid-fourteenth century, although it was founded in the late twelfth century as a leper hospital.[74] Despite the lack of documentary confirmation, it is likely that a similar change had taken place at St Bartholomew's by 1301 when its role was so fully described in the custumal. In due course it became the most exclusive almshouse in the town.[75]

6.2.3 St John's hospital

A second and somewhat less prestigious establishment founded in the 1280s was the hospital of St John, also known as the Domus Dei. Like the friary, it was established on previously uninhabited land south of the Delf (Fig. III.1) by a group of Sandwich merchants, who included Thomas de Shelving, one of the more important Sandwich wool merchants of the late thirteenth century, John de Ho, a late thirteenth-century mayor, and John Long, who may have been a shipmaster.[76] It was run from the start by the mayor and commonalty.[77] The precise year of foundation is not known, but the first deed relating to it concerns the grant by Thomas de Shelving in 1288.

The hospital was intended for twelve townspeople who were less wealthy than those who could afford St Bartholomew's, although, with an entry fee of 2 marks (26s. 8d.), or sometimes 40s., they were certainly not indigent. It probably, however, also catered for the itinerant poor, the sick and the pregnant, as it certainly did in the later Middle Ages. No medieval buildings survive, but they comprised a hall and various other rooms, and a chapel, at least by the end of the Middle Ages.[78]

6.3 Conclusion

This account of the major features of both the churches and hospitals in Sandwich during the thirteenth and early fourteenth centuries serves to show how money and work on ecclesiastical and institutional buildings by then tended to be focused on the practical needs of the increasing urban population. Church building was not so much about power and prestige, as it had perhaps been in the twelfth century, when the patrons of at least two of the churches were probably major donors to the fabric, but about enlarging the buildings in accordance with new ideas, in order better to administer the sacraments to the parishioners and to provide more space for their needs. It therefore concerned adding aisles for altars and lights, making adequate arrangements for the burial of a larger population, and enlarging the space in which to conduct the secular administration of the town. The establishment of the friary and the hospitals was equally concerned with catering for the growing and varied spiritual and material needs of different sections of society within the town.

7 Secular buildings

The houses followed by numbers in brackets have been surveyed and are listed in Appendix 2

The first domestic buildings to survive in English towns were built in stone and date from the late twelfth century. No such early dwellings have been found in Sandwich, where the earliest remains, of stone, are from the thirteenth century. They and their early fourteenth-century timber successors tell us only about domestic and commercial buildings erected by the wealthy; in medieval towns this usually meant successful merchants. The houses of most of the urban population have not survived, and in Sandwich the limited opportunities for excavation have meant that evidence for their form is lacking. But the buildings that have survived from this period are important because they not only reveal what merchants required of their dwellings, but also point the way to later developments. In towns generally, the Black Death resulted in a massive loss of life, possibly reducing the population by as much as 50 per cent. Throughout England urban building seems to have faltered between about 1360 and 1400,[1] and Sandwich was no exception, there being no surviving buildings dating from the years between *c.*1340 and the very end of the century.

7.1 Excavated buildings

In Sandwich, as in many other places, the only evidence for domestic buildings before the second half of the thirteenth century comes from archaeological excavation, and in this instance from only a single site in St Peter's Street (medieval Love Lane). The excavation (Site 20) lay at the rear of 10 Market Street (medieval Fishmarket), and the earliest building, of the twelfth century (Phase 1), has already been discussed (Chap. 4.5; Figs 4.11, 4.12). By the early to mid-thirteenth century it had been replaced by Phase 2, another clay-floored timber building with a hearth. No other internal features were discovered, but, like the earlier structure, the building lay on the street front to the east, extending back 4m, and was at least 5m wide, its north wall now disappearing into the adjacent plot.

Clay floors and timber superstructures, replaced every fifty years or so, were typical of the kind of evidence found at Townwall Street, Dover.[2] Those houses, however, were thought to be the dwellings of fishermen set at some distance from the town centre. Love Lane, Sandwich, on the other hand, was part of the central retail area where recorded occupational names suggest commercial activity in the early thirteenth century. By the mid-thirteenth century the timber-framed houses of the merchant community in central Sandwich would probably have been well-constructed, fully framed buildings with timbers set on masonry plinths and sill beams.[3] As discussed in Chapter 4.5, the fact that the Love Lane structures were more ephemeral than this suggests that they could have been buildings ancillary to properties in the Fishmarket, abutting what was then only a back lane.

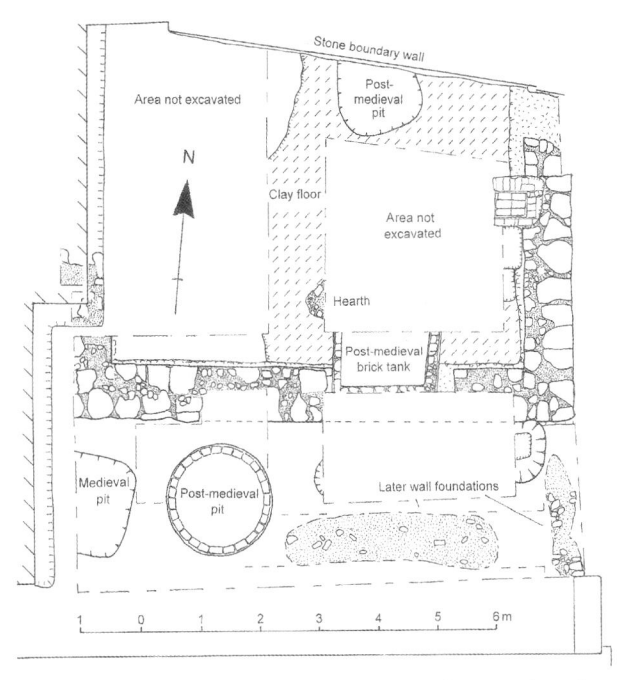

Fig. 7.1: Excavation on Love Lane at rear of 10 Market Place. Foundations of stone building of c.1300, running north into adjacent plot (B. C.)

Phase 3 of Site 20 has been dated to *c*.1300 and comprised a stone building also aligned along the street (Fig. 7.1). Rammed chalk foundations carried three surviving courses of wall, 0.85m (2ft 10in) wide, constructed of sandstone from the Thanet Beds. The internal width of the structure was approximately 7m (23ft), but its length is unknown since the walls ran into what is now a neighbouring property and therefore could not be investigated.[4] The width of the walls makes it likely that this was a stone building rather than a timber structure with stone footings, but its original purpose is unknown. An internal hearth, consisting of intensely burnt clay and peg-tile fragments, lay close to the middle of the south wall, which is not an obvious position for the main hearth of an open hall of *c*.1300, and there is little space in the yard behind for the ancillary ranges that would be expected with a large stone house. Instead, like its predecessors, it may have been an adjunct to a tenement in the Fishmarket (Chap. 4.5). Later deposits suggest that the building survived into the eighteenth century.

7.2 Stone buildings

The main building of Christ Church Priory is first documented in the thirteenth century, although possibly erected in the twelfth (Chap. 4.4). From the 1220s, when documentary evidence becomes available, it is clear that the priory was involved in erecting various new buildings. In 1224–5 £29 7s. 1d. was spent on a 'new house', the high level of expenditure indicating that it was constructed of stone. In 1229–30 rent of 51s. was received from a stone house and further rents for a stone house were received in the 1230s and 1240s. It is impossible to be certain that these references all apply to the same structure, or even what the building or buildings were used for.[5] The only other major expenditure on specifically new work, which may not have been of stone, was in 1253–4, when John Pikenoth, the cellarer, was involved in constructing a new house that was valued at 25 marks (£16 13s. 4d.). It is said to have been at least 50ft (15m) long and has been assumed to be the 'long house' that was repaired

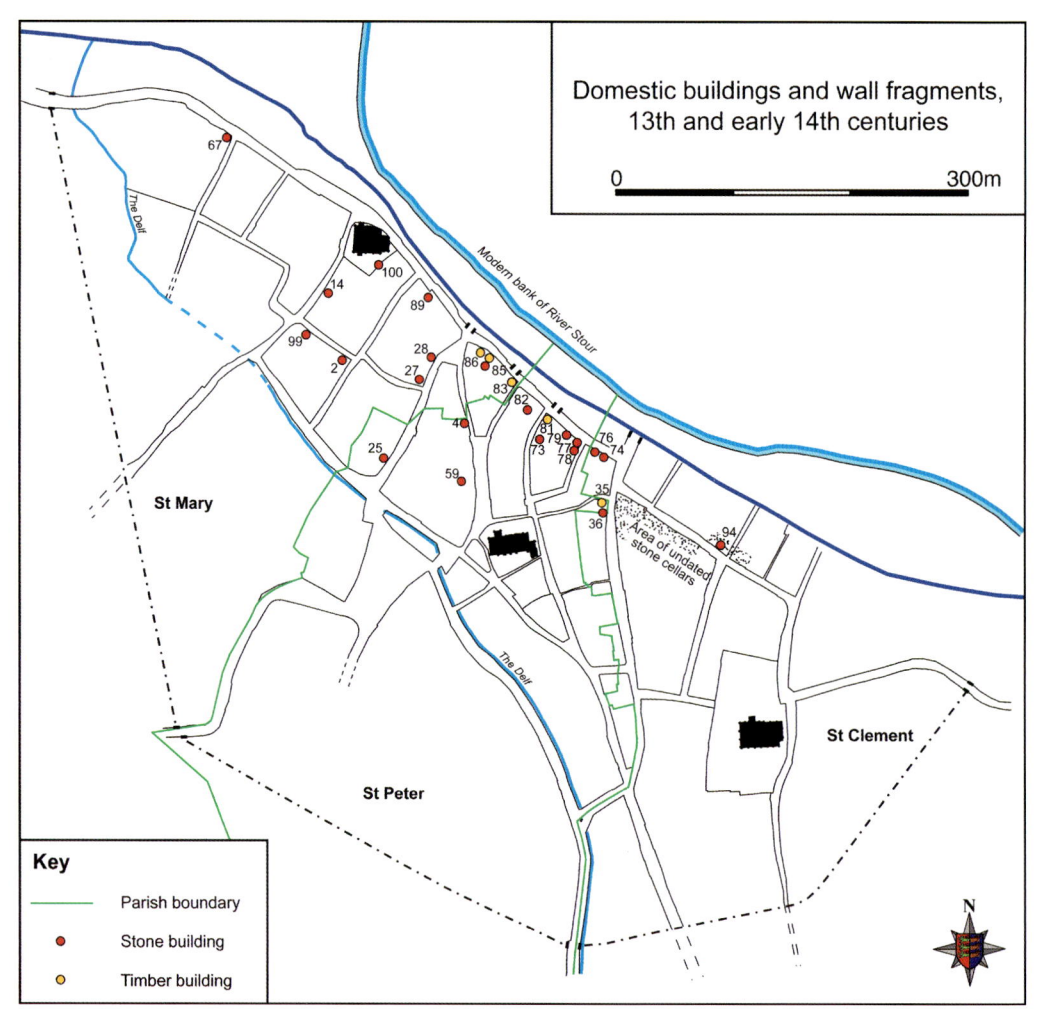

Fig. 7.2: The distribution of domestic buildings and wall fragments dating from the thirteenth and early fourteenth centuries (J. H.). Reproduced by permission of Ordnance Survey on behalf of HMSO. © Crown copyright 2009. All rights reserved. Licence number 100046522

in 1287.[6] None of these priory buildings survives, although a reset thirteenth-century stone doorway (House 67; Fig. 7.16) may have been associated with one of them.

The largest and best twelfth- and thirteenth-century urban houses in England were built of stone.[7] In contrast to the Continent, they were never common, and many of those that survive today are simply vaulted cellars or undercrofts that probably had timber superstructures that have since been demolished, as, for example, at Southampton and New Winchelsea. Given the national picture, it is no surprise to find that the earliest surviving domestic buildings in Sandwich were also built of masonry, and that, as far as the evidence allows us to say, there were not very many of them. They have few stylistic features by which to refine dating, but sufficient remains to suggest that although one or two may have been constructed in the mid-thirteenth century, most of them date from the late thirteenth century or the early fourteenth. They may be divided into three categories: large stone or flint street-front buildings, lying lengthwise to the road; small stone and flint structures set at the rear of their plots; and fragments, including reset doorways and stretches of wall between properties, which are apparently earlier than the rest of the surviving buildings. All the first two categories and many of the third are plotted on Figure 7.2.

7.2.1 Large stone or flint buildings along the street frontage

The only large stone building to survive to full height is 20 High Street, medieval 'yeldehallestrete', in St Clement's parish (House 36; Figs 7.3, 7.4). It stands on the west side of the street, at its highest point and some 90m from the present waterfront. What remains is the north part of a large open hall, just under 7m wide internally, originally set lengthwise to the street, and

Fig. 7.3: From left to right: Pellicane House (22 High Street), 20 High Street (House 36) and the former Bell and Anchor at 18 High Street (House 35) (William Henry Boyer 1827–97. © Sidery Collection, S-35)

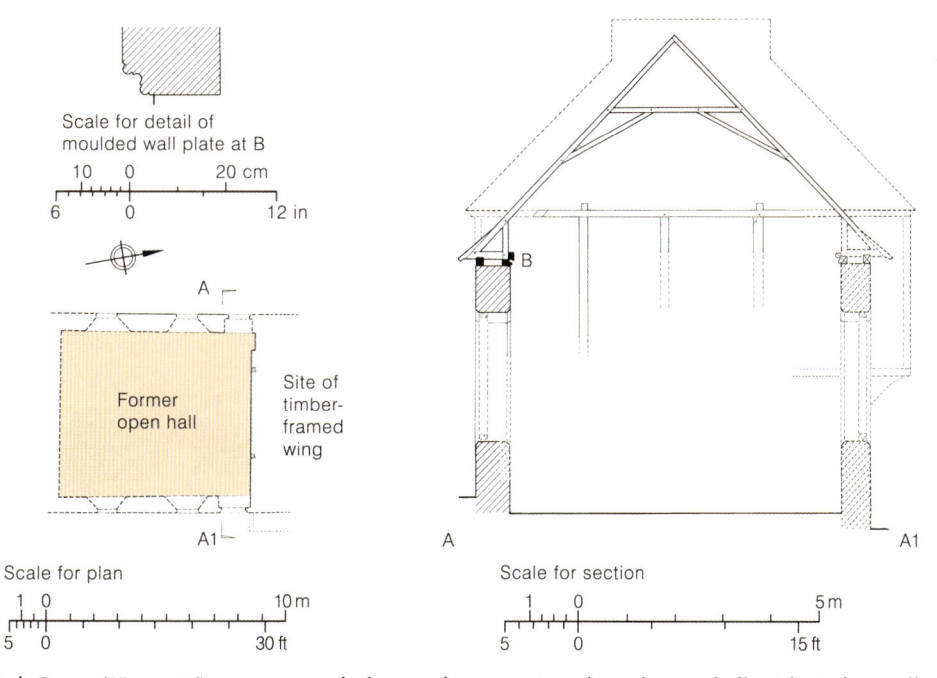

Fig. 7.4: 20 High Street (House 36), reconstructed plan, and cross section through open hall with timber wall of No. 18 behind (S. P. & A. T. A.)

Fig. 7.5: Garden wall of 29 Harnet Street (House 27), formerly a large tenement (P. W. © English Heritage DP068594)

with masonry east and west walls. Evidence for a lancet window in the west (rear) wall and the surviving collar-rafter roof with soulaces – a type of roof not found elsewhere in Sandwich – suggest a date of construction around 1300.[8] The larger part of the hall (including the east, front, wall), and whatever lay beyond it to the south in Pellicane House, were rebuilt in the early seventeenth century and later. In contrast to the stone external walls to west and east, the north wall of the hall was, and still is, timber-framed, implying that it was an internal division, and therefore that the building continued to the north. Before destruction by a fire in the 1930s, a timber range (House 35) lay at right angles, to the north of the hall, its height and steep roof suggesting that it could have been a fourteenth-century cross wing to the stone hall.

No other stone building of this kind has survived to the same extent, but another may have been aligned along the street, at the corner of Harnet Street and Guildcount Lane towards the eastern edge of St Mary's parish (House 27; Fig. 7.5). The quality of the stonework, as well as the status of its later owners, indicate that this was a major property, but the layout of the buildings on the plot is not known. All that survives today are two sections of flint walling, with Caen stone dressings used for quoins and for a two-centred doorway of thirteenth- or early fourteenth-century date. The beautifully knapped flints are tightly coursed with virtually no gaps for mortar, the technique being not dissimilar to that found in the early fourteenth-century nave aisle of St Mary's church, although the standard of workmanship in Harnet Street is even better. It must have been a highly desirable residence, and during the fourteenth century it may have belonged to a wealthy merchant family called Gibbyns or Gybon, one of whom was bailiff and mayor in the mid-fourteenth century, and another mayor in 1398–9.[9]

7.2.2 Small stone and flint buildings set to the rear of later properties

Small structures built totally or partially of stone, which make up the second category, lie to the rear of properties, all the surviving examples being behind the south side of Strand Street, between Harnet Street and the High Street.

A stone range at 27 Strand Street (House 82) now stands behind a sixteenth-century timber-framed frontage. It was not available for survey during the project, although its undercroft was recorded by Parkin in the 1970s (Figs 7.6, 7.7).[10] The upper part, of unknown date and function, is of flint and rubble. Beneath it is the only vaulted undercroft in the town, probably of late thirteenth-century date. Its precise relationship with the timber frontage and the distance of its north wall from the present street line are unclear, although it is estimated from Parkin's work that it is

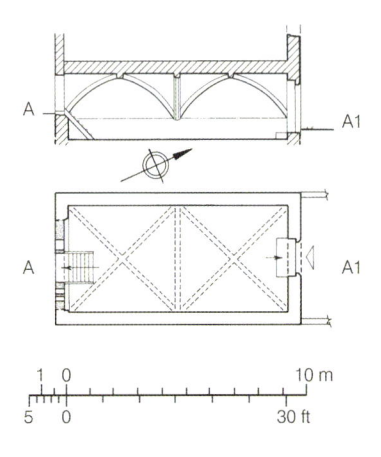

Fig. 7.6: 27 Strand Street (House 82), plan and section of undercroft (A. T. A. after E. W. Parkin)

Fig. 7.7: 27 Strand Street (House 82), view looking north (E. W. Parkin © Sandwich Guildhall Archives)

set back by 5–6m (16–20ft). The undercroft is of two bays, with large chamfered ribs, entered at its north end by a wide two-centred doorway, which appears to lie slightly below present ground level. The width of the doorway (1.97m, 6ft 6in), which opened northwards towards the waterfront, suggests use as a storehouse. Sandwich trade was vibrant in the thirteenth and early fourteenth centuries (Chap. 5.5), and cellars must have been needed for storage. Christ Church Priory rented out several from the thirteenth century onwards.[11] Those almost certainly lay at the west end of town near the priory's property, but there could have been others in private hands, particularly on the higher land to the east.[12] None of those that survive and are certainly medieval are fully sunken, and 27 Strand Street is the only one to be vaulted. If it were entered from the quay and not from a courtyard in front of the undercroft (Fig. 7.8), it provides important evidence for the development of this side of Strand Street and for the position of the south bank of the river, which must still have been progressively moving forwards. In the late thirteenth century buildings such as this one may have stood adjacent to the waterfront, but by the second quarter of the fourteenth they had been fronted by timber buildings in the position that they occupy today, on ground that must have been sufficiently consolidated to support their weight. They also must have opened onto the quays, or onto a pathway running along them, for the street itself developed only later when the ground to the north of it was reclaimed in its turn (Chap. 14.2)

The width of its doorway may indicate that the cellar was used for wine storage, although it could also have been part of a tavern, as suggested for many of the better-quality vaulted undercrofts in London, Winchester and Winchelsea.[13] It may be no coincidence that a document of 1402 seems to locate the Black Tavern in St Peter's parish in more or less this

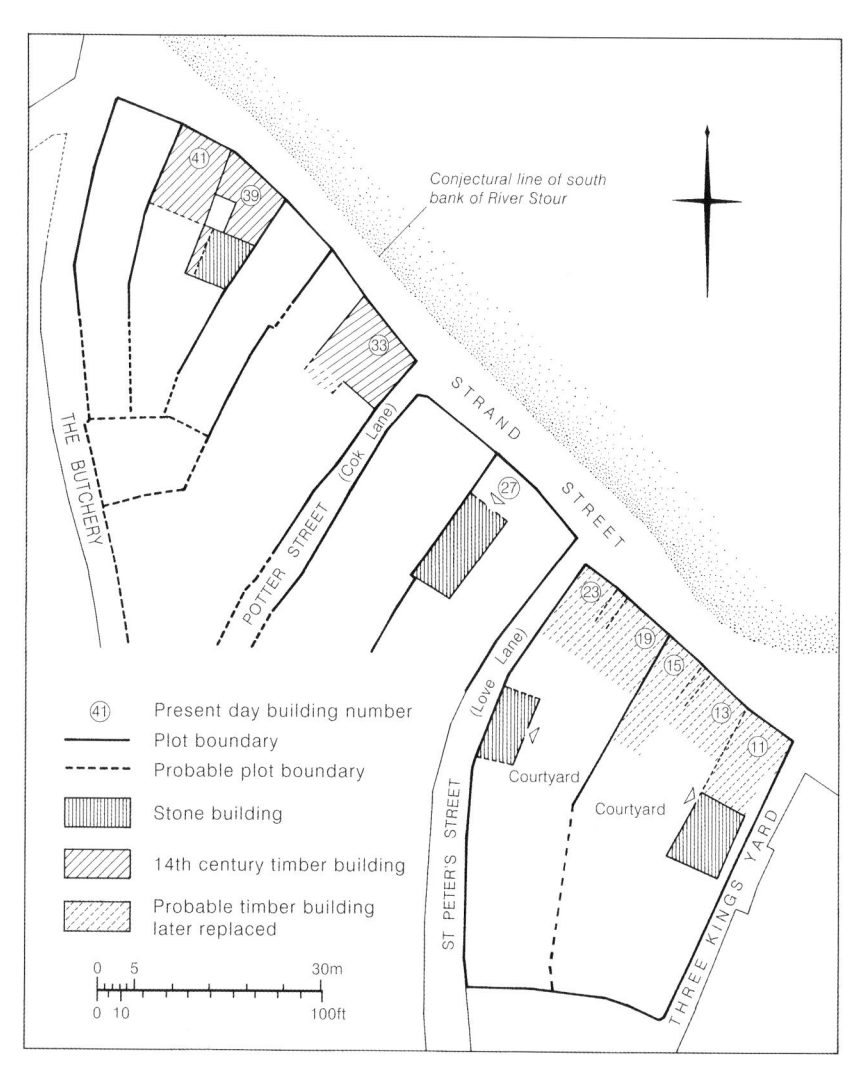

Fig. 7.8: Map of buildings and plots on the south side of Strand Street in the early fourteenth century (A. T. A. based on OS 1:500 1873 map)

position.[14] This is one of only two taverns mentioned in Sandwich records (Chap. 10.3.3).

Three other unvaulted undercrofts formed part of two-storey structures situated at the back of their plots. Two of them were reached from doorways opening from inner courtyards (Fig. 7.8). At 50 St Peter's Street (House 73), the doorway formerly led down to a relatively deep cellar (Figs 7.9, 7.10). At Three Kings Yard (House 78), which is behind 11 Strand Street (House 77), the undercroft is scarcely below street level, entered by a wide doorway with a depressed head that is set beneath a first-floor doorway with a two-centred head, which provided independent access to the storey above (Figs 7.11, 7.12, 12.35). Despite the awkwardness of one doorway lying directly beneath the other, these appear to be the original main entrances to the two storeys, although a very small internal doorway in the south wall of the undercroft may have led to a newel stair between the floors. External access to solars or first-floor chambers, common in earlier stone buildings everywhere, continued until the early fourteenth century.[15] It has previously been suggested that this and the other small buildings at the rear of the Strand Street plots were small self-contained buildings,[16] but the fact that here and at 50 St Peter's Street the stone ranges were reached through internal courtyards shows that both structures were part of much larger properties fronting the quays, although no other ranges from the same period of construction survive on the plots. Internal access also implies that they were intended to be private, probably with domestic accommodation above secure storage.[17] At 50 St Peter's Street only the courtyard wall survives and nothing can be said about the upper storey, but the range behind 11 Strand Street (House 78) has at least part of all its walls. Lancet windows, one double, light the eastern face, and there are two tiny single openings to the west (Figs 7.13, 7.14). The large internal space (8m × 6m, 26ft × 19ft 6in) was probably divided, although all sign of partitioning, which must have been in timber, has gone. Possibly the first-floor entrance led into a main chamber with an inner room to the south.

The internal access, a current right of way on the eastern plot and the line of the plot boundaries

Fig. 7.9: 50 St Peter's Street (House 73), view of east wall (P. W. © English Heritage DP044008)

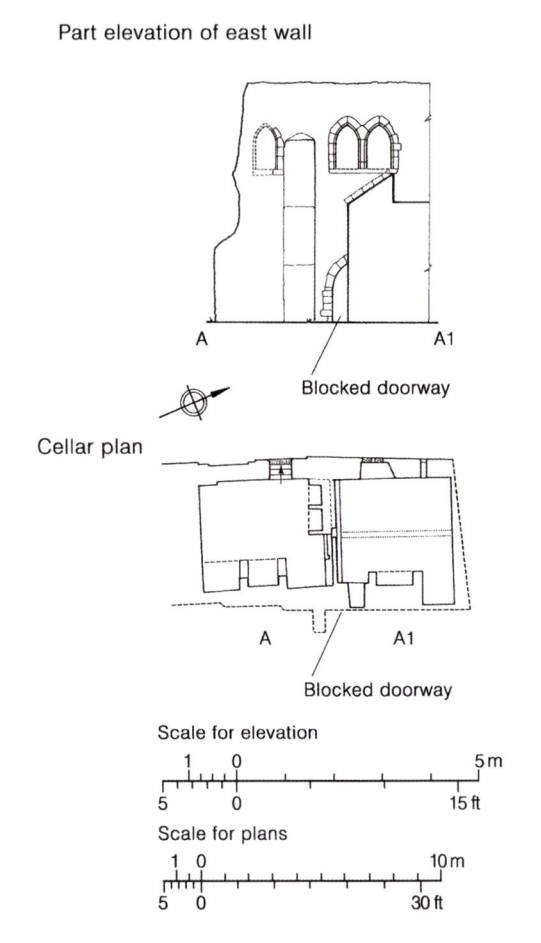

Fig. 7.10: 50 St Peter's Street (House 73), plan of cellar and elevation of east wall, showing entry and first-floor windows (S. P. & A. T. A.)

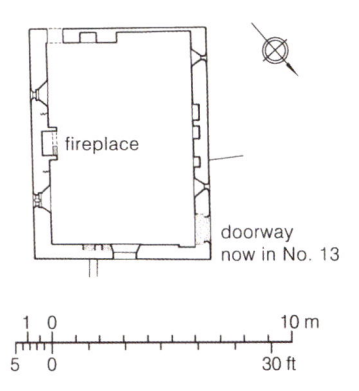

Fig. 7.11: Building in Three Kings Yard, behind 11 Strand Street (House 78), first-floor plan (S. P. & A. T. A.)

Fig. 7.12: Building in Three Kings Yard, behind 11 Strand Street (House 78), doorways to undercroft and main floor, now in 13, 15 Strand Street (P. W. © English Heritage DP032249)

Fig. 7.13: Building in Three Kings Yard (House 78), east face of first floor (P. W. © English Heritage DP044598).

Fig. 7.14: Building in Three King's Yard (House 78): a) first-floor window in east wall (P. W. © English Heritage DP044599); b) first-floor window in west wall (P. W. © English Heritage DP044604)

combine to suggest that originally there were only two plots in the stretch of Strand Street between Love Lane and Three Kings Yard (Fig. 7.8).[18] This would indicate very large merchant properties with ranges, of timber or stone, lying in front of the surviving stone buildings. By *c*.1500 these large plots had been subdivided into several tenements with a doorway apparently leading from the courtyard of Nos. 13, 15 to the building behind No. 11. This implies that even though the front was separated off, the rear range was still part of Nos. 13, 15, which by then may have become The Bull Inn (Chap. 12.8.1; Fig. 12.35).

A similar building lies at the back of 39 Strand Street (House 85; Fig. 7.15), and in this case near-contemporary

Fig. 7.15: 39 Strand Street (House 85), floor plans (S. P. & A. T. A.)

ranges survive in front. The plot is smaller than the ones further east and has only a tiny courtyard. A four-storey rear range has stone walls to its semi-sunken undercroft and part of the raised ground floor, except on the west side where the undercroft was later partially infilled to form the base of a ground-floor passage to the back of the plot. This reorganisation probably destroyed evidence for the original entrance to the undercroft and whatever lay above it. The resulting lack of evidence for an original doorway and the proximity of a niche with a two-centred head to the east window lighting the undercroft, as well as the disparity in levels between the front and rear ranges, suggest that the stonework may have been retained from an earlier building on the site. Above ground-floor level the walls are timber-framed. The timber ranges at the front have been tree-ring dated to 1334, and although the timbers of the rear range could not be dated, the similarity of details in the timber superstructures suggests that they were erected within a short space of time. Perhaps, therefore, a stone undercroft built in the late thirteenth century, and originally intended to accompany earlier buildings at the front, was later reused as part of a new rear range.

Fig. 7.16: Reset thirteenth-century doorway in Paradise Row (House 67) (P. W. © English Heritage DP043953)

7.2.3 Fragmentary stone and flint remains

The earliest evidence for stone in domestic buildings is to be found among fragments spread across the northern half of the town. They include the reset thirteenth-century doorway on Paradise Row (House 67; Fig. 7.16), which was probably associated with a building on the Christ Church Priory estate (Chap. 4.4), and a finely moulded two-centred doorway set into a later timber-framed house next to St Mary's vicarage in Vicarage Lane (House 99; Fig. 7.17). A number of other fragments of stone wall of indeterminate date occur in the western part of town, as indicated in Figure 7.2.[19] In the central area, a single lancet window in a stone wall on the west side of the Fishmarket was discovered in the 1960s when the library was built (Site 21; Fig. 7.2, House 59). Limited excavation suggested that the lancet was reset but showed that there had been early stone walls and clay floors on the site.[20] A little further north, a stretch of stone wall with a small rectangular window near ground level survives between the rear of 1 (House 3) and 3 The Butchery (House 4). This has the appearance of a window to light a storage undercroft in No. 3, similar to the range behind 11 Strand Street. In the eastern part of town, a larger, rectangular window remains at the back of 17 Upper Strand Street (House 94), overlooking Quay Lane, which leads down to Fisher Gate. Most of these fragments are undatable. Occasionally, as in the two

Fig. 7.17: Reset doorway at 3 Vicarage Lane (House 99) (P. W. © English Heritage DP032250)

doorways in Paradise Row and Vicarage Lane, they may date from the mid-thirteenth century, but what little stylistic evidence there is suggests that most are as likely to belong to the late thirteenth century or even the early fourteenth.

On Strand Street itself, some of the late medieval timber houses are separated by thick flint and stone rubble walls: between 11 and 13 Strand Street (Houses 77, 79; Figs 7.2, 12.35), to the east of 3 Strand Street (House 74), and to the west of 7 Strand Street (House 76). At No. 7 the stone wall runs as far as the present line of Strand Street, but at the first two the walls do not reach the street, stopping 2.5–3m back from the present frontage, with that at No. 3 continuing some way behind the rear of the present building (Fig. 12.34).[21] In addition, they are only one or two storeys high, even where the present building is higher. This may indicate that at least parts of the earlier front ranges were built of stone.

7.3 Timber-framed buildings

In the late twelfth century the techniques of timber building construction changed. The earliest known methods, recovered from excavation, employed earth-fast posts, which were subject to rot. Only in the late twelfth century did the main structural posts begin to be raised onto timber sills set on stone plinths, and true timber framing start to be developed. It then became possible for the first time to erect buildings that could survive for several hundred years.[22] Dendrochronology has identified a handful of houses erected c.1200. So far, all the dated survivors are rural; all are aisled buildings, that is to say, the main span of the whole building was divided into a central nave and side aisles; and all appear to have been single-storeyed throughout, both in the open hall and in any bays partitioned off at the ends. It is probable that similar aisled halls of this date existed in towns, and slightly later ones certainly occur, both surviving and excavated.[23] But the cumbersome and space-consuming aisled form, and the difficulty of introducing upper storeys without rebuilding, meant that most of those in towns were swept away in the later Middle Ages and after.

Documentary evidence indicates that multi-storey timber buildings with jetties were to be found in London by the 1240s, although they may still have been only two storeys high, and surviving urban examples have not been dated before the last quarter of the thirteenth century. Once they survive, their structural sophistication suggests that they had had a reasonably long history of development, and by the early fourteenth century three-storey examples start to survive. It is in this context that we need to consider the earliest surviving timber buildings in Sandwich. Three buildings along Strand Street, all partly of three storeys, date between c.1300 and c.1340. The hall and front range of No. 39 (House 85) have been tree-ring dated to 1334;[24] No. 41 (House 86) must be close to this in date, while No. 33 (House 83) is possibly earlier. Although varying in detail, all three have certain basic features: a three-storey range on the street frontage, an open hall heated by an open hearth behind, and service rooms or further structures at the rear or the side. Because these buildings are early survivors in national terms, and important for the understanding of the later development of Sandwich houses, they are discussed here in some detail.

No. 33 Strand Street (House 83) is on the corner of Strand Street and Potter Street (formerly Cok Lane). It had two parallel ranges, the eastern of two bays and the western of three (Figs 7.18, 7.19). The street frontages to north and east were jettied above the ground floor, and the north wall may have been jettied above the first floor as well. The roofs were probably originally arranged in a U shape.[25] Beneath the south-east quadrant is a low, rubble-walled cellar of indeterminate date, its floor 1.2m below ground level. Little of the original ground-floor arrangement remains except in the north-east corner, where the large joists and dragon beam of the jetties to the adjacent streets can be seen. Mortices for brackets along the north front suggest wide shop openings, such as can be identified at 23 Strand Street (Fig. 12.37), and a single post off-centre on the Strand Street frontage has pegs for a solid, two-centred doorhead that could have opened into a passage through to the rear. The walls and roof indicate that the south-west quadrant formed a two-bay open hall that originally projected south of the square, while the other three quadrants were floored. One unusual aspect of the building's construction is the use of a post in the centre, rising from the ground floor through the upper floors to support the central wall plate, and probably the tiebeams, of each range.[26] The post, therefore, is a crucial element of the construction, and shows that the whole building was erected at the same time.

The first-floor chambers along the north side are c.2.5m high, and ceiled with large joists that are carried on rails or bressumers only above the central windows; to either side the joists are tenoned into uprights that rise past the first-floor ceiling to a wall plate 1.5m above. The wall is then strengthened on the exterior by both downward and upward bracing. The fact that the wall plate between the two ranges has no original post supporting it at the north end suggests that this may be a modification to the original design and that the external wall on the north side was originally further forward, forming a second jetty on the north face between the first and second floors. This would make sense of the tree-ring dating discussed below.

The southern ends of the east and west ranges

were roofed north–south with king struts rising from tiebeam to apex, with collar purlins tenoned in to either side to support collars, as well as upward and downward braces. This type of roof is specific to south-east England. It is found in buildings erected in the years to either side of 1300, and provides relatively precise dating evidence.[27] At 33 Strand Street indentations or birdsmouths to support rafter feet on the central wall plate cease halfway across the northern bays, while the collar purlin surviving in the north-east quadrant has an extra peg hole just inside the northernmost collar that may have been intended for a peg to fix a collar purlin across the front of the building. The combined evidence suggests that to start with the front was roofed parallel to the street, forming a U plan, as in the schematic outline in Figure 7.19.

The details of the building are highly unusual. Medieval double-pile buildings with an open hall in one corner are not common, although they do occur.[28] First-floor joists tenoned into posts that continue upwards to wall plates a storey higher are even more remarkable,[29] and it may be that the arrangement was a result of rebuilding this frontage in the early fifteenth century. Tree-ring dating of the structure was not entirely successful, although two uprights along

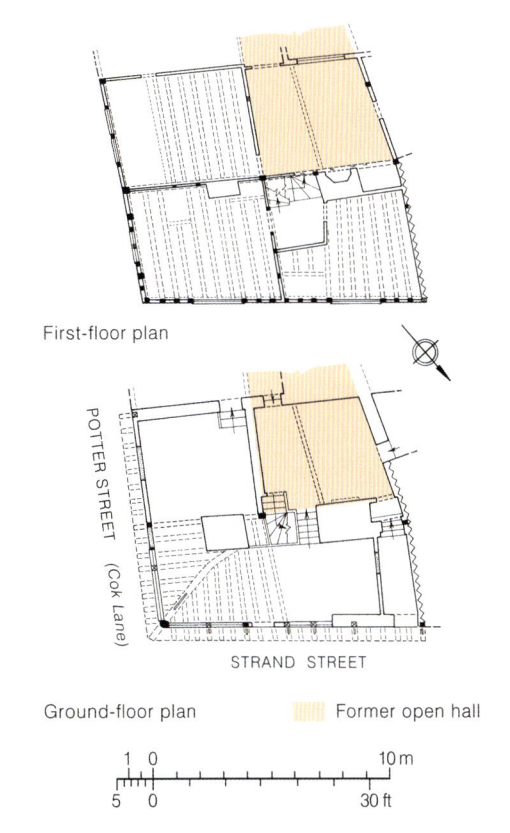

Fig. 7.18: 33 Strand Street (House 83), floor plans (S. P. & A. T. A.)

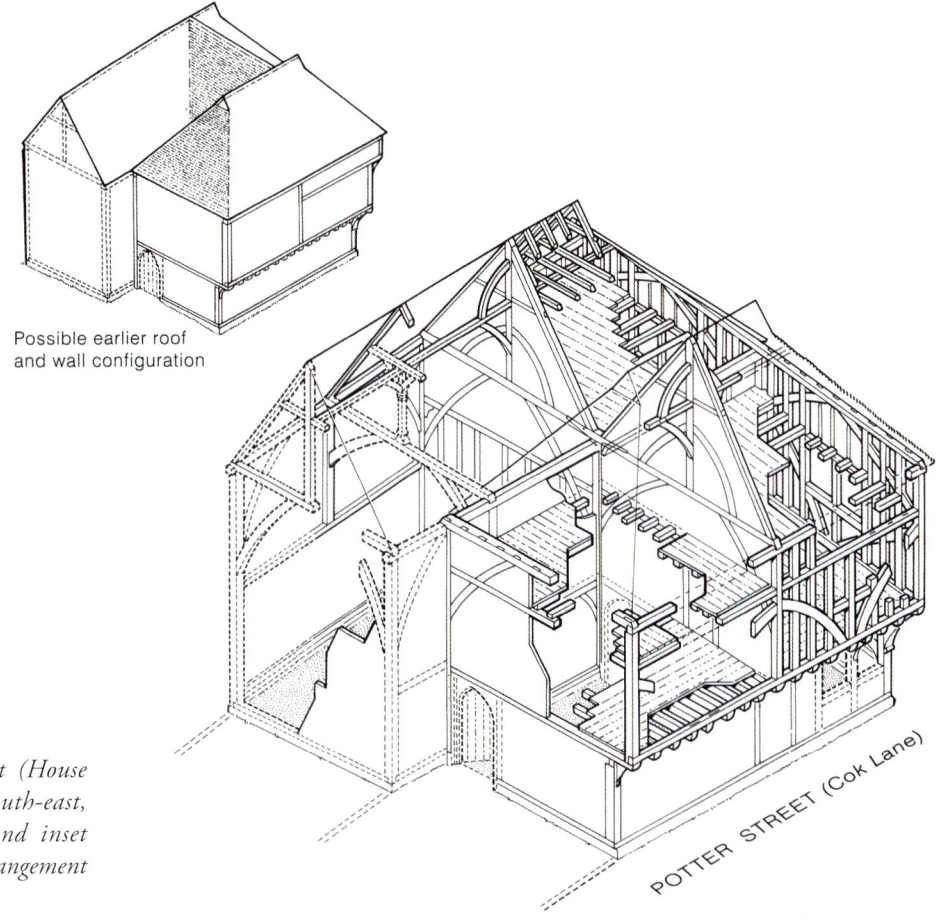

Fig. 7.19: 33 Strand Street (House 83), reconstruction from south-east, with late medieval roof, and inset showing possible original arrangement (A. T. A)

the north wall in the north-east quadrant were dated to 1433.[30] Several of the other timbers sampled cross-matched each other, but could not be dated. This, combined with the lack of evidence for a post at the north end of the central wall plate and evidence of several reused timbers on the north wall of the north-west quadrant, suggest that the original building was constructed in the early fourteenth century with a double jetty to the north, but that the wall of the first and second storeys is the result of rebuilding without a second jetty in 1433.

The large joists of the attic floor show that the roof space was used, but there is no evidence for how it was lit or reached. There is no sign of fenestration on the original east and south walls at this level, which means that the south-east quadrant at least was very dark. The tiebeams supported on the low walls must have made movement between the quadrants almost impossible until openings were cut through at a later date, so there were probably three stairs to the second floor, one in each of the storeyed bays. The only visible site for an original stair is against the north wall of the north-west quadrant, but some joists in the north-east quadrant may have been moved in the fifteenth-century restructuring, and part of the ceiling in the south-east quadrant is concealed.

The functions of the various parts of the building are not easy to deduce. It is clear that there was an open hall in the corner away from the streets, and it is likely that, located on an important junction, some if not all the ground floor was used for commerce, as suggested by the mortices for brackets on the façade, implying shop-front openings. This raises the question of where the services could have been. As discussed below (Section 7.5), there are indications that the plot was originally larger, so they could have been sited south of the hall. The first floor may have housed domestic accommodation, although that too might have been in the postulated southern extension. The low height of the walls to the upper storey, and lack of evidence for lighting, suggest that it was used for storage only, with each quadrant accessed by stairs from the chamber below. Thus this was no ordinary house. The hall indicates that it incorporated domestic functions, but the rest of what survives may have been given over wholly to business. Similar issues emerge in other Sandwich houses of this period.

The other two early fourteenth-century survivors are more conventional in form, and point the way to future construction in the town (Fig. 7.20). Tree-ring dating has established that the timbers of the hall and front range of 39 Strand Street (House 85) were felled in 1334, and it is likely that the house was constructed soon after.[31] Both here and next door at 41 Strand Street (House 86), the roofs are of the same crown-post and king-strut construction as at 33 Strand Street, proving that this form of roof construction was used as late as 1334. Both have three-storey ranges fronting onto Strand Street, although their internal arrangements are not identical.

No. 39 Strand Street is two bays wide, with a small courtyard behind the front range (Figs 7.15, 7.21, 7.22). Most of the ground-floor walls have been rebuilt, but it is likely that originally there was a way through to the courtyard and, since there is no evidence for an original doorway directly connecting the street range to the open hall, the latter was probably reached from the courtyard, possibly next to the street range where there is a seventeenth-century doorway, in a position found in a number of medieval houses in King's Lynn.[32] The absence of direct communication with the hall implies that the ground-floor rooms at the front contained shops or work-related areas rather than domestic accommodation. It is clear from the framing of the partition wall between the hall and the front range that there was no gallery across the open hall – indeed, the different floor levels at each end would have made this problematic – so any domestic accommodation in the upper storeys of the front range must have been reached by a stair within the range itself. This part of the building, therefore, could have been occupied independently from the hall and the four-storeyed block to the south.

The timber framing of the south range is structurally separate and is carried on a stone base that may belong to an earlier phase (Section 7.2.2). The timbers here were also sampled for tree-ring dating, but without success. Since the construction of both the front range and the rear one is very similar, with massive joists and splayed and tabled scarf joints, it is likely that the whole timber complex was erected over a short period in the early fourteenth century. The ground floor of the rear range, elevated over the undercroft, is higher than the floor level of the hall (Fig. 7.21), and movement between the two must have been awkward. There are now doorways on both sides of the later hall fireplace, that to the east possibly always leading to the main floor at the back (Fig. 7.22), and that to the west providing a new, later, entry to the undercroft and to a stair that lay in the north-west corner of the rear range. On the first floor a massive main beam is supported by chunky braces, and the pegged joists show that there was not only the framed stair trap, but also a square opening in the centre of the ceiling. Unfortunately, the roof of the rear range has been rebuilt, and there is no evidence for its original form.

Fig. 7.20: 39 and 41 Strand Street from the north (Houses 85, 86) (P. W. © English Heritage DP043959)

All these details pose considerable problems of interpretation. Was this just a dwelling? If it were, what ancillary domestic rooms accompanied the open hall? Although structurally of a piece with the hall, the front or north range could have been occupied separately from the rest of the building, with any domestic accommodation on its upper floors being accessible only from the probably commercial space below. At the rear, the difference in levels between the hall and the south range, presumably caused by the pre-existing stone building, made access between the two difficult – so what activities took place in the south range? The heavy joists and the square opening in the first-floor ceiling suggest that goods, perhaps wool, were hauled up for storage above.[33] But what about the lower floors? Was the undercroft for storage only – perhaps for wine – with services and chambers, perhaps combined with storage, on the first and second floors? Or was the undercroft for services alone, with chambers and dedicated storage above? Were there a detached kitchen and perhaps other service buildings further south on the plot? This kind of uncertainty over function, already

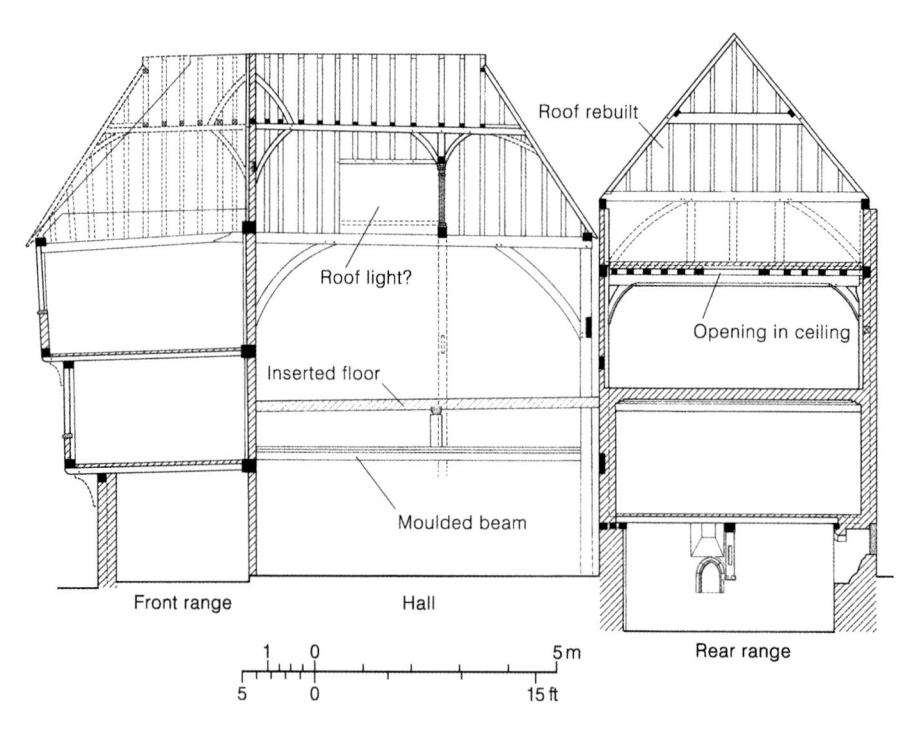

Fig. 7.21: 39 Strand Street (House 85), long section (A. T. A.)

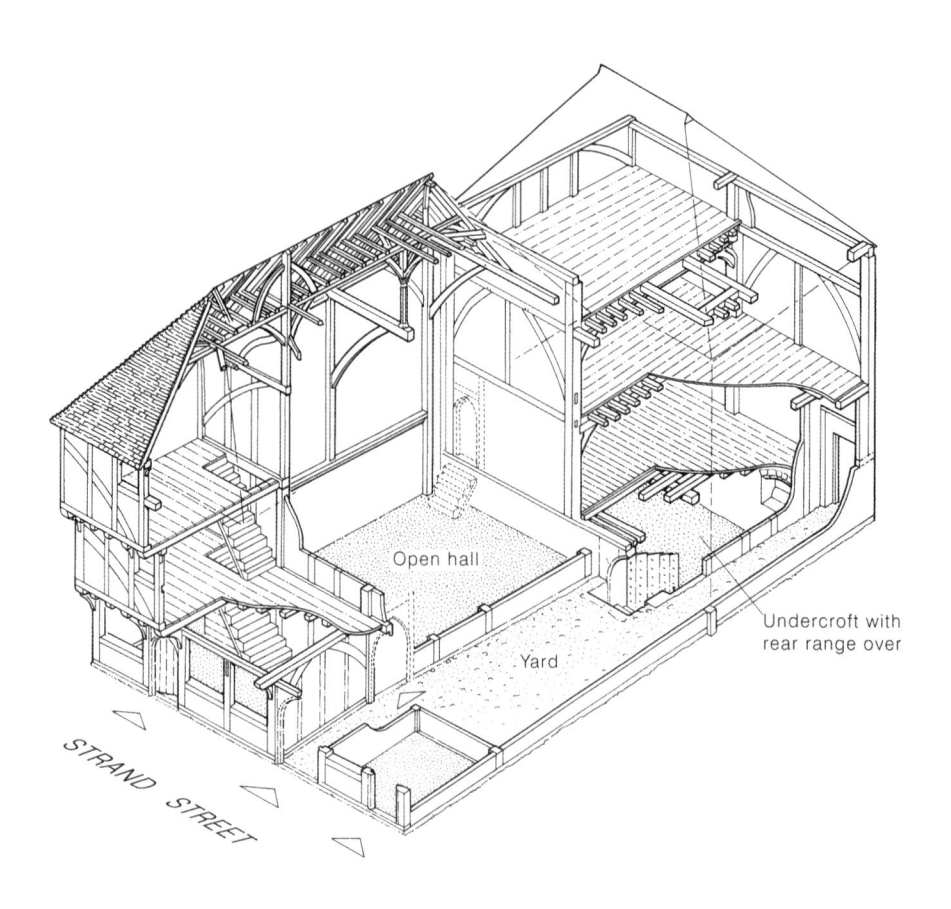

Fig. 7.22: 39 Strand Street (House 85), reconstruction (A. T. A)

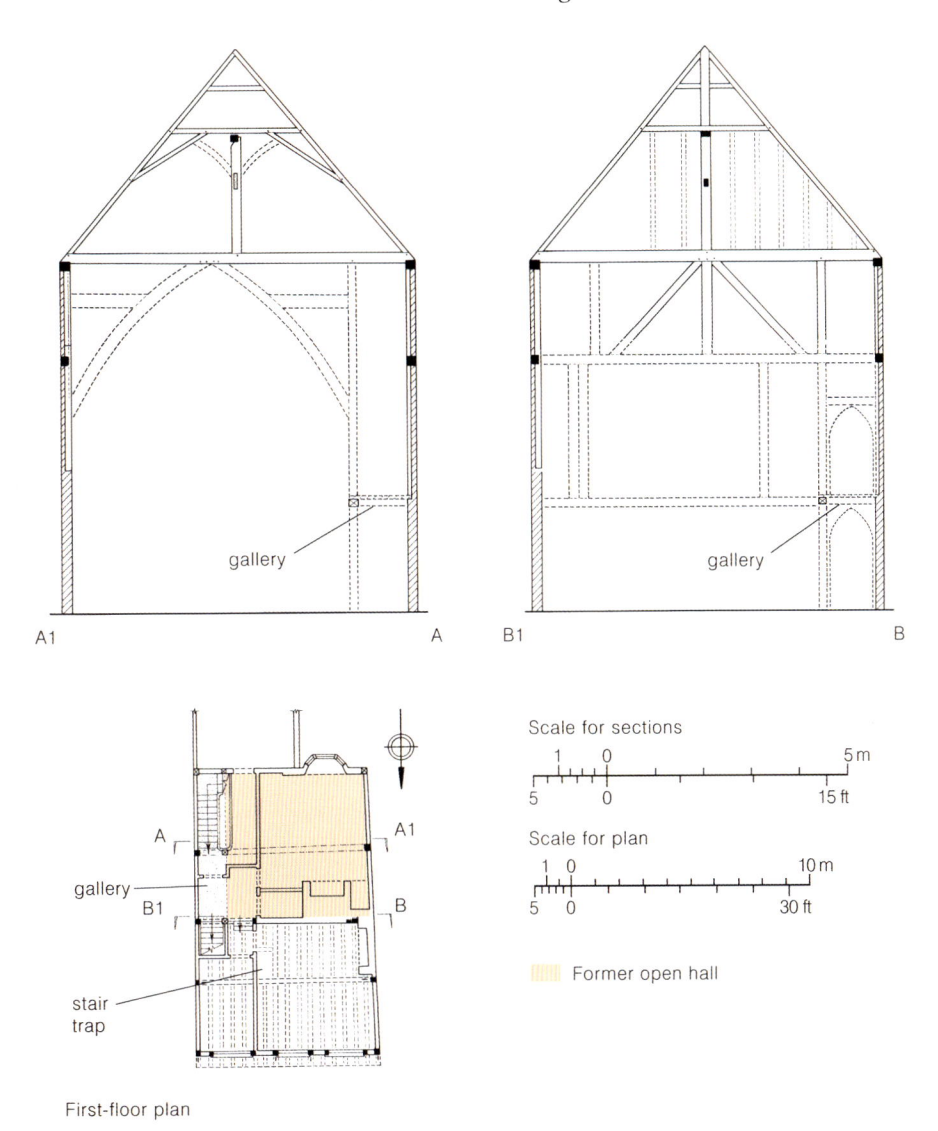

Fig. 7.23: 41 Strand Street (House 86), cross sections through open hall, showing roof structure and gallery across hall. First-floor plan showing positions of sections and stair trap in centre of the front range (S. P. & A. T. A.)

seen at 33 Strand Street, bedevils the understanding of medieval urban buildings in Sandwich and elsewhere, and will be returned to in later chapters.

No. 41 Strand Street (House 86) has structural details and roof type similar to those of No. 39, implying that it also was built in the 1330s (Fig. 7.23). It too has a three-storey jettied front range and an open hall behind, in this case with no courtyard, and there is evidence that there was further accommodation at the rear, now demolished. But there are important differences between it and its neighbour. The hall, occupying the full width of the plot, appears to have been entered at the north-east corner, probably by means of a passage through the front range. The passage appears to have continued through the hall to link with the rear range. It was defined within the hall by a post, resembling a spere post set 1m inside the east wall, but otherwise was probably entirely open to the body of the hall. Section A–A1 shows the peculiarly imbalanced result in the central open truss. The evidence suggests that long arch braces ran from the posts to an off-centre position in the tiebeam, with the crown post above set conventionally in a central position, necessitated by its function in framing the roof.

Over the passage within the hall was a gallery, reached by a stair in the rear range and linking the first-floor rooms in the front and rear ranges. The ground-floor joisting of the front range has been replaced so the evidence has disappeared, but there was probably no stair to the floor above, with the upper rooms being reached by the gallery. Galleries across open halls are found in urban buildings where the ground-floor space at the front was probably used for commercial purposes and occupied entirely separately from the rear, the gallery providing the necessary connection between the upper rooms. They became common in Sandwich during the Middle Ages (Fig. 12.9) and, although found in late medieval buildings in a number of other English towns,[34] 41 Strand Street is one of the earliest known examples. It also implies that the whole building, other than the ground-floor shop, was designed for single occupancy, in contrast to No. 39, where the upper part of the front could be reached only from within the range. On the first floor of the front range of No. 41 there is evidence for a stair to reach the second floor – essential because there was never a second, upper, gallery – but the large first-floor chamber has no sign of original partitioning, and the framed stair trap is situated in the middle of the floor rather than against a side wall, as is usually the case. On the exterior the framing has been totally renewed, but if the present pattern repeats what was there originally (Fig. 7.20), the convex braces set either side of a wide central gap might indicate the position of former loading doorways to the upper storeys. This would suggest that the upper levels of the front range might have been at least partly devoted to the storage of goods hauled up from the ground.

To the three timber buildings described above may be added the two lower floors of 23 Strand Street, on the corner of Love Lane (House 81; Fig. 12.37). The large dragon beam, solid dragon post and heavy, closely spaced joists are not dissimilar to those at 33 Strand Street. But since no evidence for doorheads or scarf joints survives and the roof has been completely rebuilt, it is difficult to date the remains with any precision. If it dates to the early fourteenth century, as opposed, say, to c.1400, it is the only building from this period with some surviving evidence for original shop windows. Small braces in the corners of the large ground-floor frames on both frontages indicate wide arched openings to a large shop space reached through the main doorway to the house, in a way that may also have occurred at 33 Strand Street.[35] It will be discussed further in the context of other shops in Chapter 12.8.2.

7.4 Building materials used in the construction of domestic buildings in Sandwich

Although flint was generally available, and sandstone from the Thanet Beds occurs round the north Kent coast (as used for the Site 20 building in Love Lane), stone is not generally quarried in north-east Kent, and was often imported; usually ragstone from Folkestone or limestone from France (mainly Caen stone). It was therefore an expensive building material, and was often supplemented by flint or, occasionally, by brick. The house in Harnet Street was largely built of knapped flints, with Caen stone dressings (House 27; Fig. 7.5). At the range behind 11 Strand Street, the quoins and the facing stones of the windows are of Caen stone, but brick relieving arches are embedded in the flint and rubble walls, and the internal window splays are of brick, which was clearly intended to be plastered (House 78; Figs 7.13, 7.14).

Early brick was also used in a highly unusual context in the timber-framed structure of 33 Strand Street (House 83). The internal timber panels are infilled with thin yellow bricks. In the open hall these are not obviously smoke-blackened and might be thought to be replacement infilling; but similar bricks occur in the apex of the closed central truss in the east range, a position where they are highly unlikely to have been replaced. The mortar between them is held in position by short stout pegs serving as wedges (Figs 7.24, 7.25), set in short mortices that also line the inner faces of timbers that have lost their infill. It therefore seems likely that this is an early use of brick nogging that was intended to be plastered, as some of the panels still are.[36] Brick at this time was almost certainly imported, as documented in the 1370s.[37] The use of such unusually early brick,[38] like the use of Caen stone, underlines the fact that the port was in a privileged location, easily able to import materials from the Continent. But it also indicates the lack of local building materials in this part of Kent.

It has been claimed that the stone structures set back from the south side of Strand Street were originally complete houses in their own right,[39] but, for the reasons discussed above, they are more likely to have been part of larger properties. It is a common misconception that stone buildings were built of masonry alone. In reality, stone and timber were frequently used together. In Southampton, for example, the absence of stone front walls in twelfth-century masonry buildings is thought to mean that those walls were of timber;[40] at New Winchelsea many houses above the surviving stone undercrofts of c.1300 were probably originally built of timber;[41] and at Winchester a number of stone buildings of the twelfth to fourteenth centuries set at the rear of plots probably had timber ranges in front of them.[42]

Stone was never commonly used in medieval towns. At Canterbury in the early thirteenth century only thirty tenements of the four hundred listed in the documents were described as 'of stone',[43] and in late thirteenth-century Winchelsea about fifty of the 723 plots that were laid out at that time are known to have had stone undercrofts.[44] Thus, in each case stone was

Fig. 7.24: 33 Strand Street (House 83), apex of central closed truss, east range, with brick filling still in place, and mortices (circled) for stud below collar and pegs on rafter, formerly to hold bricks (S. P.)

Fig. 7.25: 33 Strand Street (House 83), panel below tiebeam of north truss in hall, with brick filling and short peg or wedge (circled) to hold bricks in place (S. P.)

used in around 7 per cent of the documented buildings. In Sandwich stone remains that are probably *in situ* have been identified in fewer than twenty properties, although there are other examples of reused stone walling or of rubble and flint cellars. There are no written records indicating the number of buildings *c.*1300, but if the population were then as much as 5,000, as has been suggested, there could have been about 1,000 houses. This may be an overestimate, but even if both the population and the number of houses were lower, it is clear that stone was used in a very small proportion of the overall housing stock. Stone was a mark of distinction and considerable wealth. Occasionally, all or most of a house was built of stone, but often it was reserved for party walls between tenements or for a particularly private and important part of the property. It may have continued to be used by the elite until the 1330s, when Sandwich merchants began to experience a downturn in trade. By then timber-framed construction had anyway become capable of considerable sophistication. In Sandwich as elsewhere, stone was seldom used for domestic buildings after the mid-fourteenth century.

Even obtaining good timber must have been a problem in Sandwich. Today, east Kent has few sizeable trees, and this was probably also true in the Middle Ages, so, like stone and brick, it needed to be imported. When the bailiff's accounts begin in 1345 they include imports of between 100 and 400 'eastrishboards' from the Baltic, high-quality oak cut into planks and used for doors, shutters and screens,[45] but timber for building construction was almost certainly shipped from the Weald, where there was plenty of oak, and is therefore not listed among the foreign imports into Sandwich. When carriage was accounted for locally, as in an early fourteenth-century supply of timber from dens in the Weald to the manor of Eastry, the most expensive part of the journey was overland from the Weald to the coast, the carriage by sea to Sandwich being relatively inexpensive.[46]

7.5 The function of rooms and the size of plots

Because so little survives, it is impossible to identify the function of rooms in the large stone buildings. Possibly such houses were purely residences, and certainly 20 High Street (House 36) had a great hall on the street front, but it is unclear whether it was a standard hall house of the late medieval type with private rooms at either end. In fact, the evidence of the timber houses and the rear stone ranges suggests that early houses in Sandwich may have been more complex than this. In the timber houses the multi-storey front bays were primarily dedicated to commerce, with shops below and storage above. Open halls were set to the rear, and behind them were further ranges with chambers for domestic or even storage use placed above particularly secure storage in the stone undercrofts. That the upper floors at the front may have been used largely for storage should not surprise us, for upper-floor storage, often with external access, remained a feature of many Sandwich buildings until after the Middle Ages.

Where house frontages can be measured, the early houses in Sandwich were generally wider than those of the later Middle Ages, but there are considerable differences in both the plot sizes and the arrangement of the stone and timber buildings of this period. Some at least of the largest stone houses had halls broadside and adjacent to the street front. In Harnet Street (House 27) the plot was 13.7m (45ft) wide, and at 20 High Street (House 36) the frontage was possibly as wide as 47m (155ft). At the east end of Strand Street the small stone buildings were part of courtyard properties with frontages of 15.8m (52ft) and 22.9m (75ft). But the timber buildings of the first half of the fourteenth century run back from the street rather than along it, and their plots were only 7.5m to 11.5m wide.

Although some of the stone buildings were erected before the timber ones, both materials were probably used in the early fourteenth century, so the reason for the differences in size needs examining. It is proposed that the economic boom of the early decades of the fourteenth century meant that pressure on space near the waterfront became a critical factor in the size of merchant properties. The large stone houses broadside to the street (Houses 27, 36; Site 20) are located away from the waterfront (Fig. 7.2), on north–south streets in areas where pressure on space was probably not so great.[47] Here there was space for halls to run along the street front, as was certainly the case at 20 High Street, and there may even have been room for commercial space to the sides. On the other hand, the earliest surviving timber buildings are in prime positions on the south side of Strand Street, originally facing the quays (Fig. 7.8). The widths of 39 and 41 Strand Street (Houses 85, 86) together total 18.2m (60ft) divided in the ratio of 11:9. Only No. 39, the larger one, has a courtyard and a stone range at the rear, the latter having lost all sign of its original entrance, which probably lay to the west, next to No. 41. These features, combined with the fact that the two houses were built within a short space of time, raise the possibility that they were once part of a single plot 18.2m wide, a suggestion that is not contradicted by the length and form of the outer boundaries. Thus, when the stone range was built at the back in the late thirteenth century it could have served a single plot, entered from a courtyard in the manner of those at the east end of Strand Street. But in the early 1330s the plot was divided into two unequal halves; two houses were built where one had been before; and the stone range was modified, losing its original entrance. In the two new buildings, the ground-floor rooms at the front were reserved for commercial use; the open halls were set behind; and further ranges at the back, including the earlier stone structure, combined domestic and secure storage functions. Possibly, judging by the position of the undercroft of 27 Strand Street, the original plot was not only divided but also extended northwards as a result of newly reclaimed land on the other side of what is now Strand Street.

Elsewhere on Strand Street the wider plots persisted until the fifteenth century, when a similar process of subdivision and rebuilding took place. What originally had been two plots – present 11, 13, 15 (Houses 77, 79) and 19, 21, 23 Strand Street (Houses 80, 81) – became three, with No. 11 separated from Nos. 13

and 15. Later still, as the numbering indicates, the properties were further subdivided. No. 33 Strand Street (House 83) may also have been built on a wider plot, which possibly endured until the time of the Ordnance Survey map of 1873 (Fig. 7.8). That shows the Strand Street end of the north–south plot boundary running not along the side of No. 33, but about 9m (29ft 6in) further west, suggesting that the original plot was considerably wider. The western edge of the site is still unclear on the current OS map, even though the properties are physically divided by walls and fences. Unfortunately, the present building to the west has been totally rebuilt and its original details, apart from possibly early fourteenth-century heavy joists, are irrecoverable, so disentangling the development of the plot is not easy.

The late thirteenth- or early fourteenth-century stone party walls that separate some properties along Strand Street are all only one or two storeys high. The late medieval houses to either side, however, are mostly of three storeys, which implies that the earlier houses were lower, the third storey becoming necessary only when the plots became narrower. The earlier houses are likely to have had timber open halls, which were possibly aisled, but there is evidence neither for them nor for where they were sited on the large plots.

All the structures discussed in this chapter were erected during the thirteenth century or the first half of the fourteenth. There is no evidence for new building between *c.*1340 and *c.*1380. Once the economy and population started to decline during the middle of the fourteenth century, there was a break of about forty years before there were any signs of construction beginning again, and even in the late fourteenth and early fifteenth centuries new buildings were not common. Most of the many surviving timber buildings in Sandwich were not built until well into the fifteenth century. They will be discussed in Chapter 12.

7.6 Conclusion

The buildings in Sandwich that survive from before the mid-fourteenth century are few in number but their importance can hardly be overestimated. Although isolated buildings of the same date survive in other towns, the fact that the Sandwich examples form a group makes them highly unusual, if not unique. They were almost certainly built for Sandwich's urban elite at the turn of the thirteenth and fourteenth centuries, most of whom were merchants, as underlined by their waterfront situation and the suggested function of rooms. The positions of the various structures within their plots provide evidence of continuing subdivision at this time, and their relationship to the frontage suggests that the waterfront was still in a state of development. The structures themselves are extremely difficult to interpret, partly because so few contemporary houses elsewhere have been studied in depth, so that little comparative material is available. Nonetheless, their details indicate that residential, commercial and storage functions were inextricably mixed. Except for the open hall itself, there is no clear sign that any rooms were exclusively domestic, and commercial and storage functions appear to have been of paramount importance. The timber buildings are firmly dated by features such as the roof types and the unusual construction of 33 Strand Street (House 83), which were not repeated in later buildings, but other aspects, such as tall open halls set behind multi-storeyed frontages and often crossed by galleries, were later to become common in Sandwich houses.

8 The topography of the town by the mid-fourteenth century

For street names and archaeological sites mentioned in this chapter see Figures 1.2 and endpapers

The map in the Introduction to Part III (Fig. III.1) shows the town plan and the extent of occupation by the middle of the fourteenth century, the evidence for which is set out below. Much can be culled from documents that, although still fairly few in number and selective in survival, are more informative than in earlier centuries. More material evidence is provided by the surviving structures – domestic buildings, churches, town defences – and a few archaeological interventions. The combined evidence suggests that by the mid-fourteenth century Sandwich had achieved its greatest medieval extent both in physical size and in numbers of inhabitants. If, as has been suggested, the population reached approximately 5,000 before the Black Death, there would have been something like 1,000 households, in roughly the same number of dwellings ranged along the streets of the town.

The castle, standing in Castelmead, was still a dominating presence to the east, although the construction of Mill Wall, perhaps in the early decades of the fourteenth century, cut it off from the urban settlement. Christ Church Priory continued to occupy its headquarters in the west, even after it lost its ancient right to tolls in 1290. Meanwhile, the town itself was continuing to develop between these two entities. The northern properties were focused on the waterfront with access to quays and harbour facilities. Domestic buildings were still virtually confined to the dry land north of the Delf, although there are signs that by the end of the thirteenth century at the latest occupation had spread westwards from the Thanet Beds ridge to fill in the lower land between it and St Mary's church, and perhaps even further west. South of the Delf, much of the land newly drained and enclosed by earth ramparts must have remained open, although a new marketplace was established, St John's hospital was founded just south of the watercourse, and the Carmelites were given property closer to the southern perimeter on which to build their friary. Nonetheless, Boys's plan of the town of 1787 (Fig. 8.1) shows that even by his time the southern part of the town was almost totally uninhabited.

8.1 From the priory headquarters to Harnet Street

Documents associated with the administration of the Christ Church Priory estate provide the best information about the topography of the west end of Sandwich, especially before 1290 when its control of rights in the town passed to the crown, after which fewer priory records survive.[1] Of particular topographical interest are the accounts detailing construction costs and repairs to the priory's properties such as those outlined in Chapters 4.4 and 7.2, and also records of rents that were paid to the priory for the use of buildings, quays and so on.[2]

Thirteenth-century references have been used to propose that the main stone residence of the headquarters was built in the middle or second half of the twelfth century just south of the quay, which it overlooked. The quay was probably 'Monkenkey', not mentioned by name until 1386 but frequently referred to thereafter.[3] The quay lined the south bank of the river Stour, had at least one crane by 1336,[4] and by the early fifteenth century was 142ft 9in (43.5m) long,[5] its length probably increasing as adjoining properties were added to the estate. The priory headquarters also included a number of cellars or storehouses (not necessarily subterranean) and a herring house.[6]

The properties abutting the priory residence to east and west were owned by members of the Packer family until the priory acquired them in the 1270s and 1280s. They were long plots running back from the riverbank (or 'sea' as it is often called in contemporary sources), probably with quays to the north and a mill fleet to the south.[7] When part of the Packer messuage to the west of the priory headquarters, by then belonging to the merchant John Peny, was acquired by the priory in the 1270s, it measured 16.5 virgates (272ft 3in) in length but only 13ft in width, perhaps signifying that it was a sliver

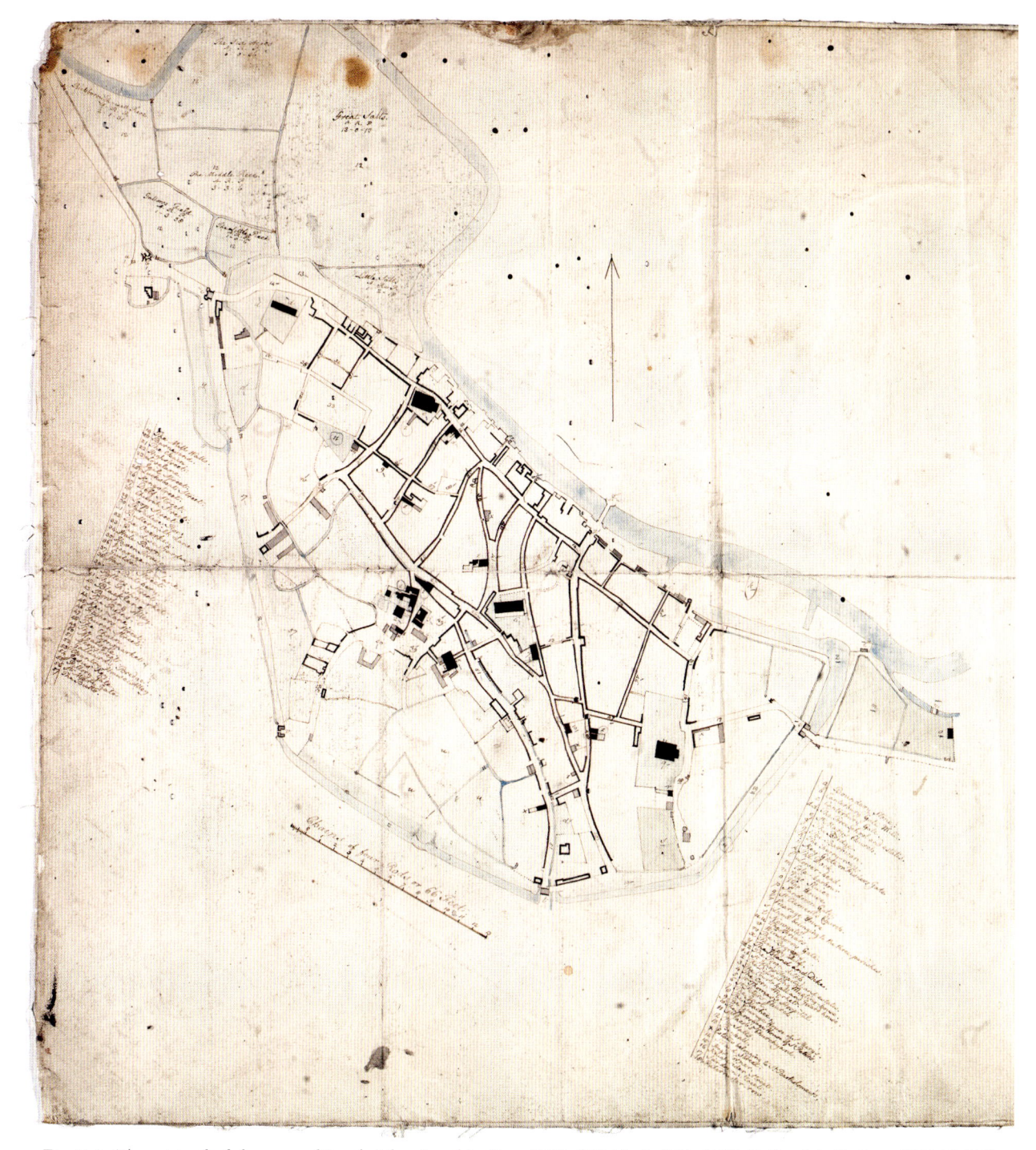

Fig. 8.1: The original of the map of Sandwich printed in Boys 1792 (EKAS: Sa/P/1; P. W. © English Heritage DP068582)

cut out of a larger messuage.[8] The priory consolidated its holding by buying the Packer property to the east in 1285; this also included a quay, which had to be repaired in 1287.[9] The positions of the priory headquarters and adjoining properties are shown on Figure III.1, but both size and location can be only tentative. Another property in the same area was that of Randal Joymer of London;[10] other wealthy owners who held land or messuages in the vicinity were the Winterlands, who, like the Penys, were wool and hide merchants, and John de Ho, who was three times mayor in the late thirteenth century.[11] The positions of their holdings are, however, too uncertain to be shown on a map, even tentatively.

In contrast to the rest of the town north of the Delf, the present street layout between Church Street St Mary and the line of The Butts cannot be taken as a model for the medieval streets since this part of town seems to have been largely abandoned in the first half of the sixteenth century and subsequently redeveloped with fewer streets with different names, suggesting considerable alteration to the layout (Chap. 14.8). It is therefore difficult to reconstruct the original streets, and almost all the surviving buildings are late sixteenth century or later. However, the fragments of stone walls or buildings that survive slightly further east, within the square defined by Strand Street, Church Street St Mary, Delf Street and Harnet Street (Chap. 7.2.3; Fig. 7.2), suggest that this area was inhabited by wealthy families at this time. This may be illusory, at least in part, since much of the stonework could have originated elsewhere, perhaps from the well-attested priory headquarters area to the west. For instance, the reset doorway in Paradise Row (House 67; Fig. 7.16) is of sufficiently high quality to have graced a masonry building constructed by the priory, although the two-centred doorway at 3 Vicarage Lane now incorporated in a timber-framed house (House 99; Fig. 7.17), while possibly deriving from the priory headquarters, could have originated as part of the original St Mary's vicarage.

The only two stone structures that can be confidently defined as *in situ* are the very high-quality knapped flint walls with Caen stone dressings (House 27; Fig. 7.5) and the stone-lined undercroft of 29 Harnet Street (House 28). They both occupy land with a present ground level of +4m OD. The level of the excavated site at The New Inn, at the southern end of Harnet Street (Site 12), was +3.60m OD, with natural waterlogged peat at +2.25m OD. The excavator concluded that that site could not have been occupied before 1400, yet only 120m further north, archaeological Site 11, inside and below 30, 32 Harnet Street (House 30), showed signs of occupation (on a dry site) from the end of the twelfth or early thirteenth century. Thus, it appears that even slight differences in the height of the ground surface may have been crucial for the dates when occupation was possible in different parts of the town.

8.2 The town centre

Less is known about the market area of the town, but documents tell us that Christ Church owned shops in the thirteenth century,[12] and although their location is not specified they were probably in St Peter's parish, perhaps in the Fishmarket, which by then may have become the town's main market at the expense of the one in the High Street. Evidence for commercial activity in the Fishmarket area is limited, but in 1227 two messuages, one owned by Adam le Erle, butcher, and one tenanted by Thomas Scissor, lay in St Peter's parish on a north–south street, with the king's highway (i.e., the street) to the west.[13] They must have been in the Fishmarket, Love Lane or the southern end of The Butchery, all of which ran south from the waterfront, and the occupational evidence suggests that the properties were shops. There is no direct evidence for when the Fishmarket received its name, but the custumal records that at some time the market for the fishmongers was moved.[14] It was argued in Chapter 3.4.2 that this may have been related to a twelfth- or thirteenth-century change to the northern end of the original marketplace, involving the creation of both The Butchery and Cok Lane (now Potter Street). Cok Lane may for a short while have become the site of the fish market, but it had been moved to present Market Street by 1300. Market Street was called the Fishmarket from then until as late as 1792,[15] despite the fact that there is a notable absence of later medieval references to fishmongers or the selling of fish there.[16] There is no direct evidence for the name of The Butchery at this time, but plenty of records indicate that it was occupied by butchers later in the Middle Ages. The custumal shows that by *c.*1300 the mayor and jurats were taking measures to keep the streets and bridges of their town in good repair, the water supply clean and the markets well regulated (Chap. 5.1.2), but at this date there are no documents to indicate whether any of the surviving buildings were owned, let alone erected, by the town authorities. As discussed in Chapter 4.5, it seems likely that several of the plots in this part of town were divided sometime between the twelfth century and the fourteenth, suggesting pressure on space in the marketplace. Many of the fifty or more occupations derived from surname evidence in the court rolls (Chap. 5.4.2) are likely to have been pursued in this area.

Because the Christ Church Priory records are the fullest source of information at this period, topographical evidence from documents is somewhat skewed towards its estate at the west of the town. There are, however, occasional references to landholdings elsewhere in the central part of Sandwich that have topographical implications. For example, as discussed in Chapter 4.5, there was a guildhall in the High Street, called Guildhall Street or 'yeldehallestrete' until the mid-fifteenth century, and in 1310 Walter Draper, wool merchant, granted a messuage on the west side of Guildhall Street to St Mary's church to pay for lights before the image of the Holy Cross. Fifteenth-century rentals indicate that this property was in St Clement's parish, possibly in the vicinity of 20 High Street (House 36), although there is no evidence that it was that particular house.[17] While the High Street continued to be used for fairs, its market function may have withered and died once the east end of town became somewhat isolated by the building of Mill Wall, blocking the two eastern entrances from Worth (Chap. 5.6.2). The Fishmarket and the Cornmarket were the beneficiaries of this change.

8.3 Strand Street and the waterfront

Documentary sources are the only evidence for the harbour installations that must have lined at least some parts of the south bank of the river Stour for more than 1km, from the priory's Monkenquay, with its crane and storehouses, at the western end of the town, to the castle which had its own shipbuilding and repairing yard. By the early thirteenth century the very short length of waterfront in St Peter's parish was occupied by private quays, probably of timber.[18] William Bucharde, John the Baker and Thomas Palmer, for example, each had a quay.[19] Traces of successive waterside revetments have been noted on Sites 52 and 72 north of Strand Street, but as no details have been published, their original appearance is unknown. They may have resembled the thirteenth-century example excavated in King's Lynn (Fig. 8.2), which was a port of similar size and importance to Sandwich at the time.

Some of the evidence for the waterfront's physical make-up can be culled from documents, but more about its appearance can be conjectured from the buildings that survive in the central section from the decades around 1300. Most of them stand in an irregular line roughly parallel to but inland from the south bank of the river (Fig. 7.8). It has been claimed that the small stone structures among them originally stood on the north side of a street, now lost, running parallel to but south of Strand Street and continuing the line of Upper Strand Street.[20] These small stone buildings, however, are unlikely to have been complete buildings in themselves (Chaps 7.2.2, 7.4), but to have contained solars above secure storage attached to larger properties to their north. If the surviving stone cellar at 27 Strand Street (House 82), which lies further north than the other stone structures, opened directly onto the waterfront (Chap. 7.2.2), the late thirteenth-century quayside may have run just south of present-day Strand Street, somewhere between the +3.5m and +3.00m contour. By the early fourteenth century, when the surviving timber buildings at 33, 39 and 41 Strand Street were built, the street frontage had been pushed further forward through reclamation, to become fixed in its present position.

There is no evidence to suggest that Strand Street was a formal street before the end of the fourteenth century.[21] The buildings described above and shown on Figure 7.8 probably faced onto an open area that separated them from the wharves revetting the riverbank a little further north (Fig. 8.3). This space could have enabled people to travel and goods to be transported along the bank and may also have served as a quayside, where goods would be loaded, unloaded or assembled. Similar arrangements, with buildings standing slightly inland of quays at the riverside end of rectangular plots, can be seen in other medieval ports in the fourteenth century. In Hull, for example, Hull Street, even named after the river, is the equivalent riverside street to Sandwich's Strand Street, with both following a sinuous line echoing the bank of the river (clearly shown in a sixteenth-century map of Hull, Fig. 11.28).[22] A similar pattern is evident in King's Lynn, where it has been shown that the east bank of the river Great Ouse once lay where the similarly sinuous King Street, Queen Street and Nelson Street are today (Fig. 8.4). King's Lynn was the first English port in which this phenomenon was observed,[23] but since then it has been demonstrated in many other waterside settlements, where the position of their waterfronts changed over the centuries through a combination of deliberate land reclamation and natural silting.[24] This process probably took place in Sandwich from the eleventh century, although it is not observable until the period under discussion here. Evidence for the land reclamation can be seen in the northern extremities of the parish boundaries in the heart of the town, where they appear to run straight across Strand Street and into the river. A little way south of the street they start to pursue a much more erratic course (Chap. 3.4.4; Fig. 3.1).

The kink in the alignment of Strand Street and Upper Strand Street has long been a matter of speculation, and was almost certainly the reason behind the suggestion that there was once another street, south of Strand Street. But, as discussed above, there is no supporting evidence for this, although the development of present Upper Strand Street may have been both earlier and different from Strand Street itself. The latter still lies little more than 3.00m above OD and on alluvial deposits that would have needed to be dried out and consolidated

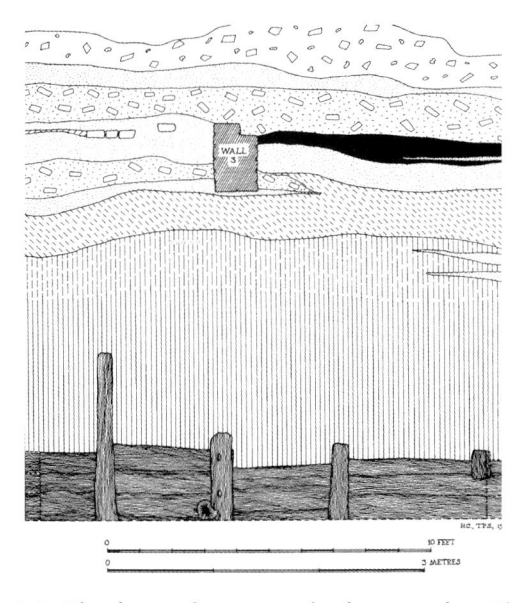

Fig. 8.2: The thirteenth-century wharf excavated at Thoresby College, King's Lynn, Norfolk (Clarke and Carter 1977, fig. 46)

Fig. 8.3: Aerial view of Strand Street between High Street (top) and St Mary's church showing reclaimed land beside the river (D. Grady © English Heritage 24073/08)

before being suitable either for buildings or for quaysides. In contrast, Upper Strand Street (itself always called merely Strand Street in medieval documents and also as late as 1833)[25] is on Thanet Beds and at an average of +5.5m OD, and therefore probably available for settlement earlier in the history of the town. Its relatively high and dry position is underlined by the presence of stone-lined cellars (although these are probably of post-medieval date) on both sides of the street (Fig. 7.2).

Fifteenth-century documents tell us that there were merchants' properties on Upper Strand Street with land stretching down to private quays on either side of Fisher Gate (Chap. 14.9), which was built in stone by the end of the fourteenth century, probably at little more than 3m above OD. For some reason, as yet not understood, the houses on the north side of Upper Strand Street were never moved forward towards the water as they were in the lower-lying Strand Street to the west.

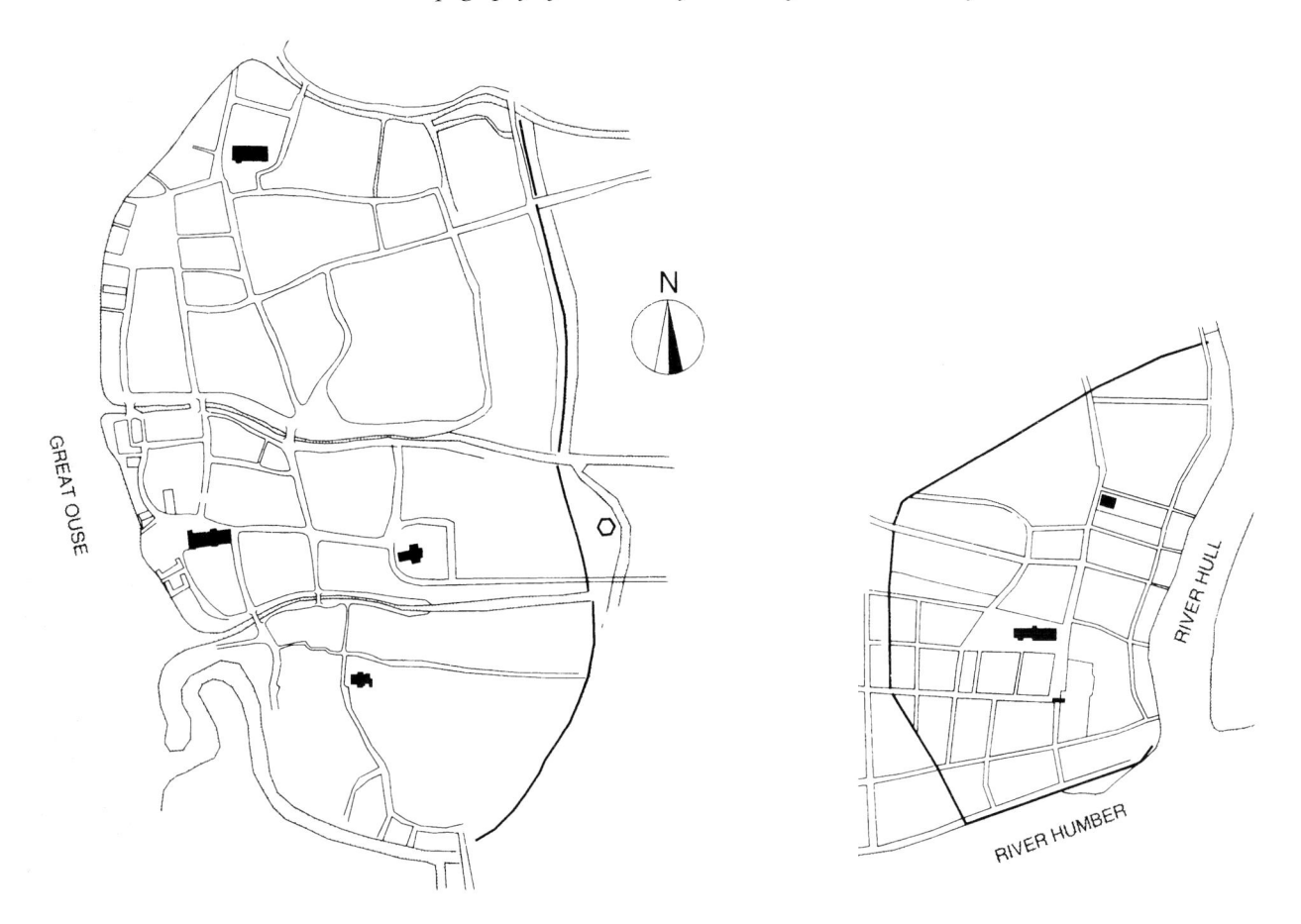

Fig. 8.4: King's Lynn, c.1350–1500 (Clarke 1987) and Kingston upon Hull, c.1350 (after Horrox 1978), reproduced at the same scale

At the beginning of the fourteenth century, Davis quay (*cayum vocatur Daviss cay* in the custumal) seems to have been the common quay, where Davis Gate also stood. It may have been developed there because of the ferry to Stonar and Thanet, with its berth at the end of the High Street since the eleventh century, and the quay probably extended along the riverbank from the ferry to the royal land to the east, perhaps as far as the place where the timbers of the Sandwich ship were found (Chap. 5.7.1). To the east of the town was the waterfront associated with the castle, where all the activities connected with the royal vessels were carried on (Chap. 5.6.1). In all, about 1,500m of the south bank of the river Stour, including the anchorage in the lee of the Deal Spit as well as the river beside Sandwich town, must have served as berths for vessels visiting Sandwich Haven.

One interpretation of the available evidence is that the waters of the haven were notionally divided into discrete areas, used by different groups and for different purposes. At the most westerly end of the waterfront stood Monkenquay, adjoining the property of Christ Church Priory. Since the priory had the right to charge tolls on ships at anchor,[26] there may have been a designated part of the haven for such vessels, perhaps near the priory's quays or even in the mouth of the Delf where it flowed into the river Stour. When the rules for 'watch and ward' appear in the custumal, one station is at *cayum monachorum*, where the guards are instructed to keep a watchful eye on what passes on the river.[27] In the centre, where the earliest buildings survive, were the private merchant quays and the public quay. At the east side there was the part dedicated to royal activities such as the maintenance, munitioning and victualling of the ships that assembled there to form the fleets for various warlike purposes. The fleets were largely made up of merchantmen impressed for duty, and gathering them together could be a protracted business. While assembling, they probably anchored in the outer reaches of Sandwich Haven, presumably in a specified area so that they did not obstruct other vessels: merchantmen bound for the town and its quays, or large cargo ships riding at anchor and awaiting transhipment. The most likely place for the war fleets to have waited was close to the royal castle, well clear of the commercial centre based on the common quay and its privately owned equivalents.

8.4 The town south of the Delf

There was probably little in the way of an urban street pattern or dwellings south of the Delf in this period. All the archaeological interventions that reached the natural subsoil have recorded it as Alluvium, with its maximum height above sea level being 2.62m. In most places it was no more than +1.20m OD. For example, the Carmelite friary was founded *c.*1268 on land where the present ground surface is *c.*2.00m OD, the top of the Alluvium being no higher than +1.20m OD (Site 3). The ground on which St John's hospital was founded was little higher, and the area that became the Cornmarket was much the same. All this must have been drained to make the land in a condition to support substantial buildings (Chaps 6.2.1, 6.2.3).

Both the priory and the town itself owned land in St Peter's parish near the bridge over the Delf,[28] which was probably situated south-west of the Fishmarket, connecting the central area to the Woodnesborough road. The bridge had been there since the mid-twelfth century, and must have been an essential element in establishing the Cornmarket and opening up the areas to either side for development (Figs 3.1, III.1). The Cornmarket may have been laid out soon after reasonably dry land had been achieved. Although not mentioned until 1338, when 'marcatfeelde' is said to lie south of the common water (the Delf),[29] the relationship of the friary and the hospital to the marketplace, from which both were reached, suggests that it was in existence by the second half of the thirteenth century, if not before. Late thirteenth-century documents relating to St John's hospital refer to a barn and to lands and messuages that probably lay in this area, but it is unclear whether these included habitations as opposed to purely agricultural buildings.[30] Archaeological Site 1, close to the Delf at 6 Cattle Market, produced some thirteenth-century pot imported from Rouen, although on the opposite side of the Cornmarket Site 4 had no evidence for intensive occupation before the late fifteenth century. The location of the market at the southern entry to the town where the Woodnesborough road came in from the arable hinterland may be significant, for local corn would have been brought to the town by road rather than by water. Grain markets were probably placed at the most convenient locations for transport, as indicated by those in London at this time, which included two on the river front, where grain from the country was unloaded, and two at major crossroads.[31]

The ramparts in this part of town (The Butts and The Rope Walk) were laid out, probably sometime in the early fourteenth century, in relatively straight stretches across low-lying Alluvium (Fig. 1.4). The former ran from where the highway from Ash entered the town (where Canterbury Gate later stood) to the road from Woodnesborough, and the latter from the Woodnesborough road to the causeway from St Bartholomew's hospital.

The third length of earth rampart, Mill Wall, crosses completely different ground. It continues north-eastwards from where The Rope Walk ends, across the Thanet Beds ridge, and at the maximum height of the ridge (+7m OD) it changes direction to continue northwards across the castle ditch (Chap. 5.6.1). In doing so it cut across the streets that were the urban continuations of the Worth and Eastry roads (Fig. III.1) and also severed the connection between the castle and the town. Built in a completely different style and on a much bigger scale than the other two ramparts, it has the appearance of being much more defensible, and must have had a different purpose. Its construction had considerable implications for the development of the town. Once it was built across the main road to the south, which was then moved westwards to New Gate, beside the Delf, the east end of town around St Clement's church became something of a backwater, no longer directly accessible from the wider world. All three ramparts will be discussed in more detail in Chapter 11.

With the creation of the ramparts and drainage ditches allowing construction south of the Delf, the town had reached its greatest medieval extent. Much of the ground between the ramparts and the Delf remained unbuilt, probably used as gardens, orchards and grazing land. This remained the case until the nineteenth century, when the Ordnance Survey surveyor's notebook of *c.*1800 shows open ground on the town side of the ramparts, and to some extent this continues to be the case today. A similar arrangement is found in many other medieval walled towns, such as Tonbridge and King's Lynn,[32] and is likely to have been a deliberate policy, not an indication that the inhabited area of the town had contracted. After the Black Death halved the population, the only increase in the urban area was caused by reclamation out into the haven. On the landward side, the developments of the later Middle Ages were simply concerned with consolidation rather than expansion.

PART IV: 1360–1560

Introduction

During the 200 years covered in this section there were many changes in the town. In 1360 it was just beginning to emerge from the catastrophic events of the mid-fourteenth century; by 1560 it looked as if it was going into terminal decline. Between these two dates, representing the impact of the Black Death and the arrival of the refugees from the Low Countries in 1561, there were many localised ups and downs in the town's fortunes, but no major events to disrupt general urban development. Thus, Part IV covers 200 years of Sandwich's history.

Our knowledge of Sandwich before the mid-fifteenth century is limited by the nature and poor survival of the source material. Before the 1430s there are some national records, a few local ones, and the evidence of buildings and archaeology. But the bulk of the documentary evidence starts only in 1432, when the town year books begin, providing a wealth of evidence about the activities and decisions of the town council, and from about this time or a little later this official record is augmented by copious material from other documents, such as treasurers' accounts, wills and deeds. Although the churches and hospitals had mostly been constructed before this period, the documentary evidence about how they functioned largely stems from the mid-fifteenth century and later. The walls and gates of Sandwich either date from the fifteenth century, or are known from fifteenth- and sixteenth-century records, and most of the surviving domestic buildings seem to have been erected from the second quarter of the fifteenth century onwards. Thus while the first seventy or more years of this two-hundred-year period are not easy to trace, there is copious evidence, both physical and documentary, from the later part of the period when many would say the town was already past its heyday (Fig. IV.1).

The question of late medieval decline in towns is one that was endlessly debated in the 1970s and 1980s, with differing and fiercely held views, the issues being well summed up by Alan Dyer.[1] Since it is clear that the population of Sandwich decreased dramatically between the early fourteenth century and 1560, and that during this period the viability of the harbour and haven was seriously damaged by silting and a changing coastline, the issue of decline is a potent one for Sandwich. But against the diminishing population and the contracting waterways must be set a number of more positive indications. The need of the crown for a south-eastern harbour to provision the armies for lengthy foreign wars had a marked effect on the prosperity of the town during the fifteenth century. The change in the types, tunnage and ports of origin of the cargo vessels that visited the harbour during the second half of the century may be indicative of a downturn in foreign trade. Nevertheless, the numbers of small freighters using Sandwich suggest that local and coastal trade made up for this shortfall. This shift in commercial emphasis led to the development of a different kind of society in the town, no longer dominated by wealthy merchants operating on an international canvas, but run by substantial middle-of-the-road merchants pursuing more humdrum livelihoods. The large storage cellars and domestic buildings of the early fourteenth century and before were not the types of dwellings they required. Instead, in the later fifteenth century smaller buildings were erected, more suited to the domestic and commercial requirements of new occupations and social levels. An unusually large number of these houses survive today. The mere fact that up to *c*.1510 what must have been seen as out-of-date monstrosities with huge maintenance problems were replaced by smaller but well-built constructions suited to the new situation suggests that at that time the inhabitants saw themselves as living in a place that was changing rather than one that was declining. More late medieval dwellings may remain in Sandwich than in any other town of its size, making it a place of national importance for the study of urban housing.

From the second decade of the sixteenth century there is more evidence of a place under stress. This is manifest in the political, economic and physical spheres. Although the problems do not surface in the trading documentation, since that evidence concerns only successful business activities, tensions can be identified in town governance. In addition, the population plummeted; almost no new buildings were erected; and many old ones were pulled down. Church activities, so central to the lives of the people, seem to have continued in much the same way as before until the catastrophic events of the Reformation. From 1540 onwards the wealth of evidence concerning the commitment of Sandwich parishioners to their churches dries up, and, in line with trends throughout

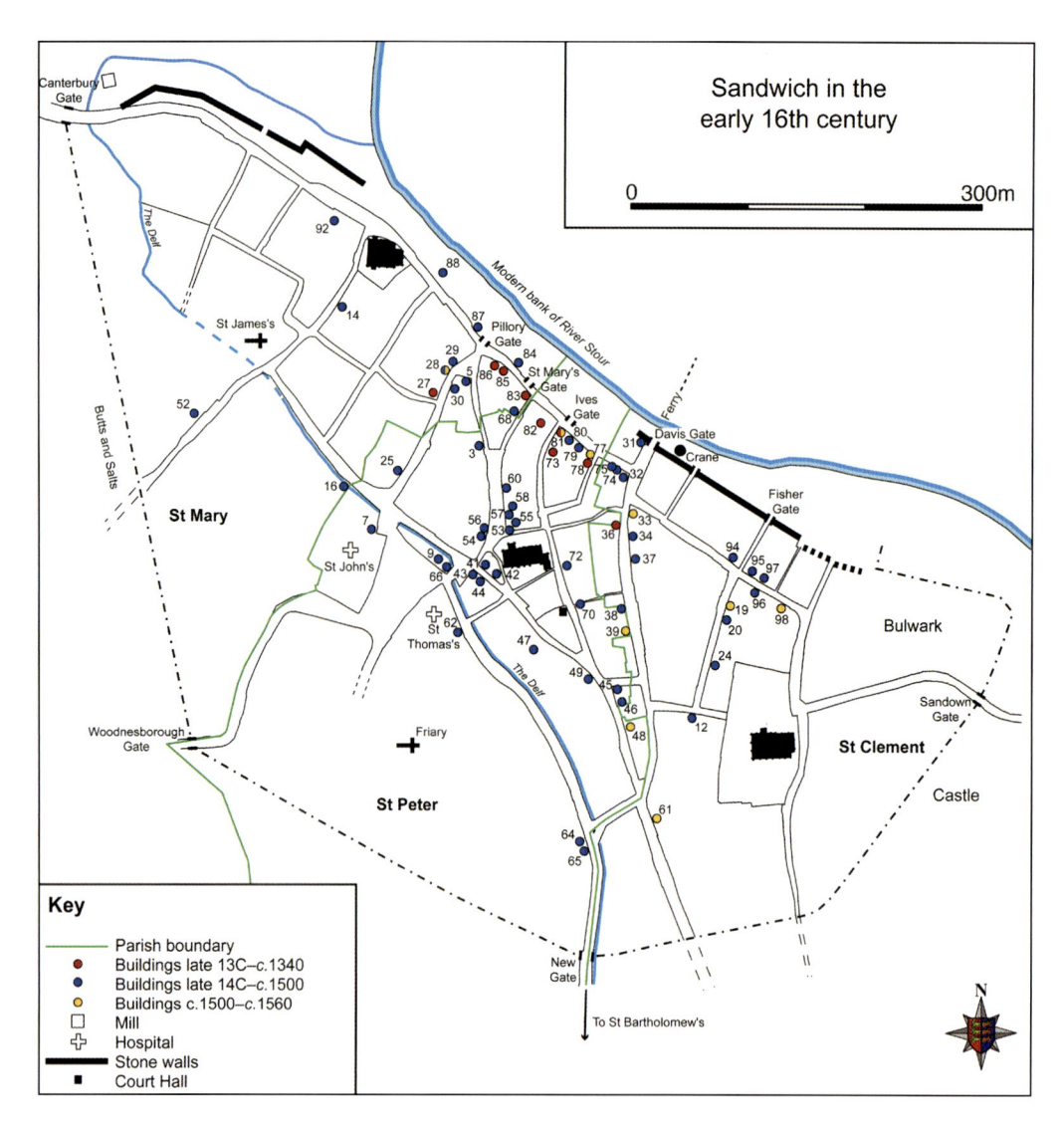

Fig. IV.1: The built environment of Sandwich in the early sixteenth century (J. H.). Reproduced by permission of Ordnance Survey on behalf of HMSO. © Crown copyright 2009. All rights reserved. Licence number 100046522

England, their wills are shorter and bleaker. But the Dissolution affected Sandwich less than it did many towns, for there was only one religious house to be closed down, the hospitals being able to continue to serve the needs of the inhabitants as before.

By 1560 Sandwich was struggling in many ways. It was far less important in national terms, but it remained a significant a regional centre, and, as we shall see in Part V, it was on the brink of an important, if relatively brief, new period of prosperity.

9 Trade and the haven

During the first half of the fourteenth century Sandwich Haven had been an assembly point both for fleets carrying troops, horses and equipment to France and for merchant vessels involved in Sandwich's flourishing foreign trade. The next two hundred years saw a gradual change both in the character of the haven, with progressively less naval activity as the Hundred Years War drew to a close, and in the nature of trade, as great Italian merchantmen gave way to smaller coastal craft. The condition of the haven and the deteriorating navigability of the waterways through the Wantsum Channel seem to have been two of the main reasons for the radical changes that affected the port and its trade for the rest of the Middle Ages, with significant effects on the kinds of people who lived the town and the buildings they constructed.

As described earlier (Chap. 2.2.2), the Wantsum Channel was greatly altered by drainage and land reclamation throughout the Middle Ages, with this human intervention leading to its navigable waterway, made up of the rivers Stour and Wantsum, becoming ever more constricted. In addition, the rivers began to silt up through natural causes, and the mouth of the Stour, the entrance to Sandwich Haven, became blocked by the inexorable northward movement of the Deal Spit. By the middle of the fifteenth century, these phenomena had combined to make the water route through the channel increasingly awkward to negotiate, and access to the port from the east more difficult. Both had serious consequences for Sandwich's long-distance trade and general economy.

Nevertheless, the increase in surviving documentation from the beginning of the fifteenth century means that much more is known about the state of the haven and the Wantsum Channel in general from this period than is the case earlier. Inferences about the extent of Sandwich's anchorage and the navigability of the rivers Stour and Wantsum can be drawn from the vessels that visited the port, and from accounts of the townspeople's attempts to keep open the access from the southern North Sea. It seems clear that during the two hundred years from c.1360 there was a decrease in waterborne traffic to and from Sandwich, and a change in the types of vessels that frequented its harbour. Trade continued as a mainstay of the port and town, but it changed in character. By the early years of the sixteenth century long-distance trade to the Mediterranean had largely been superseded by cross-Channel and local commerce, and coasters had replaced the bigger seagoing craft of before.

9.1 Sandwich Haven and its ships to the end of the fifteenth century

Much can be learnt from the foreign merchantmen that regularly visited Sandwich Haven in the fourteenth and fifteenth centuries, the best documented being those from Genoa and Venice, but many others also arrived regularly: from the Iberian peninsula, the Low Countries, France and, more occasionally, from the Hanseatic ports of the Baltic, such as Danzig (Gdańsk, Poland) and Greifswald.[1]

The Genoese had begun visiting Sandwich in their carracks by the beginning of the fourteenth century and continued to do so until the 1450s. These vessels were ideal for carrying bulky cargoes, such as wool, cloth and wine,[2] but they were large and cumbersome, rather like the cogs of northern waters (Chap. 5.7.2). They could be as much as 550 tuns burden,[3] an enormous size compared with the average of 40 to 50 tuns of the English cargo vessels of the time.[4] In addition, they depended on sails for propulsion so were not very manoeuvrable. All these features meant that the Genoese carracks could not negotiate North Foreland with its prevailing south-westerly winds, nor would they have been able to navigate the Thames up to London had they been able to reach the outer estuary.[5] Thus, the Genoese needed a transhipment port if their cargoes were to reach their destination, and Sandwich Haven was the perfect place. Its wide expanse of calm water was an ideal anchorage, and while the Genoese traffic was at its height, it had the advantage of being accessible without a pilot.[6] By 1482, however, the state of the haven seems to have made the employment of pilots more usual, and the town appointed two wardens to ensure that only English pilots were used.[7]

Cargoes may often have been transferred from carracks to the smaller vessels out in the haven itself. The earliest reference to this practice that has been found was in 1386 when a Genoese ship, anchored in the Downs on the seaward edge of Sandwich Haven, was found to be too heavily laden to attempt the London voyage, so *La Marie* of Sandwich was hired to take the goods directly to their destination.[8] This is a rare documentary record of what was probably a common occurrence – the small English coasters setting out immediately on their London voyage without calling in at Sandwich itself. They could even have taken the cargo to foreign ports from the anchorage, as happened in 1390 when the English collectors demanded that customs be paid on wine unloaded from a carrack in the Downs onto a boat 'hired for the purpose'. The boat took the wine directly to Bruges, thus not incurring liability for English customs.[9] But, as the toll figures indicate, transhipment did not normally obviate the need for paying customs, although the cranes and storage facilities provided on the Sandwich quayside may not have been in very great demand by the Genoese carracks. Sandwich's town year books and treasurers' accounts provide much information about the town crane from 1432 until the end of the sixteenth century, but the goods that it handled are seldom mentioned until the sixteenth century, and the merchants who paid for its use are never named. So it is impossible to prove, although it seems probable, that the town crane's main function was not to handle the commodities brought in by the Italian merchants, but to load and unload more local cargoes. These may have been the Kentish products, such as wool, cloth and grain, that were shipped through Sandwich, English cargoes of salt and coal that were transhipped at the port, or the herring and other fish brought in by cross-Channel and local traders.

When the Venetians frequented Sandwich Haven, which they did from the early fourteenth century to the late fifteenth, they came in galleys (Chap. 5.7.2). Even though these were much smaller, lighter and more manoeuvrable than the Genoese carracks, averaging 170 tuns, propelled by oars and sails, and capable of reaching London, they also transhipped in Sandwich, mainly loading goods that were sent there from the capital in small vessels.[10] The galleys had windlasses on board for loading and unloading,[11] but the Venetians also demanded that the port should have facilities for transhipment.[12]

Sandwich's continued popularity with the Venetians largely stemmed from the safe anchorage provided by Sandwich Haven and the Downs, where the Flanders Fleet of Venetian galleys gathered on its inward journey before splitting into two groups to go either to London or to Sluys (in Flanders, the outport for Bruges). Later in the season it gathered there again before the long journey home to the Mediterranean. Sandwich was the main assembly point until 1434, when Southampton became an alternative destination for the Venetian galley captains and gradually overtook Sandwich in popularity.[13]

Foreign vessels and luxury cargoes were not the only things to make their way in and out of Sandwich Haven during the fourteenth and fifteenth centuries. There were also smaller boats (crayers, balingers and barges) of up to 80 tuns burden. Crayers were sailing boats used in coastal waters, for short cross-Channel trips, and probably for transporting the foreign cargoes transhipped at Sandwich for London. In addition, they could serve as dual-purpose fishing boats and cargo carriers, as they also did later.[14] Balingers and barges were generally slightly larger and more heavily built, and equipped with sail and oars; although originally designed as merchantmen, they were increasingly being built as warships by the end of the fourteenth century and travelled far outside coastal waters.[15] Their names occur frequently among the arrested vessels brought to Sandwich throughout the Hundred Years War.[16]

In contrast, the vessel discovered in the silted creek by Sandown Gate (Chap. 5.7.1; Fig. 5.5) is estimated to have had an approximate capacity of 150 tuns and was of the type known in the documents without qualification as 'ship' (*navis*), with an average of 100 tuns burden.[17] This must have been a seagoing rather than a coastal craft, unlikely to have been used on voyages between Sandwich and London.

An excellent source for Sandwich Haven and many other English ports are the charts (also known as portolans) used by the Italians for their trading voyages. Some have been preserved from the beginning of the fifteenth century, many of them being drawn by chart makers working in Venice. The earliest example in the British Library is from an atlas dating from *c.*1400–25, and, although difficult to decipher, it shows that the chart maker had a good knowledge of the south and east coasts of England.[18] Sandwich Haven, the Wantsum Channel and the Isle of Thanet are shown much more clearly on another chart, drawn by the Venetian Andrea Bianco in 1436.[19] Romney, Dover and Sandwich are named, and the isles of Thanet and Sheppey are drawn, although schematically. The importance of the outer Thames estuary is indicated by its being greatly enlarged, but its treacherous nature is shown by more than twenty small symbols indicating shoals or sandbanks. The notorious Goodwin Sands outside the estuary are also marked. There is a very similar depiction on a version of 1473, where a bold red *Sanduci* puts Sandwich in the same class as Great Yarmouth ('Jarrnmua') and even London ('Londres').[20]

The portolans were supplemented by rutters, navigational directions for sailing along the coast and entering ports. A fifteenth-century English example shows a good grasp of the geography around Sandwich, mentioning Thanet, the Goodwin Sands and the Downs, and specifying Davis Gate as a landmark in Sandwich harbour.[21] Another more specific but rather opaque reference to Sandwich (*Sentuzi*) comes in Venetian sailing directions compiled by Michael of Rhodes, *c*.1435.[22] It is difficult to reconcile the 'forest' or 'wood' (*boscho*) that is said to stand on the west and north-west with the flat marshy landscape prevalent around the town then and now, and this may cast some doubt on the precision of the directions as a whole, since the author may have been 'speaking metaphorically, or conveying information based on faulty observation'.[23] Three bell-towers are mentioned as landmarks on the bank, which were almost certainly the towers of Sandwich's three parish churches, plus a fourth small one that is more problematic. It may have been the tower that probably formed part of the castle from the early fourteenth century (Chap. 5.6.1), or possibly that of the parish church of Stonar, north of Sandwich.[24]

Whether Michael of Rhodes's rutter is accurate or not, its existence suggests that Sandwich was still of significance to the Venetians during the 1430s, even though it was probably losing trade to Southampton by then. Shortly afterwards, however, Sandwich's town books start to record increasing awareness of the troubles beginning to beset the haven. The problem of access from the North Sea was recognised in the 1460s when murage was twice granted on condition that part of the sums raised from concessions on custom duties was spent on improving the entrance to the port.[25] This was presumably because of the growth of the spit, which the mayor and jurats could not do anything about, although they could attempt to counteract the obstruction of the waterway through the Wantsum Channel. The problem was primarily caused by the indiscriminate reclamation long practised by Christ Church Priory, and the 'weirs, groines and kiddles' (fish traps) constructed by St Augustine's Abbey along the rivers to the detriment of the passage. The town demanded that they should be removed, but since the same request was made in consecutive years (1468 and 1469) it seems unlikely that the demands were met.[26] By the 1480s the river had become so silted that the ferry connecting Sarre with the Kentish mainland was made inoperable, except at high spring tides.[27] Consequently, an Act of Parliament was passed for the ferry to be replaced by a bridge, but there was anxiety lest such a construction should further harm Sandwich Haven. In the event the bridge was not built, and there is no record of one having been erected until the late eighteenth century.

Other problems were caused by grounded or sunken vessels in the harbour. In one instance, sand that had built up around a ship wrecked in the haven disrupted shipping,[28] and in 1478 the town agreed to pay for a wreck, perhaps the same one, to be removed.[29] There were also obstacles to shipping further west in the Wantsum Channel, for example, the Spanish ship that foundered near Richborough in 1483 and which may still have been there twenty years later when the town demanded that 'an old ship lying in the haven at Richborough' be taken away.[30] The townspeople must have been aware of the threat to Sandwich Haven and consequently to their livelihood, for they were all required to help with dredging it, either removing stones (ballast was being illegally thrown overboard to free up space on ships at anchor as early as 1443, when a Genoese was responsible),[31] or clearing the fairway, perhaps of the accumulated shoals.[32] These measures cannot have been sufficient, for in 1477 there was an attempt to widen and divert the mouth of the North Stream (also known as Guestling; see Chap. 5.6.2) to flow into the river Stour closer to the town in the hope of scouring the haven.[33] In 1484 the mayor and commons petitioned the crown for permission to dig a new cut at their own expense,[34] and in 1487 the common council instructed the mayor to approach Henry VII once more, this time asking for a wreck in the haven to be removed.[35] In 1484 the inhabitants had been called upon to bear the cost of the work, but in 1490 some of the expenditure was transferred to landowners outside the town, probably in the Lydden Valley, who were commanded to cut dykes to encourage the flow of water into the haven.[36]

The final great fifteenth-century crisis for the haven came in 1494. Since it was considered so badly decayed that it was likely to become unusable 'over time', the revenue from taxes on coal and salt was earmarked for repairs, with elected representatives from each parish appointed to ensure that they were carried out and that a mole was built to provide deeper water for berthing.[37] The feasibility of increasing the flow of the river Stour to help scour out the haven was investigated, and Henry VII even agreed to send down a specialist in the subject, perhaps a 'Hollander', to help with the problem.[38] All this was to no avail, and the blocking of the waterways and the decay of the haven continued.

9.2 Trade through Sandwich Haven in the fourteenth and fifteenth centuries

9.2.1 Trade and the Hundred Years War

The middle of the fourteenth century saw Sandwich playing a vital role in transporting troops to France for the Hundred Years War, and after 1347 it became the chief port for forwarding supplies to Calais and the army operating in its vicinity. In addition, its significance in civilian trade was acknowledged in 1353 when it was appointed as the outport for Canterbury when the latter was established as the Staple town for Kent,[39] even though it was replaced by Queenborough on Sheppey from 1368 to 1377.[40]

Between the death of Edward III in 1377 and the accession of Henry V in 1413, there were long periods of truce and Sandwich's contribution to the war effort was less pronounced. After the war was resumed, Sandwich continued to be the place where ships were assembled for Calais and where they were victualled and maintained. For example, between December 1428 and June 1429 William Butcher of Calais imported 57 oxen and 168 sheep, and between 1445 and 1448 the Sandwich butcher John Paston traded in live animals in both places, selling 450 sheep in Sandwich and another 400 sheep and 121 oxen in Calais.[41] During the same period the official victualler of Calais bought malt and live oxen and sheep in Sandwich. His accounts show how this trade stimulated Sandwich's economy: local pasture for the animals awaiting shipment needed to be paid for, and local mariners had to be hired to convey them by ship to Calais.[42] The victualler also acquired salt and coal in Calais directly from Sandwich ships berthed there. These activities show the importance of Sandwich as a centre of distribution in wartime.

9.2.2 The predominance of alien trade in the first half of the fifteenth century

In the years between 1203 and 1482 London's share of the country's overseas trade jumped from 17 per cent to 61 per cent, while the trade of the east coast ports (notably Boston and King's Lynn) declined. At Sandwich, however, the value of its overseas trade increased, rising from 1 per cent of the nation's total in the thirteenth century to 5.5 per cent towards the end of the fifteenth, when alien shipping was crucial to the economy of the port. By 1478–82, 41.4 per cent of Sandwich's trade was in alien hands, compared to 37.1 per cent in London,[43] and this alien presence can be illustrated throughout the fifteenth century.

Details of trade through the port for several decades from the 1380s are limited, because until 1419 the bailiwick was in the hands of lessees rather than the crown so records do not survive. But there is some evidence for foreign ships carrying imports such as wine, spices, figs and raisins,[44] and exports such as wheat, wool, and tin.[45] In some cases the freight was too voluminous for the foreign vessels to carry it home, so the residue was stored in Sandwich, at unknown locations, until the ships came again.[46] During the same period local ships such as crayers were carrying wheat abroad in considerable quantities.[47]

Customs accounts are again available after 1419 when the bailiwick returned to the crown, and they show that civilian trade through Sandwich was then at a low level, with the annual revenues of about £20 during the first four years of Robert Cheldesworth's period of office as bailiff being the smallest recorded receipts since Sandwich's customs accounts began.[48] Trade revived in the late 1430s and early 1440s, when the imports of wine, which had dropped to half that of the early fourteenth century, recovered their previous level,[49] cloth exports increased, and other goods such as woad began to make their mark. All these commodities brought in and out of Sandwich Haven were largely transported in carracks and galleys by alien merchants. For example, 4,451 cloths were shipped through Sandwich by aliens in 1441–2, and 6,665 cloths in the following twelve months, whereas denizen merchants exported an average of only 272 cloths a year over the same period.[50] Furthermore, it is impossible to say how many of those denizen merchants actually lived in Sandwich itself. As a head port for customs it could have been used by merchants from Dover, the north Kent ports and even London (Fig. 9.1).

The dominance of aliens is exemplified by the trade in woad, which was imported by Genoese merchants for use in the Kentish cloth industry. Because woad was so valuable and was taxed at 2d. in the pound, it produced high revenues for the crown: £40 annually for a few years, and reaching £84 in 1433–4, when more than 3,000 small bales (*balets*) were imported.[51] In the following decade the Genoese were joined by other Italian merchants, and tolls on woad collected between 1437 and 1449 averaged £123 a year. The peak year was 1439–40, when £175 11s. 11d. was received.[52] Fortunately, the particular customs accounts

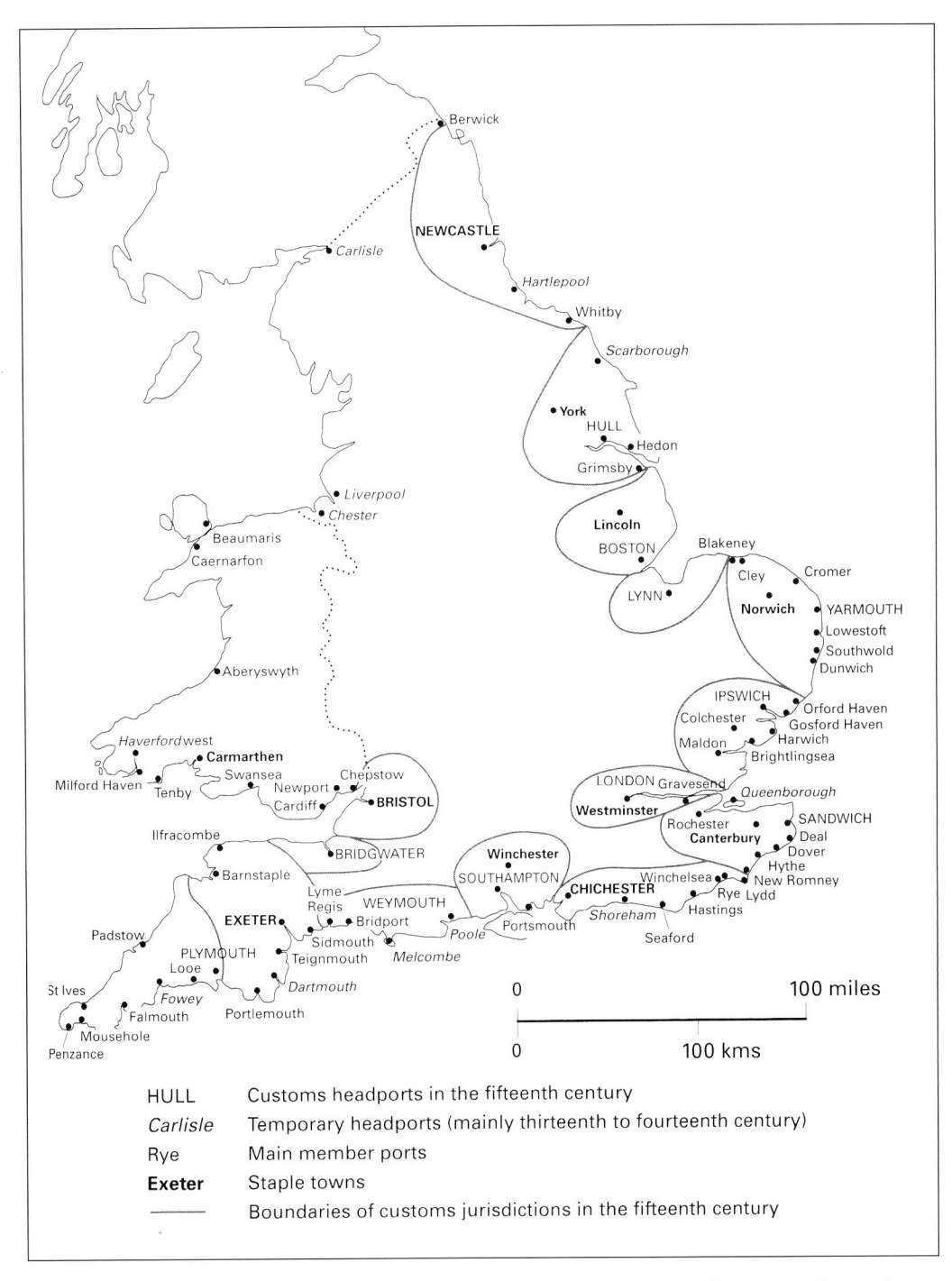

Fig. 9.1: Customs and head port jurisdictions in the fifteenth century (Palliser 2000, fig. 19.1)

for Sandwich that year have survived and show that the Genoese were still importing vast quantities of woad in consignments of up to 960 bales.[53] As before, the Genoese carracks also carried spices, fruits and sweet wine and the Venetian galleys transported similar luxury goods, sometimes freighted by twenty different shippers.[54] Italian merchants were not the only aliens using Sandwich port. Merchants from the Low Countries imported red and white herrings, bricks, saffron and madder; Hanseatic merchants brought in timber. Local merchants neither shared in nor benefited from this trade.

The early 1440s were years of great trading activity in Sandwich, with a large number of alien ships visiting from the Low Countries and Italy, and a significant number of resident aliens in the town. The alien mariners, although they may have slept on their ships at night,[55] undoubtedly spent some time in the town drinking or visiting prostitutes, and some aliens actually settled. In 1439–40 a national survey showed the presence in Sandwich of 190 men and women born outside the kingdom.[56] They included two Genoese, who were not primarily merchants, but factors or commission agents, responsible for paying the local dues, and for arranging temporary storage for goods at Sandwich.[57] Many of the other immigrants in the survey came from the Low Countries (Chap. 10.3.6).

The revival in trade was brief, for by the late 1440s the whole country was feeling the effects of a recession, with bullion famine, depopulation and deflation marking the years 1445–65. More grain, livestock and wool were produced than the declining market could absorb,[58] and rents became harder to collect. In addition, a devastating epidemic struck much of Kent in 1457. In Canterbury, sixteen Christ Church monks died between 15 July and 25 September that year; this represents a crude death rate among the priory monks of 189 per 1,000, the highest recorded there in the period 1395–1505.[59] Sandwich may have been similarly affected, so that its inhabitants were not in a position to make a robust defence when the French attacked the port in August 1457 (Chap. 11.1.3). The attack disrupted the waterborne trade of the town. The number of boats mooring in the haven dropped from one hundred in 1451–2 to thirty-six in 1457–8, and the customs accounts record a drop from £163 in 1448–9 to £19 in 1457. In that year the port was visited by not a single carrack or galley.[60]

The sharp decline in the number of Genoese and Venetian ships visiting the haven from the middle of the fifteenth century (Section 9.1) led to a diminution in the amount of overseas trade conducted through Sandwich, although outside forces such as piracy in the English Channel and the Thames (Section 9.2.3) encouraged some merchants to use Sandwich instead of London for their transactions. In 1462–3, for example, the danger of piratical raids resulted in more sacks of wool being exported from Sandwich (2,128) than from London (1,201), but once the scare had subsided export of wool and cloth through Sandwich dropped to a trickle.[61] That was the only time in the fifteenth century when Sandwich's exports outstripped those of London, but substantial amounts were still being collected as tolls in the 1470s, as much as £142 7s. 9d. for the two years 1476–8.[62]

9.2.3 The effects of piracy on waterborne trade

The luxury goods carried by Italian carracks and galleys in the first half of the fifteenth century were very vulnerable to outside raiders, and piracy flourished in the English Channel and the Thames estuary. Sandwich men had never been averse to preying on foreign vessels in the waters near the port; at the end of the fourteenth century and in the early fifteenth they may have had the excuse of forwarding the aims of the Hundred Years War when they brought five Spanish ships, two Flemish hulks and two other Flemish vessels into the port.[63] It might even have been true in 1400 when an armed barge from Sandwich captured a merchant ship carrying cargo from Spain.[64] But it can hardly have been the case in 1406 when a ship from the Baltic port of Greifswald (in Prussia and so unconnected with the war) was captured and looted by *Le Faucon* of Sandwich.[65]

'Pirates and malefactors' from Sandwich are first specifically mentioned in 1430.[66] Thereafter, Sandwich men appear regularly in the royal records as pirates. Some were of high standing in the town. John Grene, for example, was accused of piracy in 1430, yet he served as a Member of Parliament two years later and was twice mayor.[67] Piracy was not confined to the high seas: merchantmen lying at anchor and awaiting fair wind in the Downs and even in Sandwich Haven were attacked,[68] and in 1464 the master of a Venetian cargo vessel complained that the Thames itself was not safe.[69] This may have been the reason for the short-lived resurgence of the export trade through Sandwich in the 1460s, but by the mid-1470s the threat of piracy in the Thames must have decreased, for the Italian merchants returned to using London as their main stopping point.

9.2.4 The changing nature of trade in the second half of the fifteenth century

The fact that the Italian merchants no longer frequented Sandwich after *c.*1470 was not as disastrous as is sometimes suggested. Foreign trade continued until the early sixteenth century, but it was of a different character, perhaps because of the deteriorating conditions in the haven and the Wantsum Channel outlined in the introduction to this chapter. Instead of the carracks and galleys, smaller vessels such as crayers, balingers and barges, sometimes with local masters and crews, become more prevalent in the records, and the goods carried and their provenances or destinations changed. Grain, which had previously been sent to provision Calais, was shipped to Spain in the 1470s, when there were severe shortages because of a series of bad harvests in Castille. During this period more than 4,000 quarters of cereals went out through Sandwich and Faversham in Spanish ships,[70] and Sandwich merchants also benefited through buying up local produce, partly perhaps for local consumption but probably also for resale to Spain while the dearth continued. For instance, in the accounting year 1472–3 John Archer of Sandwich bought 100 quarters of barley and 58 quarters of malt from Christ Church Priory, and other Sandwich merchants acquired 60 quarters of wheat from the same source.[71] In the following year the priory sold 163 quarters of wheat and 140 quarters of barley to Sandwich merchants.[72] In the second half of the century, too, English merchants responded to changes in taste and fashion, and cross-Channel trade with the Low Countries, Normandy and Brittany expanded. The customs account for 1486–7 shows that London grocers used Sandwich to import saffron, madder, sugar-candy and onion seeds, while London mercers were regularly bringing into the port the linen goods that had become so much in demand.[73] In addition, technological improvement in the curing of fish enabled Flemish and Dutch fishermen to gut, salt and pack herrings into barrels while at sea. Herring cured this way lasted longer and could be shipped further, to England for example.[74] Hops were also imported from the Low Countries to the newly established breweries in Sandwich and other Kent towns (Chaps 10.1.3, 10.3.2).

A few Italian ships, however, still called at Sandwich, bringing in goods such as woad, alum, treacle, sweet wines and dates. In 1486–7, for example, the Genoese factor Geronimo Pinelli used an Italian carrack to bring in goods valued at more than £2,000 for himself and others. He also imported velvet, damask and taffeta from Flanders, sending two shipments into Dover as well as two into Sandwich.[75] Other Italian merchants visited the Low Countries first, and then shipped luxury fabrics, in smaller vessels with a shallower draft, from Flanders to Sandwich and other English ports.

9.2.5 The town crane as an indicator of trade and the economy of the town

Since the revival of trade in England in the early 1440s was heavily dependent on the activities of alien merchants, the customs revenues that accrued went directly to the king and not to the ports through which the commodities travelled.[76] But there were some local benefits, as illustrated by the varying amounts charged by the civic authorities for leasing the town crane: the more the price of the lease, the greater the anticipated profits on the part of the lessee. Even though some cargoes brought into Sandwich would have been transhipped in the haven without being landed, some bulky goods such as wine, cloth and bricks would have been loaded and unloaded using the port facilities provided and owned by the town, and local porters and other labourers.

From 1433, the date of the earliest surviving record of leasing the crane, to 1465 the leases were issued annually and for the crane alone. These give the best evidence for the amount of use of the crane, for after that date leases were granted either for more than one year or were combined with porterage and the collection of tronage. In 1433 it was £8 annually. By 1442 it cost the lessee £16 13s. 4d. a year, rising to £18 13s. 4d. in 1455.[77] In 1457 the French raid affected not only the number of ships visiting the port but also the amount that the crane was used, so that in 1458 the crane was leased out for £13 6s. 8d.,[78] whereas the year before it had been £19 13s. 4d.; by 1459 it was leased for £19 13s. 4d. once again. The most expensive fifteenth-century lease (£35 6s. 8d.) was issued in 1465 (during a period when more wool was being exported through Sandwich than London; see Section 9.2.2) and in 1467 the first of the combined leases cost £68 13s. 4d. for five years.[79]

Once the crane was being leased for multiple years, sometimes with and sometimes without one or more additional assets (now including the profits of the fish market), the sums charged are no longer comparable with those from the earlier years. Sometimes it is possible to extrapolate the values of the crane's annual leases, as in the 1480s and 1490s, when they were around £20.[80] The flexibility of leases is shown by the record for 1494 in which the lessee agreed to pay £22 if the carracks arrived, were unloaded in the Downs, and the cargoes brought to Sandwich; if they did not he was to pay £16.[81] By the sixteenth century combined leases were usual, so annual fluctuations in trade cannot be charted, although other information can be inferred. For example, in 1521 the lease for all was only £1 6s. 8d., possibly the result of Sandwich's trade being adversely affected by the combination of Flemish piracy (Section 9.2.3), bad harvests and rising tax levels.[82]

9.3 Sandwich Haven and its ships in the first half of the sixteenth century

By the beginning of the sixteenth century the haven needed 'substantial buoys' to mark the navigable channels,[83] and the town's efforts at keeping the waterways clear were undermined by visiting vessels still illegally dumping ballast.[84] Wrecks continued to be troublesome, with a tax being levied in 1504 for the removal of one at Richborough,[85] and in 1517 members of the town council went as far as Fordwich to check on the state of the Stour.[86] Draining and reclaiming the marshes of the flood plain (also known as 'inning'), first begun centuries earlier by the religious houses of Canterbury, was continued by secular landowners who were often absentees and apparently cared little for the state of the rivers. The first protest about this was recorded in 1506, when John Tate of London was accused of 'inning and closing the marsh' and threatened with royal intervention.[87] The problem clearly continued, for by the 1530s the crown had become very closely involved. In 1538, for example, the royal authorities ordered the town to demolish its watermill by Canterbury Gate because it was obstructing the flow of the Delf into the haven.[88] The town did not replace the mill until 1559, when it was 'next to the old crane', and so probably at Monkenquay, not far from its predecessor.[89]

An admiralty inquisition set up in 1537 reported on the injuries to the haven caused by owners of the marsh between Sandwich and Richborough, commenting also that the brethren of St Bartholomew's hospital were no longer maintaining the groynes as they had done before.[90] The groynes were breakwaters or jetties, set at an angle to the shore, against which sand and shingle accumulated, so that they needed constant maintenance. One of their functions seems to have been to provide deep-water mooring for ships, and some of the 'docks' that are mentioned frequently in the documentary record may have been such breakwaters rather than docks as we usually interpret the word today. They are often also referred to as 'groyne hedds', and references in the second half of the sixteenth century make it plain that they were used as landing places (sometimes illegally),[91] and often abused as dumping grounds for ballast.[92] They could, therefore, easily become an obstruction to passage through the haven.

In 1538 a delegation from the town reported that two sluices (or cuts) in the Monks' Wall between Sandwich and Richborough had been stopped up, and the king himself agreed to visit Sandwich to see what could be done.[93] In the early months of 1548 both the king and the archbishop were persuaded of the need for improvements,[94] which the town tried to put in train in December that year by directing merchantmen to berth at the quays at Davis Gate rather than moor out in the haven because of the damage they were doing to the harbour.[95] Since much more fundamental measures were needed, John Rogers, military engineer and surveyor of the works at Boulogne and Calais, was put in charge of building the new harbour,[96] but there were difficulties in raising the money to pay him and his workmen, and little seems to have been achieved.[97] Rogers's proposal for an artificial channel from the haven to the sea is probably that shown on a chart (Fig. 9.2), which is thought to have been drawn c.1548.[98] This may have been based on an earlier map, for in 1532 the town paid for a skin to make a parchment on which a plan of the haven was to be drawn.[99] After Rogers's scheme failed, more attempts were made to retrieve the situation, sometimes in a minor way, as in 1555 when the tolls exacted from freemen who used the Davis Gate wharf may have been dedicated to harbour clearance.[100] More petitions to royalty possibly led to experienced water engineers being recruited in Flanders in 1559,[101] but the state of the haven did not improve throughout the rest of the century (Chap. 15.1.1).

It seems that Sandwich Haven had become unsuitable for large vessels by 1520, when one of Emperor Charles V's representatives in England reported that 'Great vessels cannot come alongside there [the harbour] ... Small or middle sized ships can come to the wall of the town.'[102] The unlikelihood of carracks or galleys arriving at the harbour had been noted as early as 1498 and 1505, when the lessee of the town crane agreed to pay more to the town in the event of his having to deal with a ship of this type.[103] The carrack, probably from Flanders, that is said to have been berthed at Davis Gate in 1519 is the last such vessel to be recorded as visiting the Sandwich quayside.[104]

Most ships using Sandwich in the sixteenth century were probably coasters carrying goods such as fish, coal, salt and grain along the east coast of England and across the English Channel, and seem on average to have been smaller than their equivalents in the previous century. Ketches, which occur most frequently in early sixteenth-century records of Sandwich port, were seldom more than 50 tuns burden and often much less, although plats (or playttes) that carried miscellaneous cargoes from the Low Countries often had a carrying capacity of 60 tuns and more, and some ships transporting salt may have reached 100 tuns.[105] On the other hand, haynes, a Normandy boat type, were often as little as 18 tuns burden. Crayers continued to frequent the harbour, as they had in the previous century (Section 9.1), but were supplemented by hoys and pinks for trade with the Netherlands.[106] The customs account for the twelve months from Michaelmas 1543 records 109 pinks, all but twenty-five of them from Ostend, the rest from other Low Countries ports.[107] They carried mainly herrings, hops and beer. In the same period there were three crayers, one from Calais and two with Sandwich owners, two ketches from Ramsgate and Blankenberge, and two 'Argusyes' (Argosies). These last were large merchantmen, probably from the Mediterranean whence they carried the Malmseye and Muscadell wines purchased by three Sandwich merchants. Only four hoys were liable for customs, but such vessels may have been more common than this record suggests because they were also used to transport troops and horses, with

Fig. 9.2: Chart of Sandwich Haven, drawn probably c.1548 in connection with proposed improvements to the harbour (© British Library Board. All Rights Reserved: Cotton Augustus I.i., f. 54)

300 reputedly assembling in Sandwich and Dover for Henry VIII's abortive French expedition in 1512.[108]

Colliers, usually less than 40 tuns burden, carried only coal from Newcastle,[109] and other specialised vessels included a multiplicity of fishing boats: herring boats, mackerel boats, oyster boats, busses and, very commonly, picards. The last mentioned were not themselves fishing boats, but lighters that transported the fish to the quayside from the boats anchored further out.[110]

The ships that frequented the port in the sixteenth century seem mostly to have been small enough to berth at the quayside, where their cargoes could be unloaded by crane. This can be inferred from the tolls and wharfage recorded in the town's treasurers' accounts, and the amount of traffic led to the building of at least one more crane on the town quay by 1526.[111]

9.4 Trade through Sandwich Haven in the first half of the sixteenth century

By the first decade of the sixteenth century the wine, wool, cloth and luxury goods that had been the mainstay of the port's commerce in the previous two centuries had been replaced by less valuable or exotic cargoes. An entry in the town book in 1506, which set out the charges for loading and unloading goods at Davis Gate, shows that salt from the Bay of Bourgneuf had become the most important foreign import, and that other incoming commodities were everyday items such as coal, onions, garlic, cabbages, fish and hops.[112] Sandwich then differed from the neighbouring port of Dover in importing almost no high-value luxury goods. This can be seen from the national customs accounts for 1513–14, which show great quantities of velvet and damask being brought into Dover and only a few pieces to Sandwich.[113] Its main export was grain, followed by beer and kersey cloth,[114] some of which went across the Channel to supply markets in the Low Countries and elsewhere, although there was also brisk traffic along the English coast.

Much of the import trade in salt from France, and herrings and hops from the Low Countries, was in the hands of alien merchants and carried in the holds of alien ships, but some local merchants and shipowners were also involved. Thomas Horn, for example, imported fish and miscellaneous merchandise in a ship belonging to John Oxenbridge, whose vessel also carried cargoes for alien merchants.[115] In the 1520s and early 1530s several other Sandwich men traded in a part-time capacity while pursuing other crafts. Oliver Stromble was a brewer who imported hops and firewood for his own use but also brought in an occasional cargo of wine, linen cloth and Normandy canvas. The draper Roger Manwood imported salt, red herrings and soap, and sent out two shipments of wheat. Small cargoes were occasionally shipped in or out by others such as Thomas Lonnde,[116] and local landowners exported grain grown on their estates.[117] Early in his mercantile career, Nicholas Peake regularly shipped wheat to Calais, London and Rye, and occasionally imported herring, worsted from Saint-Omer and other Flemish cloth.[118] The most noteworthy full-time merchant in the early sixteenth century was John Master, who had his own 20-tun crayer, the *Thomas* of Sandwich, and perhaps some other vessels, in which he regularly imported sweet and non-sweet wines, hops, herrings and other salt fish, linen cloth, and salt. He also carried cargoes for alien merchants and himself used alien ships, such as the Spanish vessel in which he exported wheat, and the French boat that carried hides for him in 1518–19. In addition, he provided Calais with grain and malt.[119]

The importance of the cross-Channel grain trade to the town is indicated by the fact that in 1531 nearly 7,000 quarters of wheat, oats and malt were dispatched to Calais through the port of Sandwich.[120] Piracy in the English Channel in the late 1530s, however, led to a disruption of trade with the Continent, and this was exacerbated by a national and general ban on exporting goods without a licence.[121] When war with France was resumed in the 1540s, grain was specified in the embargo on exports, although it could still be sent to victual Calais, and this must have given some relief to Sandwich. Despite the embargo, high grain prices in the Low Countries encouraged illegal shipments, such as the beer, malt and barley reported by searchers in Sandwich, Milton and Margate.[122] Sandwich never again played the major role in provisioning troops for war in France that it had in the fifteenth century, although the need to transport troops and supplies to France for the expedition against Boulogne in 1544 diverted goods and shipping from commercial ventures. The subsequent capture of Boulogne and its need for victuals gave south-east English trade an important, albeit brief, boost.

By the early 1550s Sandwich had become the centre of a widespread grain trade, with wheat, malt and oats being shipped along the coast in every direction: to the Sussex ports, to the north Kent ports of Dartford and Maidstone, and to London, Calais and Boulogne.[123] Even after Boulogne had been handed back and Calais lost, grain remained Sandwich's main export. Although the value of goods paying customs at Sandwich naturally dropped with the disappearance of luxury commodities, the volume handled was still high enough to employ people on the quayside. Moreover, the goods exported – the grain and the beer – had either been grown or manufactured locally. This trade helped to counteract the negative effect of the downturn in the economy brought about by the drop in population and the burden of Henry VIII's war taxation. Although trading still played an important role in the town's economy, its nature had changed significantly since the fifteenth century. The ships using the port were smaller; the goods were of lesser value, and the distance they travelled was shorter. While it was still possible to earn a good living from trading, the wealthier merchants diversified their interests, investing in property (both within the town and the hinterland) as well as in trade. Sandwich was no longer a major player on the international scene.

10 The life of the town

Before the 1430s documentary evidence for people, property and occupations in Sandwich largely comes from transactions by the civic authorities and the hospitals, and from the few surviving court rolls discussed in Chapter 5. This situation changes during the fifteenth century as more documents, such as the town records, private deeds and wills, become available, enabling many more townspeople to be identified and their concerns charted. The emphasis in this chapter therefore falls on the late fifteenth and early sixteenth centuries, when documentary sources are fuller. An overview of the development of civic administration and the sort of people involved in it, of the inhabitants in different social and occupational groups, together with evidence of their property dealings where known, provides a background against which to see the domestic and commercial buildings discussed in Chapter 12. Issues concerned with the religious life of the town and its inhabitants will be dealt with, together with the churches themselves, in Chapter 13.

10.1 The governance of the town

Because of the limitations of the evidence, little can be said about the activities of the civic authorities before the 1430s, by which time the mayor and jurats met, not in St Peter's church as they had previously (Chap. 5.1.2), but in a court hall south-east of St Peter's churchyard, built on land leased from the chaplain of the Condy chantry in St Mary's church.[1] It may have been built in the late fourteenth century when work took place on the Dover court house,[2] but it could have been erected later, for in 1433 one of the earliest entries in the town year book is for a court held in the church. This may indicate that the change had been only partially accomplished, or that the move to the new court hall was so recent that the clerk made a slip when entering the location.[3]

The civic concerns illustrated by the entries in the town year books included changes in urban administration, and activities such as the organisation of the town into wards for defensive and taxation purposes, the regulation of trade and the upkeep of other features from which the town gained economic benefits and for which it therefore took general responsibility.

10.1.1 Civic administration: changes and urban unrest

Until the 1450s Sandwich was governed as it had been since the beginning of the fourteenth century, but in the mid-1450s the mayor and jurats decided to change the arrangement. The economic distress and political uncertainties early in that decade may have been behind their decision to follow the example of some other towns, such as King's Lynn and Norwich, and to share power more widely by enlarging the base of government in favour of a 'greater accountability to the commonalty'.[4] In Sandwich this entailed the creation of a common council of 'the best commoners to make all kinds of elections and levy all manner of lots and scots'. It was agreed that the mayor and jurats should choose four men from each of the three parishes, and that these four men should choose another eight or as many as seemed expedient.[5] Those initially chosen seem to have been very solid citizens and included the butchers John Paston and John Gerard, small-scale merchants and property owners like Thomas Wymark, and men such as William Claysson, who leased first the weigh beam and later the crane.[6] The methods for choosing the council were soon modified, for in 1464 sixteen men in each parish were picked by the whole community, with the mayor and jurats then selecting twelve of them to serve as councillors. This new common council was to meet in the 'guyhaldam ville', presumably the court hall, every Wednesday at 1 p.m.[7]

The move towards greater accountability was, however, short-lived because of a decision by the Brodhull court of the Cinque Ports in 1526. Henceforward, the mayors and jurats of all the ports were to be chosen by a group of twenty-four men from each town. At Sandwich, the mayor was no longer to be elected by all the freemen (Chap. 5.1.2), but instead the jurats would succeed each other to the position of mayor in order of seniority. In addition, a smaller common council of twenty-four rather than thirty-six men was set up, and appointed by the mayor and jurats rather than chosen by each parish.[8] The change from an elected to an appointed common council did not meet with general approval, since its composition was no longer in the control of the general population, and it may have had repercussions, as indicated below.

In the fifteenth century the bailiff, although a royal appointee, often delegated his responsibilities to a deputy with strong ties to the town. In 1524, however, Henry VIII appointed as bailiff Sir Edward Ringeley, a royal court official who had no previous connection with Sandwich and was determined to maintain royal rights. Soon after his appointment, the Barons of the Exchequer, who were then seeking to collect as much money as possible to finance the war with France, summoned him to produce accounts of the bailiwick, which had not been rendered since 1522. When he did, he found discrepancies, and thought that the mayor and jurats had 'wrongfully taken and yet doe receive to their own use and profit' various perquisites.[9] He drew the barons' attention to the problem, and a writ was issued to two former mayors, John Somer and Henry Bolle, to explain themselves.[10] Since Somer died before he could do so, and Bolle denied the charges, the barons ordered Ringeley fully to collect all the revenues belonging to the bailiwick until a settlement could be reached.

Trouble broke out during St Clement's fair late in November 1526, when Ringeley's serjeant was attempting to collect the king's tolls, which had been in abeyance in the early 1520s.[11] On this occasion, armed men loyal to Bolle intimidated people attending the fair to prevent them paying the toll, and also created mayhem in the streets at night. When the bailiff's serjeant came to court to protest against the uproar, he was threatened with imprisonment. Meanwhile, it was rumoured that Ringeley was arranging to call up a hundred men from the countryside to restore order. With the support of Roger Manwood (mayor in 1526) and Vincent Engeham (mayor 1528–30), however, Bolle continued to encourage the agitators. In December 1526 the protestors attacked Ringeley's house, breaking the glass in the windows, and in the late summer of 1527 they took the devotional books and beads from his wife's pew in St Mary's church. According to Ringeley, many of the townspeople would have complained to the court of Shepway, but were too afraid to do so. Traditional town government had virtually collapsed and it was probably in this context that Robert King, a barber, publicly abused the mayor and his brethren in 1529 calling them 'hedgehogs, hedgecreepers, bench whistlers, and catch polls' and that if he met the mayor in the street he 'would not doff his bonnet to him'.[12] The events suggest that the problem was centred on an overbearing governing group who had time neither for the ordinary townspeople nor for the royal bailiff. Discord between urban government and the commonalty was not new, and has been identified during the previous century in small towns elsewhere, including Lydd in Kent.[13]

The disagreements were finally put before the King's Council in 1530 and a settlement was reached, whereby Ringeley resigned and the bailiwick was taken into civic hands until his death, which occurred in 1543. Ringeley received £100 in compensation for his loss of office, £40 of this being lent by his opponent, Vincent Engeham (the mayor). Engeham was to be repaid out of the bailiwick's revenues and profits, but in 1537–8 the treasurer's accounts do not include tolls from St Clement's fair, implying that the king's rights in Sandwich were in abeyance.[14] On Ringeley's death, the office of bailiff reverted to the crown, and the king granted it to Thomas Pache, who, although a member of the royal household, had also been a jurat in Sandwich.[15]

The Ringeley affair took place against the background of Sandwich's declining economy and population, when life was hard for many townspeople. But the primary reasons for the unrest are unlikely to have been financial. Rather, it shows the anger of the elite at what they perceived as royal interference and disregard for the interests of the town, and the frustration of the ordinary people who now had less voice in local government. It also indicates how the threat and fear of law and disorder were well founded, and that, with no form of policing, an armed gang could wreak havoc.

10.1.2 The wards

One of the most important duties of the town administration was overseeing the ward system. It grew out of the night watch, formalised in the custumal of 1301, and by 1436 it had become the method whereby responsibility for guarding the town and maintaining the walls was regulated, with the townspeople being organised into 'wards'.[16] The number of wards seems to have fluctuated, perhaps as the size of population changed (Section 10.2.2). The first record, in 1435, is for two constables to be appointed annually for eight

Table 10.1: The wards in 1478

Ward number	Extent
1	Canterbury Gate to St Mary's Gate
2	Canterbury Gate to Woodnesborough Gate
3	St Mary's Gate to Ives Gate
4	Ives Gate to Fisher Gate
5	Woodnesborough Gate to New Gate
6	Fishergate to the Bulwark
7	Sandown bridge to New Gate
8	Half-ward to attend on the mayor

wards,[17] but when the first description is given in 1468, there were six and a half wards, six of which were under the control of two jurats and two constables, and a half-ward with two constables whose duty was to accompany the mayor.[18] Ten years later there were eight and a half wards (Table 10.1),[19] and by 1513, when the population had declined, a taxation document assessed by ward indicates that once more there were six.[20] Support for the equation between population size and the number of wards can be seen in the late sixteenth century after the influx of refugees from the Low Countries, when there were twelve wards (eleven plus one for the mayor).[21] In the fifteenth century the wards were usually described as extending from gate to gate. Their shifting outlines were never recorded in detail, although a mayoral ruling of 1478 indicated that at that time the Delf was to form part of all their boundaries,[22] and in 1513 the wards were definitely associated with parishes.

10.1.3 Regulation of trade

Local trade was closely regulated. Markets at which small quantities of everyday goods – butter, eggs, a loaf of bread, a few bushels of oats and the like – could be bought were held on Wednesdays and Saturdays. In 1479 the mayor and jurats specifically ordained that all victuallers should be free to sell their victuals without being menaced, beaten or hurt,[23] and in 1480 butchers and fishmongers were told that if they cut up their goods into smaller pieces for sale, they were not to keep any part of it such as the 'gobbetts' for themselves.[24]

In September 1490 it was ordained that all non-freemen living in the town and brewing beer should pay the town one penny annually for every 'bonne' (42 gallons) of beer retailed in their houses.[25] In the early sixteenth century the price for different grades of beer was fixed, and brewers were repeatedly told to be sure to brew plentiful supplies of the cheaper, single beer, 'so that the commons do lack no beer'.[26] In 1503 the price for every bonne of double beer was to be 3s., and 2s. for a similar measure of single beer, but, in times of bad harvests, when grain prices rose, brewers were allowed to charge as much as 3s. 4d. for double beer.

As the regulations regarding single beer show, the authorities in many towns, including Sandwich, were very concerned that all inhabitants should have easy access to goods, preferably in a market, and at a reasonable price.[27] By the 1520s it had become common for importers of hops and herrings to bypass the market. Hops were sold directly to brewers, taking beer in exchange, so in 1537 it was decreed that no beer brewer was to buy victuals or other merchandise directly from Flemings or strangers, and also that fish were to be sold only in a market.[28] The number of times this prohibition was reissued throughout the early sixteenth century indicates that the practice continued. The principle was also extended to other imported merchandise. In 1540, for instance, when a Canterbury merchant negotiated to purchase all the salt to be unloaded at Sandwich from a foreign vessel, several leading jurats, who believed that this action would leave the townspeople short of essential supplies, sent agents to the ship to seize nearly half the salt, intending to distribute it to inhabitants of the town. A subsequent inquiry revealed that their fears about a shortage of salt were unfounded and the confiscated salt remained in the hands of the mariners.[29]

In 1504, to supplement the long-established St Clement's fair held in November every year, Henry VII granted a charter to the mayor, jurats and whole commonalty of Sandwich, giving them the right to hold two annual fairs, one beginning on 7 February and the other on 5 June, with their revenues and fees being under the control of the town.[30] This is one of the few examples of a charter authorising specific rights to Sandwich.

10.1.4 Guilds

In Sandwich none of the formal ordinances of guild governance is known to have survived, but we can infer from what happened in other towns that during the course of the fifteenth century people working in the same trade would have formed some loose, voluntary, organisation. Gradually, town administrations sought to impose more order and structure and began to require urban craftsmen to form formal associations called guilds. Each was to be controlled by strict rules designed to protect trade and to regulate training; they had to be approved by the mayor and jurats, and enrolled in the civic records. But such recorded ordinances, which appear to show a hierarchical, male-oriented society, do not necessarily reflect the actual organisation of the craft, but what the authorities wished to see imposed on the craftsmen and women.[31]

The barbers, surgeons and wax chandlers of Sandwich were incorporated in 1482, and in 1494 wardens were appointed for the companies of tailors, shoemakers and weavers.[32] The tailors and drapers, shoemakers and bakers agreed to participate in the maintenance of the town gates; the tailors (with the drapers, responsible for New Gate in 1541) had an organisation with annual dues and at least fifteen members by 1494, but nothing is known about the early history of the drapers or of the shoemakers and bakers (both responsible for Canterbury Gate at different times). By 1559 there was also a shipmasters' guild (Chap. 15.1.3).[33]

10.1.5 Municipal responsibilities and activities

Entries in the town year books show the authorities dealing with the maintenance of the physical structure of the town. Much of the expenditure was for repairs, apparently confirming that most of the infrastructure was already in place by the time the sources begin, and probably had been so for some time. There is too much detailed information for it all to be included here,[34] so the following description will concentrate on some basic necessities of urban existence, notably public hygiene, and some structures and enterprises in public ownership, such as the town crane, the brickworks and the brothel, that have not been dealt with elsewhere in the book.

10.1.5.1 Public hygiene

Once the Delf and Guestling had been diverted, the town authorities were responsible for keeping the combined watercourses clean enough to provide drinking water for the inhabitants. Mud, reeds and weeds had to be removed periodically, as did the rubbish and dung that the inhabitants threw into the water channels. The council often paid for the work to be done, but sometimes the inhabitants, organised in wards, were required to do it themselves, as in 1451, when all householders had to bring their own tools for the purpose.[35] It appears that annual cleaning was the norm,[36] at least until 1565, when the task was leased to 'dikers' for 20s. annually.[37] This seems to have been a surprisingly good deal for the town considering that it had regularly been paying £3 and more over the previous few years.[38]

Frequent repairs were also needed to the Delf's walls, banks and designated washing and watering places.[39] Stray animals, particularly pigs and sheep, must have been a constant nuisance, for although barriers were erected to keep them away, many fines were imposed for such offences.[40] Animals were also illegally taken to drink from or to be washed in the Delf, and by 1567 washing sheep in the watering place had become so prevalent that the council began to charge for it (2d. for twenty sheep).[41]

The town was also responsible for maintaining the course of the Delf where it flowed through the Lydden Valley, past Roaring Gutter and the Pinnock Wall (Fig. 3.12). The Pinnock Wall, an embankment of earth, timber and wattles, needed a great deal spent on it, and although not mentioned until 1455, expenditure may have been going on since the twelfth century.[42] Because the Delf continued to be the primary water supply for Sandwich until 1899, maintenance of the structures in the Lydden Valley remained of paramount importance long after the end of the Middle Ages.[43]

Although the Delf was the most important water source for Sandwich, it was not the only one.[44] The Carmelite friary had had a conduited water supply since 1306,[45] but it may have been quite separate from that of the town until 1483, when agreement was reached between town and friary for it to be used more generally, and the mayor and jurats paid for a brick cistern to be built.[46] At the same time the town was digging its own conduit at great expense,[47] so by 1485 there were two conduits to be looked after.[48]

There were at least three common privies to be maintained by the authorities, all of which seem to have been constructed of timber with tile roofs. The ones beside Davis Gate and Pillory Gate certainly emptied into the harbour.[49] The location of the third, in Privy Lane, is less certain, but it probably stood in a lane running down to the river.[50] Further attempts at hygiene included making a gutter to convey foul water to the haven, through the land leading to St Mary's Gate[51] which was crossed by both path and sewer,[52] and making sure that dung hills were established in designated places and cleared out regularly.[53]

The paving of streets is less well documented, although there is evidence that stone was fairly frequently used. Private money was bequeathed for paving the Cornmarket,[54] but the town itself paved the High Street with stone in 1466, and subsequently maintained it with stone and rubble.[55] This action may reflect the importance that the street possessed, not just when it was a marketplace, but as the main route south from the haven and ferry to Sandwich's southern hinterland.

10.1.5.2 The town quay

The Sandwich waterfront was made up of a number of quays, only one of which was the common or town quay where vessels not destined for specific merchants berthed. This may have been Davis Quay, mentioned as one of the stations for watch and ward in the custumal of 1301, although the first specific evidence for this location occurs only in 1591, when the Common (Town) Quay was defined as being between Davis Gate (now the Barbican) and Fisher Gate.[56] The records from 1432 onwards show that the town financed repairs to the quay on a number of occasions.

The town quay provided not only berthing facilities but also harbour installations enabling freight to be loaded or unloaded from the merchantmen, and stored before or after shipment. Nothing above ground survives from these installations, and there is very little documentary information about any of the structures indispensable to a port, apart from the cranes. The first documented reference to a town crane is in 1432, when it was obviously already well established.[57] The year books and treasurers' accounts from that date onwards show that it was profitable, but also costly to maintain. The records of the repairs that were necessary every few years provide invaluable insights into its construction and appearance. It and neighbouring Davis Gate must have presented an imposing sight to visiting shipping in the second half of the fifteenth century. The surviving gatehouse was built in the late 1460s with money from central government,[58] but from 1483 the town authorities were responsible for its maintenance (Chap. 11.2.1.4). Its high-quality decoration suggests that it was as much a status symbol for the town as a defensive or economic structure, which may explain why the authorities expended so much on its upkeep.

10.1.5.3 The brickworks
During the early fifteenth century bricks were imported from the Low Countries,[59] and imports may have continued into the middle of the century, for in 1463–4 the town purchased 30,000 bricks from Bartholomew Brickmaker and a further 72,000 in 1466.[60] Since these transactions are recorded in the customs accounts, the bricks are unlikely to have been made locally, although local production had started by 1467 when the town established its own brickworks at Sandown, and granted the lease to John Fuller, brickmaker, who paid the town 5,000 bricks for each 100,000 that were fired.[61] This seems to be the first documentary evidence for brickmaking in Kent, following similar municipal ventures in other towns in eastern England, such as Hull, Beverley and York,[62] although the size of production and profitability of the Sandwich brickworks are unknown. In 1483 William Mason, who probably lived at 23 Strand Street (House 81), paid 40s. per annum for an annual lease,[63] and in 1488 Laurence Copley leased it for two years, agreeing to give the town 12,000 bricks in payment if he made any bricks, and 40s. if he made none.[64]

The Sandwich treasurers' accounts unfortunately do not give a very clear indication of what the bricks were used for before 1490, although 200 bricks were used to repair a house in 1469; an unspecified number were to be given to William Cok in 1475 for building a garden wall in recompense for giving up land for the town wall; and 4,000 were used for the cistern at the friary in 1483.[65] In 1490, 36,000 bricks were allocated for building a house belonging to the town at Woodnesborough Gate, while in the late fifteenth century and the first half of the sixteenth there are references to bricks being used to repair the gates, the town crane, the conduit and the watermill.[66] As far as one can tell, most of the uses were mundane in character, as indicated by the types of structures for which brick was used, although patterned brickwork occurs on the middle section of Fisher Gate, probably built in Sandwich brick under the direction of the town authorities at the end of the fifteenth century.

10.1.5.4 The brothel
In 1474 the mayor and jurats established a common house of stews called 'le galye', making it one of the rare towns in England to have an official or institutionalised brothel at this time.[67] What lay behind this decision? From the 1460s the authorities had been concerned about the sexual misbehaviour of women. Almost every year one or more women were accused of fornication, of being prostitutes or being badly governed, and were required to leave the town. In 1465, for example, nine women were escorted to the edge of town and told not to come back, and in 1468 a woman was banned because she lived 'inhoneste' with a man, against ecclesiastical law.[68] In 1474, however, the town came to an agreement with beer brewer John Kyng, whereby he received a reduction of 12s. on the rent of his main house on Strand Street in St Clement's parish, and in return gave up a barn and garden in another part of the parish that could be turned into a municipal brothel.[69] It produced some revenue, although never very much, and it brought a potentially disruptive element under supervision.[70] If the inns owned by the town were to some extent municipal inns, used by the mayor to host official functions, then the authorities may have wished to remove common women from working in them. By establishing a municipal brothel, prostitution could be regulated and controlled. In the absence of later sixteenth-century treasurers' accounts its long-term history is unclear, but it functioned at least until 1522.[71]

10.1.5.5 Other possessions and functions of the town council

In addition, the town owned other property. The most important building was the court hall, which underwent regular repair, mostly for minor matters. Little is known about its form, although it seems that the council chamber was on the ground floor. It was probably heated since there are several references to coal being purchased, and had a storehouse 'within it' and a loft above. In 1466 the council chamber was painted with red ochre, and in 1483 its window was glazed, possibly for the first time.[72] In 1506 a new ceiling, and unspecified payments to a carpenter, mason, painter and tiler suggest large-scale refurbishment; while in 1538 £8 was spent on ceiling the hall, more on boards and benches, and 13s. 6d. on painting and gilding the town's arms 'as well as the streteside without the hall dores with the antelope and the lion'.[73] Until the early sixteenth century the town gaol for freemen lay next door (non-freemen were held in the king's gaol at the castle).[74] Heavy close-set timbering, reused in the northern end of 11 St Peter's Street (now known as the Old Gaol), may come from the medieval gaol.

The mayor and jurats also devoted funds to maintaining other buildings and structures from which they hoped to gain profit through renting or leasing. These included a number of shops and shambles in the Cornmarket and Fishmarket, and several windmills, watermills and weigh beams. The earth ramparts were increasingly used as pasture, as were the Butts and Salts on the flat land outside the walls west of the town (Fig. IV.1). Less often referred to were the rope tackle ground,[75] the cross, pillory and stocks in the Cornmarket,[76] the crane (gibbet) at Davis Gate,[77] the bull ring,[78] and the pound.[79] The mixture in any one year of small quit rents for long-acquired property, economic rents for buildings such as houses in The Butchery, and changing leases for land and structures make it impossible to calculate the total value of this urban property.

When the necessity arose for extra funding for major projects of construction or repair, local taxes might be levied or the inhabitants might be asked to supply labour. In 1432 taxes were raised to complete the construction of the watermill;[80] in 1438 they were used to repair the Delf;[81] and in 1483 and 1484 they were collected parish by parish to pay for digging the conduit.[82] In 1494 money from taxes on the salt and coal trades was to be set aside for work on the haven,[83] and on a couple of occasions in the late fifteenth century the men of each ward had to undertake work on the Guestling and the haven.[84] Two assessments for local taxes survive, in 1471 and 1513 (Section 10.2.1), but in neither case is it clear what the money was to be raised for.

In the 1460s the town owned two inns, The Bull and The Bell, and also The Black Tavern. In 1519 the mayor and jurats watched a play at one of them, probably The Bell, although it had not been owned by the town since 1480;[85] at other times in the late fifteenth and early sixteenth centuries they paid for performances in private houses, the court hall, or even in the friary.[86] Throughout this time there were regular references to official payments for players, minstrels and others, including bear baiting, although the locations of these entertainments and the audiences they were aimed at are not always clear.[87]

10.2 Population and property

10.2.1 Population figures

No information survives for the number of inhabitants or households in the town in the late fourteenth century. As discussed in Chapter 5.3, it is likely that the population declined steeply in the middle years of the fourteenth century, possibly by as much as a half, leaving perhaps 2,500 inhabitants by *c*.1360. The Sandwich economy was relatively buoyant during much of the first half of the fifteenth century and the population may have recovered to some extent before the 1440s; but in 1457 the epidemic that so devastated the whole of Kent (Chap. 9.2.2) almost certainly affected Sandwich as well, and a number of economic and social problems manifested themselves in the second half of the century.

In 1471 a meeting of the common council authorised an assessment to be made in each parish of how much inhabitants should pay in taxation. The names of 523 people were listed.[88] Some of them may have come from the same household, but since there is no mention of wives, apprentices or servants, or of those considered too poor to pay,[89] the figure suggests that there could have been approximately 500 households in Sandwich at that time. In view of the large numbers not taxed, the total of those assessed has been multiplied by 7 to produce an estimated population of perhaps 3,500 people.[90] The assessment was organised by parish, with 209 people taxed in St Mary's parish, 162 in St Clement's and 152 in St Peter's. Given the small size of St Peter's parish in relation to the other two, it is probable that the figures reflect households clustering in the centre of town, that is, in St Peter's parish and the north-eastern part of St Mary's. The impression of a rise in population during the third quarter of the century is perhaps borne out not only by the figures in the survey of 1471 but also by the rise in the number of wards from six to eight, and the number of new houses that survive in the town. These are not precisely datable, but it is probable that many of them were built in the mid- or later fifteenth century.

During the late fifteenth century many of the town's inhabitants had difficulty in meeting their financial obligations, and economic distress and depopulation continued for the next sixty years. In 1497–8 twenty-five of the town's tenants who occupied houses, shops, cellars, cottages, gardens or even void ground sought a reduction in their rent,[91] and tenants of some of the cottages owned by the church of St Mary had already been in arrears for two years.[92] In addition, fines (licences that the civic authorities issued to allow traders to keep shop) were sometimes not paid on time. In 1494, when the wardens of the tailors' guild were asked to provide the names of those practising the craft in the town, fifteen proved not to have paid their dues.[93]

Outbreaks of disease affecting the whole region could have contributed to these difficulties. In Canterbury in the 1490s, for instance, rents from butchers' stalls could not be collected because the holders had died unexpectedly and therefore intestate, and tenements and plots belonging to Canterbury Cathedral Priory lay vacant because of lack of demand.[94] But a factor specific to the declining population of Sandwich was probably that the Italian ships no longer anchored there. This must have reduced the demand for casual local labour on the quays or in the haven, so fewer people may have come to the town in search of work, and there may even have been some emigration to Canterbury and elsewhere. Since the town authorities were losing income because some of their properties were unoccupied, they commissioned a new rental in 1507–8, stating that they would rent out their property at whatever rate they could get.[95]

The reduction in the numbers of inhabitants is clear in the next surviving local tax list, of 1513.[96] From this can be extracted the details of 579 adult inhabitants, including a number of those too poor to pay anything at all. Since 200 of those assessed were servants or apprentices, there are unlikely to have been more than about 380 households by this time. If multiplied by 7, this suggests a population of approximately 2,700 (Table 10.2).[97] The decline in population, however, was not yet complete. The 1540s and 1550s were turbulent decades for Sandwich and Kent as a whole. In 1544–5 Sandwich was hit by a major outbreak of disease, and in 1545 burials in St Mary's parish were double their normal level, and even higher in St Peter's.[98]

Currency manipulation, which helped to pay for the costs of the renewed struggle with France, caused prices to rise, and fundamental religious changes, such as the dissolution of the monasteries, the circulation of the English Bible and the new prayer book of 1549, must have caused unease among at least some inhabitants. However, although there was discontent in rural north and mid-Kent in 1549, there was no general uprising, and the towns seem to have been relatively unaffected.[99] In 1555 and 1556 bad harvests, followed by two years of serious influenza epidemics, reduced the population of Sandwich yet further.[100] Those people who were reliant on wages, which did not keep pace with inflation, may have suffered particularly heavily, their poverty leading to a decline in the demand for retail goods. But much of the contraction had probably taken place before this date, for in 1548 the certificates for the dissolution of the chantries indicate that the three parishes combined contained 1,020 communicants,[101] suggesting a population of approximately 1,360 living in some 215 households.[102] This is even less than the 290–300 households that are likely to have existed in 1560, a figure that has been extrapolated from the recorded 291 English households and 129 Dutch ones of 1565 (Chap. 15.2). Although all the figures are likely to be very approximate, it is clear that the population was still declining during the first half of the sixteenth century.

Table 10.2: Numbers and assessed wealth of Sandwich taxpayers, 1513

Wealth	No.	%
£50 and above	25	4
£20–£49	39	7
£4–£19	51	9
Wages and goods under £4	241	42
Servants (190) and apprentices (10)	200	34
Paupers (15), not charged, and those, excluding servants, charged elsewhere (8)	23	4
Totals	579	100

10.2.2 The effects of the declining population

From the mid-fifteenth century onwards many town authorities in England, seeking extra help from the crown, claimed that their inhabitants were having trouble paying rents and that property was empty and decaying. This happens often enough to suggests some exaggeration.[103] Each place, therefore, needs to be considered on its merits.

In Canterbury, the only other sizeable town in the region, it has been argued that a progressive downturn in the economy from the early fifteenth century onwards had led to considerable difficulties by the last quarter of the fifteenth century and the first quarter of the sixteenth.[104] In Sandwich, although the economy fluctuated during the fifteenth century, the situation there too seems to have become serious by the end of the century. The authorities were then concerned that property in the town was being abandoned, resulting in many tenements falling into decay and being replaced by gardens or void ground.[105] In March 1500 the council countermanded previously accepted practice by pronouncing that anyone demolishing a house would henceforth be fined unless he immediately built a better one.[106] This injunction was repeated in the 1520s, and since abuses continued, in 1560 it was decreed that rebuilding should take place within a year, otherwise the culprits would be fined and the building timber, tiles and the site itself be forfeit to the town.[107] As discussed in Chapter 14.8 and 14.9, the physical effect of this was a reduction in the number of habitable properties around the edge of the town and the concentration of the population in the urban centre.

By the end of the second decade of the sixteenth century not only were rental properties empty, but also the town dignitaries were prepared to make sacrifices to help the town's economy. In 1518–19, for example, the mayor agreed to give up the fee that he would customarily receive for providing a banquet on Twelfth Night and a dinner on St Bartholomew's Day.[108] Meanwhile, every effort was made to collect all the town's revenues that were due. In 1519 freemen who refused to pay their yearly fees were to lose their freedom, and inhabitants of London and Calais who claimed exemption from tolls on the export of cereals from the port were required to pay a halfpenny for every quarter of grain loaded onto ships 'for the ease of the poor inhabitants' of Sandwich.[109] In the 1520s, as in other towns, the destitute were becoming a problem, so the mayor and jurats decreed that beggars had to reside within the shelter (*harbinge*) provided by St John's hospital. They were given lodging and perhaps food, and were allowed to beg as long as they obeyed the town rules; otherwise, they were to be banished.[110] By the 1540s and 1550s the authorities were stockpiling grain for distribution to the poor.[111]

10.3 People and occupations

10.3.1 Merchants and the elite

A small group of merchant families formed the town elite in the late fourteenth and fifteenth centuries, the most notable among them being the Elyses. The family held small amounts of land in Preston and Wingham hundreds in the mid-fourteenth century, and appear in Sandwich records in the 1360s, when Thomas Elys, draper, granted a shop in the Fishmarket to St John's hospital.[112] It seems likely that it was he who served as mayor in 1370 and as a Member of Parliament in 1369–70. His son, also Thomas, who was born c.1349, was a vintner, supplying Christ Church Priory.[113] It was probably he, not his father, who served his turn as MP in 1377–8 and mayor in 1382,[114] and he was collector of customs at Sandwich in 1389. More than usual is known about him because he died in 1390, before he had time to present his final customs accounts, so there was an Exchequer inquiry for which part of his will was recorded.[115] He asked to be buried next to his father, Thomas, in the cemetery of St Peter's church and he left significant sums of money for the resurfacing (*arenadum*) of the Cornmarket and for the repair of a bridge and several roads into the town. His house, whose location can be identified as 29 Harnet Street (House 28), was left to his daughter and subsequently sold to another vintner.[116] He had built up a considerable fortune, which was devoted to charitable purposes. During his lifetime he, with his wife Margaret, gave money for a window in St Mary's church, and he directed his executors to found a perpetual chantry in St Peter's church and a new hospital dedicated to St Thomas. Elys's house and his charitable foundations are both discussed in Chapters 12.1, 13.1.3 and 13.3.1.

No other family is as well recorded, but a small group of names recur in the documents of the late fourteenth and early fifteenth centuries. Nine of the MPs who served between 1386 and 1421 are recorded as merchants who shipped wine, cloth or grain, and twelve had interests in land in the immediate neighbourhood of the town.[117] They, and others who served only as mayor, sometimes married each others' widows or daughters, served as feoffees for each other, owned property next to each other, and sold properties to each other, mostly along Strand Street or in the area around St Peter's church.[118] The careers of John Godard, William Gayler, Robert Whyte and Robert Wylde illustrate these activities.

Godard was MP five times and mayor ten times between 1379 and 1406. As a servant of the crown he was controller and collector of customs and subsidies, and of tunnage and poundage, holding these positions for fourteen years. He received at least £20 a year from his properties outside the town, and also was one of Thomas Elys's executors. Gayler acquired a tenement with a quay and a crane on the waterfront in St Mary's parish, and also owned property in Strand Street, Love Lane and Fisher Street.[119] He was mayor five times between 1417 and 1422, and when he died his widow became the wife of Robert Whyte, who was himself mayor on three occasions in the 1430s and MP on one. Whyte had property in Strand Street and the Fishmarket, and while mayor became lessee of the town's crane, fish market, weigh house and one of its watermills.[120] Robert Wylde, twice mayor and twice MP, was a merchant. In 1428 he bought Thomas Elys's old house at 29 Harnet Street (House 28) for £53 6s. 8d.[121]

As part of the exchange of 1290 with Christ Church Priory (Chap. 5.1), the king, through his bailiff, gained the right to collect tolls at Sandwich on the trade of all those who were not freemen of the port. Because records relating to these tolls have survived, more is known about the trading activities of the non-freemen than those of the freemen themselves. In the early 1440s William Kenet was recorded as importing woad, candles, hops, soap, madder and onions, plus Rhenish wine, linen cloth of Flanders, mantles of beaver, otter skins and paving stones.[122] In 1446–7 he imported 20 tons of Caen stone and the following year he brought in another 30 tons.[123] After he became a freeman in 1448 his trading activities disappear from sight, but he clearly became a man of substance in the town, serving twice as mayor and representing the town in the Parliament of 1461–2.[124] When he died in 1482 his house, possibly on the south side of Upper Strand Street, contained a hall, parlour and great chamber. In addition, he had two tenements in Fisher Street and property in Eastry, as well as silver plate, a cloak furred with miniver, and at least 100 ewes and 100 lambs.[125]

Another family that turns up regularly in the fifteenth-century records was that of the Botelers, who were drapers in Sandwich and Calais, and also barbers. Since they were all called John, Thomas or Richard, it is not always possible to work out which member of the family was which. John, a draper, was mayor four times in the 1440s. When he died in 1453 he lived in St Peter's parish, probably in a house on Strand Street, to which shops were annexed 'as far as the sea gate', and he had properties elsewhere in the town and in Eastry and Worth. These were inherited by his two sons, Richard, a draper, and John, a barber, and his brother Thomas, who was also a draper. In 1468 Thomas, or perhaps his son, another Thomas, bought a tenement next to Pillory Gate.[126] In 1494 Thomas, draper, left the dwelling place and chamber next to Pillory Gate and the Custom House, both in St Mary's parish, to his sons John and Thomas, plus smaller pieces of property to his daughters, but with the understanding that if any of them died, the property would pass to another.[127] Such a stipulation is a stark reminder of high urban mortality and the importance of female inheritance. Several families in Sandwich died out through lack of surviving male heirs, even if five or more children had been born. When more than one daughter inherited, the property was always divided rather than remaining as a single unit. Furthermore, daughters took their inheritance with them to a husband, benefiting that family and dissolving the bond between the original family and its property. Since both husband and wife had to agree to the alienation of any land held as a jointure, the town books often recorded such cases. Thus the deaths of Thomas's two sons not only led to the Boteler property ultimately passing into the hands of the Manwoods, another family of drapers, but also to the recording of the transactions in the civic records.

Useful information about the elite of the town in the early sixteenth century can be extracted from the tax assessment of 1513 (Table 10.2). The twenty-five taxpayers who had goods or land assessed at £50 or above (amounting to approximately 4 per cent of the total number of taxpayers) comprised both urban gentry – who were primarily country landowners whose wealth came largely from their property in the countryside – and merchants whose assets were mainly their goods. Some had grown rich by diversifying their activities (becoming part owners of ships, engaging in overseas trade, investing in the new industries of beer brewing or malt making, and acquiring rental property within the town). The merchants in this top category included Thomas Aldy, whose goods were assessed at £100. He was the proprietor of the New Tavern in 1493,[128] and by the time of his death in 1517 had acquired other property in Sandwich and its surroundings, and even in Calais.[129] John Worme, mayor in 1518, must have acquired his £80 worth of goods both by selling wool in Calais, where he was a merchant of the Staple, and by owning a house in Harnet Street and other property, including two malt mills, elsewhere in Sandwich, as well as land in Boston, Lincolnshire.[130] Some of the merchants who traded within the town, for example drapers who were the retailers of imported linen and luxury fabrics, could also accumulate wealth. The draper Roger Manwood was assessed on goods of £60 in 1513, and in 1514 had sufficient funds to acquire some of the property that Thomas Boteler left at his death.[131] Information about the Sandwich elite in later decades can also be obtained from other sources, such as the 'benevolence' (a royal request for money) of 1544, when the merchant John Master was sufficiently prosperous to contribute £13 6s. 8d., whereas other jurats could spare only £5 or £6;[132] Master also owned properties in Sandwich, as well as the rural manors of Stodmarsh and East Langdon.[133]

In the early sixteenth century the Sandwich elite included a few of the local landowning aristocracy who were frequently chosen as Members of Parliament for Sandwich. Their ownership of land meant that they shared the same interests as the knights of the shire, and by making useful contacts they could help to uphold the town's rights. There was considerable intermarriage between this minor aristocracy and the upper echelons of the merchant class, exemplified by the career of John Boys, who married a merchant's widow. Boys was a member of an ancient landowning family who claimed descent from John de Bosco, one of William the Conqueror's companions. He held extensive lands between Sandwich and Canterbury from Faversham Abbey, and supplemented them by purchasing two messuages from the heirs of a Sandwich merchant, John Lynch.[134] He later married Alice, widow of John Somer, merchant of the Calais Staple, living with her in Sandwich on the profits of their joint properties to the dismay of the six Somer daughters, who claimed that they had been disinherited.[135] In 1528 Boys was made a freeman of the town. In the following year he and Vincent Engeham attended Parliament and in 1531–2 he became mayor.

Vincent Engeham, jurat and gentleman, was mayor three times, and twice a Member of Parliament. He was one of the supporters of the unrest against Sir Edward Ringeley (Section 10.1.1). He bought property to lease within the town, including The Bull Inn (House 79). In 1529 he, with his co-agitator Henry Bolle, had been granted a lease of the town's watermill, which was demolished in 1538 (Chap. 14.10).[136] Towards the end of his life he concentrated on building up his landed estate, acquiring the manors of Goldstone and Lees in 1542.[137] His sheep-farming activities were clearly profitable, for in 1547 he left Goldstone manor and 200 ewes, 200 wethers and 200 lambs to his son Thomas, and the manor of Polder with all its sheep to his son Christopher, who became a freeman of the town in 1559.[138]

Despite his rough handling by the town when he was bailiff, Ringeley seems to have remained a resident of Sandwich. By the 1530s he owned a good deal of property in the town.[139] He must subsequently have become even wealthier, for when he died in 1543, in addition to many bequests of silver plate, clothing, ewes and lambs to various people, he left his wife his great house called The King's Lodging in St Mary's parish, property in St Clement's parish and the leases of the Jesus House,[140] Lydd Court and the parsonage of Goodnestone. During her lifetime she could also occupy his house called the Paradise and its adjacent barns and orchards, but on her death this was bequeathed to his nephew and godson, Edward Boys.[141]

10.3.2 Beer brewers

Hopped beer had been imported from the Low Countries into London and other English ports since the late fourteenth century, but it was only in the second half of the fifteenth that brewing on a fairly large scale and in commercialised brew-houses became established in south-east England. Since hopped beer had a longer life and travelled better than ale, it was the ideal drink to provide for crews in merchant and other vessels, and it may be no coincidence that the earliest references to brewing in the south-east come from ports.[142] The first of them is from Sandwich in 1439–40, when Giles Beerbrewer paid tax as an alien resident.[143] In 1467, another beer brewer, Derik White, was sued for debt;[144] and in 1469 John Kyng, beer brewer and later proprietor of the town's brothel, bought a property in Upper Strand Street.[145] In the local taxation record of 1471 (Section 10.2.1) the only tradesmen with high assessments were two beer brewers, Cornelius Beerbrewer (13s. 4d.) and William Giles (20s.). This puts them on the same level as the civic elite, underlining the importance and profitability of the trade, although Giles may best be described as a capitalist entrepreneur, with brewing only one of his activities. In addition to importing the hops needed in his brewery, he brought in oil, herrings, cabbages and salt fish.[146] He was able to arrange a marriage between his daughter and a London merchant, and he built up a substantial portfolio of property, including rental properties in Strand Street and the 'stonehall tenement' in Love Lane, one of the few stone buildings in the town, which he bought for £46.[147] Thus his high assessment in 1471 may have been due as much to the value of his property as to his brewery.

His brewery is one of the few in medieval Sandwich that can be located with any confidence. After his death in 1496 his two daughters were involved in a dispute over their inheritance, details of which were recorded in the town year books.[148] He had both owned and occupied a tenement on the north side of Strand Street, in St Mary's parish, which included a beer house and a quay. Today 'Giles Quay' is the name of a building on the north side of Strand Street opposite Bowling Street, which was formerly Serles Lane, and since Giles owned a stable, storehouse and cellar in Serles Lane, it is possible that 'Giles Quay' marks the site of his quay.

Each year three or four men were recorded as brewers in Sandwich, but the personnel changed fairly frequently. In 1537 four brewers paid the tax on beer: Edward Parker, John Pyham, Stephen at Wood and Oliver Stromble.[149] Two of them were also involved in making malt; Stephen at Wood and Edward Parker had their own malt-houses and, as in the case of William Giles, brewing was just one of their occupations. For example, Parker, who became a freeman by redemption in 1522,[150] was called a 'shereman' in 1532,[151] and was not described as a brewer until 1538,[152] when he and Stephen at Wood had special conduits constructed to provide themselves with their own water supplies.[153] He may also have been a grazier, for he was the lessee of Castelmead,[154] and his leasing of various vacant plots suggests that he may have had interests in property development. When he died in 1559 he had a large establishment with five male servants, a brew-house and malt-house and at least three other messuages with gardens.[155] Stephen at Wood owned a brewery by Fisher Gate, where his heir, Thomas, taking over from his father, leased the little dock in front of the gate (known as Joyses dock), perhaps to help to transport his beer by water.[156] Stephen Wood and John Pyham were jurats, and the latter was assessed on 50 marks in goods in 1513. He had inherited from his father a 'great house' in the High Street, which he in turn bequeathed to his own son John when he died in 1540.[157] Finally, Oliver Stromble was another brewer-entrepreneur. He was born in Flanders but had arrived in Sandwich by 1514, where he first worked as a haberdasher. He married an English woman, Agnes Saunder, through whom he acquired a property near Pillory Gate, on the north side of Strand Street.[158] In 1525 he was assessed as an alien worth £10, but by 1533 he was a denizen, made so by royal grant on paying 20s.[159] By 1538 he was a brewer and in debt to Hans Bleke, a brewer in Southwark, paying the debt from the rent from his tenement in Strand Street.[160] In 1546, when he and Agnes had become residents of St Bartholomew's hospital, they sold the Pillory Gate property to a Sandwich merchant.[161]

10.3.3 Retailers of food and drink in inns, taverns and alehouses

In the mid-sixteenth century there were at least thirty-one innkeepers, taverners and tipplers in Sandwich.[162]

Inns provided drink, food, accommodation, stabling for horses and occasionally entertainments such as plays. The owners, whether the town itself or a private individual, had often acquired the inn as an investment, and leased it out. Taverns resembled inns in serving wine, ale and beer, but did not always have lodgings prior to the middle of the sixteenth century. Both institutions catered for the middle orders of society. Alehouses sold only bread and beer, and were mainly frequented by poorer people.[163]

The Bull Inn (House 79), on the south side of Strand Street in St Peter's parish, is the only medieval inn to have survived in Sandwich, and this only in part. Its date and location are discussed in detail elsewhere (Chaps 12.8.1, 14.2). During the sixteenth century it was owned by a number of wealthy landlords, including Vincent Engeham, and leased with 4 acres (1.6ha) of land outside the town at Puttocks Down, which presumably served to pasture horses or provide hay for them.[164] Other inns are known only from documents, for example The Bell, probably on the west side of Love Lane, The Star in the Cornmarket (House 9) and, from 1502, The Hart and Swan at the junction of Love Lane and King Street. The earliest known tavern, referred to in fifteenth-century documents, is The Black Tavern, the abutments of which suggest that it was the present 27 Strand Street (House 82), where there is a fourteenth-century vaulted cellar.[165] In the 1460s and possibly later this seems to have been owned by the town.[166] In 1493 there was at least one other tavern in the town, the 'new tavern' owned by Thomas Aldy.[167]

There are no documentary references to specific alehouses in Sandwich, although the number of 'tipplers' who ran them, recorded in the 1520s and later, suggests that there were, as was generally the case, more alehouses than either inns or taverns.[168] The tipplers' trade seems to have been strictly regulated by the mayor and jurats. In December 1523, for instance, they were ordered to sell their double beer at the fixed rate, and by the 1530s they had to pay a levy to the town on the beer sold.[169] When they were required to be registered and licensed in 1541 and 1544, only four names were recorded in each of the years, and only one name (Widow Best) was the same both times. This suggests that the true total of tipplers was greater, perhaps much greater, as suggested by a reference in 1549 to fifteen men accused of selling drink out of doors, possibly as itinerants.[170]

In 1524 no man or woman was allowed to sell ale or beer in their houses, unless they were 'of good and honest conversation', and kept two good beds to lodge honest people.[171] In 1550 a list of beds available for visitors to the town shows that tipplers were the most frequent hosts, mostly offering two beds, although occasionally four. The list is incomplete, but shows that there were approximately seventy beds available in the town. Most (thirty-seven) were in St Peter's parish, with St Mary's next with twenty, and St Clement's with only thirteen. The beds are described as being in 'houses', although this term could include inns, for Robert Thomplynson, the lessee of The Bull, is recorded as having six visitors' beds in his 'house', that is, in the inn.[172]

Little is known about the tipplers themselves, but it may have been quite common for them to combine selling beer with other occupations: a baker, a saddler, a cooper, a tailor and a brewer are all mentioned. In these cases it was almost certainly the women of the household who dispensed the drink, leaving the men responsible for the other work. At least one tippler, Francis Gunsales, was a substantial landlord with several properties in the town, including the 'bere tenement' in Harnet Street.[173] He was a respected member of the community and churchwarden first of St Clement's church and later of St Peter's.[174] Although probably Spanish by birth,[175] he became a denizen before 1494–5, when he is recorded as a member of the common council. He must have been in the top 20 per cent of Sandwich society in 1513, for he then possessed goods worth £8 and kept three alien servants. In 1518 the mayor drank wine while minstrels played at Gunsales's house, which was probably the 'bere tenement' rather than his private house, since he was paid for his hospitality.[176] In the national tax assessment on aliens in 1523–5 the value of Gunsales's goods had risen to £20,[177] a reasonable sum for a solid citizen who continued to serve on the common council until 1532–3.

All three types of drinking establishments could have been places where so-called unlawful games such as dice, cards, 'tables', bowls, tennis and 'cloisshe' (probably skittles) were played. During the first half of the sixteenth century there was an increase in places of entertainment, such as bowling alleys where drink was sold and servants tempted to spend working hours, but where violence was likely to erupt.[178] The number of bowling alleys in Sandwich is unrecorded, but there was at least one as early as 1517, for in that year its proprietor was fined for an affray that had taken place in his establishment and in the same year the mayor and jurats reprimanded Richard Harlestone, a tiler, for various misdemeanours including bowling, and commanded him to desist and find work for himself and his assistant.[179] Later, in 1553, Thomas Patche bequeathed a bowling alley and garden at a messuage called the Sign of the White Hart.[180]

Regulations prohibiting these unlawful games were passed in 1551, and in 1552 all retailers of ale and beer in England were required to be licensed, with local justices of the peace being instructed to license only as many premises as they thought necessary for the area, and prospective licensees having to provide two sureties that they would maintain an orderly house with no gaming.[181] The rules, however, seem to have been enforced only rarely. In 1558 John Dale was accused of allowing two men to play unlawful games in his inn, and in 1560 John Smythe was prohibited from permitting games in his tippling house.[182] It is unlikely that these men were the only offenders.

This legislation was part of a national concern for regulation and order. The 1550s witnessed a marked increase everywhere in the number of people presented in local courts for being vagabonds and idlers.[183] This is not surprising, because these were years of bad harvests and high prices, and it is likely that both men and women had flocked into Sandwich, as into other towns, in the hope of finding employment.

10.3.4 Butchers and bakers

The meat trade, including both butchers and skinners, gave rise to reasonably well-to-do men like John Paston and John Gerard, who gained places on the common council in the mid-fifteenth century, and William Basyn, who may be identifiable in 1513 as a common councillor assessed in the top category, at more than £70 on goods.[184] Many butchers were based in The Butchery, where several of them owned property when they died; others lived and worked there, renting their shops from other butchers or from those who simply owned property in the street for income.[185] In the mid-sixteenth century some butchers leased the town grazing land on the Butts and Salts.[186]

Among the people in the second category of the 1513 assessment, who paid on goods valued between £20 and £49, was the baker Richard Holy, who provided ships' biscuits for overseas expeditions. Somewhat less wealthy were two of the seven bakers regularly fined for breaking the assize of bread: Henry Grandam or Brandam (£10), who was a member of the common council and lived in the High Street in St Clement's parish,[187] and Ralph Wigmore (£5), who leased a property in St Peter's parish near the Cornmarket, possibly from St Peter's church.[188] At the annual assize of bread between four and nine bakers were usually named, some of whom could have been widows taking over the bakery on the death of their menfolk. There is little evidence for the location of the bakeries themselves. In 1468 there was a bakehouse off the Fishmarket; in 1487 a butcher owned one in Harnet Street; and in 1557 one of the bakers had a 'common bakehouse' in the town.[189] William Wattes, baker, owned a house in Upper Strand Street (House 98) in an area that was not too densely populated,[190] but although he could have had a bakery at the back, some of the bakeries may have been outside the built-up area for fear of fire.

10.3.5 Building craftsmen

Building workers were divided between the master craftsmen, who owned their own tools and may have controlled a small workforce, and the labourers, who helped with the work and carried building materials and debris to and from the building site. Even when domestic building slowed, town projects must have needed repairs and maintenance involving carpenters, bricklayers and tilers. In towns such as York, Shrewsbury and Coventry, medieval building craftsmen, especially carpenters, seem normally to have worked by contract, mostly on repairs, and were among the poorest groups of skilled artisans,[191] and the same may have been true in Sandwich. In the fifteenth and early sixteenth centuries ordinary carpenters in the southeast, including in Sandwich, were normally paid 6d. a day, while master craftsmen could earn somewhat more.[192] In the 1440s and 1450s men such as the tiler Stephen Whyte, who rented a house in St Mary's churchyard for 1s. 4d. per annum, and Peter Colyn, carpenter, who paid St John's hospital 2s. 4d. per annum for a tenement in the High Street, were clearly not particularly wealthy and were probably typical of their trades.

On the other hand, from the late fifteenth century onwards some building craftsmen appear to have prospered. In 1475 Ralph Taylor, carpenter, bequeathed four properties, including two in the Fishmarket, as well as land in Folkestone.[193] In 1495 Thomas Paris, a carpenter, owned two properties.[194] Much later, in 1547, Eustace Ingram, carpenter, left two houses; the one in the Cornmarket he bequeathed to Thomas Burden or Burton, another carpenter who himself left more than one property in 1552, including a house to one of his apprentices.[195] The tiler Richard Harlestone had five tenanted houses in the High Street to bequeath in 1550.[196] The number of tenements owned by these craftsmen places them alongside the more usual owners of multiple properties, who were merchants, drapers, brewers and butchers. This suggests that by the late fifteenth century some building craftsmen may have been engaged in speculative building.

10.3.6 Other occupations

The tax assessment of 1471 is one of the few pieces of evidence for the livelihoods of inhabitants further down the social scale. In a small number of cases crafts or trades were mentioned, perhaps to distinguish people with similar names. Only two occupations are recorded in the parish of St Clement – a seaman and a pinner. In the other parishes about thirty different occupations are mentioned, fairly evenly distributed, but some that are known from other sources are lacking.[197] There is, for example, no mention of taverners, innkeepers, fishermen or carpenters. Some of these people were probably among those unidentified by their work, but others may have been omitted from the list because they were not householders, but simply rented their homes. While the list included a number of wealthy inhabitants assessed at more than 13s. 4d., only a very few tradesmen were in this class.

Ownership of property that was either sold and recorded in the town year books or bequeathed at death is among the few other ways in which tradesmen and craftsmen can be identified in the surviving documents. In the 1480s there were two men called John Broke. One was a tallow chandler in St Clement's parish, the other a cordwainer in St Peter's. Both were members of the common council and, judging by the wills that seem to relate to them, both owned property in the town. Although they were freemen and perhaps even served as jurats, none of the Botelers who were drapers in the mid- and later fifteenth century became mayor, suggesting that it was hard for tradesmen, however wealthy, to make that final transition. The reason we know about the family is because of their property dealings or those of their neighbours. Only a few other people carrying on common occupations in the town in the late fifteenth century had property to bequeath, and therefore not many are represented in the documents. Those that did included mariners (three), weavers (two), a carpenter, a baker, a capper, a cooper and a husbandman.

Mariners seldom appear in the documents except in relation to legal or regulatory matters. Several were prosecuted for affray, but few were recorded either owning or leasing property. Other tradesmen who seldom appear in property transactions were tailors, weavers, glovers, coopers, fullers, shipwrights and barbers (who sometimes included surgeons). If they worked from home, or rented separate work premises privately, the likelihood of them appearing in the records is slim. In the fifteenth and sixteenth centuries a number of smiths were recorded in the town, and there is a conspicuous group who took out leases on town shops in the Cornmarket.[198] The fact that one recurring lease was for the 'long rents of the smythes', and that the surviving No Name Shop (House 66) on the corner of the Cornmarket was probably a smithy containing four shops (Chap. 12.8.2), suggests that several smiths may have been sub-tenants of the few whose names appear in the documents.

In the fifteenth century national surveys of aliens identify some of the trades that they followed. A total of 190 foreigners lived in Sandwich in 1439–40, and in addition to the Italian factors (Chap. 9.2.2) there were fifteen married couples from the Low Countries. The occupations of these aliens were rarely given, but there are references to a baker, carpenter, mariner, stole maker and two beer brewers.[199] In some instances these newcomers may have provided new and necessary skills, but they could also have been competing with existing inhabitants for work and their numbers seem to have declined as the century progressed. By 1455–6 there were sixteen and in 1483 only seven alien householders, with a potter and a tailor identified at the latter date.[200] By the time of the local assessment of 1513 the number of possible alien householders had risen again to twenty-one.

Some occupations were recorded only infrequently, suggesting that the trade was perhaps carried on by one person at a time. Goldsmiths, for example, were rarely mentioned. John Sprynget was an alien goldsmith who became a denizen in the 1480s, William Goldsmyth rented a shop in the Cornmarket in the 1530s, and Job Pyerson, goldsmith, operated in the 1550s, but between these dates there is no mention of goldsmiths in the town, although there may always have been at least one.[201]

In many occupations the standard of living experienced by families would have depended in part on what contributions were made by wives and children, and what other sources of employment the family had. Until the late fifteenth century women, often recorded by their own names, clearly played an important economic role, but thereafter they were either squeezed out through the rise of new male-dominated trades or their contributions were hidden by the recording of the male head of household alone.[202] In Sandwich this was especially true in the tippling trade right through the period under discussion. Meanwhile, many women almost certainly worked on spinning for the Kent cloth industry, as is known to have happened in the late sixteenth century (Chap. 15.2). In addition, men, with their families, might be lured away to the harvest fields in the summer months if the wages were higher, as happened in Dover.[203]

10.3.7 The less wealthy

It is much more difficult to find details of less wealthy people. When overseas trade was buoyant there must have been plenty of work for porters and other labourers on the quayside, and at all dates the town council required men to work on their properties. But details of the individuals concerned were not recorded. Only a few of the 42 per cent whose goods were valued at under £4 in the assessment of 1513 (Table 10.2), or who were assessed on wages alone, can be identified in other documents. Marmaduke Stringer (£3 goods) was the lessee of the town's weigh house for several years, and Henry Hendon (£2 goods) had leased the town watermill in 1512.[204] It is not clear whether they profited or lost from such activity. Thomas Hochyn (£2 goods) died in 1525 owning a house in St Peter's parish and several pieces of land in the countryside, but his occupation is unknown.[205] A couple of cobblers are identifiable: Richard Archer is named as a cobbler (£1 wages), and William Jenkyn (£1 wages) may have been the cobbler who was later involved in a property dispute in The Butchery.[206] Several people assessed between £1 and £2 on goods or wages can be associated with St Clement's parish. They were probably mariners, but this cannot be proved except in the case of John Bonate or Bonatie (£1 wages), a shipmaster whose boat, with five sailors, was one of those used by the town to carry Henry VIII and his entourage to Calais in 1520.[207] Two hundred people in 1513 were assessed on wages as servants (34 per cent of those taxed), and nothing is known about them, or about the fifteen paupers.

10.4 Conclusion

During the 200 years covered in this chapter Sandwich fell from being a town of national importance to one that was of only regional significance. The population, ravaged as it was everywhere by the events of the mid-fourteenth century, seems to have made some recovery in the fifteenth, but then slowly and inexorably declined to an all-time low in 1560, when there were probably fewer than 300 households. It is not known which occupations suffered most in this drop, but the fact that thirty-one victuallers are recorded in the middle of the century suggests that this section of trade remained buoyant, perhaps at the expense of manufacturing.

During the fifteenth century the administration of the town developed; civic property and responsibilities increased; and concerns for the welfare of the citizens were manifested. But by the early sixteenth century the demands of a needy king and the economic decline of the port seem to have led to tensions and trouble between royal authority and the local elite, and between the elite and those whom they governed.

While a good deal of information is available about individuals, occupations and property in the town, it is less easy to see long-term overall trends. At the start of the period a single wealthy vintner dominated the scene with his political appointments and local philanthropy. Others at this time may have been of the same kind, but we know little about them. As time went on fewer really wealthy merchants found it worth their while to be based in Sandwich, and their places as mayors and jurats were taken by somewhat less wealthy and well-connected general merchants. Brewers and maltsters did well, but even they diversified their interests to improve their incomes, notably by acquiring property in the town and estates in the surrounding countryside. By the early sixteenth century local landowning gentry with no obvious urban backgrounds were investing in Sandwich property, becoming its Members of Parliament and playing their part in local governance. Below the level of the governing classes, there is a certain amount of information about less well-to-do traders, artisans and craftsmen, but the absence of rentals, the scarcity of local assessments and the omission of Sandwich from the lay subsidies of the early sixteenth century make it hard to identify changing trends. By the end of the period, however, there is plenty of evidence for the effects of the town's decline upon its less fortunate inhabitants.

11 War, rebellion and defence

11.1 War and civil unrest

The walls and ramparts of Sandwich are a significant feature of its topography, surrounding the heart of the town even today, with the area inside being quite distinct from the much later development outside the walls (Frontispiece). Although many of their visible features appear to date only from the late fifteenth century, they were part of the response to the troubled situation experienced by the town during the preceding two hundred years when Sandwich Haven and the town played a role, sometimes a significant one, in national affairs. Although the town itself was affected by war only during the brief French raid of 1457, and there is little surviving evidence for fortifications until the second half of the century, the economic and therefore social consequences of war played a significant part in the reactions of the inhabitants to the external developments during these two centuries.

11.1.1 The end of the Hundred Years War

During the latter part of the Hundred Years War Sandwich remained the location where troops, provisions and equipment for the war effort were assembled and from which supplies were sent to France. As discussed in Chapter 9, this formed a fundamental part of the port's overseas trade and its general economy. The castle, the administrative centre, was kept in good repair, and supplies, especially live animals, were gathered at Sandwich and corralled in Castelmead before embarkation. Ships were commandeered and brought to the port to become part of the war fleet. Orders to fortify the town or mend the defences were issued from time to time, one of them in 1435 specifying that those going to sea should erect scaffolding on their quays for defence against the enemy – presumably aimed at merchants living in the central section of the waterfront where there were no permanent defences.[1] But despite these sporadic references and the fact that the traffic to the haven must have brought trade and jobs into the town, the effect on town life is hard to trace in the documents consulted.

By the second quarter of the fifteenth century things had begun to change. The defeats that marked the ending of the war had serious economic repercussions, and the south-east of England was particularly adversely affected. The loss of a formerly friendly Normandy coast discouraged trade; royal purveyors seized, but did not pay for, livestock and grain; and disbanded soldiers roamed the lanes of Kent. Complaints about the mismanagement of affairs and the need to replace existing councillors were widespread, and in January 1450 the bishop of Chichester, Adam Moleyns, who had been sent to negotiate with angry troops, was lynched in Portsmouth. The same month a group of rebels gathered in the countryside between Sandwich and Dover and presented a list of the national figures they wanted to see beheaded and the valuables they wanted taken from religious houses.[2]

11.1.2 Cade's rebellion

The Duke of Suffolk became a catalyst for the various streams of discontent. He was accused of treachery, embezzlement, perversion of justice and of plotting with the French to invade England. After his death at the beginning of May 1450, a rumour grew that the king planned to take retribution by turning Kent into a wild forest. By the second half of May open rebellion had erupted, and by June the various risings had become organised under the leadership of John Cade. Manifestos compiled by the insurgents included complaints against abuses carried out by county officials such as the sheriff and the keeper of the Maidstone gaol, plus the seizures of purveyors and the enforcement of the statute of labourers.[3] Continued fear of French attack discouraged strong support from coastal communities, but towns such as Lydd, Rye and Romney are known to have sent lookouts to report back on the progress of the rebels, and Sandwich may have followed suit. The threat to the authorities was too great to be ignored and in July negotiations began. A general pardon was offered to Cade and his supporters, following which, and despite Cade's capture and execution, the steam ran out of the rebellion.[4]

Among those seeking pardons were fourteen from Sandwich.[5] They were men whose fortunes were clearly on the rise, although they had not yet played an important role in urban government. They included John Paston, a butcher involved in the Calais trade, who was shortly to be voted on to the newly established common council, and John Drury, reputedly an esquire, although never named as such in Sandwich documents, who was subsequently to become mayor. It is not known whether they had in fact actively participated in the rebellion or whether they simply wanted to take advantage of the free retrospective pardon for any earlier misdeeds. Unrest, however, continued in the south-east. In May 1451 a Sandwich weaver tried to raise the population of Sturry, Wingham, Canterbury and Sarre against the king, and further uncoordinated rebel uprisings clamouring for Cade's demands to be implemented continued until 1456.[6] This may have contributed to the decision by the mayor and jurats of Sandwich to establish a common council, thereby giving the people a greater say in the governance of the town (Chap. 10.1.1).

11.1.3 The French attack of 1457

In 1457 Sandwich was almost certainly affected by the outbreak of the epidemic disease that affected the Christ Church Priory monks so badly, and it may have been partly this that meant the town was not in a position to defend itself when the French attacked that year. According to the *Recueil des Chroniques d'Engelterre* of Jehan de Waurin, on 27 August a French expedition of two naval forces set out from Honfleur.[7] They landed near Sandwich, overwhelmed a newly built fort defended by a water-filled moat – perhaps the Bulwark, which was begun in 1451 – and made terms with several ships in the haven. Before attacking the town proper, the commander of the French forces ordered his men, 'sur paine de mort', to refrain from setting fire to it, damaging the churches, raping the women or killing in cold blood. They then moved in on Sandwich, on foot and by ship. There was heavy fighting, with the English valiantly defending all quarters of the town and, particularly, the gates. The number of dead persuaded the French to retreat after ten hours, but not before they had looted the town, against which there had been no prohibition. The English *Hall's Chronicle*, first published in 1548, played down the amount of loot, saying that the French authors made much of a little, 'and yet their much is in effect nothing at all'. He also emphasised that the raid was encouraged by the 'domesticall diuision and ciuile dissencion' then rife in England, and the fact that the 'chefe rulers of the towne' had deserted Sandwich as a result of 'pestilenciall plage'.[8] There is nothing of this in the contemporary French version, but the French would have known little of local circumstances, including the unrest and disease then prevalent in Kent.

How much damage and loss occurred is not clear. It has been suggested that this was the cause of the almost complete loss of medieval buildings in the outer parts of the town.[9] But since the French were only in Sandwich for ten hours, much of it involved in heavy fighting, and were explicitly forbidden to damage the churches or set fire to the town, it is unlikely that they did a great deal of structural damage. Less might have been made of the incident locally if it had not resulted in the death of the mayor, John Drury. Nonetheless, the shock to the English generally at the audacity of the attack was pronounced, and had the effect of making the royal court return to London from the Midlands, where it had been for the past year.[10]

In Sandwich itself there were certainly marked effects. Trade was disrupted; the number of boats mooring in the haven and income from the tolls both dropped (Chaps 9.2.2, 9.2.5); and property transactions in the town virtually ceased for a couple of years. In 1461 the need to repair the defences was recognised by a royal grant of £100 a year from the revenues of the customs and subsidies to the mayor and jurats, provided that they themselves contributed £20 towards the work.[11] This was changed in 1464–5 when the £20 proviso was kept, but the £100 grant was replaced by the town being allowed to ship forty sacks of wool to Italy without paying customs and subsidies. The money to be acquired in this way was to be spent on the walls and fortifications, and the entrance to the port.[12]

11.1.4 Sandwich and the Wars of the Roses

Not long after the French attack, Sandwich had a small part to play in the Wars of the Roses. Following the Lancastrian success at Ludlow in 1459, the chief supporters of Richard, Duke of York – his son Edward, Earl of March, and the earls of Salisbury and Warwick – escaped to Calais. The sheriff of Kent, Lord Rivers, therefore assembled a considerable fleet at Sandwich, with the aim of attacking Calais. Warwick, however, was well aware of all the preparations being made in the port, and when Rivers was all but ready to sail, the Yorkists made a swift and daring counter-attack. Between four and five in the morning one day in January 1460 a band of men landed and took possession of Sandwich. 'The surprise was so complete that Lord Rivers, his wife and his son were seized in their beds.' They were carried off to Calais and all the ships of the fleet, full of men and stores, were also borne off as booty.[13]

In June 1460 William, Lord Fauconberg, bastard son of William Neville, Earl of Kent, who had stayed behind at Sandwich, was joined there by the earls of Salisbury and Warwick, with a force of some 1,500 to 2,000 men. They quickly won the support of Lord Cobham and a large number of Kentishmen and, joined at Canterbury by Sir John Scott and others, they moved to London where some of the leading aldermen still supported the king. But by July the resistance had crumbled and the citizens allowed the retinues of the earls to enter the city; ultimately, Henry VI's remaining supporters were captured, and hanged, drawn and quartered. In March 1461 ordinary Londoners joined the earls' retinue, thus giving Edward popular support for his seizure of the crown,[14] and the following year, as Edward IV, he made a leisurely progress through southern towns, visiting Canterbury and Sandwich among others.[15]

When Warwick rebelled ten years later, forcing Edward to flee the country, Lord Fauconberg joined him and had much support in Kent. The Earl of Arundel, however, had been made constable of the Cinque Ports with Sir John Scott as his lieutenant, and Edward was able to rely on their loyalty and return to England, where, in April 1471, he won a significant victory at Barnet during which Warwick was slain. Fauconberg, however, continued his rebellion, finding a ready ally in Nicholas Faunt, mayor of Canterbury. Having assembled a 'formidable mob' made up primarily of men from Kent and the Cinque Ports, he marched on London. Although the populace was inclined to admit him, the Yorkist elite strongly defended the city, and after he had learned of the defeat and death of the former Henry VI at Tewkesbury on 4 May, Fauconberg retreated to Sandwich, where the Calais soldiers and sailors who had come with him returned across the Channel. Later, after Edward had returned to London in triumph, Fauconberg submitted. In June 1471, on account of their 'grete assemblees and insurrections', Sandwich lost all its privileges and was briefly taken into royal hands.[16] When their liberties were restored the following February, the populace met in St Clement's church to elect a mayor 'as of old time used and accustomed'.[17]

Sandwich was the gathering point for a final expedition to France in June 1475 when 11,000 men assembled, led by Edward IV. They took three weeks to embark, but the expedition ended in negotiation and the army returned without fighting.[18]

11.2 The defences

The Hundred Years War was probably the spur to the development of Sandwich's defences. The line of the earth ramparts around the landward side of the town seem already to have been determined by the early decades of the fourteenth century (Chap. 5.6.2), but the stone walls along its waterfront were later additions (Fig. IV.1). Records of murage grants and other information mainly from the town year books and treasurers' accounts show considerable expenditure on the urban defences throughout the fourteenth and fifteenth centuries, including the employment of masons and the purchase of building stone, some of which was for the town walls. Although the earth ramparts were neither replaced by nor supplemented with masonry, they were probably increased in volume and must have been considered sufficient for their purpose. Gates are not mentioned until the middle of the fifteenth century, by which time brick was supplementing or even supplanting stone as the favoured material, but gates onto the quayside had been a feature from at least 1300 (Chap. 5.6.2). The gates through the rampart could also have had an earlier origin, but even if this were so, they reached their apogee in the second half of the fifteenth century.

The royal castle in Castelmead remained a significant presence, for it stood where it could dominate Sandwich Haven and provide a focus for the troops who gathered there before embarking on the vessels that were to take them to France. It was, however, unusual in that it was cut off from the town by Mill Wall and is never recorded as having seen any action, not even on the day in August 1457 when the sole French attack on Sandwich took place.

11.2.1 The town walls

Although it is seldom acknowledged, the surviving town walls of Sandwich are one of the most complete defensive circuits of any English medieval town, with more than two thirds of the length being made up of earth ramparts that have survived virtually complete to the present day. There were other towns that were encircled by non-masonry walls but, with a few exceptions, the latter have usually been destroyed.[19] Tonbridge is one example of partially surviving earth ramparts, although in a poor condition.[20] Others include King's Lynn, which is also similar to Sandwich in having adjacent stretches of stone walls and earth ramparts, the latter partly following the line of pre-urban sea banks.[21]

At Sandwich, neither the earth ramparts nor the masonry walls display features that can be closely dated, but the recorded grants of murage suggest building campaigns between 1321 and 1483.[22] The potential pitfalls in using murage grants as purely chronological markers have already been pointed out (Chap. 5.6.2), but the grants remain useful as pointers to periods of construction when the surviving walls provide very little dating evidence. They can also be used with the town records to discover methods of construction, building materials and details of design that have not survived the centuries. Unfortunately, none of the surviving documentation is easy to interpret. Questions remain about building chronology, and also about the position of the stone walls in relation to the waterfront, particularly along the town quay in the east (Chap. 14.1).

11.2.1.1 The ramparts

The ramparts, which defined medieval Sandwich's landward boundary, were in place before 1360, but were clearly modified during the later fourteenth and fifteenth centuries (Chap. 5.6.2). They appear today as flat-topped earth banks along which nineteenth-century metalled paths enable virtually the whole of the circuit of approximately 1.25km to be perambulated (Figs 11.1, 11.2), with four gaps where roads run into Sandwich from its hinterland. By the fifteenth century these had been filled by gates, all of which were demolished in the late eighteenth century. The wet moat that flanks the landward side has also been modified over the years, mainly by partial infilling and subsequent clearance, most recently in 2004 when the stretches in front of The Butts and The Rope Walk were cleaned.[23] Boys's map suggests that the moat consisted of separate sections, each stopping short of the gaps so that when the gates were built only one needed to have a bridge. That exception was Sandown Gate,[24] where the moat on its east face probably resulted from modifications connected with the construction of the Bulwark in the 1450s (Section 11.2.1.2; Fig. 11.3).

The only truly informative evidence for how the ramparts were built comes from an archaeological excavation on the berm between The Rope Walk and the moat (Site 58).[25] Alluvial clay was heaped on a foundation made of rammed chalk, pebble and flint, but there was no sign of a stone or timber superstructure, although documents suggest that in 1490 the earth wall near New Gate, a little to the east

Fig. 11.1: The Rope Walk from west, with wet moat and berm to the left (K. P.)

Fig. 11.2: Mill Wall from south showing steep slope down to dry moat on east (P. W. © English Heritage DP068599)

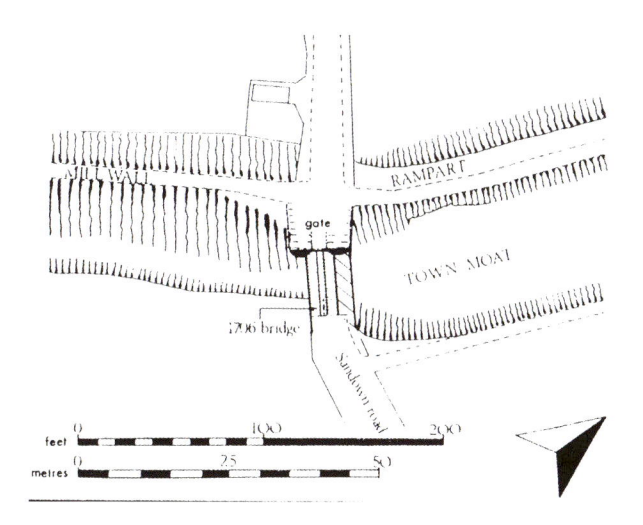

Fig. 11.3: Plan of Sandown Gate showing its connection with the moat (Tatton-Brown 1978, fig. 3)

of the excavation, was surmounted by a jettied, timber palisade.[26] Some fifteenth-century potsherds were taken to indicate the date of construction, but the build-up may rather have been a modification of the earlier structure. The profile of Mill Wall today shows that it is very different from The Rope Walk and The Butts, with an uninterrupted, steep slope running from the top of the rampart to the bottom of the ditch (Figs 5.2, 11.2). Its present condition gives no clue to the method of its construction, but observation of a shallow cable trench cut between Knightrider Street and Sandown Road showed that at least the upper part of the rampart consisted of dumps of clay, with no sign of masonry or any other superstructure (Site 71). Building it may have entailed remodelling the castle defences, because its ditch clipped the west edge of the castle ditch (Chap. 5.6.1; Fig. 5.1).

All four gates through the ramparts were demolished in the late eighteenth century, the only visible remains today being a few courses of brick from the east face of the south tower of Sandown Gate (Fig. 11.4). Some stonework from the north tower of Canterbury Gate exposed in 1929 is no longer visible.[27] Otherwise, records in the town year books and treasurers' accounts are the main sources for the history of all the gates. They give much valuable information about the structures after the middle of the fifteenth century, but because the year books do not begin before 1432 and the accounts do not survive before 1454,[28] they are of no help in determining dates of first construction, especially since the gates appear to have been well established by the time they are first mentioned in 1456 (Sandown Gate and New Gate) and 1468 (Canterbury Gate and Woodnesborough Gate).[29] Comparisons elsewhere in England and Wales show that most town gates were begun in the late thirteenth or fourteenth centuries.[30] In Sandwich, the gates along the waterfront date from at least the early fourteenth century (Chap. 5.6.2), but there is no early evidence for those through the ramparts other than the approximately dated potsherds from Canterbury Gate. The number and disparate nature of the references suggest that the gates were built at different dates, and subsequently repaired or modified in a piecemeal fashion, as and when necessary. There is no indication of an overall plan by the urban authorities for either their construction or their maintenance.

Sandown Gate guarded access to the town from the east, and may have been the gate most under threat from outside forces during the Hundred Years War. The first reference to it is in 1456, when a drawbridge was to be 'new made in all haste possible'; it was then repaired in 1459, perhaps after damage during the French raid of 1457.[31] In addition, the extensive repairs necessary in 1481 suggest that the gate may have been fairly old by then, and in 1491 it must have been irreparable, for money was collected to build it anew.[32] Archaeological excavations in 1978 and c.1980 (Site 36) revealed remains of its two towers, both of brick (Fig. 11.3).[33] There was no convincing dating evidence, however, although a date of sometime in the 1490s was suggested when the first excavation was published.[34] That dating, based on the size of bricks, is less than certain, for according to the written records, the late fifteenth-century gate was of stone. The bricks found during the excavations are more likely to date from 1538, when masons worked on the gate, using stone and brick, which they covered with rough mortar.[35] The exposed remains of the south tower suggest this, for they consist of a few courses of buff-yellow bricks with external mortar (Fig. 11.4).[36] Whatever the date, the excavated features are unlikely to have any connection with the first build of Sandown Gate.

Figure 11.5 shows a plan of the gateway reconstructed from the excavation drawings of 1978,[37] and a survey in 2006 of the visible remains. A central passageway is flanked by round-fronted towers

Fig. 11.4: Sandown Gate, exposed brickwork of its south-west tower (P. W. © English Heritage DP068600)

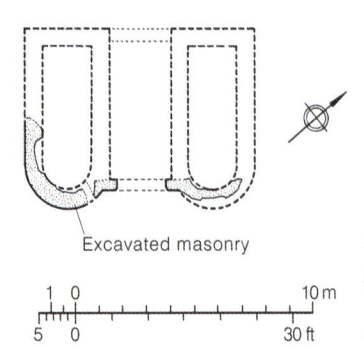

Fig. 11.5: Reconstructed plan of the excavated Sandown Gate (B. C. and A. T. A.)

Fig. 11.6: Watercolour of Sandown Gate in the early eighteenth century (Sandwich Guildhall; P. W. © English Heritage DP068611)

Fig. 11.7: Sandown Gate in the 1780s, illustrated in Boys 1792 (P. W. © English Heritage DP068586)

that project forward into the moat to the east. The position of the buried rear wall is uncertain and its location has been estimated using the tiny outline on Boys's town map and a photograph taken during the 1980s investigation.[38] Of the two eighteenth-century depictions of the gate a few years before demolition, that published by Boys in 1792 seems to show greater similarity to the reconstructed plan, although the elevation, with its curved battlements, is suspect (Figs 11.6, 11 7).

For many centuries, the main approach to Sandwich from the west (the causeway from Ash mentioned in the custumal of 1301) must have been dominated by Canterbury Gate; it was demolished in 1785.[39] The only known physical evidence of the gate is a semicircle of well-shaped, probably ragstone, blocks forming what appears to be the footing of a tower approximately 4m in diameter, revealed by road works in 1929 (Site 70; Fig. 11.8). Like the other gates through the ramparts, the date when Canterbury Gate was built is open to doubt. It was clearly a well-known landmark when first mentioned in 1468, but there is no indication of its origins. Nor are there any references to its appearance or the building materials used in its construction or repair, although some stones from it may have been preserved. They include a few blocks of Caen stone built into the garden wall of 84 Strand Street, and a possible socketed pivot stone for a door jamb, now housed at the White Mill, some 0.5km west of the site of the gate. Other evidence includes two illustrations: an oil painting of Queen Catherine of Braganza's entry into Sandwich in 1672, now in Sandwich Guildhall, and, more informatively, an engraving published by Boys in 1792 (Fig. 11.9). The latter shows the west face of the gate with two drum towers, each with a facing

of regular stone blocks and a string course roughly two thirds of the way up, above which there is a keyhole-shaped gun loop. The towers are separated by a wall pierced by a pointed archway and surmounted by a row of corbels for machicolations. It is impossible to know how accurate this depiction is (that of Sandown Gate appears to be only partly so), but if it is anything like the original, the closest local surviving parallel is the much larger West Gate in Canterbury, which was built *c*.1370–90 (Figs 11.10, 11.11).[40] This may have been the model followed at Sandwich, probably sometime during the first half of the fifteenth century.[41] That the West Gate was regarded as a template is shown by the excavated St George's Gate, Canterbury, which was built to the same plan as the former, but in 1485.[42]

Information about New Gate and Woodnesborough Gate is confined to documentary sources and illustrations. The name New Gate seems a misnomer, for the gate may have been no newer than the other gates

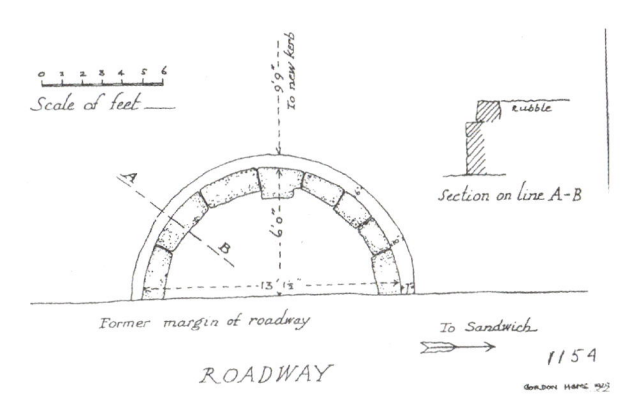

Fig. 11.8: North roundel of Canterbury Gate, Sandwich, observed in 1929 (Clapham 1930, fig. 19)

Fig. 11.9: Canterbury Gate from the north-west, illustrated in Boys 1792 (P. W. © English Heritage DP068589)

Fig. 11.10: West Gate, Canterbury, from the west (S. P.)

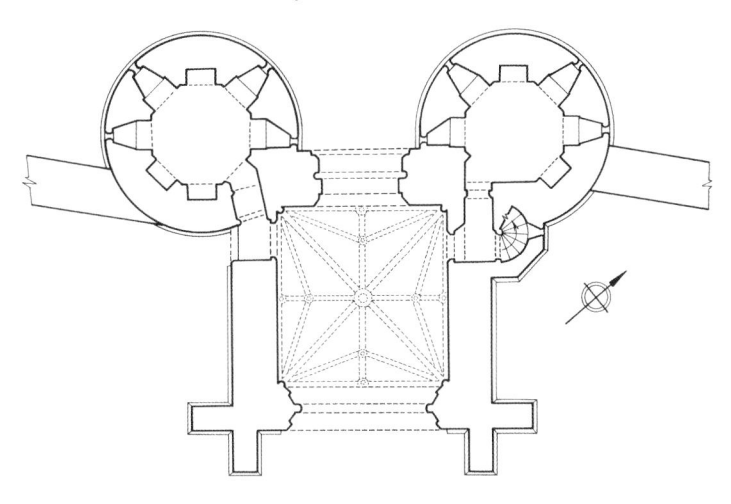

West Gate, Canterbury

Canterbury Gate, Sandwich

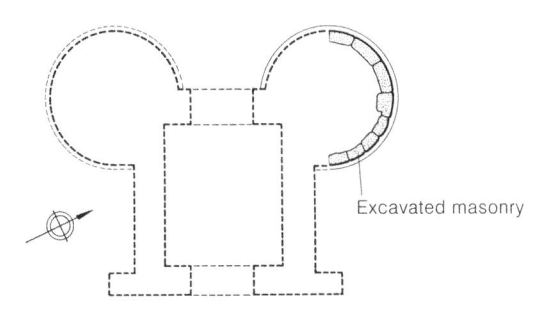

Excavated masonry

St George's Gate, Canterbury

Excavated masonry

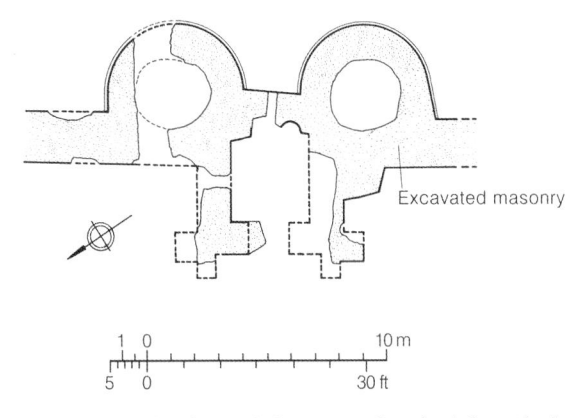

Fig. 11.11: Plan of the Canterbury Gate, Sandwich, observed during roadworks (after Clapham 1930, fig. 19), compared with the ground-floor plan of the surviving Canterbury West Gate (after Frere, Stow and Bennett 1982, fig. 53), and the excavated Canterbury St George's Gate (after Bennett and Houliston 1989, p. 18) (B. C. and A. T. A.)

through the ramparts, and had certainly been begun before its first mention in 1456, when the mayor and jurats decided that it should be completed.[43] In 1459 its custodian was responsible for keeping it wind and watertight,[44] but since it needed the same attention again only eight years later,[45] it may have been less solidly built than Sandown and Canterbury gates, perhaps a reflection of its situation in a position that was not so exposed to potential attack. Its main function may have been to guard and maintain the Delf, Sandwich's medieval water supply (Chap. 14.10). Woodnesborough Gate seems to have played a similar role, not for the Delf but for a conduit carrying water from a spring in Woodnesborough village into Sandwich town through the gateway.[46] Records of repairs shortly after its first mention in 1468 suggest

Fig. 11.12: The town side of Woodnesborough Gate, illustrated in Boys 1792 (P. W. © English Heritage DP068588)

that the gate was a timber structure until 1490, when it was rebuilt in stone, brick and tile, and adorned with battlements and paint.[47] The only illustration is the engraving in Boys (Fig. 11.12), which seems to show rectangular towers with a partial stone or brick facing and diaper brickwork of possibly sixteenth-century date. This may have been the gate erected in brick in 1575 to replace the one built in 1490, which was then too dilapidated to be repaired.[48]

11.2.1.2 The Bulwark

The north-east corner of the town is defined by a structure that appears to be a modification of the earth rampart, and which was an artillery fortification made predominantly of earth and timber in 1451.[49] When first mentioned it was called the 'new wall', but it soon became known as the 'Bulwark', a name that seems generally to have been somewhat loosely applied to a variety of defensive structures but which in this chapter is used only for the fort at the north-east corner of the town.[50] Today Sandwich's Bulwark consists of two lengths of earth rampart forming an L-shape, with an 80-degree angle at the junction effectively forming a pointed bastion. Potential information about the area on the west side of the ramparts has been obliterated by twentieth-century landscaping, but early maps suggest that it was originally bounded by walls or ditches that created an almost square enclosure with an entrance at its south-west corner, to which the present course of Sandown Road appears to be heading.

The ramparts making up the corner are predominantly of earth but differ from those around the rest of the town in that they are revetted in masonry in places, partly with yellow-buff bricks (Fig. 11.13).[51] A little further south, towards Sandown Road, a previously unrecorded blocked arch fronts the rampart (Fig. 11.14). It also is built of yellow-buff bricks of similar size. No detailed archaeological examination has been possible, so the origin, date and purpose of neither the revetment nor the arch are certain. They may have been constructed in 1545 when the side of the moat beside the bulwark was 'muryd up', presumably meaning that it was revetted with stone or brick, or both.[52]

In 1451 the Bulwark was described as a wall for guns, but by 1465 it must have been taking on the semblance of a fort behind the rampart, for its foundations were stabilised with piles and it had a timber roof.[53] More work was undertaken in 1469 when piles were sunk for foundations, scaffolding was erected for completing a tiled upper storey and a bridge was built, perhaps to connect what must have been a free-standing building to the rampart.[54] The bridge is unlikely to have led from the Bulwark to the town because there is no evidence that there was a moat on its townward side. By 1478 the fort was defended by guns, which were sited to

Fig. 11.13: Bricks from the east face of the Bulwark rampart (P. W. © English Heritage DP068603)

Fig. 11.14: Recently exposed brick arch on the east face of the Bulwark rampart (P. W. © English Heritage DP068602)

give protection to the quayside. Their location led to a prohibition against ships anchoring beside Fisher Gate and eastwards to the Bulwark itself, presumably the stretch of the town quay that was considered particularly vulnerable and where lines of fire had to be kept open.[55]

In 1483 the Bulwark's upper storey was used to store small arms (crossbows and bolts, spears, hand guns and gunpowder), body armour, helmets and long and round shields. Beneath it there was the arsenal, with about thirty breech-loading guns, including a 'grete gun of the speynards' brought off a Spanish ship. All were secured behind a locked door. At the entrance to the fort, perhaps in its south-west corner nearest the town, there was a great gun known as the 'murderer'.[56] Considerable sums were regularly spent on maintenance of its walls and gates, with particularly large outlays in 1519, 1532 and 1539.[57] Its armaments were also kept up to date with a substantial purchase in 1546.[58] An inventory in 1553 listed the weaponry, which included two small cannon ('port pieces'), a large calibre stone-thrower ('slang') and a considerable number of hand guns ('forlockes and bases').[59]

11.2.1.3 The stone walls[60]

The masonry walls, which are confined to the north side of the town along the south bank of the river Stour, are both shorter in length and less well preserved than the earth ramparts. Even though they are in generally poor condition, greatly damaged, repaired and rebuilt, their line can be traced for much of their length. The first documentary reference to the use of stone in the town walls was in 1386.[61] The fabric of the walls themselves contains no dating evidence to confirm this as a starting date, but it is consistent with defending the town during the Hundred Years War and also with the erection of Fisher Gate, the earliest surviving masonry gatehouse in the town. The gate still stands on the quayside and may originally have been part of a general plan for waterside defences at the end of the fourteenth century. Records of murage grants and the shipping in of stone throughout the fifteenth century suggest that there was then a lengthy campaign of wall building over a hundred years or so. No precise chronology of construction can be offered.

In the west of the town, the wall probably started at or near the bridge over the Delf east of Canterbury Gate and ran for approximately 300m along the south bank of the Delf to its confluence with the river Stour near modern Guestling Mill (Fig. IV.1). There it stopped, and despite published suggestions that it originally extended unbroken along the waterfront,[62] no traces of the wall have ever been found along the roughly 360m from the Delf mouth to Davis Gate. In 2001 an archaeological observation at the entrance to the Gazen Salts car park east of Guestling Mill (Site 9) failed to locate any signs of it, and the same was true of an earlier excavation at Aynsley Court, further east on Strand Street (Site 52).[63] Both sites were situated across what would have been the most likely course of the wall, had there been one. The absence of defences from waterfronts is not unusual in medieval river or sea ports, as evidenced by London, King's Lynn, Boston, Hull and Great Yarmouth (Figs 11.22, 11.28).[64] At Sandwich it may partly have been due to the low-lying, waterlogged nature of the ground (Figs 1.3, 1.4), but more important was probably the fact that the central section was lined with private quays interspersed with public gates, and the demands of loading and unloading vessels and storing merchandise – there may have been warehouses here – was of more pressing importance than defence. The stone wall starts again on the west side of Davis Gate (The Barbican), whence it continued eastwards for at least 225m, until it was probably interrupted by the mid-fifteenth-century Bulwark.

The most detailed information about how the stone walls at Sandwich were built has been provided by a small-scale excavation that was carried out in 1977 on what was then the boundary wall between Nos. 62 and 66 Strand Street (Site 46). Figure 11.15 is an

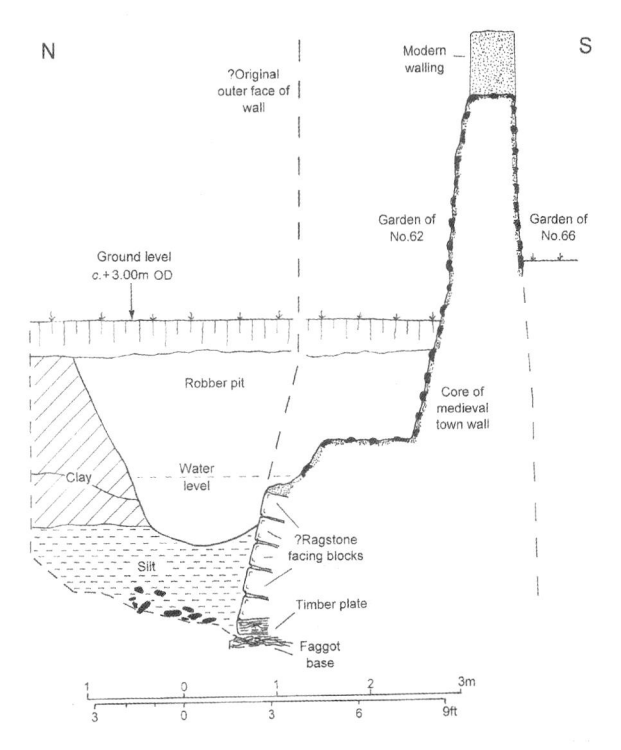

Fig. 11.15: Reinterpreted section through the town wall, now the boundary between 62 and 66 Strand Street (K. P. and B. C.).

interpretative section through the excavated wall, based on a brief published account and field notes housed in the Guildhall Archive, Sandwich.[65] Re-examination of the field notes in the light of more recent archaeological observations and investigations along the wall line (Sites 9, 49, 52) have led to a modification of the excavator's conclusions. He believed that he had discovered a stone wharf (Monkenquay) backed by the town wall. It is now clear that what he had found was not the remains of Monkenquay but the base of the town wall with its north (outer) face intact, and a part of the wall core above it. The wall rested on a wooden base plate on top of bundles of faggots placed directly on water-laid Alluvium some 3.30m below present ground level. This method of construction may have been common for the walls against the waterfront; for example, both timber and faggots were used in building and repairing the town walls in 1459 and 1517.[66] The wooden base plate in Site 46 supported five courses of large, mortared ragstone blocks forming a slightly battered front. Above these the wall seems to have been robbed of its facing and cut back to produce what now appears to be a rubble garden wall. Silt had accumulated in front of the surviving facing stones, which showed signs of having been regularly washed by tidal waters. Thus in effect the wall had been the south bank of the Delf.

More evidence for the waterside location of the wall at the western end of town was found at 76 Strand Street (Site 49). Excavation revealed the square mouth of a culvert or conduit on the north face of the wall there, at approximately 1.80m above OD. It had originally been provided with a flap that would have closed off the culvert at high tide.[67] Further signs of the culvert itself were later located south-west of the excavated site.[68] This discovery shows that tidal water came up to the north face of this stretch of the town wall during the medieval period and that high water mark was above +1.80m. In addition, the external wall face revealed in Sites 46 and 50 was comparable with excavated stretches of the town wall of Dover, where the lowest courses of ragstone were water-worn. Thus it can be assumed that, at least in some places, Sandwich's town wall ran alongside the mouth of the Delf, where, in 1485, the water was still deep enough to enable a carrack to be berthed and a dock to be built.[69] The problem that this appears to present for access to the quayside is discussed in Chapter 14.1.

The town wall in the east has been very heavily repaired, and substantial stretches removed. For example, a short stub projecting from the west tower of the Barbican seems to be integral with the mid-fifteenth-century Davis Gate (Fig. 11.21), although it may have been a buttress rather than part of the wall, but the short length now joined to the eastern tower can have been part of the gate only since 1873, when the 1:500 OS map depicted it as a detached fragment. Investigation of a sewer trench under the street just to the east of the gate (Site 67) revealed masonry that must have been from the town wall,[70] its line being perpetuated in the four fragments of rubble core that survive in the cellar of The Bell Hotel (Fig. 11.16)[71] and in the above-ground stretch extending, with interruptions, for approximately 33m from the hotel to the building now known as The Keep. Although this piece of wall is 3.40m high in places, only its lowest courses of Folkestone rag and Thanet Beds sandstone remain *in situ* (Fig. 11.17). Records in the town year books suggest that in the fifteenth century the wall stood in much the same place as it does today, but that there has been considerable land reclamation north of it since then. In 1475 and 1478 it was said to stand on the foreshore,[72] with tenements between it and Upper

Fig. 11.16: The core of the town wall in the cellar of The Bell Hotel (K. P.)

Fig. 11.17: Surviving town wall along the quay, the lowest four courses in situ (P. W. © English Heritage DP068610)

Strand Street. When the wall between Fisher Gate and the Bulwark was repaired in 1517, sharpened piles and bundles of wood were used as foundations (cf. Site 46 and Davis Gate, below), suggesting that it there stood on reclaimed ground and perhaps against the water.[73]

11.2.1.4 Surviving gates and possible boom tower

The earlier of the two surviving gates is Fisher Gate, at the north end of Quay Lane (Fig. 11.18). It consists of a rectangular tower of flint with stone dressings, the ground floor forming a passageway flanked by a stair and perhaps a guardroom (Fig. 11.19). The architectural details of its north face indicate that the gate was built in the late fourteenth century, and the groove for drawing up the portcullis between the two faces of the arch shows that the first floor was part of the original design. Two small windows in the north wall of the portcullis chamber and one in its west wall are also likely to be original. The main windows in the centre of the north and south walls, and the second storey below gable level, were added in yellowish brick in the fifteenth and sixteenth centuries. The walls in which they are set are decorated with glazed bricks in black diaper patterns, a form of decoration associated with work of the late fifteenth century. The gable itself was erected or repaired at a later date. It has tumbled brickwork, and a plaque at its apex, which, although now not easily decipherable, in 1851 read '1581 RPM'.[74]

The second surviving quayside structure is Davis Gate (Figs 11.20, 11.21), now known as the Barbican, a name not ascribed to it in the Middle Ages, although from the end of the fifteenth century there was a structure beside or attached to the gatehouse that was variously called 'barbican' or 'barbican house'.[75] In 1579 both Barbican and Davis Gate are mentioned in the same document, but it is impossible to establish whether they were alternative terms for the same place.[76] The first time that they are unequivocally the same is in 1776, when 'David's-gate, called Barbican' occurs in an antiquarian account of Kent.[77]

The present structure dates from the second half of the fifteenth century, but Davis Quay was a landmark by 1301 when it is mentioned in the custumal, and Davis Gate itself is recorded from the early fourteenth century onwards.[78] Its precise position at that date is unknown, but it stood at a strategic point, near the ferry to and from Thanet, and at the north end of the High Street, which originally led out of town towards Worth, Eastry and Dover. Neither its physical appearance nor its precise site can be established before 1467, when Davy Dyker and his workmen dug foundations and sunk piles (presumably into the foreshore at low tide) to prepare for the construction of a new Davis Gate.

Fig. 11.18: The north face of Fisher Gate (P. W. © English Heritage DP026001)

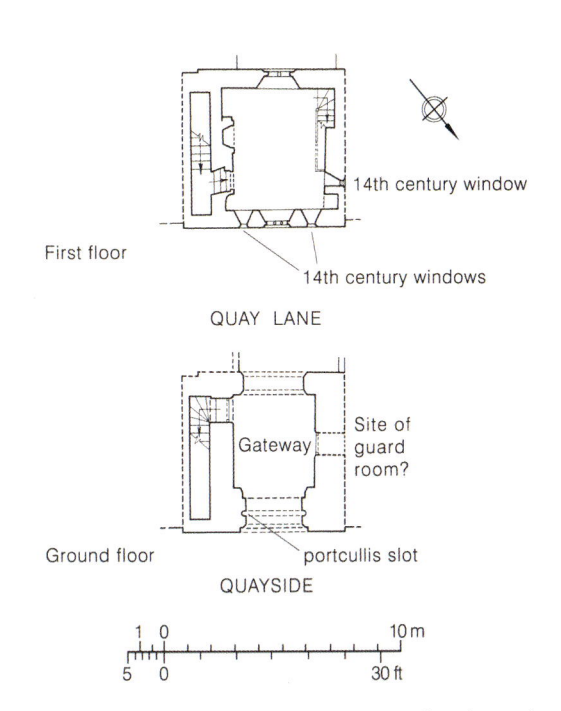

Fig. 11.19: Fisher Gate, plans (A. T. A., based on plans by Duncan+Graham Partnership)

Fig. 11.20: Davis Gate (the Barbican) from the north (P. W. © English Heritage DP043972)

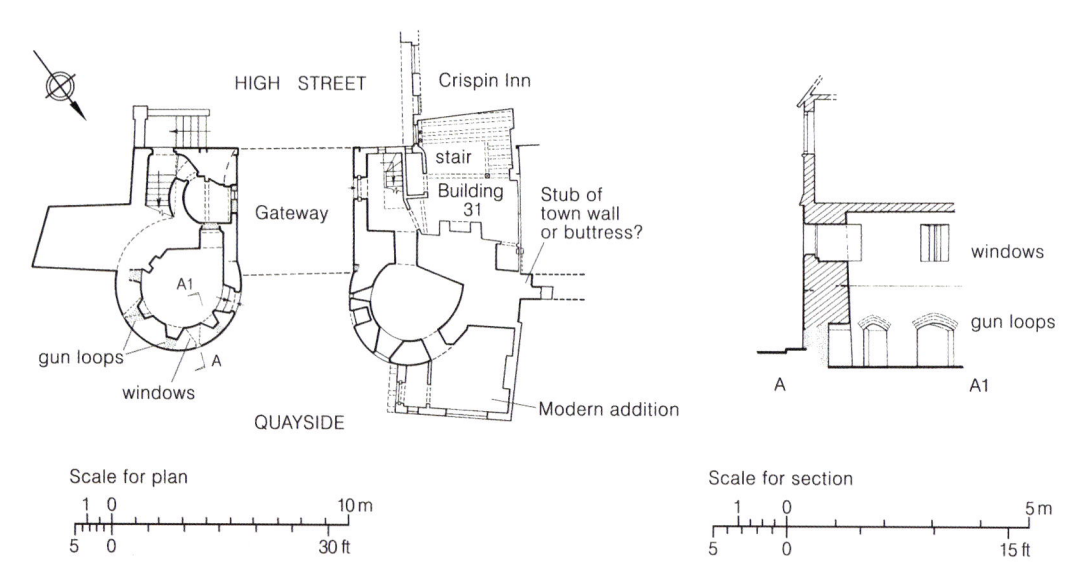

Fig. 11.21: Plan and section of Davis Gate (S. P. and A. T. A.)

Three years later the mason Thomas Whyteler was employed to make 'jambs and arches', perhaps using some of the 1,000 'great ashlars' that he sold to the mayor and jurats for £111. The considerable quantities of ragstone, chalk, flint, hewn stone, sand and lime that were brought from Folkestone in the same year indicate a vigorous building programme somewhere in the town, and all those materials are still visible in the gate.[79] Davis Quay also received attention while the new gate was being constructed, and became an integral part of a waterfront complex, home to the town crane and other harbour installations (Chap. 14.1).

In 1483 the town expended a considerable sum on Davis Gate. The mayor and jurats must have taken their responsibilities for such a fine gate seriously, for the area around the gate was paved with stones and gravel; battlements were added to the two towers (the first time they are mentioned), and both were provided with 'great guns', some of which rested on trestles, presumably in the still-surviving gun-loop embrasures (Fig. 11.21). By 1490 there were two gated passageways through the gatehouse, one for wheeled transport, where the archway is today, and another, probably a walkway, known as the postern, at one side.[80] This pedestrian path may have led to the timber-built latrine or privy, already in existence by 1439, and repaired four times between 1478 and 1520.[81]

As little as thirty years after Davis Gate was built in stone, this weighty masonry building may have been proving too heavy for its substructure, for both the foundations and the wharf to the north of it needed extensive repairs on five occasions between 1507 and 1532.[82] The town authorities also continued to spend freely on the superstructure throughout the first half of the sixteenth century, underlining the likelihood of its being as much a status symbol as a fortification or toll station. Caen stone brought from Fordwich (perhaps surplus building material from Canterbury) in 1513 may have been used in the chequerwork of the drum towers, perhaps supplemented by the stone that was purchased from Stonar at the same time.[83] Stonar could not itself have been the source of this stone, unless it were flint cobbles from Stonar Bank, so it must have been brought in from elsewhere, perhaps from the Roman forts of Reculver or Richborough. More aboveground work took place in 1519 and 1532.[84] The gate itself seems to have needed little repair during the rest of the sixteenth century, although the Davis Gate wharf demanded frequent attention.

Another important feature of Davis Gate was the conduit, which must have been in existence sometime before 1490, since it and its lead pipes were repaired while other work was going on at the gate.[85] New pipes were laid in 1513.[86] This conduit was one of several that ran through the town, often through the gates, and there may have been two through Davis Gate, for the 'little conduit' is specifically mentioned in 1537 when James Hall became responsible for keeping the main one in good order from Davis Gate to 'the conduit head at Woodnesborough'.[87] The larger of the two conduits must have carried clean water from the source, so perhaps the smaller was used to dispose foul water into the harbour.

The decorative treatment of the gate's two towers is very rare in medieval town gates elsewhere; it reinforces the idea that Davis Gate was a symbol of urban pride, not merely a defensive gateway. The same may have been true of the only surviving comparable example, Burgess Gate in Denbigh, Gwynedd,[88] and of the now demolished South Gate at Great Yarmouth

Fig. 11.22: Part of the map of Great Yarmouth of c.1580 showing the decorated South Gate and mural towers, the town crane and the unwalled waterfront (© British Library Board. All Rights Reserved: Cotton MS Augustus I.i.74)

Fig. 11.23: Blackfriars Tower, Great Yarmouth (S. P.)

Fig. 11.24: The Round House (present Keep), Sandwich, from north-east (K. P.)

depicted on the mid- or late sixteenth-century view of that town (Fig. 11.22).[89] That illustration seems to show the same use of chequerwork, but one of the surviving mural towers indicates that a different technique was probably used (Fig. 11.23).

About 20m east of Fisher Gate stands what may have been a mural tower. This is now known as The Keep, called Round House on Boys's map (Fig. 8.1); neither name appears in the medieval documents. Today it is a plain rectangular three-storey building 8.33m × 5.27m in plan, with lower walls of uncoursed flint, brick and ragstone, the upper part being rebuilt in modern brick (Fig. 11.24). Wall stubs protrude at slight angles, consistent with curving walls making an apsidal north end, as illustrated in eighteenth- and nineteenth-century paintings and maps, and which presumably gave the building its name (Fig. 11.25). A watercolour of 1791 shows the curved wall, built of chequered flint work above plain stone walling (Fig. 11.26) in a style similar to that of Davis Gate.

The Round House is popularly supposed to have been a tower housing the mechanism for a boom chain slung across the harbour.[90] That there was a boom, although not made up of a chain, is indicated in 1480 when the council proposed buying a cable with windlass, to go across the haven from Sandwich to the

Fig. 11.25: Wall scars on the north face of the Round House (P. W. © DP068609)

north bank of the river Stour.[91] The associated windlass would have needed to be housed on the quay, so it may have been located in the Round House, which seems to have been the only structure of any height in roughly the right situation. Thus, Sandwich's Round House may have been a medieval boom tower, of which there are many examples elsewhere. Some survive as towers, for example Lendal Tower and North Street Postern in York (Fig. 11.27).[92] Others are depicted on near-

Fig. 11.26: Watercolour of the Round House (Keep) and Fisher Gate, 1791 (KAS Kent Drawings III, p. 46)

Fig. 11.27: Boom tower at Lendal Bridge, York (H. C.)

Fig. 11.28: Detail from a mid-sixteenth-century map of Kingston upon Hull showing the river Hull protected by a boom chain, the west bank with cranes and Hull Street slightly further west (© British Library Board. All Rights Reserved Cotton Augustus I.i., f. 83)

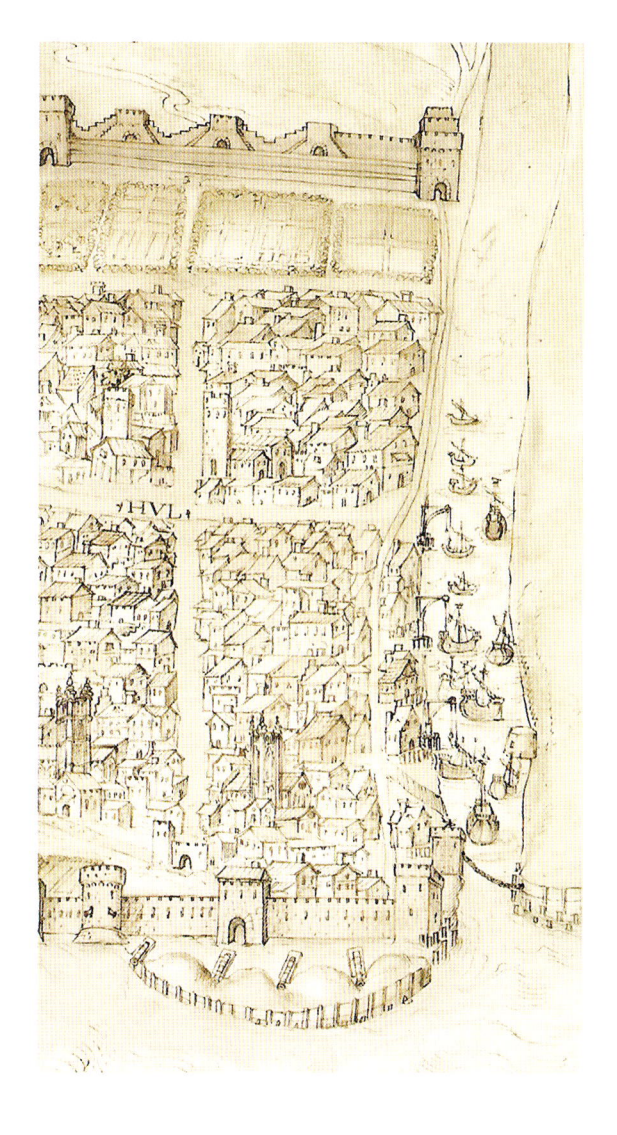

contemporary maps (Fig. 11.28), and there are many documentary references.[93]

11.2.2 The Castle

Throughout the Hundred Years War and until the end of the fifteenth century the castle seems to have remained a royal administrative centre for the gathering of troops. In 1385 masons, carpenters and other workmen were employed digging foundations, constructing walls and making an audience chamber (*consillion*) using stone, perhaps greensand, shipped from Kingston upon Thames, and lime obtained from an unspecified source.[94] The stone walls revealed during archaeological excavations in 1996 could be the remains of that chamber, although their date is imprecise (Chap. 5.6.1).[95] A drawbridge was built at the entrance in 1386 when there was also work on the moat, a new gate, and a 'turret',[96] possibly the tower first mentioned in 1303. Although the castle appears in the records as the seat of the king's bailiff throughout the first half of the fifteenth century,[97] there is no mention of its physical fabric until 1440, when 'stonecutters, masons, carpenters, plumbers . . . and other workmen and labourers' repaired the castle.[98] They may have been preparing it for the final stage of the Hundred Years War, but they could equally have been employed because the structure had been damaged, for reasons unknown, by two Sandwich men six years earlier.[99]

The land surrounding the castle probably continued to be used for accommodating troops and horses awaiting embarkation on the numerous vessels that were to take them across the English Channel. On thirty occasions between 1383 and 1453 ships ranging from 20 to 140 tuns burden were arrested in English east coast ports, from Newcastle southwards, and assembled at Sandwich. Some were loaded with provisions to be taken to Calais. In 1393, for example, '100 quarters of wheat, 80 quarters of malt, 50 barrels of ale, 20 carcases of beef, 80 quarters of flour, 60 carcases of mutton, 40 carcasses of pork' were put on board *La Cristofre*,[100] and in 1454 'all manner of goods . . . whatever they may be' were brought to Sandwich from its environs.[101] Other ships summoned to Sandwich Haven carried men-at-arms and mounted archers, or were horse transports.

Ships bound for royal service were also repaired at Sandwich, with carpenters and other labourers being dispatched to the port specifically for this purpose.[102] All these activities are likely to have taken place in Castelmead, and yet the castle itself seems to have played no active part in warfare, and is not even mentioned in accounts of the notorious French raid on Sandwich in 1457.[103] An illustration of the attack in a French manuscript (*Vigiles de Charles VII*), said to depict the castle,[104] is unlikely to be other than a standard representation of fifteenth-century warfare. Even if the castle were threatened in 1457, it can hardly have been badly damaged, because there are no definite references to subsequent repairs, although the fortifications mentioned in the murage grant of 1464 may refer to the castle as well as town walls and gates.[105] Fauconberg is reputed to have seized the castle in 1471,[106] but there is no evidence for this even though Sandwich played its part in the events of 1459–61 and 1471 (Section 11.1.4).[107]

The town cannot have had many dealings with the castle during its greatest period of activity for it remained in royal hands until 1483,[108] when the civic authorities paid for artillery to defend the castle and, presumably, the eastern approaches to the town. Subsequently, the town seems to have taken over all responsibility, for in 1490 the mayor and jurats appointed one of their own to be in charge of the castle and gave him some men from the town wards to defend it.[109] Until then the relationship between castle and town must have been somewhat anomalous, for once Mill Wall had been built the two were effectively separate units.

As the construction of the Bulwark indicates (Section 11.2.1.2), by the middle of the fifteenth century the mayor and jurats had become aware of the increasing need to defend their town by the most up-to-date methods available. This may have been part of the reason why the town took on responsibility for the castle after 1483, even though it was much less formidable than the Bulwark. Although there are signs that the castle stood until the end of the century (Chap. 15.3.5), the last reference in which it was mentioned by name is in 1537 when the town paid for the gate into Castelmead to be repaired.[110] From then until the end of the century the 'castle next to Sandwich' that is referred to on several occasions is probably Sandown Castle,[111] built for Henry VIII in 1539–40 at North Deal. The tower demolished in the 1890s (Chap. 5.6.1) may have been the only visible sign of the castle left after the mid-sixteenth century.

11.3 Conclusion

By the end of the period covered in this chapter Sandwich had acquired much of the plan as shown in Boys's map (Fig. 8.1). The ramparts had been supplemented by stone walls along the eastern and western ends of the waterfront, and the artillery fortification of the Bulwark had been completed. The castle was no longer a significant factor, with its omission from the eighteenth-century map indicating that it was soon forgotten once it had fallen out of use.

During the late fourteenth and fifteenth centuries a great deal of money and effort was spent on the defence of both the harbour and the town. But by the mid-sixteenth century the harbour was ceasing to be the huge, safe haven easily accessible to great ships of the royal fleet, and the threat of foreign invasion was being met by modern defensive structures built elsewhere along the coast. The withdrawal of the royal presence, typified by the town's acquisition of the castle, must have contributed to the gradual decline of the port's importance, adding its weight to the general downturn in overseas trade that was apparent by the end of the fifteenth century.

12 Secular buildings

The houses followed by numbers in brackets have been surveyed and are mapped in Figure IV.1 and listed in Appendix 2

As discussed in Chapter 7, an important group of early secular buildings survives in Sandwich, among them some of the earliest urban timber-framed structures in the country. The number of these buildings is small, no doubt partly because later demolition has removed other examples, but also perhaps because relatively few people were in a position to construct substantial dwellings before the mid-fourteenth century. Very many more buildings survive from the later Middle Ages and their form and function will be described in this chapter.

Relating the construction of buildings closely to the ebbs and flows in the history of the town depends upon confidence in accurate dating, but it has to be stated that a clear chronology of building has not emerged from this study. There are a number of ways in which buildings or parts of buildings may be dated. Dendrochronology is a widely applied technique that often provides extremely accurate results, but it depends upon the presence of suitable timbers. These are generally lacking in Sandwich for the fifteenth century, prohibiting the establishment of a reliable framework for establishing a firm chronology. Typological dating may be used with caution: the widespread change from the open hall of the medieval period to the floored hall of the following era provides a broad indication of typological progression, but it is probable that, in Sandwich as elsewhere, the adoption of one form or the other was dependent on a range of considerations – social, functional and cultural – and that both options were available simultaneously in the late fifteenth and early sixteenth centuries.

Stylistic and structural features provide a further method of dating, and for Kent an extensive body of comparative material is available to assist with the chronology of Sandwich's late medieval houses.[1] Good-quality vernacular buildings of the late fourteenth or very early fifteenth century in Kent are easier to identify than their successors because they used relatively archaic features that are not found in buildings that can be securely placed in the later fifteenth century.

These include the aisled form, unjowled posts, splayed scarf joints and decorative details such as quarter-round mouldings.[2] The absence of these features in Sandwich suggests that few buildings can confidently be attributed to *c.*1400. The development of new roof types in Kent in the late fifteenth century also provides a guide to dating some of Sandwich's buildings. There is, however, a problem in that stylistic and structural comparisons provide relative rather than absolute accuracy outside a firmly established framework of reliably dated features. The construction of such a framework, well established in the study of rural buildings in Kent and Sussex, would be a useful medium-term research objective for the urban buildings of the same area.

Sandwich's late medieval buildings seem to fall into a number of clear chronological groups. No new houses appear to have been erected between *c.*1340 and *c.*1380, and certainly none survives. A handful of buildings may have been built between *c.*1380 and *c.*1420, but there are fewer than ten of them (see Appendix 2). The Sandwich evidence conforms to a general picture across England, in which there is a marked decline in the number of urban buildings known from the four decades after 1360,[3] but it is in contrast to evidence from some other south-eastern coastal towns, such as Rye and Faversham, where the survival of several houses of *c.*1400 seems to buck the national trend.[4]

Only from about the end of the first quarter of the fifteenth century did construction appear to pick up momentum. From then until *c.*1500 a great many new houses were built, of which around fifty still survive in Sandwich. This profusion was followed by another period, from *c.*1500 to *c.*1520, in which only about six new houses have been identified. There is some overlap in periods, in that some of the last group, although fully storeyed and therefore typologically advanced, may not have been chronologically later than the latest of the previous group, which had, or probably had, open halls. By 1510 or shortly thereafter, however, new building virtually ceased so that few structures can confidently be dated between *c*.1520 and *c*.1560. This decline, which was ostensibly caused by local factors, is in line with an apparently general reduction in the number of tree-ring-dated urban buildings across the country after 1500.[5]

The suggested chronology of building construction is important because, if accepted, there appears to be a discrepancy between the periods of economic prosperity and the periods of building construction. The implications of this are considerable, not only for the interpretation of Sandwich's late medieval development, but also for the study of the link between architectural evidence and economic and social history. The relationship between building activity and economic prosperity will be explored at the end of this chapter.

12.1 Large courtyard houses

Sandwich has few houses of the wealthy surviving from this period, with only three timber-framed examples of large courtyard houses well enough preserved to have been investigated. One is 29 Harnet Street (House 28; Fig. 12.1) with a frontage of 16m (52ft 6in), or 23m (75ft 6in) if one includes 31 Harnet Street (House 29), which was part of the same property in the early fifteenth century. Deeds and other documents identify it as the home of Thomas Elys, vintner and one of the most prominent Sandwich inhabitants of the fourteenth century (Chap. 10.3.1). Later deeds, combined with the surviving parts of the building, allow a map to be drawn of the site and surrounding properties (Fig. 12.2).[6] The house was of two storeys only and in plan consisted of a long, early sixteenth-century street range with a continuous jetty (now underbuilt) and a utilitarian crown-post roof (these are the only retrievable medieval features because the whole house was gentrified in the eighteenth century). This frontage may have been dedicated to commercial use, and before the sixteenth-century rebuilding its predecessor may have been shorter, allowing access at the south end to the extensive grounds behind. The northern rear wing is among the few late fourteenth-century structures in Sandwich, dated by the heavy scantling of its timbers, crown-post roof, and quarter-round mouldings to the arch braces of the first-floor chamber. On the ground floor of the southern wing a large room with finely moulded early sixteenth-century ceiling joists[7] may replace an earlier open hall. Behind it and formerly detached, a post-medieval range stands above a shallow stone undercroft, which would appear to be the foundations of the 'great kitchen' that was documented as in this position. Elys is known to have had a wine cellar, and this could have been the deep, but now inaccessible, cellar under the front of 31 Harnet Street (House 29) to the north, which the deeds indicate was once part of the same property.[8]

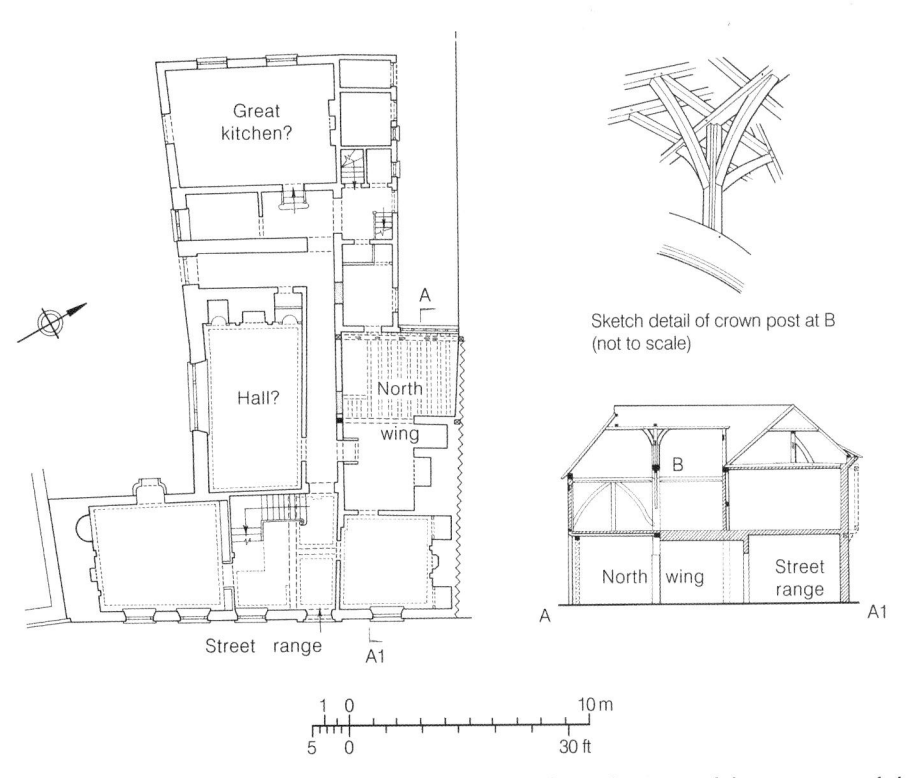

Fig. 12.1: 29 Harnet Street (House 28), ground-floor plan, section through north wing and front range, and detail of crown post above north wing (S. P. & A. T. A.)

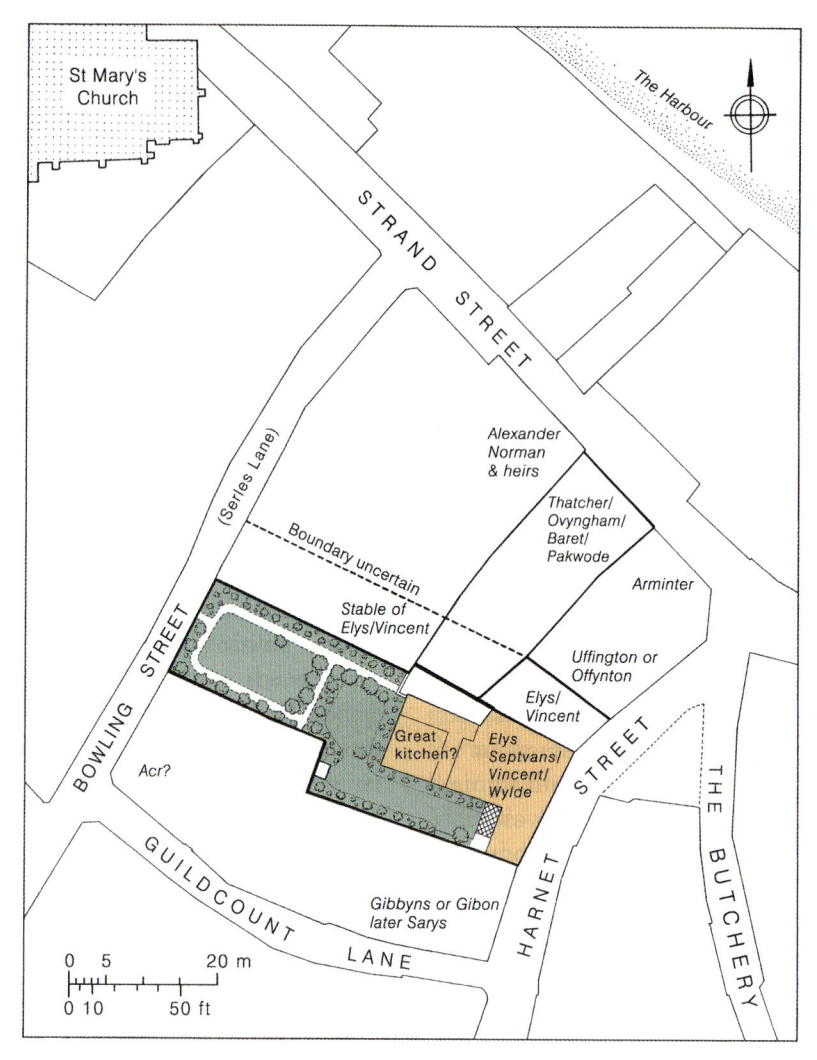

Fig. 12.2: 29 Harnet Street (House 28), location plan derived from contemporary documents showing relationship of the Elys property to its surroundings, and the descent of the properties in the late fourteenth and early fifteenth centuries (A. T. A., based on 1: 500 OS map of 1873)

A slightly smaller example, only 15m (49ft) wide, is 19, 21 and 23 Strand Street (Houses 80, 81), which, together with 50 St Peter's Street (House 73), formed a single large property (Fig. 12.3). This would appear to have formed another large courtyard property fronting Strand Street. It was created in the thirteenth century or even earlier, largely rebuilt in the fifteenth and sixteenth centuries, and subsequently split into several occupations. No. 50 St Peter's Street, a late thirteenth-century stone chamber block over an undercroft entered from the courtyard, and the lower part of No. 23, built in the fourteenth century as a timber-framed shop with chamber over (Fig. 12.37), have already been discussed (Chaps 7.2.2, 7.3). No. 23 lay next to a wide entrance into the courtyard, and in the fifteenth century whatever formerly lay to the east of that was rebuilt as a plain three-storey range of indeterminate use, now Nos. 19, 21 Strand Street (House 80). In the early sixteenth century a third storey was added to No. 23 and the rear was rebuilt (Fig. 12.46). If there were an open hall, as seems likely, it probably lay at the back, along one side of the courtyard, possibly on the site of the later rear range (Section 12.8.1). No owners are identifiable before 1482, when it was in the hands of William Mason, the lessee of the Sandwich brick ground (Chap. 10.1.5.3). Subsequently, both 23 Strand Street and a cellar in Love Lane (50 St Peter's Street) came into the possession of William Baly, one of the wealthiest men in the town in the local assessment of 1513, who was likely to have been responsible for building the rear range of No. 23. A third large courtyard property was 11, 13 and 15 Strand Street (Houses 77, 78, 79; Chap. 7.2.2, Fig. 7.8; Section 12.8.1). The Strand Street ranges of all these buildings are illustrated in Figure 12.4 (there is no No. 17).

These houses are not in the class of the great

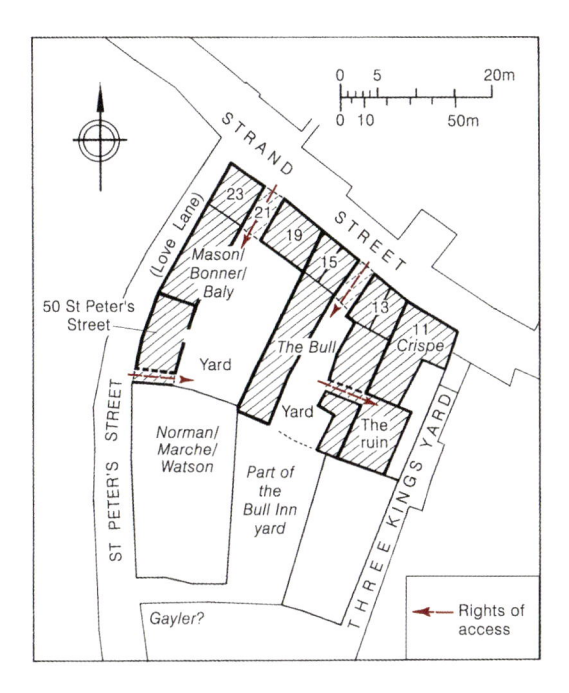

Fig. 12.3: Suggested layout of 11–23 Strand Street and the ranges behind in the fifteenth and sixteenth centuries, based on the evidence of surviving buildings and documentary sources, and the sequence of known owners (A. T. A., based on 1: 500 OS map of 1873).

aristocratic and institutional medieval houses documented in London and Bristol,[9] but are smaller versions of this type such as survive in Salisbury and York,[10] in which shops, sometimes rented out, stood in front of the property owner's dwelling. In the fourteenth and early fifteenth centuries they probably included open halls at the back, but none survives in Sandwich. Their front ranges are plain, with no signs of the grand chambers that might be expected if they formed the main domestic accommodation of wealthy owners, suggesting that they were either built for storage (Section 12.8.3) or were designed to be separately occupied.

12.2 Open halls

The large courtyard houses excepted, plots in Sandwich were relatively narrow, usually ranging in width between 3m and 8m (10–26ft). The one constant factor was the open hall, the main room, which was open from the ground to the roof, although other parts of the house were of two or more storeys. Such halls have already been discussed (Chaps 7.3, 7.5), and remained standard in the town until the end of the Middle Ages, recognisable in thirty out of fifty-seven timber-framed buildings built before c.1500. Although a number of fifteenth-century houses no longer have remains of their open halls, there is little definite evidence that they did not originally exist. Only two houses show possible evidence for halls raised on to the first floor (Section 12.3.4), and ground-floor halls built to be ceiled did not occur before c.1500 (Section 12.7.1). Instead, it is likely that at all social levels, most medieval houses in Sandwich were centred upon halls open to the roof, whether they were the dwellings of the town elite or the hovels of the urban poor.

The open hall was heated by an open hearth, probably laid on a foundation of clay and tiles like the

Fig. 12.4: Houses in Strand Street. From left to right: 11 (House 77); 13 and 15 (House 79); 19 and 21 (House 80); and 23 (House 81) Strand Street (P. W. © English Heritage DP043963)

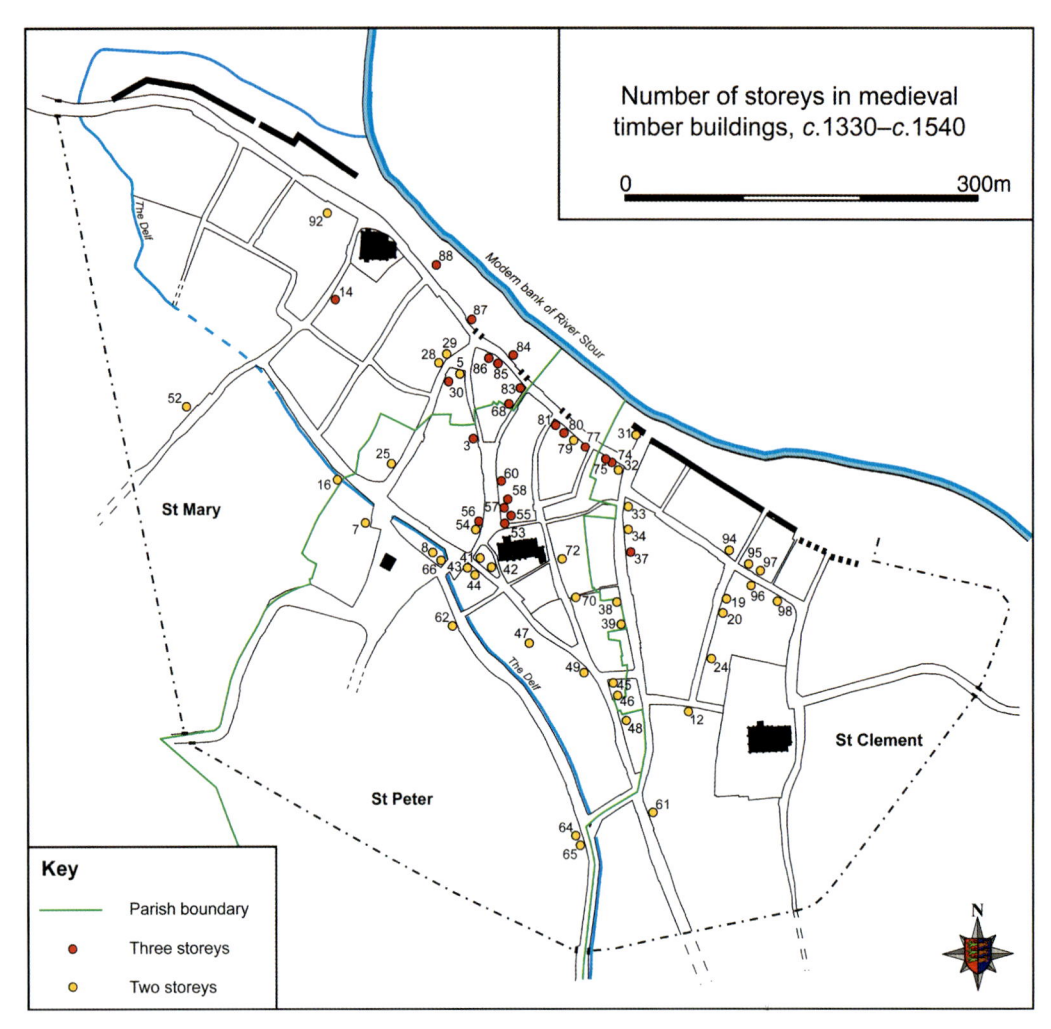

Fig. 12.5: The distribution of the number of storeys in medieval timber buildings, c.1330–c.1540 (J. H.). Reproduced by permission of Ordnance Survey on behalf of HMSO. © Crown copyright 2009. All rights reserved. Licence number 100046522

excavated hearth at Site 20 in St Peter's Street (Chap. 7.1). Where hearths have been found in rural houses they were situated towards the upper end of the hall, designed to heat the best seating at the dais end, with a louvre or smoke outlet, when there was one, located towards the entrance end of the hall so that the smoke drifted away from the dais.[11] There is no direct evidence for the position of hearths in Sandwich, and, as discussed below (Section 12.9), the layout of urban halls may have been different from their rural counterparts. Nonetheless, the presence of open hearths is clear from the heavily smoke-blackened roofs found in all open halls except for three late examples, which were probably always heated by enclosed fireplaces.[12]

Surviving open-hall houses in English towns have been divided into two basic types by the relationship of the hall to the street frontage. In the first, the dwelling lay parallel to the street, either on the street or behind a front range, with ancillary accommodation at one or both ends. In the second, the open hall lay at right angles behind a multi-storeyed bay or bays on the street frontage.[13] In the centre of Sandwich, almost all halls were set behind and at right angles to the street range, which could then be used entirely for business purposes. This makes sense where pressure for street space was intense; most of these houses were also three storeys high, thereby making maximum use of the site (Fig. 12.5). In the outer parts of town, however, most dwellings were only two storeys high and the open hall was aligned along the street frontage. Since rooms in houses in this part of town were generally much smaller than those in dwellings in the central area, a hall and at least one other room could be squeezed into the width of a narrow plot. The division into hall types was therefore normally related to size and location, and the following discussion concentrates first on those that lay in the town centre, followed by those somewhat further out.

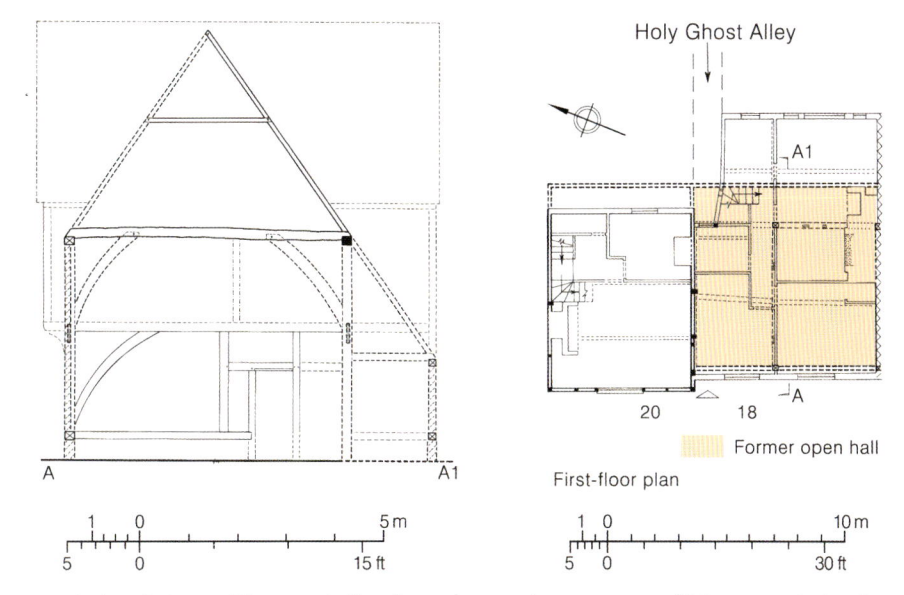

Fig. 12.6: 18, 20 St Peter's Street (House 70), first-floor plan, and cross section of No. 18 at A–A1 (S. P. & A. T. A.)

12.3 The town centre: open-hall houses

12.3.1 An open hall parallel to the street

Only one house surviving in the town centre, 18, 20 St Peter Street (House 70), had its hall parallel to the street frontage. What are now two houses were originally a single timber-framed building, comprising an open hall and a two-storey cross wing beyond the entry passage, giving a total length of 13.5m (44ft). The fragmentary open hall, primarily identifiable at roof level, extended 7.5m (24ft 6in) along the street and seems to have had a rear aisle (Fig. 12.6).[14] A hipped roof to the south marks the end of the hall and of the building. At the north end of the hall is a doorway on the street front with a solid, two-centred head of a type that does not survive elsewhere in the town (Fig. 12.7). It is now the entrance to a public right of way (Holy Ghost Alley), although the fact that the hall roof continues across the alley, and that the doorway to the alley is rebated for a door, imply that this was originally an entry passage within the hall. The form of doorway and the simple collar-rafter roof indicate a date no later than the late fourteenth century.[15] The wall along the north side of the alley was once the end wall of the hall, probably with doorways leading into what is now No. 20, although the present blocked doorways here are sixteenth-century replacements. No. 20 is largely of sixteenth- and seventeenth-century date, but has a heavy wall plate and brace on its north wall apparently surviving from an earlier, probably fourteenth-century, build. Evidence for the position of a main post suggests this was the side wall of a wing. Several first-floor joists are reused rafters with cuts for lap joints, indicating a

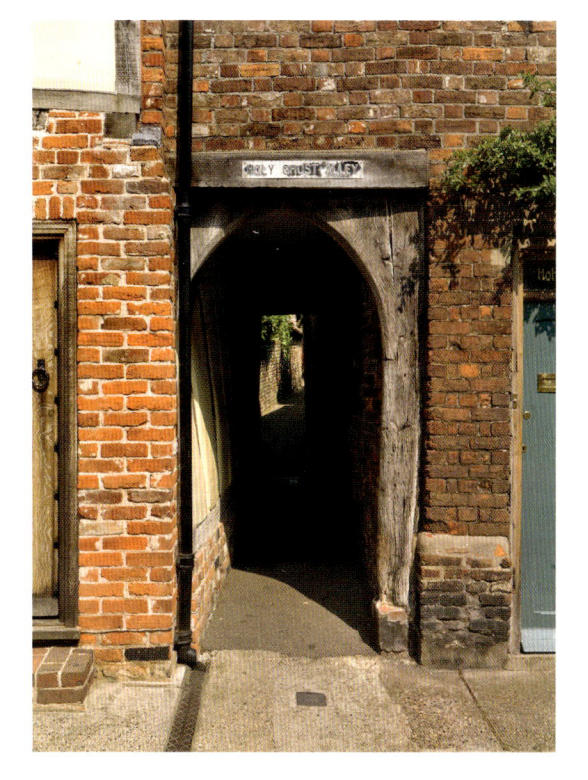

Fig. 12.7: Doorway to Holy Ghost Alley, formerly into the hall of 18 St Peter Street (P. W. © English Heritage DP068618)

fourteenth-century or even earlier date. Thus, despite the fragmentary nature of survival, it is possible that Nos. 18 and 20 together formed an open hall with a single aisle, accompanied by a two-storey cross wing beyond the entry passage. It was probably built in the late fourteenth century, although the wing could have been earlier.

Halls of *c*.1400 arranged parallel to the street were common in other towns, such as Rye and Faversham. At Rye, ancillary rooms in storeyed bays tend to be under the same roof as the hall.[16] In Faversham, the normal form is for the storeyed accommodation to be set in cross wings at right angles to the hall.[17] But these were smaller towns than Sandwich, with nearly all their medieval houses being of only two storeys arranged parallel to the street, suggesting far less commercial pressure on the town centre. Except for 18, 20 St Peter's Street, this arrangement does not occur elsewhere in central Sandwich. The wing of what might have been a similar building of the late fourteenth century at 10 Church Street St Clement (House 12) is some distance from the centre. The question of whether 18, 20 St Peter's Street was built in this way because after the Black Death there was generally less pressure on plots in the centre, or whether it was possible to build such a house in St Peter's Street because it was not considered a main commercial street, is unclear, and at present the form of this house remains a puzzle.

12.3.2 Open halls set back from the street frontage

Twenty-two out of a total of thirty known open halls occur in houses that run back from the street front, with the hall set behind a multi-storey bay. Three were built in the early fourteenth century (Chap. 7.3), fourteen during the fifteenth century and a further group of five are judged to have been constructed around 1500. None was built in the period between *c*.1360 and *c*.1410. Twelve of those in the Fishmarket and on or just off Strand Street rise through three storeys. The rest are two storeys high, and are located slightly further away from the centre: in the Cornmarket, on Luckboat or on Strand Street west of St Mary's church. Leaving aside the early fourteenth-century examples, the plots on which these houses were constructed ranged from just under 7m (22ft) at 10 Market Street (House 58), to the diminutive 3.2m (10ft 6in) width of 9 Cattle Market (House 8), with most being 4–5m (13–16ft) wide. Such widths do not allow decent sized open

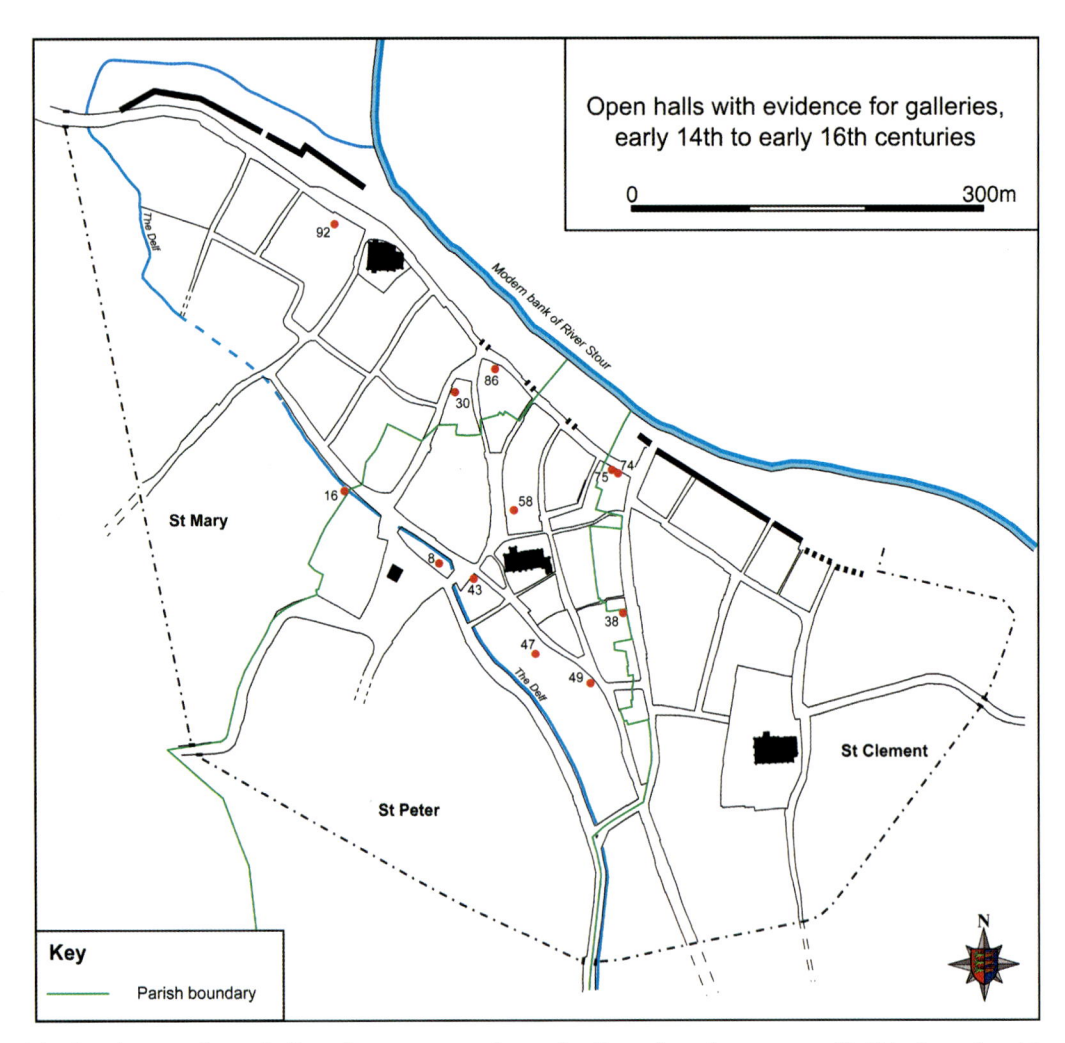

Fig. 12.8: The distribution of open halls with surviving evidence of galleries from front to rear (J. H.). Reproduced by permission of Ordnance Survey on behalf of HMSO. © Crown copyright 2009. All rights reserved. Licence number 100046522

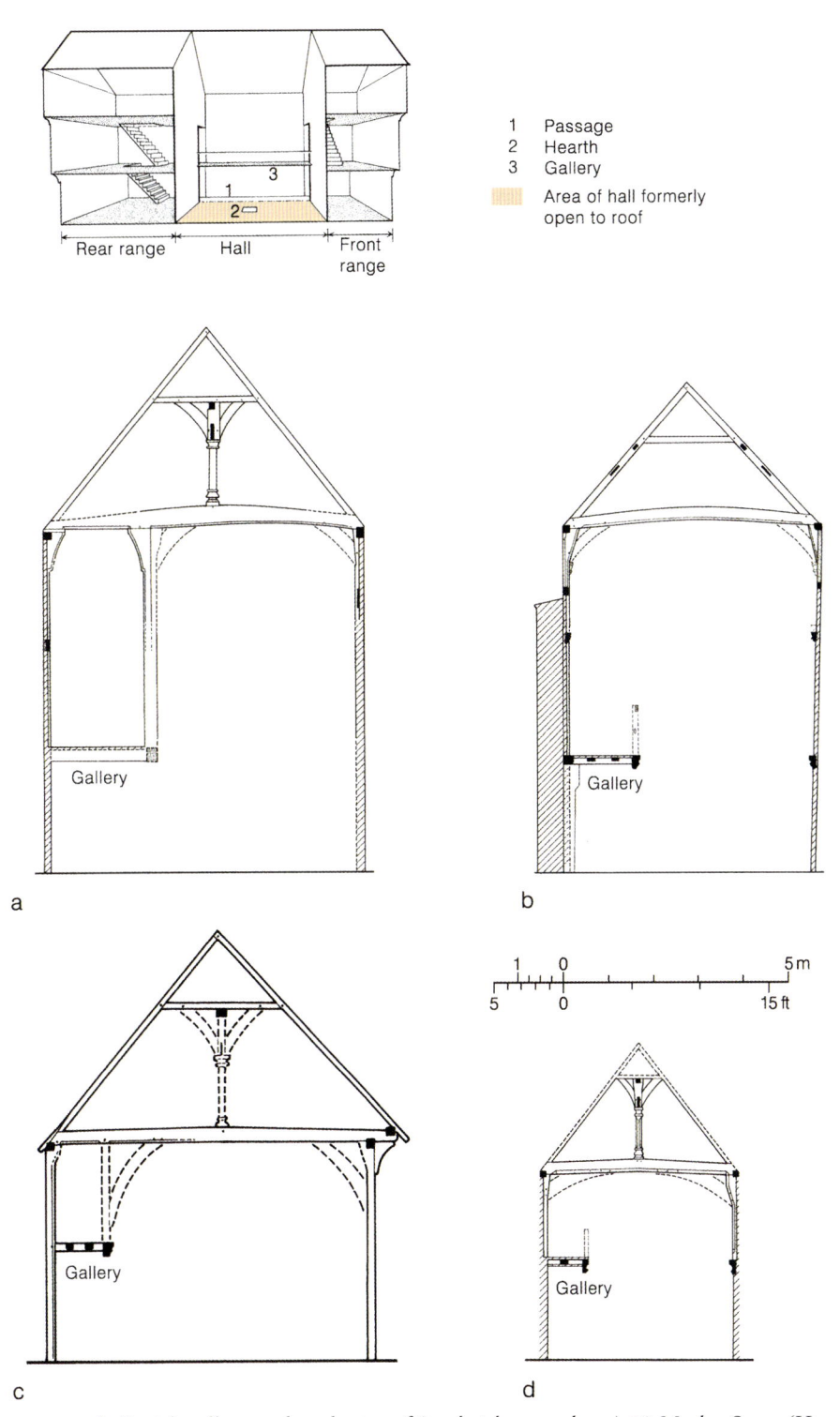

Fig. 12.9: A schematic open hall with gallery, and a selection of Sandwich examples: a) 10 Market Street (House 58), mid- to late fifteenth century, b) 3 Strand Street, c.1500 (House 74), c) 71 Strand Street, mid-fifteenth century (House 92), d) 38 King Street (House 49), mid-fifteenth century (S. P. & A. T. A.)

halls and storeyed bays to be ranged along the street frontage, so the houses had to extend backwards.

None of the fifteenth-century examples had external access from the front to the rear of the plot, for the street frontages were fully built up. Instead, the hall, the rear accommodation and the back yard were reached by an internal passage through the front range, as occurs in houses in other large towns.[18] In some houses, the internal passage continued across the hall below a gallery at first-floor level (Figs 12.8, 12.9). The earliest is the early fourteenth-century 41 Strand Street (House 86; Fig. 7.23); the latest are probably those at

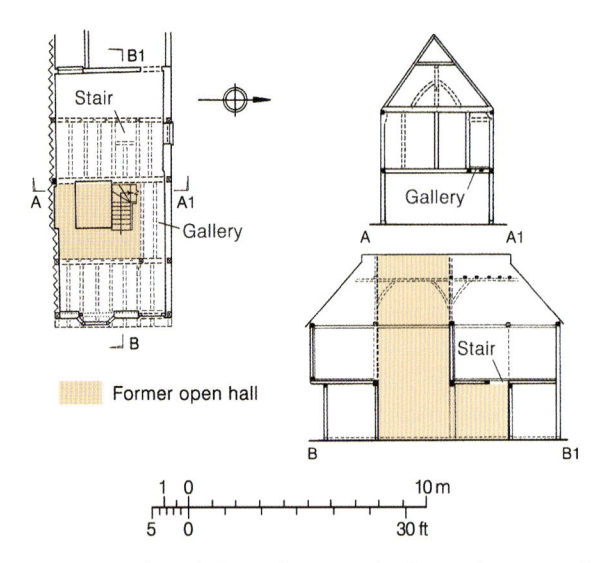

Fig. 12.10: 34 High Street (House 38), plan and sections of a late open hall with a gallery (S. P. & A. T. A.)

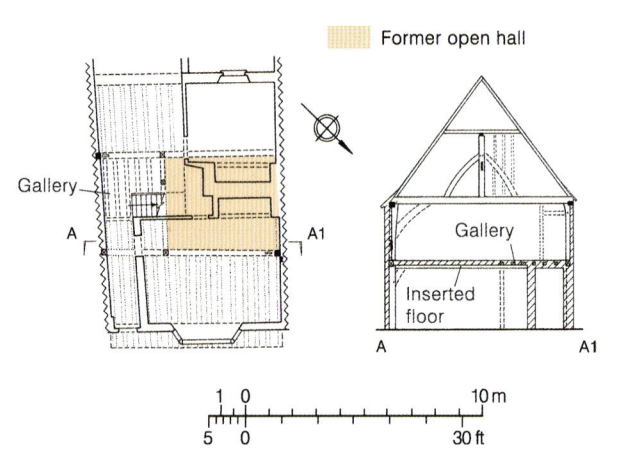

Fig. 12.11: 17 Delf Street (House 16), plan and cross section of a late open hall with a gallery (S. P. & A. T. A.)

Fig. 12.12: 38 King Street (House 49), view of the gallery from the east, showing the doorway to the first-floor rear accommodation (P. W. © English Heritage DP044065)

34 High Street (House 38) and 17 Delf Street (House 16), small houses probably built in the early sixteenth century in which the open hall was little more than a smoke bay (Figs 12.10, 12.11). The galleries are usually now embedded within later work, identifiable only by the size of their floor joists compared to the later ones inserted into the open area of the hall, or by the first-floor doorways opening from the galleries to rooms at the front or the rear of the house. Two fine examples, however, can be illustrated at 38 King Street and 3 Strand Street (Houses 49, 74; Figs 12.12, 12.34). The presence of galleries is significant in several ways. In the first place they indicate that the stairs, and perhaps other accommodation, lay in a rear block beyond the open hall, as at 38 King Street. Secondly, they show that the upper storeys at the front formed an integral part of the main dwelling. And finally they suggest that the ground-floor front was used as a shop or workshop that could be occupied separately from the rest of the house.

12.3.3 Lighting the open hall

In the central part of town open halls were usually hemmed in by buildings to each side (Fig. 12.13), raising the question of how they were lit. In some cases, as at 7 Market Street, the three-storey house was clearly taller than at least one of its neighbours, and a roof-level window in the gable shed light down into the hall below (House 56; Fig. 12.14). In this instance the contiguous rear range was only two storeys high, and there is also evidence for high windows at the back, placed either side of the rear extension. At 3 Strand Street (House 74) the hall must have been higher than its neighbours *c.*1500 since windows existed at the top of the wall on both sides. One of them is now blocked by another, slightly later, open-hall house (House 75); the other is still in use today (Fig. 12.15). An alternative way of lighting the hall may have been by roof lights. Two houses have framed openings in the rafters suggesting this, presumably originally with small gables to provide protection against the weather. The earlier example (from 1334) is framed into the east roof slope of the hall of 39 Strand Street (House 85; Fig. 7.21). The other, probably of the mid-fifteenth century, occurs at 8 Cattle Market (House 7; Fig. 12.16). Curiously, they are among the only buildings where there could have been open space to one side of the hall.[19] If such openings existed elsewhere they have either been destroyed or perhaps reused as apertures for inserted brick stacks, in which case they may have escaped detection. After the Middle Ages, when open halls were ceiled over and two or three storeys created where one

Fig. 12.13: 4, 6, 8, 10 Market Street (Houses 58, 57, 55, 53). Medieval houses in the former Fishmarket (P. W. © English Heritage DP068619)

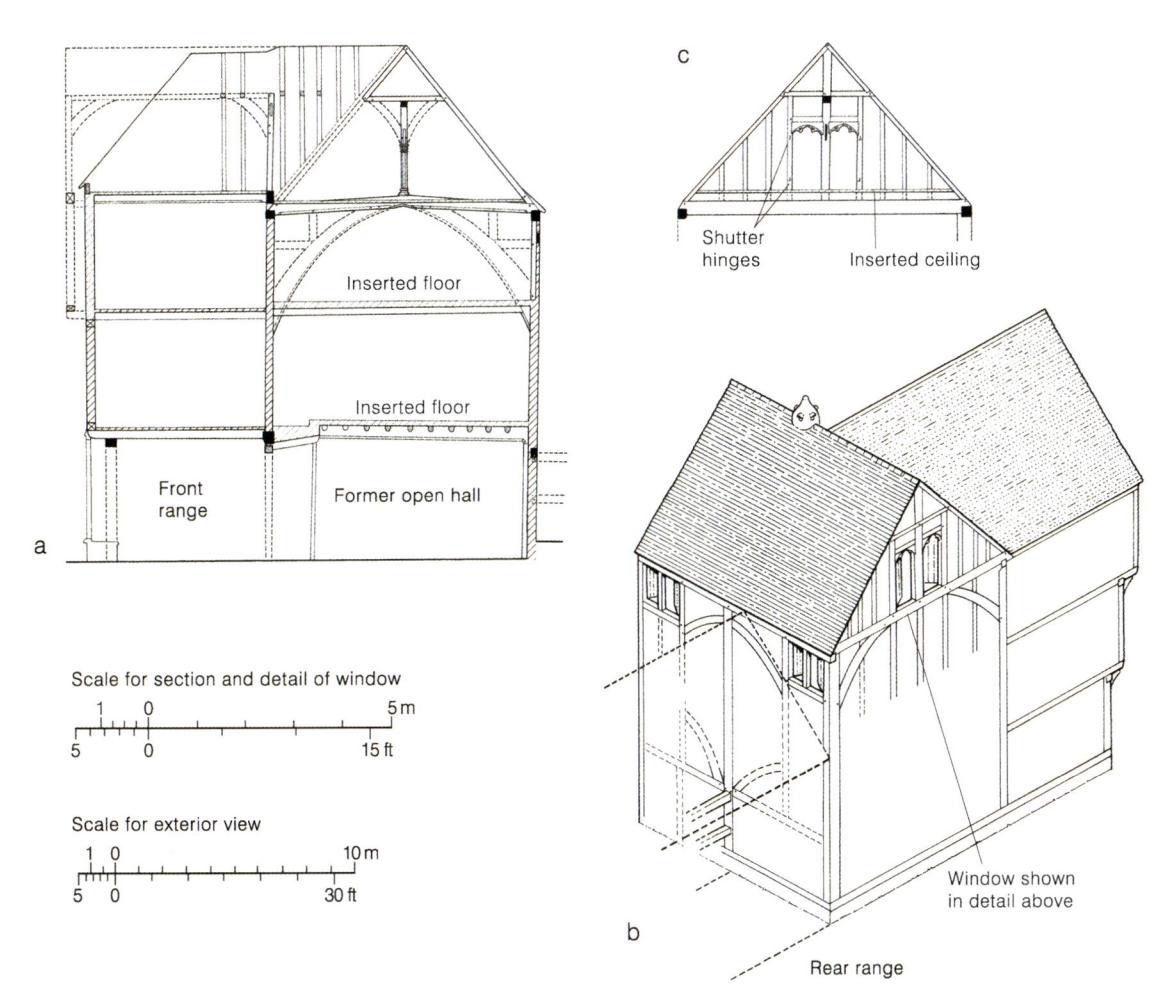

Fig. 12.14: 7 Market Street (House 56): a) long section through front range and hall, from north; b) reconstruction from south-west, showing probable two-storey range at rear; c) detail of window in south gable of hall (S. P. & A. T. A.)

Fig. 12.15: 3 Strand Street (House 74), window at top of side wall of hall (P. W. © English Heritage DP026005)

Fig. 12.16: 8 Cattle Market (House 7), top of former roof light at attic-floor level (P. W. © English Heritage DP026097)

quatrefoils decorating the spandrels formerly opened into the passage leading to the hall behind (House 30; Fig. 12.17).

Some houses, however, had two bays at the front. The only one to have a surviving open hall behind it is the two-storeyed 8 Cattle Market (House 7; Fig. 12.18). Although the decorative details of the two parts are not dissimilar, the front bays were constructed entirely independently, so if the hall had been destroyed, as it has in some houses, there would have been no evidence for its former presence.[20]

Others examples come in two forms. The first, exemplified by the two-storey 30 St Peter's Street (House 72), and the three-storey 7 Potter Street (House 68; Fig. 12.19) and 1 The Butchery (House 3; Fig. 12.39), have single good-quality chambers of two bays on the upper floors. Thus, as surviving, these buildings have only one room on each upper floor. There are signs that all three continued backwards, but no conclusive evidence for or against open halls.[21] It is probable that the best chamber was at the front, and noticeable that these buildings are on relatively shallow plots. At 8 Cattle Market there was room for only a single bay behind the hall (now rebuilt); elsewhere, the line of the back of the plot is less

had been before, the lower floors had no light at all. Probably as a result, the rear accommodation was totally demolished and rebuilt on a narrower footprint, leaving space for windows to be added at one side to light the rooms created in the lower part of the former open hall. This development may account for the almost total lack of surviving original rear accommodation.

12.3.4 The storeyed front bays

The 'classic' central Sandwich open-hall house, found from the early fourteenth century onwards, usually had a single multi-storey bay in front of the hall, as at 7 Market Street (House 56; Fig. 12.14) and 34 Harnet Street, where a rare surviving doorway with

Fig. 12.17: 34 Harnet Street (30), former front doorway opening into a passage leading to the open hall behind (P. W. © English Heritage DP068595)

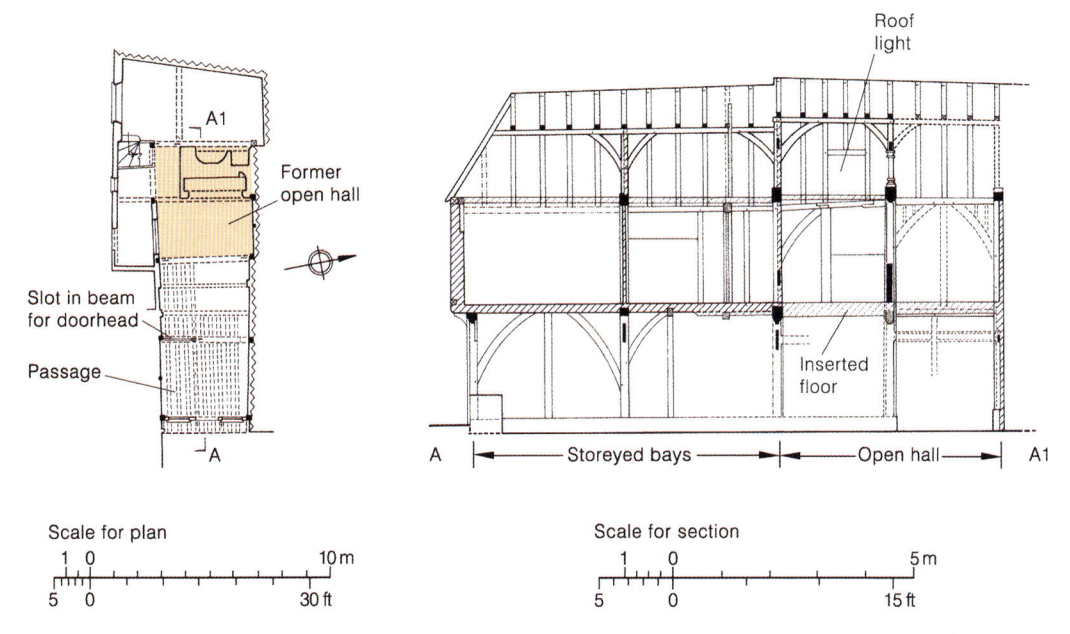

Fig. 12.18: 8 Cattle Market (House 7): a) ground-floor plan; b) long section from north (S. P. & A. T. A.)

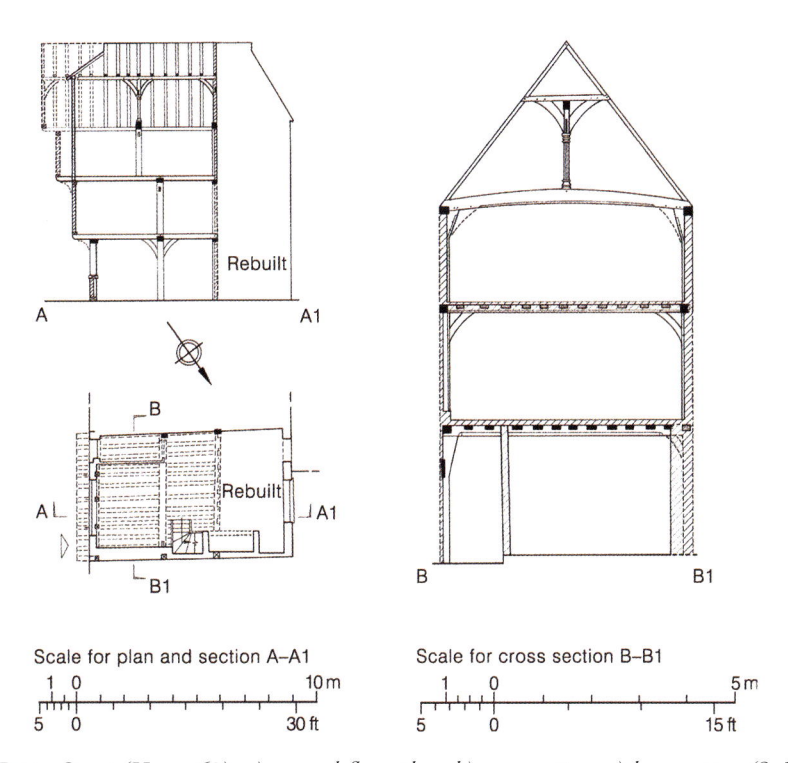

Fig. 12.19: 7 Potter Street (House 68): a) ground-floor plan; b) cross section; c) long section (S. P. & A. T. A.)

clear, but if a household required a detached kitchen, a cesspit or any outhouses in the back yard, it may have been more economical of space to have two bays at the front, with integral accommodation behind the hall being severely restricted or non-existent.

The second form has more and smaller rooms. At 8 Market Street (House 57) both upper floors are divided into two rooms, one behind the other. The rear wall has entirely disappeared, so it is not certain whether the building continued further back or not. If it did, then the inner room, sandwiched between two medieval rooms, must have been lit by borrowed light from the front.[22] The second building is 14, 16 Market Street (House 60). Here, only part of the first floor survives from a formerly three-storey house occupying two bays, running across rather than back from the street. Two adjacent doorways formerly led from No. 14 into No. 16, indicating that the two were once a single unit parallel to the frontage. The doorways have segmental heads, solid spandrels and chamfered surrounds, suggesting a date in the second half of the fifteenth century. Two related bays side by side across the front of a building occur nowhere else in the town centre, and the two doorways are reminiscent of paired service doorways in halls. This could imply that the first floor of No. 14 contained an upper hall or main room with two smaller rooms to the north (in the rebuilt No. 16), the whole probably situated above one or two shops.

Both 8 and 14, 16 Market Street had at least four rooms on the upper floors. Although adjacent houses of apparently much the same date have evidence for open halls, the features in these two may indicate that the domestic element of some marketplace buildings was moving from behind to above the shop during the second half of the fifteenth century. This arrangement had been known in the centres of London and other large towns such as Winchester and Salisbury since the fourteenth century.[23]

12.3.5 Rear accommodation

Where the plots were longer it is likely that there was further accommodation behind the open hall. But apart from the rear block at 39 Strand Street (House 85; Chap. 7.3), only two such ranges remain, at 38 King Street (House 49) and 34 High Street. No. 38 King Street (Fig. 12.20) occupied a long plot on the south side of Luckboat, where documents show that plots were defined on the south by the Delf – in other words, the medieval plots ran back as far as modern New Street (Fig. IV.1). Here, a single front bay and part of the hall were rebuilt in the nineteenth century, but one bay of the hall with its gallery survives, as does a separately constructed rear range of three bays. The ground floor is greatly altered. It contains an added double stack next to the hall, a large heated parlour or kitchen and a small room beyond, but since the ceiling timbers have been moved about this arrangement may have been achieved only once the stack had been inserted. The first floor has fewer alterations, and a single bay next to the hall may have been the original site of the stairs, leading to a fine two-bay chamber at the back spanned by a crown-post roof with a decorative post to the open truss. At 34 High Street (Fig. 12.10) there was originally a two-bay chamber behind the hall, and although it has no distinctive features it was the largest room in the house after the hall. In other words, the best chamber, found at the front of 30 St Peter's Street and 7 Potter Street, was here located at the rear of the house. All the houses with evidence for galleries across the hall must have had the stairs to the rear, but in the absence of firm evidence it is impossible to say whether they had such a generous amount of rear accommodation as found at 38 King Street.

12.4 The outskirts of town: open-hall houses parallel to the street

In the outer parts of town, notably on Upper Strand Street, Fisher Street and near New Gate, several open-hall houses were arranged parallel to the street frontage. They were probably built in the middle or second half

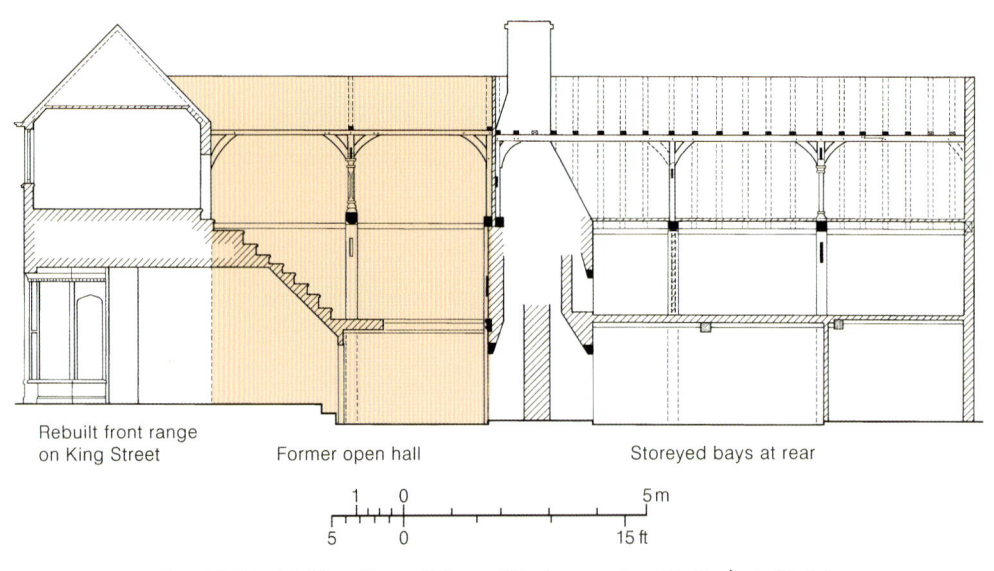

Fig. 12.20: 38 King Street (House 49), long section (S. P. & A. T. A.)

of the fifteenth century, although there is little by which to date them closely. All are of two storeys and were originally of wealden form, that is, the storeyed end bay or bays were jettied to the front, with a single roof, parallel to the street, running over them and the open hall, resulting in the hall appearing to be recessed.

No 22, 24 Upper Strand Street may be the earliest of them (House 96; Fig. 12.21). The plot was 10m (33ft) wide and was occupied by a hall with one two-storey end bay and a chamber over half the hall. One short bay of the hall (3m/10ft long) was open to the roof; the other, to the west, does not survive but has evidence to show that it had a chamber over, as in the reconstruction. The entry passage lay to the east with a chamber above in the manner termed 'overshot'.[24] In the open bay a false and structurally unnecessary 'tiebeam' carrying a moulded crown post was placed along the axis of the roof rather than across it, suggesting that despite the small size of the open bay this was the home of a well-to-do family, keen to adorn its miniature hall with high-status display features.

No. 19, 21 Upper Strand Street (House 95; Fig. 12.22) is another example of a hall with two two-storeyed end bays. The house is 11m (36ft) in length along the street, with a tiny 'upper' end bay, short hall, and longer 'lower' end bay with the entry passage again set under the first-floor chamber. High-quality seventeenth-century plasterwork has covered much of the detail making dating difficult, and a further storeyed bay, which formed part of the initial construction, now No. 23, makes the interpretation of functions uncertain. In these instances it was clearly possible for relatively wealthy people to obtain plots wide enough to build across the breadth of the plots, but to do so they had to live outside the centre of town.

The other houses of wealden form are on smaller plots, all less than 6m (20ft) in width along the street. The houses are less pretentious and possibly later, although still probably built in the fifteenth century. Each has only one two-storeyed end, with an 'overshot' entry passage beneath a first-floor chamber. At 7 Fisher Street the hall and passage take up the full (5m/16ft) length of the house (House 20; Fig. 12.23). The same arrangement occurs at 70 and 72 New Street, each built independently but with No. 70 (4.9m/16ft long overall) relying on the end wall of No. 72 (5.8m/19ft long) for its gable (Houses 64, 65; Fig. 12.24). Each house had a single-bay open hall, a wide cross passage that partially served as a room, and a single chamber upstairs. In No. 70 a first-floor doorway in the partition wall suggests that the chamber was accessed by ladder from the hall. 'Contracted' wealdens of this type have been found in terraces, as in the Spon Street area of Coventry, some

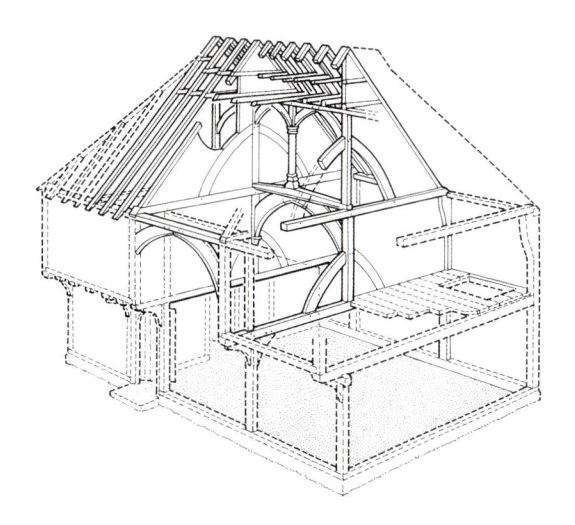

Fig. 12.21: 22, 24 Upper Strand Street (House 96), reconstruction of a wealden house with storeyed bays at each end (A. T. A.)

Fig. 12.22: 19, 21, 23 Upper Strand Street (House 95), view from the west (P. W. © English Heritage DP044044)

of the latter being built in 1454 or possibly earlier.[25] But in small towns they were also built in pairs or even singly.[26] While the builders of terraces were usually institutional landlords, the smaller developments may have been erected by private individuals, as was probably the case in Sandwich (Chap. 10.3.5). The New Street houses, which stand in what was known as Newgate in the Middle Ages, might even be those bequeathed in 1471 by Thomas Jekyn, husbandman, who left 'my tenement in the street called Newgate next the Delf, and another annexed to the same . . . ' to his wife, or other 'little' tenements recorded in the area in the early sixteenth century (Chap. 14.9).[27]

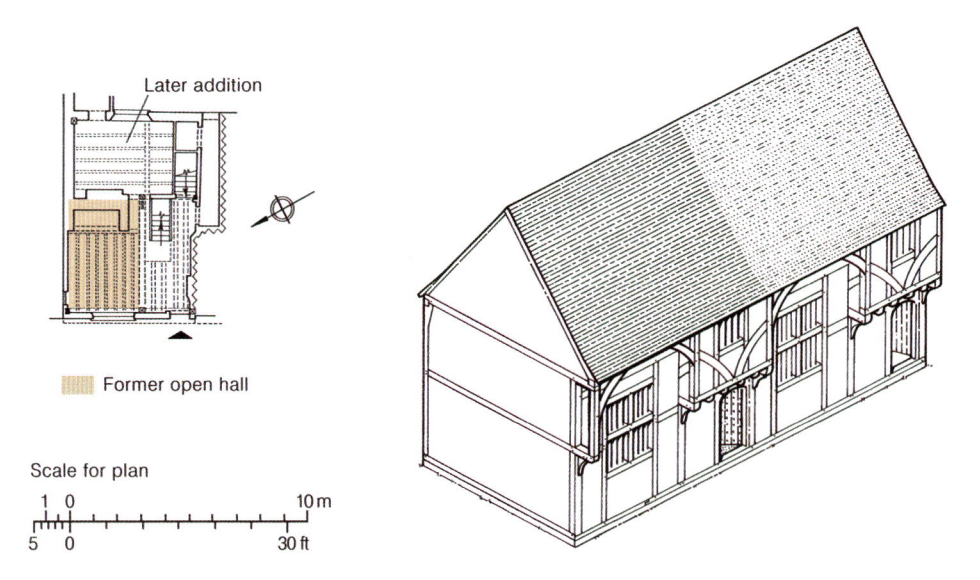

Fig. 12.23: 7 Fisher Street (House 20): a) plan with added joists in hall and later addition at rear; b) reconstruction showing how it, and its next-door neighbour, might have looked in the fifteenth century (A. T. A.)

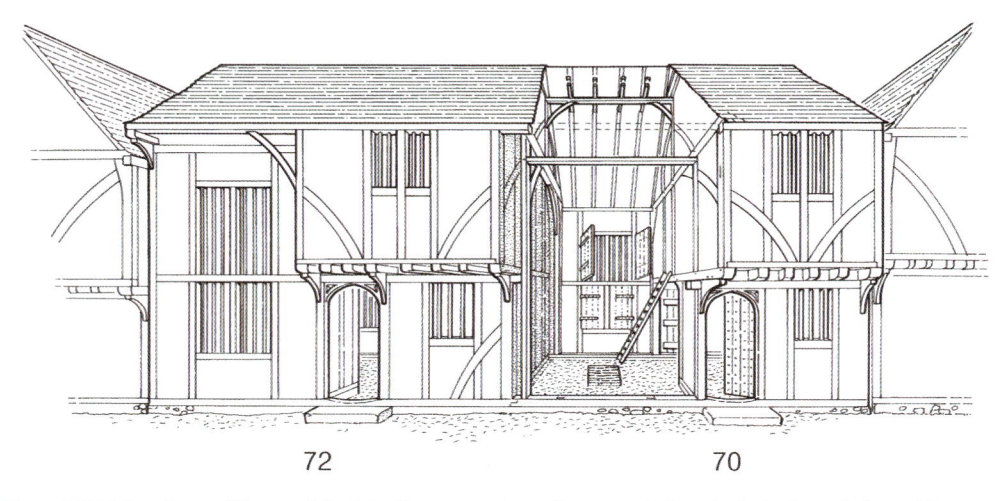

Fig. 12.24: 70 and 72 New Street (Houses 64, 65). Reconstruction of two semi-detached single-ended wealden open-hall houses (A. T. A.)

12.5 The size of houses

Some idea of both the development of the town's buildings and the distribution of house sizes within that development may be gained by examining the sizes of houses from the early fourteenth century to the early sixteenth. Since few of the open-hall houses survive in their entirety, it is impossible to make comparisons of overall size. The size of the hall alone, however, is often ascertainable, and since hall sizes were normally related to house sizes, they provide some idea of how large the houses were (Fig. 12.25).[28]

In the first place there was usually a relationship between the floor area of a hall and its height. In Sandwich, the open halls (including any passage area) of houses of all dates that were otherwise of three storeys (eleven examples) range in size between 12m^2 and 38m^2 (129ft^2 and 409ft^2), with an average and median size of 27m^2 (290ft^2), while open halls in houses of only two storeys (sixteen examples) range between 12m^2 and 41m^2 (129ft^2 and 441ft^2), with an average of 23m^2 (247ft^2) and a median of 24.5m^2 (264ft^2). Thus, although few in number, and allowing for unusually large or small halls at either end of the scale, the halls of two-storey houses were somewhat smaller than those of three-storey ones; in addition, the two-storeyed houses obviously had fewer rooms in relation to floor area than did the three-storey ones.

Secondly, the size of halls in surviving houses

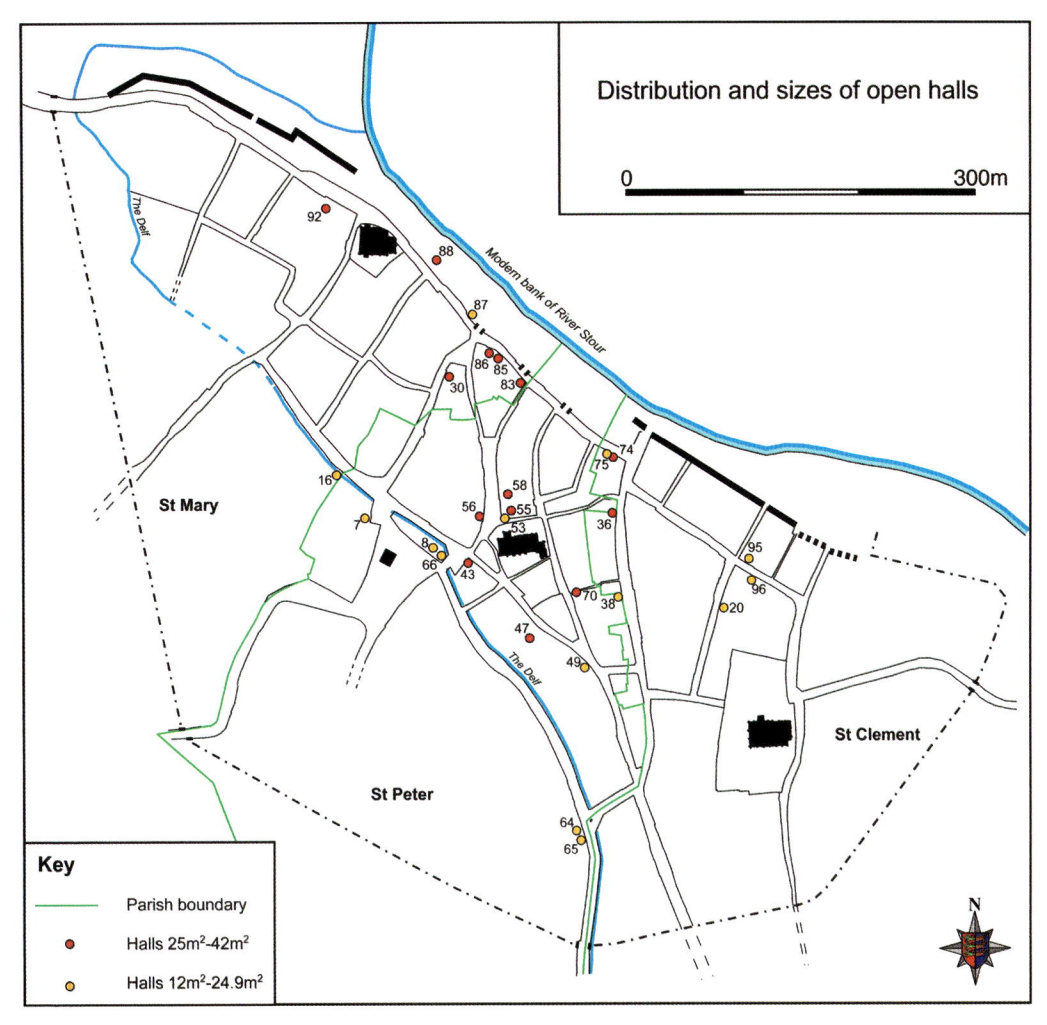

Fig. 12.25: Distribution of open halls by size (J. H.). Reproduced by permission of Ordnance Survey on behalf of HMSO. © Crown copyright 2009. All rights reserved. Licence number 100046522

decreased over time, dropping from an average of 30m² (323ft²) in the fourteenth century, through 24m² (258ft²) in the fifteenth century, to 22m² (237ft²) by the early sixteenth century. Finally, there is a difference in the distribution of house sizes: the largest houses with halls rising through three storeys are located in the central sections of the town, in or near the Fishmarket and St Peter's church and along Strand Street, while smaller houses, of two storeys, are located further out, in Fisher Street and Upper Strand Street, near New Gate, and in the Cornmarket. Open halls in houses that were otherwise of two storeys, therefore, were not only smaller but were also found in different parts of the town.

The issue of why houses decreased in size during the Middle Ages is a tricky one, and is not confined to Sandwich or to an urban context.[29] Since owners and occupiers are unidentifiable we can only guess that the majority of later and smaller houses were built for occupation by the less wealthy, and that the diminution in size in Sandwich means that no houses were built for the very wealthy in the fifteenth century, but that good-quality housing was gradually becoming available to sections of society not previously represented by standing structures. House size, like house height, may therefore be used to indicate zoning suggestive of social status, wealth and occupation. If the poor were accommodated in small single-storey houses, these no doubt stood at the margins of the town in the areas where so many houses were lost during the first half of the sixteenth century for the reasons outlined in Chapter 14.8 and 14.9.

12.6 Houses of the poor

There is little reason to suppose that the poorer or smaller houses, which do not survive, were arranged very differently from the small open-hall houses discussed above. In early fourteenth-century Winchester a row of three cottages, measuring about 5m × 5m (16ft × 16ft), seem to have contained a heated hall, passage and tiny inner chamber.[30] Later examples of such buildings may have had an upper chamber over the passage and part of the hall, as at 70, 72 New Street, Sandwich, whose dimensions are very similar to the Winchester properties. There is now a consensus of opinion that by the fifteenth century most people were occupying professionally built, well-constructed houses. In York, for example, some of the fourteenth- and fifteenth-century 'Rows' – purpose-built one-up/one-down rows of tenements erected by the ecclesiastical authorities for relatively poor tenants,[31] – were constructed well enough to survive today, 600 years after they were built. York may have been unusual in the form taken by its poorer housing, but it is likely that many of the houses erected elsewhere for poor people in the late fifteenth and sixteenth centuries could have survived if other factors had not intervened. Among the reasons that led to the destruction of poorer houses and cottages were the general decline of some towns, lack of maintenance, the need to cram people more tightly into towns that prospered, and the problems of adapting medieval buildings, whether to take more people or to satisfy later standards of living.

There is some debate about whether the York tenements and others like them were heated. If they were, with no open hearths, they must have had enclosed stacks from the start,[32] and in Sandwich there is little evidence for storeyed tenements of that sort except possibly in the central market areas (Section 12.8.2). Instead, it is probable that the poorer sections of society lived in single-storey dwellings with an open hall or main room, heated by an open hearth, and perhaps a small unheated inner room or chamber on the ground floor, exactly as excavated in Winchester. Their distinguishing features would have been that they were of low overall height and had no upper chamber. Turning such buildings into two-storey dwellings in the sixteenth century and later would have involved either total demolition, since the main posts would have been too short to reuse in two-storey buildings, or rebuilding on a scale that would have disguised earlier features.

12.7 Changes in the late fifteenth and early sixteenth centuries

The change from houses with open halls to those that were multi-storeyed throughout was slow and complex, and no precise dates can be given. In rural Kent, the process began at upper social levels in the second half of the fifteenth century, but smaller open halls continued to be constructed at least until the 1530s. A little later, earlier open halls were adapted by having ceilings and enclosed hearths inserted.[33] But what occurred in the countryside is not necessarily a guide to what happened in towns, for in Hampshire, in Rye, East Sussex, and in Farnham, Surrey, it has been suggested that the change came earlier in towns than in the countryside. In Hampshire, using only houses whose timbers were dated by dendrochronology, Edward Roberts has shown that the earliest town house without an open hall was built in 1477–8; the conversion of urban open halls began in the 1520s; and the last precisely dated open-hall house in an urban context was constructed in 1533. In Rye most of the open halls were ceiled by the mid-sixteenth century.[34] Thus in Sandwich one might expect significant evidence for fully floored houses and the flooring of formerly open halls from the years around 1500.

The evidence needs to be divided into two strands: first the introduction of fully floored houses, and second the ceiling of open halls. Since the latter can be seen as emulating the new forms introduced in fully floored houses, the introduction of fully floored houses will be discussed first.

12.7.1 Fully storeyed houses before c.1560

The details of the three-storeyed town-centre properties discussed in Section 12.3.4 are very similar to the open-hall houses surrounding them, implying that they were all built in the mid- or second half of the fifteenth century. They were, if interpreted as fully storeyed houses, almost certainly the earliest houses without open halls to have been built in the town. Not until around 1500 did some town-centre open-hall houses have their halls completely rebuilt with upper floors, and it was probably at much the same time that a few completely new fully floored houses were built towards the outer parts of town.

One of the earliest and finest of the new houses is 27, 29 King Street, formerly St Peter's rectory (House 48; Fig. 12.26). It lies away from the centre, ranged along the street with two rooms to either side of a double brick stack (the passage cut through it is much later), and well-detailed timber lintels and stone jambs to the fireplaces (Fig. 12.27). On the ground floor the hall, which was entered by a passage at the north end, has hollow-chamfered joists, and the beam and joists in the parlour are moulded in a manner normally associated with early sixteenth-century buildings (Fig. 12.28). The two upstairs chambers were also heated by brick fireplaces and the roof is of crown-post construction. Despite a lack of precise dating, the combination of structural and decorative details suggests a date around or a little after 1500; it is possible that it was built for Master Leonard Eaglesfield, clearly an educated and travelled man, who was rector from 1501 to c.1510.

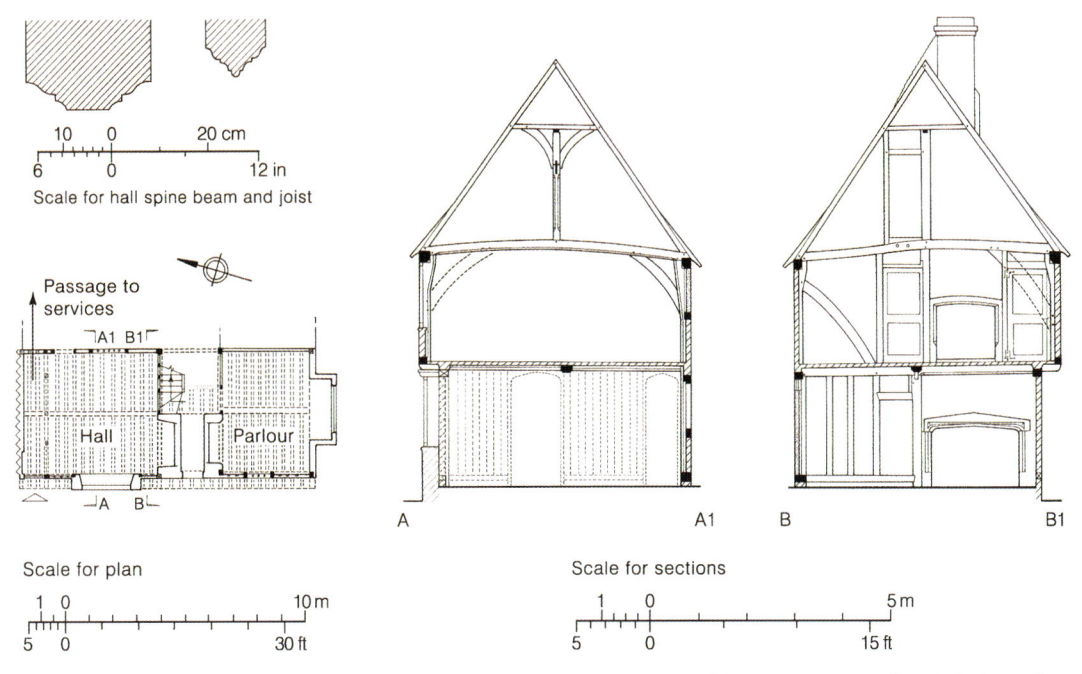

Fig. 12.26: 27, 29 King Street (House 48; St Peter's rectory), ground-floor plan of front range (rear demolished) and cross sections in hall (S. P. & A. T. A.)

Fig. 12.28: 27, 29 King Street (House 48; St Peter's rectory), parlour beam and joists (P. W. © English Heritage DP026212)

Fig. 12.27: 27, 29 King Street (House 48; St Peter's rectory), parlour fireplace (P. W. © English Heritage DP026206)

Thomas Pauley, the rector in 1565, had eight rooms, including a study, which was probably cut out of one of the upper chambers, as well as a buttery, a heated kitchen and another chamber, the last three almost certainly situated at the rear and now demolished.[35]

The two large courtyard houses exhibit the same high-quality decorative features in the rebuilding of what may have been their former open halls (Section 12.1). At 23 Strand Street the front was heightened by the addition of a third storey above the earlier shop, and the range behind was rebuilt with a finely moulded ceiling beam and joists (House 81; Fig. 12.46). It was probably the hall to a large house that at the time still occupied what is now No. 19, 21 (House 80), as well as 23 Strand Street. By 1505 the owner was William Baly, mayor in 1509 and one of the twenty wealthiest men in the town in 1513.[36] At 29 Harnet Street (House 28) the front range and southern rear wing were rebuilt, and the large room in the wing, which may replace a former open hall, was provided with roll-moulded joists.[37] The owner in the early sixteenth century is unknown, but the extent and sophistication of the work imply that the house was still in the hands of a wealthy family. By 1551 it was the home of Thomas Pinnock, a maltster in 1534 and mayor in 1548.[38]

The decorative details of these houses stand out from the much plainer work encountered in other buildings, the remains of which are often difficult to interpret. At 15 Upper Strand Street (House 94) hollow-chamfered joists in the large ground-floor room are similar to those in the hall at St Peter's rectory, but little else survives from which to understand the rest of the house. Next door, at 17 Upper Strand Street, two fine stone fireplaces (House 94; Fig. 12.33d) must have been built at much the same time. The remains of a sixteenth-century door frame between Nos. 15 and 17 imply that by the second quarter of the century the two houses may have formed one large property, possibly owned by William Crispe, jurat,[39] but they were independently constructed and may have had two different owners *c.*1500.

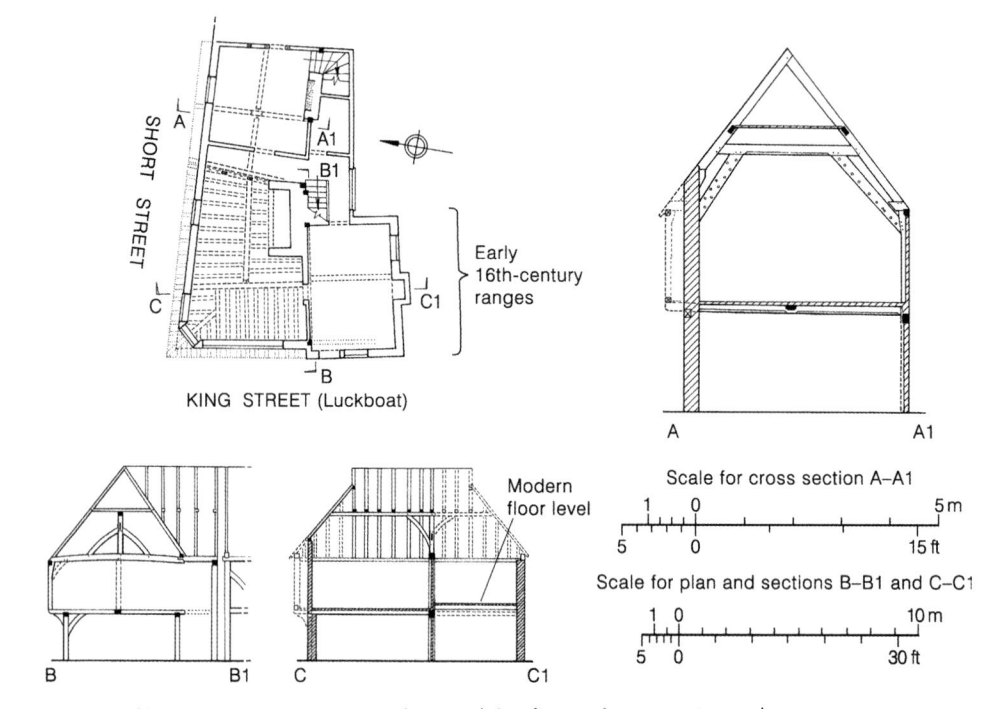

Fig. 12.29: 21 King Street (House 45), plan and sections (S. P. & A. T. A.).

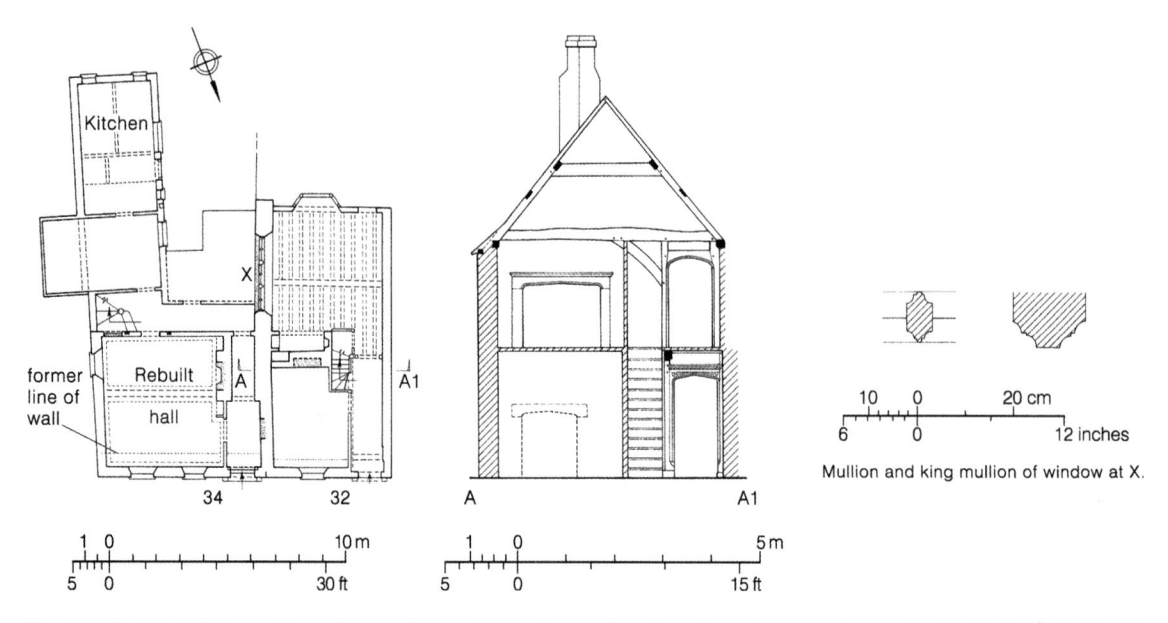

Fig. 12.30: 32, 34 Upper Strand Street (House 98), plan and section through cross wing at A–A1 (S. P. & A. T. A.).

Fig. 12.31: 32 Upper Strand Street (House 98), window in rear ground-floor room of cross wing (P. W. © English Heritage DP044048)

Fig. 12.32: 32 Upper Strand Street (House 98), details of doorway in cross wing (P. W. © English Heritage DP044046)

Other fully floored houses with wide joists and crown-post roofs likely to date from the first two decades of the sixteenth century are 21 King Street (House 45; Fig. 12.29), with three floored bays of indeterminate function on a corner plot; 3 Fisher Street (House 19), where only a single large room remains; and 11, 13 High Street (House 33), which probably had a central hall and additional rooms at either end. By *c*.1520 almost no new houses were being constructed in Sandwich. A rare example of a house probably built during the 1520s is now divided between 32 and 34 Upper Strand Street (House 98). It consists of a hall and a wing. The latter, No. 32, contains two rooms on each floor, separated by an original, double, brick stack (Fig. 12.30). A thick stone and flint wall to its east, almost certainly remaining from an earlier structure, was partially rebuilt in brick and provided with windows with hollow-chamfered mullions lighting the rear parlour and chamber over (Fig. 12.31). The hall range in No. 34 has been mostly rebuilt, although some framing and beams from *c*.1520 survive. At the back, a formerly detached timber building, now largely reconstructed, may be the remains of a detached kitchen of uncertain date. In No. 32 a doorway (Fig. 12.32) between the front and rear rooms has a four-centred head, double chamfers to the jambs, and leaf mouldings and the initials WW in the spandrels. It is tempting to suggest that these refer to William Wattes, baker, who owned a property on this side of Upper Strand Street between 1518 and 1529. He was an incomer who became a freeman in 1522, and had a mill at Sandown when he died in 1529. Positive proof that he owned this house, as opposed to the plot to the west, is lacking, but the coincidence of the initials is suggestive. This sort of decoration is unusual in Sandwich, except perhaps in inserted fireplaces, and suggests that little new construction took place between *c.*1520 and *c.*1560.[40]

12.7.2 *Heating and flooring of open halls*

As mentioned earlier, at Rye and in Hampshire towns many open halls are thought to have acquired enclosed fireplaces and ceilings during the first half of the sixteenth century. There is, however, remarkably little evidence for such changes in Sandwich. A number of fireplaces with shaped and moulded lintels date to the years either side of 1500 (Fig. 12.33a–d), but few of these are found in halls. Admittedly, one survives in the hall of 39 Strand Street (House 85; Fig. 12.33a), but the present ceiling is later, perhaps added in 1606 when a new hall window and doorway were introduced. An early sixteenth-century fireplace in a formerly open hall is also found, most surprisingly, at 7 Fisher Street (House 20), a small wealden in an outer part of the town, where the wide ceiling joists may be contemporary with the fireplace. But these are exceptions. Where visible, the inserted ceilings in open halls have beams with simple chamfers ending in runout stops and small, plain and widely spaced joists that are unlikely to date from before the middle of the sixteenth century; some may even date into the seventeenth century. The fireplaces that accompany these ceilings are of brick with plain timber lintels, also suggesting dates in the middle of the sixteenth century or after. In Sandwich, therefore, there is a gap between the dates when the earliest fully floored halls occur and the date when most of the surviving open halls appear to have been ceiled.

a

b

c

d

Fig. 12.33: Late fifteenth- and early sixteenth-century fireplaces: a) 39 Strand Street (House 85), hall (S. P.); b) 7 Potter Street (House 68), chamber; c) 20 St Peter Street (House 70), ground floor wing; d) 17 Upper Strand Street (House 94), chamber (P. W. © English Heritage DP044040, DP026056, DP068620)

Elsewhere in England it is clear that enclosed fireplaces were sometimes inserted prior to the hall being ceiled over. The best evidence lies in the presence of wall paintings on inserted brick or stone chimneys that were cut in half by the later introduction of ceilings.[41] Nothing quite so obvious survives in Sandwich, but it is worth exploring whether ceilings and fireplaces were inserted at different times, with the latter built into still-open halls. Three open halls with structural and decorative details dating to c.1500 or slightly later have honey-coloured roof timbers with no smoke blackening, suggesting that they were heated by enclosed fireplaces from the start. No. 3 Strand Street (House 74; Fig. 12.34) is the best example. There is no firm evidence for the suggested stack, but gaps in the moulded cornices that surround the room at two levels imply that it lay in the south-west corner, next to the rear extension, which is indicated by the presence of a first-floor gallery. In some houses it seems that the open halls were never completely ceiled. At 38 King Street, for example, although a late sixteenth-century fireplace with a chamfered and stopped lintel was inserted to heat one bay of the hall, this bay has no evidence for an inserted ceiling and still remains open today (House 49; Fig. 12.12). At 24 King Street (House 47) the front range was rebuilt c.1600, but half the hall behind was left open and seems to have been provided with an enclosed fireplace only in the nineteenth century; whether it remained in use as a hall or became a service area, as it is today, is not entirely clear. Both these halls had galleries that permitted access between the upper chambers at the front and back.

Corroborating evidence for the practice of inserting a fireplace but leaving the hall open comes from Sandwich's late sixteenth-century probate inventories.[42] Accurately identifying fireplaces from probate inventories is a risky business. They are never mentioned per se, and can be inferred only from the itemised goods associated with them. Even if the 'hall chamber' is not mentioned in an inventory, it does not necessarily mean that a hall was still open to the roof, since goods were frequently listed in chambers with terms such as 'the', 'another', 'his' or 'best', making deductions about their position impossible. As we have seen, however, several Sandwich open halls were crossed by galleries, and where these are mentioned in inventories, and combined with no reference to a hall chamber, it is likely that the hall remained open.

This conjecture is particularly compelling in eleven examples, ranging in date from 1572 to 1597, where the accompanying first-floor chambers include the 'fore chamber' or the 'chamber next the street', conjuring up an image of an open-hall house with the hall set behind

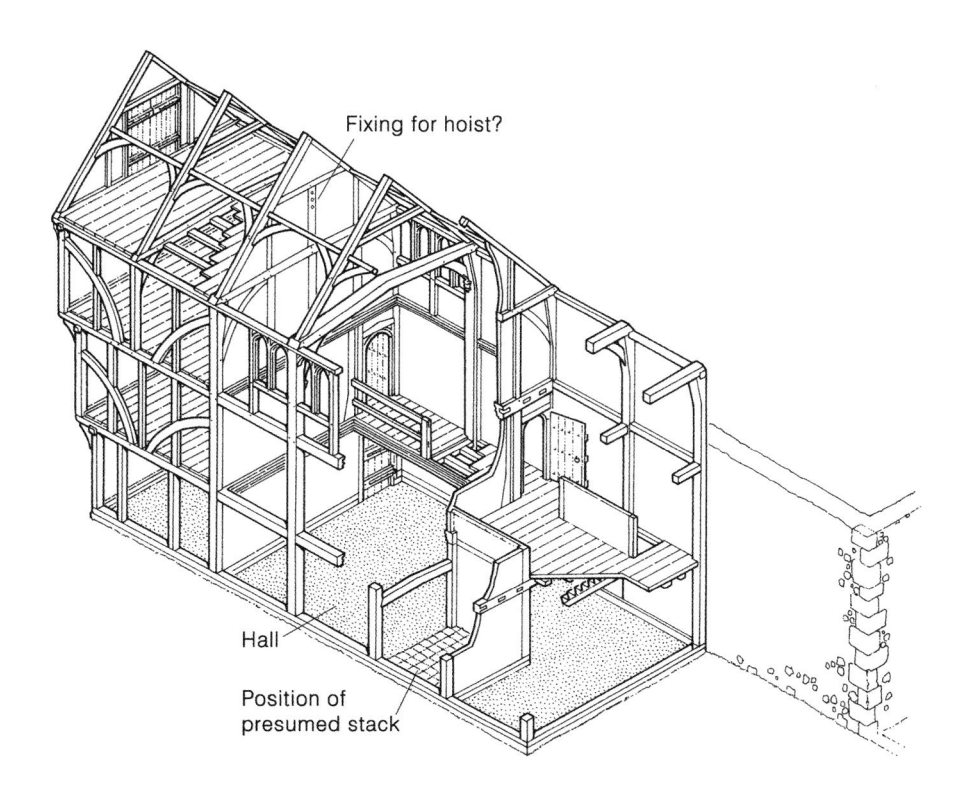

Fig. 12.34: 3 Strand Street (House 74), reconstruction showing storeyed front bays with reconstructed gable and fixing for possible hoist pegged to far side of the central strut. It also shows the open hall with high windows and gallery across, and the suggested rear bay, including a timber stack to heat the hall (A. T. A.)

a storeyed street range whose first floor was reached by a gallery.[43] All eleven inventories have evidence of fireplaces in the hall, but it is fairly clear that these were not open hearths: two people listed coal, a fuel unlikely to have been used in open hearths; one had a 'cole iron'; two had fire 'backs'; and another actually listed the goods 'in the chimney' in the hall. Thus the inference is that the hearths in these open halls were set in some kind of enclosed space.

So what form did the fireplaces take during the sixteenth century? Not only is evidence for early fireplace lintels sparse, but also the existing brick stacks, despite being notoriously difficult to date, mostly seem to have been built in the late sixteenth century or later. Although bricks were certainly imported into or through Sandwich in considerable numbers from the early fourteenth century and the town brickworks were in operation by the 1460s (Chap. 10.1.5.3), there is little firm evidence that brick was much used for private houses during the fifteenth century. The few documentary references include one to 200 bricks that were needed to repair a house in 1469, and one to the removal of bricks when a house was being demolished in 1513.[44] Since the documents are municipal this is perhaps not very convincing evidence in itself, but the scarcity of identifiable early brickwork suggests that the earliest stacks may have been built not of brick but of timber and plaster, and this is what is shown in the reconstruction drawing of 3 Strand Street (Fig. 12.34).

The presence of timber and plaster stacks should come as no surprise, for although surviving evidence for them is limited, they were common in the late Middle Ages. Where they were not part of the main frame they could be inserted easily, and subsequently removed with little trace.[45] Carpenters and daubers are recorded as constructing chimneys in London in the fifteenth century, indicating that they could occur in towns just as easily as in the countryside.[46] In Sandwich, fragments of a first-floor hearth seem to survive at 6 Market Street (House 55), where a three-storey open hall, perhaps built in the fourteenth century, was remodelled several times, leaving the remains of a narrow (1.8m) smoke bay at roof level and a mortice for a possible fireplace lintel on the first floor. Timber stacks, however, seldom served more than one fireplace,[47] and the fact that many brick stacks of the late sixteenth and seventeenth centuries were built with multiple flues, as at 38 King Street (House 49; Fig. 12.20), may indicate that their predecessors were not built of brick (which could have been added to) but had single fireplaces heating only the hall, with large timber and plaster hoods above. It is important to consider the possible presence of timber stacks when reviewing evidence for early fireplaces.

The most convincing evidence for the use of a brick chimney stack in an open hall is found at 39 Strand Street (House 85; Fig. 12.33a); here the fireplace opening has moulded timber jambs and a shallow-arched lintel, all apparently original although the brick side and back walls have been rebuilt. Similarly early lintels are found in other houses, but they appear to have been reused, either from original timber or brick stacks in a hall (Fig. 12.33c) or, if smaller, from fireplaces in parlours or chambers (Fig. 12.33b). In the roofs of several houses the presence of former timber chimneys is suggested by the fact that the area of rafters and collars cut away to accommodate the present brick stack is larger than strictly necessary for the purpose. The suggestion is, therefore, that by c.1540 most halls had been provided with enclosed fireplaces, although some of the halls remained open until at least the end of the sixteenth century. The late retention of open halls in Bristol has been linked to high-status ownership.[48] Up to a point this is true in Sandwich – the late sixteenth-century testators living in the eleven houses with open halls were all relatively wealthy in Sandwich terms, but they were by no means of aristocratic or gentry status (Section 12.9).

12.8 Commercial and industrial buildings

12.8.1 Inns

Inns were often large establishments, providing accommodation for travellers and their horses. The largest among them probably had a hall, and certainly had a kitchen, services, parlours and lodging chambers, the rooms frequently being set around a courtyard with galleries along the sides from which the various first-floor rooms could be accessed. They also incorporated stabling at the rear and often had shops along the street frontage.[49] In Sandwich, The Bull Inn seems to be the sole medieval survivor, and that only in part. It is known to have stood on the south side of Strand Street in St Peter's parish, and was almost certainly one of the medieval buildings, now 11–23 Strand Street, that still line the short stretch of Strand Street between Three King's Yard to the east and Love Lane to the west (Fig. 12.4).

The Bull Inn was first mentioned (as 'la Bolle') in 1466, when the town owned both the Belle and the Bolle; and is known to have continued in existence at least until 1549.[50] In 1482 a messuage called 'le Bole' formed an abutment to the east of a property on Love Lane,[51] and from other information it is almost certain that it lay east of the large building occupying 19, 21

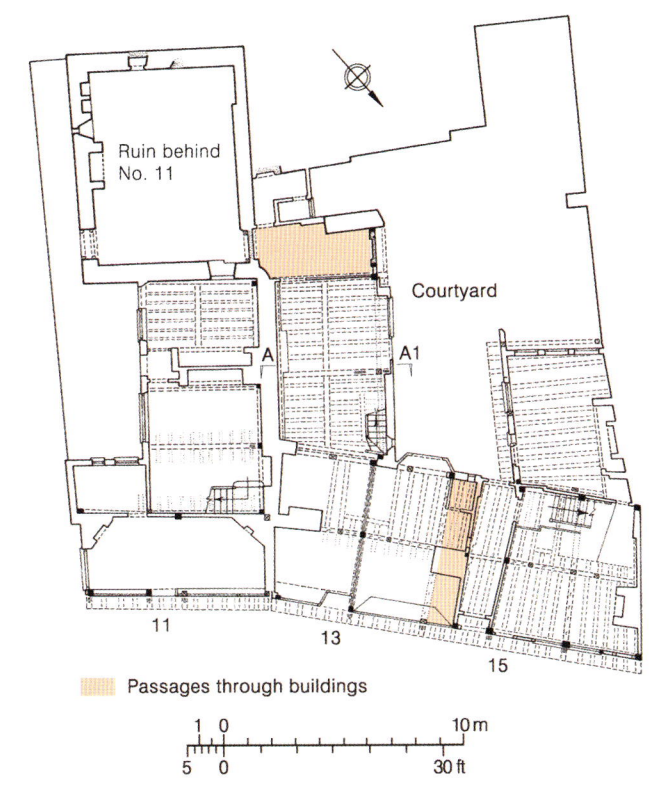

Fig. 12.35: 11, 13, 15 Strand Street (Houses 77, 78, 79), ground-floor plan (S. P. & A. T. A.)

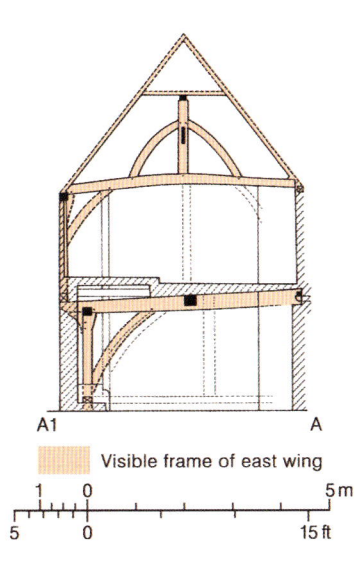

Fig. 12.36: 13 Strand Street (House 79), cross section through east wing of 13, 15 Strand Street at A–A1 on plan (S. P. & A. T. A.).

and 23 Strand Street (Houses 80, 81). A complicated series of documents confirms this identification, and suggests that the inn was 13, 15 Strand Street (House 79), with a wide archway leading through a street range of shops into the inn yard (Figs 12.3, 12.35). One might therefore have expected high-quality ranges at the rear, but, surprisingly, the partially surviving rear ranges do not provide evidence of either lodgings or communal areas.

The complex was constructed *c.*1500, and with four shops at the front was typical of many medieval inns (Figs 12.42, 12.44; Section 12.8.2). But the partially surviving courtyard ranges behind the shops show few of the features associated with inns. Both ranges have large two-bay rooms on each floor with no evidence for galleries or lodgings. On the east side, the presence of a heavy brace in the middle of a ground-floor room (Fig. 12.36) is more in keeping with a storage, service or even stabling function than a domestic room in an inn. Behind that was a passage from the courtyard to the undercroft of the stone range of *c.*1300 at the back of 11 Strand Street (House 78). The fact that a timber doorway of *c.*1500 was constructed leading to this from the courtyard of Nos. 13, 15 indicates that it was still part of that property, although the documents suggest that the front range of No. 11 (House 77) by then belonged to someone else.

It was suggested earlier (Chap. 7.2.2) that in the fourteenth century Nos. 11, 13, 15 Strand Street formed part of a large merchant property that ran much further to the south than it does today (Fig. 12.3). This may have still been the case in 1500, when the original building, no longer required as a private dwelling, was largely rebuilt. If the plot were as extensive as it may have been earlier, the inn would have occupied a long rectangular site in the manner of some more famous medieval inns in other towns. Since the south ends of the side ranges and any structure across the south side of the courtyard have been demolished, valuable evidence for its use as an inn may have been destroyed. A lack of diagnostic features in the structure does not in itself prove that this site was not an inn, for there are problems of interpretation in many of the well-known inns published by Pantin. He found that the hall, for example, was often small and difficult to locate.[52] If there were a hall at 13, 15 Strand Street, it could well have been to the south of the surviving north-west range and no longer open to the roof by 1500. More perplexing is the lack of evidence for galleries, or for a series of stairs (another way of reaching first-floor lodgings), or for smart chambers in the side ranges. As pointed out by all who have examined the construction of medieval inns, however, many buildings known from documents to have been inns are hard to identify as such from surviving medieval remains.

12.8.2 Shops and workshops

The earliest surviving shops in the town are found in fourteenth-century buildings along Strand Street. All the timber houses discussed in Chapter 7 may have had them, and their conjectural arrangements can be

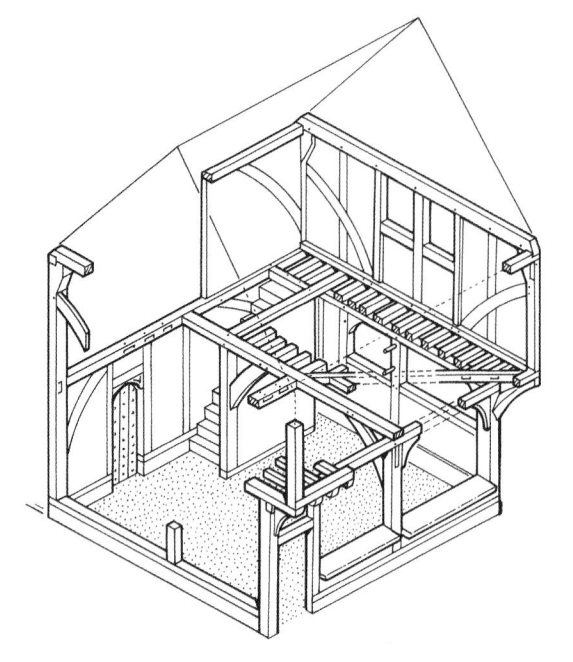

Fig. 12.37: Reconstruction of front of lower two storeys of 23 Strand Street (House 81), illustrating shop window openings (A. T. A.)

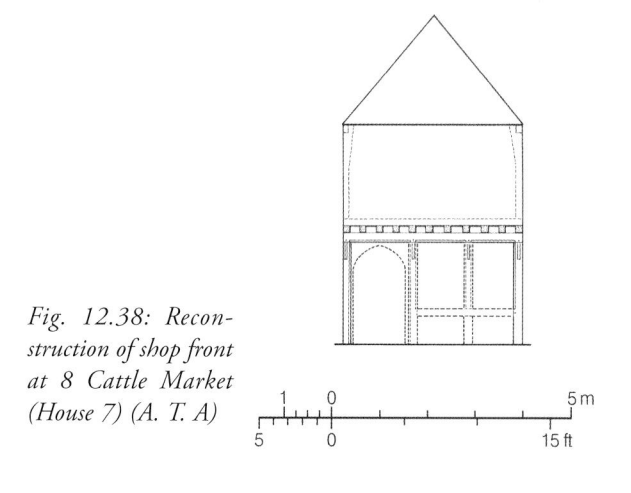

Fig. 12.38: Reconstruction of shop front at 8 Cattle Market (House 7) (A. T. A)

seen in the reconstruction of No. 39 (House 85; Fig. 7.22). Evidence for shop windows, probably of the fourteenth century, is visible at 23 Strand Street (House 81; Fig. 12.37), and the framework for the windows of a fifteenth-century shop was found at 8 Cattle Market (House 7; Fig. 12.38). In the last two examples the shops appear to have been single and sizeable, and because they were entered through a doorway that also led to the hall behind, it is likely that they were integrated with the domestic accommodation. No survivors have evidence for an independent shop doorway of the type well known in East Anglia,[53] although houses in which there was a gallery across the hall could have had a ground-floor shop in separate occupation from the dwelling above and behind.

A second type of shop, not found surviving before the fifteenth century, had several units grouped in one building.[54] No. 1 The Butchery (House 3), in St Peter's parish on the edge of the Fishmarket, is a single structure containing two mirror-image shops with dwellings above and behind. Although the street frontage has been replaced, and the back of the house destroyed in a fire, the rear half of the front bays of two single-bay shops survives, the back walls retaining evidence for small doorways leading to further accommodation beyond (Fig. 12.39). Property in The Butchery was valuable and was sometimes owned entirely for rent, but some butchers were owner-occupiers and had more than one house. In 1474 William Joynte bequeathed his own house in The Butchery, in St Peter's parish, and one 'new built' where his son John lived.[55] In 1542 John Basedon, son of William, butcher, had 'two tenements together', one of which he dwelt in, further along the street in St Mary's parish.[56] These documented examples are unlikely to relate to the surviving structure, but they probably describe very similar buildings.

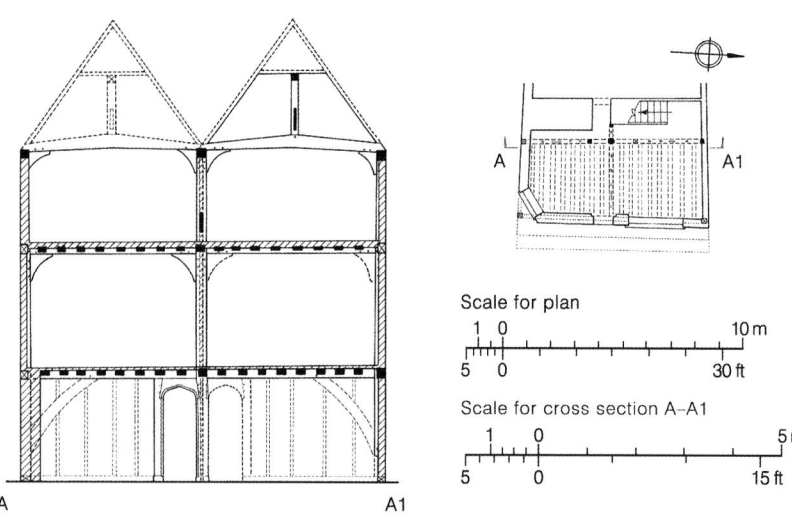

Fig. 12.39: 1 The Butchery (House 3). Two semi-detached shops, cross section and ground-floor plan of front bays (S. P. & A. T. A.)

Fig. 12.40: No Name Shop, No Name Street (formerly 11 Cattle Market) (House 66) from the north-east (P. W. © English Heritage DP043984)

In other examples more than two shops were involved. The No Name Shop (formerly 11 Cattle Market), on the corner of the Cornmarket and No Name Street, with the Delf to the north, is a two-storey building of wealden form, that is, with an apparently recessed hall, built in the mid- or later fifteenth century (House 66; Fig. 12.40). The ground-floor walls and shop windows have gone, but the layout can be reconstructed from the partition mortices and the roof (Fig. 12.41). The building had four small spaces around two sides, which could have been entered only from the street and must have been shops or workshops. A passage between two of them led to a tiny open hall with a smoke-blackened roof behind, and from there doorways led to an inner room and stairs to two upstairs chambers. A third chamber has no visible evidence for an internal doorway but evidence for an external loading doorway in one wall. The west wall of the building has been rebuilt and it is impossible to tell whether it always had an abutting neighbour, as at present, or whether it was originally free-standing on that side.

Because of its clearly defined position on the edge of the marketplace, with the Delf at the back and the road to the east, this building should be identifiable in the records. From 1444 onwards documents show that the town owned a number of shops in the Cornmarket. In 1444 a smith leased two of them on the corner of the marketplace, and in 1497 rent was received from another smith. In the mid- and later sixteenth century both the 'long rents of the smythes' and the corner shop

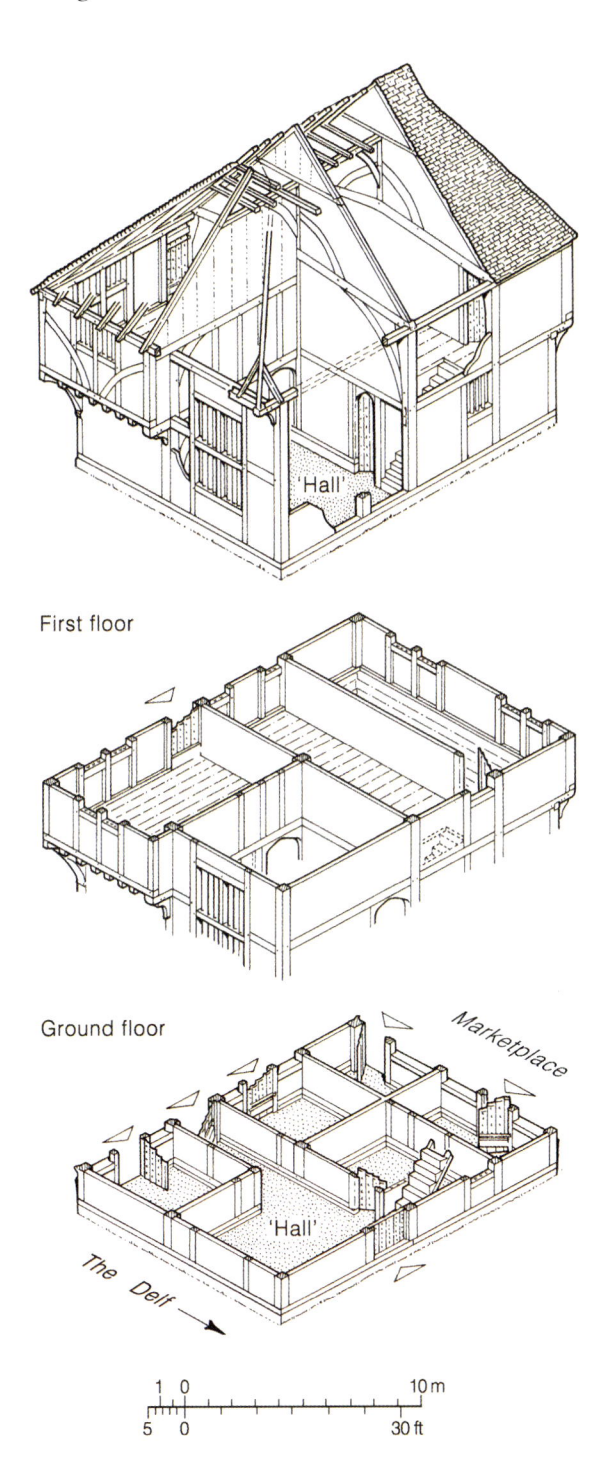

Fig. 12.41: No Name Shop, No Name Street (formerly 11 Cattle Market) (House 66). Three-dimensional drawing and reconstructed plans of both floors showing arrangement of 'hall', shops, stair and storage chambers with arrows indicating likely positions of doorways (A. T. A)

next to it were tenanted by smiths, with the 'corner shop' possibly referring to the surviving building.[57] But there was also a privately owned corner tenement that is an even more likely candidate, for when it was sold by the pewterer William Cokyn in 1522 it was described as having 'the Cornmarket to the south, the Delf to the north and the highway to the east'.[58] Thus, the documents suggest that, whether owned by the town or privately, the No Name Shop was occupied by metalworkers during the fifteenth and sixteenth centuries.

Although large-scale smithing was probably more often pursued in smithies outside town centres, the making and retailing of metal household wares were often associated with marketplaces, for example at Tonbridge and Cambridge.[59] Could the tiny open hall of the No Name Shop have been not a domestic room but a forge, with a hearth used by a number of smiths whose trading premises lay on the street frontage? The water essential for smithing could have been extracted from the Delf, which still runs just beneath the 'hall' window on the north side of the building. A later building to the west has destroyed any evidence for the west wall of the No Name Shop, but it is not beyond the bounds of possibility that a doorway on this side originally opened into an alley between it and 9 Cattle Market (House 8), providing direct access from the forge to the water. The three chambers on the first floor may have been used purely for storage – as the one accessed only by external ladder must have been – so the building may have contained no domestic accommodation at all. Another building in which workspace and storage were probably combined, and with no domestic accommodation, is 3 Mill Wall Place (House 61), a four-bay building of the early sixteenth century recently identified as a workshop heated by a smoke bay.[60]

Documents indicate that shops were common in the Cornmarket, the Fishmarket and on the central section of Strand Street, and a row of four occupy the front range of 13, 15 Strand Street (House 79), built c.1500 and already tentatively identified as part of The Bull Inn. The plan and elevation can be reconstructed, and show that there were two shops or workshops either side of a central archway (Figs 12.42–12.44). Each had two rooms on the ground floor, the back one having no evidence for either a doorway or a window to the courtyard but containing stairs to an unheated chamber above. Although this is the only row of shops still identifiable on Strand Street, there must have been others on the north side, for in 1453 John Boteler, draper, bequeathed a messuage 'with all the shops annexed to the same as far as the sea gate (*ad portam maris*)', and in 1491 two workshops with garrets above were sold.[61]

Shop ranges of this kind have been found in other towns, and have sparked debate about whether they contained unheated domestic accommodation on the

Fig. 12.42: 13, 15 Strand Street (House 79), possibly The Bull Inn, front range of four shops (P. W. © English Heritage DP043964)

Fig. 12.43: 13, 15 Strand Street (House 79), detail of archway to courtyard of possible Bull Inn (P. W. © English Heritage DP032245)

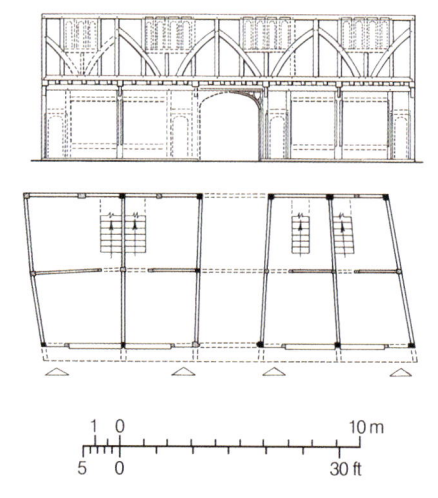

Fig. 12.44: 13, 15 Strand Street (House 79), reconstructed plan and elevation of shops (S. P. & A. T. A.)

upper floors or were used entirely for business and storage purposes.[62] It has been argued that craftsmen did not need much room for storage, and that poor people, the assumed occupants of such buildings, did not need warmth and bought their food from cookshops. The first point may be true, but the assumptions about poor people are open to question. It can be argued that structures of a quality able to survive for several hundred years are unlikely to have been intended for domestic occupation by tenants who were so poor that they were unable to afford to heat their homes. In addition, the evidence for sales and rents on Strand Street suggests that property there was among the most valuable in the town (Chap. 14.2). It is more likely, therefore, that the absence of signs of heating demonstrates that this range was divided and rented out for purposes of craft, trade and storage alone, as suggested at the No Name Shop. Comparisons may be drawn with some properties in London and several East Anglian towns with storage both behind and above the shops.[63] This leads to another point, which is that the occupiers of shops or workshops of this kind must have lived elsewhere, possibly in some of the cottages mentioned in the documents. Unfortunately, we have no information on this matter, for the tenant or sub-tenant of a shop space was probably also a tenant of his home, and there is little surviving documentation about such people.

Although there is limited evidence for shops in Sandwich, it is noticeable that the fourteenth-century survivors are different from those of the later fifteenth century. In the earlier period, identifiable shops were single or perhaps double spaces in front of what were almost certainly single dwellings. They could have been either owner-occupied or tenanted. By the second half of the fifteenth century, however, some surviving shops were built in units of two or more, clearly intended for rent. This may reflect a changed social structure. Nos. 13, 15 Strand Street was certainly rebuilt on a site that had been occupied in the fourteenth century, if not earlier. Although there is no evidence for its fourteenth-century appearance, it is likely to have been part of a large owner-occupied property, possibly of three storeys like other fourteenth-century buildings on Strand Street. In the late fifteenth century whatever occupied the site was replaced by a complex of two-storey buildings, with a row of shops on the street front and what may have been an inn behind, the whole site owned by a member of the Sandwich elite but entirely occupied by tenants. That the original was replaced suggests both that the use of the site had changed and that there was no longer any need for the kind of buildings that had been appropriate a hundred and more years earlier, and

Fig. 12.45: 1, 3 King Street (Houses 41, 42), with St Peter's church behind (P. W. © English Heritage DP044036)

that, at least until 1500, the ruling class in Sandwich still had enough confidence in the future of the town to invest in new building.

The function of 1 and 3 King Street (Houses 41, 42) was probably similar. This is a long, narrow structure on the edge of St Peter's churchyard (Fig. 12.45), erected during the fifteenth century. It was built in two stages, both of two storeys, and jettied on three sides. The bay divisions on the ground floor have been destroyed and there is no visible sign of stairs or original heating. On the first floor there was possibly a two-bay chamber in the earlier, western, half, and two chambers in the later half to the east. Large ceiling joists above the first floor of the west end imply that, despite having intrusive crown posts, the roof space (which was not a proper loft) was used for storage. Partial though the evidence is, it seems likely that this was a range on the edge of the churchyard containing both shops and storage. It may originally have been owned by the church, since ecclesiastical authorities are known to have built speculative developments on the edges of churchyards,[64] but by the late fifteenth century the building was almost certainly in private hands, forming part of the nine messuages on the corner in the west part of St Peter's churchyard that were bequeathed by Henry Bolle, brewer, in 1481.[65] A three-storey building of the same sort may be shown in the late eighteenth-century engraving of the Fishmarket (Fig. 14.5), which was probably the 'corner house at St Peter's church stile in the Fishmarket' given to the Jesus Mass in St Mary's church in 1494.[66]

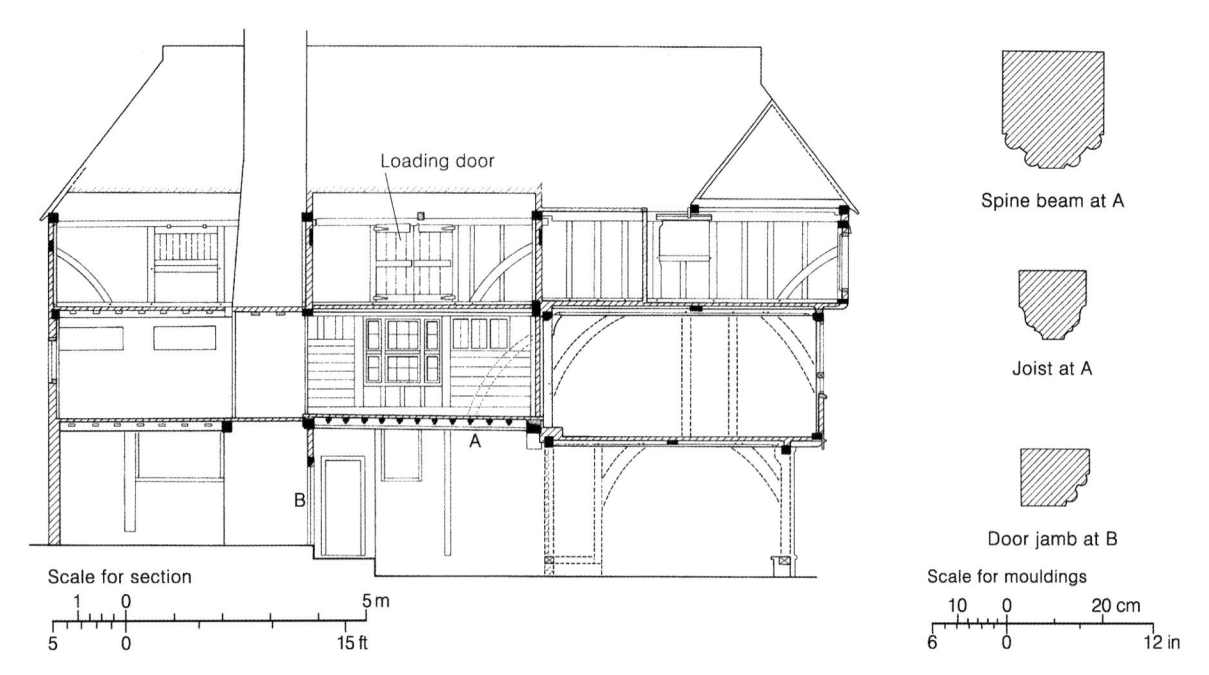

Fig. 12.46: 23 Strand Street (House 81), long section from the east showing early sixteenth-century additions above and behind the earlier building, and top-storey loading doorway to middle bay (A. T. A.)

12.8.3 Storage facilities

No storage building in Sandwich equals the splendour of the merchant warehouses in King's Lynn,[67] or the fifteenth-century timber warehouse built by the town on the quay in Faversham. Wine and cured fish were important trading goods in Sandwich in the thirteenth and fourteenth centuries, and during that time a number of cellars that would have been suitable for storing such goods were available for hire.[68] They probably lay along the waterfront, but none appears to survive. Occupying valuable commercial sites, they may have been replaced by new buildings with a different function after the decline of the wine trade in the second half of the fifteenth century.

On the other hand, there is evidence for relatively small-scale storage incorporated into the later medieval buildings of the town. This includes not only the multiple shop-cum-storage units already discussed, but dwellings, particularly along Strand Street, designed to include storage on the upper floors. Early fourteenth-century examples have already been discussed (Chap. 7.3), and such houses continued to be erected throughout the Middle Ages. At 23 Strand Street the early sixteenth-century alterations included the addition of an upper storey lit by large shuttered openings without mullions, some of them starting at floor level and remaining unglazed until the late twentieth century (House 81; Figs 12.4, 12.46), suggesting that the upper storey was devoted to storage, the openings used for hoisting goods up from the street.

No direct evidence for shops below or storage above is visible in the front range of 19, 21 Strand Street (House 80), which was part of the same complex as 23 Strand Street and situated on the far side of a wide entrance bay, or in the front range of 29 Harnet Street (House 28), but the plainness of the structures and the fact that they formed the most accessible parts of large courtyard houses owned by wealthy inhabitants suggest that they may not have served domestic functions. Storage on upper floors must have been for dry goods, perhaps initially wool and later grain; in the late sixteenth and early seventeenth centuries the wills of farmers in the surrounding countryside refer to grain stored in lofts in Sandwich, perhaps upper floors of this type.[69]

A clearer example of roof storage above domestic accommodation occurs at 3 Strand Street (House 74), dated c.1500. Heavy joists survive above the second storey, and the queen strut in the closed truss between the storeyed front and the open hall is reinforced on the front by what appears to be a piece of original timber, which may be the remains of the fixing for a hoist to draw up goods from the street below (Figs 12.34, 12.47). This is a unique survival of what may have been a common feature. The front sections of almost all the roofs of medieval houses in Sandwich have been rebuilt, often because the jettied upper storeys have been cut back. Most of the present roofs have hips (examples illustrated here can be seen in Figs 12.13, 12.14, 12.19, 12.34, and there are many others), and it is possible that they replace gables through which bales and sacks could have been hauled up.

12 Secular buildings

Fig. 12.47: 3 Strand Street (House 74), timber block on street face of closed roof truss at north end of the hall. It is suggested that it was put here as part of a hoist to draw goods up from the street to the left (S. P.)

Occasionally, surviving timber buildings seem to have been devoted entirely to storage. The few known examples are situated some distance from the waterfront and their purpose may have been different from that of the Strand Street houses. No. 6 King Street is one of the few buildings erected *c*.1400, the date indicated by the heavy timbering and the splayed and tabled scarf joint to the central collar purlin of the roof (House 44; Fig. 12.48). It is of two storeys, floored throughout with no internal partitions, and with large, heavily braced timbers carrying both the first and attic floors. Instead of the usual intrusive crown posts, the collar purlin in the roof is supported by extra collars, allowing more space for storage. The front hip to the roof has been rebuilt and probably replaces a gable in which there could have been a hoist. The Delf runs just south of this property, and a late fifteenth-century will of one Thomas Colman refers to 'my corner house at St Peter's church stile in the Fishmarket . . . and a storehouse to the same standing upon the Delfside in the same parish';[70] this could well have been 6 King Street, but there is no evidence for Colman's trade or what he was using his storehouse for. Evidence of heavy first-floor joists at the outbuilding to 21 King Street (House 46; Fig. 12.49) also suggests attic storage, despite the presence of a crown-post roof, although whether the whole building was a storehouse is unclear.

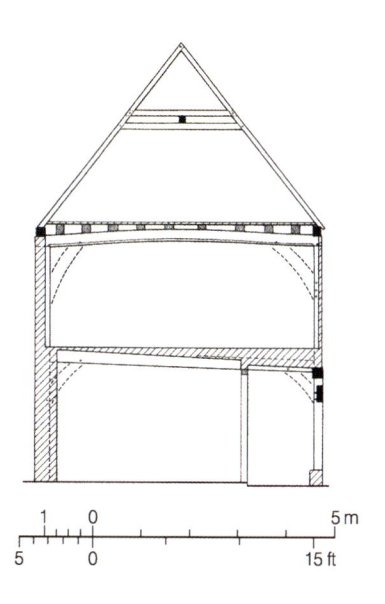

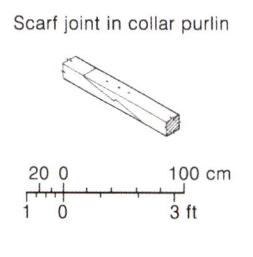

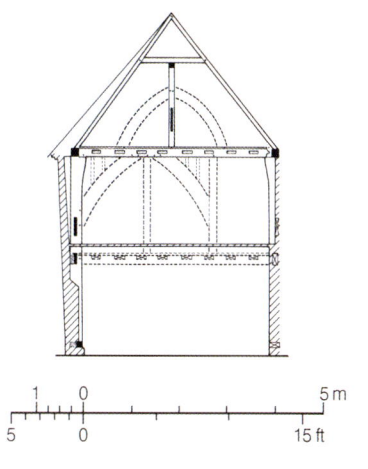

Fig. 12.48: 6 King Street (House 44), cross section showing reinforced flooring and method of carrying collar purlin (S. P. & A. T. A.)

Fig. 12.49: 21 King Street (House 46), cross section of outbuilding showing large mortices for joists at roof level (S. P. & A. T. A.)

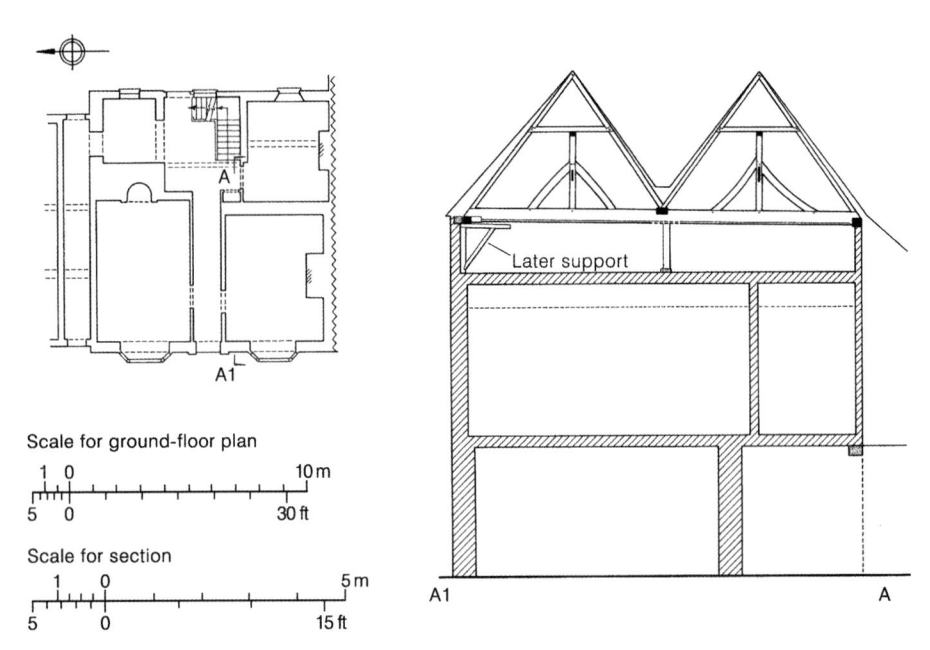

Fig. 12.50: 25 High Street (House 37), ground-floor plan and cross section showing two ranges of crown-post roofs parallel to the street (S. P. & A. T. A.).

The only other structure that may have been a purpose-built storehouse is 25 High Street (House 37), a double-pile house with three storeys and attic that appears from the front and lower storeys to have been erected in the nineteenth century. On the second floor, however, there is detailing of domestic character of *c.*1600, and the attic suggests an even earlier origin. It forms one huge space roofed in two parallel ranges with crude crown-post trusses (Fig. 12.50). Each range contains three plain crown posts perhaps dating to the first half of the sixteenth century, with the sheer size of the structure suggesting that the building was erected as a multi-storeyed warehouse converted into a dwelling *c.*1600. Since no floor joists or wall posts are visible below roof level, this conclusion must remain untested.

12.9 The function and use of medieval houses

A great deal has been written above about open halls, heating, shops and storage, all of which are identifiable from the physical remains, but the frequently asked question of how the houses were used has only been touched upon. Except in the hall, medieval buildings have few diagnostic features for the original uses of many of their rooms. Furthermore, most Sandwich houses survive only in part, so discussing room functions from physical evidence is tricky, and documentary sources, notably probate inventories, are needed if more is to be learned about the functions that the buildings served. The inventories do not start to survive until 1564, so detailed analysis and the problems associated with interpreting them will be discussed in Chapter 16.5. The question here is whether some information in the inventories may be relevant to earlier buildings. It has already been argued (Section 12.7.2) that at least eleven inventories describe houses with medieval open halls; it is this core group that is discussed below in relation to the surviving buildings.

Among surviving houses, 39 Strand Street, 34 High Street and 38 King Street are the only ones with rear halls that may be complete (Figs 7.22, 12.10, 12.20). The first, of the early fourteenth century, has evidence for eleven rooms, but, as discussed in Chapter 7, it is unclear how much was occupied by the owner or occupant of the hall himself, how much may have been occupied by someone else, or how much was used for non-domestic purposes. No. 38 King Street, the only fifteenth-century house in which both the hall and the rear domestic accommodation remain, is of two storeys but has lost its front bay. Overall, the house seems to have contained seven rooms. The number of rooms in the early sixteenth-century 34 High Street was probably five. In all three cases there could have been a detached kitchen at the back for which no evidence remains. In other houses, although the front and the hall survive, the rear has gone, or what may have been a cross wing survives with no hall range. Most are likely to have contained between five and eight rooms, depending upon whether they were of two or three storeys and how many bays lay beyond the hall. Of the 165 houses with room names in the probate inventories, and leaving aside for the moment the problem of completeness discussed in Chapter 16.5, the median number of rooms in the houses is 5, and the average 5.6. Thus, whatever the shortcomings of the documents, the surviving houses with rear halls, mostly within the town centre, represent the larger houses in Sandwich.

Of the eleven houses in the probate inventories that had galleries, suggesting that they were medieval in origin, and still had open halls, five were of three storeys (normally indicated by the term garret), and six were of only two. They contained from six to fifteen rooms, and the fact that the values of their goods were all in the upper two quartiles of the inventories in the late sixteenth century (Chap. 16.5.1) indicates that the inventories are for the homes of the well-to-do. All had halls, ten had kitchens, eight had parlours, seven had butteries and six had shops. The other rooms were largely chambers of varying kinds. Of course, even if the late sixteenth-century probate inventories are describing medieval buildings, the houses may have been updated and enlarged by then.

The hall in most medieval houses was a general-purpose room with tables, trestles, benches, forms and stools for sitting and eating. It was heated by an open hearth, where cooking often took place, although in larger houses at least some cooking was done in a separate kitchen. In crowded towns with houses running back from the street frontage, the normal diagnostic features of the 'standard' hall of medieval houses in south-east England, that is, a cross entry at one end with services beyond and the 'dais' at the opposite end, are seldom found. This includes the houses described in the eleven Sandwich inventories, for their galleried halls must have taken up the entire width of the building, with the passage beneath the gallery running from front to back along the side wall. Thus, the relationship of passage to services had to have changed, and since in Sandwich halls there is no sign of the twin service doorways of the 'standard' medieval plan found in rural Kent, there is little architectural evidence for where the services lay. There is also little evidence for moulded dais beams marking the 'upper' or superior end of the hall, a common feature in better quality houses in Kent. Some halls, for example 38 King Street (House 49; Fig. 12.20) and 3 Strand Street (House 74; Fig. 12.34), had moulded cornices similar in style to dais beams, but they go right round the hall and do not distinguish a seat of honour in the manner of rural buildings. At 39 Strand Street, dated 1334, a hollow-chamfered beam set into the east wall opposite the entrance may be a dais beam (House 85; Fig. 7.21), and a similarly simple moulding to a cross beam at 4 King Street, opposite the galleried passage, may not have been repeated on the other walls. Although these are the only examples in which there is any architectural clue for how the hall might have been arranged, they may show that the seat of honour, if there were one, was usually set against the side wall opposite the passage and gallery.

By the mid-sixteenth century houses of any pretension would everywhere have had a parlour,[71] but wills and inventories suggest that in fifteenth-century rural Kent parlours were still rare and confined to the homes of wealthy owners. They were always on the ground floor; they might contain beds, but were sometimes used only for sitting and entertaining, not for sleeping.[72] The only parlour mentioned in Sandwich in the late fifteenth century (1482) was in the house of a former mayor, William Kennet, and there is no evidence as to how it was furnished.[73] A large house such as 29 Harnet Street (House 28; Fig. 12.1) almost certainly had a parlour, perhaps in the surviving north wing, but in the crowded town centre there was little ground-floor space left over once a shop, a hall and a service room of some kind had been accommodated. No parlours have been clearly identified in fifteenth-century houses, and it is possible that most ground-floor rooms at that time were devoted to business, storage or service functions. By 1500, however, the situation may have been changing, and in new-style, fully floored houses, at least in the outer parts of town, parlours were definitely coming in, as indicated by the southern room at 27, 29 King Street and the rear room at 32 Upper Strand Street (Houses 48, 98; Figs 12.26, 12.27, 12.30, 12.31).

On the other hand, butteries, where comestibles and utensils were stored and food may have been prepared, were probably common in the fifteenth century and penetrated further down the social scale (despite the popular belief that medieval houses had pantries and butteries, few inventories below a very high social level ever list pantries).[74] As an example, in Canterbury in 1497 four houses were to be erected with shops and butteries at the front, and halls and kitchens behind; the single upper chamber, reached from a stair in the hall, clearly lay at the front, indicating that the hall and kitchen were single-storeyed, probably to be heated by open hearths.[75] This not only shows that small open halls were still being constructed in 1497, but also indicates that butteries and even kitchens were required in houses that had no parlour, and that the buttery might be placed at the front of the building. This was clearly not possible where there was a single shop across the front, but may have occurred in other houses running back from the street in parts of town for which there is no evidence for shops, for example in the small houses at 17 Delf Street and 34 High Street (Houses 16, 38; Figs 12.10, 12.11).

Of the eleven sixteenth-century inventories discussed here, all but one, belonging to a widow and therefore perhaps not reflecting the whole property, had a kitchen. It may be argued that these kitchens were sixteenth-century additions to medieval houses, but this is unlikely to be the case. Not only do we have rare glimpses in other Sandwich documents of detached fifteenth-century kitchens, normally belonging to larger houses,[76] but their position in the later inventories, usually at the end of all the rooms and often without a chamber above, suggests the continued presence of medieval detached kitchens, which were probably rebuilt only gradually and incorporated into rear wings. Evidence before the mid-sixteenth century is too limited to tell whether all the cooking was done in a kitchen, where one existed, or whether, as later on, some cooking also took place in the hall.[77] Detached kitchens in town houses rarely survive,[78] and fragments of only two have been found in Sandwich: at the rear of the great house of Thomas Elys at 29 Harnet Street, which is also known from the documents (House 28; Section 12.1; Fig. 12.1), and an undatable timber example behind 34 Upper Strand Street (House 98; Fig. 12.30). We do not know for how long kitchen hearths remained open; gradually, during the later fifteenth and sixteenth centuries, they were probably confined within timber chimneys or brick stacks.

Thirty-one per cent of all the probate inventories include shops, and the physical evidence for these has been described in Section 12.8.2. If the householder was a man of means, he might also have had an office and saleroom on the ground floor, as was specified in a London contract of 1410.[79] In this London house the hall and kitchen were raised to the first floor, but in Sandwich they were more likely to have been placed to the rear, at least until the late fifteenth century, when the remains at 14, 16 Market Street (House 60) and perhaps even 1 The Butchery (House 3) may indicate the introduction of more modern arrangements.

As discussed above (Section 12.4), houses with the open hall on the street frontage occur on the outskirts of Sandwich. They are of two, not three, storeys overall, and often survive more completely than their contemporaries in the centre. The larger of the wealden houses at 19, 21 and 22, 24 Upper Strand Street (Houses 95, 96; Figs 12.21, 12.22), with first-floor chambers at either end of an open bay, are likely to have had five or even six rooms. They could have had what is thought of as the 'standard' plan of two rooms opening off the cross passage, one being a buttery.[80] This cannot, however, be proved from surviving evidence in either of these examples, and indeed the fact that so few houses of this plan remain means that there is no way of demonstrating that such a plan was in common use in Sandwich.

The smaller wealden houses in Fisher Street and New Street (Figs 12.23, 12.24) had only a hall, a wide passage-cum-room and a single upper chamber. These appear to survive in their entirety, and if they are represented in the probate inventories they are likely to be among the four two-room, or fifteen three-room houses, that contained a hall and perhaps a buttery, if the passage were counted as a room – the Canterbury butteries of 1497 were to be only 4ft (1.2m) wide – and a chamber or loft over the passage and buttery. Whether they had detached kitchens as well, or cooked in the hall, is unclear. In the late sixteenth century 26 per cent of all testators cooked in the hall, and the surviving small wealden houses may have been used in the same way.

The inventories of the houses with galleried halls seem to reflect the alternative possibilities for the location of the best chamber (Sections 12.3.4, 12.3.5). In one, belonging to the widow of a baker, there was a 'great chamber', but it was not over the parlour, which simply had a loft above it, suggesting that this may have been a house with a two-bay chamber at the front above the shop and a parlour behind the hall.[81] Smart front chambers are also indicated in the houses of two mariners, one of whom had the most valuable items in his 'fore' chamber, and the other a fireplace and expensive linen in the chamber over the shop.[82] On the other hand, in some cases the best goods were definitely in the 'back' chambers.[83] Elsewhere, the situation is less clear: a haberdasher had two chambers 'next the street', one of which contained linen, giving it a high valuation of £28 8s., but the 'best' chamber, which was extremely well furnished, including a great bed, cushions, carpet and buckram curtains totalling £13 16s., was obviously at the back.[84] In 1585 Alexander Cobb, jurat, would appear to have had his most valuable goods in his 'fore' chamber (£21 5s.), but when his widow died four years later the value of the goods in the fore chamber (£28 16s.) was exceeded by those in the chamber over the parlour (£37 15s.), which had not been mentioned in her husband's inventory.[85] These examples illustrate the difficulties of understanding houses from inventories, but also suggest, as the buildings do, that there was no fixed position for the best chamber in the house.

The late sixteenth-century inventories do not help us to understand why there is so much physical evidence for commercial storage in the surviving open-hall houses. By that time there is no sign of one or two floors being devoted entirely to storage; rather, as is commonly found elsewhere, beds and some household storage were combined in the upper chambers and garrets. The reason is probably because the economic status of the town had changed by then, and the way people used their houses reflected a somewhat different lifestyle. The wealth and ambitions of Sandwich inhabitants were becoming more limited as the fifteenth century drew to a close. Richardson's research on household objects bequeathed by Sandwich householders between 1460 and 1520 reveals that in comparison with other towns, notably those in the orbit of London, there was little luxury on display, leading to the conclusion that the town was 'in decline, with narrow geographical and commercial horizons'.[86] As discussed in this book, this contraction became even more pronounced by the middle of the sixteenth century. Prior to c.1500–10, however, when open halls went out of fashion, the types of structures changed very little. In the past, assumptions have been made about the uses to which rooms in medieval town houses were put,[87] but the more we know about surviving buildings the more it seems likely that many of them, and certainly those in Sandwich, were intended to be multi-functional, their rooms serving domestic, craft, commercial or storage purposes as the situation required. Unfortunately, however, the contemporary wills used by Richardson do not shed light on the actual structure of houses, and there is no other documentary evidence to enlighten us.

12.10 The proportion of surviving medieval houses

Figure IV.1 plots the distribution of the sixty-nine houses that are thought to date from before 1560, almost all of which were constructed by 1520 and certainly before c.1540. It excludes the stone fragments discussed in Chapter 7.2.3, and is almost certainly not complete since more buildings probably still await discovery. But the map shows that a large number of houses in the town today retain a good deal of medieval work. The port may have enjoyed its greatest prosperity before the Black Death, but at that time wealth was confined to a few. In Sandwich as in other towns, it was only later that buildings substantial enough and of a type capable of being adapted for later living spread to a wider section of society.

If there were as many as 1,000 households in the early fourteenth century (Chap. 5.3), the surviving houses of that period represent only a tiny proportion of their dwellings. But by 1471 the number of households had dropped to somewhere around 500 (Chap. 10.2.1), suggesting that something over 11 per cent of their dwellings may remain. By 1513, when the number of households had dropped yet further to approximately 380, it is likely that almost all the buildings on the map had been erected. Since there are possibly more houses surviving than are shown here, and since some households probably shared a house, it is possible that around 20 per cent of the dwellings needed to accommodate the early sixteenth-century population survive today. No doubt there were many more well-constructed buildings in Sandwich than remain today. But although perhaps 50 per cent or even more of the population lived in such houses, the figures are a stark reminder that there were almost certainly many poor people living in crowded, shared accommodation or in single-storey cottages that had no hope of surviving for 500 years.

12.11 Conclusion

This account of late medieval buildings in Sandwich raises some questions concerning the integration of evidence obtained from buildings with that from other sources. Although the dating of buildings in Sandwich is somewhat imprecise, there are enough datable features among the survivors to suggest that after a gap in the late fourteenth and early fifteenth centuries, new building began again around the second quarter of the fifteenth century. There may have been a break in the middle of the century, when the economic evidence suggests that people in the town faced a difficult time, but construction certainly picked up shortly after, for a number of houses have late medieval features normally associated with buildings erected after c.1470. In rural Kent the period between c.1460 and c.1510 was one of considerable building activity, which was most intense between 1480 and 1500.[88] Towns, however, may not always have followed the rural pattern. In Hampshire, there was a marked increase in urban construction between 1425 and 1450, followed by a slight levelling off for the rest of the fifteenth century, before a slump in the early sixteenth,[89] and it has been suggested that in Rye the introduction of fully floored houses may have begun before c.1490, that is, earlier than in the Sussex hinterland,[90] and earlier than seems to have occurred in rural Kent. These comparisons, together with the evidence of datable features in the Sandwich buildings themselves, suggest that while some building may have taken place in the town just before the middle of the fifteenth century, it is likely to have recommenced during the second half of the century and into the early sixteenth. As discussed in other chapters, however, the effect of the harbour silting up, along with other problems, meant that Sandwich trade was much diminished by the end of the fifteenth century. The population, drastically reduced after the Black Death, recovered somewhat during the fifteenth century, but steadily declined from the 1470s. So how can one account for the continued construction of substantial buildings after that date?

In the first place, it seems likely that until the early sixteenth century the inhabitants retained their confidence in the future. Although the international merchants had left the town, it remained a centre of regional significance, with a thriving malting and brewing industry, and it served as an entrepôt for shipping goods and produce around the coast and across the Channel. Houses were no longer built for the wealthiest kind of merchant, but there were plenty of men making money who needed good homes and wished to invest in property for income.

One result of the decreased population after the Black Death was a rise in the wealth and spending power of those that survived, and a demand for higher standards of living. It led to a notable expansion in the consumption of all kinds of possessions, including houses. Patterns of production are not necessarily the same as patterns of consumption, and it is the latter that are important when considering the rapid growth of new houses across the country in the mid- to late fifteenth century.[91] In Sandwich, with the disappearance of the major merchants, there was by this time less disparity between the very wealthy and the middle ranks of society, and many of the surviving houses must represent the homes of those whose forebears had lived in houses known only from excavation.

Finally, the mid- and late fifteenth-century buildings of Sandwich are subtly different from earlier ones in ways that probably reflect declining economic expectations. In the fourteenth century the large open-hall houses discussed in Chapter 7 can be compared with those in major towns across the country, but this became less true later. In a thriving city like Salisbury, open halls became rare during the fifteenth century, replaced it seems by fully storeyed buildings usually located in prominent positions in the town centre and often marked by display framing.[92] This is a type of structure for which evidence in Sandwich is limited, if not missing altogether (Section 12.3.4). The fifteenth-century members of the merchant and commercial classes who lived in Sandwich town centre were content to continue constructing old-style dwellings with open halls, now of smaller size than the earlier ones. They did not change to new fully storeyed structures and the different lifestyle that this would have implied. Some two-storey rental properties, containing shops and no open halls, occur in the commercial district, but new fully floored houses that were probably purely dwellings are identifiable only from the very end of the century, and were built away from the town centre and along the street frontage. Although the basic infrastructure and topography of the town had not changed, and new houses continued to be erected at least into the early sixteenth century, there are glimpses that the social structure and mentality of the inhabitants were rather different from those of 150 years before.

13 Churches and hospitals

As discussed in the previous chapter, many secular buildings were erected in the fifteenth and early sixteenth centuries, but they differed somewhat from the earlier structures in size and form. Changes in form occurred everywhere, due to general typological and chronological development, but in Sandwich the reduction in size was probably caused by the declining fortunes of the town, which led fewer very wealthy inhabitants to make their homes there, and by the survival of dwellings of those of far lower social status. This chapter will examine whether Sandwich's churches and hospitals reflect similar subtle changes in their buildings in the later Middle Ages.

By the end of the fourteenth century the inhabitants of Sandwich had recovered sufficiently from the catastrophic events earlier in the century to turn their attention again to the physical embellishment of their churches. In the 1390s, thanks to the philanthropy of a single individual, a major chantry and a new hospital were added to the earlier religious foundations. As surviving documents become more prolific in the later fifteenth and early sixteenth centuries, evidence becomes available for the parishioners' involvement with their churches. In particular, bequests in wills towards the provision of fixtures and fittings provide details of work on the fabric of the churches and also information about their internal layout.

Later, the records illustrate the abrupt changes brought about by the Reformation. In Sandwich the friary and chantries were dissolved and their property sold off, but the hospitals were not affected because they were administered by the town or by secular trustees. By this date religious houses from outside Sandwich seem to have held little property in the town, so there seems to have been no appreciable redistribution of assets at the Dissolution. A few records chart the divisive nature of the old and new beliefs, and the wills of the period illustrate the effects of the Reformation on parishioners who must have been raised in one tradition but died in another.

13.1 The churches

13.1.1 The architecture and layout of St Clement's

In 1403 John Stylle bequeathed enough timber to cover the roof of the great chancel of St Clement's,[1] and we can therefore take it that the crown-post roof over the chancel, with soulaces, moulded tiebeams and crown-post capitals, was added shortly afterwards (Fig. 13.1). This seems to be the last of the major building programmes at the east end of the church. The western arm, however, was rebuilt in the first half of the fifteenth century, perhaps because the almost 200-year-old aisled nave, with its narrow aisles and lack of clerestory, was considered inadequate to the needs of the time. The windows in the south aisle indicate that it had been widened during the fourteenth century, but in the early fifteenth the nave itself was reconstructed and the north aisle enlarged to match the south one (Fig. 13.3). The finely moulded piers and capitals of the new arcades, and the new west doorway and windows, are in the decorative style found in Kent parish churches after the rebuilding of Canterbury Cathedral nave c.1400. In a separate and later phase the nave was heightened by the addition of a clerestory and a shallow panelled ceiling with foliate bosses and carved angels in the centre – a feature unusual in Kent (Fig. 13.2). None of this work is precisely dated, but it was probably completed by the 1460s since no bequests for work on the nave were made in the wills that start to survive in some numbers from that time

The last important building project at St Clement's before the Reformation concerned the tower. The work, carried out around 1500, involved general repairs to the twelfth-century structure and the insertion of a floor to create a bell-ringing chamber.[2] The tower was occasionally referred to as a campanile (bell-tower), but was more usually called the 'steeple', the normal word for a church tower in the Middle Ages.[3] There was also a steeple or spire (in the modern sense), although the date

Fig. 13.1: St Clement's church, chancel roof looking west (P. W. © English Heritage DP044054)

Fig. 13.2: St Clement's church, nave roof looking east (P. W. © English Heritage DP044038)

of its construction is unknown.[4] All the church towers in Sandwich served as landmarks used by mariners, as illustrated by the portolan of *c.*1435 compiled by Michael of Rhodes (Chap. 9.1),[5] thus keeping the towers in good repair must have been extremely important to the maritime economy of the town. At St Clement's, Nicholas Burton, a wealthy merchant, left £4 for the bell tower (*campanilis*) in 1492. Four years later Richard Trysham left his son four tenements on condition that when he reached the age of 21 he gave £3 6s. 8d. to the repair of the 'steeple'.[6] Through the early years of the sixteenth century more funds were bequeathed both for making bells and repairing the steeple (presumably the tower). The work dragged on and costs probably soared out of control, for in 1529 William Wattes gave 6s. 8d. to the church to redeem the church plate and pay his contribution towards a local subsidy for building the 'steeple'.[7] This is the last of the fifteen bequests specifically made to the tower or steeple, so presumably the work was completed soon after, although the church plate was redeemed only in 1533.[8]

By combining the evidence of wills with the extant fabric of a church, many of the chapels, altars and other fixtures and fittings can be identified and located. In Sandwich, St Clement's is the only church that has survived sufficiently intact for this exercise to work satisfactorily. The results are illustrated in Figure 13.3. At the east end there is no evidence for an image of the patronal saint, although, as in all late medieval churches, there would have been one, paired with an image of Our Lady on the other side of the high altar.[9] To the north of the chancel is St Margaret's chapel. It may always have been in this position, and in 1492 Nicholas Burton requested that he should be buried in the body (*corpus*) of the church, specifically between the chapels of St Margaret and St James the Apostle,[10] suggesting that the latter may have been the next chapel to the west, where there is a change in the roof construction, north of the crossing tower. No evidence for an original piscina serving either chapel has been found, although a fifteenth-century squint on the south side of St Margaret's chapel has a later (possibly nineteenth-century) piscina inserted into it, perhaps a replacement for one in the east wall, unless a simple bowl was used.[11] The squint provides a view from the chapel to the high altar, allowing the priests to coordinate the celebration of multiple Masses and the elevation of the Host so that everyone in the congregation could benefit from seeing this critical moment (Fig. 13.4).[12]

The Lady chapel was probably always sited to the south of the chancel, where it was later, and the fine early to mid-fourteenth-century piscina in the south wall probably marks the site of the altar (Fig. 6.12). To the west of this, beyond a break in the roof structure and more or less in line with the east crossing pier, another fourteenth-century piscina in the south wall indicates a second chapel on this side, in an area now known as the chapel of St George. Although the present altar of St George was brought here from St Peter's church

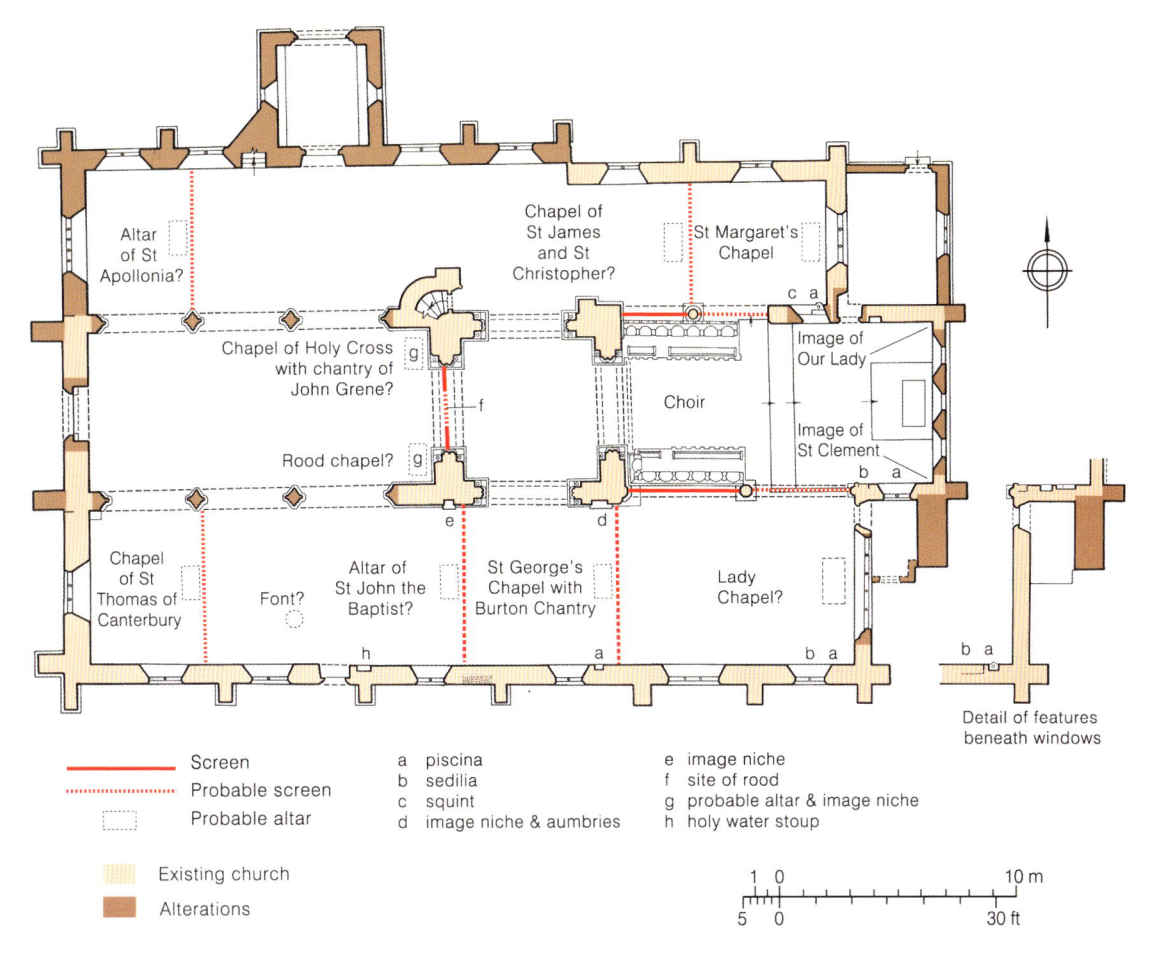

Fig. 13.3: St Clement's church, reconstructed plan and arrangement (S. P. & A. T. A.)

Fig. 13.4: St Clement's church, squint from St Margaret's chapel to the high altar (P. W. © English Heritage DP044055)

only in 1951, a medieval chapel and altar of St George are mentioned in wills between 1480 and 1534, and a perpetual chantry at the altar of St George was established by Nicholas Burton.[13] The south side of the east tower pier contains a fine fourteenth-century image niche, originally with a cusped head and surrounded by a broad band of foliage. Below are two small aumbries, originally closed by hinged doors (Fig. 13.5). These features probably served St George's chapel.

Since a will of 1525 makes clear that there was an image of St John the Baptist over the south door, the altar of St John the Baptist may have been west of St George's chapel, with the image niche on the south side of the south-west crossing pier being associated with its altar. In the south-west corner of the church, beyond the south doorway, was the chapel of St Thomas of Canterbury. Nothing now remains to identify this area as a chapel, but several wills make clear that it lay in this corner.

In the centre of the church was the rood. In 1487 Thomas Clerke, chaplain, asked to be buried before the door of the rood chapel, which was possibly situated at the foot of the stairs to the rood loft, or even in the loft itself.[14] The rood was clearly highly decorated, for

Fig. 13.5: St Clement's church, image niche and aumbries in St George's chapel (P. W. © English Heritage DP044052)

in 1507 Thomas Toller left £3 6s. 8d. to gild it, a piece (*sic*) to make a crown for the image, and enough broken silver for a pair of gloves. He may have been following the example of his father, a smith who in 1490 had given his white silver girdle to the *figura crucis*.[15] There was a second rood, referred to in 1526 as the rood of Sandown, which was presumably above a screen on the west side of one of the chancel chapels.[16]

Both piers on the west side of the central tower have flat stretches of wall facing the nave, gouged with marks where fixtures have been torn away; they could have been altars and consoles for images. If it were at ground level, the rood chapel could have been here, with the chapel of the Holy Cross on the other side. The latter is mentioned in the 1450s when John Grene established a chantry there, and several references to the lights of the Holy Cross were probably associated with this altar. One altar that remains unaccounted for is that dedicated to St Apollonia; it was not mentioned in the wills, but the gutter above it was in need of repair at the time of Archbishop Warham's Visitation of 1511.[17] It could have been at the west end of the north aisle, the only area that has neither documentary nor physical evidence for late medieval fixtures, except for the bulk of the nave, which would have been used by the congregation, but also may have been where the mayoral elections took place.[18]

The present font, decorated with armorials and five-petalled roses, was made in the early fifteenth century and bears close similarities to fonts at Margate, Herne

Fig. 13.6: St Clement's church, choir stalls with holes for acoustic jars below (P. W. © English Heritage DP044030)

and Sittingbourne. On the basis of the arms it has been dated to 1405–7, and certainly not later than 1414.[19] It is now situated north of the crossing but has been moved several times, as shown by James Hall's will of 1540 in which he asked to be buried in the church 'afore the font stone on the south side of the church'.[20] A plan of the church drawn in 1767 shows the font at the west end of the nave, on the line of the north arcade, whereas on Boys's slightly later plan it was in the north transept. By 1869 it had been moved into the north-east chapel.[21] Given the description in 1540 it seems reasonable to assume that it was on the south side of the church in the late Middle Ages, perhaps between the south doorway and the chapel of St Thomas in the south-west corner.

A second fine feature is the carved choir stalls (Fig. 13.6). These have cusped panel fronts and a single surviving misericord, and originally carried parclose screens separating them from the aisles. The stalls are set on stone bases that appear to have been made for them, even though the stalls have been much modified. The bases have holes for acoustic jars, and there are similar jars high up in the chancel walls. These were inserted to amplify sound,[22] and indicate that St Clement's had a choir, as we also know from the fact that money was bequeathed in 1497 to pay the parish clerk to teach boys pricksong (written vocal music).[23]

13.1.2 St Mary's

Perhaps partly as a consequence of the almost total destruction of the interior of St Mary's when the tower collapsed in the seventeenth century, the only physical remains of the fifteenth-century church are fragments of a carved reredos embedded in the east wall of the south nave aisle, possibly the chapel of St Lawrence, and the south porch. Thus documentary sources provide the bulk of the information. The late fourteenth- and early fifteenth-century benefactions listed in the bede roll include donations of altar furnishings and vestments, and also gifts to the church fabric.[24] In the late fourteenth century Thomas Elys with his wife and Thomas Rolling (vicar of St Mary's and Elys's executor) gave the west window of the church (possibly the glass rather than the masonry). John Gylling, who owned an inn in the parish in the early fifteenth century, and his wife gave the north window.[25] The surviving south porch and a south window were donated by Alexander Norman, wax chandler and owner of property in St Mary's parish. He, like Henry Dyery, who gave six couples of the south roof of the church, was a member of St Katherine's guild in St James's church in 1416.[26] Finally, the processional porch, possibly outside the west door, was paid for by Thomas Chyn and Thomas Barbor.[27] The scale of these gifts suggests that the main part of the building was more or less complete and there were no major additions, such as the nave at St Clement's. This impression is reinforced by the churchwardens' accounts, which begin unusually early, in 1444,[28] and by wills that survive from 1450 onwards. From then to 1558, but mostly in the 1470s and 1490s, 33 out of 121 testators (27 per cent) left money for the fabric of the church without specifying the target, so the funds were probably used for general repairs rather than new building.

The only large-scale fifteenth-century building project was the construction or reconstruction of the tower, which involved obtaining Caen stone and Folkestone rag and paying for advice from a mason from Canterbury Cathedral. It was first mentioned in 1444 when the churchwardens' accounts begin, and building went on continuously until 1459, when banners were hung from the 'steeple' on dedication day. Its position and whether there was a separate bell-tower for the bells are subjects of debate, but since the accounts show that the great bell was rung and all the bells were frequently repaired while the tower was being constructed, a separate bell-tower seems possible.[29] By 1445 there was a church clock, presumably on the tower, with a chiming mechanism that frequently required repair.[30] There is some evidence for music in the church. Although a choir is not specifically mentioned, the fact that a form for children was set up in the chancel in 1463 implies one,[31] and in the Visitation of 1511 the priest of the Condy chantry was reproved for not singing a weekly Jesus Mass as his predecessors had done.[32] In addition there was organ music, for in 1444 the church was bequeathed a pair of organs, and in 1496 both the great organ and the little organs were in need of repair.[33]

Other entries in the churchwardens' accounts and in the wills relate to chapels and altars. An aumbry was made behind the statue of the Virgin at the high altar, and the east window above was repaired. The chancel of St John the Evangelist was re-roofed and had a tabernacle and alabaster image of the saint installed in 1445. The chapel of St Mary at the East Head, the chancels and altars of St James and St Lawrence (possibly with the reredos mentioned above), and the altars of St Christopher and the Morrow Mass were all mentioned during the first half of the fifteenth century. Later, the Jesus altar and chapel became extremely important, and the altars and chapels of St Thomas of Canterbury, St Ursula and the Salutation of Our Lady are mentioned in the early sixteenth century.

Sometime during the fifteenth century, a Mass in the Name of Jesus was established. The Feast of the Name of Jesus was a new feast that appeared in England early in the fifteenth century,[34] and the first reference to it at St Mary's is in a will of 1466 when the chaplain and clerk of the Jesus Mass are mentioned. Since it was not listed in the bede roll written *c*.1447, it was probably introduced in the 1450s or 1460s.[35] In 1511 the priest of the Condy chantry was responsible for the weekly Mass. The cult became extremely popular in Sandwich, with at least thirty-one testators leaving money, land or goods to the Mass or the altar between 1466 and 1551. In the first half of the sixteenth century there are several references to the Jesus chapel and its associated rood. This was separate from the high rood of the church and, at least by 1551, was on the north side of the church.[36] Since the greatest enthusiasm for this cult was among the laity, Jesus altars were usually in the western part of the church, and if that were the case here it could have been in the surviving north nave aisle. Its position on the north side of the church is likely to be the reason why the quay north of the church was known as Jesus Quay by the mid-sixteenth century.[37] Throughout England the Jesus Mass tended to be supported by the well-to-do, and this seems to have been the case in Sandwich. This was particularly noticeable in the sixteenth century when the Jesus chapel was singled out as a place of burial by some prominent parishioners, such as the former mayors William Salmon, Benett Webbe and Vincent Engeham and, above all, by Sir Edward Ringeley and his widow in 1543 and 1551.[38]

The subject of seating and segregation in churches has been little studied since the nineteenth century and is still one in which disentangling myth from fact is tricky. Nonetheless, it is clear that by the late Middle Ages seats in churches were becoming more widespread.[39] In Sandwich, more information is available for St Mary's than for the other two churches, with brief references to settles or pews occurring in the churchwardens' accounts on several occasions.[40] In 1482 the chaplain, Thomas Norman, asked to be buried in the Lady chapel 'below the seats of the women over against the south window',[41] suggesting that there were seats for women on the south side of the church (the opposite of the traditional view that women were confined to the north). Private pews had been legislated against in the late thirteenth century, but were becoming common in many churches by the middle of the fifteenth.[42] How soon they were found in Sandwich is not clear, but in St Mary's church Lady Jane Ringeley had her own pew in 1527 (Chap. 10.1.1), and in the 1550s both Thomas Pache and John Master wished to be buried beneath their pews at the east end, in the chancel and the Lady chapel.[43]

The chapel and hermitage of St James stood south-west of St Mary's church, opposite the junction of Church Street St Mary and Vicarage Lane (Fig. IV.1). It has long since gone and there are no records to indicate when it was founded, although it must have been well established by the early fifteenth century when St Katherine's guild was based there. In the late fifteenth and early sixteenth centuries it was often mentioned in wills, and its cemetery was frequently used as a place of burial.

13.1.3 St Peter's

Little remains in St Peter's church from this period, despite the fact that a major chantry was set up in 1392. This was the perpetual chantry of Thomas Elys, financed by lands in Eastry and elsewhere, and established for three priests – an exceptionally large number known elsewhere in Kent only in Canterbury and at the Rochester Bridge chapel.[44] Various references make clear that the chantry was situated in the Lady chapel,[45] which is usually thought to have been in the destroyed south aisle. If so, it must have been just west of the raised floor over the undercroft, from where the high altar was visible through the southern of two late fourteenth-century squints (now turned into a doorway) (Fig. 6.13). Since the only sign of the chapel is the undatable jamb of a high east window above the undercroft, there is no evidence that the chantry was decorated with any architectural embellishments.

Elys's endowment included a house for the chantry priests to the east of the church. It has been suggested that this stood in and above the undercroft of the two-storey structure built in the first half of the fourteenth century to the east of the Lady chapel.[46] As discussed in Chapter 6.1.5, the undercroft was probably used as a charnel house, with the floor above being its chapel, so Elys's priests' house was more likely to have been the tenement on the west side of Love Lane held by his heirs in 1410.[47] It has also been claimed that one of the priests was to act as a schoolmaster, with the school held in the undercroft or the room above.[48] Although one of the priests served as schoolmaster in the sixteenth century, and earlier priests may have acted in like manner, there was nothing in the foundation charter about this duty, and no recorded upper chamber.[49]

Little can be said about the fabric or internal layout of St Peter's church in the fifteenth and early sixteenth centuries. By April 1432 the mayor's court had been moved from the church (probably its north aisle) (Chap. 6.1.6) to a purpose-built court hall in or next to the churchyard (Chap. 10.1), and there is no evidence for how that aisle was used after the move had taken place. Large-scale construction seems virtually to have ceased by the fifteenth century, although many people left small amounts of money for unspecified work in the church. The only specific bequest was made by John Coke, who in 1490 left lead to repair the roof of the Lady chapel.[50] In 1511 the Visitation reported that a beam in the chancel should be taken down and that 'the reparacion of the stepille [tower] is ylle mayteigned',[51] but there is nothing to indicate that any action was taken. The tower collapsed in 1661 and its rebuilding destroyed all physical evidence for its earlier form.[52]

The documents are also tantalisingly uninformative about the positions of chapels and altars in the church. The only chapels identifiable from the wills are the Lady chapel, the site of the Elys chantry, and the chapel of St John the Baptist, both of which may have been on the south side of the church, and the chapel of St Erasmus, the position of which is unknown.[53] In addition to the high altar dedicated to St Peter, there were also altars to the Holy Trinity, St Thomas, St John of Bridlington and St Margaret. There were also numerous images and lights, some of which had fraternities connected with them. In the late fifteenth century many people wished to be buried near, or gave money or gifts to, the cross or rood, its images and its lights. As at St Mary's, there is no direct evidence for a choir, but there were organs, for in 1534 William Auger bequeathed 20s. towards the purchase of a new pair.[54]

13.1.4 *The Carmelite friary*

The friary seems to have prospered during the fourteenth century, with twenty-four friars by 1331. By the end of the century some of those who began as friars in Sandwich but had subsequently moved elsewhere came back to the town at the end of their lives. The friary also attracted interest outside Kent, as indicated in 1370 by the indulgences granted by the bishop of Exeter to anyone in his diocese who visited Sandwich to venerate the Carmelites' image of St Katherine, and also by donations to the friary by several non-Sandwich testators, including John of Gaunt, who left it 40s. in 1372. In 1398 and 1436 the provincial chapter of the Carmelite Order was held at Sandwich.[55] It is clear that the activities of the friary were a forum for interaction between Sandwich and the wider world at this time.

Scant details of the later history and architecture of the church survive. Many testators bequeathed small sums for repairs in the late fifteenth and early sixteenth centuries or left money for Masses to be said for them by the friars, the latest recorded being in 1537. The excavated remains of a possibly fourteenth-century wall tomb may have been the grave of a Sandwich resident who chose to be buried in the church.[56] That this was not unknown is shown by twelve later bequests in the wills of ten parishioners from St Peter's and two from St Clement's, who asked for burial within the friary church, some of them specifying in the choir or before named images.

Henry VIII may have stayed at the friary when he visited Sandwich, probably in 1532, possibly resulting in his gift of 15 crowns in November of that year.[57] The house was dissolved in 1538 and the site, together with all its lands, dovecotes, fishponds, fruit gardens and orchards, was taken into crown hands. Thomas Pache, a former mayor, was appointed collector of rents for the property. Some of the land and buildings were sold locally, but in 1540 most of the five-acre site was acquired by Thomas Arden of Faversham and no more is known of it until much later.[58]

13.2 The religious life of the town

13.2.1 *Lay associations*

In the late Middle Ages religious fraternities, guilds or brotherhoods (the last being the term usually used in Sandwich) played an important part in parish life. They were associated with specific saints who had altars and images in the churches. Many parishioners belonged to them, often to more than one, and information about them is largely provided by bequests to the lights associated with the saint. The most obvious functions of each fraternity were to maintain the lights of the altar, to hold feasts, and to arrange funerals and make sure Masses were said for former brothers and sisters.

Membership of a religious guild, however, provided other important benefits. The sense of belonging was central. Some fraternities may have been aimed at specific segments of the community, but usually parishioners of both sexes and all occupations and ages, including the clergy who often figured prominently, could join on payment of an entry fee. This inevitably meant that the very poor were excluded, an exclusiveness that was apparently highly prized. On the saint's day, a procession was organised and a feast was held, binding the brothers and sisters together in a social as well as a religious sense. Reputations were established and contacts were made, without which it was difficult to get financial credit; membership may also have been valuable in finding work, patrons and even marriage partners. In addition, the fraternity might care for those who had fallen on hard times. Although members might be drawn from a wider constituency, fraternities were largely parish-based organisations, providing essential lay support for the parish church, the clergy and the parishioners in an organised and controlling manner.[59]

There is no clear evidence in Sandwich of fraternity involvement in major church construction, but when work such as the new nave at St Clement's took place, it is likely that the brotherhoods were involved,[60] but by the time the parishioners' wills start to survive only the tower of St Clement's still needed funds. The scale of most bequests was small; they were made to at least six brotherhoods attached to altars, images or lights in St Clement's church: Corpus Christi, St Thomas, the Holy Trinity, St Peter, St John the Baptist and, most importantly of all, St George. For example, in 1480 the mayor and commons gave the wardens 6s. 8d. a year for their annual procession in which the image of St George was paraded around the town, an event that no doubt ended in a feast,[61] and in 1497 Henry Pyham left the wardens of the Light and Mass of St George 5s. from the rent of a tenement to pay for the parish clerk to teach the children to read pricksong, to be sung weekly at the St George's Mass.[62]

On several occasions in the fifteenth century, the St Mary's churchwardens' accounts refer to payment for carrying banners on festivals and feast-days, indicating the importance of processions and feasts during the year, some of which may have been related to the religious guilds. There are few testamentary references to brotherhoods in St Mary's parish. The Jesus Mass was sometimes referred to as a brotherhood when money and property were bequeathed for maintenance of the Mass and its chaplain and clerk,[63] and the Jesus House may have been its meeting place.[64] In 1466 Richard Bilton left 2d. to 'each light of which I am a brother', emphasising his multiple membership and suggesting that many of the lights may have had brotherhoods attached. But this may not have been true of them all, for in 1492 John Fuller's bequests distinguished between two brotherhoods (of the Jesus Mass and the Assumption of the Virgin) and two lights (of St Christopher and St John the Baptist).[65] None of the wills makes it clear that there was a St Katherine's guild in St James's chapel in St Mary's parish, yet as many as fourteen men were named as wardens for the brothers and sisters of the guild in 1478.[66] References in wills do not, therefore, provide a complete picture of the religious associations existing in the parishes.

In St Peter's church a number of testators clearly belonged to several fraternities. For example, in 1459 Simon Ruddock left money to the brotherhoods of the Holy Cross, St Peter, the Holy Trinity and St John the Baptist, and in 1484 John Catour made bequests to those of St Mary, Corpus Christi and St John of Bridlington. Apart from a mention of the brotherhood of St Erasmus in 1534, the evidence is mainly from fifteenth-century wills, although a so-called 'Brotherhood of the Poor' flourished for a short time in the mid-1540s (see below).[67] As has been noted elsewhere, fraternities reached their maximum importance in the fourteenth and fifteenth centuries.[68]

In Sandwich, testators left bequests exclusively to brotherhoods in their own parish churches. In other places, such as East Anglia, some fraternities had extra-parochial members,[69] and while there is no firm evidence that this occurred in Sandwich it may explain the bequest of Thomas Colman of St Peter's parish, who in 1495 left two properties to the Jesus Mass in St Mary's church, a bequest that suggests a strong attachment, perhaps amounting to membership of the brotherhood.[70]

13.2.2 Burial

Table 13.1, compiled from wills in which the testators specified where they wished to be buried, indicates that the pattern of burial in the three parishes varied. Most St Clement's testators, including wealthy men such as Nicholas Orpathe (1533) and William Crispe (1543), asked to be buried in the large churchyard.[71] They probably wished to be buried next to previously interred members of their family, a pattern that also held good for many of the 26 per cent who sought burial within the church. In St Peter's parish, despite the small size of the churchyard, almost as high a proportion asked for burial in it, suggesting that the

Table 13.1: Locations of burial in Sandwich wills[*]

Parish	In church		In churchyard		Elsewhere in Sandwich		Outside Sandwich		Total
	No.	%	No.	%	No.	%	No.	%	
St Clement	35	26	94	70	4	3	1	1	134
St Mary	42	37	44	39	22	20	4	4	112
St Peter	53	25	137	65.5	18	9	1	0.5	209

* This table and the following two are based on evidence in wills transcribed by Arthur Hussey and held in Sandwich Guildhall Archive.

fourteenth-century charnel house may have been in frequent use. Favoured places were by a stone cross on the south side or under a palm tree (probably yew or box[72]). Since a number asked to be buried elsewhere, including nine people who opted for the friary church, only a quarter, as at St Clement's, desired burial inside the church. In contrast, far fewer St Mary's testators specified the churchyard, although a number requested burial in the chapel or churchyard of St James, which remained popular even after the chapel was destroyed in 1543.[73] Instead, 37 per cent asked to be buried in the church itself – a rather higher proportion than in the other two churches.[74]

Most internal burials specified particular chapels or before particular images, often in the same grave as, or near to, family members. Such references enable some of the chapels and altars to be located, with additional information about the church and its fittings emerging occasionally, as for example from the small number who asked for burial next to the pew where they had sat. The trend for prosperous parishioners to request burial inside the church increased throughout England during the fifteenth century, and from the later fifteenth century became common in Kent, including Sandwich.[75]

Only a few people asked for any kind of memorial. In St Peter's, John Brayne (1528) wished to be buried under a white stone in the chapel of St Erasmus, and Henry Bolle (1533) asked to join his wife in a brick tomb with a stone capping. Of the St Mary's testators, a butcher, William Garrard (1497), specified that his grave in St James's churchyard should be covered by a marble slab with a 'convenient scripture' added, probably in brass. Roger Manwood (1534) directed that his tomb in St Lawrence's chapel in St Mary's church should have a stone with brass (*coopra*) images of himself, his wife and six children. He also said that there should be four escutcheons, two containing the arms of the port, one depicting St George and the fourth displaying the 'token of death'. By the 1460s brasses could be made relatively cheaply,[76] and this rare instruction is almost certainly an indication that many graves of wealthier parishioners were embellished by brasses. Several stone slabs bearing their outlines remain in the churches, but as the brass figures and inscriptions have been removed the interred are unidentifiable.

13.2.3 Wills and the character of the parishes

An analysis of the wills suggests that the three parishes had rather different characters (Table 13.2). Despite being the smallest parish of the three (Fig. 3.10), far more wills survive for St Peter's than for the other two parishes. Most are after 1500, almost certainly reflecting the fact that when the population of the town declined during the early sixteenth century the remaining inhabitants tended to be concentrated in the town centre. That is, the whole of the northern part of St Peter's parish plus small areas in the north-east of St Mary's and the north-west of St Clement's.

Furthermore, the religious bequests in the wills imply that the parishes attracted rather different kinds of people (Table 13.3). Although all the wills surviving from before 1558 have been scrutinised, they were most numerous between about 1460 and 1540. Since the friary was the recipient of many bequests before

Table 13.2: Sandwich wills, 1402–1558

Parish	Pre-1500 No.	Pre-1500 %	1501–58 No.	1501–58 %	Total No.
St Clement	54	41	79	59	133
St Mary	62	51	59	49	121
St Peter	59	26	166	74	225

Table 13.3: Bequests to religious institutions in Sandwich wills, 1460–1538

	St Clement 104 wills	St Peter 162 wills	St Mary 97 wills
Bequests to Sandwich churches or institutions other than parish churches	31.7%	30.8%	32.9%
Bequests to churches or institutions outside Sandwich	6.7%	17%	11.3%

the Dissolution, the following analysis of religious bequests covers only the period 1460–1538. Nearly 80 per cent of those from St Mary's and St Clement's parishes fall between these dates, dropping to 72 per cent for St Peter's because there are more wills for later years. It must be remembered that the surviving wills provide insights only into the allegiances of the wealthier inhabitants of the town, and exclude most of the poor.

In all three parishes, just over 30 per cent of Sandwich testators left bequests to the churches of parishes other than their own, to the friary or the hospitals (including the leper hospital), and, in variable amounts, to churches and religious institutions outside the town. The impression given by the external donations is that the parishioners of St Mary's and St Peter's were much more cosmopolitan than those of St Clement's, with many having links to places outside Sandwich. In particular, St Mary's was home to a number of wealthy merchants, some of whose bequests suggest business connections in London or even as far away as Newcastle upon Tyne.

St Peter's was the parish in which most testators (17 per cent) left bequests to external bodies, but their contacts were of a different nature from those of St Mary's parishioners. The St Peter's bequests went to other churches in Kent, particularly in the east of the county, where many of the testators also owned land, perhaps in areas from which they or their families had migrated to settle in the commercial heart of Sandwich, that is, in St Peter's parish.

On the other hand, St Clement's parishioners were more parochial and largely concerned with life in the parish itself. Table 13.1 shows that almost all parishioners were buried in the church or churchyard, and Table 13.3 indicates that they made few bequests outside the town. This may have been because so many mariners lived there; their livelihoods depended upon the sea rather than the ownership of land outside the town, and their profession was less likely to be swelled by migrants from the neighbouring countryside.

13.2.4 The Reformation

In the 1530s and early 1540s Kent was noted for the struggles between the old and new religions, and signs of tension were apparent throughout the east of the county, including in Sandwich.[77] The trouble may first have come to the fore in 1532, when the clergy of St Peter's refused to fulfil their traditional role of leading the annual procession of civic dignitaries to St Bartholomew's hospital. They were imprisoned and, possibly as a result, all had either died or left the town before 1538 when Edmund Grene became rector of St Peter's.[78] Grene had pronounced Protestant views, which resulted in his church becoming the most fervently Protestant of the three. In 1554, after the accession of Queen Mary, the civic authorities placed the then rector of St Peter's, William Powes, under house arrest for continuing to conduct services in English.[79] The vicar of St Mary's, John Croft, appointed in 1532, also held reformist views and married as soon as this was possible. When Mary came to the throne there were no unmarried ministers at all in the town. Croft was replaced by the religious conservative John Steward, who had been the hermit of St James's chapel and then chantry priest of the Condy chantry, and so may have been without employment since 1548, when the chantry was abolished.[80]

Sandwich had no local monastic house, and the records do not provide much information about the effect of the redistribution of monastic property. As discussed above, the friary was dissolved in 1538, but its five-acre site was soon in the hands of a Faversham merchant (Section 13.1.4). There is no record of what happened to most of the property in the town centre once owned by Christ Church Priory and St Augustine's Abbey, although it is clear that the Dean and Chapter became owners of the priory's enclave at the west end of St Mary's parish, stretching from St Thomas's Lane (present Paradise Row) to Canterbury Gate. In 1563 they granted it to Sir Roger Manwood for the site of the new grammar school (Chap. 16.1). The priory's main house, however, may have survived the building of the school and come into civic ownership, for as late as 1585 Edward Wood, a wealthy jurat, was paying rent for a garden next to 'St Thomas's house',[81] and the treasurers' accounts record the mending of the sewer at the house in the following year.[82] The lands that had supported the four chantries – Grene's and Burton's in St Clement's, Elys's in St Peter's and the Condy chantry in St Mary's – were sold in 1549 to men living elsewhere in Kent, in London, and even in Wiltshire.[83] It is unknown whether this had any effect on the locals who rented the former chantry properties in the town.

A concomitant to the number of people crowding into the centre during the difficult years of the early sixteenth century may have been that a high proportion of the poor resided in that part of town. Such people did not leave wills, but their presence is perhaps noticeable in St Peter's parish where the early sixteenth-century wills were the most likely to specify bequests to the poor. A 'Brotherhood of the Poor', whose precise purpose is unknown but which may have been connected with relief of the poor, seems to have been set up shortly before 1545. It was mentioned again in 1546, although it must have been suppressed along with all the other brotherhoods in 1547.[84] Later, bequests of money or food were made directly to the poor, or money was left for the poor box.[85] How this was distributed is not clear. Admittedly, concern for the poor is evident in all three parishes, probably because bequests were the only form of charity actively encouraged by the authorities once there were no religious guilds, but it is more evident in St Peter's parish in this period.

The dissolution of the chantries and destruction of the brotherhoods in 1547–8 must have had the same significant impact on the religious life and social structure of the parishes in Sandwich as it had throughout England. Masses for the dead ceased to be said; images were destroyed; all lights but those on the high altar were put out; liturgical books were abolished, and religious feasts and processions abandoned.[86] Although there is little record of the effect in Sandwich, these must have been confusing times for the people. It is hard to gauge the parishioners' views from their wills, and it is only through other activities that one can sometimes obtain a glimpse of their religious beliefs. There seem to have been no clear-cut distinctions between Catholic and Protestant by political or civic affiliation. Some, such as the royal bailiff Sir Edward Ringeley and his wife, were clearly conservatives, and several of the leading townsmen who opposed Ringeley politically, such as Henry Bolle, Roger Manwood and Vincent Engeham, were of his mind on religion. Among the jurats on the reforming side were Alexander Aldy and Richard Boteler, who was one of the iconoclasts of the 1540s, mentioned below. Other reformers held less socially dominant positions, in particular William Norrice, who left money to the Brotherhood of the Poor in 1546, and Thomas Holy, tenant of some of the lands of Grene's chantry, lessee of the town crane, and water bailiff in the 1520s and 1530s. Both men were iconoclasts, involved in the destruction of images, and seem to have been friends of the reforming clerics Edmund Grene and John Croft.[87] Most of the reformers were inhabitants of the socially mixed and tightly packed parish of St Peter's, while several of the conservatives, such as the Ringeleys, Roger Manwood and Vincent Engeham, lived in St Mary's. Few men prominent on either the conservative or the reforming side are known in St Clement's.

13.3 The hospitals

13.3.1 St Thomas's

In addition to endowing a chantry in St Peter's church in 1392, Thomas Elys also made provision for the foundation of St Thomas's hospital, an almshouse for

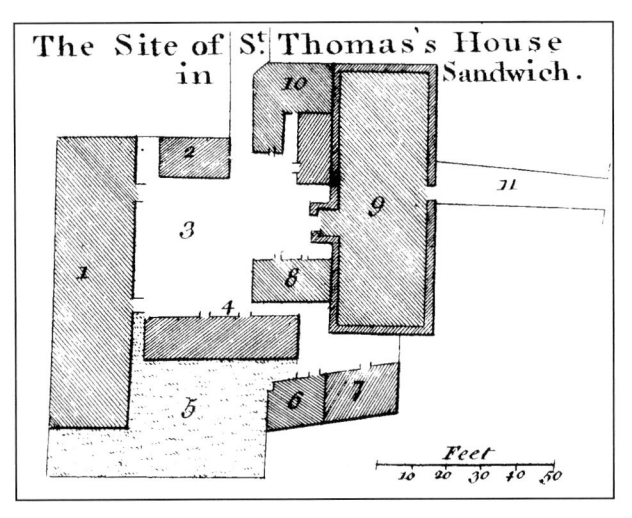

Fig. 13.7: St Thomas's hospital, plan of buildings. The access from the Cornmarket is at the top, and that from New Street is to the right; see endpapers (Boys 1792, 171; P. W. © English Heritage DP046236)

twelve poor people: eight brothers and four sisters.[88] It was administered by Elys's feoffees (later trustees), and since it was not an ecclesiastical institution it was able, like St Bartholomew's and St John's hospitals, to survive the Dissolution. The buildings were situated on the south-east side of the Cornmarket, from which they were almost certainly approached. There was probably also rear access from New Street; this may later have become the main entrance (Fig. 13.7). The complex consisted of a great hall and private accommodation, surrounded by outbuildings and a garden. There was no chapel, the inmates simply being parishioners of St Peter's church.[89] The medieval buildings were demolished in 1857–8 when the almshouses were moved to a new site in Moat Sole.

Much of our information about the accommodation comes from Boys's description: 'A passage through the middle of the house divides it into two parts. On the south side is the hall, open to the roof; beyond which are the women's apartments, two above stairs and two below. The men's rooms are on the north side, four above and four below.' Two sketches published by Rolfe in 1852 (Fig. 13.8)[90] show that there was far more building to the left (north) of the cross passage than to the right, where the great window lighting the still-open hall was situated.

A few fragments of the great stone hall survived the demolition of 1857–8. The south-east corner still stands in its original position, forming part of the party wall between 14 and 16, 18 New Street (Houses 62, 63). Although no decorative elements remain, it confirms that the hall was built of stone. The hall window shown by Rolfe now stands in front of the west end of St

Fig. 13.8: St Thomas's hospital, drawing of south-west side of the great hall (Rolfe 1852, 3, pl. 66, copy from Roget Collection, Dover Museum and Bronze Age Boat Gallery).

Fig. 13.9: Window from St Thomas's hospital, re-erected at the west end of St Peter's church (P. W. © English Heritage DP044012)

Fig. 13.10: Archway of the porch from St Thomas's hospital, re-erected at the new hospital in Moat Sole (P. W. © English Heritage DP 068621)

Peter's church (Fig. 13.9), and the porch has been re-erected in the new St Thomas's almshouses in Moat Sole (Fig. 13.10). In default of other physical remains, the drawings must be relied on for an understanding of the hospital buildings, although, as discussed below, they confuse rather than illuminate their origin and form.

The great sweeping roof of the hall with upper rooms set into it, and the roof's immense depth, suggests a date in the early fourteenth century rather than the late, although this is hardly proof in itself. The tracery of the window on the south-west side has a square head and cusped detailing of a type normally found in the first half of the fourteenth century, being very similar to one in the claustral ranges at Davington Priory, near Faversham, which has been dated to that period.[91] The porch is shown in the drawing as having been entered through a timber archway, with what might be a stone doorway beyond, opening into the hall itself. The timber arch seems certainly to have been the one reset at the rear of the gateway to the Moat Sole almshouses. It has a two-centred arch in which the head is formed by narrow brace-shaped timbers rather than the solid arches normally found in early timber doorways. The only other example known to the writer is at Hurst Farm, Chilham, of early fourteenth-century date.[92] The stone arch now on the street side of the almshouse gate seems more likely to date from the thirteenth century than the fourteenth and it is less certainly from the medieval St Thomas's hospital.

Thus, the surviving window and the fabric of the porch seem to date from before the hospital was founded. Two explanations may be proposed. The hospital building may originally have been an early fourteenth-century hall house, perhaps owned by the Elys family and given by Thomas to his new foundation in 1392. Against this is the lack of documentary evidence, both for Elys's actions and for the presence of any private dwellings built by the Sandwich elite in this part of town, south of the Delf. Alternatively, ignoring the inconclusive depth of the roof, the hall could have been constructed in the late fourteenth century with the window and the archways of the porch later being rescued from another building and inserted – brought, for example, from the neighbouring friary after the Dissolution. Neither explanation is entirely satisfactory, so that questions remain.

13.3.2 St Bartholomew's

By the fifteenth century St Bartholomew's was an almshouse for better-off Sandwich inhabitants and the chapel, which may have been a chapel-cum-infirmary hall when built (Chap. 6.2.2), was almost certainly used

Fig. 13.11: Photograph reputedly of a building at St Bartholomew's hospital, possibly the hall (William Henry Boyer 1827–97 © Sandwich Guildhall Archive BP/C-00195)

exclusively as a chapel. The original north aisle had been extended a little to the west, blocking a window in the nave. A crown-post roof over the north aisle probably dates from the late fourteenth century; those over the nave and chancel have been renewed.

From at least 1301, as mentioned in the custumal, there was a communal hall where the inmates met at least once a week, and a photograph of the 1870s, purportedly recording the demolition of a building at the hospital, may illustrate this hall (Fig. 13.11). The photograph shows a large two-storey building of stone, flint and brick, already stripped of its roof and partitions. On the two visible walls there are four two-centred aumbries of possible fourteenth-century date. If it were the hall, then it later must have been converted to individual dwellings and had an upper storey inserted. Unfortunately, the building cannot be identified on the plan of the hospital published in Boys in 1792 (Fig. 13.12). The hall remained in use through the fifteenth and early sixteenth centuries, for in 1543 payment was made 'for making a buttery in our great hall'.[93]

By the fifteenth century the inmates were provided with individual dwellings arranged around the west, south and east sides of the chapel as shown on the plan of 1792. Almost all of them have been rebuilt, although some survived long enough to be drawn in the eighteenth century.[94] In addition, the basic structure of one timber-framed open-hall house remains at No. 2 (House 17; Fig. 13.13), marked '4' on Boys's plan at the south-east corner of the courtyard, opposite the east end of the chapel. Now refaced in brick, it was originally built during the fifteenth century, although not enough remains to make more precise dating possible. It contained a hall, open to the roof (since replaced), including an undershot cross

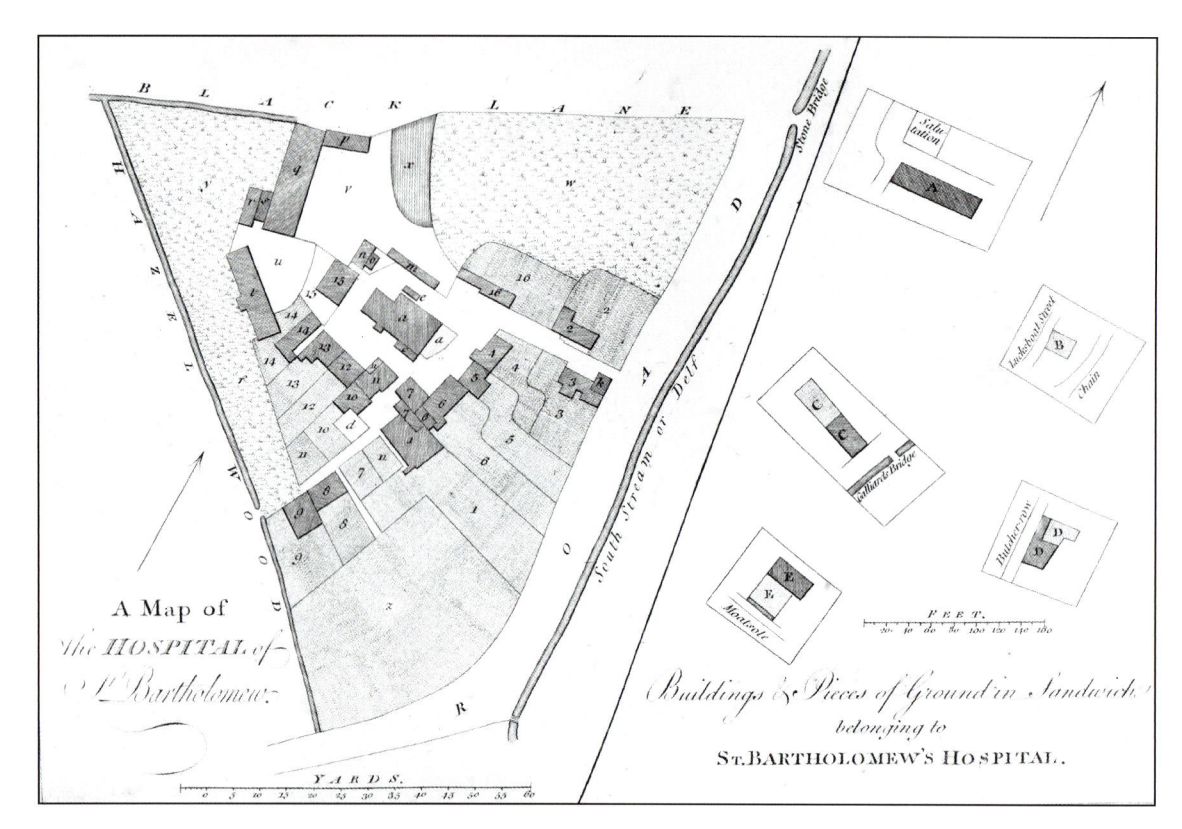

Fig. 13.12: St Bartholomew's hospital, detail of plan (Boys 1792, 113; P. W. © English Heritage DP046234)

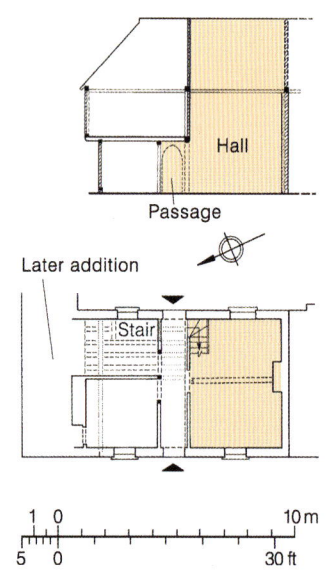

Fig. 13.13: 2 St Bartholomew's hospital, plan and long section showing form of original almshouse (S. P. & A. T. A)

passage at the north end, with two doorways leading to two small rooms beyond, one of them containing a stair to a single chamber above. The end bay was jettied to the north, and the sizeable chamber above extended across the passage. The house was thus of 'end-jetty' form, a type common in the Kentish countryside but otherwise unknown in Sandwich. In addition, the arrangement of hall, passage and two end rooms is the 'standard' medieval plan so conspicuously lacking within the town itself.

The provision of a living room and bedroom for each inmate occurs in almshouses elsewhere. Sometimes, as at St Mary's, Chichester, they were added inside the original infirmary hall; sometimes they were built to a unified design around a courtyard, as at St Cross, Winchester.[95] At St Bartholomew's, each house appears to have been *sui generis*, possibly erected at different times (as their refacing or rebuilding certainly was). We have no substantiating documentary information for the dwellings in the fifteenth century, but between 1568 and 1593 fifteen probate inventories for hospital residents mention the names of rooms within their dwellings.[96] They all list a hall and a chamber, and most of them had a buttery as well. In addition, several had other rooms such as a parlour, kitchen, milk house and two chambers upstairs, one of which may have been over the open hall, which by that date was probably ceiled over. That most of the residents of the hospital were by no means indigent is illustrated by the fact that their inventory goods, including debts owed to them, ranged in value between £5 and £82 8s. 4d. In addition, in 1475 one inmate owned four cottages in town,[97] and in the 1540s, when the brewer Oliver

Stromble and his wife had become residents, they still had valuable property to sell in Strand Street (Chap. 10.3.2). Both documentary evidence and the surviving almshouse suggest that there was a generous amount of accommodation for each inhabitant.

13.4 Conclusion

After the rebuilding of the nave of St Clement's church in the first half of the fifteenth century, the major items of church expenditure in Sandwich during the later fifteenth and early sixteenth centuries were the renovated towers at St Clement's and St Mary's. Apart from these, work seems to have concentrated on the provision of internal fittings, particularly on woodwork and the elaboration of the various altars and chapels. But donations were small. Even though Thomas Elys left money to found an unusually lavish chantry in St Peter's in the late fourteenth century, there is no evidence that a new chapel, or finely carved stone screens, were ever built to enclose it, and the later perpetual chantries in St Clement's seem to have been much smaller affairs. Elys also founded St Thomas's hospital, but this was the last major charitable foundation in the town. St Bartholomew's hospital was not distinguished by any addition to its public buildings in the fifteenth century, but by the erection of new and better accommodation for individual inmates.

The scale of religious bequests was small and personal, reflecting what we know of the gradual downturn in the fortunes of the town and its inhabitants during the later fifteenth and sixteenth centuries. This was not peculiar to Sandwich and its particular history. Small-scale bequests were a feature of churches everywhere at this time, and while church architecture flourished in some parts of England – notably East Anglia and the West Country – Kent was not among them. As Newman put it when discussing various aspects of later medieval churches, 'Kent has plenty to show, but little that is really outstanding.'[98]

Sandwich may not have been unusual, and what has survived is not particularly distinguished, but the copious evidence of the active participation of the laity in the routine life of their parish churches provides some idea of the immense importance of religion in their lives. It also brings out the different character of each parish and dovetails with what we know about secular buildings and Sandwich society. We can see that at the time when the construction of major projects on the churches was coming to an end, the scope of pious bequests was changing. Donations were now focused on the furnishing and servicing of churches, stopping short of the grand private gestures of earlier periods. Ordinary people made donations to altars, images, lights and Masses, which benefited both themselves and their neighbours, and their bequests were often channelled through the brotherhoods to which all but the poorest belonged. The impression that this development began in the late fourteenth century and went on to affect nearly all the will-making community by the late fifteenth may be due to differential survival, but it is unlikely to be erroneous. It is worth noting that it occurred at the same time as the number of surviving private houses increased, and it leads to the conclusion that as material expectations improved, more and more people were trying to have the best of both worlds: better quality houses and the lifestyle that went with them in this world, and better provision for their souls in the next.

There is not enough information to paint an accurate picture of the effects of the Reformation on the town. By 1540 Sandwich was in a depressed state. A silting harbour and declining economy affected all the inhabitants; the population was steadily shrinking, and there was considerable decay in the housing stock. Although there was no major religious upheaval, since only one religious house had to be dissolved, it must have been a grim period for most of the inhabitants. The year 1560 may seem an odd date at which to close a chapter on the religious life of the town, but by then the religious changes could be seen as just one of the many problems for which there seemed to be no solution.

14 The landscape of the town

For the medieval and modern street names mentioned in this chapter see the endpapers. For the distribution of buildings surveyed see Figure IV.1.

This chapter describes the physical aspect of Sandwich during the two centuries between 1360 and 1560, drawing on the information that has been discussed in Chapters 8 to 13 and supplementing it with some new evidence. It is possible here to take a long view of urban development, for by the mid-fourteenth century the town had reached its maximum walled area and street pattern (Fig. III.1), and topographical development henceforth concerned minor variations and how the fixed features – the walls, gates, quays, streets, marketplaces and major buildings – dictated the distribution of occupations and people (Fig. IV.1). Documents describe the activities that went on along the waterfront, and they and the few surviving fifteenth-century buildings north of Strand Street illuminate how that area developed. The extant buildings, which are distributed over a much wider area than hitherto, are of different types in different parts of the town, reflecting a zoning of wealth and occupations. Evidence for this is less in the western half of St Mary's parish because of the absence of surviving medieval buildings there, and this is also true of all three parishes south of the Delf. The reasons for these discrepancies will be discussed below.

14.1 The waterfront: access and facilities

There are indications of waterside development at the west end of town (near the Christ Church Priory headquarters) as early as the thirteenth century, and to the east (in the Fisher Gate area) by the early fourteenth century, but the first signs of houses on the north side of the central stretch between the junction of the Delf and the Stour and Davis Gate are no earlier than 1387. This suggests that the riverbank was consolidated at different periods (Chap. 8.3), and that the central area was the last to be developed. Most of the waterfront was occupied by merchants' properties fronted by private wharfs, with public access to the water limited to a few lanes that ran from Strand Street to gates with their own wharfs. The town owned and maintained Ives Gate, St Mary's Gate and Pillory Gate in the central section, and Fisher Gate to the east. Monk's or Monkenquay Gate was associated with Christ Church Priory at the west end of town. It may not have been a waterside gate, but rather to have led from the priory grounds into the town,[1] although in 1461 it was cited as one end of the ward that was responsible for the area between it and Canterbury Gate, suggesting that it stood close to the water.[2]

Ives Gate and St Mary's Gate are known only from brief documentary references which imply that they were built of timber,[3] but Pillory Gate is better recorded. It stood on the north side of Strand Street opposite the junction of Harnet Street and The Butchery. In 1385 the phrase the 'place leading to Pillory Gate' suggests that it was not on the street frontage, but set a little way back from it.[4] In 1494 a 'dwelling with a chamber belonging to it' may refer to Pillory Gate,[5] and by 1514 it was of at least two storeys, with an adjacent privy and tenements abutting on both sides.[6] In the sixteenth century the illegal disposal of offal at the gate by butchers caused concern, and by 1522 the Butchers' Guild had become responsible for cleaning and maintaining it.[7] It cannot have been used only for depositing butchers' waste, however, for in 1523 it was named with Davis Gate and Fisher Gate as one of the three wharfs where herrings could be landed.[8] Nevertheless, rubbish continued to accumulate,[9] and by 1558 the butchers had misused Pillory Gate to such an extent that it needed thoroughly refurbishing, involving the construction of an 'overshoot' through which the offal could be dumped further offshore (although still in the harbour).[10] It continued to be a nuisance and a source of noxious smells throughout the rest of the century.

At the junction of Strand Street and High Street lay the town quay, on which stood Davis Gate, the town crane and probably one of the town's weigh beams. Both the quay and the gate are known from the early fourteenth century, but their precise location at that time remains in doubt. It can only be said that because of the gradual reclamation of the waterfront they may have stood a little further south than the current gate and quay. The present gatehouse dates from the 1470s (Chap. 11.2.1.4), being constructed right beside the haven, probably mainly on newly reclaimed land. A two-storey timber building (House 31) is attached to the south side of its western tower. This is now of two bays, one bay forming part of the modern dwelling inside the tower, the other forming part of the Crispin Inn (Fig. 11.21). Originally, there was one large room on each floor of the dwelling, with an internal stair; the crown-post roof and close-studded walls suggest that it was built in the mid- or later fifteenth century, and it could have preceded the erection of the new gate. But since its northern end has been destroyed, the relationship between the two structures is uncertain. By the 1550s it might have been the building called the Barbican next to Davis Gate itself, its ground floor being the 'little storehouse under the barbican'.[11]

The wharf in front of Davis Gate must have been built when the present gatehouse was put up, presumably being regarded as part of the town quay. Its upkeep entailed much expenditure until the middle of the sixteenth century. As early as 1497 it was paved with stone and the side facing the water reinforced with timber and bricks.[12] In 1517 the brickwork needed mending,[13] and the town levied a tax for more repairs in May 1528.[14] A new wharf, however, is recorded in the treasurers' accounts for the same year, possibly an additional quay rather than a replacement,[15] for the dilapidated state of the original remained a continuing cause for concern to the civic authorities.[16] The surplus beer money used for repairs throughout the town in 1536 may have helped to shore it up until the end of the century.[17]

The town crane stood on the town quay, very close to Davis Gate and probably more or less where one is marked on the Ordnance Survey map of 1873, although none is shown on Foord's plan of the quay of 1833 (Fig. 14.1). The crane was an important contributor to civic finances (Chap. 9.2.5) and so was scrupulously maintained. It was probably also a model of its kind, for in 1555 it was studied by a carpenter from Rye who was to build a new crane in that port.[18] It seems to have been a substantial structure, consisting of an upright mast with a manoeuvrable wooden beam, block and tackle, rope and grab, and its mechanism depended on a pair of tread wheels rotated by horses. The whole appears to have been encased in a crane house, two storeys high, with a stair between a cellar

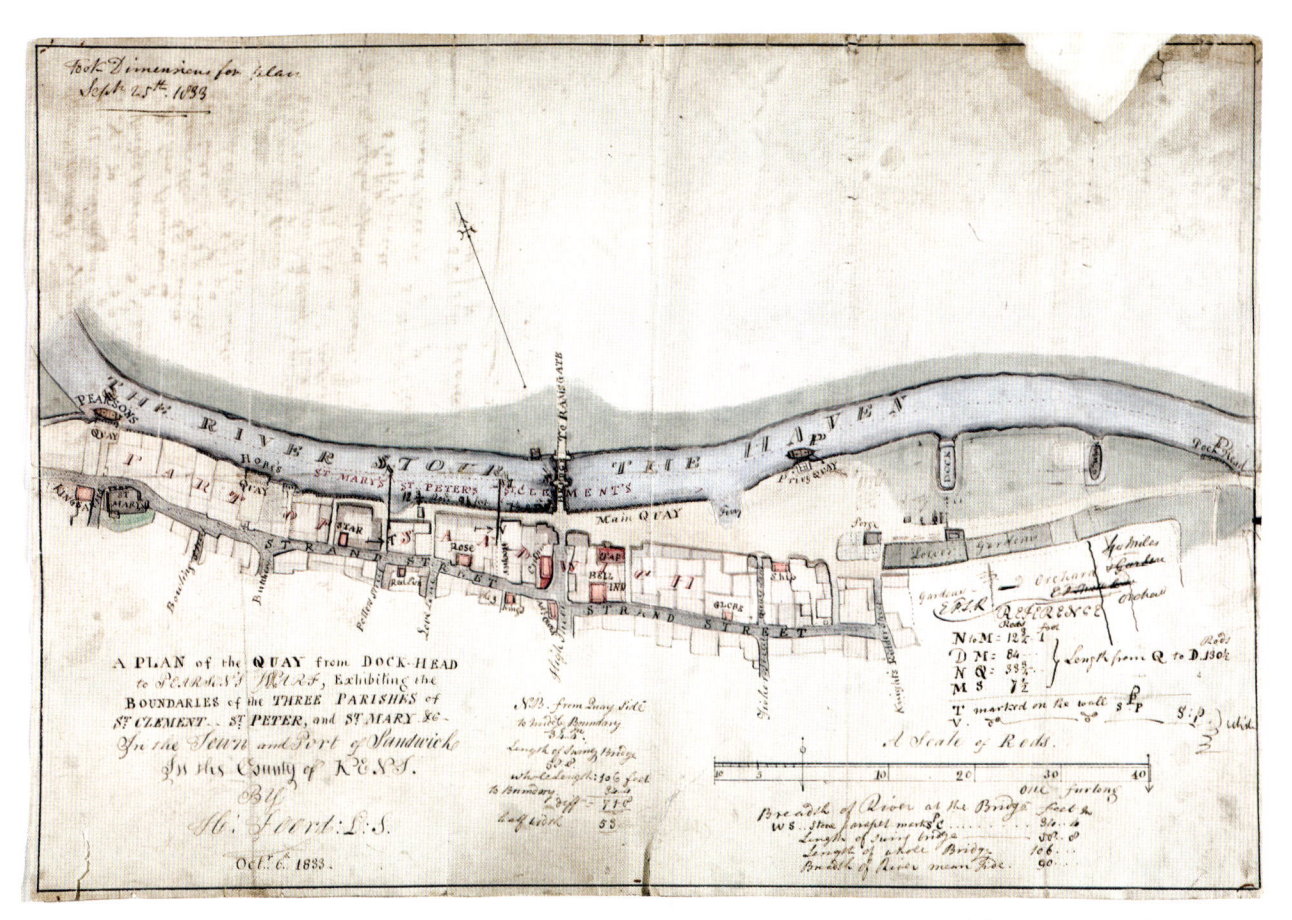

Fig. 14.1: Plan of Sandwich quay drawn by Foord in 1833 (EKAC: Sa/P/6; P. W. © English Heritage DP068581)

and an upper floor, brick walls and a tiled roof.[19] The cellar served as a storehouse at various times, and there are references to the crane 'with appurtenances', indicating the likelihood of other buildings nearby.[20] It seems to have been a much more robust structure than those known from documents of other medieval ports or depicted on sixteenth-century maps (Fig. 11.22). It was not unusual for a port to have a number of harbour cranes at work simultaneously, as shown in Figure 11.28, with this being true in sixteenth-century Sandwich, where two cranes were built on the quay in 1526 and 1530, and the crane on Monkenquay (Chap. 16.4.1) was still being referred to as the 'old crane' until 1597.[21]

That mentioned in 1530 was called a crane with bulwerk (tower) at Davis Gate, which may mean that a crane was incorporated into one of the gatehouse towers,[22] which were also referred to as 'bulwerk' on occasions. If this were so, Davis Gate may have been a 'crane gate', as it is called in a single reference in 1490.[23] Combined gatehouses and harbour cranes were not unknown in the Middle Ages. The only surviving example is in the Hanseatic port of Danzig, but it is on an altogether more massive scale than Davis Gate, although its design is similar and it stands on the quay fronted by a revetment or wharf, as did Davis Gate.[24]

There is less evidence of other harbour facilities in the vicinity. There may have been a weigh beam for checking cargoes somewhere nearby, for as early as 1372 'balances, weights and other instruments appointed for weighing wool' were shipped from Queenborough, when wool was once again loaded onto vessels at Sandwich (Chap. 9.2.1).[25] This equipment was presumably erected on the quay for convenience to shipping, but no town records specifically state this.[26] The custom house was not located on the public quay, but in the middle of private wharfs two plots west of Pillory Gate, where the remains of a decorative brick facade of c.1620 at 40 Strand Street faces the waterfront.[27]

One of the main surviving features on the land between Strand Street/Upper Strand Street and the south bank of the river is the stone town wall that ran continuously from near Canterbury Gate to the mouth of the Delf (Chap. 11.2.1.3). At the west end of town it partially survives in house walls and gardens no less than 20m from the present south bank of the Guestling (Figs 14.2, 14.3). In the Middle Ages the waterway (then known as the Delf or merely 'the creek') flowed much closer to the wall's northern face, apparently right against it in one place (Site 46, garden of 66 Strand Street; Fig. 11.15). Further west it was fronted by Monkenquay, for which there is good documentary

Fig. 14.2: Town wall in garden of 62 Strand Street, from north (K. P. DSCN2058)

Fig. 14.3: Town wall in garden of 68 Strand Street, from north, showing possible medieval gateway (K. P. DSCN2077)

evidence from the early thirteenth century, some two hundred years before the wall was built.[28] The wall's construction must have cut across the quay, and also probably some of the thirteenth-century merchants' wharfs.[29] Presumably there were gates through it to the water, and a small archway in the wall at 68 Strand Street may perpetuate a medieval opening (Fig. 14.3). The wall's presence may have been at least part of the reason why fifteenth- and sixteenth-century evidence for private quays is concentrated east of St Mary's church, where there was no intervening wall.

There must have been a similar relationship between wall and quayside in its eastern stretch. For much of its length there it was fronted by the common quay, with the main access from the town being through Davis Gate (at least from c.1300) and Fisher Gate (at least from c.1385). By the middle of the fifteenth century the latter was flanked by merchants' tenements, with houses fronting onto Upper Strand Street and their land running north towards the water. Some of them had private wharfs, for in 1458 it was agreed that Richard Cok should retain his access to his quay when a brick revetment was built on the north-west side of the gate.[30] There was no town wall there at the time, for when the wall was built in 1475 William Cok (probably Richard's son) was recompensed for giving up part of his property.[31] Most of the tenements north of present Upper Strand Street probably had ways onto the waterfront, as suggested by an entry in the year book for 1479, when the town authorities ordered repairs to the wall east of Fisher Gate, stipulating that all its gates should be secure and lockable.[32] In 1519 John Somer and John Cok were given permission to construct a stone wall between their properties and the quay;[33] perhaps the town wall had become dilapidated in the years since John Cok's father had lost part of his property to it.

Fisher Gate stands at the north end of Quay Lane (Site 74; Figs 11.18, 11.19) with access to the quay provided by a stone-paved passageway with a portcullis integral with the late fourteenth-century structure (Chap. 11.2.1.4). The present paving was probably laid down in the nineteenth century, with its surface at approximately +3.20m OD, the lowest point in the area. The passageway is still occasionally flooded at particularly high tides (which reach between +3.00m and +3.50m OD), suggesting that before the revetment was built in 1458 it may have opened directly onto the foreshore, with dry access at low tide and possibly partial flooding at high tide.[34] It was, however, certainly fronted by its own wharf after that, for in 1487 ships and boats berthing there were in danger of obstructing the artillery in the Bulwark,[35] and in 1490 a dock was built so that a Flemish ship could be berthed there to be broken up.[36] The dock is not referred to again until 1557, when the town leased 'Joyses dock outside Fisher Gate'.[37] The same record refers to a groyne against which ships were tied – evidence to suggest that the 'dock' was a breakwater or jetty (Chap. 9.3).

By the 1450s the far eastern end of the riverbank must have been consolidated enough to support a very substantial structure, which, beginning as a gun emplacement, developed into formidable defensive feature – the Bulwark (Chap. 11.2.1.2). Its construction differed from the rest of the wall along the waterfront by being built of earth and timber, with only a facing of stones, forming the north-east corner of the earth ramparts that surrounded the rest of the town.

14.2 Strand Street between Pillory Gate and Davis Gate

This short stretch of Strand Street has land in all three parishes. By the fifteenth century waterfront properties in this area, especially those with quays, were among the most desirable in the town. The first reference to property on the north side of the central section of the street occurs in 1387, when the corporation granted a vacant piece of land in St Mary's parish to a tallow chandler.[38] The fact that the adjacent plot was also vacant at the time suggests that this may have been when the land reclaimed from the river was becoming sufficiently consolidated for building. No convincing evidence for more extensive development there occurs until 1414, when tenements next to Pillory Gate are mentioned.[39] From that time onwards there were regular references in all three parishes to waterfront tenements, several with quays. They were owned mainly by prominent townsmen, some of whom were discussed in Chapter 10.[40] Only three medieval buildings have survived the later development of this stretch of waterfront and none dates from before the middle of the fifteenth century. The earliest is probably the short two-storey range attached to Davis Gate, now partly in the Crispin Inn (House 31). The others are of three storeys. No. 42 (House 87), just to the west of Pillory Gate, is a house of *c*.1500, and No. 34 (House 84) has few remaining features, is not precisely datable, and may not have been domestic.

Although the south side of the street possibly became less desirable to those occupied in overseas trade because it no longer had direct access to the waterfront, it was still a significant area of the town, lined with private houses, shops, inns and taverns (Fig. 14.4). The

Fig. 14.4: South side of Strand Street from the east (P. W. © English Heritage DP043982)

Black Tavern (Chap. 7.2.2), in St Peter's parish, was possibly 27 Strand Street (House 82), where there is the only surviving vaulted cellar in the town. It was first mentioned in 1402, and seems to have become town property in the 1460s when it was leased for 13s. 4d.[41] Nearby was 'Le Bolle' (The Bull Inn), occupying at least part of the large courtyard property at 11–15 Strand Street (Houses 77, 78, 79), and leased out by the town for 53s. 4d. in 1466. We do not know the form of the building at that date, but by the early sixteenth century the main part of The Bull had been rebuilt with a row of shops at the front (Chap. 12.8.1; Figs 12.42, 12.44). There were also shops on the north side of this central section of Strand Street, as mentioned in the bequest of a row of shops in 1453, and the sale for £15 of two shops with garrets above in 1491.[42] But the presence of shops did not drive away wealthy inhabitants. In 1509, 23 Strand Street (House 81; Figs 12.3, 12.4, 12.46) is likely to have been the house of William Baly, mayor in 1509 and one of the richest men in Sandwich in the tax assessment of 1513.[43] Unfortunately, it has not been possible to identify the later owners or occupiers of any of the fine fourteenth-century houses surviving at 33, 39 and 41 Strand Street (Houses 83, 85, 86).

14.3 The Fishmarket

There are still a number of medieval houses in the Fishmarket, all having three storeys of accommodation on the street frontage, probably with shops on the ground floor (although no evidence for them survives) and in several instances medieval open halls behind (Fig. 14.5). No individuals can be connected to surviving buildings but there is a wealth of information about property owners. In the 1360s Thomas Elys the elder owned property here.[44] In the 1440s and 1450s Robert Whyte, a former mayor, and John Drury, the unfortunate mayor who was killed by the French in 1457, both owned property in the street.[45] In the early sixteenth century a Londoner sold a property on the corner of the Fishmarket and Cok Lane, and much later, Edward Parker, beer brewer and entrepreneur, bequeathed a tenement in the Fishmarket when he died in 1559.[46] Most of these men almost certainly lived elsewhere, renting out their valuable marketplace properties. In 1385 one tenement was rented for 26s. 8d.; in 1445 a messuage and two shops were rented by a couple from Dover for 15s. 6d. a year, presumably to be sub-let, and in 1446 another fetched 20s.[47] In 1513 the town let a tenement in the Fishmarket for 12s. a

Fig. 14.5: Fishmarket and St Peter's church at the end of the eighteenth century, from Boys 1792, facing p. 297 (P. W. © English Heritage DP068587)

year and two shops for 4s. a year,[48] suggesting that the shops were rented out separately from accommodation above and behind them. The drop in rent perhaps reflects the difficulty of finding tenants at this time of population decline, and is mirrored in other towns at this period.[49]

Not all the buildings in the Fishmarket were owned by the town's elite or people from outside Sandwich. In 1475 Ralph Taylor, carpenter, had two properties in the Fishmarket, and in 1484 Alice Tanner left two properties to her husband William, a barber. One of Alice's properties was occupied by Thomas Sole, the sexton of St Peter's, who may later have bought it jointly with his son.[50] The stalls or shambles in the marketplace were owned by the town and in 1433 they were leased for an annual sum of £8 1s. 8d.; on the same day the town let vacant land there to another man on the understanding that he would repair the stalls that occupied it.[51] Although it is never stated, the shambles in the Fishmarket were presumably used for fish rather than for meat, which was sold in The Butchery or from butchers' standings in the Cornmarket (Sections 14.4 and 14.6). Likewise, the weigh beam in the Fishmarket, leased by the town for £8 a year in 1434, may have been connected with the marketing of fish.[52] There is little information about the trades in the permanent shops on either side of the street. In 1385 a baker paid 26s. 8d. free rent (quit rent) to St John's hospital, and in 1468 a dispute between two owners involved a right of way leading to a bakehouse.[53] But apart from these references there is little evidence for the trades practised.

14.4 The Butchery

The Butchery, as its name implies, was largely occupied by butchers. Some, like William Joynte and Thomas Janyn, lived in owner-occupied property,[54] but others rented their premises. Stephen Gerard paid 10s. a year to St Bartholomew's hospital, and for several years in the mid-fifteenth century John Brownyng had difficulty paying St Mary's churchwardens his annual rent of 13s. 4d.[55] The connection with butchers continued during the sixteenth century, as exemplified by Thomas Goodbarn, a yeoman and butcher, who in 1557 willed that William Fulwood, also a butcher, should continue to occupy his house in The Butchery with all the tools in his shop.[56] Others bought property in The Butchery purely as investments. For example, William Cok, gentleman, bought two tenements from a Dover couple in 1470,[57] and Vincent Engeham, gentleman, who died in 1547, owned a tenement occupied by Thomas Thorne, butcher.[58]

14.5 Love Lane

An impressive property called 'stonehalle tenement' lay on the west side of the street in the late fifteenth century. In the early 1480s it was owned by the Kenet family, who sold it for £46 to William Giles, beer brewer, who then settled it on his daughter and her London husband.[59] It is tempting to suggest that this was the large excavated stone building of *c.*1300 that survived on the west side of Love Lane until after the Middle Ages, but as discussed in Chapter 7.1, it is more likely that that was an adjunct to a tenement in the Fishmarket. Another important building on this side of Love Lane was The Bell Inn, privately owned in 1435, but town property in the 1460s when it was leased for 54s. 4d.[60] On the opposite side of the street, 50 St Peter's Street (House 73) was part of a large courtyard property fronting Strand Street owned by successive prominent townsmen (Chap. 12.1; Fig. 12.3). Thus, around the junction of Strand Street and Love Lane, and extending a short way down the latter, were clustered a number of important properties. Between these buildings and nearer to St Peter's church, cottages and workshops were owned by men such as Thomas Elys and William Gayler in the late fourteenth and fifteenth centuries.[61] A couple of timber-framed houses survive on the east side: No. 30, and the possible aisled hall and cross wing at Nos. 18 and 20 (Figs 12.6, 12.7). Around 1600 new small houses (House 69) replaced some of the earlier buildings. Further south, at the junction of Love Lane and Luckboat, The Hart and Swan was established at least by *c.*1500.[62] The documents and the survivors suggest that Love Lane was a mixed street, with dwellings belonging to the wealthy lying cheek by jowl with poorer commercial or semi-commercial properties.

On the opposite side of Love Lane was St Peter's church, with the court hall, built sometime before 1432, to the south. The site marked on the 1:500 Ordnance Survey map of 1873 is in part of the churchyard,[63] but in the Middle Ages the hall probably stood outside it (Fig. IV.1). In 1776 St Peter's bought land from the town to enlarge its extremely small graveyard, and this possibly included the site of the old court hall.[64] Court or guild halls were often located in or near marketplaces. The fact that the Sandwich hall was built in Love Lane rather than in the marketplace may indicate that by the time it was decided to have a purpose-built hall rather than use the church for meetings there was no space for it in the Fishmarket. At that time the Cornmarket was not yet considered the centre of town activities. The building has gone, but we know that in the fifteenth century there was a council chamber, with a storehouse 'within' it and a loft above, and that in 1560 a new council chamber was ordered to be made above the old one, which was to be turned to a treasury.[65] Thus it would seem to have been a fully enclosed building of two storeys, rather than the kind that had an open trading space below.[66]

One of the functions of the mayor was to mete out justice to wrong-doers, sending them to prison if needs be. In 1467 it was decreed that he should send any non-freeman to the king's prison, which lay in St Clement's parish, either in the castle or near Sandown Gate, while any freeman should be sent to the 'house of the common wardman'.[67] It is unknown where the latter was at this time, but by the early sixteenth century the town gaol lay in Love Lane beside the court hall,[68] almost certainly where there is now a seventeenth-century building, 3, 5 and 11 St Peter's Street. It is still called The Old Gaol and No. 11 reuses a considerable number of large medieval timbers.

14.6 The Cornmarket

The southern part of St Peter's parish, south of the Delf, contained the Cornmarket. With its generous layout (first mentioned as 'marcatfeelde') and lower buildings it had a very different character from that of the Fishmarket, and was perhaps established to provide space for trading grain and livestock brought into Sandwich from the hinterland before being shipped to other parts of England or to the Continent (Chap. 8.4; Fig. 14.6); since there were only two marketplaces in the town by this time each must have had more than one function. The Cornmarket had probably been laid out in the late thirteenth century when the friary and St John's hospital were founded, and they and the later St Thomas's hospital were approached from it. In 1390 and 1453 money was bequeathed for paving.[69] Although the first reference to small buildings in or around the marketplace dates only to 1435,[70] and none survives before the mid-fifteenth century, they are likely to have existed earlier.

The importance of the Cornmarket as a focal point is perhaps underlined by the fact that it was part of a punishment route in 1465, when a woman was sentenced to be carried round the town before being banished. She was taken from the court hall, up the High Street to Davis Gate, along Strand Street to Cok Lane and into the Fishmarket; whence they went round the cross in the Cornmarket, up Harnet Street to Pillory Gate, along Strand Street to Monkenquay, and thence to the stone cross at the windmill (on the west side of town outside Canterbury Gate), and so out of the Liberty of Sandwich.[71]

From the 1440s onwards the town itself owned a considerable amount of property in the Cornmarket, which it had to keep in repair and for which it received rent. Substantial new butchers' standings, perhaps relating to cattle that were to be transported as carcases, were erected in 1469 when they were walled and tiled,

Fig. 14.6: Painting of the Cattle Market from the south with St Peter's church behind. The building to the left is the seventeenth-century Guard House (H. Maurice Page 1906, Sandwich Guildhall; P. W. © English Heritage DP068612)

costing the town 17s. 6d.[72] Dung from the cattle was deposited on a dunghill at the friary gate.[73] In the centre of the marketplace was the cross, which formed part of the punishment route.[74] This probably began as a simple cross, but by the early sixteenth century it had become more elaborate, roofing materials being required for repairs that took workmen eleven and a half days to complete, and in 1549 a platform or loft was constructed within it to take 'commons', presumably grain, for the poor,[75] such as was housed in a barn in the marketplace in 1554.[76] By the sixteenth century both the stocks and the pillory were located in the Cornmarket.[77]

The town owned several shops around the edge of the marketplace. In 1455 the sum of 29s. 4d. was received for rent from 'shops and pasturage' there,[78] but in 1497 the shops seem to have been let individually for 2s. or 3s. a year, with the rents reduced in 1498 and 1499.[79] In 1513 shop rents in the Cornmarket fetched 7s. 6d., and in the 1530s William Goldsmyth and another man paid 6s. 8d., but these may have been for several shops that the tenants then sub-let.[80] Although the evidence is limited, it appears that around 1500 rents of 2s. a year were being charged for individual shops both in the Fishmarket and the Cornmarket. Privately owned property around the marketplace included The Star Inn (House 9; Fig. 16.8), no doubt established to serve the traders. It stood on the north-west side in front of St John's hospital, on what may have been an encroachment.[81] Other privately owned messuages nearby included a barn[82] and 8 Cattle Market (House 7; Figs 12.18, 12.38), which may have been built on St John's hospital lands. It comprised a single shop in front of an open hall (Chap. 12.8.2). Two medieval buildings survive from a 'middle row', an encroachment on the north-east side backing onto the Delf. No. 9 Cattle Market (House 8) had a single bay, probably a shop, in front of an open hall, but the No Name Shop (House 66; Figs 12.40, 12.41), on the corner of the marketplace and No Name Street, originally contained four shops, a small open hall and two separate areas of storage on the first floor. This might have been one of the two shops 'upon the corner of the corn market' that Roger Parker, smith, rented from the corporation in 1444, or it might have been the privately owned 'corner messuage' with the Cornmarket to the south and the Delf to the north that was sold by William Cokkyn, a pewterer, in 1522.[83] Either way it seems to have been occupied by smiths of varying kinds who appear to have operated from several premises round the marketplace, as indicated also by William Goldsmyth, who rented from the town in the 1530s.

14.7 Luckboat[84]

There is plenty of evidence for commercial property in Luckboat. In the late fifteenth century two coopers had shops there, one of them asking in his will that his shop and two rooms (*camerae*) be sold, hoping they would fetch 40s., and William Garrard, butcher and accumulator of property, had a malthouse and two small tenements there.[85] At the west end, the brewer Henry Bolle bequeathed nine messuages in the west part of St Peter's churchyard in 1481.[86] These were almost certainly rental properties and a couple survive as 1 and 3 King Street (Houses 41, 42; Fig. 12.45). They probably date from the second half of the fifteenth century, were originally jettied to the churchyard as well as King Street, and have evidence for shops or storage, or a combination of both (Chap. 12.8.2). Opposite them is 6 King Street (House 44; Fig. 12.48), a dedicated storehouse of *c*.1400 (Chap. 12.8.3). It seems likely that this area, close to the junction of Luckboat with the Fishmarket and the Cornmarket, was densely packed with buildings largely devoted to trade. This continued throughout the sixteenth century, for the town had two tenements in Luckboat that were rented together for 6s., and a labourer took up a ninety-nine-year lease on a shop next to his existing house, agreeing to pay 18d. a year to St John's hospital.[87]

Some houses in the street were substantial, although all the survivors are only two storeys high. On the south side, where tenements had gardens that stretched back as far as the Delf, a number of fifteenth-century houses with galleried open halls remain, as at 4, 24 and 38 King Street (Houses 43, 47 and 49; Figs 12.12, 12.20). In 1521 two tenements on this side were sold by a gentleman of Whitstable to a Sandwich baker for £35 6s. 8d., which suggests that the buildings involved were of above-average quality,[88] and from around or just after 1600 52 King Street (House 51) was built with fine plaster ceilings dating from 1610–12.[89] On the north side, St Peter's rectory (House 48; Figs 12.26–12.28) is one of the best surviving buildings of *c*.1500 anywhere in the town. Thus the evidence suggests a street with property of mixed value. The north-west end was largely devoted to commercial buildings, many of which were tenanted; the south-east end, further from the centre of town, was occupied by good-quality houses with gardens running back to the Delf. Some at least of these may have been owner-occupied.

14.8 The streets and property in the west end of town

Wealthy merchants holding messuages with quays along the waterfront towards the Christ Church Priory headquarters were documented in the thirteenth century (Chap. 8.1), and gentry held property near the water in the later sixteenth century. But between these dates there is little documentary or building evidence for houses on the waterfront west of St Mary's church. The only fifteenth-century timber-framed houses to survive in the neighbourhood are 22 Church Street St Mary (House 14), a three-storey wing that was probably originally part of a larger house, and 71 Strand Street (House 92; Fig. 12.9c), a wealden lying on the south side of Strand Street not far west of St Mary's church. These, and the earlier stone fragments in Bowling Street and Vicarage Lane (Houses 2 and 99; Figs 7.17, 16.14) and the churchyard (House 100), suggest that there was some good property in this area throughout the fourteenth and fifteenth centuries.

Because the houses in the centre and west of St Mary's parish have largely been replaced, one has to turn to documents for a picture of what was there before the late sixteenth century. Much of the evidence for the first half of the fifteenth century derives from the accounts of St Bartholomew's hospital and the churchwardens of St Mary's church, both having been given property in the parish,[90] while other buildings were in the hands of the town. Some houses, in Dreggers Lane, Painters Lane, by the Delf, near St Jacob's churchyard, in St Mary's Lane or Street, and in St Mary's churchyard, or listed as several cottages together, had low rental values of between 6d. and 4s. a year. Few of the tenants' occupations are known, although the sexton of St Mary's, a tailor, a tiler and a labourer are mentioned. Periods of recession in the 1450s and 1460s, in 1498, and after 1518, led to many of these tenants having difficulty paying the rent. It is impossible to identify precisely the locations of these dwellings, since the street layout probably changed in the sixteenth century, when Christ Church Priory and St James's chapel were dissolved and the land redistributed. Many of the earlier names for streets fell out of use at that time.

By the sixteenth century the decline in population resulted in property in the western half of St Mary's parish being abandoned. In 1518 and 1527 the St Mary's churchwardens' rental acknowledged that several gardens in St Jacob's Lane and Dreggers Lane had previously contained cottages, and other references in the documents to void land may also indicate former dwellings.[91] If there had been dwellings near the walls, they were abandoned at this time, and the inhabitants became concentrated in the centre, in St Peter's parish and the neighbouring parts of the parishes to either side. The effect is graphically illustrated by a comparison of the maps in Figures 14.7 and 14.8 illustrating the distribution of properties bequeathed in wills dating from 1458 to 1558. In the fifty years after 1458, eighty-six people bequeathed 220 dwellings. Forty-three per cent had only one property to leave, and a further 16 per cent left two. Two testators each left nine tenements, and three bequeathed eight, all but one of the five being resident in St Mary's parish, where most of their property lay. Figure 14.7 illustrates those properties in the first period where the sites can be approximately identified (125 examples), showing that up to 1508 there were many buildings in the western part of town. Between 1509 and 1558 eighty-seven people left 183 properties, of which 48 per cent had only one property, 32 per cent had two, and no one had more than six. Figure 14.8 illustrates the changed distribution of the 114 identifiable properties, with only Strand Street and The Butchery in St Mary's parish being reasonably well represented on the map, and only one of the eleven people with five or six properties to leave living in St Mary's parish. The change illustrates the way in which much of the western part of town was virtually abandoned during the first half of the sixteenth century.[92]

East of St Mary's church property values were higher and there is less evident sign of distress during periods of recession. In 1447 a privately rented messuage in Serles Lane fetched 16s. a year;[93] Thomas Norman, chaplain at St Mary's between the 1440s and 1460s, paid 8s. a year for a cellar with a chamber over lying adjacent to his capital messuage in Serles Lane,[94] and Simon Ruddock, who died in 1459, owned five tenements in the same street, four of them 'new-built'.[95] In the late fifteenth century the beer brewer William Giles owned a house, quay and brew-house on the north side of Strand Street opposite Serles Lane. A modern house called Giles Quay may indicate where his quay lay (Chap. 10.3.2). It is also possible that 46 Strand Street (House 88), a fine fifteenth-century open-hall house with a parallel three-storey range, which lies immediately to the east, could have been his house. In the mid- and later sixteenth century this might have become the Sign of the White Hart, which likewise lay in this area.[96] On the south side of Strand Street, just east of Serles Lane, four tenements were rented in 1473 for the high sum of £5 6s. 8d. a year.[97] Most tenements to the east and south of these were owned by wealthy families (Fig. 12.2). One passed through the female line to owners in Southampton and London,[98] and 29 Harnet Street was the 'great house' of Thomas Elys' (House 28; Fig. 12.1), which was later owned by a succession of elite Sandwich families (Chaps 12.1, 10.3.1). Further south in the same street, in St Peter's parish, a widow, Joan Worme, whose husband and son were maltsters, left another 'great house' in

14 The landscape of the town 223

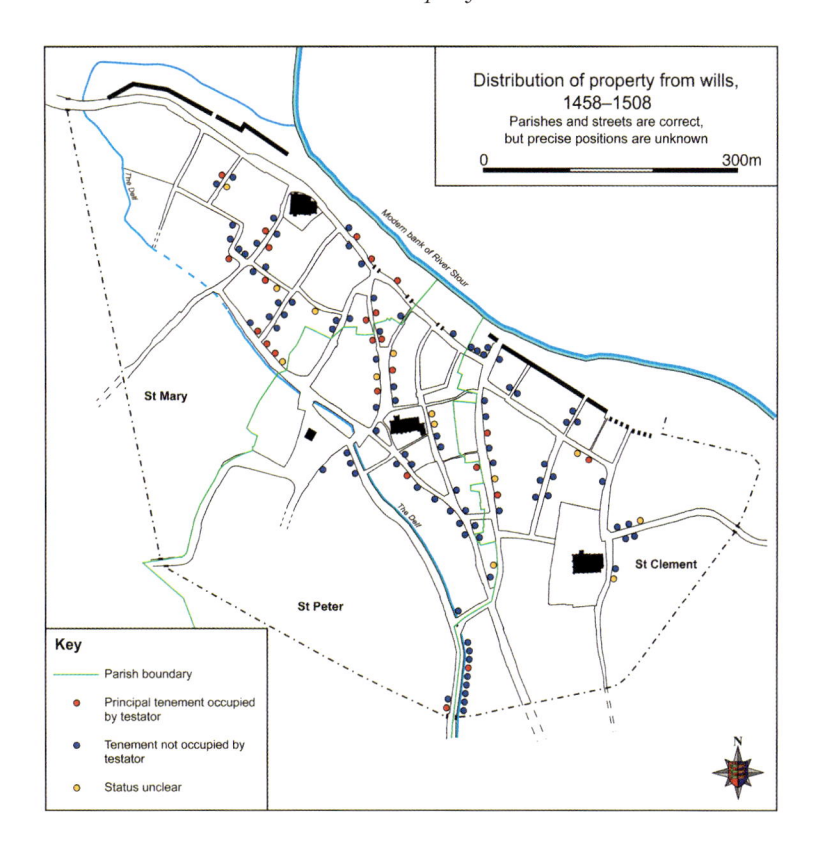

Fig. 14.7: Map showing approximate distribution of identifiable properties bequeathed between 1458 and 1508 (J. H.). Reproduced by permission of Ordnance Survey on behalf of HMSO. © Crown copyright 2009. All rights reserved. Licence number 100046522

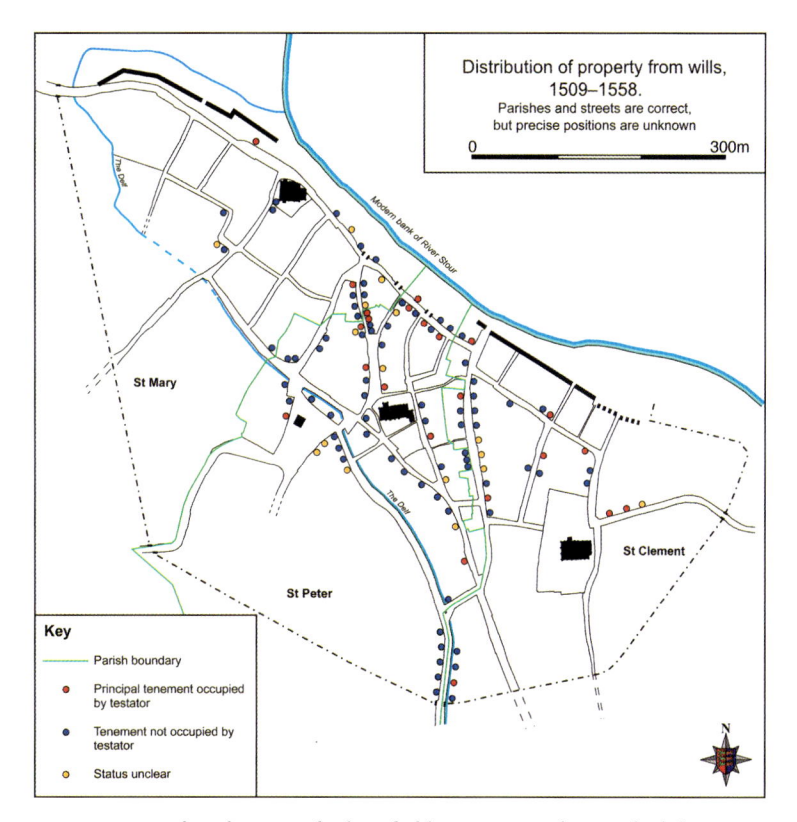

Fig. 14.8: Map showing approximate distribution of identifiable properties bequeathed between 1509 and 1558 (J. H.). Reproduced by permission of Ordnance Survey on behalf of HMSO. © Crown copyright 2009. All rights reserved. Licence number 100046522

1531, although that may not have been where she lived,[99] and from the 1550s onwards Harnet Street is the likely location of a large house, a brew-house and a malthouse, all of which belonged to wealthy owners connected with the brewing industry.[100] The inhabitants of Harnet Street lived just outside, but conveniently close to, the town centre.

14.9 The streets and property in the east end of town

In St Clement's parish a few high-status houses lay towards the waterfront. There was a cluster around Davis Gate at the junction of the two Strand streets and the High Street. No. 3 Strand Street (House 74; Fig. 12.34), for example, was in St Clement's parish. Others lay further east, including a tenement with a quay on the north side of what is now Upper Strand Street adjacent to the lane leading to Fishergate, now 17 Upper Strand Street (House 94). In 1434 this property was owned by Hugh Rys, merchant, who sold it to a London mercer.[101] Surviving fifteenth-century houses in the street are not large but all are of good quality (Chap. 12.4; Figs 12.21, 12.22), and the description of a house, possibly an inn, in Upper Strand Street in 1525 mentions two parlours, a buttery and several chambers.[102] In 1431 and 1468 houses in the street sold for £30 and £20, and rents of 13s. 4d. were recorded in the fifteenth century and of 10s. in the sixteenth.[103] Although property values declined, they remained considerably higher than those found in some parts of town. Several property transactions in this area involve names that turn up in other contexts, such as Robert Cheldesworth, the bailiff, and his son Richard;[104] William Garrard, the butcher who bought a number of buildings in town; and John Kyng, the beer brewer who supplied the barn that was converted to a brothel.[105] The town also owned property there in the sixteenth century, in 1550 renting a house to John Manwood, jurat, and granting void land and a cellar (probably where a house had been pulled down) to Nicholas Peake, another jurat.[106]

The market in the High Street seems to have ceased to function by the fifteenth century, although St Clement's fair was still held there at least until the early sixteenth century.[107] The only mention of shops was in 1449, when a tailor, tenant of St Mary's church, who had a long lease on a messuage with shops annexed in 'yeldehallestrete street', failed to pay his rent.[108] Two bakers, Thomas Grandame and Henry Pyham, lived there, but it is not clear in either case whether their bakeries were attached to their houses.[109] The small number of shops documented in the whole of St Clement's parish suggests that by the fifteenth century the commercial centre had irrevocably shifted westwards to the Fishmarket and Cornmarket. Both the town and St Mary's churchwardens owned property in the High Street, charging rents of between 6s. and 7s. per year in the fifteenth century. But in 1517 one of the town rents was reduced to 3s. 4d.,[110] and in the mid-sixteenth century three references to houses in the High Street having been demolished and requiring rebuilding suggest that some of the property there had become very neglected.[111] Few late medieval dwellings remain and those that do survive are relatively small (Houses 34, 38; Fig. 12.10).

The two small wealden hall-houses that survive in Fisher Street (Houses 20, 24; Fig. 12.23), known as Tareshestrete in the fourteenth and most of the fifteenth centuries,[112] may have been occupied by mariners or fishermen. In 1467 John Tannar, probably one of the most prosperous mariners of the period, left four tenements, two of them tenanted properties in Fisher Street. After his wife's death these passed to St Clement's church, but the family connection with the street continued, for in 1478 his son William was involved in buying another messuage there.[113] In 1561 John Lowe, another mariner, left a tenement in Fisher Street that was occupied by John Clark, a seaman who was recorded that year serving on the *Grace of God*, a bark involved in the Newcastle coal trade.[114] This was probably typical of the tenants in this part of town, but since few seamen are likely to have owned the houses they occupied, very few turn up in property documents. In most other cases tenements or cottages in Fisher Street, often in groups of two or three, were owned by wealthy people who lived elsewhere.[115] The only known rent, for a cottage on the southern corner of the street, was a mere 20d. a year in 1427.[116]

Another location for small dwellings was near New Gate, along the short stretch of street from Luckboat and Galliardsbridge to the gate itself. Further northwest, what is now New Street has no evidence for medieval buildings between the bridge and St Thomas's hospital. Since property in Luckboat ran back to the Delf, which still flows along the east side of New Street, and it is possible that the friary land reached the watercourse on the south side, taking in the property now known as Whitefriars, which abuts New Street, there may have been no road here at that time. The name New Street does not appear in the documents, and Nos. 14, 70 and 72 (Houses 62, 64, 65; Fig. 12.24), the only surviving medieval buildings, lie either at the north end in front of the hospital or at the south end just south of the bridge. Among the few inhabited buildings mentioned near New Gate are two tenements bequeathed by Thomas Jekyn, husbandman, in 1471 and three or four 'little' tenements owned by William Morpathe and his son Nicholas in 1509 and 1533.[117] In 1549 Richard Orpethe (sic), perhaps son of Nicholas, sold four tenements opposite Galliardsbridge to John Parker, draper and jurat, who bequeathed one of them, described as 'little', to a widow in 1556.[118] The descriptions and location suggest that these houses could have included 70 and 72 New Street (Houses 64, 65), and imply that they were primarily used as rental properties.

In 1427 St Bartholomew's hospital owned a number of poor properties in the area east of St Clement's church. The vicarage was rented for 3s.; a tenement in Capel Street was let for 2s. 6d.; two cottages in Knythenstrete together fetched 2s. 4d.; and three other cottages, including the one on the corner of Fisher Street, were worth a rent of only 20d. each. In 1458, the date when the rental of 1427 was written up, some of these cottages were held by wealthy townsmen who presumably sub-let them.[119] By the 1480s the town owned unoccupied land in Capel Street.[120] This was the last time the street was referred to in the documents and the abutments suggest that it may have become known as Sandown Street. Three people left property in Knythenstrete after that date, but it, too, disappears from the records in 1525.[121] Property in Sandown Street leading to the Sandown Gate is identifiable three times in the documents, between 1493 and 1517,[122] but a will of 1540 shows that there were empty plots there by then.[123] No medieval houses remain, and the land is now largely occupied by gardens. The area seems to have suffered the same early to mid-sixteenth-century depopulation as occurred at the far west end of town and indicated on Figures 14.7 and 14.8.

In 1474 the mayor and jurats established the galey or town brothel.[124] It has sometimes been suggested that this was in Galliard Street, the street being called after the galey. The street name, however, came from the bridge and was already in use by 1383 (*galyottesbregde*).[125] Although we cannot be sure of the original location, later documents indicate that the brothel first lay on the west side of a north–south street in St Clement's parish, which suggests either Barnsend (now Mill Wall Place) or Knightrider Street, east of the church. It was possibly a lack of dwellings belonging to the elite that determined the location of the brothel in this area. By 1484 this site was empty again and the brothel must have been moved, although it continued to function at least into the early sixteenth century.[126]

14.10 The ramparts, watercourses and land south of the Delf

In the fifteenth century the Delf still defined the south edge of the main built-up area of the town, although some of the land between it and the earth ramparts had been taken up by institutional establishments, and by small tenements round the Cornmarket. In common with other medieval walled towns the ground close to the ramparts was possibly not occupied by houses but mostly given over to gardens, orchards, barns and dovecotes. In St Mary's parish, these are mentioned at Moat Sole, 'walls end' with the Delf to the north, and around St James's churchyard.[127] There were a number of gardens near St Clement's vicarage, near Galliardsbridge, and in Capel Street and Knightrider Street to the far east of St Clement's parish.[128] 'Barnsend' is a name found in all three parishes,[129] always in association with barns, gardens or even marshland, indicating that sometimes the property may have been beyond the walls. The ramparts themselves were extensively used as pasture. The authorities initially considered this a nuisance, as in 1436 when they attempted to prevent it.[130] Grazing animals on the ramparts was still an offence in 1522,[131] but ten years later the council appears to have accepted that the practice could not be stopped, so they leased out the walls with the proviso that cattle should not be allowed on Mill Wall (perhaps because it was so high and its sides very steep), but that it should be open to the townsmen for their 'pastime and sport', as had been the custom.[132]

After Mill Wall was built, cutting off the main routes into Sandwich from the south-east, traffic to and from Eastry and Worth must have been diverted to join the road that ran on a causeway from St Bartholomew's hospital through New Gate to Luckboat and the High Street via Galliardsbridge. Eventually, this may have influenced the development of New Street, for which there is neither documentary nor building evidence during the Middle Ages (Section 14.9). To the east of Mill Wall, the castle and Castelmead came into the hands of the town in the late fifteenth century (Chap. 11.2.2), the latter probably being used for grazing.

The Delf continued in the same course as in previous centuries, both from its source through the Lydden Valley and within the town itself. It flowed beside a causeway from St Bartholomew's,[133] and entered the town through a gap in the ramparts at New Gate. The road went through the gate without needing to cross a bridge, showing that there was no moat,[134] so that the Delf could flow on without interruption. One of the main functions of the New Gate custodian must have been guarding the Delf and ensuring that its sweet water was not contaminated by noxious substances or the infiltration of seawater.[135] Where the Delf flowed through the gate it was edged on its east side by a stone wall reinforced by wattles and underpinned by piles, which protected it from pollution by the seawater in the Mill Wall moat.[136] The water in that moat was tidal until 1479, when a dam between the Bulwark and Sandown Bridge was built to prevent the ingress of salt or brackish water.[137]

Woodnesborough Gate was also an important feature of the town's water system. Like New Gate, the town moat stopped short of it so that there was no need for a bridge for either people or waterways. By the late fifteenth century the conduit leading from a spring near Woodnesborough village (perhaps present-day Convent Well) to the Carmelite friary was supplemented by another, this time for the town's use (Chap. 10.1.5.1). Both conduits had a common source, where there was a 'conduit head',[138] from which the water was led approximately 2km to Woodnesborough Gate, whence it was piped to the Fishmarket and then to Davis Gate.[139] The precise course of the main town conduit is unclear, although there are some clues, such as the repairs to the pipe for which a plumber from Canterbury was employed in 1491. That work took place at Robert Yves's corner and Thomas Iden's corner,[140] probably near Davis Gate.[141] The materials used included lead for the pipes, and also stone, brick, tile and timber in great quantities.[142] These suggest that there were associated structures above ground, perhaps to protect junctions in the pipes, but more probably to allow access for drawing water. The 'roundhouse' in the Fishmarket may have been one of these,[143] and there could have been a similar building at or near Davis Gate, which was also part of the conduit system (Chap. 11.2.1.4).

Canterbury Gate was also connected with the town's water system, although less directly than the other two gates. Figure 14.9 shows that in the late eighteenth century the gate (number 17 on the map) stood approximately 20m west of the Delf (by then called the Guestling) and adjacent to the moat, which did not continue in front of the gate. In contrast to the New and Woodnesborough gates, however, Canterbury Gate had a bridge, albeit some distance away, which crossed the Delf and carried the main road from Ash, Wingham and Canterbury, Sandwich's main land route to and from the west. It must have been heavily used and was frequently in need of repair, with its timbers being renewed roughly every ten years throughout the sixteenth century.[144] But the bridge was also instrumental in keeping the water supply unpolluted, since the mouth of the Delf opening into the river Stour was tidal. Whereas at the east end of the town the problem was solved in 1479 by building a dam across the end of the Mill Wall moat, at the west end it was resolved by having a sluice under the Canterbury Gate bridge. Although there is no record of one before 1528, the 'new sluice' mentioned then could well have been a replacement, perhaps for one constructed at roughly the same time as the eastern dam.[145]

One of the town's watermills stood by the mouth of the Delf near Canterbury Gate. Keeping salt water out of its mechanism was a problem; in 1482 the solution was to build at least two sluices and a mill.[146] It seems to have been the most important of several watermills owned by the town,[147] all of which demanded considerable funding for repairs recorded from 1455 onwards,[148] with the Canterbury Gate mill receiving most of them. In 1535 it and its pond were leased to Vincent Engeham for thirty-six years at 13s. 4d. per year, but the lease was clearly not honoured, for in 1538 the town was ordered to demolish the mill because it was considered to be a factor in the deterioration of the haven (Chap. 9.3).[149] Five years later the timbers of the demolished mill were still obstructing the Delf.[150] As a result, workmen were paid to clear the watercourse, sluices belonging to the former mill, and various now unidentifiable mill leats (generally called 'loopes') on the west side of the town, particularly by The Butts.[151] By 1559 the town had decided that a new mill needed to be built. It was probably erected on much the same site as the previous one.[152]

14.11 Conclusion

After several hundred years of growth, Sandwich's role as an important international port came to an end in the late fifteenth century, resulting in the town's decline during the first half of the sixteenth. But this future could not have been foretold by the inhabitants during the fifteenth century, when we can, for the

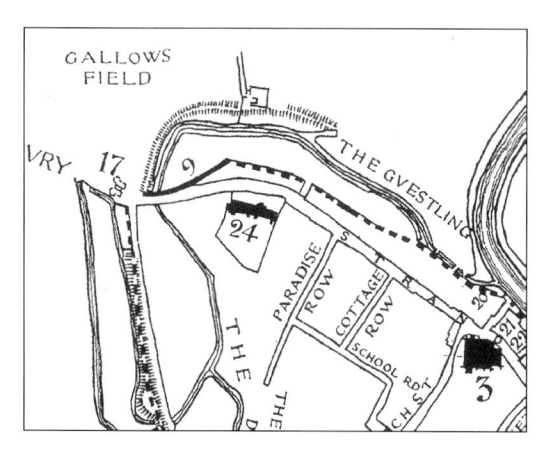

Fig. 14.9: The area around Canterbury Gate in 1787 (detail from Clapham 1930, pl. XIV)

only time, obtain a wide-ranging picture of life in the town while it was still prosperous. Topographically, it had achieved its greatest extent within the encircling walls and ramparts. The streets had all been laid out; many quayside facilities served bustling quays; the watercourses were being improved and maintained; and new medieval buildings, which still survive, were in the process of being erected. While rich and poor no doubt lived cheek by jowl in places, the quality of property clearly varied across the town, caused by the clustering of both social and occupational groups, with different categories occupying different types of building. The Sandwich elite mostly had their main dwellings on or near the waterfront, although they might own rental property almost anywhere in town. Mariners and fishermen, who also needed ready access to the water, congregated in the northern half of St Clement's parish, most of them probably tenants rather than landowners. The commercial centre of town and most densely occupied area was in St Peter's parish, indicated by the clustering of three-storey buildings along the central section of Strand Street, and in The Butchery and the Fishmarket. Throughout the Middle Ages, most of the known inns also lay in this area. The Cornmarket, and streets such as the High Street, the northern end of Luckboat and the southern end of Love Lane, seem to have been home to craftsmen and minor traders, living in smaller houses than those in the centre. To the west and east of this busy central area, on Strand Street and Upper Strand Street, and in Harnet Street and the southern end of Luckboat, lay a ring of good houses, some larger than others, perhaps owned by those who had no need to live in the busy commercial centre. Yet further out, to west and east, property values were considerably lower, and surviving houses were smaller. Finally, storehouses, barns and gardens belonging to the wealthy lay close by the ramparts. These determined the edge of the inhabited town, and beyond them, apart from the castle, St Bartholomew's hospital and a number of mills, lay agricultural land, mostly used for grazing.

This lively picture was to change around 1500. Maintenance of public facilities continued, but new building became scarce and many dwellings, largely perhaps the cottages of workmen and labourers, were demolished altogether. As discussed in earlier chapters, by 1560 the town had reached its nadir in terms of economy, population and property.

PART V: 1560–1600

15 The town

The story of Sandwich in the second half of the sixteenth century is one of contrary forces at work. On the negative side were circumstances over which the townsmen had no control: these included the increasing dominance of London in national commerce and trade, and the forces of nature, which led to the increasing silting of Sandwich Haven. London's growth at the expense of provincial towns and ports was felt by many other places, but in the case of Sandwich it was exacerbated by declining waterborne trade brought on by the increasingly difficult access to the port caused both by coastal change and human intervention.

By 1560 the situation for the town was looking bleak, with a visible decline in population as well as in trade. In that year, however, the mayor and jurats sought to reverse Sandwich's fortunes by offering to provide homes for some of the religious refugees who were starting to arrive in England from the Low Countries. As a result of a successful petition to the crown, from 1561 refugees came in increasing numbers, bringing with them their skill in weaving new kinds of cloth. Many English towns were revitalised during the second half of the sixteenth century, but in Sandwich the advent of the 'Strangers', as they were known locally, was probably the catalyst for change. The records of the late sixteenth century show that a significant amount of trade passed through the port, albeit in relatively small vessels, with the export of the new draperies being additional to the grain and beer trade of earlier years. The results of the rejuvenated economy had implications far beyond providing for the well-being of the immigrants themselves, many of whom did not prosper markedly. The population more than doubled, and the elite of the English population gained a great deal from the influx, enabling them to rebuild civic buildings and provide themselves with new and up-to-date dwellings. Whether the less well-off English also benefitted is perhaps open to question.

As might be expected, the arrival of a large number of new inhabitants led to a shortage of accommodation and to the need for new regulations relating to their trade. As in other parts of the country,[1] social tensions arose, and a great deal of attention was also paid to law and order and managing the conduct of individuals for the good of the whole community By this time Sandwich was run by a small elite, most of whose names occur regularly in documents. Even below this level, however, more is known about the lives, wealth and occupations of many other Sandwich people, although it remains difficult to find comparable details for the Strangers. They stayed in Sandwich for several decades beyond 1600, the closing date for this book, but the effects that the first forty years of their sojourn had on the town are illustrated in this and the following chapter.

15.1 Trade and Sandwich Haven

15.1.1 The state of the haven

The appeals to the crown for the improvement of Sandwich Haven, which had been a feature of the first half of the sixteenth century, continued into its final years. In 1560 a newly built dock between Sandown Gate and the Bulwark was leased out by the mayor and jurats, who remarked at the time that it would soon be necessary to make a new cut there to repair the haven.[2] The mayor then travelled to London to put this proposition to the crown.[3] In March 1561 Queen Elizabeth was said to be looking favourably on the town's appeal,[4] and her officials may even have given advice, for a person who practised a new method of excavating was recommended for harbour works in both Sandwich and Dover.[5] In 1562 the Commissions of Sewers (set up in 1531)[6] showed signs of interest in Sandwich by suggesting that water from the Chislet stream should be diverted through the haven to help in scouring the channel.[7] This may not have been put into practice because the situation had become even worse by 1565, when the breakwaters or groynes (Chap. 9.3) were again causing obstruction. Once more, the town council forbade the deposition of ballast on the groynes, and allowed merchant vessels only restricted access to the quayside.[8] The number of landing places seems to have been reduced, with passengers being permitted to embark or disembark from specified jetties only.[9] This must have been a continuing problem, for the prohibition was reiterated in 1576, when the building of unlicensed quays or breakwaters was forbidden,[10] and fines of 10s. per vessel were instituted for ships lying within 30ft (approx. 9m) of the quay.[11]

When Queen Elizabeth visited Sandwich in 1573 she was not allowed to leave before having been presented with a letter asking for help with the haven.[12] This must have borne fruit, for two years later an Italian engineer presented her with a report on the state of the havens of both Sandwich and Rye, with suggestions for the repairs that were necessary.[13] This resulted in yet another proposal for a new cut, this time to carry the waters of the Stour through a channel south of that proposed by Rogers thirty or so years before (Fig. 9.2). The engineer Andrian Andrison laid out the scheme in impressive detail, but its estimated cost of £13,000 meant that it was doomed to failure.[14] Although there continued to be minor measures against throwing rubbish into the harbour,[15] no further substantial works were proposed or undertaken until 1591, when the town authorities suggested that a new breakwater should be built on the north side of the haven to encourage a stronger flow of water along the quay at Davis Gate at ebb tide;[16] there is no evidence that this was ever built. At the same time, ships were instructed not to approach the quayside, and not to ground (settle on the mud at low tide) any closer than 20ft (approx. 6m) from it.

The late sixteenth-century map in Figure 15.1 shows that by then the western stretch of the river Stour had been straightened in places to facilitate navigation as far as Fordwich, and that the river Wantsum itself was still open as far as Northmouth, where a 'Newe haven' is marked. The significance of this can only be guessed at; was it part of a new scheme to supplant Sandwich as the dominant port on the Wantsum Channel, and a further indication of the dire state of the haven? Fears about its condition continued into the seventeenth century, but nothing was done to alleviate those worries. By the 1620s it must finally have become obvious that the haven could not be saved except with enormous

Fig. 15.1: Map of the Wantsum Channel drawn by William Lambarde, c.1585, extending from Sandwich (top left-hand corner) to Northmouth and Newe Haven (centre foreground) (© British Library Board. All Rights Reserved: Royal 18 D III, f. 22)

expenditure, and the estimated £50,000 must have been considered far too much to save the port and its faltering economy.[17]

15.1.2 The haven and its ships

The last four decades of the sixteenth century seem to have continued the trend in shipping that was discernible during the previous sixty years. Small vessels were the norm, although on one occasion a hulk from Lübeck of 400 tuns burden came as far as the quayside.[18] This, however, was an exception, and most references are to hoys, crayers, barks and lighters (including a lighter belonging to the town)[19] carrying cargoes such as fish, grain, malt, beer and wood. Salt was one of the few commodities brought from farther afield than the Low Countries, either from France[20] or occasionally from Spain.[21]

In 1565 the Privy Council responded to repeated complaints about English pirates by ordering ships to be licensed and their cargoes scrutinised. This resulted in a survey of 'all portes, crekes and landing places', which included the quantity, size and type of vessels and the number of seamen dwelling in the town; there were sixty-two mariners, many more than earlier records suggest.[22] Sandwich's home fleet comprised seventeen vessels in all, nine crayers, five boats and three hoys, varying from 40 to 60 tuns burden.[23] Six were recorded as solely for fishing, but eleven claimed to be cargo ships carrying commodities such as coal and wood.[24] By 1571 there were thirty-six ships and by 1587 the fleet had risen to forty-three, an indication of increased coastal trading during the twenty intervening years.[25] There may, however, have been a sharp decline in the number or size of Sandwich ships later. When the town was required to find five ships for the fleet against the Spanish Armada in 1588 they seem to have been provided without difficulty,[26] but when five were again demanded in 1595 there were problems,[27] not perhaps about the number of vessels but about the size of them. In 1596 the provision of one ship of 160 tuns necessitated the imposition of a local tax.[28] The following year the authorities called upon some of the wealthier inhabitants to pay for the rigging and artillery on the ship,[29] and the debt that the town incurred was such that auditors were called in at the end of August 1597.[30]

15.1.3 Waterborne trade

Throughout the sixteenth century Sandwich remained the head port for the Kentish ports from Milton Regis to Dover. But, like all the east coast ports in England, it experienced a reduction in international trade at this time, albeit partly compensated for by an increase in coastal shipping.[31] The aliens' dominance of trade through the Kent ports that had been a feature of Sandwich's early sixteenth-century commercial activities (Chap. 9.4) came to an end in 1559, when the mayor and jurats, at the request of the shipmasters' guild, ordered that all cargoes for Rye or London should be loaded onto ships owned by guild members or be fined.[32] A Sandwich port-book from 1565–6 shows that the London market was of prime importance, but that Sandwich merchantmen, freighted mainly with wheat and malt, also had other destinations such as Newcastle, the West Country ports of Dartmouth, Plymouth and Falmouth, and Arundel and Pevensey in Sussex.[33] Some ships seem to have specialised in certain journeys, such as that between Sandwich and London or across the Channel. The *Mathew of Sandwich*, for example, sailed to and from London on four occasions in August 1565, and in the same year the *Lion of Sandwich* arrived from Middleburgh and from Dieppe, although her usual ports of call were Rye and London. London was the main commercial contact, with Sandwich sending out grain to the metropolis,[34] and being visited by its coasters carrying cargoes of miscellaneous groceries, pewter ware and Spanish salt.[35]

For the rest of the century, grain and beer remained the staple products exported through Sandwich, both officially and unofficially. In 1588 a group of Sandwich merchants were accused of illegally shipping grain to supply the queen's enemies at Dunkirk, Graveling and Newport. Grain was also legally shipped to cross-Channel ports and southern Spain,[36] and beer was exported to northern France and the Netherlands. In the 1590s the government expressed concern that too many licences had been issued for the export of beer, and that small boats from towns like Sandwich, Dover and Ipswich were either carrying away more beer than they paid customs duties for, or avoiding duties altogether by bribing customs' officers. This is illustrated by the case of Sandwich, where there were four brew-houses (three of them held by Dutchmen) producing fifty barrels at a time, chiefly for sale to the Low Countries. Thus, a great quantity of beer must have been exported annually from the town, although almost no evidence of this was found in the customs books.[37] At the time there was only one brewing licence. On being urged to grant more, the customs official stated that the trade had decayed once Gravesend had begun shipping beer and that other licences that had been issued previously had not yet expired.

In times of dearth, such as 1585–6 and the mid-1590s, the needs of the metropolis competed with other parts of the county for Kent supplies. Londoners, who had preferred to purchase from factors and shipmasters at the London quayside, began to travel into Kent to make purchases directly at the ports. Malt exports to London from the customs head port of Sandwich, which reached almost 4,000 quarters in 1586–7, more than doubled to 9,000 quarters in 1598–9 and continued to rise.[38] An account of grain brought into London in 1595–6 placed Sandwich as third, after the north Kent ports of Faversham and Milton.[39]

By the 1590s a considerable number of cloths, including kerseys and new bays, were being exported. Between 2,000 and 5,000 bay cloths were exported each year, nearly half of which were produced by Flemish immigrants from wool brought from Romney Marsh and prepared by combers in Sandwich.[40] Jan Carboneel, a Flemish merchant residing in Sandwich, was amongst the exporters, employing the Sandwich ship *Saloman* with William Wolters, its master, for this purpose.[41] In 1595 the customs port of Sandwich was second among English provincial ports in the revenue raised, its total of £3,126 outstripping Bristol, Hull, Newcastle and Southampton and second only to Exmouth.[42] It is small wonder that the crown took the matter of the haven's deterioration seriously.

15.2 The influx of religious refugees

The town had always housed a sizeable number of aliens, some of whom remained within the town and contributed to the government as members of the common council (e.g., Francis Gunsales, Chap. 10.3.3). Others left after a few years, but while they stayed they sometimes paid a fine to set up a shop and carry out a trade. In 1537–8 there were sixteen foreign tradesmen – three coopers, two tailors, two shoemakers, two skinners, two weavers and a joiner, painter, glover, shearman and barber.[43] Violence between aliens and local men occasionally broke out, but it is hard to tell whether it simply arose out of drunken brawls, or was part of a deep-seated animosity or jealousy against newcomers.[44]

In May 1561 a small group of Flemish families who had migrated to Sandwich from London asked for official recognition. The town council immediately approached the Privy Council, and Lord Burghley, who was anxious to promote the development of new industries, convinced the queen to grant permission.[45] The newcomers, or 'Strangers', had to be skilled in making 'light draperies', that is, bays and says.[46] The initial group comprised twenty-four say workers and fifty-seven bay workers, and in 1562 they were given space in the hall of the market cross (Chap. 16.2) to sell their products on Wednesday and Saturday mornings.[47]

Plague was still endemic within the town. In 1564 the mayor and jurats instructed the Flemings that, due to the disease amongst their community, they were no longer to attend divine service at the church of St Clement. In recompense, they were given sole use of St Peter's, a move that was partly made possible, no doubt, because of the reduced number of English parishioners in the town.[48] Thus the two communities had less chance to meet and integrate.

The Privy Council report of 1565 counted a total of 420 households, of which 129 belonged to immigrants.[49] The 290 English households suggest that just prior to the start of the immigration there had been only 1,500–2,000 people in the town, considerably fewer than in 1513 (Chap. 10.2.1). But the number increased dramatically within a few years because the collapse of the Calvinist uprising in Flanders sent religious refugees flooding into England, with the 420 households of 1565 probably indicating a population of at least 2,500 and perhaps more.[50] In addition, between 1567 and 1575, 450 French-speaking Walloons arrived. By 1574 it has been estimated that there were about 2,500 or more Strangers resident in the town, out of a total population of around 5,000.[51] By the 1580s Sandwich contained the third largest community of Strangers after London and Norwich, and, according to Backhouse, the only town where the Strangers outnumbered the native population.[52] The increase in population was not, however, simply due to the immigrants, for as occurred in most towns in Kent, examination of the parish registers suggests that during the second half of the sixteenth century the native population was also growing again, albeit by a smaller amount.[53]

The establishment of a new cloth industry had important ramifications, not only for the town itself but also for the surrounding countryside, as the demand for spinners and wool-combers spread. Although much of the yarn used for making bays and jersey cloth was spun upon wheels by Flemish women and children in Sandwich itself, they could not produce enough and the weavers turned to English spinners in parishes such as Wingham and Ash in the hinterland. Nonetheless, the output of the industry at Sandwich was far below that of East Anglia. Whereas in the 1570s and 1580s between 11,000 and 13,000 cloths a year were produced in Norwich, in Sandwich between 2,000 and 5,000 cloths were made annually.[54]

The new immigrants could not all find employment in the cloth trade and many started to do other work, bringing them into competition with townsmen. In February 1570 severe restrictions were placed on their activities. For example, they were not allowed to sell English butter, cheese or bacon by retail; Stranger shoemakers were no longer allowed to sell or make new shoes; no Stranger hosier or tailor could continue working without a licence; no Stranger carpenter, bricklayer or mason could work other than as a hired hand without official permission unless an Englishman had already refused the job; and Stranger bakers were no longer allowed to bake ordinary bread for sale. A few men were fined for breaches of the regulations, but it is not clear how rigorously they were enforced.[55]

In 1570, and again in 1571, surveys were carried out listing the occupations and places of residence of the Stranger community. Thirty-six occupations were mentioned, of which the most common was that of tailor (nineteen in total).[56] Although the seven bakers and seven cobblers undoubtedly did compete with local inhabitants, the purse maker, basket maker, shuttle maker and pot maker probably introduced new trades. Some of the newcomers, moreover, were highly skilled – three surgeons, two goldsmiths, a bookbinder and two apothecaries (John Reglesbert, 'pottyscary', and Victor Bowdens, 'pottycary'). It is also possible that some of the five gardeners working in 1571 introduced new vegetables and subsequently sent the seeds from these plants all over the country.[57]

Opposition to the immigrants intensified in the 1580s. In 1582 they were reminded that when they first arrived in the town they willingly agreed not to practise any trade or occupation then used by any inhabitant of the town. But they had become denizens and recently, 'of greedie desire to enrich themselves', they kept open shops as mercers, tailors, chandlers, shoemakers and other trades 'to the great impoverishment of all the inhabitants' of the town and its 'utter undoing'.[58] It was therefore enacted that no Stranger should keep open any shop without a licence, and as a result ninety-five Strangers sought permission to trade.[59]

The Strangers complained to the Privy Council about the restrictions, and Lord Cobham was asked to investigate. He reported that most of the native town dwellers were content to let the Flemish refugees reside and trade in the town, but a few leading townsmen objected to the success and wealth of some of the Strangers, who 'serve all the country towns within 30 miles'.[60] Backhouse investigated these complaints and found that some of the newcomers did indeed prosper. Jan Carboneel, for example, who exported bay cloths during the 1590s (Section 15.1.3), arrived with his wife and two children in 1565, became a denizen in 1581, and at his death left £693 10s. Another was Willem Even, who left at least £467 in money, but also possessed property in Sandwich.[61] On the other hand, the vast majority of Strangers were of modest means and just managed to achieve a minimum standard of living.[62]

The Privy Council, having summoned the mayor and jurats and a delegation of Flemings, made the following resolutions: that Strangers who made bays and says, those who had been admitted to the freedom of the town, and those who were brewers and joiners could stay, but that the others had to leave and settle at least 8 miles (approx. 13km) away. Tension between the two groups continued: in 1584 the native tailors of Sandwich complained that the Flemish tailors continued to work, contrary to the order of the Privy Council. Four Sandwich men raided the house of a Flemish tailor, searching for other foreign tailors whom they believed were working there. The Flemish settlers then requested that they be allowed to retain an appropriate number of their own tailors to make and mend Dutch apparel. This was agreed, but they had to pay an annual fee of 40s. to the town and £4 to the warden of the corporation of tailors.[63]

A considerable number of immigrants, however, preferred to leave, and either returned to the Low Countries or settled in another part of England. Thus between 1582 and 1585 the size of the Stranger community in Sandwich declined. It has been suggested that an additional cause for a reduction in population in the 1580s and 1590s was the prevalence of marshland fevers, in particular malaria, arising from the salt marshland that surrounded the town and exacerbated by the crowded living conditions of the rising population. Almost every year the number of burials exceeded the number of baptisms, with peak years of mortality in 1594 and 1597.[64]

15.3 The governance of the town

15.3.1 Urban administration

Over the course of the sixteenth century central government increased its control over local administrations throughout the country.[65] By the 1590s the justices of the peace in Sandwich not only regulated the common alehouses, but also in times of bad harvests intervened in local trade to ensure that adequate grain supplies were available and provision had been made for poor relief. Nonetheless, the most important forum of town government remained the town council – the mayor, jurats and common councillors. It was this body that issued by-laws, leased structures such as the cranes and the weigh beams, authorised expenditure on civic functions and urban improvements, appointed the majority of local officials and, sitting as a court, heard and fined offenders for offences such as making an affray or stealing a purse.

During the later sixteenth century Sandwich also followed a general urban trend,[66] which saw the power of the mayor and jurats gradually consolidated, and that of the common council eroded. In 1568 there were again thirty-six members on the council (Chap. 10.1.1), and they were once more elected by all the freemen so the government of the town was relatively open; but by 1595 it had become a self-selecting body of forty-eight, with most of the common people excluded from political power. Although in 1599, when the number reverted to thirty-six, the commonalty was again involved in electing the council, this reintroduction was short lived, and in 1603 the practice of self-selection was resumed and the number reduced yet further to twenty-four.[67] By that time the council had become little more than a 'rubber stamp'.[68]

15.3.2 The queen's visit

Knowing that Elizabeth I was planning to visit Sandwich in August 1573, the mayor and jurats wanted everything to be spruced up in readiness. In July they ordered an inspection of the state of buildings in the town. Houses and stables in disrepair were to be made good, the streets and lanes to be paved, the town walls tidied up with the weeds cut down and the muck buried, and the houses in Strand Street to be painted black and white.[69] In mid-August the butchers were ordered not to dump offal at Pillory Gate until the queen had gone, and one Richard Stone was ordered to remove his pigs from near St Clement's churchyard.[70]

When the queen arrived she was met outside the Sandown Gate by the mayor, John Gilbert, in a scarlet gown. She was taken 'over against' the house belonging to Mr Crispe, which was probably on the west corner of Upper Strand Street and Quay Lane, and then went almost as far as the Pelican Inn in the High Street, where, according to the town book, 'stood a fine house, newly built and vaulted over on which the queen's arms were'. She stayed at the King's Lodging further west on Strand Street, in St Mary's parish (Fig. 16.7), opposite the present King's Arms pub (House 91).[71] It belonged to the Manwoods, and the furnishing of the rooms, including the queen's chamber, is described in an inventory of 1590. During her visit she attended a banquet in her honour, held in the new schoolhouse (Chap. 16.1).[72]

15.3.3 Problems at the end of the century

In the 1580s and 1590s the whole country faced serious economic distress caused by bad harvests, repeated outbreaks of epidemic disease, and the financial and military levies of the crown. In addition, manipulation of coinage and the growth in population were causing prices to rise, so that by 1580 prices were three times as high as in 1500.[73] Overall, the price of consumables in Sandwich increased between 40 and 50 per cent, whereas, between 1563 and 1598, the wages of artisans, labourers, maids and servants remained static.[74] The Privy Council was very concerned to alleviate the distress of the common people and frequently complained about the failure of the Sandwich town government to make adequate provision when harvests failed. In the 1590s the jurats there ordered a watch to be kept on the town gates to keep out vagrants, although it is not clear whether this arose from fear about the spread of disease or was to prevent poor migrants from entering the town.[75] In the winters of 1596 and 1597 there was considerable agitation within the town against those who exported the grain that might otherwise have fed the inhabitants.[76]

An analysis of the prices of staple goods in Sandwich shows that the prices of butter, cheese and beef seem to have been the least affected by the problems of the 1590s, probably because the demand for these goods was very elastic, and when a bad harvest hit, the poorest consumers ceased to make any purchases. On the other hand, the prices of tares, hay and bran rose because they were essential fodder for livestock. The number of English families receiving charity is illustrated by St Peter's parish in 1598, when £17 19s. 4d. was disbursed to its poor (comprising twenty-four families, probably about a quarter of the English population of the parish) and bread was provided for forty English parishioners. Similar information is lacking for the Strangers because they were responsible for looking after their own poor.[77]

Occasionally, wealthy men made specific provision in their wills for poor relief. For instance, in 1589 the jurat Roger Manwood bequeathed a little house near St James's churchyard to a dependant, stating that on her death it was to pass to the vicar and churchwardens of St Mary's church. They were to use it to house one or two poor folk rent-free on condition that the church at all times helped parishioners suffering from the plague and other diseases.[78]

15.3.4 The quayside and harbour facilities

The Privy Council report of 1565 recorded that Sandwich was a port with two creeks and two landing places.[79] A creek was a narrow inlet where small vessels could be berthed and loaded, the two recorded for Sandwich being named as Old Crane Creek and

Guestling Creek. The former was Monkenquay, by then a public or common quay where the old crane stood and therefore at the west end of the town,[80] and the latter must have been at the eastern extremity of the harbour, at the mouth of the North Stream where there had been a royal fishery by the beginning of the fourteenth century (Chap. 5.6.2; Fig. 3.12), and which is shown as 'the Gestlyngs' on the map of 1548 (Fig. 9.2). The two landing places were Davis Quay and Jesus Quay. Their mention in this national survey confirms that both were public quays. Davis Quay had certainly been so from its first occurrence (Chap. 8.3). It is less clear whether Jesus Quay, north of St Mary's church and first mentioned in 1553,[81] had always been so, but it must have been a town quay by 1565. Merchandise could also be landed east of the town, on the coast of the Sandowns 'between the castles', presumably between Sandwich Castle to the west and Sandown Castle, where the 'oude haven' is later shown on the Boycote map of 1615 (Fig. 2.5).

The 1565 document gives a more detailed picture of the condition, and particularly the extent, of the haven at that time. Vessels were able to load and unload at specified sites along a stretch of town and coast up to roughly 1 mile (approx. 1.25km) long, although the best facilities must still have been on the waterfront of the town itself. Davis Gate and the adjacent town crane and common quay seem to have been most frequently used by cargo vessels. In 1576 a charge of 4d. per ship was made to pay for removing the mud (or ooze) that had accumulated against the quay,[82] but silting must have continued to be a problem until the end of the century.[83] The town records do not mention repairs or modification to the quayside itself until 1593, when its edge was straightened to run in line with the rest of the quay as far as mayor Edward Peake's house.[84]

The town crane on the town quay was leased out as it had been for generations. Its housing may have become more elaborate over the course of time, for a storehouse, a two-storey crane house and a garden were all mentioned when the leases were being arranged in most years from 1560 to the late 1570s.[85] A glimpse of the structure of the crane house is given in 1567, when the town records charged Edward Wood 40s. for repairing some of the principal timbers that had been cut down by the tenants to whom he had sub-let the property.[86] In 1575 it underwent considerable repairs and the town paid St Thomas's hospital 20s. rent for using its crane while this took place.[87] The civic and hospital authorities had come to a similar arrangement at the beginning of the century.[88]

The old crane and adjacent open ground at Monkenquay were also leased out by the town. The crane house there included a warehouse in which part of the civic artillery was stored in 1572.[89] These were mainly small-calibre anti-personnel weapons, many of which could have originally been carried on ships.[90] The 'portuigall bases of brass with their carriages' may, for instance, have been looted from a Portuguese vessel that was wrecked in the Downs in 1565.[91]

Davis Gate and Fisher Gate both retained their importance and were repaired when necessary, although the only record of repairs to Davis Gate in this period is for 10d. spent on the stairs in 1575, the carpenter employed for that task also being paid 3s. for the barbican next to the gate.[92] A new privy was built beside the back door of Davis Gate in 1577, but six years later there were instructions that it should be removed.[93] Fisher Gate may have needed more upkeep than did Davis Gate, for in 1560 the coopers' guild agreed to pay 2s. each year for its repairs in exchange for incorporation.[94] It seems unlikely that the guild incurred this obligation for many years, for by 1582 the gate was leased to Thomas Harrison with the proviso that he paid 30s. per year rent and took responsibility for repairs.[95] In the previous year the lease of the gate had been linked with that of 'the old tower on the east side', which was presumably The Keep (Chap. 11.2.1.4).[96] By 1568 both the gate and the dock in front of it (Joyses dock) were leased by Thomas Cripps, who agreed that Sandwich freemen could freely repair their vessels in it, a rare record of such an activity in the port.[97] The gable of the gate, above the diamond-patterned brickwork, was repaired in 1581, in small yellow bricks with tumbling on the outer edges, and at the same time a plaque was built into the north face carrying the date and the initials RPM, which were those of Richard Porredge, mayor during that year.

A new dock near the Bulwark and Sandown Gate, built in 1560,[98] was also leased out by the authorities, with the lessee John Tysar undertaking to maintain it.[99] The impression given by the records is that by the second half of the sixteenth century most of the waterfront was in the hands of the town and that private quays were no longer of much importance.

The stone wall along the harbour seems to have been pierced by several new postern gates during this period, suggesting that the wall was regarded as much a hindrance as a defence. In 1563 Oliver Frende agreed to contribute towards building a new schoolhouse if he were allowed to construct a postern gate,[100] and in 1579 John Bartholomew was granted permission to do the same, with a door 5ft (1.5m) wide and 7ft (2.1m) high through the wall near Davis Gate.[101] Both had to agree to provide a strong door with locks, bars and bolts, particularly in time of war, so the defensive potential of the wall was not entirely overlooked. This concern was also shown in 1575, when the stretch of wall between Davis Gate and Fisher Gate was reinforced with shingle.[102]

15.3.5 Maintaining the defences

Defence was high on the agenda in 1563, when all walls and gates were repaired where necessary 'for the preservation of the town',[103] and the next year the crown insisted that a tax should be levied to finance 100 men to defend Sandwich.[104] By 1570 a survey for the crown ordered that the garrison be further increased, and made an estimate of the cost.[105] In 1572 the artillery at the Bulwark was reviewed,[106] and in later years more guns were positioned on the ramparts around the town.[107] Troubles at the end of the century led the Privy Council to demand that the Flemish immigrants in Sandwich should contribute to its defence.[108]

The castle probably continued to play a small part in the defence of the town,[109] although it must have been in a fairly poor state by 1568, when the castles and forts of the Cinque Ports were all noted as having deficiencies.[110] The order of 1570 about the garrison was one result, but there are no records to indicate the condition of the castle itself. A recommendation in 1588 that special care should be taken with the defence of Sandwich may have referred to both the town walls and the castle,[111] as may the proposal to strengthen Sandwich and Great Yarmouth against possible attacks by the king of Spain in 1596.[112]

Woodnesborough Gate was the only gate through the town ramparts that received much attention during the second half of the sixteenth century. In 1575 its probably late fifteenth-century structure was demolished, and rebuilt in brick and timber.[113] Boys's late eighteenth-century engraving (Fig. 11.12) may depict part of this rebuild. Sandown Gate is mainly mentioned because of the dock that was dug between the gate and the Bulwark in 1560, but there are records of its wall being repaired with 5,000 bricks in 1575,[114] and probable repairs using sand and gravel in 1585.[115] The gate was still of significance as the east entrance to the town through which the road from Deal ran, and where the queen entered the town in 1573. The road must have carried considerable traffic, for in 1566 a metalled surface 16ft (approx. 4.5m) wide and suitable for horses and carriages was laid, using cobbles and shingle.[116]

There were few changes in the walled circuit after the end of the sixteenth century, the only ones of any significance being the addition of gun emplacements along the ramparts in 1643,[117] and the demolition of the gates in the 1780s.[118]

15.3.6 Municipal responsibilities

Although waterborne access to the town became increasingly restricted, the amount of trade passing through the customs port remained high; small coasters still frequented Sandwich, and the town cranes and weigh beams still produced some income for the urban authorities. Much of the money raised in this way was spent on the upkeep of urban facilities, such as keeping the Delf clean and free from debris,[119] and ensuring that the pipes for the conduits were in good repair,[120] that the streets were paved,[121] and the rubbish removed, especially during times of plague.[122] Although the economy took a downturn towards the end of the century, the mayor and jurats continued to make every attempt to maintain the standards set by their predecessors.

15.4 Sandwich society

15.4.1 The urban elite

It was the jurats who ran the town, and, as in the past, their families frequently intermarried. In the sixteenth century the most important family was that of the Manwoods. In the first four parliaments of Elizabeth's reign, Roger Manwood (later Sir Roger) had served as senior member for the town, accompanied by a jurat on each occasion. In 1571, however, the warden of the Cinque Ports, Lord Cobham, nominated his secretary, John Vaughan. This nomination was rejected by the mayor and jurats on the grounds that they had always chosen one, and sometimes two, men who were inhabitants of the port, and who would swear to abide by its customs and liberties. They were willing, as in the past, to choose Roger Manwood, even though he was not a resident, and Vaughan's name was not even put before the assembly. Instead, John Manwood, the brother of Roger, was chosen for the Parliament of 1571.[123] The following year the warden did not attempt to interfere, and the recorder, John Boys, was elected. After Roger Manwood became a judge, his cousin, Edward Peake, was chosen in his place. The Peake family held dominant positions in the town for three generations.[124]

Other jurats included men like Alexander Cobb, who held land in the countryside as well as property within Sandwich, and Edward Wood, whose garden the queen walked through on her way to the school when visiting the town. One of the wealthiest jurats was William Richardson, who had acquired much of the property of the gentleman Richard Cooke, who in 1574 had offered to buy the friary for £100.[125] When he died in 1590 Richardson also held other property in

Sandwich and the surrounding area. If account is taken of all the debts owing to him, the value of his inventory was just over £754.[126]

15.4.2 Occupations

As the guild structure within the town became formalised, some, but not all apprenticeship agreements were recorded in the town books. It is not clear what criteria determined inclusion, since occupations such as baker, brewer and carpenter had many more known practitioners than the three whose names were recorded as taking apprentices. Nonetheless, the 213 agreements that are mentioned give an idea of how the occupational structure of the town was changing.

In the 1550s and 1560s the cloth industry was important, with Christopher Kempe and Thomas and Christopher Skott working as cloth makers, shearmen and weavers. By the 1570s perhaps because cloth working had become concentrated among the Stranger community whose members who were not freemen,[127] Sandwich clothiers disappeared from the records. At the same time grocers are mentioned for the first time, pointing to the growing importance of Sandwich as a regional distribution centre. Even more significant is the increase in the number of master mariners or shipmasters in the records, suggesting that they and their occupation may have grown in importance and prestige. In 1565, when there were seventeen ships belonging to the port, there were sixty-two seamen in the town, working on ships carrying general 'merchandise', coal and/or engaged in fishing (Section 15.1.2). In 1574 the town book recorded the names of eighteen shipmasters, some of whom were able to attract apprentices from a considerable distance, such as Exmouth, Devon, and Eye, Suffolk.[128] In addition, apprentices can be found binding themselves to the 'ropier' or shipowner Robert Prior, and to a shipwright named William Collard, who was responsible for undertaking repairs on a boat from Rye, in order to carry malt there.[129] Many ships were not owned or operated by a single person, so that the cost, responsibilities and profits were shared with others, including family members. Several of the wealthier mariners' probate inventories list part shares in ships,[130] including that of Richard Hurlestone, who died in 1596 with shares in four ships, including a new hoy, which was still being built in London and was valued at £100.[131]

No new trades took apprentices in the 1580s, although new masters appeared among existing trades. The busiest (or most highly regarded) shoemaker was Christopher Clarke, who is known to have taken on six apprentices. Unfortunately, there is no surviving will or inventory for him. During the whole period, 1558–1600, just eight women were recorded as being apprenticed. In some cases these were clearly intra-family arrangements: Susan Pynnock, the daughter of John Pynnock, became an apprentice of Jeremy Pynnock, grocer. In other cases, such as that of Mary Wybrand, who was apprenticed to William Silvertopp, ale brewer, the record specifically states that she was an orphan.[132] But occasionally, as in the case of Susan Haycock, apprenticed in 1581 to a cooper, who was not a relative, the agreement appears to have been similar to that granted to young men. In the 1590s, however, the wife of the master was included in the agreement, as in the case of Elizabeth Atkins, the daughter of a shoemaker, who became the apprentice of Edward Smallwood, shoemaker, and his wife.[133]

15.4.3 Beer brewing and retailing

Brewing equipment was expensive, so that beer brewers often leased their brew-houses. One brewer might also sell to another, so that no more than four to six brewers were working in any one year. In the 1560s Adrian Collens, who himself was leasing a brew-house and other buildings where he lived, then sub-let them to John Carsee, brewer, and also sold him all manner of brewing implements for £100.[134] When Thomas Wood died in 1581, he requested that his brew-house and equipment, including 'ledes, pipes, and a pot gallery', should be sold for cash and from the money £100 should be paid to his wife and £60 should be used to pay off a mortgage.[135] Leasing also provided an opportunity for the immigrants to enter the trade. In 1579 the brew-house owned by Joyce Buskyne was occupied and run by John Bone and the Stranger Bernard Lent.[136] The two men also cooperated in cattle rearing, for Lent's inventory of 1584 mentions cattle worth £400 held in partnership with Bone. By this time Lent had been able to buy his own brew-house in Harnet Street.[137]

Brewers generally had good relationships with innkeepers. In 1572 the beer brewer Thomas Parker got together with his fellow brewer John Thomas (or John Bartholomew) to pay off the debt of the innkeeper John Dale for his new inn.[138] In 1588 the tipplers and innkeepers together petitioned the mayor and jurats to ban others than themselves from keeping people's horses on market days in the stables at the rear.[139]

The passing of the licensing act of 1552[140] meant that thereafter the town kept yearly records of the names of those who received licences. Initially, some butchers, bakers and vintners were also licensed as victuallers, but by the mid-1580s they had largely disappeared. As in earlier years (Chap. 10.3.3), some licensees are known to have had other occupations, such as tiler, cooper, glover and shoemaker. Sometimes this may have been because a husband took out a licence for his wife. One case is recorded of a woman who was married five times. Twice she applied in her own name, but at least three of her husbands also took out licences, almost certainly on her behalf.[141] Recording practices varied a great deal from one community to another,[142] but all licensees had to promise not to allow illicit games such as dice and tables, and to arrange for two bonds of £10 for their good behaviour.[143] This effectively limited the occupation of victualler/tippler to people of ample means, although at least three had probate inventories valued at less than £18, thus falling into the fourth quartile of Table 15.1 by the time of their deaths.[144]

In April 1576 it was enacted that brewers should buy malt only from merchants and maltsters within the town.[145] Consequently, some of the aspects of brewing and victualling were combined in the hands of a single household. By the 1580s many licences were issued to men who were making and then brewing their own malt, before retailing the drink. John Ballard, for example, maltster in some documents but called merchant when he died in 1595, leased and lived in The Star Inn in the Cornmarket (Fig. 16.8), and had on his account-books bills and bonds for debts totalling £326 18s., as well as malt and barley in an outhouse.[146] John Chilton, yeoman and beer brewer, shared with his son the lease of The Bell Inn (by then moved from St Peter's parish to St Clement's), where he lived in some style, with malt worth £55 in his malt house and brewing vessels, utensils and implements valued at £40.[147]

Other men seem to have run alehouses. They did not manufacture the beer that they sold, but bought it from the brewers. Thomas Yeoman appears on all the lists of tipplers/victuallers from 1578 until 1591, just before his death, when his inventory was valued at £12 15s. and he owed £2 12s. for barrels of beer.[148] Another tippler, John Neame, whose goods were valued at £33 15s. 4d., had fourteen barrels of beer in his buttery (worth £14 13s. 4d.).[149] The goods of these men placed them within the third and fourth quartiles of wealth.

15.4.4 The evidence of probate inventories

Probate inventories for Sandwich inhabitants start to survive from 1564. They are immensely valuable for understanding both society and houses of the late sixteenth century, but using them is fraught with problems. Inventories were compiled in order to prove wills, and wills were made only by people who had goods or property to bequeath. Since these were members of the middle and upper sections of society, the very poor were inevitably excluded. The aim was to take an inventory of the deceased's possessions. Real estate that was not rented or leased was not necessarily included; settlements of property made before death were not always noted; and debts, especially those owing by the deceased, were not always recorded. Thus the overall value of the inventory might bear little relation to the true state of a person's wealth.[150] Connected with this is the fact that people's fortunes undoubtedly changed over the course of their lifetimes – many inventories reflect the circumstances at the end of a testator's life, which may have been very different from the situation when he or she was younger. In Sandwich this is implied by the inventories of some relatively poor men who, other documents suggest, had been wealthier ten or so years earlier.

Since the purpose of analysing Sandwich inventories for this project was to reveal information about late sixteenth-century houses, only the 168 examples with room names were analysed.[151] Nonetheless, they provide useful information about the relative standing of the will-making section of the population. In Table 15.1 they have been divided into four equal quartiles according to their total value (i.e., including debts to or by the testator where these are shown); the table also shows some general points

Table 15.1: Inventory values (168 examples, divided into four quartiles)

Quartile	No. of associated wills	Range in value	Values Mean	Values Average	No. owning property or leases No.	%	No. with known occupation No.	%	No. women No.	%
1st	34	£112–£754	£212	£277	30	71	34	81	2	5
2nd	24	£46–£111	£69	£71	14	33	33	79	1	2
3rd	21	£19–£45	£30	£31	10	24	34	81	6	14
4th	8	£2–£18	£9	£9	4	9	27	64	4	6

concerning occupations, and property holding where these are known. Some information on property and occupations was supplied by the accompanying wills or other documentary sources rather than by the inventory itself. Because of all that may have been left out, this is no more than a rough and ready impression of Sandwich society gleaned from this source. It nevertheless suggests that the value of the inventory, whether or not the testator owned or had leases of property, and the size of the house occupied, were normally related (Chap. 16.5).

The first quartile included seven jurats. Among them were a merchant and a cooper, although the source of the wealth of the other jurats remains elusive. Six men in this quartile were labelled merchants, four were master mariners, and six were styled yeomen, which tended to indicate either an interest in farming (an activity that meant that the value of goods could vary according to the season) and/or involvement in malting and beer brewing. Five men were maltsters or had enough malt to show that this was their occupation. Others in this quartile were a hackneyman, a baker, a tanner, a haberdasher, a draper, two butchers, five mariners – whose wealth resided largely in the ownership of boats – and three Dutch wool combers, the simplicity of whose homes was belied by their wealth. Only two widows made this grade. Joan Wilson, who died in 1585, was the widow of a baker. She lived in, perhaps renting, a property that included a working bakehouse and a shop full of wheat and meal. She owed more than £200 in debts, suggesting that it was difficult continuing the business on her own, but even with the debts included, her inventory was valued at £156. She gave all she had, including the upbringing of her children, to her father, William Jacob, another baker, who later took two of her sons as apprentices.[152] Jacob had gained his freedom through apprenticeship and rose to become a jurat, founding a dynasty whose members became jurats and common councillors through three generations.[153] Unfortunately, we do not know where his daughter Joan lived, but the fact that hers was one of the houses with a gallery, which was likely to have crossed an unceiled open hall (Chap. 12.9), and that she had a garret over the parlour loft, suggests that it was a three-storey medieval house in the centre of town.

Seventy-one per cent of people in this first quartile held property, either through leasing or by ownership. Such buildings were often intended for rental, although few testators appear to have lived from property investment alone. Trade was of paramount importance. The ten wealthiest inventories in the town included those of a maltster, a haberdasher, a draper, a tanner and four merchants. Sandwich was not a town with a large gentry class, even though one or two jurats may have had aspirations, such as the Roger Manwood who lived in the 'King's Lodging', which belonged to his relative Sir Roger Manwood and where Queen Elizabeth stayed.[154]

The second quartile also had five merchants as well as one maltster and five tipplers. In addition, there were four grocers and a number of other traders, such as chandler, currier, painter, tailor, two butchers and two carpenters. Two mariners were also included, as was a parson, a town clerk and a ferryman. This quartile was the only one in which two people were actually termed 'gent', although that title must have been appropriate for some of the wealthier jurats in the first quartile. A third of the testators are known to have owned property, although the houses were mostly smaller than those in the first quartile (Chap. 16.5, Table 16.2).

Merchants (two) and maltsters, beer brewers and tipplers (three) were still found in the third quartile, indicating that these occupations were carried on at several levels. Three inventories belonged to clergy, three to shoemakers and two to bakers. Nearly a quarter of the testators in this quartile are known to have owned property, although, as in the case of a grocer, Jacob Bery, it might be only a fourth part received through gavelkind or partible inheritance.[155] Widows (six) were more prominent, including the widow of William Wodcoke, 'a poor labouring man in the occupation of shipwright', who, however, with part of a small boat to her name, was worth £19 15s.[156]

In the fourth quartile the number of known occupations decreases. This is because the testators, whose inventories were valued between £2 and £19, are less likely to turn up in other documents. The number of associated wills that can be identified with confidence drops sharply to only eight. Nonetheless, there were four men who may have been beer brewers and/or tipplers, three mariners (including a lighterman), a shoemaker and a cobbler, two clerks, a shearman, a weaver, a turner, a hackneyman and a labourer. The poorest man of all, worth £1 19s. 8d., was a tailor whose goods, including bed, shop board and cooking equipment, all lay in a hall, the only room he had. It is at this level that references to the same names in other documents sometimes suggest that people who had begun with higher expectations had fallen on hard times. George Ham, whose goods were valued at £5 1s. 6d. in 1571, may have been the shipmaster who sailed a 50 tun hoy with coals from Newcastle in 1561.[157] Andrew Lee, whose inventory of 1569 totalled £3 8s. 10d., was probably the grocer who received property from his father that he had to sell in 1559.[158]

A labourer, Jerome Furner, who had goods valued at £2 17s. in 1598, left a will that makes clear that he owned his house in The Butchery, which he shared with a butcher who was to pay his widow rent,[159] and Richard Marback, whose inventory of 1586 was worth only £2 13s. 8d., was a beer brewer until at least 1580.[160]

This probate evidence underscores the variety of late sixteenth-century town life. There was by no means always a direct correlation between occupation and wealth. Merchants, mariners, beer brewers and innkeepers could be very prosperous or just surviving adequately, and fortunes often changed during a person's lifetime. Nor was there necessarily a connection between wealth and new building, since it was common to live in a rented dwelling rather than build a new house. It also shows how many people of different kinds diversified their interests, renting out property and owning shares in ships.

16 The buildings

In the second half of the sixteenth century, as the religious turmoil of the mid-century eased and religious refugees poured into Sandwich, the economy began to revive. The number of English inhabitants was also increasing, and people were starting to build again, although changes to the built environment took place slowly. The earliest signs of new confidence were manifested by public buildings: a purpose-built school and a new court hall. At the same time there is documentary evidence for the erection of new dwellings to accommodate the growing population, but none of these has survived, suggesting that the majority may have been cheap, poorly constructed and in parts of the town that were later abandoned once more. Nonetheless, the wealthy Englishmen who built them invested some of their profits from these developments in fine new houses for themselves, probably turning their old homes into rented accommodation for immigrants. Alongside the smart new residences a few well-built small houses survive, and there is evidence for the reconstruction of some of the smaller medieval dwellings. Dating these modest buildings accurately is tricky, and some may not have been erected until the early years of the seventeenth century.

During this period probate inventories describing houses, including the dwellings of some relatively poor people, at last provide insights into their layout and use, something that was lacking earlier. Sandwich was not at the forefront of architectural change in the late sixteenth century, and the descriptions in the inventories, together with the evidence of the surviving buildings, suggest that many testators still lived in medieval houses that had not been fully converted to modern living standards. Since the immigrants had mostly left before the middle of the seventeenth century, leaving the town to decline again, there was never any wholesale modernisation of medieval property.

16.1 The school

Prior to the Reformation, there was a school in Sandwich attached to the chantry of Thomas Elys in St Peter's church (Chap. 13.1.3). Documents relating to the closure of the chantry in 1548 specifically say that no grammar school was kept there,[1] but Edmund Grene, the chantry priest with Protestant leanings, is known to have been its schoolmaster in the 1530s, before he became rector of St Peter's,[2] and Holinshed stated that Roger Manwood (later Sir Roger) attended this school in that decade.[3] After the dissolution of the chantry there was no school until 1563, when Manwood and the town council decided to found a new grammar school worthy of the educational aspirations of the period. It was to be paid for by subscriptions raised in the town.[4]

A royal licence for the foundation was granted in October 1563,[5] and Manwood obtained the support of Archbishop Parker.[6] He in turn persuaded the Dean and Chapter of Canterbury Cathedral to grant Manwood the buildings and land of the Christ Church Priory headquarters on Strand Street, towards the west end of town, for its site.[7] Leading citizens, including the mayor, Henry Boteler, collected money for the construction, which was to be under their supervision,[8] while Manwood promised a substantial endowment to fund the running of the new school. The surviving building bears the date 1564 on the façade, suggesting that work began immediately, although, since there is no record of a schoolmaster being appointed before 1570, it is uncertain how soon it became operational. Despite this, it may have opened its doors in 1564 or 1565, for already in 1569 the mayor and jurats were complaining that the structure was much decayed, and so appointed an usher at a salary of £10 a year.[9] The early history of the school seems to have been fraught with problems over funding, finding suitable staff and endowing scholarships.[10] In 1570, for example, it was reported that there were not enough scholars, so the usher was dismissed.[11] There was trouble finding an

Fig. 16.1: Manwood School, 91, 93 Strand Street (House 93) (P. W. © English Heritage DP043948)

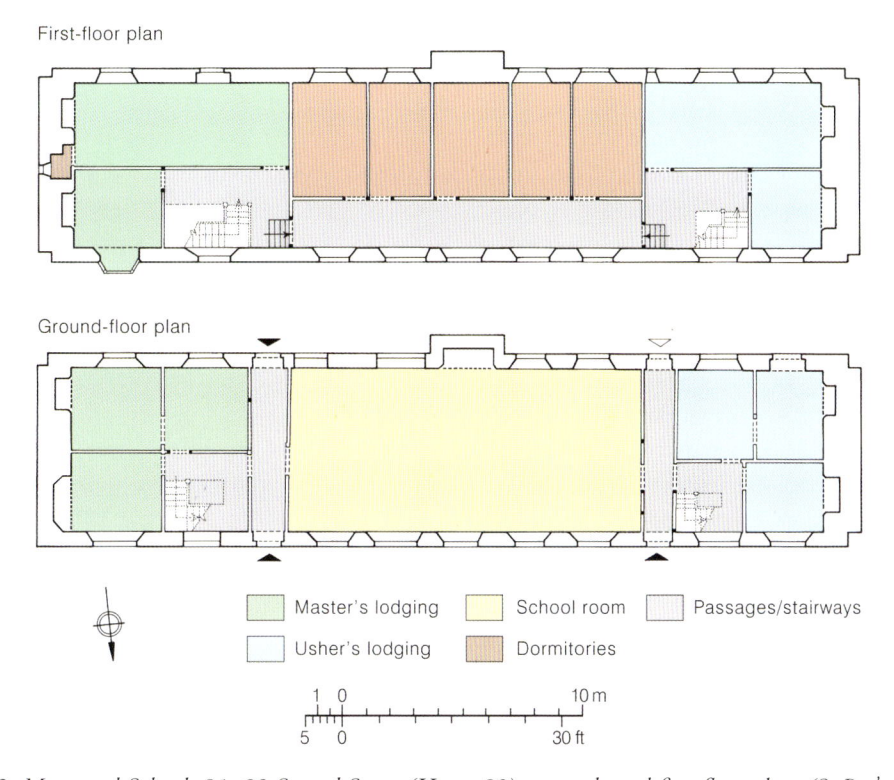

Fig. 16.2: Manwood School, 91, 93 Strand Street (House 93), ground- and first-floor plans (S. P. & A. T. A)

appropriate master, and when Queen Elizabeth visited in 1573 the vicar of St Clement's church was acting in this position. Shortly afterwards, Richard Knolles of Lincoln College, Oxford, was appointed and things ran more smoothly. He was a distinguished scholar and remained at the school for the next forty years.[12]

In 1580 Manwood drew up regulations that made clear that the school was to be free for Sandwich residents, but that the parents of those who lived outside the town were to pay. There was to be an usher in addition to the master, and the master should not board more than twelve scholars and the usher not more than six – that is, eighteen boarders in all, presumably boys from the countryside who could not attend daily.[13]

The two-storey building with attics (Figs 16.1, 16.2) was constructed of buff or pale yellow bricks, very similar to those used for the top of Fisher Gate in 1581, and perhaps obtained from the town's own brickworks. The style, with crow-stepped gables above the attic windows, has been considered Flemish or Dutch,[14] but it may simply be a case of being fashionable and up-to-date, since crow-stepped gables occur throughout Kent at this time.[15] The windows were originally mullioned and transomed, and are now much altered, although many of the moulded hoods above them survive. Large chimney stacks dominate the gable ends and there is another in the middle, at the back.[16] The date of 1564 is formed with iron ties set between the ground and first floors in the centre of the building.

The long, narrow plan conforms to school designs of the period, with a tall, heated school room in the centre separated by cross passages from domestic blocks at either end.[17] An outline plan, published by Boys in 1792, indicates that the master's lodging lay in the eastern domestic block and the usher's in the west one.[18] Some partitions and the stairs have been moved, but surviving doorways suggest that each end had three chambers on the ground floor, two of which were heated, and two heated chambers on the first floor. In the centre of the first floor, reached from each end by short flights of steps and a passage along the north side, were four chambers – one large heated one and three smaller unheated ones. It is not clear whether the unheated attic was also used for accommodation. The four central rooms, perhaps combined with the attic or with one room from each end, would certainly have provided enough dormitory space for eighteen boarders.

In 1640 an inventory of all the goods for which the master was responsible makes clear that at that time he had a kitchen, buttery, best chamber (with a bed) and two other chambers, plus a chest in the gallery. The usher had a little chamber, a study and a parlour. The 'common school' was mentioned, but contained no furniture. Since the inventory was concerned only with goods for which the master was responsible, it was not a list of all the contents, and the absence of any mention of rooms off the gallery or in the attic, or their contents, means very little. The school continued with fluctuating fortunes on the site until the 1890s, when it was moved to new buildings at the east end of town. The old school was then sold and transformed into a dwelling.[19]

16.2 The new court hall and related buildings

During the sixteenth century the old court hall in St Peter's churchyard, built sometime before 1432, had undergone considerable repairs and improvements. In 1560 the original council chamber was converted into a treasury and the loft above it rebuilt as a new council

Fig. 16.3: The mayor's chair, 1562, council chamber, court hall, now Sandwich Guildhall, Cattle Market. Details of the armrests (P. W. © English Heritage DP044591)

chamber.[20] But this was not used for long, for in 1577 the decision was taken to build a totally new hall. As a result the old building was leased, the lessee being instructed to hire it out for storage, charging rates such as 6d. per week for a tonne of wine and 2d. a week for 100 salt fish.[21]

It was probably in connection with the refurbishment of 1560 that Simon Lynch, mayor in 1561–2, commissioned a new mayoral seat (Fig. 16.3). It is likely that at an earlier period the mayor sat on a bench with the jurats, but seating was an important aspect of the mayor's dignity and authority, and a new chair with armrests, albeit still fixed to the wall, would have enhanced his special status. Surviving medieval chairs are rare, and even sixteenth-century civic seats are not common.[22] In the mid-sixteenth century an earlier piece of fixed furniture was adapted to form the surviving mayor's chair in Coventry Guildhall; one is known to have been made for the mayor of York in 1577–8; and another, which still survives, was made for Salisbury Guildhall in 1585.[23] Thus Sandwich's mayoral seat is an unusual and important survival. The chair, now in the council chamber of the new hall erected in 1579, has largely been rebuilt, but the two armrests survive, decorated with satyrs and scrolls, with 'Simon Lynch 1561' on the side of one arm and '1562: SL: M: AC: T' carved in descending order on the top of the other. The carving is of high quality, far more elaborate than on the free-standing mayoral chairs in the other halls mentioned above, and is thought to be English work, although the design is almost certainly based on Flemish pattern books.[24]

In December 1577 the mayor (Edward Wood) and jurats decided to build an entirely new and more convenient court hall in the centre of the Cornmarket near the old market cross.[25] Unfortunately, the treasurer's accounts for this period do not survive, so we have no information regarding the building costs or financing arrangements. We know that progress was swift, however, for in July 1579 (when John Iden was mayor) a meeting was held to decide on the ordering of the new hall, and the council moved in before the end of the year.[26]

The building lies at the heart of the present Guildhall.[27] It was constructed of timber, of two storeys with an attic above, and comprised a single range of four bays with a projecting stair turret at the rear or west side (Fig. 16.4). The long east wall was originally jettied, but this has been rebuilt several times (Fig. 16.5). Inside it contained a courtroom on the ground floor, the council chamber and an inner chamber on the first floor, and an attic above that. Various additions have since been made to north and south.

In the eighteenth century the entrance lay at the north end of the east wall,[28] and by analogy with sixteenth-century buildings elsewhere, it is likely that this was the position of the 1579 doorway, with an opposing one on the west wall opening into the stair turret. The ground floor appears to have consisted of one large room. The rear or west posts are still in place, the ceiling beams, decorated with simple ovolo mouldings and supported on decorative brackets, indicating a large undivided space. This was presumably the courtroom, and it has been suggested that some of the movable, low, balustraded screens dividing the space may have been there from the start.[29] If so, they are extremely rare early survivals.

The rear doorway opens into a closed-well stair with clustered mouldings to the posts at the corners. This type of stair came into use during the second half of the sixteenth century, replaced by open-well stairs in the early seventeenth.[30] On the first-floor landing a doorway opens into the council chamber above the large room below, with the stairs going on up to the attic. The first floor was jettied to the east, and the council chamber occupied three bays, with similar detailing to the room below (Fig. 16.6). The joists in this room are of varying shape and size with nail holes underneath, indicating that they were always intended to be plastered.[31] There may have been a fireplace on the

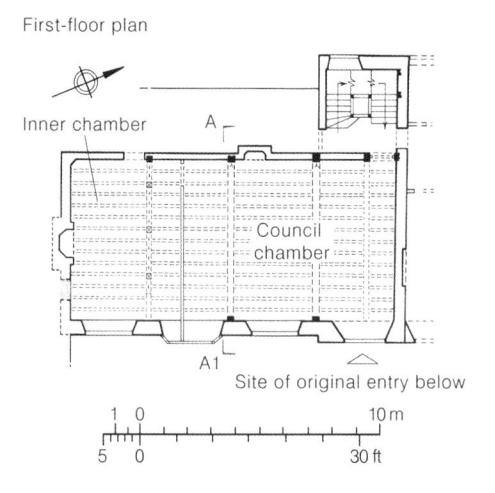

Fig. 16.4: The court hall, Cornmarket, now the Guildhall, Cattle Market. First-floor plan (S. P. & A. T. A.)

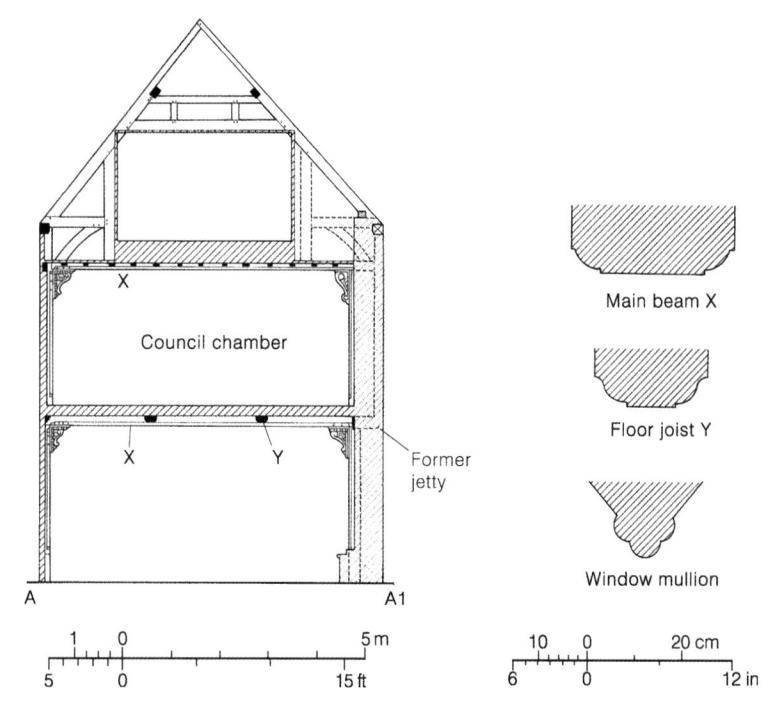

Fig. 16.5: The court hall, Cornmarket, now the Guildhall, Cattle Market. Cross section looking north, showing former jettying to the east and the attic roof construction (S. P. & A. T. A)

Fig. 16.6: The court hall, Cornmarket, now the Guildhall, Cattle Market. Decorated bracket of 1579 in council chamber (P. W. © English Heritage DP044589)

west wall, but if so it has been rebuilt. The mayor's seat was reset in the new council chamber, apparently with an inscription reading 'Justicia virtutum regina 1579' on the back.[32]

The north bay of the building was partitioned off to form a small inner chamber, originally smaller than at present and possibly always heated by a gable-end fireplace. No document referring to a 'mayor's parlour' in Sandwich during the sixteenth century has so far been found, but this could have been its function, since mayors' parlours are known in court halls as early as the fifteenth century, the one in Canterbury being documented in 1438.[33] On the other hand, this room could have contained the treasury once it had been transferred from the old court hall.

The fact that the stair continues upwards indicates that there was a useable attic from the start. Much of the roof has been rebuilt, but a short section survives to show that it was divided longitudinally into three, with two inaccessible 'aisle' areas to either side of a central section. The roof is of clasped side-purlin and queen-strut construction, and the tiebeam was dropped below wall-plate level to provide adequate head room. The east side of the roof was largely rebuilt when the jetty was cut back, so the original means of lighting the attic has been destroyed, but it is likely that on this side the windows were set in large gables in each bay. Dropped tiebeams creating attic storeys are known from the 1560s onwards and were usually accompanied by gabled windows.[34] Presumably, this area was always used as an archive and storage area, although it may also have contained the treasury and counting chamber if they were not on the floor below.

The court hall was sited near the earlier market cross, which was probably one of the fourteen places in the town from which proclamations were made. By the sixteenth century it had become a roofed structure: in January 1562 the Dutch refugees were given space 'within' the cross to sell their wares, and a few months later the place where they held their market was referred to as a 'hall'.[35] It is hard to know exactly what this structure was. By the sixteenth century many market crosses elsewhere had had pillars or columns placed around and a roof built above so that the traders had somewhere dry to set out their wares in inclement weather. An example of this kind is known from the Tuesday Market Place in King's Lynn, built in 1580 as 'a place . . . for persons resorting to the market to stand and walk dry'.[36] In some cases, the fine line between market crosses and market houses became blurred, as at Halstead and Rochford in Essex, which had upper rooms but continued to be called market crosses.[37] In Sandwich, unfortunately, no illustration survives to make the layout clear. The immigrants still used the hall in 1589 when they were given permission to erect a maypole on the top – implying that it was not very large.[38] In fact, the original space was probably too small for the very many immigrants who arrived during the 1570s, and they may have rebuilt the structure. In 1593 it was reported that the cross house, which had lately been 'removed and enlarged', was now confirmed for the use of the chandlers.[39] This suggests that by 1593 the Strangers had moved elsewhere, and although no document has been found to prove it, this may have been when a specialised bay (or baize) hall was erected at the old crane on or near Monkenquay in St Mary's parish. Bay hall is not mentioned in the pre-1600 documentation examined for this project, but the site is shown on Boys's map of the town in 1789 (although he says that it had been taken down in 1693).[40] The cross house in the Cornmarket was sold and probably pulled down in 1795.[41]

16.3 Homes for the increasing population

During the preceding half-century both the population and the prosperity of the town declined, so few new houses were built. Instead, as noted earlier (Chap. 10.2.2), houses were abandoned and often pulled down, so that in July 1560 the council decreed that anyone not rebuilding within a year should be fined, and the materials and ground should be confiscated.[42] By May 1561, however, the situation changed with the first influx of Flemish refugees and it became necessary to find homes for them.

To start with many probably lodged with the native population, and they may also have lived in some of the empty and perhaps derelict properties abandoned by their previous occupiers. Analysis of wills during the first half of the sixteenth century suggests that most of these may have been relatively mean houses or cottages on the outer edges of the town (Figs 14.7, 14.8), where vacant and decaying dwellings, formerly liabilities, must suddenly have become valuable assets. Unfortunately, there is no documentation to show this process at work, but equally there is very little evidence of new building before the late 1560s, and the new families must have lodged somewhere. The Privy Council inquiry of 1565 shows that there were 129 foreign households in the town and that there were seven persons 'lacking proper habitation'.[43] Since these comprised three merchants, a scrivener, two surgeons and a master of fence, it appears not only that pressure on housing was becoming intense, but also that the problem did not just affect the poor.

Most evidence of immigrants renting property comes from the 1570s and later; it usually took the form of private arrangements and was mentioned in wills where the property occupied by the Dutch was left to family members of the English landlord.[44] But in 1564 a merchant and haberdasher, Walter Shetterden, who owned the former chantry houses in Love Lane, granted a ten-year lease to a Dutchman, who in turn handed it on to a Dutch preacher, who in his turn passed the remaining interest to a Dutch merchant, Gerrard Motte. Shetterden meanwhile sold the old chantry properties to Thomas Thompson. The transactions came to court because Thompson molested Motte, with the result that Shetterden had to pay Thompson extra money.[45] The story indicates how complicated the ownership and leasing of these buildings might be, and how likely it was that older houses such as these were used for housing the Dutch, with others, both English and Dutch, making money from the transactions.

The size of the influx, however, meant that the housing problem could not be solved by simply using old buildings and it was essential that new ones were erected. In 1566 void ground near to and outside the gates was leased to several leading townsmen on ninety-nine-year leases, with the understanding that they would build new houses. Thus, land outside and adjoining Canterbury Gate was granted to John Manwood, who was to build a house upon the gate for an English gatekeeper, but was also allowed to erect other houses in any place that he wanted so long as he enclosed an acre of ground with each house. Nearer the town centre, void ground in Luckboat, beyond St Peter's parsonage, was leased to Roger Peake, whose new house was to be finished within two years, and to the east, land outside Sandown Gate was leased to William Sowthaike, who was expected to build 'a fair house' there by Michaelmas 1568.[46]

More, however, was required than the odd houses these documents imply, so in 1567 the town granted land specifically for building, and ordered that on every 6 perches of land a 'sufficient dwelling' was to be made. The documents suggest that each house was to be set in a plot of 6 perches, with the house on the street frontage occupying 1 perch (5m) and land behind. Thus on 60 perches John Tyssar was to build ten reasonable houses; Thomas Parker, brewer, was granted 30 perches from the end of Tyssar's garden to the Loop; and the Winchelsea merchant Thomas Thompson was also granted permission to build at the same rate between Barraway's Garden and the Canterbury Gate. The houses were to be in a new street called Thomson's Street, which was to run from Barraway's garden, which lay between the Canterbury and Woodnesborough gates, alongside the Delf to the Canterbury Gate, with 24ft to be left from the side of the town wall to the front of the houses to allow for the street.[47] These buildings were probably to be constructed on the south-west side of the Delf where neither street nor houses survive today (Fig. 16.7). A few months later, John Gilbert leased land for house building between the old crane house and the stone house of Simon Lynch, probably along Strand Street in St Mary's parish.[48] All the men involved in these new developments were among the elite of the town, most of them being jurats at the time they acquired their plots of land.

As the number of immigrants continued to rise, peaking in the 1570s when there were around 2,400 Dutch-speaking Flemings and 500 French-speaking Walloons,[49] more evidence survives for private house-building initiatives. John Dale, innkeeper and taverner, erected a new house before he fell into debt in 1572.[50] The parishioners of St Peter's wanted to rebuild the house that belonged to the church in 1575, borrowing £30 from the town and promising to repay in two years.[51] William Molland, carpenter, together with Leonard Kene, glazier, received permission to vault 36ft of the Delf for building in 1579, and in 1584 Molland built three tenements in the Cornmarket behind the new court hall, adjacent to the late sixteenth-century Star Inn (Fig. 16.8). When Molland died in 1586 these were left to his three children, possibly as investments.[52] Many wealthy testators left multiple properties. In 1590 John Chilton, yeoman, beer brewer and lessee of The Bell Inn, where he lived, left a large property portfolio including a messuage at Luckboat occupied by the town clerk and certain Dutch people. He also left his wife £5 per annum from all his houses, barns and stables on the walls (i.e., ramparts) in St Clement's and St Peter's parishes, on condition that she finish the new buildings begun there.[53]

During the 1570s several surveys of the immigrant populations reveal more details of how and where they were accommodated. In 1571, 142 immigrant ratepayers and their landlords were listed.[54] Fifty-one landlords, some of whom appeared more than once, housed 102 families. Properties were distributed between twelve wards in the town – the number of wards having increased since the late fifteenth century. Identifying the precise location of the wards is as difficult as earlier, but it is clear that wards 1, 2 and 3 lay to the far west around the Canterbury Gate and the Loop. Ward 5 included the old court hall in Love Lane, ward 7 The Butchery, ward 8 the church stile, which was probably to the west of St Peter's church, while ward 9 included part of the High Street, as well as The Hart and Swan Inn, which lay at the junction of Love Lane and Luckboat. Ward 11 lay near the Sandown Gate to the far east of the town, and ward 12 included St Clement's vicarage, south of that church. The largest number of immigrant families lived towards the west, where the new houses on land granted by the town had been built. Manwood, Thompson, Tyssar, Gilbert and Lynch were among the names of the property owners, some of them renting to two or three families, a few of the houses being described as 'upon the walls'. Another cluster of properties lay around St Peter's church and in the Luckboat area, in wards 8 and 9, and another group were located in the far east of the town.

In 1573 and 1574 further lists distinguished between Flemings and Walloons, the former being concentrated in wards 1, 3 and 12 – that is, towards the edges of the town – and the Walloons in wards 3, 4, 5 and 8 – that is, towards the centre.[55] The list of 1574 provides details of Walloon families and the houses they occupied in the fifth ward (in the Love Lane area). This shows four families totalling ten people occupying the house of John Bartholomew, three families totalling eight people in Mr Gilbert's house, three families with ten

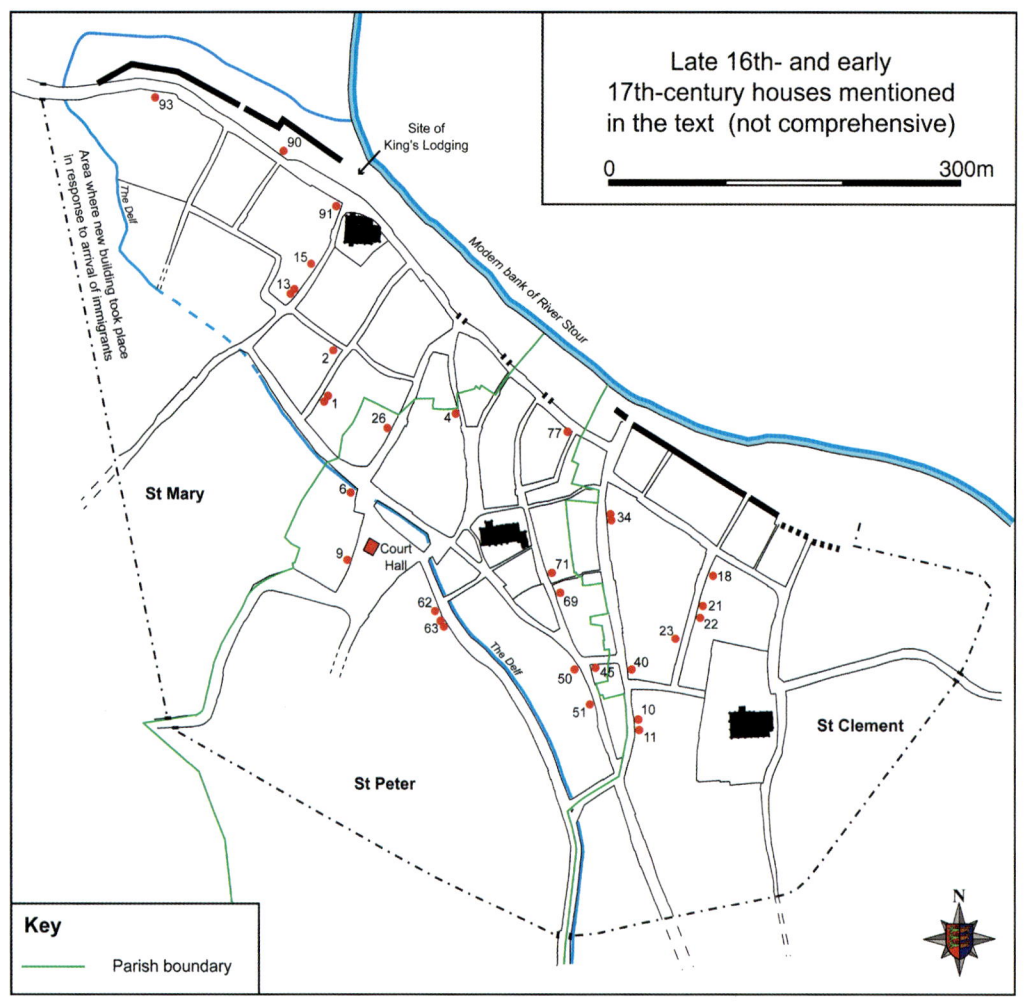

Fig. 16.7: Distribution of some of the late sixteenth- or early seventeenth-century buildings in the town (J. H.). Reproduced by permission of Ordnance Survey on behalf of HMSO. © Crown copyright 2009. All rights reserved. Licence number 100046522

people in Pynnock's house, and seven families with thirty-one people in Goodman Tripps's house. Tripps, who was a merchant, and Bartholomew, who was a beer brewer, are mostly associated with property in St Clement's parish in the Strand Street area; their connections with ward 5 are not clear, although the ward, which must largely have been in St Peter's parish, may have included the western edge of St Clement's. Gilbert, who was mayor in 1572 and probably the shipowner of that name, had property that he let to immigrants in several wards, including the fifth, which was also where the Pynnock family had their main dwelling and other houses.[56] The Walloons, who did not arrive in Sandwich until 1567, may have had the worst accommodation of all. The document of 1574 suggests that some of them must have lived in one or two overcrowded rooms in large, old properties in the centre of town. Those Flemings who lived towards the edge of town in the newer houses on large plots built especially for renting must have been in much better circumstances. Only a few of the wealthiest Flemings came to own their own houses, and evidence for this does not begin until the mid-1580s.[57]

16.4 Surviving houses

New dwellings in the late sixteenth century can be divided into three categories. First, there are large houses built on the profits of the expanding economy; second, a few completely new, good-quality, small dwellings, possibly built for occupation by immigrants; and finally, there are houses that were reconstructed reusing material from older ones. Surveying houses of this period for this project was less systematic than in the earlier periods. It is often difficult to judge the precise dates of the buildings other than to say that they fall into the general period 1570–1640, and since the prosperity brought to the town by the immigrants was not over until the latter date,[58] many houses built for them may have been erected in the early seventeenth century rather than earlier.[59] The map in Figure 16.7 shows some, but almost certainly not all, of the houses of this time.

These new dwellings are of a form strikingly different from the houses discussed earlier. They were well heated, the ground floors of the larger examples containing halls, parlours and service areas, including attached kitchens, whereas single rooms served as general-purpose living rooms in the smaller houses. Almost all were of two main storeys only, although they tended to have well-lit attics for servants, household storage and possibly work space (sometimes these are now simply roof spaces). Stairs were no longer straight flights of medieval type, perhaps placed

Fig. 16.8: The Star Inn, Cattle Market (House 9, now demolished), at the back of the Guildhall (© Sandwich Guildhall Archives BP/V-00106)

Fig. 16.9: Detail of Elizabethan house off Strand Street (Rolfe 1852, 3, pl. 40, copy from Dover Museum and Bronze Age Boat Gallery)

in different parts of the building on different floors, but continuous from ground to top floor. In the larger structures they were constructed with dog-legs, and in smaller buildings they wound round a newel beside the stack. Unless otherwise mentioned, the houses continued to be built of timber, with brick used only for nogging, chimney stacks or, occasionally, a gable wall. The larger among them have ovolo mouldings to beams and to window mullions, and probably originally had attic gables and projecting bay windows supported on carved brackets, as indicated in the now-demolished houses shown in Figures 16.8 and 16.9. Crown-post roofs were replaced by ones of clasped side-purlin construction with wind braces, some with sling braces. The larger houses lay along the street frontage, and most of the surviving smaller ones were also paired along the street. All these features can be used to help date buildings, but some of the revamped dwellings, often reusing earlier timbers and with no decorative features, are difficult to date precisely.

16.4.1 Large houses

Some of the wealthier English inhabitants, probably the same men who were involved in the new housing developments, were able to build new dwellings for themselves, while no doubt renting out their old homes to immigrants. An instance of this practice may have occurred when John Streating, a yeoman of St Clement's parish, died in 1586 bequeathing to his wife his new house in Strand Street, in which he dwelt, as well as leaving a rented house next to it and half of a brick house in Luckboat that he and his son had purchased from Thomas Parker (the brewer who was building near the Canterbury Gate).[60]

The largest houses from this period have been lost. These include the King's Lodging, which had formerly belonged to Sir Edward Ringeley. It was owned by Sir Roger Manwood in the later sixteenth century and was where Queen Elizabeth stayed in 1572. It stood on the north side of Strand Street, opposite the present King's Arms (Fig. 16.7). Edward Wood's house called Paradise, on the opposite side of the street, nearer the school, through whose garden the queen walked to the school in 1572, is another casualty. But some slightly more modest houses built in St Mary's parish in the late sixteenth century survive to indicate that, as in earlier periods, the parish was home to many of Sandwich's most prominent families.

The Long House, 62 Strand Street (House 90), just to the west of the King's Lodging site, was probably built on part of the property formerly owned by Christ Church Priory. It has been tree-ring dated to 1562–78,[61] and was therefore constructed quite early in the new period of prosperity. The identity of the owner is not known for certain, but it may have been John Gilbert, jurat, shipowner and probable merchant (Section 16.3). The house lies near the site of the old crane, on land leased to Gilbert in 1567.[62] The new buildings, of which there was more than one, were a cause of dispute five years later, but in 1597 one of John's descendants, Thomas Gilbert, bequeathed a 'great house' and adjacent tenements near the old crane to his son.[63] It could have been the Long House.

The house is of two storeys, ranged along the street frontage, jettied to the south and probably originally to the east, with brick nogging in the exposed panels of the timber framing at the rear. There are four main rooms on each floor, and further rooms in a wing at the rear beside an eastern stair turret (Figs 16.10, 16.11). Possibly there was another, larger, stair turret towards the west end since that is where the best rooms on both floors were situated. The evidence is somewhat ambiguous, but there appears to have been a parlour to the west, a three-bay hall, a separate entrance passage leading directly to a kitchen at the rear, and an unheated room that might have been for services or have had a commercial function. The hall, parlour and kitchen were heated and the former two had moulded ceiling beams. On the first floor the three western chambers had fireplaces, the eastern one sharing a rear stack with the kitchen behind. Three of the four front chambers were richly decorated. Grisaille wall paintings of griffins, fruit and flowers, of two qualities, still cover the walls of the chamber over the parlour, the paint

Fig. 16.10: The Long House, 62 Strand Street (House 90), from the south (P. W. © English Heritage DP032006)

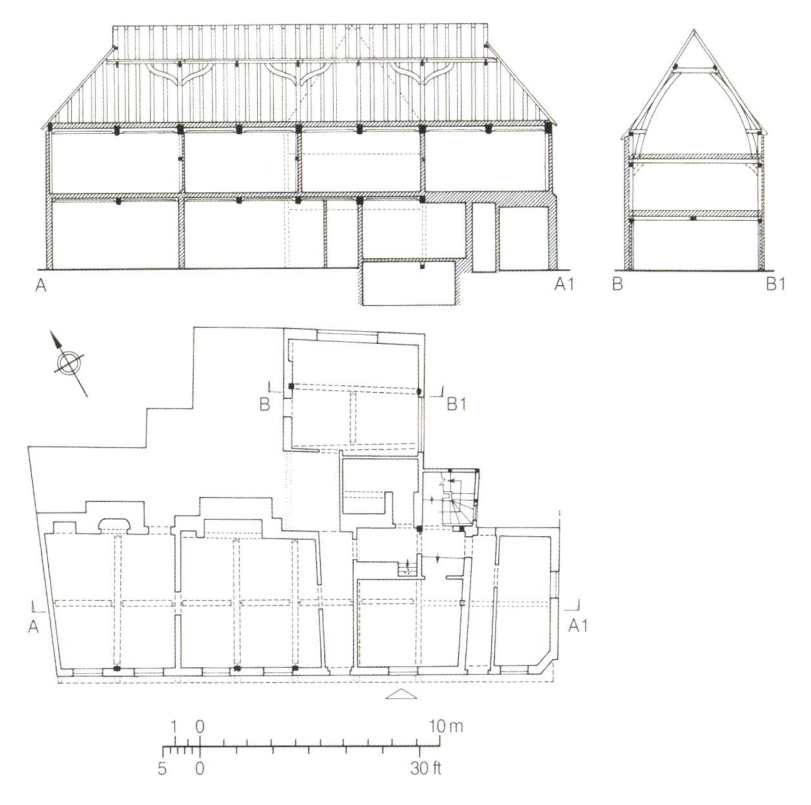

Fig. 16.11: The Long House, 62 Strand Street (House 90), plan and sections (S. P. & A. T. A.)

Fig. 16.12 (above): The Long House, 62 Strand Street (House 90), wall painting on west wall of west chamber (P. W. © English Heritage DP032224)

Fig. 16.13 (left): The Long House, 62 Strand Street (House 90), plasterwork border in east chamber (P. W. © English Heritage DP032228)

extending across the timber framing where necessary (Fig. 16.12). In the other chambers plaster panels, set inside the framing, have narrow bands of plaster decoration stamped round the borders in a highly unusual manner (Fig. 16.13).[64] The roof space was usable from the start. Only the rear slope of the main roof survives, with clasped side purlins and wind braces; the front has been rebuilt and was probably originally lit by gabled dormers that have since been removed, as have any bay windows lighting the first floor. The rear wing has a sling-brace truss (Fig. 16.11) of a type also found elsewhere in the town. With its long street frontage, rear chimney stacks, stair turret or turrets and attic roofs, this is a far cry from the open halls of the Middle Ages, and the first truly 'modern' building to survive in Sandwich.

Most of the other surviving large houses seem to have been built later, perhaps only in the 1580s or 1590s, and none took up so much frontage or had such fine decoration. Richborough House, 7 Bowling Street (House 2; Fig. 16.14), also of two storeys with attics, has only two rooms at the front, originally with an outshut and stair at the rear (largely rebuilt as a wing). The stone and flint of the external north wall have been reused from an earlier building. Above the stonework this wall is of brick with 'tumbling' in the gables (used in the upper part of Fisher Gate in 1581), and at the back there is a decorative brick chimney stack, typical of *c*.1600,[65] serving the hall and its chamber. The formerly jettied and timber-framed east front was probably infilled with brick nogging, a couple of the panels being exposed beneath the plaster today, and lit by bay windows. The interior has been enlarged and altered, but it is likely that the parlour to the north was heated, as well as the hall and best chamber above (Fig. 16.15). The poor finish to the framing of the latter and the deep overhang of the beam on the south wall suggest that this chamber was intended to be panelled. The first floor was reached by a stair in the north-west corner of the outshut, with a smaller stair beside the main stack going up to the attic.

At the King's Arms, on the corner of Church Street St Mary and Strand Street, the date of 1592 is carved on a caryatid supporting the dragon beam of the two jetties (House 91; Figs 16.16, 16.17). Two short ranges, of two storeys each, probably formerly with gables and bay windows of the types discussed above, were added to an earlier range to the west at this date. The northern room was heated and has ovolo-moulded ceiling beams. Slightly later in date was a large and well-detailed house on the Cornmarket, at 2, 4 Cattle Market (House 6), with the date 1601 carved on the jetty bressumer. Along the Delf Street frontage there appear to have

Fig. 16.14: Richborough House, 7 Bowling Street (House 2), from the east (P. W. © English Heritage DP032215)

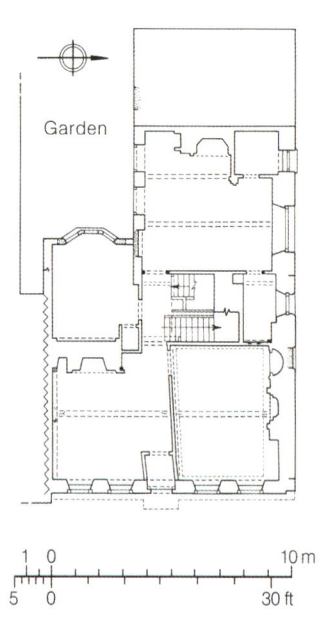

Fig. 16.15: Richborough House, 7 Bowling Street (House 2), ground-floor plan (A. T. A.)

been two rooms heated by a central stack and ceiled with ovolo-moulded beams, with a smaller unheated room to the south. 52 King Street (House 51) has a two-bay, two-storey and attic frontage (remodelled in the eighteenth century) and a wing behind, which, with decorative plaster ceilings on both floors, was certainly not a service wing. The ground-floor beam is plastered

Fig. 16.16: The King's Arms Public House, 63, 65 Strand Street (House 91) on the corner of Church Street St Mary, from the east (P. W. © English Heritage DP032221)

and decorated with the feathers and motto of the Prince of Wales, which must date to c.1610–12,[66] suggesting that the house may have been built only in the early seventeenth century. The roof is of dropped tie beam construction (see the new court hall) and has archbraced collars similar to those in 2, 4 Cattle Market.

Some earlier houses in the town were renovated at this time. The fifteenth-century house now called the King's Lodging (formerly the Old House) at 46 Strand Street had a highly decorated plaster ceiling and several late sixteenth-century overmantels (House 88; Figs 16.18, 16. 19), some of which were shipped to an unknown destination in the USA in the twentieth century.[67] This house may have been the White Hart Inn, a leased property occupied during the 1580s by the jurat and former mayor John Iden and his wife Richardine, who ran the business. When he died in 1587 the house had a hall and three parlours, and he left the rest of his lease to his wife with instructions that she was not to carry away any of the long settles or the glass windows, leaving the house destitute.[68] The fireplaces probably date from his time or shortly after. Richardine lived on into the seventeenth century and remarried three times, once to a wealthy London mercer who moved to Sandwich, and twice to local Sandwich jurats. They continued to take out licences for her to tipple, although whether they also took over the lease of the White Hart is not known.[69]

The owners or occupiers of these houses are mostly

Fig. 16.17: The King's Arms Public House, 63, 65 Strand Street (House 91), caryatid carrying dragon beam (P. W. © English Heritage DP032252)

Fig. 16.18: Fireplace in the King's Lodging, formerly the Old House, 46 Strand Street (House 88) (photographed 1920–29, reproduced by permission of English Heritage, NMR cc001235)

Fig. 16.19: Fireplace in the King's Lodging, formerly the Old House, 46 Strand Street (House 88) (photographed 1920–29, reproduced by permission of English Heritage, NMR cc001233)

unknown, but such evidence as there is suggests that they were jurats, wealthy merchants, mariners or maltsters, probably among those in the first quartile identified in the probate inventories (Chap. 15.4.4), who were building homes for their own use. The ground floor is often largely disguised by later alterations, but the presence of fireplaces in most front rooms and the use of moulded ceiling beams imply that the fronts were usually occupied by a hall and parlour and that none of these houses had shops. Apart from 2, 4 Cattle Market, no large building of this period has been identified in the town centre where properties incorporating shops were most likely to have been located.

16.4.2 Small houses

None of the houses built as part of the large-scale development that took place at the west end of town in the late 1560s and early 1570s survives, although one or two buildings elsewhere may date from this time. Nos. 6 and 8 Bowling Street (House 1; Fig. 16.21) form a pair of semi-detached houses of two storeys and attics, with a single room on each floor and a central

Fig. 16.20: 8 Bowling Street (House 1), ground-floor fireplace (S. P.)

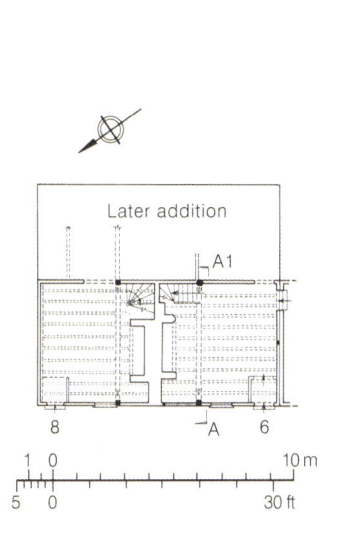

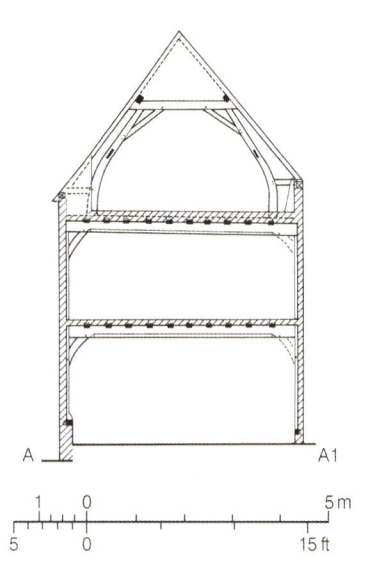

Fig. 16.21: 6, 8 Bowling Street (House 1), ground-floor plan, and cross section of No. 6 (S. P. & A. T. A.)

stack with two fireplaces to each side. The structure cannot have been jettied to the front, and there is no sign that there were ever end jetties. Thus this house is something of an innovation in the development of timber houses in the town. There were once outshuts at the rear where now there are two-storey extensions, but it is unclear whether they were original. The stairs, although remade, must always have been behind the fireplaces. Dropped tiebeams and sling braces give extra head height to the attic floor. The fireplace in No. 8 probably has its original thin bricks, almost tiles, at the back (Fig. 16.20).

A second example is 16, 18 New Street (House 63; Figs 16.22, 16.23). This building was erected just in front of St Thomas's hospital, the corner of whose hall forms the rear wall of its tiny back yard. It is three full storeys high with no attic, each storey jettied to both front and rear, thus providing more space on each floor as one moves up the house. Later alterations make it

Fig. 16.22: 16, 18 New Street (House 63), view from north (P. W. © English Heritage DP044003)

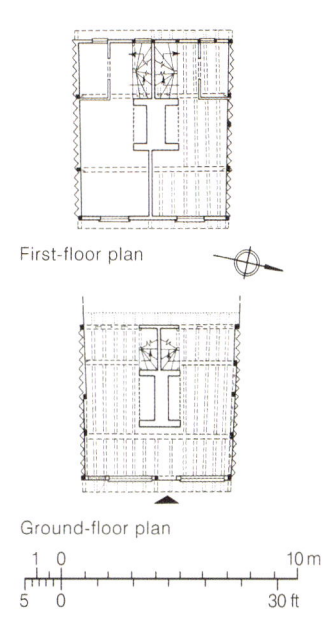

Fig. 16.23: 16, 18 New Street (House 63), ground-floor and first-floor plans (S. P. & A. T. A.)

Fig. 16.24: 19, 21 Church Street St Mary (House 13), two single-bay houses, now of two storeys, but brackets at eaves level show where attic gables have been removed (P. W. © English Heritage DP068593)

name for the south end of the High Street, their present brick stacks built into larger bays that probably once contained timber stacks.

Sometimes new building took the form of an addition to an older house. At 21 King Street the fully storeyed bays of *c*.1500 were untouched, although a fireplace was inserted, but at the side facing Short Street a new two-storey bay was added at the east end with a form of sling-brace truss on the first floor (House 45; Fig. 12.29, section A–A¹). Whether such head height was required for a special purpose, notably for looms and weaving, and why the braces are studded with large holes, remain unclear.

In other cases older houses were partially rebuilt. Nos. 17 and 19 High Street are now two cottages of much the same size, formerly with one room to either side of a central double stack (House 34; Figs 16.25, 16.26). Medieval, lightly smoke-blackened rafters were reused in No. 17 when constructing the present clasped side-purlin roof with wind braces, while a beam in No. 19 has an arched shape suggesting a reused tiebeam.

difficult to be certain whether it was intended as two dwellings (as it became later), heated by a central stack with two fireplaces on each side and stairs at the rear, or whether the subdivision is secondary (the timbers provide conflicting evidence). If it were a semi-detached pair, each with a hall and perhaps a small buttery at the rear and two chambers on both the first and second floors, the dwellings could have had six rooms each on a very small footprint.

Another semi-detached pair of houses is 19 and 21 Church Street St Mary (House 13; Fig. 16.24). Here, the large ground-floor rooms were heated by rear fireplaces. The houses are now of two storeys only, but the brackets of late sixteenth-century character set under the eaves originally carried bressumers supporting overhanging gables facing the street, indicating that originally there were well-lit attic rooms.

Sometimes small houses were built individually, as at 57 High Street (House 40), a single-cell house of two storeys, jettied to the front and heated by a stack against one gable wall. The beams suggest that the stack may initially have been of timber, later reduced in size and rebuilt in brick. Here as elsewhere, the roof is of clasped side-purlin construction with diminishing principals and wind braces. Other single or double versions of this form are in The Chain (Houses 10, 11), the modern

Fig. 16.25: 17, 19 High Street (House 34) (P. W. © English Heritage DP026082)

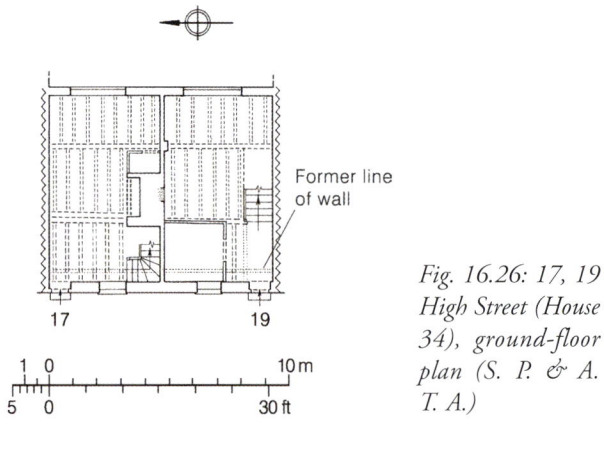

Fig. 16.26: 17, 19 High Street (House 34), ground-floor plan (S. P. & A. T. A.)

16 The buildings

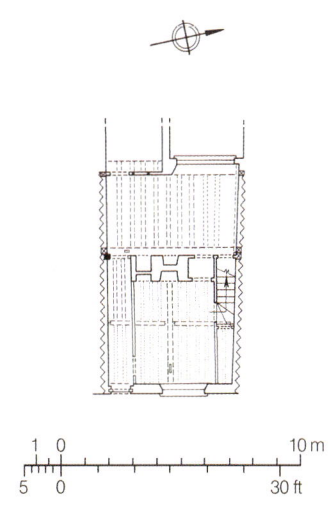

Fig. 16.27: 27 Church Street St Mary (House 15), ground-floor plan (S. P. & A. T. A.)

The current layout is *c.*1600, but the large scantlings of the visible joists at the front, with evidence for a former front jetty, look earlier. They are the only ones to be pegged to the main beams, which have no evidence for joisting on their rear faces, suggesting that the present arrangement may be the result of partially rebuilding two small houses with open halls of *c.*1500 set behind storeyed front bays, probably of the type surviving at 34 High Street (House 38; Fig. 12.10). Possibly the street was once lined with small open-hall houses of this sort, only recognisable here because rebuilding was less drastic than usual. A similar sequence may be represented at 27 Church Street St Mary (House 15; Fig. 16.27), where the rear bay has features suggesting an early sixteenth-century date, whereas the front bay was rebuilt *c.*1600. It is possible that this is an example of what is known as 'alternate rebuilding': the house may originally have consisted of a medieval front range with a small open hall of wealden form as found in Fisher Street and New Street (Chap. 12.4). In the early sixteenth century a range was added to the back, and at the beginning of the seventeenth the open hall in front was rebuilt in the new style, with a hall and chambers above. In most of these small buildings the façades are now heavily disguised, so there are likely to be others as yet undiscovered.

Many of the late medieval plots in the town were approximately 5.00m wide (16ft 5in or 1 perch), or multiples of this measure. On the 5.00m plots, most of the houses that were rebuilt in the late sixteenth century and later had side stacks. Only occasionally, as at 27 Church Street St Mary, were rear stacks added to houses of this width. Where the plot was narrower, perhaps because of earlier subdivision – as at 13 and 24 Fisher Street (Houses 22, 23: 4.00m and 3.9m)[70] and 16 St Peter's Street (House 69: 3.7m; Fig. 16.28) – the stack tended to be placed at the rear.[71]

Where visible, the thin timbers, square framing and simple details of most of these houses make it unclear whether they were rebuilt shortly before or just after 1600. Where decorative details survive they tend to indicate that rebuilding did not take place until the seventeenth century. At 28, 30 and 32 Church Street St Mary, a row of three single-cell, two-storey cottages was built reusing earlier timbers internally, but the small square-panelled framing of the front wall, thin brackets supporting the jetty, and strap work and circular motifs carved on the jetty bressumer, indicate that the rebuild took place after 1600. Likewise, the flat moulding of the bressumer, carved barge boards and central pendant of the attic gable to 16 St Peter's Street (House 69; Fig. 16.29) – probably built with No. 14, not seen – belong

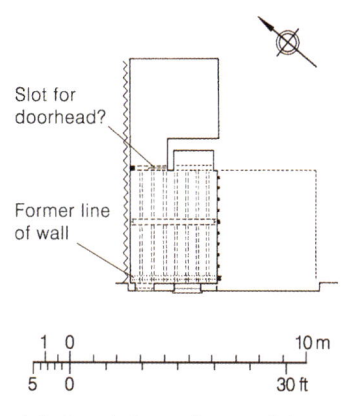

Fig. 16.28: 16 St Peter's Street (House 69), ground-floor plan (S. P. & A. T. A.)

Fig. 16.29: 16 (and 14) St Peter's Street (House 69) (P. W. © English Heritage DP068617)

255

to the early seventeenth century. Such diagnostic details seldom remain among the smaller buildings.

The occupiers of these smaller houses are even more difficult to trace than those of the larger houses. Parkin believed that the unusual roof construction in some dwellings, such as 6, 8 Bowling Street (Fig. 16.20), indicated that they had once housed looms, and he suggested that they were occupied by Flemish weavers.[72] Unfortunately, it has proved impossible to verify his claim. Similar roof constructions occur at 11 Harnet Street, in the late sixteenth-century addition to 21 King Street (House 45; Fig. 12.29), and in the rear wing of 62 Strand Street (House 90; Fig. 16.11), built before 1578. Later, it was a type of roof used in single-cell houses in the Rows at Great Yarmouth.[73] Even if weaving took place on the upper floors, it is unclear that it required either the extra ceiling height or the large holes sometimes found along the timbers in this sort of roof. If lighting was as important for weaving as is sometimes claimed, houses like 6, 8 Bowling Street were not particularly well lit on the top floor, unless the gable ends were less hemmed in than is the case today. Thus the attics may simply have been made this way to provide decent accommodation on the top floor. Not many surviving late sixteenth-century small houses have been identified, and if most of them were inhabited by immigrants, the homes of the native craftsmen and artisans are missing. Since their houses are more likely to have survived than those of the immigrants, it is probable that the small houses discussed in this chapter were built for those whose probate inventories fall into the third and fourth quartiles, a few of whom may have been immigrants, but most of whom were local people. This is in stark contrast to Rye, where it is thought that the influx of Protestant refugees in the 1570s resulted in considerable evidence for surviving late sixteenth-century buildings.[74]

16.5 Probate inventories and the function of rooms

The 168 probate inventories used to consider the wealth and social standing of Sandwich inhabitants in the late sixteenth century were primarily consulted for the information they contain about dwellings. When used for interpreting the layout of houses, one must remember that the inventory was concerned with itemising goods, not with the rooms themselves; so if a room was empty, or at least held no goods belonging to the deceased, then it would not be mentioned.[75] Thus many inventories may relate to only part of a house.

For example, some inventories, such as that of Roger Manwood of 1590 for the original King's Lodging, with fourteen rooms, is invaluable for its list of polite rooms, but is clearly incomplete since no service rooms other than the kitchen are mentioned.[76] In other cases independent evidence indicates incompleteness where none might have been suspected from the inventory itself. Alexander Cobb, jurat, left his house with seven rooms to his widow Agnes in 1585, but when she died in 1589, apparently living in the same property (both houses, for example, had a gallery with a chair and hangings in it), she had eleven rooms.[77] In 1579 Joyce Buskyn had a hall and two chambers, and while one might be tempted to think this was a whole house, his will makes clear that he left 'that part of my mansion house in which I dwell' to his widow, to be passed to his two sons after her death. When one son died in 1586 his goods were listed in two chambers and a buttery. If this is the same house, then it was again probably only part of it.[78] Widows often lived only in part of a house, as was presumably the case with Avice Denbowe, who had goods in the hall chamber but none in the hall itself,[79] and sometimes an inventory makes clear that the testator was renting a single room, as in the case of the maltster David Jones, whose goods all lay in 'his lodging chamber'.[80] Other authors have excluded inventories that they judged not to list all the rooms in a house.[81] But since it is likely that many inventories that at first sight appear to mention all the rooms were in fact incomplete, the decision was taken here to include all those inventories in which named rooms are mentioned.

In order to allow comparisons to be made between Sandwich and other towns where inventories have been analysed, Table 16.1 indicates the range of room numbers during this period without regard to quartiles. The result is strikingly similar to Norwich in much the same period, with Sandwich having only a slightly higher proportion of houses with three rooms or fewer, and a slightly lower proportion of those with more than fourteen rooms.[82] This is surprising, since the wealth and social character of the two towns must have been very different. It may be partly because the Norwich figures do not include buildings suspected of having been inns, whereas they are included in the Sandwich sample (see Section 16.5.5). For most other purposes the Sandwich inventories have been divided into the four quartiles used in Table 16.2, since this provides a clearer picture of what the houses of different social levels were like.

Table 16.3 illustrates the incidence of the commonest room types in houses in the four quartiles. The rooms will then be discussed in turn.

Table 16.1: Numbers of rooms overall

	Sandwich 1564–1600		Norwich 1580–1604	
No. of rooms	No.	%	No.	%
1–3	41	24	24	20
4–6	63	38	45	38
7–9	38	23	30	25
10–14	21	12	15	12
More than 14	5	3	6	5
Totals	168	100	120	100

(Figures for Norwich taken from Priestley and Corfield 1982, 10.)

Table 16.2: Number of rooms in Sandwich (168 examples, divided into four quartiles)

Quartile	Range in value	Values		Range of room nos.	No. of rooms in inventory	
		Mean	Average		Mean	Average
1st	£112–£754	£212	£277	1–23	9	9
2nd	£46–£111	£69	£71	3–14	6	6.6
3rd	£19–£45	£30	£31	1–10	5	4.9
4th	£2–£18	£9	£9	1–7	3	3.2

Table 16.3: The incidence of commonest rooms

	Quartiles							
	1st		2nd		3rd		4th	
Rooms	No.	%	No.	%	No.	%	No.	%
Hall	36	86	42	100	37	88	37	88
Galleries	7	17	4	10	0	0	0	0
One or more parlours	32	76	21	50	18	43	12	29
Buttery	25	59	22	52	14	33	12	29
Kitchen	33	79	30	71	18	43	13	31
Shop/workhouse	14	33	14	33	13	31	9	21
Cellar	7	17	5	12	1	2	0	0
At least one chamber	41	98	40	92	38	90	33	79
At least two chambers	37	88	29	69	24	57	13	31
At least three chambers	27	64	15	36	11	26	2	5
More than three chambers	16	38	5	12	4	10	0	0

16.5.1 Halls

Ninety per cent of all houses had a hall, and where none was listed that was probably because the testator lived in only part of a house. While halls may have been ubiquitous, the way in which they were used varied considerably. The incidence of specialised equipment such as spits, jacks, frying and dripping pans indicates where cooking took place. Table 16.4 shows that the number of halls used for cooking was highest in the fourth quartile and lowest in the first. In some houses there is evidence that both hall and kitchen were used in this way, but this diminishes as the value of the inventory and the number of rooms increases. There is little identifiable change as the sixteenth century progressed, probably because the date range of 1564 to 1600 is too short. Indeed, some surprisingly wealthy

258 Part V: 1560–1600

Table 16.4: Location of cooking

	Quartiles							
	1st		2nd		3rd		4th	
	No.	%	No.	%	No.	%	No.	%
No cooking in hall	31	*74*	28	*67*	20	*48*	13	*31*
Cooking in hall	4	*10*	11	*26*	13	*31*	16	*38*
Cooking in kitchen	30	*71*	29	*69*	14	*33*	12	*29*

people continued to cook in the hall. John Ballard, a malster who owned and lived in The Star Inn (House 9), died in 1595 with an inventory valued at £415; he had no kitchen and all his cooking equipment was in the hall. Roger Raw, probably a draper, who died in 1594 with an inventory worth £475 had both a kitchen (cooking) and an old kitchen (used for lumber), but despite having window curtains and a looking-glass in his hall, he also kept a jack to turn a spit there.[83] Sandwich inventories are said to display more evidence for cooking in halls than those of other towns in Kent.[84]

In addition to tables, forms, chairs and stools, which were found in all halls, the best of them might have had cupboards, cushions, window curtains, looking-glasses, pictures, hangings or painted cloths, as well as various items of armour and weaponry. The last were sometimes present in even some of the poorest households, since all men had to serve in the militia.[85] The poorest halls might also contain a bed, a linen chest or a spinning wheel, and such halls were clearly the main living room of the dwelling. But for the wealthiest testators the hall now served as a reception room only, with other activities moved to parlours, chambers and kitchens.

It is difficult to be sure of the number of halls that were ceiled, because the only evidence is when a 'chamber over the hall' is mentioned in an inventory. There are eighteen such references in the first quartile, sixteen in the second, nine in the third and eight in the fourth, but many other houses, especially in the top three quartiles, had enough chambers for one to have been over the hall, even if not called that by name. On the other hand, as discussed in Chapter 12.9, eleven inventories, all in the first and second quartiles, had galleries, and none of these lists a chamber over the hall.[86] As we know from the surviving buildings, not all open halls had galleries, and there are other inventories where open halls can be surmised, sometimes because all the other ground-floor rooms had chambers above them. No. 39 Strand Street was one of the larger houses in the town; the ceiling beams and the windows in a new brick wall lighting the hall and room above suggest a date around 1600, the alteration possibly dated precisely by a date stone of 1606, which was set above the new entrance doorway. In poorer dwellings in particular there is sometimes evidence for two or even three rooms downstairs but only one or two chambers above, suggesting that the hall may still have been open.

In the fourth quartile, four inventories mention a hall and chamber only, possibly indicating single-storey structures with an open hall and an inner room. But surviving buildings from the second half of the sixteenth century, for example 6, 8 Bowling Street (House 1) and 16, 18 New Street (House 63), show that the chamber could have been above the hall, so caution in interpretation is required. Thus, although they may be represented but not stated in the inventories, there is no incontrovertible evidence that Sandwich had the high proportion of houses without upper floors as suggested for Coventry and Derby.[87] In addition, no dwellings in Sandwich, and indeed only two in Canterbury,[88] have any sign of having been wholly on the first floor, such as is known to have occurred in London.

Despite the uncertainties, when the information about ceiled halls is set in a chronological sequence (Table 16.5) it indicates that the number of halls that definitely had chambers above them increased during the second half of the sixteenth century. This supports the proposition that some halls may have remained open into the second half of the century, if not beyond. There were probably two reasons for this. Wealthy people may have chosen to keep their halls, perhaps particularly those with galleries, open as a mark of status.[89] On the other hand, open halls may have survived in the homes of the poor where it may have been structurally impossible to insert a chamber above, or when the occupier was in no a position to undertake such a major alteration. Although the documents are silent on the matter, the amount of money necessary to alter or rebuild a hall must have been considerable, and it would hardly be surprising if this had been beyond the means of some, who left such niceties to the next generation.

Even if a hall remained unceiled, its formerly open hearth is likely to have been enclosed in a fireplace below a chimney stack, as at 39 Strand Street (Fig. 12.33a). Ordinances against open hearths in towns had begun

Table 16.5: Chronological table of chambers over the hall

	No. houses	**No. with chamber over hall**	**%**
1564–70	17	1	6
1571–80	27	7	30
1581–90	57	17	30
1591–1600	68	26	38

as early as the fourteenth century in London, although they were not always obeyed.[90] In Sandwich, iron fire backs for use in enclosed fireplaces were referred to from the 1580s onwards, with two houses in the fourth quartile owning them in 1586 and 1596, and more in the upper three quartiles. Two people who had galleries and no chambers over their halls clearly had chimneys, one specifically mentioning the chimney, the other the 'coal iron'.[91] At the same time coal, which was almost certainly used only in enclosed fireplaces, gradually became commoner. Being expensive, its presence is more prevalent in wealthier inventories, although it occurred in all the top three quartiles and occasionally in the fourth.

The chimneys, however, may not always have been of brick. In some surviving houses evidence has been adduced for larger fireplaces and stacks than the brick ones that now survive, and these were probably constructed of timber and plaster. The dangerous nature of some chimneys in Sandwich is indicated by an ordinance in 1564 that stacks of straw and thatch were forthwith to be used only in those areas of the town where the authorities decreed that there was no risk of fire.[92] Not everyone complied, however, for in 1576 John Molland, a yeoman who had been in court once or twice before, was ordered to demolish his thatch stack.[93]

16.5.2 Kitchens

Kitchens are present in more than 30 per cent of all houses in the inventories and in more than 70 per cent of those in the top two quartiles (Table 16.3).[94] Table 16.4 shows that when there is a kitchen it is usually the place used for cooking, although sometimes there are second kitchens, often termed 'old', which seem simply to have become overflow storage space.

Whether kitchens were always integrated into the house, as has been suggested for Midland towns from 1530 onwards, is unclear.[95] In some cases the order in which rooms are listed, with the kitchen in the middle, suggests that it was integrated,[96] as is clear at 62 Strand Street (House 90). But sometimes the kitchen is near the end of the inventory, and is perhaps the only ground-floor room not to have a chamber above

it, leaving unclear whether it might still have been detached, as was usual for most medieval kitchens.[97] The only possible surviving late sixteenth-century detached kitchens are at 7 Bowling Street (House 2) and 34 Upper Strand Street (House 98), where what may have been previously detached kitchens were later attached to the rest of the house. It is therefore difficult to be categorical about the location of kitchens.

16.5.3 Butteries and other service rooms

More than half of the houses in the top two quartiles (Table 16.3) have butteries, which are sometimes 'in the hall', suggesting that they were simply partitioned spaces rather than structurally separate rooms. Where butteries are not listed, the pots, platters, bowls, pewter and brass that were usually kept in them are either located in a kitchen or are not mentioned at all. This adds to the difficulties in interpreting the inventories, since such items were essential household goods. In the bottom two quartiles, the number of butteries drops to around a third, their normal contents occurring in the kitchen, hall, or what appears to have been a ground-floor chamber. In larger houses other service rooms listed include larders, milk houses, back rooms, outhouses, wash rooms and bunting houses, where flour was kept.

16.5.4 Cellars

Cellars, or 'sellers' as they were always termed, occur in thirteen houses (8 per cent). All except one are in the first or second quartiles. In the first quartile they occur in the inventories of wealthy men and are either empty of all but shelves, or contain essentials such as salt, coal, wood, tubs and milking vessels, or simply lumber. The cellars belonging to the vintners John Elnor and John Iden, the occupant of the White Hart Inn, are the only ones to contain wine.[98] In the second and third quartiles, two cellars are also full of disparate objects, but four, probably belonging to tipplers, contain wine, beer, sack and malmsey.[99] It is not clear whether these are sunken cellars, as at 27 and 39 Strand Street (Houses 82, 85), or are little more than secure storage areas in a back yard.

16.5.5 Parlours

As Table 16.3 shows, parlours were present in 49 per cent of all houses, a figure that would have been higher still if not masked by some inventories that clearly refer to only part of a house.[100] Five houses from all the quartiles had two, or in one case three, parlours. Other than in houses belonging to the wealthiest jurats, the presence of more than one parlour may indicate that the house was an inn. These have not been excluded, as has been done elsewhere,[101] since in Sandwich almost all the evidence for inns comes not from inventories but from other sources, such as victualling and tippling licences, of some years prior to the inventory. The White Hart, which was occupied as an inn by Thomas Gull in 1572, was by 1586 perhaps also the private dwelling of John Iden, jurat, even though his wife was a tippler.[102] Furthermore, in the fourth quartile, some of the poorer houses had parlours where none might have been expected. In these cases it is only additional evidence that suggests that the testators were involved in beer brewing or tippling, and that the occupants may have been running drinking establishments.[103]

The total number of parlours, as distinct from the number of houses with parlours, is shown in the top line of Table 16.6. They all have seating, and the best among them have window curtains and painted cloths, as well as other signs of elegant living. The percentages of those with beds, without beds, and with evidence for heating are calculated from the total number of parlours rather than the number of houses in each quartile. The actual number of parlours falls from thirty-six in the first quartile to only thirteen in the fourth. In the latter some are present in the houses of people who seem to have fallen on hard times, suggesting that the testators were living in larger houses than might be expected from their inventoried wealth.

In the town centre many parlours were situated behind the hall, except in inns with more than one parlour, in which case one might be on the street front. For example, both the tippler Griffyn Amoore in St Peter's parish, and John Iden, at the White Hart, had one of their parlours 'next the street'.[104] This could, however, also have been true of single parlours in dwellings in the outer parts of town where houses stood lengthways to the street. An example in an inventory is that of William Crispe (d. 1599), who may have lived in 15, 17 Upper Strand Street (House 94). This house lay parallel to the street, and the parlour was probably beside the hall.[105] The fireplace in the presumed parlour chamber is illustrated in Figure 12.33d.

At the top end of the social spectrum, well over half the parlours were used for sitting or dining only, and all of these were heated. The overall number of parlours decreases as wealth declines, along with the proportion of those without beds or with fireplaces. But the picture is skewed by evidence from two occupational groups. On the one hand, several parlours without beds in the third and fourth quartiles appear to have been in tippling houses. On the other, parlours were often absent among shop keepers, with only half having one in the first quartile and none in the fourth, suggesting that their private living space was either in chambers upstairs or, in the case of the less wealthy, severely restricted.

16.5.6 Chambers and garrets

A high proportion of all houses had at least one chamber. Most of them, designated by the term 'over', were clearly first-floor rooms, but where a single chamber has no adjective, or the term 'low' is used in an inventory that also had chambers 'over' other rooms, it may have been on the ground floor.[106] The term might also be used of an innkeeper's bedchamber, which was often placed on the ground floor beside the entrance to the inn.[107]

In the first quartile (Table 16.3) nearly all testators had first-floor chambers, and many had several, often bearing descriptive names. Thirty-eight per cent of houses at this level had more than three chambers, with the number rising to eight, nine and ten in a few cases. The number of chambers declines through the quartiles, and only two people in the fourth quartile had more than two chambers. In all houses, chambers

Table 16.6: Parlours, beds and heating

	Quartiles							
	1st		**2nd**		**3rd**		**4th**	
No. of parlours	36		22		19		13	
	No.	**%**	**No.**	**%**	**No.**	**%**	**No.**	**%**
Parlours with beds	14	*39*	13	*59*	13	*68*	9	*69*
Parlours without beds	22	*61*	9	*41*	6	*32*	4	*31*
Heating in parlours	22	*61*	6	*27*	6	*32*	3	*23*

usually contained beds. Only the great chamber of the original King's Lodging, which may have been fitted up for Queen Elizabeth's personal use, was solely a sitting room.[108] In addition to having beds, however, many of the better chambers were also withdrawing or sitting rooms, provided with seats, cushions, hangings and window curtains.[109] A few of the wealthier houses also had a study, which seems to have been on the first floor, sometimes 'within' another chamber. In the larger houses some of the less well-equipped chambers were clearly where servants slept, and some were reserved for the storage of crops, cheese and apples.

As the century progressed more and more chambers were heated. This is a tricky area, for the registration of fireplaces in inventories, particularly those in secondary rooms, is often incomplete.[110] In Sandwich this can be illustrated by the case of Thomas Pauley, the rector of St Peter's, who died in 1565 with an inventory value of £47 8s. The rectory, 27, 29 King Street, largely survives (House 48; Chap. 12.7.1; Figs 12.26–12.28), and clearly had fireplaces in the hall, parlour and two chambers above. But the inventory lists the implements for a fireplace only in the kitchen, which has been demolished.

Nonetheless, analysis of first-floor fireplaces indicates both that they were more prevalent in the upper quartiles, as might be expected, and that they became commoner after 1580 (Table 16.7). Bearing in mind that many fireplaces are not mentioned, a third, or perhaps even a half, of all houses in the upper quartiles probably had at least one chamber fireplace by the 1580s.

In most houses upper rooms were called chambers, and if there was another floor above, the rooms were called garrets (Table 16.3). These were commonest in the first quartile, sometimes occurring with galleries, probably meaning that the houses in which they were situated were medieval survivals. But some late sixteenth-century houses, such as the large Richborough House, 7 Bowling Street (House 2; Fig. 16.14), and the small dwellings at 6 and 8 Bowling Street (House 1; Fig. 16.20) had attics, so the term 'garret' used in the 1590s could refer to these. Usually garrets contained old beds, and perhaps discarded household items. In houses with more chambers than ground-floor rooms, some of the chambers, especially those for servants, may also have been in attics even when the term garret was not used.[111] Lofts were less common but more evenly distributed throughout the quartiles. Although the term was sometimes used for domestic rooms on the first floor, suggesting a low, relatively mean, house with a first floor partly in the roof, this was also the term used for storage space, possibly even in an unlit roof, where wheat or wool was kept.

16.5.7 The embellishment of rooms

The probate inventories indicate that during the second half of the sixteenth century the number of hangings used to decorate the walls of parlours and chambers began to decline, although painted cloths became increasingly common.[112] Since hangings were presumably woven and expensive, and painted cloths were both cheaper and more generally available, this trend illustrates the rising popularity of wall coverings generally but probably also conceals the growing desire among the wealthy for new and more permanent forms of wall covering: paint, plaster and panelling, which would not feature in probate inventories. Rooms decorated in such a manner would have had fine fireplaces as well.

Not many examples of permanent decoration remain in Sandwich houses. The surviving paint- and plasterwork of the chambers at the Long House have been noted above (House 90; Figs 16.12, 16.13), and there is evidence that the main chamber was panelled in Richborough House, 7 Bowling Street (House 2). The fireplaces photographed in the 1920s in 46 Strand Street, possibly once the White Hart Inn, were rare survivors of the best-quality work of the period (House 88; Figs 16.18, 16.19). The pride that their owners took in these new embellishments can be seen from wills, such as that in which John Iden in 1587 gave instructions to his wife about the fittings in the White Hart Inn (Section 16.4.1). In 1596 the wealthy mariner William Gayny stipulated that all the glass and wainscot in his mansion house, together with a joined bedstead in the best chamber, and a joined court cupboard and table, which he had bought in London and intended to place in his parlour, should remain in his house as heirlooms.[113]

16.5.8 Shops

About 30 per cent of all inventories list shops, or sometimes a chamber over a shop, perhaps in the inventory of an elderly occupant who had passed on the business to someone else. Shops were fairly evenly

Table 16.7: Heating in chambers

	No. houses	No. examples	%
1564–70	17	1	*6*
1571–80	27	3	*11*
1581–90	57	15	*26*
1591–1600	67	14	*21*

distributed through all the quartiles (Table 16.3). In the lowest quartile two blacksmiths, a cobbler, a weaver and a turner all had appropriate goods in their shops. In the next quartile there were two shoemakers, two coopers and two butchers. In the upper quartiles were wealthier butchers and bakers, a haberdasher, a Dutch joiner and a Dutch wool comber, a tanner and a currier. There were also people of various occupations who specialised in selling luxury goods, like the chandler who lived in the Fishmarket and had both a workhouse/workshop for making candles and also a shop full of prunes, raisins, spices, ribbons, silk, buttons, pots and glasses.[114] On the other hand, three merchants, one of whom was certainly also a grocer, had nothing but weights and scales in their shops, suggesting either that they had retired, or the premises were used only intermittently when the merchants had imported goods to sell.[115]

Just over half of all the shops belonged to testators whose parishes can be identified and, not surprisingly, nearly three-quarters of them lived in St Peter's parish. No parish is given for two of the butchers, but they almost certainly resided in The Butchery, either in St Peter's or St Mary's parish. Those shops in St Clement's parish, or in St Mary's other than in The Butchery, were probably located on the fringe of the central commercial area.

16.5.9 Outside the house

Buildings in the town centre lay side by side, often sharing party walls. At the back, there was sometimes not much space before the boundary of a neighbouring property, but probably enough for a small yard containing outbuildings such as 'the little cove in the yard'. If kitchens, or former kitchens, were detached, they must have been in the yard, as no doubt were some of the outhouses listed: stable, backhouse, milk house and 'the place' where wood and coal were kept. Occasionally, there are references to capon coops, and Richard Hurlestone, mariner, who lived in the High Street and died owning much property, kept five 'kyne' and two 'fatting pigs' as well as capon coops, in the 'yard in the backside'.[116]

There was little space for gardens in the centre of town, and the wills imply that they were often detached from the houses, lying out near the town walls, as in the case of John Chilton, who left several gardens 'at or near the town walls', including a place for stalling bullocks.[117] But in the outer parts of town where the properties were large, gardens could have been part of the main holding. Here pigeons were kept and fruit trees and herbs grown, as indicated by Walter Shetterden's wish that his daughter should have access to the garden in order to keep pigeons. John Clerke, who lived in the High Street, had a tenement with a garden that he wanted his wife to inherit so she could grow and increase herbs at her pleasure. John Chilton left his wife a house and garden at Luckboat, while Oliver Warson, tanner, bequeathed to his son his tan house and stable near the Delf in St Mary's parish.[118] All these properties lay on the fringes of the town centre. Large storehouses and barns are also likely to have been sited away from the town centre, next to the ramparts or near St Clement's church. Many of the wealthier inventories itemised growing crops, cattle, sheep and horses. It is not always possible to tell where these were, but some were clearly located on estates in the surrounding parishes.

16.6 Probate inventories, houses and Sandwich society

The inventories used for this study cover just less than forty years, a length of time too short to establish the early modern trends that have been adduced for towns where longer runs of inventories, from the sixteenth to eighteenth centuries, have been analysed.[119] Nevertheless, the information obtained from the present analysis can be supplemented by Richardson's work on late fifteenth-century wills and late sixteenth-century wills and probate inventories,[120] and by evidence from the surviving domestic buildings in the town, to allow comparison between the medieval period and the late sixteenth century in Sandwich.

Bequests of household objects in the late fifteenth-century wills, and their locations as stated in late sixteenth-century probate inventories, highlight some of the differences between the two periods. The inventories show that by the late sixteenth century rooms in wealthier houses, notably those in the top two quartiles, were becoming more specialised. Halls were furnished as reception rather than general living rooms; cooking was relegated to separate kitchens; parlours were becoming places to sit rather than to sleep; and chambers were heated and provided with fine furnishings. Ownership of valuable items such as silver, and of goods linked to comfort and embellishment, became much more widespread than in the previous century.[121] Non-domestic storage, which may have been spread through many rooms in medieval houses, was now largely kept outside the dwelling or was consigned to lofts and garrets. At the lower end of the social scale, where houses of fewer than five rooms were the norm, there were fewer opportunities for the separation of functions other than keeping cooking out of parlours and chambers, and beds out of halls and kitchens, and the families of these testators may still have been living much as their forebears had.

Analysis of the surviving buildings in Sandwich has confirmed that there were differences in lifestyles between the fifteenth and late sixteenth centuries. In the latter period, although some people still lived in houses of basically medieval type, most of them were being modified and some new dwellings were built. Some old ones still retained their open halls, but in others ceilings were inserted and new chambers created above. As a result, daylight must often have been cut off from the ground floors of the formerly open halls (Chap. 12.3.3), necessitating the complete rebuilding of rear ranges. In these houses and the large newly erected ones there had to be changes to the internal circulation and use of rooms. Meanwhile, the evidence for storage space, so noticeable in many houses built before *c.*1510, is no longer found. These differences are hardly apparent in the smaller houses, where fewer rooms meant that functions must still have been combined.

Research into late sixteenth-century inventories from several other Kent towns has shown that, despite the modifications outlined above, there is more evidence of dwellings in Sandwich still being used for multiple activities, and of being more old-fashioned than urban houses elsewhere in Kent.[122] Sandwich society was also somewhat limited, with few gentry and none of more than local significance. The highest total inventory value in the sample studied here was under £800, and the largest surviving late sixteenth-century houses are relatively small in national, or even county, terms. By this time there were wealthier inhabitants and finer late sixteenth-century houses in other Kentish towns such as Maidstone, Rochester and Canterbury (where, tellingly, Sir Roger Manwood, Sandwich's most famous son of the period, chose to spend most of his adult life). Also, many members of the local elite made do with refurbished and modified medieval houses. This is in contrast to some prosperous late sixteenth-century towns in other counties where medieval houses were totally replaced. In Norwich, for instance, there was a 'dramatic rebuilding of many mercantile residences' in the sixteenth century,[123] and in Totnes, Devon, merchant properties were completely rebuilt at the end of the sixteenth century and later, so that no medieval houses have survived.[124] Medieval houses in Sandwich may have been kept because they were of better quality than those in other towns, being substantially built and adaptable enough for the needs of their late sixteenth-century inhabitants, but their survival may also be due to the relative decline in wealth and status of the town's elite at that time.

PART VI: CONCLUSIONS

17 Sandwich in the context of wider studies of historic towns: an assessment

17.1 Archaeology and topography

The story told here begins with the rise of Sandwich from a small early medieval trading settlement to a flourishing port with a national reputation and sizeable population. Its rapid growth seems to have started at the turn of the tenth and eleventh centuries, when its original site was abandoned and a new settlement grew up around a stone-built church (St Clement's). From then until the crises of the fourteenth century, it thrived, but thereafter, and despite a partial recovery, it was gradually overtaken by other towns and ports in Kent and beyond. By the end of the Middle Ages Sandwich was no more than a regional centre, facing a variety of problems ultimately stemming from the changing coastline and from its location at the very edge of England – a position of strength in the early days of expansion and international operations, but ultimately one of weakness regarding internal communications and a viable hinterland. The events it experienced were perhaps not so dissimilar, although less extreme, to those that affected other prominent towns that sank into obscurity once the features that had made them important ceased to be significant. Thetford, Wallingford and the unfortunate Dunwich are all examples of prosperous early medieval towns that either sank to relative obscurity or collapsed altogether by the end of the Middle Ages, and even Winchester, once one of the most important centres of England, became little more than a county town.[1]

The history of Sandwich was greatly influenced by its geographical position on the south bank of the river Stour and at the south-east entrance to the Wantsum Channel. In the first centuries of its existence, the rivers Stour and Wantsum were navigable, providing a route between the river Thames and the English Channel, while the calm anchorage in the lee of the Deal Spit offered a sheltered haven to merchantmen and warships alike. These advantages enabled Sandwich to become one of the premier ports in the kingdom, but once the rivers began to silt up and the spit to accrete, the formerly international trading centre became little more than a harbour for local traffic. Few other English ports had such problems to contend with.

The medieval defences that still encircle Sandwich's historic core are some of the most complete in the country, although often overlooked in general surveys of urban fortifications, perhaps because the town's landward side is cut off from the hinterland not by stone walls but by more than 1km of earth ramparts. It is usually thought that earth ramparts were merely precursors of masonry walls, to which all medieval walled towns must have aspired but which could not always be afforded. This seems not to have been the case at Sandwich, where the only stone walls ever to be built were two short stretches at the east and west ends of the waterfront. There is nothing to suggest that the earth ramparts remained unmodified because of financial constraints, and other examples such as King's Lynn suggest that towns could deliberately decide to combine earth and stone defences, not necessarily to save money.[2] The absence of stone walls along the central section of the river should also not be regarded as unusual. In England, Southampton is a rare example of a port with complete harbour-side walls, contrasting with London, and smaller medieval ports such as Hull, King's Lynn and Great Yarmouth, which are comparable in size to Sandwich, none of which has a wall along its quayside. The operations of the major merchants with their requirements for ready access to their quays and to the water were presumably of more pressing importance than occasional threats of invasion.

Sandwich also resembles the above three east coast ports in other aspects of its topographical development, particularly in the formation of its waterfront. Comparisons have been drawn between the position of Sandwich's Strand Street in regard to the riverbank and the equivalent streets in Hull and King's Lynn (Chap. 7.3), and land reclamation in all the ports seems to have followed very similar lines. There have been fewer published archaeological excavations in

Sandwich than in the other two places, but the evidence that is accessible at present suggests that the processes whereby land was claimed from the water along the south bank of the river Stour were very similar to those discovered and postulated in Hull and King's Lynn. The economic base of all these east coast ports was also comparable, with waterborne trade and fishing being of paramount importance. The scale and fluctuation in prosperity differed in detail, but nevertheless there are sufficient similarities for direct comparisons to be made. A detailed study of Hull and King's Lynn using the multidisciplinary methods employed at Sandwich would surely throw much new light on the workings of medieval ports on the North Sea coast and provide a context into which to fit the results already obtained through the current study of Sandwich.

17.2 Surviving buildings

Discussion of medieval urban houses is often based upon a mere handful of examples from each town, but the remarkable survival of houses in Sandwich makes the study much more meaningful. More than seventy buildings may be dated before 1520 (Appendix 2), and while some of the earliest are fragmentary stone structures, sixty-seven are timber-framed buildings erected from the early fourteenth century onwards. In 1513 there may have been around 380 households and a population of 2,700 in the town, reducing to approximately 290 households by 1560. Discounting the stone buildings, some possibly already ruinous by 1560, and also those that seem never to have been dwellings, there are still fifty-seven probable houses dating from before c.1520. If houses may be roughly equated with households, the Sandwich statistics shows that 15 per cent of the dwellings required in the early sixteenth century, and 20 per cent of those needed by 1560, are still standing.

This phenomenal proportion of surviving buildings is matched in no other major towns in England, even though the total numbers of houses may be greater in places such as York, Salisbury and Shrewsbury.[3] In Salisbury, seventy-three houses of early sixteenth-century or earlier date have been identified, yet the population in 1524–5 is thought to have been more than 5,000. Early sixteenth-century Shrewsbury had approximately 3,500 inhabitants but there are only around thirty surviving medieval houses. Even if the numbers are underestimates, they suggest survival rates of 8–10 per cent for Salisbury and 5–6 per cent for Shrewsbury, far smaller than Sandwich's 15 or 20 per cent.[4]

There are even fewer extant medieval buildings elsewhere. In Southampton, and Chester, although stone undercrofts survive well, the timber-framed superstructures of medieval date rarely remain.[5] In the case of King's Lynn, which was not so very much larger than Sandwich by this time, about a dozen houses survive in the port area, giving a good picture of late medieval merchant housing in Lynn, but few buildings remain in the heart of the town, particularly in the crowded shopping streets, or on the outskirts, so survival is both more limited and not strictly comparable.[6] In Coventry many medieval houses existed until the twentieth century, but damage during World War II and the rationalisation of the 1950s and 1960s destroyed most of the city centre before the buildings had been properly recorded; although some remain in the outer streets and suburbs, they do not provide a picture of the full range of medieval buildings. In the even larger centres of London, Norwich and Bristol, few if any buildings below extremely high-status social levels survive today.

The existence of shops and workshops has been discussed at length in the preceding chapters, including evidence for commercial and industrial buildings in the market areas, and shops and storage accommodation throughout the town centre. Sandwich has little sign of the thirteenth- and early fourteenth-century vaulted undercrofts found in Southampton, Winchelsea and elsewhere. Its low-lying position may have been unfavourable for the construction of subterranean cellars, and if there were more, they have largely been replaced. But there is notable evidence in about a dozen timber-framed buildings for above-ground warehousing, either on its own or combined with domestic, commercial and industrial accommodation. This is an aspect of urban building that has perhaps not received the attention it deserves. Although there have been specialist studies on medieval shops as a class of building,[7] only one article on late medieval workshops in the small cloth towns of East Anglia has considered all aspects of urban domestic and working space.[8] In order to understand how people ran their lives and businesses and how town houses were intended to be used in the Middle Ages, it is essential that all the activities that may have taken place in the buildings are considered together. This has to be done through structural analysis, for by the time buildings were described in late sixteenth-century probate inventories, in Sandwich and probably elsewhere, uses had changed. Much more information is required from other towns across the country and we hope that the Sandwich evidence will encourage others to look for clues elsewhere.

Even though the survival of so many medieval houses in Sandwich is remarkable and important, it may be thought presumptuous to discuss the buildings of what ultimately became a small regional town in terms of places that continued to be very much larger. But there is a reason for so doing. The medieval houses in the centres of smaller towns, whether market towns or ports, for example Rye, Faversham, and Lavenham in Suffolk, are very different from those of Sandwich. In those, all the surviving buildings are two storeys high and arranged parallel to the street, suggesting that the demand for commercial space in their centres could be satisfied without dividing the plots. Division into smaller units forces buildings to become taller and to extend backwards from the street frontage. In Sandwich the pressure on space must have been intense, as indeed it was in the centre of larger towns and cities. The date when this pressure began in Sandwich is unclear, although the discussions of plot division in the Fishmarket and Strand Street (Chaps 4.5, 7.5) suggest that it may have begun during the twelfth century and continued into the early fourteenth.[9] By the fifteenth century, when so many of the surviving Sandwich houses were erected, the high point of the town's prosperity had passed but the legacy of its past survived in the form of its buildings. In some cases when towns declined, plots were amalgamated,[10] and that may well have happened in Sandwich when the elite of the town were building new houses in the outer parts of St Mary's parish in the sixteenth century. But in general it seems that as Sandwich's population dwindled it contracted into the centre. That appears to have been the most desirable area, presumably since that was where trade was likely to attract most custom. Space here remained at a premium, and there is no evidence that town-centre plots were combined to form larger holdings during the sixteenth century. Furthermore, there was no need to destroy and reconstruct the substantially built houses of the previous century, many of which remain in large part today. Thus, the three-storey right-angled houses in the centre of Sandwich provide important evidence for what houses in the centres of larger and wealthier towns may have looked like. The comparisons for these buildings are to be found in places like Southampton, not in small ports or market towns across the country. Only on the outskirts of Sandwich, beyond the highly prized central core, were buildings aligned along the streets in the manner of all houses in smaller towns and of those on the outskirts of larger ones. These findings emphasise the need to study urban buildings in the context of their location within a town and in relation to the history of the town itself. Surviving historic buildings in all towns would benefit from detailed analysis similar to that carried out here.

Since the peak of Sandwich's prosperity had passed by the late fourteenth century, it is legitimate to ask why so many of its medieval houses were erected after that time. Indeed, more than one historian has queried whether the dating of buildings proposed in this book can possibly be correct. But this is to assume that surviving houses were built only during periods of economic prosperity. In all towns, whatever their history, surviving buildings erected before 1400 are few, and may be associated with leading citizens and wealthy institutions, usually in the period before the Black Death. Not until the fifteenth century do the houses of what one may term the middling sort begin to survive, erected by those who prospered as a result of the opportunities presented by a severely reduced population. In Kent generally this process began around 1460, reaching a peak towards the end of the fifteenth century, and this seems to have been true in Sandwich as well. That the people occupying the late medieval buildings were different from their early fourteenth-century predecessors is suggested by the smaller – in some cases far smaller – size of the buildings, and by the fact that the most up-to-date urban forms were not adopted. These rather old-fashioned houses survive precisely because Sandwich went into decline and post-medieval rebuilding was kept to a minimum.

The architecture of the churches and hospitals of Sandwich is not particularly worthy of note in a national context, and the study of late medieval parish life could be mirrored in many other places. Nonetheless, the inclusion of the churches and hospitals in this study has been invaluable to the project. Analysis of the development of each building has provided important insights into the developing topography and prosperity of the town, while consideration of the architecture, the liturgical functions, the roles of parishioners and their differences in each parish, has mirrored work on the pattern of secular buildings, contributing to a greater understanding of the social structure of the town in the Middle Ages.

17.3 Heritage management and future research

The first archaeological assessment of Sandwich was compiled for English Heritage by the Heritage Conservation Group of Kent County Council (it is frequently called the Extended Urban Survey and shortened to EUS) and completed immediately before the start of the current project.[11] The assessment took into account previously published research, outlined Sandwich's urban characteristics, proposed a series of research questions and included a short appendix on supplementary planning guidance. The current project has attempted to answer some of the research questions posed in the assessment and has also extended lines of enquiry into the history and development of the town by incorporating detailed evidence from documentary sources. It has also been able to expand some of the aspects tackled in the appendix to the EUS.

The project's research into the archaeology and topography of Sandwich has shown that the area of historical significance for the town is not confined to within the surviving earth and stone walls, but extends much further into its immediate hinterland, particularly on the east towards the Sandowns. The urban archaeological zones shown on figure 16 of the EUS document need to be expanded to encompass the area dealt with by the present project, as illustrated by Figures 3.1 and III.1. Two examples can be cited here. First, the site of the royal castle and the land in which it stood, including the proposed positions of its waterside features, are of vital importance for the understanding of Sandwich's development, and should be included as a sensitive area in any redrawn archaeological zones map. Second, the road running south from the town to the still surviving St Bartholomew's hospital and the properties flanking it are of potential archaeological significance. The project's work on the standing buildings has also supplemented the EUS. It has become evident from the study of surviving medieval buildings in the town that architecturally Sandwich was a place of more than regional significance until the middle of the fourteenth century, and that even its later medieval buildings can play a national role in understanding the development of urban housing in the Middle Ages.

But a great deal remains to be learnt about the archaeology and buildings of this important medieval town, and the future management of its heritage will be critical. All areas or buildings affected by planning proposals, both within the walls and in the surrounding hinterland, need to be properly assessed in order to evaluate their potential significance for the history of the town, and to provide the basis for informed decisions on what action should be taken. The recommended process of assessment, evaluation and informed decision making is clearly set out in PPGs 15 and 16, in the supplementary planning guidance provided in the Sandwich EUS, and also in English Heritage's more recent policy and guidance on historic buildings.[12] The work undertaken by the current project has provided new background information for Sandwich, against which informed decisions and appropriate action to the highest possible standards can take place. This is not just a plea for information that may lead to a better understanding of the town for academic purposes. Informed planning decisions, based on the most up-to-date knowledge and research questions and taken before any work has been started, can minimise potential damage, and influence the outcome of modern development for the benefit of the heritage and the community. Such action can increase understanding of the historic environment and enable the introduction of better planning policies in the future. Medieval Sandwich survives far better than most medieval towns and enchants all who come in contact with it, whether they have a deep knowledge of its past or not. Modern planning policies understand that the unique qualities of such a place, with its finite and often fragile archaeological and historical resources, need to be treasured, preserved and enhanced for the enjoyment and education of future generations. Opportunities have been lost in the past, but we sincerely hope that the more than regional significance of the town, as suggested in this study, will mean that planners in the future will be sensitive to the responsibility of making the correct decisions.

It was argued in Chapter 2 that the origins of Sandwich should be sought on the east side of the town, where the road from Eastry met the south bank of the river Stour. This hypothesis could be tested by excavations in the area, where there has never been extensive urban development and where silting or land reclamation may have preserved waterlogged remains. A little west of this stood the royal castle in its grounds of Castelmead, where there have been three rather limited interventions since the 1970s. Those raised more questions than they answered, particularly in relation to when the site was first occupied, the date and form of the earliest castle, and the stratigraphic relationship between Mill Wall and the castle ditch. Tantalising documentary references to shipbuilding and repairing in Castelmead could also be tested here. The timbers from the so-called Sandwich ship were discovered nearby, indicating that preserved organic material might be expected in the area, including wood from another vessel, which is said still to be *in situ*.[13]

Every opportunity should be taken to investigate the earth ramparts in order to confirm their methods and date of construction. The sites of Canterbury, Woodnesborough and New gates are known, and would benefit from observations of any road works that might be undertaken there. Sandown Gate has had some investigation, but no convincing dating evidence was unearthed. The ramparts surrounding the Bulwark, apparently a mid-fifteenth-century artillery fortification, need to be investigated, particularly because they are part of a Scheduled Ancient Monument and, at the time of writing, parts are deteriorating badly. Although the land that they define, which formed the main body of the Bulwark itself, suffered from landscaping in the early twentieth century, its potential must not be overlooked.

Investigation of any part of St Mary's parish, where the medieval street pattern was apparently disrupted in the sixteenth century, might produce evidence from which the earlier topography could be reconstructed. The land north of Strand Street is of crucial significance both for the dating of the masonry walls and for the process of land reclamation. At the west end of town the town wall runs through private property, and some stretches are currently in danger of collapse. If repair work were to be carried out, this might both save the above-ground structure and provide a chance of investigating the ground between the wall and what has been postulated as the course of the Delf, while the vexed question of where Christ Church Priory's 'Monkenquay' stood throughout the Middle Ages might be answered. There is also a potential site for excavation just north of St Mary's church, where Jesus Quay was located, which could produce much-needed evidence for the waterfront, quays or revetments, and the original junction of the Delf (present Guestling) and the Stour. In the other parishes, opportunities may be more limited but should be seized upon when they occur. Rumours of redeveloping the present town quay may be unfounded, but if it were to happen it would provide an occasion for excavating a potentially extremely productive waterfront site.

Sites that may become available in the areas south of the Delf, where there have already been some interventions with inconclusive results, should also be watched with care. For much of the Middle Ages, the land around the inside of the walls was clearly occupied by industry, gardens, and small-scale agriculture and associated buildings. But it is possible that some of this ground was used for dwellings c.1300 when the population was at its height and before the walls were built, and it is certain that parts were occupied by the new buildings erected for the late sixteenth-century immigrants. These buildings have gone, but the gardens in the western end of the town bring up large quantities of pottery, and chances to explore further should not be missed.

Within the area of the town walls it is essential that archaeological investigation forms part of any ground disturbance, whether or not planning permission is necessary. Even if no datable finds or structures are discovered, information about the depth below ground level of the subsoil and its composition would be invaluable. This may not always be possible, however, since work generated through PPG 16 must aim for the conservation of archaeological deposits and thus the lowest stratigraphy or subsoil may never be reached, which makes it difficult to pursue targeted research on crucial issues such as urban origins.

Speedy publication of all results is and will always be essential. Unfortunately, several large sites excavated in Sandwich during the 1970s and 1980s, before the introduction of PPG 16 in 1990, are still unpublished due to lack of resources, and their results have been inaccessible to the members of the present project. Everything possible must be done in future to avoid this recurring, since it is detrimental both to the interpretation of the history of the town and to the process of informed planning in the future.

Outside the walled town, survey and field-walking on the rising ground immediately to the south and south-west might well be productive in terms of identifying further evidence for early habitation in the area. Larger-scale excavations at the important late Iron Age and Roman settlement site identified on the Sandowns, near Archer's Low Farm, would no doubt be highly informative, especially if these could be extended to locate and investigate the contemporary coastline. The nature of the remains previously recorded on Mary-le-Bone Hill west of the town continues to be enigmatic and more excavations are needed here to establish the true significance of this place.

Where standing structures are concerned, the present study of the medieval houses has shown there to be clear distinctions between those in the inner and those in the outer parts of the town. It has also raised a number of questions relating to their completeness and their functions. We need to know more about the type and extent of accommodation required by the inhabitants at different periods and at different social levels. We also need to establish, either through building analysis or archaeology, or both, how the back ranges of the buildings and their yards were used. Many of the buildings have clear evidence of commercial and storage functions, and the information provided by them needs to be strengthened by further research. The fact that the front terminations of so many of the roofs in surviving houses have been rebuilt may be related to the function of their top storeys and roof spaces. The sort of questions raised about functions are not ones that concern Sandwich alone, but since they have not yet been adequately considered in relation to urban buildings generally, further and more detailed recording of some houses surveyed early in the project could provide new clues that would help to clarify matters, both for Sandwich and elsewhere.

The scope of this project has allowed us only to scratch the surface of enquiry into the development of buildings in the post-medieval period. Far more research and recording is required to elucidate the various forms of building erected after 1560, to understand the overlap in form and style between the late sixteenth and the seventeenth centuries, and to identify what was built in the eighteenth and nineteenth centuries. It is clear that there was a revival of building construction in the town, probably towards the end of the eighteenth century, but no work has been undertaken to discover what the houses were like, or to consider their distribution, sizes and social status. Thus, the study of the historic buildings in the town is by no means finished.

In the absence of any future research projects on buildings in the town, all these areas of enquiry need to be advanced through the medium of informed planning policies, as outlined above. Dialogue between the applicant and the planning authority at an early stage should always be encouraged for it may lead to changes in the application that are of benefit not only to the heritage but also to the developer. In the case of building recording, the advantages of such a dialogue have been discussed on many occasions, but seldom acted upon.[14] It is to be hoped that the recently published English Heritage policy and guidelines on historic buildings will rectify this.[15] Once action has been agreed, it is vital that the correct procedures are followed throughout the development.

A final point concerns the dissemination of the accumulated knowledge. The results of all work on the history of the town in its widest sense should be made available for the benefit of the inhabitants and the wider public. Ideally, Sandwich needs a larger museum and archives centre to reflect its status as an important historic town.

17.4 Evaluation of the methods used in the project

The database of archaeological interventions within the town expands and updates the entries in the Historic Environment Record (HER) for Kent and the list of archaeological data in the Sandwich EUS. It has proved to be a very useful overall statement of what has so far been achieved and also highlights the problems of working in an historic town where so many medieval buildings remain standing and in regular use. Opportunities to undertake large-scale excavation within the historic town centre have been few, and this situation is never likely to change. Many interventions have been confined to observations of relatively small pits and trenches, often too shallow to expose the earliest occupation levels and to establish the nature of the underlying natural subsoil. The resulting gaps in the story are particularly unfortunate from the perspective of understanding the origins of Sandwich, which have long been of special interest to Kentish scholars and have been one of the main themes of the present study.

The almost total absence of Anglo-Saxon discoveries from within the town has been reconfirmed by the archaeological database. This is a curious blank in a region in which early Anglo-Saxon remains survive in profusion, and are regularly being increased both through excavation and other activities such as metal detecting.[16] Much of the evidence consists of grave goods from fifth- to seventh-century cemeteries, with very little suggestive of occupation sites. More importantly, perhaps, virtually all the early medieval sites and artefacts have been found on higher and drier land to the south and east of Sandwich, where the ground was probably more conducive to settlement than was the low-lying Alluvium on which most of medieval Sandwich lies. In view of the lack of physical remains, the search for earliest Sandwich has had to depend largely on critical evaluation of the available documentary evidence, with the resultant suggestion of a site for a possible early medieval settlement or trading centre outside the area later enclosed by the town defences (Chaps 2.3.5, 2.4). This suggestion could be tested only by detailed excavation of the earliest occupation levels on a number of sizeable sites across the town and east of Mill Wall. This was far beyond the terms of reference of the present study, although the close contour and geological surveys carried out for the project have suggested some likely areas that could be targeted in the future.

At present, the quantities and types of data provided by archaeological interventions in Sandwich are not in themselves sufficient to reconstruct its history and development, but by combining them with close-contour surveys of the town and its surroundings, information from excavations in the hinterland, and documentary and cartographic sources, a totally new view of medieval Sandwich emerged. The contours in the walled area have been used to establish the sequence of settlement on the Thanet Beds and Alluvium, these subsoils often being confirmed by archaeology, and also to suggest where the south bank of the river Stour may have run before it became more formalised through reclamation.

The multidisciplinary approach and the principle of viewing Sandwich in its geographical area, and not just as a discrete unit, has also been rewarding. Previous historically based research into Sandwich has focused on the walled town, whereas archaeological writing, particularly by Tatton-Brown, has concentrated on

Sandwich's early, pre-wall, centuries. The two approaches have not been coordinated. The current project has attempted to do that, one of the by-products being an increased awareness of Sandwich's connection with its hinterland. Roman roads and early medieval routes ran to the banks of the river Stour, where the original settlement was founded and near where the medieval town subsequently developed. In addition, the combined use of disciplines has shown that the castle was an integral feature in the townscape until the fourteenth century, when Mill Wall cut it off from the urban scene, and remained a significant royal presence until the sixteenth. Any map of medieval Sandwich should therefore include it.

There have been significant benefits from integrating archaeology and topography with buildings and documentary history. The pre-Conquest date of St Clement's church has been cited as one strand of evidence for the early development of the east part of the town, and its architectural features, combined with an analysis of the contours and geology, street formation, parish boundaries and documentary evidence, clearly reveal the importance of the east end of the town throughout the eleventh and twelfth centuries. Furthermore, the date and form of all three churches provide almost the only material evidence of the town's prosperity in the twelfth century. The twelfth-century work at St Peter's, viewed in conjunction with puzzling modifications to the street pattern at its west end, suggests significant changes to the street layout in the town centre during the twelfth century. Archaeological input into secular building development has been small, but such as there is has been combined with study of the town plan to show that plots in the town centre were probably originally larger and subdivided later. Some of these changes took place before the surviving buildings were erected, thereby giving rise to the narrow house types suggestive of a packed central area, a form of building that was perpetuated long after the prosperity of the town had declined.

The unpublished and published historical sources proved to be of exceptional interest and use for the physical history of the town. The unpublished documents were investigated in detail in the various archives mentioned in Chapter 1, and the printed versions trawled for all references to Sandwich. They were then entered in searchable databases which became invaluable tools for they enabled the members of the project to consult documentary information otherwise inaccessible to them, and thus to incorporate much local historical evidence into their research. It is worth emphasising, however, that the databases were designed specifically for this project, deliberately intended to capture data primarily relating to urban structures, with events and broad social and economic developments being included less systematically. During the course of the project this remit proved too restrictive in some cases, so the early court rolls, original town year books and treasurers' accounts were consulted again for information on occupations, but other aspects, such as government, community, economy and social structure, have been explored only in part and will benefit from future research. Thus the present publication does not aspire to be a definitive history of the town drawn from all sources; it is, rather, an attempt to write the history of Sandwich based largely on its physical features.

In the absence of published accounts of relevant archaeological interventions, most of the new evidence for the waterfront and harbour installations has been obtained from documentary sources, gathered together in the database described above. The treasurers' accounts are particularly valuable for details of structures such as harbour cranes, which were owned by the town and repaired at frequent intervals. Physical remains of such installations are seldom found through excavation, although the wooden axle from a harbour crane has been discovered in waterlogged conditions beside the quayside in Dordrecht in the Netherlands.[17] The Sandwich waterfront is likely to display similarly favourable conditions for preservation, so it is possible that some such remains may one day be discovered.

Documents and buildings together have been critical in picturing how various parts of the town were used, and illuminating a variety of issues. Both are required to explain the lack of medieval buildings in the west, to elucidate the possible function of the tiny open hall and lock-up shops on the edge of the Cornmarket, and although there can be no straightforward correlation between the medieval houses still occupied in the late sixteenth century and the dwellings described in probate inventories of the same period, studying the two together provides the best chance of understanding how houses were used at varying social levels during the fifteenth and sixteenth centuries.

As discussed above, documents and buildings may appear to provide contradictory evidence for the prosperity of the town in the late fifteenth and early sixteenth centuries, but it is hoped that these pages have shown that by using both sources the discrepancies can be reconciled. Although by the late fifteenth century Sandwich was past its peak in terms of national significance, there is evidence that it was still an important regional centre, its economy underpinned in particular by the brewing industry and the export of grain. There was still enough confidence in the future for some new houses to be erected by the well-to-do for their own use, and for many of them to develop dwellings and shops as rental properties for people whose homes have not survived from an earlier period. During the first half of the sixteenth century, however, conditions became extremely difficult for everyone, and were resolved only when the economy was reinvigorated by the introduction to the town of the Strangers and their weaving skills. This action, initiated in 1560, led directly to increased prosperity, both for the town's elite who built fine new houses and, more gradually, for lower social levels. The departure of the immigrants *c.*1640 led to Sandwich's final decline.

The town inspires fierce and understandable loyalty among its inhabitants, and its narrow streets lined by beautiful historic houses are both a revelation and instantly appealing to any visitor. Given its undoubted importance during much of the Middle Ages, it is astonishing that it is almost disregarded by the historical, archaeological and architectural literature on medieval towns. It deserves to be far better known than it is, and we hope that this book will go some way towards enabling Sandwich to take its rightful place among the towns and ports of medieval England.

APPENDIX 1

Sandwich Archaeological Sites, 1929–2007

Details taken from the database of archaeological sites compiled for the project

Published reports are cited here in bold, and may be found in the References. Copies of unpublished reports (shown here in regular typeface) are available for inspection at the offices of KCC Heritage Conservation Group or the appropriate excavation unit.

Abbreviations
Type of intervention
EX: excavation; EV: evaluation; WB: watching brief

Excavation unit
CAT: Canterbury Archaeological Trust; DAG: Dover Archaeological Group; DoE: Department of the Environment; KARU: Kent Archaeological Rescue Unit; SAG: Sandwich Archaeological Group; SEA: South-east Archaeology

Site No.	Address	Type	Dated finds	Subsoil	Top of Sub-soil (metres +OD)	Ground surface (metres +OD)	Unit	Reference
1	6 Cattle Market	WB	13C, 16C	—	below 1.44	c.2.44	DAG	KCC: Holman 1994
2	25 Cattle Market	WB	—	—	—	c.2.36	TTA	KCC: Perkins 2000
3	45 Cattle Market	EV	—	Alluvium	c.1.20	c.2.11	DAG	Parfitt 1999
4	27/29 Cattle Market	WB	15–16C	Alluvium	1.01–1.33	2.37–2.43	CAT	Parfitt 2003
5	adjoining Cattle Market, fronting The Rope Walk	EV	—	Alluvium	1.28–1.74	1.98	TTA	KCC: Boast 2003
6	Cricket Pavilion, The Butts	WB	—	Alluvium	1.47	1.77	DAG	KCC: Holman 1993
7	Delf Stream House, Delf Street	WB	—	Alluvium	c.1.20	c.1.65	DAG	KCC: Parfitt 2002c
8	Fisher Street	EX	13–14C	—	—	c. 6.30	KARU	**Philp 2002**, 138
9	Gazen Salts (a & b)	WB	—	Alluvium	2.20	2.60–2.95	CAT	KCC: Parfitt 2001a
10	Guildhall car park / 27 Moat Sole	WB	—	Alluvium	1.42	2.17	DAG	Parfitt 1993
11	32–8 Harnet Street	WB	12–13C	Blown Sand?	2.58	3.82	CAT	KCC: Parfitt 2002
12	New Inn, Harnet Street	EV	14C	Peat	2.25	3.60	TTA	KCC: Perkins and Boast 2000
13	28 High Street	EV	13C	Thanet Beds	4.27	5.59–6.29	DAG	KCC: Parfitt 2004

Site No.	Address	Type	Dated finds	Subsoil	Top of Sub-soil (metres +OD)	Ground surface (metres +OD)	Unit	Reference
14	39 High Street	WB	14–15C	—	below 5.40	6.25	DAG	KCC: Parfitt & Holman 1997
15	26 King Street	WB	16C and later	Alluvium	2.18	3.10–3.50	DAG	KCC: Parfitt 2004
16	14 Knightrider Street	WB	—	Thanet Beds?	4.50	5.75	CAT	**Houliston 1996**
17	Loop Street	EV/WB	12C, 15C	Alluvium	1.30	2.36–2.55	CAT	**Keller 1987**; KCC: Hutcheson 1993; **Hutcheson 1995; Corke 1995**
18	Manwood House, Strand Street	WB	13C	—	below 2.00	c.3.00	DAG	KCC: Jones 1992
19	8 Market Street	WB	13C and later	—	below 3.15	c.4.50	DAG	Holman 1999
20	10 Market Street	EX	10–13C	—	below 3.62	4.40–5.00	DAG	Parfitt, in prep.
21	13 Market Street	EX	13C and later	—	—	c.3.38	SAG	KCC: Southam & Trussler, c.1970
22	Mill Wall	WB	—	—	—	—	KARU	**Philp 2002**, 136
23	6 Millwall Place	WB	—	—	below 2.55	c.3.25	DAG	KCC: Holman 1995
24	18 Millwall Place	WB	—	—	below 2.82	3.72	DAG	KCC: Parfitt 2002
25	10 Moat Sole	WB	—	—	below 1.78	c.2.10	DAG	KCC: Holman 1993
26	17 Moat Sole	WB	—	Alluvium	1.22	2.17	DAG	Parfitt 2003
27	33 Moat Sole	WB	—	—	below 1.85	c.2.55	DAG	KCC: Holman 2002
28	Co-op, Moat Sole	EV	13C	Alluvium	1.00–1.40	1.80–2.20	CAT	**Herdman 1996**
29	29 New Street	WB	—	—	below 2.05	3.05	DAG	Parfitt 2003
30	38 New Street	WB	—	Alluvium	1.65	2.79–2.89	DAG	Parfitt 2003
31	56a New Street	WB	—	Alluvium	1.40–1.65	c.2.30	TTA	KCC: TTA 2002
32	84 New Street	WB	—	Alluvium	1.68	2.50	DAG	Parfitt 2001
33	Plum Orchard	EV	16–17C	Alluvium	0.27–0.43	1.57–1.91	DAG	KCC: Parfitt 2000
34	6 Potter Street	EX	9C, 13C and later	Alluvial Sand	2.62	3.88–4.45	DAG	KCC: Parfitt 2000
35	Quay Cottage, The Quay	EV	—	—	—	c.3.53	CAT	KCC: CAT 2002
36	Sandown Gate	EX	—	—	—	4.80	KARU	**KARU 1978; Tatton-Brown 1978; Philp 2002**, 135–7
37	Castle Field, Manwood Road	EX	Medieval, 17C, 18C	Thanet Beds	—	4.50	CAT	**Bennett, Blockley & Tatton-Brown 1983**
38	Sandale House, Manwood Road	EX	9C, 12C, 17C, 18C	Thanet Beds	3.25	4.50	CAT	**Stewart 2000**
39	'Bridge End', St George's Lees	WB	—	Thanet Beds	4.62	5.62	DAG	Holman 2001
40	2 St Peter's Street	EX	8–11C, 13C and later	Alluvium (?)	3.15	4.04	DAG	**Parfitt 2003**
41	24/28 St Peter's Street	EV	—	Thanet Beds	c.4.73	c.5.50	DAG	Parfitt 1993
42	34 St Peter's Street	WB	—	—	below 4.95	c.5.50	DAG	Parfitt 2001
43	Barlow's Yard, St Peter's Street	EV	Medieval and 18C	—	—	5.50–4.60	SEA CAT	KCC: Greatorex 1994; KCC: CAT 1996

Sandwich Archaeological Sites, 1929–2007

Site No.	Address	Type	Dated finds	Subsoil	Top of Sub-soil (metres +OD)	Ground surface (metres +OD)	Unit	Reference
44	41 Strand Street	EX	12–19C	Wind-blown sand	below 2.22	3.79	DAG	KCC: Parfitt 2004
45	The King's Arms, 65 Strand Street	WB	—	—	—	c.4.00	CAT	**Stewart 1999**, 26
46	66 Strand Street	EX	—	Alluvium	-0.35	c.3.00	SAG	**Southam 1980**
47	67 Strand Street	WB	—	—	below 3.50	c.4.00	DAG	KCC: Parfitt 1997
48	72 Strand Street	EV	—	—	below 1.35	3.05	DAG	KCC: Parfitt 1997
49	76 Strand Street	EX	—	—	below 0.23	3.05	DAG	KCC: Parfitt 1997
50	80 Strand Street	EX	—	—	below 2.26	3.26–3.46	DAG	KCC: Parfitt 1997
51	87 Strand Street	WB	13–18C	—	below 2.50	c.4.00	DAG	KCC: Parfitt 1997
52	Aynsley Court, Strand Street	EX	—	Alluvium	—	3.25–3.45	KARU	**Philp 2002**, 136–7
53	Guestling Mill, Strand Street	EV	—	—	below 3.50	c.4.00	CAT	Allen 1997
54	Town Moat, The Bulwarks (ship)	EX	14C	Alluvium	below -2.75	1.84	SAG KARU	**Youngs & Clark 1981; Philp 2002,** 136; **Milne 2004**
55	6 The Butchery	EV	12–13C	—	below 2.80	3.80	CAT	**Willson 2005**
56	11 Harnet Street	WB	17C and later	—	—	c.3.75	DAG	KCC: Holman 1994
57	The Butchery	WB	—	—	below 3.70	c.4.00	DAG	KCC: Holman 1998
58	The Rope Walk	WB	—	Alluvium	—	c.2.00	KARU	**Philp 2002**, 136
59	19–21 Upper Strand Street	WB	13–14C, 16–17C	Thanet Beds?	below 4.09	4.96	CAT	Parfitt 2001; **Parfitt 2003**
60	1 Vicarage Lane	WB	—	—	below 2.35	c.3.20	CAT	KCC: Linklater 2004
61	Whitefriars	WB	—	Alluvium	—	2.20–2.50	KARU	**Parfitt 1993**
62	Whitefriars	EX	12–14C	Alluvium	1.33–1.50	2.20–2.50	KARU	**Parfitt 1993**
63	Whitefriars Meadow, car park	WB	—	—	—	c.2.50	DAG	KCC: Holman 2002
64	Whitefriars Meadow, Flats	WB	—	—	—	c.2.50		**Rigold 1965**
65	Gate House Cottage Sandown Road	WB	—	—	below 4.40	c.5.20	TTA	KCC: Boast 2001
66	28 Fisher Street	EV	9C, 13C and later	Thanet Beds	5.00	6.58	CAT	KCC: Parfitt 2005
67	Strand Street, near Barbican	WB	—	—	—	3.00–4.36		**Philp 2002**, 136–7
68	Loop Street	WB	—	—	—	c.2.85		**Philp 2002**, 137
69	Town Moat, The Bulwarks	WB	19C	—	—	c.1.85	DAG	KCC: Parfitt 1992
70	Canterbury Gate	EX	Probably 14C or 15C	—	—	—		Clapham 1930
71	Knightrider Street, pipe trench	WB	15–16C	Sand?	5.72?	6.30–6.85	CAT	KCC: CAT 2005
72	Strand Street	WB	—	Alluvium	—	c.3.16		**Southam 1980**, 309
73	26 Upper Strand Street	WB	—	—	below 5.81	6.13	CAT	KCC: Parfitt 2005
74	Fisher Gate, Quay Lane	WB	—	—	below 2.32	3.15	CAT	KCC: Parfitt 2005

Site No.	Address	Type	Dated finds	Subsoil	Top of Sub-soil (metres +OD)	Ground surface (metres +OD)	Unit	Reference
75	'Sandworth', St George's Lees	WB	—	Thanet Beds	3.36	4.06	CAT	KCC: CAT 2005
76	14 Knight rider Street (rear of)	EV	—	Thanet Beds	5.90	6.88	CAT	KCC: CAT 2006
77	Luckboat House, 52 King Street	WB	—	—	below 2.07	3.07	CAT	KCC: CAT 2005
78	St Mary's Churchyard	WB	—	—	below 2.00	3.72	CAT	KCC: Parfitt 2006
79	37–43 Cattle Market (rear of)	EV	13–14C	Alluvium	0.96–1.69	2.00–2.45	CAT	KCC: Parfitt 2006
80	Land between Knightriders & The Gate House, Sandown Road	WB	12–16C	Thanet Beds	4.28–4.62	5.22–5.74	CAT	Parfitt, in prep.
81	3 Millwall Place	WB	—	Thanet Beds	c.3.45	3.75	CAT	KCC: Parfitt 2007

APPENDIX 2

Sandwich houses (municipal and religious buildings excluded) that appear on the maps

Those listed have been recorded or are known through publication or illustration. They do not necessarily constitute all houses of these dates in the town; in particular, no attempt was made to investigate and record all buildings dating to c.1600 or the early seventeenth century. All buildings above Level 1 have an archived report as well as the drawings listed.

Copies of the original buildings survey reports and drawings (and some for later buildings surveyed in the town) are held in Sandwich Guildhall Archive, indexed by street and name or number.

House No.	Address	Original materials	Dates of main phases	Type*	Level of drawn record#
	Bowling Street (Serles Lane)				
1	6, 8 Bowling Street	Timber-framed	Late 16C	D	Level 3 1P, 1S
2	7 Bowling Street (Richborough House)	Stone, timber, brick	?13C wall; late 16C	D	Level 3 1P
	The Butchery				
3	1 The Butchery	Timber-framed	Mid-/late 15C	D + S	Level 3 1P, 1S
4	3 The Butchery	Stone; timber-framed	c.1300 wall; late 16C	?	Level 1
5	17 The Butchery (38 Harnet Street)	Timber-framed	Early 15C	D	Level 3 1P, 1S
	Cattle Market (Cornmarket)				
6	2, 4 Cattle Market	Timber-framed	1601	D	Level 3 1P, 2S
7	8 Cattle Market	Timber-framed	Mid-/late 15C	D + S	Level 3 1P, 2S, D
8	9 Cattle Market	Timber-framed	Mid-/late 15C	D + S?	Level 3 1P
9	The Star Inn (demolished)	Timber-framed	Late 16C	Inn	Level 1
	The Chain				
10	3 The Chain	Timber-framed	Late 16C	D	Level 1
11	7 The Chain	Timber-framed	Late 16C	D	Level 1
	Church Street St Clement				
12	10 Church Street St Clement	Timber-framed	Late 14C	D	Level 2
	Church Street St Mary				
13	19, 21 Church Street St Mary	Timber-framed	Late 16C	D	Level 2
14	22 Church Street St Mary	Stone; timber-framed	?13C wall; mid-/late 15C	D	Level 3 1P, D
15	27 Church Street St Mary	Timber-framed	Early/mid-16C; late 16C	D	Level 3 1P
	Delf Street				
16	17 Delf Street	Timber-framed	c.1500	D	Level 3 1P, 1S
	Dover Road				
17	2 St Bart's, Dover Road	Timber-framed	Mid-/late 15C	D	Level 3 1P, 1S
	Fisher Street				
18	1 Fisher Street	Timber-framed	Late 16C	D	Level 3 1P, D
19	3 Fisher Street	Timber-framed	Early 16C	D	Level 3 1P, 1S

House No.	Address	Original materials	Dates of main phases	Type*	Level of drawn record#
20	7 Fisher Street	Timber-framed	Mid-/late 15C; early/mid-16C	D	Level 3 1P, 1S
21	9 Fisher Street	Timber-framed	Late 16/early 17C	D	Level 2
22	13 Fisher Street	Timber-framed	Late 16/early 17C	D	Level 2
23	24 Fisher Street (George and Dragon PH)	Timber-framed	Late 16/early 17C; 17C	D	Level 2
24	23 Fisher Street	Timber-framed	Mid-/late 15C; early/mid-16C	D	Level 3 1P
	Harnet Street				
25	5, 7 Harnet Street	Stone; timber-framed	?c.1300 wall; c.1400, later rebuilt	St.?	Level 2 1P
26	11 Harnet Street	Timber-framed	Late 16C	D	Level 2
27	29 Harnet Street, garden walls	Stone and flint	c.1300 walls	D?	Level 1
28	29 Harnet Street, Haven House	Stone; timber-framed	?c.1300 cellar; c.1400; c.1500; early/mid-16C	D	Level 4 1P, 1S, D
29	31 Harnet Street	Timber-framed	15C	D	Level 2
30	30, 32, 34, Harnet Street	Timber-framed	Early/mid-15C	D	Level 3 1P 1S D
	High Street (Guildhall Street)				
31	2 High Street (N bay Crispin Inn, S end of Barbican)	Timber-framed	15C	?	Level 3, 2P
32	8 High Street (Admiral Owen PH)	Timber-framed	15C	D	Level 1
33	11, 13 High Street	Timber-framed	Early 16C	D	Level 3 1P, 1P, 2S
34	17, 19 High Street	Timber-framed	c.1500; late 16C	D	Level 2 1P
35	18 High Street (Masonic Hall, formerly Bell and Anchor Inn, demolished)	Timber-framed	?14C	D	Level 1
36	20 High Street	Stone; timber-framed	c.1300	D	Level 31P, 1S, D
37	25 High Street	Timber-framed	c.1500	St.	Level 3 2P 1S
38	34 High Street	Timber-framed	c.1500	D	Level 3 1P 2S
39	42 High Street	Timber-framed	Early 16C	D	Level 1
40	57 High Street	Timber-framed	Late 16C	D	Level 1
	King Street (Luckboat)				
41	1 King Street	Timber-framed	c.1500	S + St.	Level 2 1P, 1S
42	3 King Street	Timber-framed	c.1500	S + St.	Level 2 1P, 1S
43	4 King Street	Timber-framed	Early 15C	D	Level 3 1P, 1S, D
44	6 King Street	Timber-framed	c.1400	St.	Level 3 1P, 1S, D
45	21 King Street	Timber-framed	15C; late 16C	D	Level 3 1P 3S, D
46	21 King Street, Outbuilding	Timber-framed	15C	St.	Level 3 1P, 2S, D
47	24 King Street	Timber-framed	15C	D	Level 3 1P, 2S
48	27, 29 King Street (St Peter's rectory)	Timber-framed	c.1500	D	Level 3 1P, 2S, D
49	38 King Street	Timber-framed	Early/mid-15C	D	Level 3 2P, 3S, D
50	42 King Street	Timber-framed	?Late 16C	D	Level 1
51	52 King Street	Timber-framed	Early 17C	D	Level 3 1P, 1S
	Loop Street				
52	The Old Cottage, Loop Street (no. 21)	Timber-framed	15C	D	Level 1
	Market Street (Fishmarket)				
53	4 Market Street	Timber-framed	Late 15C	D + S?	Level 2 1S
54	5 Market Street	Timber-framed	15C	D + S?	Level 1
55	6 Market Street	Timber-framed	c.1400; late 15C	D + S?	Level 3 1P, 1S
56	7 Market Street	Timber-framed	Early/mid-15C	D + S?	Level 3 1P, 2S, D

House No.	Address	Original materials	Dates of main phases	Type*	Level of drawn record#
57	8 Market Street	Timber-framed	Early/mid-15C	D + S?	Level 2 1P
58	10 Market Street	Timber-framed	Mid-/late 15C	D + S?	Level 3
59	13 Market Street (Library)	Stone	14C remains	?	Level 3 1P, 1S, D
60	14, 16 Market Street	Timber-framed	Late 15C	D + S?	Level 2 1S
	Millwall Place				
61	3 Millwall Place (demolished and rebuilt)	Timber-framed	Early 16C	Ind.	Austin & Sweetinburgh 2007
	New Street				
62	14 New Street	Timber-framed	15C; early 17C	D	Level 3 1P
63	16, 18 New Street	Timber-framed	Late 16C	D	Level 3 2P
64	70 New Street	Timber-framed	Mid-/late 15c	D	Level 3 2P, 3S
65	72 New Street	Timber-framed	Mid-/late 15C	D	Level 3 1P, 1S
	No Name Street				
66	The No Name Shop (formerly 11 Cattle Market)	Timber-framed	Early/mid-15C	Ind. + St.	Level 3 2P, 2S
	Paradise Row				
67	Paradise Row (corner of Strand St)	Stone	13C, reset doorway	?	Level 1
	Potter Street (Cok Lane)				
68	7 Potter Street	Timber-framed	Early/mid-15C	D	Level 3 1P, 2S
	St Peter's Street (Love Lane)				
69	16 St Peter's Street	Timber-framed	Early 17C	D	Level 3 1P
70	18 20 St Peter's Street	Timber-framed	c.1400; 17C	D	Level 3 1P, 1S, D
71	22 St Peter's Street	Timber-framed	Late 16/early 17C	D	Level 1
72	30, 30A St Peter's Street	Timber-framed	Mid-/late 15C	D	Level 3 1S
73	50 St Peter's Street	Stone	Late 13C	D	Level 3 2P, 1S
	Strand Street				
74	3 Strand Street	Stone; timber-framed	?c.1300 wall; c.1500	D + St.	Level 3 2P, 1S, D
75	5 Strand Street	Timber-framed	c.1500	D	Level 3 2P, 1S, D
76	7 Strand Street	Stone; timber-framed	?c.1300 wall; 17C	D	Level 2 1P, D
77	11 Strand Street	Timber-framed	Early 16C; 17C	D	Level 3 1P
78	11 Strand Street, rear (ruin in Three Kings' Yard)	Stone	Late 13C range	D + St.?	Level 3 2P, D
79	13, 15 Strand Street	Timber-framed	c.1500	Inn? + S	Level 3 2P, 1S, 1E, D
80	19, 21 Strand Street	Timber-framed	Mid-/late 15C	D	Level 3 1P, 1S
81	23 Strand Street	Timber-framed	?14C; early 16C	D + S	Level 3 1P, 1S, D
82	27 Strand Street	Stone	c.1300 undercroft	St. + ?	Level 1 1P
83	33 Strand Street	Timber-framed	Early 14C	D + S	Level 3 2P 2S 1E
84	34 Strand Street	Timber-framed	15C	D?	Level 2 1P
85	39 Strand Street	Stone; timber-framed	?13C; 1334	D + S + St.	Level 3 3P 2S
86	41 Strand Street	Timber-framed	1330s	D + S +St.?	Level 3 1P 2S
87	42 Strand Street	Timber-framed	c.1500	D	Level 3 1P, 1S
88	46 Strand Street (The King's Lodging)	Timber-framed	15C	D + inn?	Level 1
89	57 Strand Street	Stone	c.1300	?	Level 1
90	62, 62a Strand Street (The Long House)	Timber-framed	1562–78	D	Level 3 1P 2S
91	63, 65 Strand Street (King's Arms PH)	Timber-framed	1592	D	Level 1
92	71 Strand Street	Timber-framed	Mid-/late 15C	D	Level 3 1P 1S
93	91, 93 Strand Street (Manwood School)	Brick	1564	School	Level 3 2P

House No.	Address	Original materials	Dates of main phases	Type*	Level of drawn record#
	Upper Strand Street				
94	15, 17 Upper Strand Street	Stone; timber-framed	*c.*1300; *c.*1500	D	Level 3 2P, D
95	19, 21, 23 Upper Strand Street	Timber-framed	Mid-/late 15C	D + ?	Level 3, 2P
96	22, 24 Upper Strand Street	Timber-framed	Mid-15C	D	Level 3 2P, 2S, D
97	25 Upper Strand Street	Timber-framed	Mid-/late 15C	D	Level 2 1P
98	32, 34 Upper Strand Street	Timber-framed	1520s	D	Level 3 2P, 1S
	Vicarage Lane				
99	3 Vicarage Lane	Stone	13C doorway	D	Level 1
	St Mary's churchyard				
100	East wall, St Mary's churchyard	Stone	13C wall	?	Level 1

* Type: the identified functions of the building: D = Domestic; Ind. = Industrial; S = Shop or workshop; St. = Storage; ? = uncertain.

\# Level of drawn record: the levels refer to the English Heritage levels of record published in Menuge 2006. The number of drawings is indicated by P = Plans, S = Sections, E = Elevations, D = Details

Notes

Chapter 1

1. Lincoln: Jones, Stocker and Vince 2003; St Albans: Niblett and Thompson 2005.
2. Sandwich Survey Reports 9 and 10.
3. Sandwich Survey Report 5.
4. Sandwich Survey Report 1.
5. Sandwich Survey Report 10.
6. Conzen 1968 and literature cited in Palliser, Slater and Dennison 2000.
7. Dates were obtained for 39 Strand Street (House 85) and 62 Strand Street (House 90), but only for a secondary phase of 33 Strand Street (House 83).
8. Pearson 1994, 148–61.
9. Menuge 2006.
10. For example, *Itinerary*; *Perambulation*; *Britannia*, Kilburne 1659; Lewis 1736.
11. EKAC: Sa/ZT 14, 1–35.
12. Gardiner 1954.
13. Tatton-Brown 1984, 1988a.
14. Butcher 1977; Croft 1997a, 1997b.
15. Sweetinburgh 2004a; Richardson 1999, 2003; Ollerenshaw 1990.
16. Backhouse 1991, 1995; Andrewes and Zell 2002.
17. Martin 1974, 1979, 1980; Wanostrocht 1993, n.d.; Richardson 2004.
18. Sandwich Survey Reports 2, 3 and 8.
19. Boys 1792, facing p. 869; Boys thought the Worth site was a Roman lighthouse or watchtower, but it later proved to be a Celtic temple: Klein 1928.
20. Hardman and Stebbing 1942, 42; Parfitt 2001.
21. Roach Smith 1882; Dowker 1900, 111; Laker 1917, 14.
22. Dowker 1884; Rolfe's work proved invaluable to later excavators: Bushe-Fox 1926.
23. Holman 1999.
24. Published by Boys in 1792, facing p. 868.
25. Matson 1961, 184; Gibson and Wright 1988, 12, 122.
26. Gatty 1883.
27. By the Society of Antiquaries of London; Bushe-Fox 1926.
28. Most physical traces of Stonar were quarried away between 1897 and 1974 and all that survives is its south-eastern corner (Scheduled Ancient Monument, Kent 204).
29. Hardman and Stebbing 1942; Dunning 1941.
30. Macpherson-Grant 1991.
31. Ogilvie 1960.
32. By-pass: Bennett 1978; Parfitt 1980, 1982; Archer's Low: Holman 2005, 10–13.
33. Rolfe 1852, 1853.
34. Parkin 1984; his material is deposited in the Sandwich Guildhall Archive.
35. Parkin's article is not mentioned in Quiney 2003.
36. Tatton-Brown 1993.
37. Chichester 1887; Bulmer-Thomas 1959, 1960, 1962.
38. Tricker 2002.

Chapter 2

1. Shephard-Thorn 1988; Sandwich Survey Report 4.
2. High tides in the river Stour at Sandwich generally reach an approximate height of 2.5m above OD, occasionally +3m OD and very exceptionally +3.5m OD. Were it not for modern flood barriers, much of the town would still be subjected to flooding at very high tides.
3. The numbering of the Roman roads follows Margary 1955.
4. Hicks 1998, 92–3.
5. Klein 1928; Holman 2005, 8–10.
6. Spurr 2005.
7. *HE*, Bk I: XXV, 72.
8. *HE*, Bk V: VIII, 474.
9. EKAC: Sa/LC 1; Sa/AC 1, f. 185v.
10. Lewis 1744, 81–2.
11. Rickman 1840, 399.
12. Walker 1927; Hardman and Stebbing 1940, 1941, 1942; Ward 1943.
13. Halliwell 1981; Ogilvie 1983; Halliwell and Parfitt 1985.
14. Robinson and Cloet 1953; So 1963, 164–96; Shephard-Thorn 1988, 37; LVRG 2006, fig. 6.
15. *Life of Wilfrid*, XIII, 28.
16. *HE*, Bk I: XXV, 72.
17. Brooks 1994, 21.
18. From King Eadberht II of Kent to the abbess of the convent of Minster-in-Thanet; Sawyer 1968, no. 29; Kelly 1995, no. 53.
19. Brookes 2007, 12–18, fig. 3.
20. *AS Charters* (E), *s. a.* 851; early medieval sea battles were fought in inshore waters where vessels could be blockaded and boarded: Pullen-Appleby 2005, 110, 115.
21. *AS Charters* (E), *s. a.* 1009.
22. Lewis 1736, 8–9; Lewis 1744, 80–82.
23. Battely 1745, 6–7.
24. Seymour 1776, 700.
25. *Ammianus*, Bk XXVII: 8, 6, p. 5.
26. Cunliffe 1968, 251.
27. Blockley *et al.* 1995, 19.
28. Bushe-Fox 1949, 80.
29. Richardson 2005, II: 3.
30. Augustine and his band of followers supposedly landed there in 597, with the saint's miraculously preserved footprint being kept for many years as a sacred relic in a chapel on the site; *Thorne*, 4.

31. Bushe-Fox 1928, 34–40.
32. Rigold 1968a.
33. Parsons 1994, 316–17.
34. Tweddle, Biddle and Kjølby-Biddle 1995, 168–71.
35. Richardson 2005, map 10.
36. We are very grateful to the late Dr Margaret Gelling for commenting on this section.
37. *Life of Wilfrid*, XIII, 28; Kirby 1983; *Oxford Dictionary of National Biography*, 52.423.
38. Reynolds 1977, 18; and see also Coates 1999, 91.
39. His ship would have resembled that reconstructed from the Sutton Hoo ship burial (Gifford and Gifford 1996, figs 2 and 8) or the Kvalsund ship excavated in Norway (Greenhill 1995, 181–2).
40. Sandwice, Sondwic, *c*.720; Sandwic, 851; Sandwich, 993; Sanduuich, *c*.963; Sanduuic, 1006; Sanduich, 1015.
41. Clarke and Ambrosiani 1991, 15–23. See also Hodges 1982, 67–74; Hodges 1988, 5–7; Coates 1999; Hill and Cowie 2001; Ulmschneider and Pestell 2003, 1.
42. But see Schütte 1976, 15–18, 78–81, 196–7.
43. Coates 1999, 87, 89–90.
44. Verhulst 1999, 45–7.
45. Reynolds 1977, 24–7; Hodges 1982, 67–74; Hill and Cowie 2001; Pestell and Ulmschneider 2003.
46. Quentovic: Hill *et al*. 1990; Clarke and Ambrosiani 1991, 16–18; Coupland 2003; Dorestad: van Es and Verwers 1980, 2009; Verwers 1988.
47. Including Sandwich, Fordwich, *Sandtun*, Sarre and Seasalter in Kent: Hill and Cowie 2001, Appendix 2.
48. Rumble 2001.
49. Tatton-Brown 1984, 1988a; Holman 2001.
50. Stewart 2000, 69.
51. See references to Ipswich, London, Southampton and York in Hill and Cowie 2001.
52. Bennett, Blockley and Tatton-Brown 1983, 246.
53. *Symeon*, 3–10; the reliability of the account is questioned by Gransden 1974, 149.
54. Wallenberg 1931, 73.
55. Hawkes 1979, 95; 1982, 75; for Eastry as 'an early Saxon or Jutish estate-centre', see Everitt 1986, 8, 73, maps 3, 101.
56. Everitt 1986, 194–5; Blair 2005, 254.
57. Arnold 1982.
58. Parfitt 1999; Parfitt and Sweetinburgh 2009, 313–14.
59. Sawyer 1968, nos. 128 (for 788), 1264 (for 811), 1636 (for 979), 914 (for 1001), 1047 (for 1042); Parfitt and Sweetinburgh 2009, 314–17.
60. Kilburne 1659, 237–41; Boys 1792, 327, 839; Hasted 1797–1801, VIII, 197.
61. Kilburne 1659, 238–9.
62. *Chronica*, 100; *Thorne*, 233–6; Jenkins 1878; Rollason 1979; Hollis 1998.
63. Rollason 1982 and personal communication.
64. Parfitt 1999; Parfitt and Sweetinburgh 2009.
65. Everson and Stocker 2003.
66. Ogilvie 1960.
67. CKS: S/EK/Ch 10b/A10.
68. Shephard-Thorn 1988; Fordham and Green 1973.
69. Holman 2005, 10–13. An article on the significance of Archer's Low and the development of early medieval Sandwich is in preparation.
70. For recent discussions of early medieval Sandwich, see Tatton-Brown 1984, 1988a; Clarke 2005a, 2005b.
71. For example, Andrews, Birbeck and Stoodley 2005, 204; for Continental examples, see Clarke and Ambrosiani 1991.

Chapter 3

1. Reynolds 1977, ix.
2. Astill 2006, 233.
3. This idea was proposed by Justin Croft in a talk at the University of Kent, Canterbury, in 1998.
4. For the importance of the building of the first stone churches in towns, see Astill 2000, 41.
5. Parfitt, in preparation.
6. Boys 1792, 728; Hasted 1797–1801, X, 154; Tatton-Brown 1984, 19.
7. Sawyer 1968, nos. 808 and 1636.
8. Brooks 1984, 293.
9. *ASC* (E), *s. a*. 1009.
10. *ASC* (A), *s. a*. 991.
11. *ASC* (E), *s. a*. 1014.
12. *Encomium*, 20–21; Stafford 1997, 28–40.
13. Brooks 1984, 297.
14. *ASC* (C), *s. a*. 1044; *ASC* (E), *s. a*. 1045; *ASC* (C, D, E), *s. a*. 1049; *ASC* (C, D, E), *s. a*. 1052; Rodger 1996, 649.
15. We are grateful to Paul Barnwell, Howard Jones, Hugh Richmond and Tim Tatton-Brown, each of whom visited St Clement's and contributed to discovering the form of the eleventh-century church. Hugh Richmond was the first to spot the fact that St Clement's still contained evidence of a pre-Conquest stone church.
16. Tim Tatton-Brown, personal communication; Tatton-Brown 1990, 73–4. Pieces of Marquise stone were also discovered in the 1996 excavations of the castle; their original function is unknown (Stewart 2000, 68).
17. Napier 1908. For Edward's visits to Sandwich, see *ASC* (C), *s. a*. 1044; *ASC* (E), *s. a*. 1045; *ASC* (C, D, E), *s. a*. 1049; *ASC* (C, D, E), *s. a*. 1052. Gatch 1993, 229, and Baxter 2007, 269n, suggest that 1052 is the most likely date.
18. Baxter 2007, 1–4, 154n.
19. Gatch 1993, 243.
20. Gatch 1993, 243–51.
21. Taylor and Taylor 1965, 94–6, 214–17; Fernie 1983, 113, 115; Tatton-Brown 1988b, 110; Gem 2004, 295.
22. *Michael of Rhodes*, f. 125b.
23. Everitt 1986, 232–3; Tatton-Brown 1988b, 109; Tatton-Brown 2006a, 25 and fig. 1; Brooks 2006, 16.
24. Crawford 2008, 204–8.
25. Crawford 2006, 278.
26. Tatton-Brown 1988b, 110; Blair 2005, 355.
27. Gem 2004, 324–55.
28. *EHD I*, Athelstan II, 14, 14.2.
29. Holman 1990, 194–5; Metcalf 1998, 54.
30. Freeman 1985, 518, lists only thirty-nine coins.
31. Holman 1989, 186.
32. Brooks and Kelly, forthcoming, no. 151 (amending the judgement in Brooks 1984, 292–4).
33. For example *Early Charters*, nos. 27–9; *AS Charters*, nos. 158–60; Sawyer 1968, charter no. 959.
34. Northmouth is recorded as an anchorage in 1049 and an exit from the Wantsum Channel in 1052; *ASC* (C), *s. a*. 1049; *ASC* (E), *s. a*. 1052.
35. EKAC: Sa/LC 1; for a translation and discussion, see Clarke, forthcoming.
36. Brooks 1984, 298; Brooks and Kelly, forthcoming, no. 164; Sawyer 1968, no. 1467.
37. Kelly 1995, xx.
38. Kelly 1995, xx.
39. For details of the complex history of Sandwich between 1037 and 1086, see *Regesta*, nos. 69 (1a), 71, 72.

40. *DB Kent*, f. 1.
41. *DB Kent*, f. 11.
42. *DM*, 89.
43. Eales 1992, 32; the territorial dispute between the two houses culminated in 1127.
44. Reynolds 1984, 306; Reynolds 1998, 210; Dyer 1985, 91–2; Holt 2000, 83.
45. Both the thirty and the thirty-two were included in the figures used by Dyer 2000, 752.
46. Darby and Campbell 1962, 550, 553, 554.
47. Dyer 2000, 752.
48. *DM*, 89.
49. Reynolds 1998, 215.
50. *DM*, 89; *DB Kent*, f. 3.
51. *DB Kent*, ff. 1a, 2.
52. *DB Kent*, f. 1a; Reynolds 1987, 307; Reynolds 1998, 212.
53. Eales 1992, 32.
54. Ward 1933, 84, 86; Tatton-Brown 1988b 114.
55. *DM*, 89.
56. CCA: DCc/Lit. MS E19; Ward 1933, 84; Tatton-Brown 1988b, n. 2; Eales 1992, 6.
57. Kelly 1995, xix–xx; Williams 1997, 58; Eales 1992, 32.
58. We are grateful to Paul Barnwell for this suggestion.
59. Tatton-Brown 1980, 214.
60. Late eighteenth-century signs for parish boundaries are marked on several buildings in the town. The outlines on the maps have been taken from nineteenth-century OS maps. Parish acreages are given in *VCH* Kent 1974b, 370. See Campbell 1975, 23, for the warning that parish boundaries can change; in Sandwich a minor change to the St Peter's/St Mary's boundary on the west side of Harnet Street was recorded in 1632 (CCA: U3/173/6/46).
61. A small detached portion of Worth parish lies to the south-west of St Mary's parish, carved out of it or of Woodnesborough parish; the reason for this has not been discovered.
62. Baker and Holt, 2004, 240–41.
63. Rogers 1972, 63; the same was true in Norwich: Campbell 1975, 4, 23–4; Ayers 2004b, 4.
64. Reynolds 1984, 81–90; Morris 1989, 169–71, 222; Baker and Holt 1998, 210; Barrow 2000, 140.
65. CCA: DCc/Reg. G, f. 50v; we are grateful to Barney Sloane for drawing this reference to our attention.
66. Boys 1792, 295.
67. Milne 2003, 45, fig. 17.
68. Fenwick 1978, 181; Milne 2003, 43, fig. 15; personal communication Keith Wade.
69. Parfitt, in preparation.
70. *Laws*, no. 254.
71. Aston and Bond 1976, 87–9; Palliser, Slater and Dennison 2000, 167.
72. Morris 1989, 212–13; Barrow 1992, 89–93.
73. Hutcheson 1995; Corke 1995.
74. Philp 2002, 137; unfortunately, no dating evidence was published.
75. See also OS map, 1st edn, 1872, sheet XLVII.6.
76. EKAC: Sa/P5/3.
77. CCA: DCc/Reg. H, f. 15v.
78. The Great Cockey stream at Norwich was also never led through pipes and was not conduited until the nineteenth century: Ayers 2003, 11; London acquired its first conduit for piped water in 1260: Lewis 2004, 39.
79. LVRG 2006, 46–7.
80. As in 'Rhee Wall' in Romney Marsh; Eddison 2002.
81. For instances of the medieval modification of river channels, see Rhodes 2007.
82. Rippon 2002, 91.
83. Today, the top of the water in the Delf is up to 1m below ground surface.
84. Watercourses were controlled and diverted for the benefit of religious houses as early as the ninth century, both on the Continent (Wijntjes 1982, 196 and 199) and slightly later in England, where *c*.960 Abbot Æthelwold of Abingdon had a drain dug from the abbey's reredorter to the river (*Chronicon*, 278).
85. Keene 2001, 174, 176.
86. Ayers 2004a, 32; Ayers 2004b, 7–9 and Map 1.
87. Urry 1986; Woodman 1992.
88. Morris 1989, 193, discusses similarly jagged boundaries at Colchester, and suggests that the outer areas, where the boundaries are straighter, were less built up, or remained in undivided ownership when the parishes were established.

Chapter 4

1. *Laws*, no. 254.
2. Murray 1935, 6, 11–15, 233–4; Campbell 2000, 66–7, 69.
3. *Pipe Roll* 11 Henry II, 108.
4. *CCR* iii, 221.
5. Murray 1935, 11–12.
6. Murray 1935, 19–20.
7. CCA: Reg. H, f. 15v.
8. Canterbury had a guild in the ninth century, and a merchants' or burgesses' guild in the late eleventh century; Brooks 1984, 28–9; a *gilhalla* at Dover was recorded in 1086: *DB Kent*, f. 1a.
9. Reynolds 1977, 80–84; Reynolds 1998, 212.
10. Members of the assembly were described as 'barons' in 1205; *Rot. Litt. Claus.* I, 29.
11. Tait 1936, 291; Campbell 2000, 71.
12. The Burgate in Canterbury has been a gate in the accepted sense of an entrance through walls since Romano-British times. The street leading to it was called Burhstraet in AD 1002; Frere, Stow and Bennett 1982, 34–40.
13. Brooks 1984, 293.
14. *Thorne*, 59; *Laws*, no. 137.
15. In 1037 a wharf in Sandwich Haven had protected vessels against rough water.
16. In 1579 the town experienced an earthquake that was said to 'shake and cleave fower arches in St Maries church' (Boys 1792, 695–6). The church was no doubt weakened by this event, and its state was causing concern by the mid-seventeenth century. After the tower collapsed in 1668, the building was reported to be a ruinous heap (Bulmer Thomas 1960, 38, 41).
17. This was also noted by Robertson 1886, lv.
18. Levels taken within the church show that the bases of the twelfth-century structure vary between 3.38m and 3.45m OD. Given the build up of the ground outside, and the troubles from collapsed masonry and rebuilding after the Middle Ages, there is no reason to doubt that the surviving bases all belong to one campaign of construction.
19. Robertson 1886, lv; Chichester 1887, 340–43.
20. Hoey and Thurlby 2004, 175.
21. Bulmer-Thomas 1959, 36; Newman 1987, 448.
22. Kahn 1991, 107.
23. Fernie 2000, 228.
24. Bennett and Tatton-Brown 1992.
25. Chichester 1887, 341. Unfortunately, the architect, Joseph Clarke, who undertook the reseating, left only a plan of what was there (now in Lambeth Palace Library), and no notes of what he found.
26. We are grateful to Howard Jones for explaining exactly how this could have been achieved.

27. Tatton-Brown (1993) thought that the upper two stages, which are of sandstone and rubble on the interior, were additions, but since the external detailing is all of a piece, and the interior of these two stages was not visible from below, it seems more likely that the tower was constructed in a single campaign, even if over a period of time.
28. Dating of the Canterbury towers is a little uncertain. The towers are not shown on the famous waterworks drawing commissioned by Wibert, which is generally agreed to have been made *c.*1160. They are, however, illustrated on a seal of the priory, first used in 1158. The implication is that the towers had been decided upon by the late 1150s, but may not have been built until a few years later. Heslop 1982, 94; Kahn 1991, 102, 114; Fernie 2000, 142; Tatton-Brown 2006b, 92.
29. Kahn 1991, 114, 120–27.
30. Kahn 1991, 124–5.
31. Morris 1989, 287.
32. Morris 1989, 279, 282–3, 290–91.
33. Mary Berg, personal communication.
34. St Mary's and St Clement's came to be held by the archdeacon of Canterbury, but it is unknown at what date this occurred.
35. Rosser 1988a, 32; Morris 1989, 285–6; Draper 2006, 50, 178–9.
36. Reynolds 1984, 81–90; Davidson Cragoe 2005, 39; Draper 2006, 179–80. Details of mid-twelfth-century lay involvement in a London church are discussed by Brooke and Keir 1975, 132–3.
37. Barnwell 2004, 55–6.
38. Reynolds 1984, 91–2.
39. *Thorne*, 543.
40. Smith 1943, 14–17.
41. Gardiner 1954, 41.
42. BL: Add. MS 33511, ff. 60–64, 73–7 (1585); EKAC: Sa/ZB4/11 (1586); the second document, which is a town treasurer's account, mentions work on the schoolhouse, and payment for cleaning the sewers at St Thomas's house. That the main house still existed is supported by the fact that Edward Wood, to whom the town had leased vacant land and a lane next to St Thomas's house in 1563 (EKAC: Sa/AC 4, f. 240), was asked to return most of it in 1564 because it was wanted for the site of the school.
43. Mills and Scrogg, n.d., 4:11, citing *Carte Antique* X. 17. In the current catalogue in CCA, document DCc/Chartae Antiquae X. 17, of *c.*1220, was recorded as missing on 14 November 2003; it was 'possibly recatalogued as DCc/AS1', but this is a document dated 1225. Since Mills and Scrogg refer to both the *c.*1220 and 1225 documents, it suggests that they saw two separate items.
44. CCA: DCc/AS7.
45. CCA: DCc/Chartae Antiquae S.282, 266c, 266d; DCc/Treasurer 36.
46. Blair 1993; Quiney 1999.
47. Urry 1967, 192–4.
48. CCA: DCc/Reg. H, f. 15v; U3/173/6/11
49. The establishment of new markets, leading to a shift in the focus of towns, occurs elsewhere, as at Northampton and Norwich (Palliser, Slater and Dennison 2000, 154).
50. Boys 1792, 534, 537.
51. Parfitt, in preparation.
52. Much earlier at Worcester for example (Baker and Holt 2004, 171–2).
53. Parkin 1984, fig. 4. Tatton-Brown 1984, 19, also thought that this area was an extension, but probably already in existence by the time of Domesday.
54. Herdman 1996.

Part III: Introduction
1. Dyson 1981.

Chapter 5
1. *Rot. Chart.* 1: 1, 153; *Rot. Litt. Pat.* 1: 1, 50; *Pipe Roll* 7 John, 117.
2. *Pipe Roll* 16 John, 145.
3. Croft 1997a, 33 c.2; EKAC: Sa/Ch 10B A1, 30.
4. CCR 1247–51, 106; Gardiner 1954, 14–15.
5. CPR 1281–92, 345.
6. TNA: E101/3/18; Gardiner 1954, 27.
7. *Coram Rege Roll* 16, 13–14.
8. CPR 1281–92, 358; CPR 1292–1301, 35. The events leading up to the exchange are discussed in Gardiner 1954, 33–8.
9. TNA: E163/2/26, printed as an appendix to Croft 1997a, 33–6.
10. CPR 1292–1301, 525, 551.
11. Croft 1997a.
12. Murray 1935, 70.
13. Boys 1792, 435–40.
14. Croft 1997a, 16–17.
15. EKAC: Sa/LC 1; for a concise resume of the contents of the custumal, see Croft 1997b, 348–50.
16. EKAC: Sa/LC 2; Boys 1792, 432–547; Croft 1997b, 145–7.
17. TNA: E122/124/5, E122/124/6, E122/124/12. It is not known for how long the division of proceeds continued. For details of the court rolls, see Chap. 5.4.2.
18. Boys 1792, 426–503.
19. EKAC: Sa/LC 1, ff. 105r–107r; Boys 1792, 533–8.
20. Clarke, forthcoming.
21. CPR 1272–81, 136.
22. Boys 1792, 500–04.
23. Fairs were always associated with one of the main feasts in the Christian year, since 'predictable crowds meant a certain amount of predictable trade'; Britnell 1993, 15–17.
24. Gardiner 1954, 38–9.
25. CChartR 1257–1300, p. 368, no. 18. The first was held from 1 January to 2 February; the second was on the fifteen days either side of the Nativity of St John the Baptist (24 June); and the third was held on the fifteen days either side of Michaelmas (29 September).
26. CCR 1302–7, 55.
27. CCR 1313–18, 415.
28. Murray 1935, 77.
29. Reculver ceased to be a limb during the Middle Ages, although it is named with Fordwich, Sarre and Deal in a thirteenth-century manuscript that belonged to St Augustine's Abbey (CCA: Lit MS E19, f. 30v) and again in a sixteenth-century transcript (Rye Old Custumal, f. 55b) printed in Jeake 1728, 25; Murray 1935, 43, 240–43. The five were joined, *c.*1373, by Ramsgate and Walmer.
30. First recognised *c.*1150; Murray 1935, 60.
31. Murray 1935, 63.
32. Murray 1935, 69–71.
33. Murray 1935, 139–59.
34. The decisions of the 1357 court were deemed important enough to be included in full in a revised version of the Sandwich Custumal; Boys 1792, 560–62; see also Croft 1997b, 116–17, 361–2.
35. Dyer 2002, 190.
36. TNA: E363/4.
37. Butcher 1987, 94–5.
38. CCA: DCc/Reg.G, f. 50v.
39. Croft 1997b, 359.

40 For Henry de Sandwich, see Gardiner 1954, 14 (quoting *Rot. Litt. Claus.* I, 29), and for Thorold de Kyvilly, see Gardiner 1954, 20–21 (quoting *Rot. Litt. Claus.* II, 40b).
41 Lloyd 1977, 25–9.
42 There were two merchants called Thomas Shelving, one known as 'junior'.
43 TNA: E122/124/2, E122/124/4.
44 EKAC: Sa/Ch 10J T1.
45 TNA: E122/124/2; Pelham 1932, 224–6.
46 Several Penys were exporting wool through Sandwich in the late thirteenth century (TNA: E122/124/2; Gardiner 1954, 86; Pelham 1932, 224).
47 John de Wynterland, Gardiner 1954, 86; William Winterlond, EKAC: Sa/Ch 10J T1.
48 For their land, see CCA: DCc/Chartae Antiquae S.244, 252.
49 Adam Wyberd, *CPR* 1272–81, 18; *CCR* 1272–9, 384; EKAC: Sa/Ch 10B A1, f. 17. Walter Draper, EKAC: Sa/Ch 10B A1, ff. 3v, 4; CCA: U3/173/6/11, U3/173/6/13; Pelham 1932, 225–6.
50 On his resignation, William was granted £30 per annum from the Canterbury fee farm for himself and his heirs. Sweetinburgh 2004a, 197–8; Croft 1997b, 120, 122.
51 TNA: E179/123/14; E 363/4.
52 TNA: E 363/4.
53 Gardiner 1954, 68–76.
54 Gardiner 1954, 54.
55 Mid-thirteenth century to 1285: CCA: DCc/Ch Ant S242, 243, 244, 245, 247, 248, 249, 250, 254, 255, 266A, 266B, 268, 278/1, 278/2, 278/3, 278/4, 276/1, 276/2, 281; DCc/SVSBiii/485, 486; U15/29/19, 20, 22; DCc/Register C, ff. 55v, 56, 56v; EKAC: Sa/Ch 10B; TNA: E122/124/5, 6, 12 (1298–1307).
56 TNA: E122/124/12.
57 Bennett 1986, 1996.
58 The Middle English Dictionary defines 'hore' as whore.
59 TNA: E122/124/5, E122/124/6, E122/124/12.
60 TNA: E122/124/5.
61 In peacetime ninety to a hundred passengers a year used the port to cross to or come back from the Continent. TNA: E122/124/5, E122/124/6.
62 Boys 1792, 555–9; Croft 1997b, 127, points out that the list may be an ideal list of occupations, rather than a real one, and that there is no evidence as to whether it was present in the custumal of 1301 or added in the late fourteenth-century version.
63 CCA: DCc/Reg. H, f. 176v.
64 TNA: E363/4.
65 This was not unusual: Britnell 1986, 16–17, found that in 1296 and 1301 as many as two-thirds of all taxpayers in Colchester probably had at least some land outside the town.
66 *Pipe Roll* 6 John, xliii–xliv.
67 Butcher 1977, 26, 29.
68 TNA: E122/124; SC6/894, 895.
69 '£36 15s. 6d. for almonds . . . wax . . . rice . . . raisons and figs, bought for the king's use at Sandwich': *CLR* 1226–40, 170; see also *CLR* 1245–51, 133.
70 *CLR* 1226–40, 257, 446.
71 Gras 1918, 66.
72 *CFR* 1272–1307, 47.
73 Lloyd 1977, 25–9.
74 Carus-Wilson and Coleman 1963, 36–7.
75 Butcher 1977, 29–31.
76 CCA: DCc/Chartae Antiqae S.242–245, 279; DCc/Treasurers 36.
77 TNA: E101/5/28; Sylvester 2004, fig. 2.6.
78 At the end of 1294 Canterbury Cathedral Priory had thirty-six sacks of wool in its warehouses. The next year some of the new crop was sold locally, but the monks still ended the year with forty-one sacks and nineteen great pounds in store. It is not known whether the priory officials were unable to find buyers or whether they were holding back in the hope that prices would improve (Mate 1982, 763).
79 *CCR* 1296–1302, 108–11; Lloyd 1977, 85–9.
80 For a good discussion on the burdens imposed by the various kinds of taxation, see Ormrod 1991.
81 Prestwich 1972, 121.
82 *CCR* 1296–1302, 61; *CPR* 1292–1301, 348.
83 *CCR* 1296–1302, 150.
84 Butcher's fear about the impending decline of the port seems to have been unfounded; Butcher 1977.
85 Pelham 1930.
86 Sylvester 2004, 9.
87 Pelham 1930, 129–33, 136–41.
88 James 1971, 98–104 (Appendix 14).
89 Mate 2006a, 16.
90 *CCR* 1307–13, 421.
91 The rights of the Gascons to be exempt from customs duties had arisen in the reign of Edward II, probably because the king was also lord of Gascony (James 1971, 74).
92 TNA: E159/109.
93 For further details, see Mate 1991, 91.
94 Maddicott 1987, 329.
95 *CCR* 1333–7, 643–4.
96 *CCR* 1339–41, 237.
97 Gardiner 1954, 100.
98 *CFR* 1347–56, 440; *CPR* 1354–8, 300.
99 TNA: SC6/894/24; 894/29.
100 TNA: E101/22/37. Other men buying salt fish were Simon Hereward, Thamas Fraunceys, William Berte, Roger le Ku, William Serle, John Parson and Roger Baron.
101 TNA: E101/22/37.
102 TNA: SC6/895/1.
103 TNA: SC5/895/2.
104 TNA: E122/193/15.
105 First mentioned as 'Castelmed' in 1364; *CPR* 1361–4, 471.
106 The date of the earthwork makes it unlikely that this was a motte, as sometimes suggested; Bennett, Blockley and Tatton-Brown 1983; Stewart 2000, 54, 72.
107 Stewart 2000, fig. 2.
108 See Chap. 11.2.2 for the suggestion that the stone walls may be from a building constructed in 1385.
109 Bennett, Blockley and Tatton-Brown 1983, fig. 2. Note that the line of the ditch was extrapolated from a small excavated trench.
110 TNA: E101/3/18.
111 *Pipe Roll* Edward I, 143 m.36.
112 *CFR* 1272–1307, 397; *CPR* 1292–1301, 335; *CCR* 1296–1302, 150.
113 EKAC: Sa/LC 1, ff. 110v–111v; Boys 1792, 540.
114 *CCR* 1302–7, 55.
115 *CFR* 1272–1307, 500; *CPR* 1301–7, 266–7.
116 *CCR* 1318–22, 39.
117 *CPR* 1313–17, 106; *CFR* 1307–19, 238, 326; *CCR* 1323–7, 237.
118 *CCR* 1343–6, 634.
119 *CPR* 1358–61, 48.
120 *CCR* 1288–96, 295; *CCR* 1296–1302, 266.
121 *Deal Telegram*, 22 January 1881.
122 Stewart 2000, fig. 2.
123 Martin and Martin 2004, 55–9; 2009, 47–50.
124 We are grateful to Paul Everson for this suggestion.
125 Forces could have been billeted on locals or housed in camps,

126 *CCR 1337–9*, 508.
127 TNA: E101/22/28; *CPR 1358–61*, 350; Hewitt 1966, 53–4.
128 Hewitt 1966, 83.
129 *CPR 1429–36*, 133.
130 Hewitt 1966, 79.
131 *CCR 1354–60*, 564.
132 In 1355: *CPR 1354–8*, 203; in 1388: *CPR 1385–9*, 449.
133 *CPR 1358–61*, 26; for medieval docks, see Friel 1995, fig. 3.10.
134 Brooks 1928, 28.
135 Bellamy and Milne 2003.
136 Creighton and Higham 2005, 67, 84.
137 Sweetinburgh 2004b, 186–7.
138 Scheduled Ancient Monument, Kent 57, 58, 59; for a detailed description, see Sandwich Survey Report 6.
139 TNA: E101/3/6, E101/3/9; Lewis 1939, 200–01.
140 *Coram Rege Roll* 16, 13–14.
141 *CPR 1321–4*, 14.
142 EKAC: Sa/LC 1, ff. 110v–111v; Boys 1792, 540.
143 Boys 1792, 504.
144 EKAC: Sa/Ch 10B A1, f. 48; Sa/Ch 10B T1.
145 Boys 1792, 537.
146 TNA: E122/124/5.
147 *CCR 1339–41*, 237.
148 Creighton 2002, 133–74.
149 *CPR 1281–92*, 206.
150 There was a royal fishery there by the beginning of the fourteenth century; *CFR 1307–19*, 191, 259.
151 *CPR 1321–4*, 25.
152 EKAC: Sa/TB 1, f.4.
153 W. H. Cronk's map of land belonging to Sandwich corporation, 1776: EKAC: Sa/P2.
154 *CPR 1324–7*, 25.
155 Sylvester 2004, 13.
156 Trussler 1974; Milne 2004.
157 Milne 2004, 250; the poor evidence for medieval shipbuilding in Sandwich makes it impossible to be certain that the so-called Sandwich ship was built there.
158 *CMem Rolls 1326–7*, no. 892 (o).
159 Rodger 1996, 639.
160 Hutchinson 1994, 10–15; Hutchinson 1995; Friel 1995, fig. 1.2.
161 Friel 1995, 81.
162 *CPR 1258–66*, 283–4.
163 Crumlin-Pedersen 1983; Hutchinson 1994, 15–20, fig. 1.8.
164 Carpenter 1990, 43–4.
165 Tipping 1994, 9–11.
166 *CPR 1313–17*, 501–2.
167 Ruddock 1951, 21.
168 Colvin 1963, 42–9, 55.
169 Unger 1980, 221.
170 TNA: E122/69/5.
171 *CCR 1318–22*, 692; *Dromundus* must have been an Anglicisation on the part of the scribe, the vessel no doubt being a dromond, originally a Byzantine term for a vessel of the 'great galley' type.
172 *CPR 1321–4*, 259, 317.
173 Tinniswood 1949; Unger 1980, 176–82; Hutchinson 1994, 151.
174 Unger 1981.

Chapter 6

1 Draper 2006, 50–51, 178–9.
2 Barnwell, Cross and Rycraft 2005, 13–14.
3 Parsons 1986; Davidson 1999.
4 The southern chancel arcade has piers and a central column of Purbeck and Hythe stone. The date has been debated. Tatton-Brown (1993 and pers. comm.) believes that the use of Purbeck means it is early to mid-thirteenth century. But Purbeck continued to be used later, as discussed by Blair 1991, 49, and the style here is more in keeping with a mid- or late thirteenth-century date.
5 Tatton-Brown 1993.
6 Hoey 1995, 45.
7 Drew 1954, 6–8; Mason 1976, 23–6; Draper 2006, 179–80.
8 Morris 1989, 284–96; Davidson 1998, 204–6, 234–6; Draper 2006, 185.
9 Rosser 1988a, 33.
10 Marks 2004, 86–9. The only documented thirteenth-century image in Sandwich was one of St Thomas, bought by the priory for 20s. in 1253, but it was probably intended for the chapel in the residence rather than for one of the parish churches. CCA: DCc/Reg. H, f. 176v.
11 Hoey 1995.
12 *Thorne*, 594–5.
13 Denton 1993, 2005.
14 Lloyd 1977, 71; CCA: U3/173/6/11.
15 *CPR 1343–5*, 378; Hussey 1936, 256–60; Sweetinburgh 2004a, 196–7.
16 The details are given in the bede roll, a list of early benefactors to St Mary's church written c.1447; Boys 1792, 372–3.
17 Sweetinburgh 2004a, 197. In his will of 1481 Deryk Roke (CKS: PRC 17/3/386) asked the chaplain, John Cristofer, to say Masses at the 'chantry of St Mary', thereby firmly associating the chantry with a chapel of St Mary.
18 The words used in wills indicate that the chapel was near rather than within the church: 'iuxta' (CKS: PRC 17/3/475) and 'contigua' (CKS: PRC 17/6/53).
19 Boys 1792, 416; a Thomas Loveryk was also mayor in 1409, 1411 and 1415, but this was presumably another generation since the bede roll seems to be listed chronologically and the Loveryks are listed before Thomas Elys, who lived in the late fourteenth century.
20 Boys 1792, 186, 308. Parkin 1984, 210, perhaps following Boys, also thought it was a priest's house. The question of whether this structure was used in connection with the chantry will be discussed in Chap. 13.1.3.
21 Thomas Sole, sexton (1498): CKS: PRC 17/7/117; Joane Worme, widow (1531): PRC 17/19/205; Alexander Alday, jurat (1534): PRC 17/19/207.
22 Worcester Cathedral (1224) and Old St Paul's, London (c.1282): Bloxham 1855, 4; St Augustine's, Canterbury (1287–99), and Bury St Edmunds Abbey ('before 1300'): Gilchrist and Sloane 2005, 37–8, 41–3.
23 There are examples at Higham Ferrers, Oundle and Rothwell in Northamptonshire (Paul Barnwell, pers. comm.), and at Great Yarmouth and King's Lynn (Norfolk), St Albans (Herts) and Hythe (Kent): Bloxham 1855; Cook 1954, 130; Gilchrist and Sloane 2005, 42. For the conversion to charnels of vaulted undercrofts in London, see Schofield 1997, 43–9.
24 CCA: DCc/Register G, f. 50v.
25 Boys 1792, 443; Croft 1997a, 17–18.
26 Davies 1968, 57–9.
27 Draper and Meddens 2009, 43.
28 In 1368 the civic authorities paid rent to Dover Priory, but also received rent for the cellar under the hall; BL: Add. MS 29615,

ff. 6, 7, 9v; Haines 1930, 284; Sweetinburgh 2006, 176.
29. Murray 1935, 73, 102–6, 163; Sweetinburgh 2006.
30. Sweetinburgh 2006.
31. For a discussion of this hall and the one that succeeded it, see Chaps 10.1 and 16.2.
32. Newman 1980, 433.
33. Tricker 2002, 7, suggests *c*.1330–40, which is possible, although it could have been started a little earlier.
34. Gardiner 1954, 54.
35. Tricker 2002, 15; Boys 1792, 307–8.
36. Binski 1996, 74–5.
37. Blair, Goodall and Lankester 2000; Harding 2002, 121.
38. Sweetinburgh 2004a, 199.
39. CCA: DCc/DE 26.
40. Sweetinburgh 2004a, 187–8.
41. Knowles and Hadcock 1971, 233–6; VCH Kent 1974a, 204–5; Rigold 1965; Deighton 1994, 317n.
42. Butler 1984, 123.
43. The others were Aylesford and Lossenham (Rigold 1965). For a detailed history of Sandwich friary, see VCH Kent 1974a, 204–5; Knowles and Hadcock 1971, 233–6; Rigold 1965; Deighton 1994.
44. Sweetinburgh 2004a, 193–5.
45. *CPR* 1272–81, 404. John de Sandwich had, by his father's marriage, acquired the barony of Folkestone; Hasted 1797–1801, VIII, 157–8.
46. Rigold 1965, 5–6, who discussed and corrected Boys and others on the identities of the founders; Deighton 1994, 317. For the Crawthorne family in the later thirteenth century, see *CPR* 1272–81, 19, 34, and CCA: DCc/Chartae Antiquae S.266a. Both the Sandwich and Crawthorne families had also been connected with founding St Bartholomew's hospital in the early thirteenth century; see Chap. 6.2.2.
47. VCH Kent 1974a, 204; Deighton 1994, 321.
48. The basic outlines of the church and some accompanying buildings were established by Stebbing in 1936; the results were augmented and amended by Rigold in the 1960s. Rapid and inadequate salvage recording was undertaken by local groups in advance of a major housing development on the site in the 1970s, when no provision for a proper examination had been made. This was followed in 1992–3 by excavation of a small area by Keith Parfitt and the Dover Archaeological Group. Parfitt then undertook a re-analysis of all the previous excavation work; Parfitt 1993.
49. See comparative plans in Woodfield 2005, figs 4–6. Rigold (1965, 15) thought the best analogy was with the Franciscan church at Gloucester, which, although later in date, probably preserves a thirteenth-century plan.
50. Aisled naves were developed in urban friary churches between 1270 and 1320; Butler 1984, 129.
51. Rigold 1965, 15–16.
52. Evidence for the lane from the marketplace has been discovered (Site 3); Deighton 1994, 318.
53. Butler 1984, 132.
54. Rigold 1965, 16–17; the planning of friary cloisters varied considerably (Butler 1984, 131–3).
55. Stebbing 1936; Rigold 1965.
56. Rigold 1965, 13–14.
57. Parfitt 1993.
58. Cannon 1912, 667.
59. Boys 1792, 1.
60. Gardiner 1954, 19; *CPR* 1216–25, 563; *CPR* 1225–32, 151, 293, 306, 307 333, 364.
61. EKAC: Sa/LC 1, f. 19v; Croft 1997b, 348; Boys 1792, 3–115; Wanostrocht, n.d., 9.
62. EKAC: Sa/Ch 10B A1, f. 1.
63. An important annual procession from St Peter's to the hospital had been established by 1301; Sweetinburgh 2004a, 190.
64. Boys 1792, 17–21, 87–90.
65. The possibility of a changed role for the hospital is also discussed by Sweetinburgh 2004a, 189.
66. The chapel had fallen into disuse in the eighteenth century: Wanostrocht, n.d., 40–41; Newman 1987, 449.
67. Hoey 1995, 60–63.
68. Gilchrist 1995, 20.
69. Orme and Webster 1995, 88–9.
70. Godfrey 1929, 107.
71. *Itinerary*, 250; Boys 1792, 2.
72. Godfrey 1929, 101; Rubin 1989. The situation in Kent is well described and put into a wider context in Sweetinburgh 2004a, chaps 1 and 2.
73. Sweetinburgh 2004a, 136.
74. Butcher 1980, 25.
75. Sweetinburgh 2004a, 224–8, discusses the type of people who became corrodians.
76. EKAC: Sa/Ch 10J T1. The manor and family of Shelving were of Woodnesborough parish (Hasted 1797–1801, X, 125–6), and in 1306 Thomas de Shelving gave the Carmelite friars a spring of water in Woodnesborough with permission to make a conduit through his land to their house in Sandwich (VCH Kent 1974a, 204); Boys 1792, 416; EKAC: Sa/Ch 10J T1ad, ae.
77. The account in the custumal is reprinted in Boys 1792, 126–31; the history and organisation of the hospital around 1300 is discussed in Sweetinburgh 2004a, 190–92.
78. Sweetinburgh 2004a, 207–8.

Chapter 7

1. Pearson 2001a.
2. Parfitt, Corke and Cotter 2006, 27–44.
3. Milne 1992, 135–6; Pearson 2005, 47–50.
4. Parfitt, in preparation.
5. CCA: DCc/AS1, DCc/AS2, DCc/AS4, DCc/AS5, DCc/AS6, DCc/AS16. Butcher 1977, 30–31, assumes that the new house and the stone house were the same building.
6. Gardiner, 1954, 42. The house is mentioned on several occasions, with different lengths, because there was some dispute over the payment for its construction; CCA: DCc/Reg. H, ff. 179, 185, 197; DCc/Chartae Antiquae S.279. In recent times this has been equated with the present 'Long House', 62 Strand Street (Parkin 1984, 198–9), although the length of this house (20.5m or more than 67ft) does not agree with the documented measurements and the house has no identifiable features earlier than *c*.1570.
7. For an overview, see Grenville 1997, 175–81.
8. For a discussion of roof types in Kent at this period, see Pearson 1994, 50–52 and fig. 40.
9. For the mid-fourteenth-century Gybon, see Gardiner 1954, 106. For the family's connection to the plot, see CCA: DCc/Chartae Antiquae S.256 and deeds in possession of present owner. In 1759 the plot was occupied by four cottages called Plockys. Parkin (1984, 196–8) believed that this was a fortified dwelling of the early thirteenth century with a hall in the corner away from the streets, a chapel at the front, a tower in the north-west corner and a gatehouse straddling Guildcount Lane; no evidence has been found for this interpretation.
10. Drawings in NMR, no. 39752. Photographs in Parkin Collection, Sandwich Guildhall Archives.
11. CCA: DCc/Chartae Antiquae S.275, 282; DCc/treasurers 36.
12. Deep, unvaulted and stylistically undatable stone and flint-walled cellars are present in Upper Strand Street at Nos. 15, 17

288 Notes to pages 97–115

13 (House 94), 19, 21 and 23 (House 95) on the north side, and Nos. 4 and 12 on the south side, and in Nos. 11, 13 (House 33) and 15 High Street. The fact, however, that they are set inside the walls of the houses above suggests that they may not have been dug until after the Middle Ages.
13 A recent discussion of the literature on this subject may be found in Martin and Martin 2004, 125–7.
14 St John's hospital deed, EKAC: Sa/Ch 10J T1, p.
15 A number of rural examples in Kent and elsewhere are discussed in Pearson 1994, 19–23.
16 Parkin 1984, 193–5.
17 The type was distinguished in twelfth-century town buildings by Harris 1994, 26–36, who listed examples in Winchester, Canterbury, York and Colchester, among other places.
18 We are grateful to Terry Slater for his views on these plots. See also Pearson 2003, 417–18.
19 For example, stone blocks, in some cases reused, also occur in the north wall of 7 Bowling Street, the rear walls of 5 Harnet Street and St Mary's churchyard walls.
20 Notes by Southam and Trussler c.1970, Sandwich Guildhall Archives.
21 A thirteenth-century piscina set into this wall within the house seems to have given rise to the story that there was a chantry here. The piscina has clearly been set into the wall at an unknown but later date, and no documentary evidence has been found to support the claim of a chapel in this area.
22 Milne 1992, 131–7; Smith 2000, 157–9.
23 The argument is more fully set out in Pearson 2005, 47–50, on which this and the following paragraph are based.
24 Arnold et al. 2001a; Arnold, Howard and Litton 2003.
25 Warm thanks are due to David and Barbara Martin who helped to unravel some of the more complicated aspects of the structure of this building.
26 Slippage of timbers and a crude repair have made it difficult to be certain of the original construction at the junction of post, plate and tiebeams, but it is possible that the post was intended to carry all the timbers directly.
27 Munby, Sparks and Tatton-Brown 1983, where the roofs are largely associated with buildings erected in the late thirteenth century by ecclesiastical landlords. But since the same construction occurs at 39 Strand Street, Sandwich, in 1334, it is clear that the type went on being used in private dwellings at least into the 1330s.
28 For example, King's Head, Mardol, Shrewsbury, dated 1404; Moran 2003, 227–30.
29 At 37 Long Wyre Street, Colchester, Essex, of c.1400, first-floor uprights continue up to the second-floor level, but all the joists are supported by intermediate rails. We are grateful to Dave Stenning and Richard Shackle for information about this building.
30 Arnold, Laxton and Litton 2002.
31 Arnold et al. 2001a; Arnold, Howard and Litton 2003; for the use of timbers soon after felling, see Miles 1997, 50–54.
32 Parker 1971, 49, 56–66.
33 Alston 2004, 49. See also the late sixteenth- and early seventeenth-century London surveys of Ralph Treswell (Schofield 1987) where warehouses are common, often set behind shops, sometimes set by themselves in rear courtyards.
34 E.g., in Southampton (Faulkner 1975, 94, 104–7, 115–16), where it is suggested that 58 French Street also dates to the early fourteenth century. Later examples include 33, 34 High Street, Winchester, tree-ring dated to 1463–4 (Roberts 2003, 183–4), and 36 and 38 North Street, Exeter (Portman 1966, 6–7).
35 For small brackets to large shop windows, see a house in Bures St Mary, Suffolk, of the mid-fourteenth century; Alston 2004, fig. 4.3.
36 The pegging is similar to that found in 29 The Bail, Lincoln, of the mid-fourteenth century, where the pegs are used to hold panels of gypsum covering thin slabs of limestone rubble (Jones et al. 1996, 28–9). Flat tiles, documented as having been used for the walls (*parietibus*) of Sheppey Castle in 1365, might be for nogging of this sort, but it is impossible to be certain (Salzman 1952, 141). In York, 'walteghill' was first documented in 1358 in the undercroft of the Merchant Adventurers' Hall; and stone and brick infilling to timber framing was used from the fourteenth century onwards (RCHM 1981, lxii–lxiii, xcvi).
37 TNA: SC6/894–896.
38 In Kent, brick was used in vault construction at Allington Castle c.1280, but is more normally associated with the fourteenth century and later. See Smith 1990, 171.
39 Southam 1980; Parkin 1984, 194–5.
40 Faulkner 1975, 81.
41 Martin and Martin 2004, 108, 156.
42 Keene 1985, 156.
43 Urry 1967, 192–5.
44 Martin and Martin 2004, 105–6.
45 TNA: SC6/894/25–30. Sandwich was simply the port of entry, and most of the boards were probably taken on to London, Canterbury or elsewhere. Estrichbords were commonly bought in London during the fourteenth century (Salzman 1952, 245–6).
46 The cost of overland transport from Hawkhurst and Benenden to the coast was 7s. for 140 logs, but transporting 100 tree trunks and 1,000 logs from Small Hythe to Sandwich cost only 10s., plus wharfage; Witney 1990, 29.
47 For the point that larger medieval houses tended to be set behind commercial frontages in town centres or situated away from the main commercial areas, see Keene 1989, 223–4. Surviving medieval examples can be found in most large towns.

Chapter 8

1 *CPR* 1281–92, 358; *CPR* 1292–1301, 35.
2 CCA: DCc/AS 6, 7, 16, 18; DCc/Reg. H, ff. 176v, 179, 182, 185, 188v, 190, 197, 202v, 207v, 214v; DCc/Chartae Antiquae S. 279, S 282; DCc/DE 118; DCc/Treasurer 36.
3 CCA: DCc/Treasurer 33.
4 CCA: DCc/Chartae Antiquae S.252.
5 CCA: U3/173/6/36: 'from the town wall to Monkenkey bridge'.
6 CCA: DCc/Regi. H, f. 176v; DCc/Chartae Antiquae S.275, 282; DCc/Treasurer 36. The cellars are not individually identified at this time, and we do not know how many there were until the late fourteenth century, when fourteen different ones were named.
7 CCA: DCc/Chartae Antiquae S.242–244, S.254; Reg. E, ff. 200v–201v.
8 CCA: Reg. C, f. 56.
9 CCA: DCc/Chartae Antiquae S.245, S.279.
10 CCA: DCc/ Chartae Antiquae S.254.
11 EKAC: Sa/Ch 10J T1, ae.
12 CCA: DCc/AS 9, 16.
13 EKAC: Sa/Ch 10B A1, 30.
14 Boys 1792, 534, 537.
15 Boys 1792, 297.
16 There were shambles in the Fishmarket, but no evidence as to what was sold from them.
17 CCA: U3/173/6/11, U3/173/6/13.
18 Those owned by the priory needed constant maintenance, suggesting that they were timber structures; CCA: DCc/Reg. H, ff. 176–214; DCc/AS18; DCc/Chartae Antiquae S.242–245, 279; Lambeth MS 242 1272–1326, f. 163; CCA:

[19] DCc/treasurers 36. This was probably true of the other quays, although no documents survive to confirm it.
[19] EKAC: Sa/Ch 10B A1, 1.
[20] Southam 1980; Parkin 1984, 194–5.
[21] Although the first known reference to the name Strand Street dates only from 1426 (EKAC: Sa/AC 1, f. 35 [dated 1434, but said to be a late feoffment of a document of 28/2/4H6]), it is probably referred to in 1385 (EKAC: Sa/TB1, 13), with land north of it in 1387 (EKAC: Sa/TB 1, 15).
[22] Horrox 1978, map facing p. 184; Horrox 1983, 53–90.
[23] Clarke 1973, 1981; Clarke and Carter 1977, fig. 191.
[24] Schofield and Vince 1994, 54–62.
[25] Foord's Plan of the Quay, EKAC: Sa/P6.
[26] TNA: SC6/894/24–27.
[27] Boys 1792, 503.
[28] CCA: DCc/Reg. H, f. 15 (1152–67); DCc/Reg. K, f. 47v (c.1216).
[29] EKAC: Sa/TB 1, 5.
[30] EKAC: Sa/Ch 10J T1, ae, ad.
[31] Campbell *et al.* 1993, 28–31.
[32] Tonbridge: Wragg, Jarrett and Haslam 2005, 130; King's Lynn: Clarke and Carter 1977, fig. 195.

Section IV: Introduction

[1] Dyer 1991.

Chapter 9

[1] *CCR* 1385–9, 538 (Danzig); *CPR* 1405–8, 237 (Greifswald).
[2] *CInqMisc* IV, nos. 56, 88.
[3] Wallace 1974, 118.
[4] Burwash 1947, 121.
[5] Ruddock 1951, 47.
[6] Burwash 1947, 157.
[7] EKAC: Sa/AC 1, f. 278v.
[8] *CCR* 1385–9, 181.
[9] *CCR* 1389–92, 203.
[10] *CCR* 1399–1402, 372; *CSPV* 1202–1509, p. 59, no. 220.
[11] *CSPV* 1202–1509, p. 62, no. 230; pp. 148–52, no. 492.
[12] *CSPV* 1202–1509, p. 61, no. 228.
[13] *CSPV* 1202–1509, p. 63, no. 247.
[14] In 1565, for example, Sandwich reported that 'its sea-faring men were employed sometimes for merchandising, sometimes for fishing, as the time of year requireth . . . and as masters will have them'; EKAC: Sa/ZB 24.
[15] Hattendorf *et al.* 1993, 43; Rose 2002, 70.
[16] *CPR* 1396–9, 52–3; *CPR* 1429–36, 353; *CPR* 1441–6, 105.
[17] Friel 1995, 202, table 2.
[18] BL: Add. MS 19510, ff. 2v–3.
[19] *CSPV* 1202–1509, frontispiece.
[20] BL: Egerton MS 2855, ff. 7v–8.
[21] Gairdner and Delmar Morgan 1889, 12–13; BL: Lansdowne MS 2850.
[22] *Michael of Rhodes*, f. 125v. The relevant text from the manuscript of Michael of Rhodes was kindly provided by Alan M. Stahl; it is the source of these translations of the term *boscho*, which might otherwise, in a Sandwich context, have been assumed to mean scrub or bushes.
[23] Personal communication, Alan M. Stahl, 26 September 2007.
[24] Only the plan of the church is known, from which it is impossible to say whether there was a tower; Parfitt 2001.
[25] *CPR* 1461–7, 63, 465.
[26] EKAC: Sa/AC 1, ff. 180v, 185v.
[27] CCA: DCc/Chartae Antiquae T.
[28] *Itinerary*, 250: 'in the time of Pope Paul (1464–71)'.
[29] EKAC: Sa/AC 1, f. 241.
[30] EKAC: Sa/FAt 8; Sa/AC 1, f. 291v; Sa/AC 2, f. 111.
[31] EKAC: Sa/AC 1, f. 60v.
[32] EKAC: Sa/AC 2, f. 24.
[33] EKAC: Sa/AC 1, f. 233v.
[34] EKAC: Sa/AC 1, f. 290v; it is not clear whether this was a new cut or a reinforcement of the work done in 1477.
[35] EKAC: Sa/AC 1, f. 316.
[36] EKAC: Sa/AC 2, ff. 7v–8.
[37] EKAC: Sa/AC 2, ff. 26v, 27v, 28.
[38] EKAC: Sa/AC 2, ff. 32v, 33.
[39] Kowaleski 2000, 472.
[40] *CCR* 1364–8, 478–9.
[41] TNA: SC6/895/13; SC6/895/14.
[42] TNA: E101/194/6.
[43] Kowaleski 2000, 477–83.
[44] *CPR* 1385–9, 261; *CPR* 1399–1401, 263; *CCR* 1385–9, 542; *CCR* 1402–5, 243.
[45] *CCR* 1385–9, 360; *CCR* 1392–6, 143; *CCR* 1409–13, 378 *CSPV* 1202–1509, p. 53, no. 189; *CPR* 1413–16, 147.
[46] One example is recorded in 1417: *CSPV* 1202–1509, p. 59, no. 220.
[47] *CCR* 1385–89, 360; *CCR* 1392–96, 143.
[48] TNA: SC6/895/7–8.
[49] James 1971, 57–9.
[50] Carus-Wilson and Coleman 1963, 95.
[51] More than 3,000 bales of woad were imported in 1433–4; TNA: SC6/895/17.
[52] TNA: SC6/895/22–SC6/896/4.
[53] TNA: E122/127/18.
[54] In 1449, for example, a Venetian ship was loaded in Sandwich with sixty bales of woad, eight buttes of sweet wine and other goods; *CPR* 1446–52, 285.
[55] In 1402 the captain of a Venetian galley was granted special dispensation to visit St Thomas's shrine in Canterbury, but he had to return to Sandwich to sleep on board; *CSPV* 1202–1509, p. 64, no. 257.
[56] TNA: E179/242/9. For the introduction of stricter regulations for aliens, see Kowaleski 2000, 493.
[57] TNA: SC6/895/17.
[58] Hatcher 1996.
[59] Hatcher 1986, 28.
[60] TNA: SC6/896/10.
[61] Carus-Wilson and Coleman 1963, 64.
[62] TNA: E364/112 m. 2.
[63] *CPR* 1385–9, 236, 253; *CCR* 1385–9, 196; *CCR* 1399–1402, 173.
[64] *CPR* 1399–1401, 271.
[65] *CPR* 1405–8, 237.
[66] *CPR* 1429–36, 75.
[67] EKAC: Sa/AC 1, f. 43v.
[68] *CPR* 1452–61, 176; *CPR* 1461–7, 35.
[69] *CPR* 1461–7, 347.
[70] Childs 1978, 98.
[71] CCA: DCc/Prior/12.
[72] CCA: DCc/Prior/13.
[73] TNA: E122/129/3; by 1500 many people, even those with limited means, were wearing linen underclothes and using linen bed sheets and table cloths. For an excellent account of the role of London mercers in Sandwich, see Sutton 1999.
[74] Unger 1978; Mate 2006a, 81–2.
[75] TNA: E122/129/3.
[76] The lack of benefit of this form of trade to a port has been charted for Southampton by Coleman 1963–4, but see Thick 1997, 226–7.

77 EKAC: Sa/AC 1, f. 14v; Sa/FAt 2.
78 In 1458 the lease of the weigh beam was reduced from £12 to £6 13s. 4d.; EKAC: Sa/AC 1, f. 104
79 EKAC: Sa/AC 1, f. 175.
80 EKAC: Sa/AC 1, f. 300 (1485); Sa/FAt 24 (1490).
81 EKAC: Sa/AC 2, f. 25.
82 EKAC: Sa/AC 2, f. 276v; Britnell 1997, 228–41.
83 EKAC: Sa/AC 2, f. 117; ships were being charged 'buoy money' in 1508: EKAC: Sa/FAt17.
84 EKAC: Sa/AC 3, f. 28; Sa/FAt29; Sa/AC 3, ff. 99, 150; Sa/AC 4, f. 114.
85 EKAC: Sa/AC 2, ff. 111, 121v.
86 EKAC: Sa/FAt 22.
87 EKAC: Sa/AC 2, f. 146v.
88 EKAC: Sa/AC 3, f. 109; the watermill was leased by Vincent Engeham at the time of its demolition.
89 EKAC: Sa/AC 4, f. 136.
90 L&P XII: ii, p. 46, no. 136.
91 EKAC: Sa/AC 5, f. 184v.
92 EKAC: Sa/AC 4, f. 283.
93 EKAC: Sa/AC 3, ff. 98, 99v.
94 Boys 1792, 732–5; EKAC: Sa/AC 3, ff. 204, 207v, 209.
95 EKAC: Sa/AC 3, f. 213.
96 EKAC: Sa/AC 3, f. 215v; Shelby 1967, 112–15.
97 EKAC: Sa/AC 3, ff. 217, 219, 243, 247v, 251; Sa/FAt 35.
98 BL: Cotton Augustus I.i, f. 54.
99 EKAC: Sa/FAt 29.
100 EKAC: Sa/AC 4, f. 79.
101 EKAC: Sa/AC 4, ff. 140v, 142v, 144; the town sent John and Edward Wood to seek suitable engineers; Henrique Jacobson of Amsterdam was proposed, at a cost of £10,000 'or thereabouts'; Boys 1792, 736.
102 L&P III: i, pp. 228–30 no. 689.
103 EKAC: Sa/AC 2, ff. 61, 139v.
104 EKAC: Sa/AC 2, f. 168v.
105 Burwash 1947, 137; in 1506 ships carrying salt were up to 100 tuns burden and colliers 40 tuns, EKAC: Sa/AC 2, ff. 142v, 143.
106 Burwash 1947, 131.
107 TNA: E122/130/15; printed in Hyde 1996, 164–73.
108 L&P I: i, p. 805 no. 1768.
109 EKAC: Sa/FAt 23.
110 Burwash 1947, 125–6.
111 EKAC: Sa/AC 2, f. 366v.
112 EKAC: Sa/FAt 20–29.
113 TNA: E122/130/2.
114 TNA: E101/5/45; EKAC: Sa/AC 2, ff. 142v–143.
115 TNA: E122130/4, E122/208/2, E122/130/8; at first Horn imported knitted hose, woollen cloth, kettles, nails, glasses and earthenware, but in the 1530s he changed to importing salt, figs, paving tiles, paper, pepper and other spices.
116 TNA: E122/208/2, E122/208/3, E122/30/8, E122/30/10. In 1537–8 Thomas Lonnde imported hops, herring, soap, Norwegian bowstaves and ten bushels of apples; John Strode and George Webbe also participated in such trade.
117 Thomas Aldy of Ash, for example; Mate 2006a, 88.
118 TNA: E122/208/2, E122/131/3, E122/130/8.
119 TNA: E122/208/2, E122/130/10, C1/1146/13.
120 TNA: E36/257.
121 TNA: STAC 2/20/188.
122 TNA: STAC 2/27/32, 2/27/40, 2/27/42, 2/27/64.
123 Mate 2006a, 41, 92–3.

Chapter 10

1 A quitrent of 10s. was paid to the priest of the Condy chantry until the Reformation, after which the corporation paid the crown for what had been chantry lands. The first reference to payment occurs in 1469 (EKAC: Sa/FAt 6), and is thereafter recorded fairly regularly.
2 BL: Add. MS 29615, ff. 33, 34v.
3 EKAC: Sa/AC 1, f. 9.
4 Rigby 1995, 172–3.
5 EKAC: Sa/AC 1, f. 96v.
6 EKAC: Sa/AC 1, ff. 42, 85, 96v.
7 EKAC: Sa/AC 1, f. 126v; Gardiner 1954, 148.
8 Green 1894, 432–3.
9 BL: Lansdowne MS 276, f. 167. The following account is based upon this source.
10 John Somer was mayor in 1512, 1514, 1523 and 1524, and Henry Bolle in 1522 and 1525.
11 The original fair of St Clement's had continued to be part of the perquisites of the bailiwick, and the revenues were traditionally collected by an agent of the bailiff. These had averaged 18d. a year in the early fifteenth century.
12 EKAC: Sa/AC 3, f. 14.
13 Dimmock 2001.
14 EKAC: Sa/AC 3, f. 25v; Sa/FAt 34.
15 TNA: E101/518/45.
16 EKAC: Sa/AC 1, f. 29.
17 EKAC: Sa/AC 1, f. 5.
18 EKAC: Sa/AC 1, f. 175v.
19 EKAC: Sa/AC 1, f. 240.
20 BL: Add. MS 33511, ff. 33–44.
21 BL: Add. MS 3351, ff. 150–84.
22 EKAC: Sa/AC 1, f. 241.
23 EKAC: Sa/AC 1, f. 249.
24 EKAC: Sa/AC 1, f. 255v.
25 EKAC: Sa/AC 2, f. 7v.
26 EKAC: Sa/AC 2, f. 280.
27 Mate 2006a, 23–38.
28 EKAC: Sa/AC 3, f. 95; Mate 2006a, 32.
29 TNA: STAC2/6/202, STAC3/3/10/34; the confiscated salt was estimated to be worth £19 15s. 3d.
30 CPR 1494–1509, 402; EKAC: Sa/AC 2, f. 124v.
31 Swanson 1988.
32 Green 1894, 150–55; Boys 1792, 680.
33 EKAC: Sa/AC 4, f. 151v.
34 Articles on some individual structures, such as the town crane, will be published elsewhere after the conclusion of the Sandwich Project.
35 EKAC: Sa/AC 1, f. 87v (1451); Sa/AC 2, f. 24 (1493); Sa/AC 3, f. 76v (1536); Sa/AC 5, f. 102 (1572).
36 EKAC: Sa/FAt 22, 24.
37 EKAC: Sa/AC 4, f. 274.
38 In 1553, for instance, the town paid Robert Haddock £3 13s.4d. for cleaning and scouring the Delf; EKAC: Sa/AC 4, f. 31.
39 Washing places: EKAC: Sa/AC 1, f. 87v (1451); Sa/FAt 12 (1498); Sa/AC 3, f. 171v (1544); Sa/AC 6, f. 282 (1600). Watering places: CCA: U3/11/5/1, 101–8 (1457); EKAC: PRC 17/9/311 (1506); Sa/AC 4, f. 345 (1567).
40 EKAC: Sa/AC 2, f. 190v (1511); Sa/AC 2, f. 367 (1526); Sa/AC 3, f. 36 (1532); Sa/AC 3, f. 68v (1535).
41 EKAC: Sa/AC 4, f. 345.
42 For example, EKAC: Sa/FAt 2.
43 LVRG 2006, 47, 88.
44 We are grateful to Ray Harlow for drawing attention to the MS 'Notes on the watercourses of Sandwich', Sandwich Guildhall Archive, Fretton 34/16.

45 *CPR* 1301–7, 440.
46 EKAC: Sa/FAt 8; Sa/AC 1, f. 284.
47 EKAC: Sa/AC 1, f. 255v.
48 EKAC: Sa/AC 1, f. 305v.
49 EKAC: Sa/FAt 25 and 29.
50 EKAC: Sa/FAt 5, 6.
51 EKAC: Sa/AC 2, f. 28.
52 EKAC: Sa/AC 4, f. 143v.
53 EKAC: Sa/AC 1, f. 255v.
54 TNA: E159/167; CKS: PRC 32/1/62.
55 EKAC: Sa/FAt 5; Sa/AC 1, f. 209v.
56 EKAC: Sa/AC 6, ff. 152–3.
57 EKAC: Sa/AC 1, f. 4; the mayor and jurats gave a robe to the crane keeper.
58 TNA: E122/124/5–6.
59 The cost was 4s. for 1,000 bricks; TNA: SC6/894–896.
60 TNA: E101/481/26–28.
61 EKAC: Sa/AC 1, f. 168.
62 Smith 1985, 31, 60.
63 EKAC: Sa/FAt 8.
64 In addition he was to give St Bartholomew's hospital 1,000 bricks each year; EKAC: Sa/AC 2, f. 2.
65 EKAC: Sa/FAt 6, 8; Sa/AC 1, f. 223.
66 Sa/FAt 8, 9, 12, 20, 22, 25, 33.
67 The other places were Southampton and the London suburb of Southwark; Karras 1996, 35.
68 EKAC: Sa/AC 1, ff. 130, 186.
69 EKAC: Sa/AC 1, f. 217v.
70 In 1498 the town treasurers accounted for 9s. 9d. received from the mistress of the 'galye'; EKAC: Sa/FAt 12. In 1508 nothing was received, and in 1513 the treasurers accounted for the receipt of 19s.; Sa/FAt 17, 20.
71 In 1522, the last mention in the accounts, only 8d. was received; EKAC: Sa/FAt 27.
72 EKAC: Sa/FAt 5, 8, 14, 32; Sa/AC 4, ff.18, 170v.
73 EKAC: Sa/FAt 14, 32.
74 EKAC: Sa/AC 1, f. 170; Sa/AC 2, ff. 158, 317v, 361; Sa/FAt 33. For the record of the king's prison being in St Clement's parish, see Sa/AC 1, f. 253v.
75 This may have been what was later called The Rope Walk, but there is no documentary evidence for its medieval location; EKAC: Sa/FAt 5, 6, 12, 33; Sa/AC 2, f. 76.
76 EKAC: Sa/FAt 21, 29, 30; Sa/AC 3, f. 47v; Sa/AC 4, f. 68.
77 EKAC: Sa/FAt 12, 32; Sa/AC 3, ff. 86–7, 89.
78 EKAC: Sa/FAt 24, 33.
79 EKAC: Sa/FAt 7, 9, 32.
80 EKAC: Sa/AC 1, f. 5.
81 EKAC: Sa/AC 1, f. 41v.
82 EKAC: Sa/AC 1, ff. 284, 293v.
83 EKAC: Sa/AC 2, ff. 26v, 27v, 28.
84 EKAC: Sa/FAt 12.
85 EKAC: Sa/FAt 24. In 1480 The Bell seems to have been sold to meet the costs of constructing the conduit; EKAC: Sa/AC 1, f. 255v.
86 EKAC: Sa/FAt 8, 14, 21, 23.
87 Gibson 2002, 824–52.
88 EKAC: Sa/AC 1, ff. 163, 163v The reason for the assessment is not specifically stated, but circumstantial evidence points to the Commons granting a whole 'maltote, howserent and frerent' in that year to pay for bringing back Queen Margaret and Prince Edward from France.
89 Britnell 2006, 483, points out that fifteenth-century local urban taxes seldom list as many people as were assessed for royal taxes, so that account must be taken of the number who fell below the threshold of assessment.
90 A. Dyer used a multiplier of 6.5 in Dyer 1991, 64, and of 6.0–7.0 in Dyer 2000, 764. We have used a multiplier of 7 to compensate for those who may not have appeared in the assessment.
91 EKAC: Sa/FAt 12.
92 CCA: U3/11/5/1, 182–94.
93 EKAC: Sa/AC 2, f. 35v.
94 Mate 2006a, 125.
95 EKAC: Sa/AC 2, f. 161.
96 BL: Add. MS 33511, ff. 33–44.
97 Based on a figure of 379 households (i.e., the 579 of the list minus the 200 servants and apprentices, who were likely to have been part of households) multiplied by 7. This is higher than the total suggested by Mate 2006a, 239, since she did not treat the servants separately. The multiplier of 7 is the upper end of the range chosen by Dyer 2000, 764.
98 Andrewes and Zell 2002, 81, figs 2 and 3. There is no surviving information for St Clement's.
99 TNA: E133/6/815; Beer 1982, 152–3.
100 Andrewes and Zell 2002, 81, figs 2 and 3.
101 Hussey 1936, 251, 262, 270.
102 The approximate figure of 1,360 is arrived at by counting children as a quarter of the population, and therefore one third of the number of communicants. See Wrigley and Schofield 1981, 565–6, who estimate the number of households from communicants by dividing the total by 4.75.
103 Dyer 1991, 35–42.
104 Butcher 1979, 42–3.
105 EKAC: Sa/AC 2, f. 67; CCA: U3/11/5/1, 262–5.
106 EKAC: Sa/AC 2, f. 66v.
107 EKAC: Sa/AC 4, f. 161v.
108 EKAC: Sa/AC 2, f. 263.
109 EKAC: Sa/AC 2, ff. 267v, 268.
110 Sweetinburgh 2004a, 208.
111 EKAC: Sa/FAt 21; Sa/AC 3, f. 226v.
112 TNA: E363/4; EKAC: Sa/Ch 10J Tl, ac.
113 CCA: DCc/Chartae Antiquae S.283. In 1390 he imported 13 tuns of wine; TNA: E122/126/27.
114 Boys 1792, 406, 416.
115 TNA: E159/16. He gave evidence about the capture of wine from a Portuguese ship and stated that he was 40 years old. This means that he was born c.1349 and would presumably have begun his career about 1370.
116 CCA: DCc/ Chartae Antiquae S.256.
117 Roskell, Clarke and Rawcliffe 1992, 764.
118 For lists of mayors and MPs, see Boys 1792, 406–9, 416–18. Short biographies of the MPs can be found in Roskell, Clarke and Rawcliffe 1992.
119 Sandwich Guildhall Archive, Fretton 34/16; EKAC: Sa/Ch 10J T, m, t1p; Sa/AC 1, ff. 49, 94.
120 EKAC: Sa/AC 1, ff. 28v, 92v, 93.
121 CCA: DCc/Chartae Antiquae S. 258.
122 TNA: E122/127/18.
123 TNA: SC6/896/3, SC6/896/4.
124 Wedgwood 1936, 513.
125 In 1471 he owned a house adjacent to one that was probably on the south side of Upper Strand Street; EKAC: Sa/AC 1, f. 200; CKS: PRC 17/3/479.
126 1468: private deed, present location unknown; 1470: HLS deeds: bcb6675, 122.
127 CKS: PRC 17/6/39.
128 EKAC: Sa/AC 2, f. 23v.
129 CKS: PRC 32/12/117.
130 EKAC: Sa/AC 3, f. 35v; for the details, see his will (1524) and that of his wife (1531): CKS: PRC 32/14/64, PRC 17/19/205.
131 EKAC: Sa/AC 2, f. 222v.

132 TNA: E179/125/290.
133 Bindoff 1982b, 587; EKAC: Sa/AC 2, ff. 350v, 372v.
134 TNA: C1/113/12.
135 TNA: C1/601/12.
136 EKAC: Sa/FAt 33, Sa/FAt 34.
137 Bindoff 1982a, 99.
138 CKS: PRC 17/26/136; EKAC: Sa/AC 4, f. 145.
139 EKAC: Sa/AC 3, f. 79.
140 The Jesus House, which may have been the headquarters of the Jesus brotherhood, may have been located beside Jesus Quay, which lay just north of St Mary's church. This would have been more or less adjacent to Ringeley's house, The King's Lodging, which lay a little further west (Fig. 16.7).
141 CKS: PRC 32/19/8.
142 In the Cinque Ports: Sandwich (1439–40), Rye (1475), New Romney (1477), Winchelsea and Hastings (1483); Mate 2006a, 62.
143 TNA: E179/242/9.
144 EKAC: Sa/JB 2.
145 EKAC: Sa/AC 1, ff. 190, 200.
146 TNA: E122/128/19, E122/128/11, E122/128/14.
147 EKAC: Sa/AC 1, ff. 271v, 272; Sa/AC 2, f. 47–47v.
148 EKAC: Sa/AC 2, ff. 47v–48, 73; CKS: PRC 32/3/326.
149 EKAC: Sa/AC 3, f. 76.
150 EKAC: Sa/AC 2, f. 309v.
151 EKAC: Sa/AC 3, f. 34.
152 EKAC: Sa/FAt 33.
153 EKAC: Sa/AC 3, ff. 118v–119.
154 EKAC: Sa/FAt 34.
155 EKAC: Sa/AC 2, f. 371v (void ground); EKAC: Sa/AC 4, f. 10 (garden); CCA: U3/11/5/1, 293–4 (void ground); U3/11/5/1, 324–8 (void ground); CKS: PRC 17/34/273.
156 EKAC: Sa/AC 4, ff. 95 120, 130, 133.
157 CKS: PRC 17/6/291, 17/23/16.
158 EKAC: Sa/AC 2, ff. 232, 350v, 378.
159 EKAC: Sa/FAt 27, 31; Sa/AC 3, f. 37v; TNA: E179/124/197.
160 EKAC: Sa/AC 3, f. 97.
161 EKAC: Sa/JH 3, 48.
162 EKAC: Sa/AC 3, f. 250; the number taken from an ordinance forbidding the playing of unlawful games in their houses.
163 Hunter 2002.
164 CKA: PRC 17/21/17, 17/26/136; EKAC: Sa/FAt 35.
165 EKAC: Sa/Ch 10J T1, p.
166 EKAC: Sa/FAt 5, 6.
167 EKAC: Sa/AC 2, f. 23v.
168 According to the *Oxford English Dictionary*, tipplers were 'retailers of intoxicating liquors'.
169 EKAC: Sa/AC 3, f. 51v.
170 EKAC: Sa/AC 3, f. 220.
171 EKAC: Sa/AC 2, f. 328.
172 EKAC: Sa/AC 3, ff. 232–3.
173 EKAC: Sa/AC 2, ff. 121v, 170v, 257, 317v.
174 Ford 1997.
175 Gunsales must be an anglicisation of Gonzales.
176 EKAC: Sa/FAt 23.
177 TNA: E179/124/197.
178 McIntosh 1998, 96–7; Mate 2006b, 288–9.
179 EKAC: Sa/AC 2, f. 249; this Richard Harlestone might well be the youngest son of the wealthy property owner mentioned above.
180 CKS: PRC 32/25/33. It is possible that The White Hart in St Mary's parish was either where the house called Giles Quay stands, or next door at the present King's Lodging (House 88), which may have been part of the same property. Both houses are more or less opposite Bowling Street, which may have taken its name from the bowling alley (see also Chaps 14.8, n. 96 and 16.5.5 n. 102.
181 Hunter 2002, 65–70.
182 EKAC: Sa/AC 4, ff. 128v, 163v.
183 Jones 2001, 244.
184 BL: Add. MS 33511, f. 33v; Basyn is likely to have been William Basylver of St Peter's parish.
185 CKS: PRC 17/2/112, 17/2/304, 17/2/411, 17/6/267, 17/19/205, 17/22/204, 17/26/136, 17/30/126.
186 EKAC: Sa/AC 3, ff. 190, 225.
187 Grandam inherited a property from his father, also a baker, in the High Street, St Clement's (CKS: PRC: 17/3/463), and also rented from St Mary's churchwardens (CCA: U3/11/5/1, 248–5 and subsequent years).
188 EKAC: Sa/JH 3, 3. The other four bakers whose names are known may have lived outside the town and so not have been assessed in 1513.
189 EKAC: Sa/Ch 10J T1, r; Sa/AC 1, f. 183; Sa/AC 4, f. 107v; CKS: PRC 17/6/267.
190 CKS: PRC 17/19/3.
191 Swanson 1989, 82–9, 152–3, 170.
192 Mate 2006a, 142–5.
193 CKS: PRC 17/2/418.
194 CKS: PRC 17/7/51.
195 CKS: PRC 17/25/176, 17/30/144, 17/30/261.
196 CKS: PRC 17/29/243.
197 Tailor (seven), corveser (four), cook (three), smith (three), brewer (three), tallow chandler (two), butcher (two), weaver (two), miller (two), hosier (two), gardener (two), baker, barber, cooper, shipwright, cutler, tiler, turner, mason, glover, draper, clerk, capper, shoemaker, fuller, soap maker, sumptnor (?), wax chandler, skinner, rippier; EKAC: Sa/AC 1, ff. 163, 163v.
198 EKAC: Sa/AC 1, f. 33; Sa/AC 2, f. 239; Sa/AC 3, ff. 208, 225; Sa/FAt 11.
199 TNA: E179/242/9.
200 TNA: E179/235/55, E179/230/200C. The same documents record alien non-householders or servants: twenty-five in 1439–40, twelve in 1455–6 and eighteen in 1483.
201 EKAC: Sa/AC 1, f. 313v; Sa/FAt 30.
202 Goldberg 2004, 66, 101–3, McIntosh 2005, chaps 6 and 7.
203 Mate 2006a, 148.
204 EKAC: Sa/FAt 22–5; Sa/AC 2, f. 203v.
205 CKS: PRC 17/17/62; EKAC: Sa/JH 3, f. 2.
206 EKAC: Sa/AC 3, f. 34.
207 EKAC: Sa/FAt 25.

Chapter 11

1 *CPR* 1385–9, 175; *CCR* 1402–5, 412; EKAC: Sa/AC 1, f. 24v.
2 Harvey 1991, 63–5.
3 For various of these demands, see Harvey 1991, Appendix A.
4 Harvey 1991, 67–101.
5 Harvey 1991, 157; Cooper 1868, 255, 269.
6 Harvey 1991, 131–75, especially 157.
7 *Jehan de Waurin*, 384–8.
8 *Hall's Chronicle*, 235.
9 Parkin 1984, 211–13.
10 Harriss 2005, 637.
11 *CPR* 1461–7, 63.
12 *CPR* 1461–7, 465.
13 Scofield 1923, 41–50.
14 Barron 1981.
15 Ross 1974, 26, 48.
16 Scofield 1923, 522–3, 589; EKAC: Sa/AC 1, f. 201.
17 EKAC: Sa/AC 1, f. 204.

18 EKAC: Sa/AC 1, f. 223.
19 Barley 1976, 58–60; Creighton and Higham 2005, 158.
20 Streeten 1976; Wragg, Jarrett and Haslem 2005.
21 Smith 1970, 61, 72–4; Clarke and Carter 1977, 436.
22 *CPR* 1321–4, 14 (1321); *CPR* 1381–5, 534 (1385); *CPR* 1385–9, 268 (1387); *CPR* 1401–5, 489 (1405); *CPR* 1408–13, 425 (1412); *CPR* 1461–7, 63 (1461); TNA: E101/481/27, E101/481/28 (1466); E344/112/m/B. 16–18 (1468); *CCR* 1476–85, p. 48, no. 159 (1477); EKAC: Sa/AC 1, f. 255v (1480); *CPR* 1476–85, 405 (1483).
23 It was deepened as an anti-tank obstacle in World War II.
24 EKAC: Sa/AC 1, f. 100; Sa/FAt 7.
25 Webster and Cherry 1980, 253; Philp 2002, 136.
26 EKAC: Sa/FAt 9.
27 Clapham 1930.
28 One surviving roll, from *c*.1385, is badly damaged and almost totally illegible.
29 EKAC: Sa/AC 1, f. 100 (Sandown Gate and New Gate); Sa/AC1, f. 175v (Canterbury Gate and Woodnesborough Gate).
30 Turner 1970, 67; RCHM 1972, 41; Creighton and Higham 2005, 139.
31 EKAC: Sa/AC 1, f. 100; Sa/FAt 3.
32 EKAC: Sa/FAt 7 (1481); Sa/AC 2, ff. 13–14v (1491).
33 Tatton-Brown 1978; Philp 2002, 137, fig. 31–I.
34 The bricks used in the north-eastern tower were said to be comparable to those in Bell Harry tower, Canterbury Cathedral; Tatton-Brown 1978, 153.
35 EKAC: Sa/FAt 33; Sa/AC 3, f. 96v.
36 Bricks 24 × 11.5 × 7cm in size.
37 Tatton-Brown 1978, figs 4 and 5.
38 Philp 2002, fig. 32–I; no plan of the excavation is available.
39 EKAC: Sa/AC 9, ff. 329.
40 Tatton-Brown *et al.* 1982.
41 The potsherds found in 1929 are simply said to have dated from the fourteenth or fifteenth century.
42 Tatton-Brown 1989.
43 EKAC: Sa/AC 1, f. 100, 'performed up as hit begynne'.
44 EKAC: Sa/AC 1, f. 108.
45 EKAC: Sa/AC 1, f. 172.
46 EKAC: Sa/FAt 30, 32; Sa/AC 3, f. 90.
47 EKAC: Sa/AC 1, f. 175v; Sa/FAt 6, 8; 9.
48 EKAC: Sa/AC 5, f. 165.
49 EKAC: Sa/AC 1, f. 86.
50 In the early fifteenth century bulwark could be interchangeable with 'barbican', as in 'a strong defensive work which we call a barbican but the common people bulwerkis'; *Gesta Henrici Quinti*, 219. In medieval Sandwich 'bulwark' was sometimes used to mean the tower of a gatehouse.
51 Bricks 21–22 × 10–11 × 5–6cm in size.
52 EKAC: Sa/AC 3, f. 179.
53 TNA: E101/481/29, 5 Edw IV.
54 TNA: E101/481/29, 9 Edw IV.
55 EKAC: Sa/AC, 1 f. 241.
56 EKAC: Sa/FAt 8; thanks are due to the late Andrew Saunders for advice on the Bulwark and its armament.
57 EKAC: Sa/FAt 24, expenditure on 'mud walls' (1519); Sa/FAt29, both storeys of the Bulwark were cleaned, and tiles, lime and sand used in repairs (1532); Sa/AC 3, ff. 104v–5, masonry was brought in, including 'old bricks' (1539).
58 EKAC: Sa/AC 3, f. 187.
59 EKAC: Sa/AC 4, f. 40: '3 brass pieces, 8 forlockes and 1 broken, 9 chambers, 37 chambers, 8 bases, 1 curtall base, 1 portingale base, 2 port peces 1 stocked the other not, 1 hoole slang, 2 half slanges, 2 basys with 4 chambers'.
60 Scheduled Ancient Monument, Kent 56; for detailed descriptions, see Sandwich Survey Reports 7a and 7b.
61 *CPR* 1385–9, 140.
62 Southam 1980.
63 Philp 2002, 136–7.
64 See Creighton and Higham 2005, figs 3–7, for many other examples.
65 Southam 1980, site B.
66 EKAC: Sa/FAt 3, 22.
67 The opening, 0.15m square, was lined with ragstone slabs that projected 0.15m northwards from the wall face. The top of each side slab had a circular socket drilled into it, presumably designed to support a flap; Southam 1980, 309.
68 Personal communication the late J. Trussler.
69 EKAC: Sa/AC 1, f. 304v.
70 Philp 2002, 136.
71 Published erroneously as the base of a mural tower; Parkin 1984, 200.
72 EKAC: Sa/AC 1, ff. 221v, 223 (1475); see also Sa/AC 1, ff. 105v, 243 (1478).
73 EKAC: Sa/FAt 22.
74 Drawn by H. W. Rolfe. See Rolfe 1852, 4, pl. 55.
75 EKAC: Sa/FAt 8, 9; Sa/AC 4, ff. 76v–78.
76 EKAC: Sa/AC 5, f. 245.
77 Seymour 1776, 699.
78 TNA: E122/124/5–6.
79 E344/112/m/B. 16–18.
80 EKAC: Sa/FAt 9.
81 EKAC: Sa/AC 1, ff. 49, 24; Sa/FAt 11, 22, 25.
82 EKAC: Sa/FAt 16, 20, 22, 24, 29.
83 EKAC: Sa/FAt 20; this is the first time that the term 'bulwark' is used of Davis Gate's drum towers.
84 EKAC: Sa/FAt 29.
85 EKAC: Sa/FAt 9.
86 EKAC: Sa/AC 2, f. 215.
87 EKAC: Sa/AC 3, f. 90.
88 Butler 1990, 35.
89 BL: Cotton MS Augustus I.i.74.
90 Parkin 1984, 200, but citing no authority.
91 EKAC: Sa/AC 1, f. 257.
92 RCHM 1972, 45.
93 Daniels 1986, 71 (Hartlepool); Pye and Woodward 1996 (Plymouth); Horrox 1983, 112, 177 (Hull).
94 TNA: E101/481/24; *CPR* 1385–9, 4.
95 Stewart 2000, 61–4 and fig. 3.
96 TNA: E101/481/259.
97 *CPR* 1399–1401, 532–3; *CPR* 1436–41, 159.
98 *CPR* 1436–41, 362.
99 EKAC: Sa/AC 1, f. 6.
100 *CCR* 1392–6, 143.
101 *CFR* 1452–61, 95.
102 *CPR* 1385–9, 449; *CPR* 1422–9, 362.
103 *Hall's Chronicle* 1809, 235; *Jehan de Waurin*, 384–8.
104 Richardson 2004, pl. 6.
105 TNA: E101/481/26–27.
106 For example, Stewart 2000, 57.
107 Richmond 1970, 681–3.
108 EKAC: Sa/FAt 8: 'a grete gun with 3 chambers, a myche + a bolt + a forlock; 3 serpentyne guns with 6 chambers, 3 mychis, 3 bolts + 3 forlocks'.
109 EKAC: Sa/AC 2, f. 6v.
110 EKAC: Sa/FAt 32.
111 *L&P* 1540–41, p. 168, no. 372; p. 224, no. 465; p. 460, no. 745; *CSPDom* 1557–80, p. 510, no. 77; *CSPDom* Add. 1580–1625, p. 280, no. 45.

Chapter 12

1. Large numbers of rural houses in Kent have been dated using a framework provided by dendrochronology; Pearson 1994, 148–61. The difficulties of precise dating without such a framework are discussed in a Sussex context by Martin and Martin, 2009, vi–vii.
2. Barnwell and Adams 1994, 12–25.
3. Pearson 2001a.
4. For Faversham, see Pearson 2003, 412–15; for Rye, see Martin and Martin, 2009, 105–6.
5. Pearson 2001a.
6. CCA: DCc/Chartae Antiquae S. 256, 257, 258; EKAC: Sa/AC1, ff. 35, 78v, and deeds in possession of the current owner.
7. The ceiling is concealed, but Nick Dermott kindly made available photographs of the joists taken during restoration some years ago.
8. CCA: DCc/ Chartae Antiquae S.283. It was not possible to record this building, which is now independently owned.
9. Schofield 1994, 34–52; Leech 2000, 6–7.
10. RCHM 1980, 82–4, 85–8; RCHM 1981, 128, 138–40.
11. Pearson 1994, 30. This is also supported by work from elsewhere, e.g. Martin and Martin 2009, 96.
12. The three examples with no smoke-blackening are 3, 5 and 42 Strand Street (Houses 74, 75, 87).
13. The two types were first classified by W. A. Pantin, particularly in his influential article of 1962–3.
14. The timbers on the rear wall of the hall, now within a sixteenth-century wing, are flush with the interior, and were never part of an external wall. This suggests an aisle, but the presence of a mortice for a vertical post in the centre of the 'arcade plate' is puzzling and may indicate that a rear aisle was separated from the hall proper, forming more of an outshut than a true aisle.
15. The solid durns of the doorway are tenoned into the posts in a manner found at The Tudor Lodge Gift Shop, Chilham, which has been dated to 1370–1410 (Barnwell and Adams 1994, 94–5; Pearson, Barnwell and Adams 1994, 37).
16. Two late fourteenth-century examples are 16 East Street and Lamb Cottage, West Street, Rye; Martin and Martin 2009, 95–8. See also Tudor Lodge Gift Shop, Chilham; Pearson, Barnwell and Adams 1994, 37.
17. Pearson 2003, 415–17.
18. E.g., The Red Lion, High Street, and 58 French Street, Southampton (Faulkner 1975, 94–6, 104–7); 33 and 34 High Street, Winchester (Roberts 2003, 183–4).
19. A similar opening in the rafters occurs at The Red Lion, High Street, Southampton; Faulkner 1975, 94. We are grateful to David Martin for pointing out some rural examples with gables that leave the same evidence in the roofs.
20. Evidence can be found for and against the hall and front bays having different construction dates. We are grateful to Peter Lambert for his views on this difficult building.
21. No. 7 Potter Street must have been larger for there is no evidence for a stair, but evidence for smoke-blackening on the ground-floor beam at the rear, and a lack of partitioning to the south. These features suggest that there may have been an open hall or, more likely, a smoke bay and other accommodation at the back, and that there was an earlier or contemporary building to the south, possibly in the form of a mirror-image building as found at 1 The Butchery (House 3).
22. See 19 High Street, Charing, Kent; Pearson, Barnwell and Adams 1994, 27.
23. Salzman 1952, 418–19, 483–5; Keene 1990, 36; RCHM 1980, xlvi, 59–60, 64, 68–9, 82, 99–100; Roberts 2003, 186.
24. Barnwell and Adams 1994; Pearson 1994.
25. Charles 1978–79; Nos. 119–23 Upper Spon Street, tree-ring dated to 1454 and erected by Coventry Priory, await publication by Nat Alcock and Bob Meeson; we are grateful to them for information prior to publication.
26. Gibson 1973, 127–30; Andrews and Stenning 1989; Smith 1992, 148–9; Gibson 1998, 93–8.
27. CKS: PRC 17/2/116, 17/11/67, 17/20/3.
28. Pearson 1994, 123–5.
29. Pearson 1994, 69–75.
30. Keene 1985, 164–5, 758–66, fig. 88.
31. Short 1980.
32. For a summary of the debate and details of the buildings, see Grenville 1997, 121–33.
33. Pearson 1994, 114–15.
34. Roberts 2003, 148–50; Martin and Martin 2009, 118. Work on Farnham is currently ongoing. Thanks are due to Martin Higgins and Rod Wild for information in advance of publication.
35. CKS: PRC 10/1/76v.
36. For William Baly/Baily/Bayley in this property in 1505, see EKAC: Sa/AC 2, ff. 133–133v; for his mayoralty and wealth, see Boys 1792, 418, and BL: Add. MS 33511, f. 33.
37. We are grateful to Nick Dermott for showing us photographs of the hall ceiling joists, visible when the house was being restored.
38. Abstract of title in the possession of the present owners; EKAC: Sa/FAt 30.
39. Will of William Crispe (1543), CKS: PRC 17/23/109, where his house, which he left to his son William, was said to be in 'Strand Street next to Fisher Gate'. That it was on the west side of the lane to Fisher Gate is suggested by the route taken by Queen Elizabeth I when she came to Sandwich in 1572 and rode westwards along Strand Street 'until she came directly over against Mr Cripps house, almost as far as the Pellicane'; Boys 1792, 692.
40. Thanks to Linda Hall for visiting this house and agreeing that a date in the 1520s is feasible.
41. Mercer 1975, 20–21, 203; Moran 2003, 227–30, 323–5.
42. These are discussed in more detail in Chaps 12.9 and 16.5.
43. CKS: PRC 10/5/286 (1572); 10/8/158 (1575); 10/8/36v (1575); 10/9/161 (1577); 10/16/350 (1585); 10/15/38 (1586); 10/15/240 (1587); 10/17/299 (1587); 10/19/46v (1589); 10/19/113 (1590); 21/14/316 (1597). Six other inventories, which have no hall chambers but 'chambers next the street', may also describe houses of the same form, but since some of them have terms such as 'middle' or 'next' chamber, they have been excluded from the analysis.
44. EKAC: Sa/FAt 6; Sa/FAt 20.
45. Barnwell and Adams 1994, 133–5; Pearson 1994, 111–12; Harrington, Pearson and Rose 2000, lxv–lxix. In Sandwich, in 1556, Thomas Burden, carpenter, was contracted by John Parker, jurat, to make 'a frame to stand within the house' of one of his tenants, possibly suggesting the insertion of a timber chimney; CKS: PRC 17/30/98.
46. Keene and Harding 1987, 137–49, 5D, 5F.
47. Barnwell 2006, 178–9.
48. Leech 2000.
49. Pantin 1961; Smith 1992, 150–53; Roberts 2003, 179–82.
50. EKAC: Sa/FAt 5; Sa/AC 3, f. 219.
51. EKAC: Sa/AC 1, ff. 274v, 275.
52. Pantin 1961, 186.
53. Alston 2004, 40–49.
54. For a general discussion of survivors, see Clark 2000. A catalogue of remaining medieval shops in England is currently being prepared by Dave Stenning.
55. The name 'Joynte' is not listed among butchers, although a William 'Joynce' and a John 'Joyne' were butchers in the late 1470s and early 1480s; CKS: PRC 17/2/411; EKAC: Sa/AC 1, ff. 171, 253, 274; CKS: PRC 17/15/118.

56 CKS: PRC 17/22/209.
57 EKAC: Sa/AC 1, f. 33; Sa/FAt 2, 11; Sa/AC 3, ff. 208, 225; Sa/ZB 4, 12.
58 EKAC: Sa/AC 2, f. 305.
59 Personal information on Tonbridge from Gill Draper; for Cambridge, see Bryan and Wise 2002, 76, 83 and fig. 1.
60 Austin and Sweetinburgh 2007.
61 CKS: PRC 32/1/62; EKAC: Sa/AC 2, f. 20v.
62 Keene 1990; Smith 1992, 143–5; Grenville 1997, 190–93; Pearson 2003, 425–30; Pearson 2005, 57–9.
63 Schofield 1987, 16, 100–03; Keene and Harding 1987, 351–63, 421–5; Keene 1990, 36; Alston 2004, 54–8.
64 Schofield 1994, 70–71; Grenville 1997, 190–92.
65 EKAC: Sa/AC 1, f. 265.
66 CKS: PRC 17/6/90.
67 Parker 1971, 40–42, 113–18.
68 CCA: DCc/treasurers 33; DCc/Chartae Antiquae S.266d.
69 CKS: PRC 20/5/464, PRC 21/4/265, PRC 28/15/31: see Andrewes 1991, 217. In Suffolk large first-floor rooms, open to the roof and with shops or workshops below, were relatively common. It has been suggested that they were storage areas for wool, woad and cloth; Alston 2004, 49. In Winchester in the 1480s an inventory describes the house of a wealthy man with two shops, a hall, buttery, parlour, study and four chambers, as well as a wool chamber and a warehouse; Keene 1985, 176.
70 Will of Thomas Colman, 30 January 1495: CKS: PRC 17/6/90. In 1403 the heirs of an earlier Thomas Colman owned a tenement north of the Delf in St Peter's parish, which could be this building; EKAC: Sa/Cn 10J T1, j.
71 They were known in London as early as the fourteenth century; Keene and Harding 1987, 118–25, 299–312.
72 For the incidence of late fifteenth-century parlours and their contents in Kent, see Pearson 1994, 100.
73 CKS: PRC 17/3/479.
74 Pearson 1994, 103–4.
75 Salzman 1952, 554–6.
76 EKAC: Sa/TB 2, 21; Sa/AC 1, ff. 35, 78v, 308v; Boys 1792, 59.
77 Pearson 1994, 104–7.
78 Two may have existed at 36 and 38 North Street, Exeter; Portman 1966, 7–8 and fig. xii.
79 Salzman 1952, 483–5.
80 This type was common in Rye. See Martin and Martin 2009, 95–6.
81 CKS: PRC 10/15/38.
82 CKS: PRC 10/8/158, 10/15/240.
83 CKS: PRC 10/9/161, PRC 21/14/316.
84 CKS: PRC 10/5/286.
85 CKS: PRC 10/16/350, 10/19/46v.
86 Richardson 2003, 437, 446.
87 Pantin 1962–3.
88 Pearson 1994, 67–9, fig. 64.
89 Roberts 2003, 193.
90 Martin and Martin 2009, 114–115.
91 Dyer 2005, 128–57.
92 RCHM 1980, xlvi, 59–60, 64, 68–9, 82, 99–100.

Chapter 13

1 CKS: PRC 32/1/14.
2 Tatton-Brown 1993.
3 See *Oxford English Dictionary* definitions.
4 It was judged unsafe and dismantled between 1670 and 1673; Boys 1792, 285.
5 *Michael of Rhodes* I, f. 125b.
6 CKS: PRC 32/3/368–70, 32/4/212.
7 CKS: PRC 17/19/3.
8 CKS: PRC 17/20/3; Sweetinburgh 2004a, 218n.
9 Marks 2004, 73–85.
10 In 1494 the altars of St James and St Christopher were combined.
11 Jessiman 1957–8, 67–8.
12 Duffy 1992, 97–8; Cross and Barnwell 2005, 13–14. We are grateful to Paul Barnwell for visiting Sandwich and discussing the layout of the late medieval church.
13 CKS: PRC 32/3/368.
14 CKS: PRC 17/4/123. Chapels in rood lofts are not unknown; Jessiman 1957–8, 67.
15 CKS: PRC 17/5/308, PRC 32/9/20.
16 CKS: PRC 17/17/302.
17 Wood-Legh 1984, 111.
18 The change from elections in St Clement's to elections in the town hall was not made until 1683, by order of Charles I; Boys 1792, 345.
19 Rosseter 1986; Blake 1987.
20 CKS: PRC 17/23/60.
21 The 1767 plan of the church: copy held by St Clement's church; the original is said to be in Canterbury Cathedral Archives, but cannot at present be located. Plan of 1869 by Joseph Clarke, drawn in connection with alterations to the seating (Lambeth Palace Library, ICBS 06891). Boys 1792, facing p. 284.
22 Harrison 1967–8, 49; Lewcock 1980, 54–6.
23 See *Oxford English Dictionary* definitions; will of Henry Pyham, CKS: PRC 17/6/291, and Sweetinburgh 2004a, 223.
24 Boys 1792, 372–3.
25 EKAC: Sa/AC 1, ff. 5, 127.
26 CCA: U3/173/6/35.
27 Bulmer-Thomas 1959, 49.
28 The churchwardens' accounts survive for 1444–50, 1456–65, 1495–7, 1499–1503, 1504–23, 1526–32, 1542–9, 1558, 1568, 1582.
29 Bulmer-Thomas 1959, 50–51, discusses the evidence for and against a separate bell-tower, possibly located in the north-east corner between the choir and the crossing.
30 CCA: U3/11/5/1, pp. 262–5, 364–6.
31 CCA: U3/11/5/1, pp. 145–56.
32 Wood-Legh 1984, 112.
33 CCA: U3/11/5/1, pp. 3, 175–82.
34 Pfaff 1970, 62–83, especially 62–3; Duffy 1992, 115–16.
35 For a discussion of the popularity of the Jesus Mass in St Mary's and the status of those who contributed to it, see Sweetinburgh 2004a, 222–3.
36 CKS: PRC 17/29/7.
37 Will of Thomas Pache, 1553; CKS: PRC 32/25/33. In 1579 the Jesus Quay was owned by St Bartholomew's hospital, but its earlier history is unknown; EKAC: Sa/Ch 10B A1, 85.
38 For the relevant parts of most of the wills connected with the Jesus Mass, see Hussey 1907, 285–6.
39 Aston 1990.
40 CCA: U3/11/5/1, pp. 5, 18–36, 364–6.
41 CKS: PRC 17/3/475.
42 Cox 1916, 3–10; French 2000, 170.
43 CKS: PRC 32/25/33, PRC 17/32/104.
44 EKAC: Sa/AC 1, ff. 88–9; Boys 1792, 185–6, 190–93; Hussey 1936, 263–71.
45 Papal Bull of 1404 (EKAC: Sa/AC 2, f. 88) and confirmation of the establishment in 1509 (Sa/AC 2, f. 166).
46 Parkin 1984, 210.
47 EKAC: Sa/Ch 10J T1, m.
48 Boys 1792, 186; Parkin 1984, 210.
49 Boys 1792, 185–6. The reference to the school is only in the

sixteenth-century manuscript, now lost, which Boys relied upon. Draper 2007, 78–9, is mistaken in saying that the foundation charter specified that one of the priests was required to teach but there must have been a schoolmaster in Sandwich in the early fifteenth century since one called Thomas gave 40d. to St Mary's church when he died in 1449; CCA: U3/11/5/1, pp. 64–84.
50. He left the lead 'that is shot . . . and the other lead that is to be shot for the regeying of Our Lady Chancel'; CKS: PRC 17/5/297.
51. Wood-Legh 1984, 113–14.
52. Tricker 2002, 3.
53. A combination of evidence from wills of the Broke family suggests that the altar of St John the Baptist may have been on the south side near the south door; CKS: PRC 17/5/82, 17/6/301, 17/9/311.
54. CKS: PRC 17/20/215.
55. This paragraph is largely based on VCH Kent 1974a, 204–5, and Deighton 1994.
56. Recorded by Denis Harle in 1971; see Parfitt 1993, 60–61.
57. Deighton 1994, 325.
58. Rigold 1965, 7; Deighton 1994, 326; Hyde 1996, 48, 198.
59. Rosser 1988b; Rosser 1997, 141–54; Duffy 1992; Farnhill 2001, 48–50, 60–80.
60. Palliser 2006, 8.
61. EKAC: Sa/AC 1, f. 261v.
62. CKS: PRC 17/6/291.
63. CKS: PRC 17/5/344, 17/6/27, PRC 32/18/.
64. We are grateful to Caroline Barron for this suggestion. In 1543 the lease of the house was bequeathed by Sir Edward Ringeley to his wife; CKS: PRC 32/18/8. It still existed after the Dissolution when it was owned by the town; BL: Add. MS 33511, ff. 60–64, 73–7.
65. CKS: PRC 17/1/256, 17/5/344.
66. CCA: U3/173/6/22.
67. CKS: PRC 32/2/118, 32/3/39, PRC 17/20/4.
68. Rosser 1988b, 33.
69. Farnhill 2001, 96–7.
70. CKS: PRC 17/6/90.
71. CKS: PRC 17/20/3, 17/23/109.
72. Duffy 1992, 23.
73. Boys 1792, 843.
74. The number of Sandwich testators requesting burial inside is relatively low when compared with the fifteenth-century wills of the parish of All Saints, North Street, York, where 85 per cent of testators specified burial inside (Barnwell 2005, 81–3).
75. Duffy 1992, 331–2; in many places in Kent there was a preference for being interred near the image of Our Lady of Pity or near a family pew.
76. Norris 1977, 154; Badham 1990, 6–8.
77. Clark 1977, 60–68; Duffy 1992, 433–47.
78. Clark 1979; Sweetinburgh 2002.
79. EKAC: Sa/AC 4, f. 42.
80. Boys 1792, 687; Hussey 1936, 260; Bulmer-Thomas 1960, 24–7.
81. BL: Add. MS 33511, ff. 60–64, 73–7.
82. EKAC: Sa/ZB 4, 11.
83. Hussey 1936, 249–71.
84. CKS: PRC 17/25/76, 17/24/241; Duffy 1992, 504–5.
85. EKAC: Sa/AC 4, f. 46v.
86. For the general picture, see Duffy 1992, 379–523.
87. Sweetinburgh 2002.
88. Boys 1792, 149–71.
89. Sweetinburgh 2004a, 200–01.
90. Rolfe 1852, 3, pl. 66; Rolfe 1853, 4, pl. 2.
91. Tester 1979. We are grateful to Christopher Wilson for alerting us to this resemblance, and for discussing the date of the window.
92. Barnwell and Adams 1994, 95; Pearson, Barnwell and Adams 1994, 35.
93. Martin 1974, 20.
94. Boys 1792, facing p. 7; Roget Collection, Dover Museum and Bronze Age Boat Gallery: Eng./R/17.35, T1985.921; KAS: *Topographica Cantiana*, 7, 10.
95. By 1424 Whittington's hospital in London provided each resident with 'a little house with a chimney and other necessaries', and by 1443–6 each person at St Cross in Winchester had a lobby, a sitting room and a bedroom, both with fireplaces, a privy and a storeroom; Orme and Webster 1995, 91.
96. CKS: PRC 28/2/109, 28/2/130, 28/3/166; 21/2/45v, 21/7/15, 21/2/178, 21/7/233, 21/8/45, 21/8/185, 21/9/66, 21/9/284, 21/10/7, 21/11/22v, 21/12/306.
97. CKS: PRC 32/2/326.
98. Newman 1987, 68–71, quote on p. 70.

Chapter 14

1. CCA: U3/173/6/36.
2. EKAC: Sa/AC 1, f. 98.
3. EKAC: Sa/AC 1, ff. 30, 175v, 240; Seymour 1776, 700.
4. EKAC: Sa/TB 1, 13.
5. CKS: PRC 17/6/39.
6. EKAC: Sa/AC 2, f. 222v; in 1514 Roger Manwood was granted the 'chamber upon Pillory Gate'; EKAC: Sa/FAt 29.
7. EKAC: Sa/AC 2, f. 310v.
8. EKAC: Sa/AC 2, f. 320.
9. EKAC: Sa/AC 3, f. 27v.
10. EKAC: Sa/AC 4, f. 134v.
11. EKAC: Sa/AC 4, ff. 79, 100v, 119, 150.
12. EKAC: Sa/FAt 11.
13. EKAC: Sa/FAt 22.
14. EKAC: Sa/AC 2, f. 7.
15. EKAC: Sa/FAt 28; Sa/AC 3, f. 213; there is a suggestion of more than one wharf by 1548.
16. EKAC: Sa/FAt 29, 30.
17. EKAC: Sa/AC 3, ff. 63v, 78. No further structural repairs seem to have been needed until 1591; EKAC: Sa/AC 6, f. 147v.
18. Mayhew 1987, 29.
19. EKAC: Sa/FAt 2, 5–7.
20. EKAC: Sa/AC 1, f. 14v; Sa/TB 2, 39; Sa/FAt 8.
21. EKAC: Sa/AC 2, f. 366v; Sa/AC 3, f. 25v; CKS: PRC 17/50/195. For cranes at Southampton see Thick 1997, 177–200.
22. 'Bulwerk' and 'tower' seem to have been interchangeable terms, for example, at Fisher Gate in 1458 (EKAC: Sa/AC 1, f. 105v) and Davis Gate in 1491 (EKAC: Sa/FAt 10).
23. EKAC: Sa/FAt 9.
24. Salemke 1967; it was built in 1443 and is much restored.
25. *CCR* 1369–74, 399.
26. There was a weigh beam in the Fishmarket from 1434 to the end of the sixteenth century, and there was also a weigh beam in The Butchery; EKAC: Sa/AC 1, f. 20v; Sa/TB 1, 19.
27. EKAC: Sa/AC 1, f. 209v.
28. EKAC: Sa/Ch 10B A1, 1.
29. CCA: DCc/Chartae Antiquae S.243 (1281)
30. EKAC: Sa/AC 1, f. 105v.
31. EKAC: Sa/AC 1, f. 223.
32. EKAC: Sa/AC 1, f. 248.
33. EKAC: Sa/AC 1, f. 268v.
34. Site 74; unpublished CAT Report, 2005.
35. EKAC: Sa/AC 1, f. 313v.
36. EKAC: Sa/FAt9.

37 Sa/AC 4, f. 120.
38 'With the seashore to its north, the king's highway to the south, and another piece of vacant land to its east'; EKAC: Sa/TB 1, 15.
39 HLS: apz1324, bbz2861.
40 CKS: PRC 32/1/61 (1452); EKAC: Sa/AC 1, f. 101 (1456); private deed (1468); HLS: bct5773 (1517).
41 EKAC: Sa/Ch 10J T1, p; Sa/FAt 5, 6. Perhaps, as has been discovered at Boots, St George's Street, Canterbury (information Sheila Sweetinburgh), the cellar was occupied separately from the building above.
42 CKS: PRC 32/1/62; EKAC: Sa/AC 2, f. 20v.
43 BL: Add. MS 33511, f. 33.
44 EKAC: Sa/Ch 10J T1, ac (1366).
45 EKAC: Sa/AC 1, f. 93; Sa/TB 1, 25–8.
46 CKS: PRC 17/34/273.
47 EKAC: Sa/Ch 10J T1, r (1385); Sa/AC 1, f. 68 (1445); Sa/TB 1, 26 (1446).
48 EKAC: Sa/AC 2, f. 220v.
49 Mate 2006a, 24–5.
50 CKS: PRC 17/2/418, 17/4/38, 17/5/382, 17/7/117.
51 EKAC: Sa/AC 1, f. 14v.
52 EKAC: Sa/AC 1, f. 20v.
53 EKAC: Sa/Ch 10J T1, r; Sa/AC 1, f. 183.
54 CKS: PRC 17/2/411, 17/2/112.
55 EKAC: Sa/Ch 10b B1, 73 (1427); U3/11/5/1, pp. 18–36 (1445); U3/11/5/1, pp. 110–17 (1458).
56 CKS: PRC 17/30/126.
57 EKAC: Sa/AC 1, f. 193v.
58 CKS: PRC 17/26/136: Engeham owed the town 10s. annual rent for this property, but in 1518, in recompense for a loan of £7, the town agreed give up its annual rent.
59 EKAC: Sa/AC 1, ff. 271v, 272v; Sa/AC 2, f. 47.
60 EKAC: Sa/AC 1, ff. 25v, 115, 246; Sa/FAt 6.
61 EKAC: Sa/Ch 10J T1, p (1402); Sa/AC 1, f. 34 (1408); Sa/Ch 10J T1, m (1410).
62 The location has been identified from abutments in various documents: EKAC: Sa/AC 2, ff. 102, 121v; CKS: PRC 17/8/94; 32/11/49; 17/47/2.
63 Its position next to the churchyard is indicated in sixteenth- and seventeenth-century documents: EKAC: Sa/AC 3, f. 55v; Sa/AC 4, f. 176v; Sa/ZB 4, 7, 9–10 (town rents for 1760–61), where the old court hall is still mentioned.
64 Boys 1792, 295.
65 EKAC: Sa/FAt 6; Sa/AC 4, ff. 18, 170v.
66 Rigold 1968b; Tittler 1991, 25–33.
67 In the castle in 1460 (CPR 1452–61, 556), but possibly later in a special building in St Clement's parish (EKAC: Sa/AC 1, ff. 170, 253v). The growing complexity of prison arrangements and the distinction between the incarceration of freemen and strangers were not unique to Sandwich; Tittler 1991, 122–8.
68 EKAC: Sa/AC 2, ff. 158, 317v, 361; Sa/FAt 33.
69 TNA: E159/167; CKS: PRC 32/1/62.
70 EKAC: Sa/AC 1, f. 17v.
71 EKAC: Sa/AC 1, f. 130.
72 EKAC: Sa/FAt 6.
73 EKAC: Sa/AC 1, f. 216v.
74 EKAC: Sa/AC 1, f. 130.
75 EKAC: Sa/FAt 21; Sa/AC 3, f. 226v.
76 EKAC: Sa/AC 4, f. 46v.
77 EKAC: Sa/AC 3, f. 47v; Sa/AC 4, f. 68. The pillory may once been beside Pillory Gate, but of this there is no evidence.
78 EKAC: Sa/FAt 2.
79 EKAC: Sa/FAt 11–13.
80 EKAC: Sa/FAt 20, 30, 33.
81 CKS: PRC 32/2/512; EKAC: Sa/AC 1, f. 247v.
82 EKAC: Sa/AC 1, ff. 17v, 247v.
83 EKAC: Sa/AC 1, f. 33; Sa/AC 2, f. 305.
84 In modern times the name 'Luckboat' has been applied only to the south-east end of King Street, from its junction with St Peter's Street (medieval Love Lane) to the crossroads at its southern end. In the Middle Ages, however, Luckboat was used for the whole street, and the name King Street is mentioned in only one document, a will of 1492: CKS: PRC 17/5/335.
85 CKS: PRC 17/2/355, 17/6/267; EKAC: Sa/AC 1, f. 312v.
86 EKAC: Sa/AC 1, f. 265.
87 EKAC: Sa/AC 2, f. 210v; Sa/Ch 10J T1, n.
88 EKAC: Sa/AC 2, f. 285v.
89 The ground-floor plaster ceiling is decorated with a pattern of roses and fleur-de-lis flanking the Prince of Wales's feathers and his motto 'ich dien'. This was almost certainly done in honour of James I's eldest son, the popular Prince of Wales who died in 1612. Similar motifs are used elsewhere in Kent, including 40 High Street, Sandwich. (We are grateful to Claire Gapper for her opinion on the motifs.)
90 EKAC: Sa/Ch 10B.
91 CCA: U3/11/5/1, pp. 262–5, 286–9.
92 Winchester is a very clear example of a town contracting to its centre between the fourteenth and sixteenth centuries; Keene 1985, 143–7, figs 153–5.
93 EKAC: Sa/AC 1, f. 72v.
94 CCA: U3/11/5/1, pp. 18–36; U3/11/5/1, pp. 110–17.
95 CKS: PRC 32/2/118.
96 Unfortunately, No. 46 could not be investigated for this project, and although published by Parkin 1984, 205–8, its layout is not easy to understand. The Sign of the White Hart, along with a bowling alley and a quay next to Jesus Quay, was first mentioned in 1553 (CKS: PRC 32/25/33) and thereafter its history is well documented Chaps 10.3.3, 16.4).
97 EKAC: Sa/AC 1, f. 213v.
98 EKAC: Sa/AC 1, ff. 35, 78v.
99 CKS: PRC 17/19/205.
100 CKS: PRC 17/34/273, 17/30/122; 32/30/226; 17/45/273v, 17/43/254.
101 EKAC: Sa/AC 1, f. 17v.
102 EKAC: Sa/AC 2, ff. 243, 344v.
103 EKAC: Sa/AC 1, ff. 17v, 187, 190; Sa/AC 3, f. 234.
104 EKAC: Sa/AC 1, ff. 17v, 190.
105 EKAC: Sa/AC 1, ff. 217v, 258.
106 EKAC: Sa/AC 3, ff. 234, 234v.
107 From 1452, and perhaps earlier, the bailiff of Sandwich was charging non-freemen for the right to sell goods at the fair; TNA: SC6/896/8. In the years 1476–8 the Exchequer was collecting the profits of lastage and of St Clement's fair; TNA: E344/122mB. In 1501 John Wodbrand was to have the profits of the fair stalls that were against his house, which he rented from the town (EKAC: Sa/AC 2, f. 95); and a will of 1509 (CKS: PRC 17/11/67) indicates that he lived in the High Street.
108 This was the property that Walter le Draper had given to St Mary's church in 1312; CCA: U3/173/6/11; U3/173/6/13; U3/173/6/14.
109 CKS: PRC 17/3/463, 17/6/291; EKAC: Sa/AC 1, f. 287v.
110 EKAC: Sa/TB 1, 16; Sa/AC 2, ff. 160v, 245v; CCA: U3/11/5/1.
111 EKAC: Sa/AC 3, f. 135; Sa/AC 4, ff. 161, 209v, 213v; CCA: U3/173/6/17.
112 In 1598 the street was called 'Taresheafe or Fisher Street'; EKAC: Sa/AC 6, f. 248.
113 CKS: PRC 17/1/213; EKAC: Sa/AC 1, f. 242v.
114 EKAC: Sa/ZB 3, 68.
115 CKS: PRC 17/1/213, 17/2/33, 17/3/479; EKAC: Sa/AC 1, ff. 83, 227, 242v.

116 EKAC: Sa/Ch 10B A1, 73.
117 CKS: PRC 17/2/116, 17/11/67, 17/20/3.
118 EKAC: Sa/JH 3, 49; CKS: PRC 17/30/98.
119 EKAC: Sa/Ch 10B A1, 73; Sa/AC 5, f. 106.
120 EKAC: Sa/FAt 8; Sa/AC 1, f. 316v.
121 CKS: PRC 17/6/39, 17/12/572, 17/17/39.
122 EKAC: Sa/AC 2, f. 86v; CKS: PRC 17/5/376, 17/12/568.
123 James Hall, yeoman, bequeathed a piece of enclosed ground 'among the void grounds in Sandown Street'; CKS: PRC 17/23/60.
124 EKAC: Sa/AC 1, f. 217v.
125 EKAC: Sa/ChB A1, f. 72.
126 EKAC: Sa/AC 1, ff. 274, 289v.
127 CCA: U3/11/5/1, pp. 18–36; U3/11/5/1, pp. 38–61; EKAC: Sa/Ch10 T1, y.
128 EKAC: Sa/Ch 10B A1; Sa/AC 1, ff. 6v, 34v, 35, 41.
129 EKAC: Sa/Ch 10B A1, 73; Sa/AC 1, f. 48; CKS: PRC 17/29/221.
130 EKAC: Sa/AC 1, f. 29v.
131 EKAC: Sa/FAt 27; Sa/AC 2, f. 301v.
132 EKAC: Sa/AC 3, f. 36.
133 It was repaved in 1475, suggesting that it was subject to heavy wear and therefore presumably carried much traffic; CKS: PRC 32/2/326.
134 The same is true of both Canterbury Gate and Woodnesborough Gate.
135 For example, in 1498 the town paid for a dam to be built at New Gate to prevent salt water polluting the Delf; EKAC: Sa/FAt 12.
136 EKAC: Sa/FAt 2.
137 EKAC: Sa/AC 1, f. 246.
138 EKAC: Sa/FAt 30.
139 EKAC: Sa/FAt 10, 32; Sa/AC 2, ff. 103, 234.
140 EKAC: Sa/FAt 10.
141 EKAC: Sa/AC 2, f. 103.
142 EKAC: Sa/FAt 20, 22, 24, 34.
143 EKAC: Sa/FAt 20.
144 EKAC: Sa/FAt 23, 28, 33.
145 EKAC: Sa/AC 3, ff. 13, 168.
146 EKAC: Sa/AC 1, f. 272.
147 There were two by 1432; EKAC: Sa/AC 1, f.4.
148 EKAC: Sa/FAt 2.
149 EKAC: Sa/FAt 33, Sa/FAt 34.
150 EKAC: Sa/AC 3, f. 165.
151 EKAC: Sa/AC 3, ff. 171v, 179.
152 EKAC: Sa/AC 4, ff. 136, 143.

Chapter 15

1 McIntosh 1998.
2 EKAC: Sa/AC 4, f. 168v.
3 EKAC: Sa/AC 4, f. 162.
4 EKAC: Sa/AC 4, f. 175v.
5 *CSPDom* 1547–80, p. 171, no. 25.
6 Bowler 1983, 29.
7 *CSPDom* 1547–80, p. 201, no. 35.
8 EKAC: Sa/AC 4, f. 283.
9 EKAC: Sa/AC 4, f. 372v;.
10 EKAC: Sa/AC 5, ff. 184v, 193.
11 EKAC: Sa/AC 5, f. 184.
12 EKAC: Sa/AC 5, f. 137v.
13 *CSPDom* 1547–80, p. 491, no. 41.
14 Boys 1792, 736–40, gives the whole of Andrison's admirable report.
15 EKAC: Sa/AC 5, f. 219.
16 EKAC: Sa/AC 6, ff. 152–3.
17 Gardiner 1954, 207.
18 EKAC: Sa/AC 5, f. 253.
19 EKAC: Sa/AC 5, f. 262v.
20 *APC* ns 1, 1575–7, 214; in 1576 a ship from Marseilles was shipwrecked outside Sandwich.
21 EKAC: Sa/AC 5, f. 141v.
22 BL: Stowe MS 570, ff. 16–19.
23 Gibson 1993, 347.
24 EKAC: Sa/ZB 3, 24.
25 *CPSDom* 1581–90, p. 384, no. 5.
26 EKAC: Sa/AC 6, f. 94v.
27 EKAC: Sa/AC 6, f. 210.
28 EKAC: Sa/AC 6, f. 215.
29 EKAC: Sa/AC 6, f. 224.
30 EKAC: Sa/AC 6, f. 231v.
31 Sacks and Lynch 2000, 387–8, 393–8.
32 EKAC: Sa/AC 4, f. 151v; in return, the guild agreed to carry cargoes at the rate of 8d. a quarter for wheat and 6d. a quarter for malt.
33 TNA: E190/638/1.
34 By the 1580s nearly 75 per cent of London's grain supply came from Kent; Fisher 1954, 139.
35 EKAC: Sa/AC 5, f. 141v.
36 Hipkin 2008, 102–6.
37 BL: Lansdowne 71/46, ff. 89, 89v.
38 Hipkin 2008, 115–16.
39 *CSPDom* 1594–7, pp. 324–5, no. 30.
40 Backhouse 1995, 105–8.
41 TNA: E190/645/15.
42 Bower 2000, 164.
43 EKAC: Sa/FAt 33.
44 EKAC: Sa/AC 4, ff. 111v, 114, 167v.
45 Backhouse 1995, 17, 75; *CPR* 1560–3, 336.
46 Bays were tissues fabricated with the use of carded wool: says were crossed tissues made with threads of combed wool.
47 EKAC: Sa/AC 4, f. 204v, at the Wednesday market freemen only were allowed to buy, but on Saturday both freemen and strangers could buy.
48 EKAC: Sa/AC 4, f. 248v.
49 BL: Stowe MS 570, ff. 16–19; Gibson 1993, 347.
50 Andrewes and Zell 2002, 81 and n. 9, use a multiplier of 4.75, with allowances for under-registration, to arrive at 2,500 in Sandwich; Dyer 2000, 764, more generally uses one of 6–7, which would give a higher figure.
51 Backhouse 1991, 77–8; Andrewes and Zell 2002, 81–6.
52 Backhouse 1995, 31–2.
53 Tables in Backhouse 1995, 31, and Andrewes and Zell 2002, 86; for Kent in general, see Bower 2000, 142, 149–59.
54 Andrewes 2000, 117–18.
55 Backhouse 1995, 83–4.
56 EKAC: Sa/AC 5, ff. 53–54v, 83–85v.
57 Bentwich 1971, 37.
58 BL: Add. MS 27462; Backhouse 1995, 84–5.
59 EKAC: Sa/AC 5, ff. 267v, 278.
60 TNA: SP12/152/14; SP12/152/40.
61 Backhouse 1995, 87–8.
62 Backhouse 1995, 132–4.
63 Backhouse 1995, 90.
64 Andrewes and Zell 2002, 87–9.
65 Archer 2000, 238–41.
66 Archer 2000, 241–6.
67 Ollerenshaw 1990, 65–79, 139–42.
68 Clark 1977, 139.
69 EKAC: Sa/AC 5, f. 135.
70 EKAC: Sa/AC 5, f. 136v.

[71] The site was identified from eighteenth- and nineteenth-century deeds still in existence in the 1880s; Dorman 1886, 59–60.
[72] The visit is recorded in the year book (EKAC: Sa/AC 5, f. 137v) and recounted in detail in Boys 1792, 691–5. The furnishing of the King's Lodging is described in the probate inventory of Roger Manwood, jurat, who was a nephew of the owner Sir Roger (d. 1592), and was living in the house when he died; CKS: PRC 10/19/113.
[73] Backhouse 1995, 98–9.
[74] Backhouse 1995, 121–2.
[75] EKAC: Sa/AC 6, f. 245v; Bower 2000, 161.
[76] Hipkin 2008, 30.
[77] Backhouse 1995, 119–20.
[78] CKS: PRC 17/48/55.
[79] EKAC: Sa/ZB 3, 24.
[80] EKAC: Sa/AC 4, f. 355v.
[81] CKS: PRC 32/25/33.
[82] EKAC: Sa/AC 5, f. 179.
[83] EKAC: Sa/AC 6, ff. 152–3.
[84] EKAC: Sa/AC 6, ff. 179, 184.
[85] For example, EKAC: Sa/AC 4, ff. 167, 218, 296v; Sa/ZB 4, 12.
[86] EKAC: Sa/AC 4, ff. 350v, 355v.
[87] EKAC: Sa/ZB 4, 12.
[88] EKAC: Sa/FAt 22, 24.
[89] '4 sacres of cast iron on their carriages; 1 mynion of iron on carrg; 2 falcons & 2 falconettes on carrgs; 3 portuigall bases of brass with their carrgs; 3 fowlers of iron; 2 quarter slinges with carrgs; 2 old single bases & 1 cast base; 3 robenettes of brass with carrgs; 30 chambers; 6 ladells, 5 spunges, 1 worme; good and bad shovells; 12 mattocks; 4 iron crows; 6 short pitchforks; a searching auger with the podd broken from the shank; 10 stores hewen; certain slate and shot of lead and stone'; EKAC: Sa/AC 5, f. 102v.
[90] We are grateful to the late Andrew Saunders for his comments on this subject.
[91] EKAC: Sa/AC 4, f. 271v.
[92] EKAC: Sa/ZB 4, 12.
[93] EKAC: Sa/AC 5, f. 203v; Sa/AC 6, f. 17v (1583).
[94] Sa/AC 4, f. 170v.
[95] EKAC: Sa/AC 6, f. 2v.
[96] EKAC: Sa/AC 5, f. 272v.
[97] EKAC: Sa/AC 5, f. 3v.
[98] EKAC: Sa/AC 4, f.168v.
[99] EKAC: Sa/AC 4, ff. 168v, 188v, 218, 240, 259v, 296v.
[100] EKAC: Sa/AC 4, f. 223v.
[101] EKAC: Sa/AC 5, f. 245.
[102] EKAC: Sa/ZB 4, 12.
[103] EKAC: Sa/AC 4, f. 231v.
[104] EKAC: Sa/AC 4, f. 244.
[105] *CSPDom* 1547–80, 389 no. 22.
[106] EKAC: Sa/AC 5, f. 102v.
[107] EKAC: Sa/AC 5, f. 135; Sa/AC 6, f. 33.
[108] *APC* ns 1, 1595–6, 443.
[109] Stewart 2000, 55, suggests that the castle was demolished during Henry VIII's castle building programme in 1536, but later references, although ambiguous, imply that it continued in existence at least until the end of the sixteenth century.
[110] *CSPDom* 1547–80, p. 310, no. 77.
[111] *CPSDom* 1581–90, p. 506, no. 69.
[112] *CSPDom* 1595–97, p. 179, no. 70.
[113] EKAC: Sa/AC 5, f. 165.
[114] EKAC: Sa/ZB 4, 12.
[115] EKAC: Sa/AC 6, f. 33.
[116] EKAC: Sa/AC 4, f. 291.
[117] EKAC: Sa/AC 8, ff. 27, 33–4.
[118] EKAC: Sa/AC 9, ff. 204, 297, 304, 329.
[119] £5 was spent in 1586, for instance; EKAC: Sa/ZB 4, 11.
[120] Major work was undertaken in 1575 (EKAC: Sa/ZB 4, 12) and 1586 (EKAC: Sa/ZB 4, 11).
[121] EKAC: Sa/AC 6, f. 134v.
[122] EKAC: Sa/AC 4, f. 204v.
[123] Eales 2000, 292; see also Hasler 1981, 306.
[124] Ollerenshaw 1990, 200–11.
[125] EKAC: Sa/AC 5, f. 155.
[126] CKS: PRC 17/48/49, 10/18/433.
[127] Bower 2000, 165.
[128] EKAC: Sa/AC 5, ff. 147v, 171.
[129] EKAC: Sa/AC 5, f. 169.
[130] Such as William Gayney, CKS: PRC 10/25/182; John Coxe, PRC 10/15/240, and Thomas Hurlestone, PRC 10/20/177.
[131] CKS: PRC 32/37/261, 28/3/199.
[132] EKAC: Sa/AC 5, f. 153; Sa/AC 6, f. 114.
[133] EKAC: Sa/AC 5, f. 264v; Sa/AC 6, f. 169.
[134] EKAC: Sa/AC 4, f. 255.
[135] CKS: PRC 17/43/321.
[136] CKS: PRC 17/43/254.
[137] CKS: PRC 17/45/273.
[138] EKAC: Sa/AC 5, f. 116.
[139] EKAC: Sa/AC 6, f. 102.
[140] Hunter 2002, 65.
[141] Ollerenshaw 1990, 118–19.
[142] For an excellent discussion of the changing role of women and men in the food and drink trades, see McIntosh 2005, chapters 6 and 7.
[143] EKAC: Sa/AC 6, f. 65.
[144] William Skynner, CKS: PRC 10/4/163; Thomas Yeoman, PRC 10/22/432; William Silvertopp, PRC 10/27/56.
[145] EKAC: Sa/AC 5, f. 185.
[146] EKAC: Sa/AC 6, f. 120v; CKS: PRC 10/23/438, 17/50/406.
[147] CKS: PRC 10/18/109, 17/47/362v.
[148] CKS: PRC 10/22/432.
[149] CKS: PRC 10/25/532.
[150] Spufford 1990.
[151] Overall, 291 inventories survive for this period, analysed by Richardson (1999) for their goods and domestic bequests.
[152] CKS: PRC 10/15/38, 17/46/83; EKAC: Sa/AC 6, ff. 119v, 199v.
[153] Ollerenshaw 1990, 191–211 and appendix 3.
[154] CKS: PRC 10/19/113.
[155] CKS: PRC 10/27/62.
[156] CKS: PRC 10/18/548.
[157] EKAC: Sa/ZB 3, 68.
[158] CKS: PRC 10/3/271v; EKAC: Sa/AC 4, f. 137.
[159] CKS: PRC 10/24/56, 17/51/115.
[160] CKS: PRC 10/15/275; EKAC: Sa/AC 5, ff. 221, 253; Ollerenshaw 1990, 128–9, notes several common councillors and jurats who had fallen on hard times in the early seventeenth century.

Chapter 16

[1] Hussey 1936, 270.
[2] Boys 1792, 186.
[3] Holinshed 1586–7, vol. 3, p. 1377.
[4] Cavell and Kennett 1963, 6; Seaborne 1971, 12–32; EKAC: Sa/AC 4, f. 224v.
[5] *CPR* 1560–63, 613.
[6] Manwood was steward of the liberties to Archbishop Parker until 1572, when he became a judge. Earlier, he had been Solicitor of the Cinque Ports and Recorder of Sandwich (1555–66);

Backhouse 1991, 74; Hasler 1981, 15.
7. Boys 1792, 199, 207–13.
8. EKAC: Sa/AC 4, f. 232v.
9. EKAC: Sa/AC 5, f. 13v.
10. Boys 1792, 199–275; Cavell and Kennett 1963. These sources document what is known about the early running of the school.
11. EKAC: Sa/AC 5, f. 44.
12. Cavell and Kennett 1963, 34–40.
13. Boys 1792, 223–5.
14. Cavell and Kennett 1963, 20–21.
15. See, for example, Hoad Farm, Patrixbourne, of 1566; Bax Farm, Tonge, of 1567; and Boughton Malherbe Place of 1584.
16. Described in an article in the *Deal, Walmer and Sandwich Mercury*, 14 October 1893.
17. See Berkhamsted School of 1541, Ashbourne School of 1585 (Seaborne 1971, 15, 19–21), or, more locally, Tonbridge School of 1553 (Summerson 1969, 105).
18. Boys 1792, facing p. 275.
19. *Deal, Walmer and Sandwich Mercury*, 14 October 1893.
20. In 1552 various town charters found in the vestry of St Peter's church were so 'putrified' that it was ordered that they should be placed in the best of three chests in the church and moved to the loft over the council chamber; EKAC: Sa/AC 4, ff. 18, 170v.
21. EKAC: Sa/AC 5, ff. 246, 259–259v.
22. Chinnery 1990, 240–41; Tittler 1991, 113.
23. Chinnery 1990, 448; Tittler 1991, 113–17.
24. Perhaps based upon designs by Vredeman de Fries or Cornelis Bos. We are grateful to Victor Chinnery, Tarq Hoekstra and Charles Tracy for these suggestions.
25. EKAC: Sa/AC 5, f. 214v.
26. EKAC: Sa/AC 5, f. 241.
27. The building has been greatly enlarged over time, and the following account deals only with the original phase of work.
28. Boys 1792, facing p. 788.
29. Linda Hall, personal communication. Their style suggests a date between *c.*1580 and the very early seventeenth century.
30. Hall 2005, 103–4.
31. Ornate plaster ceilings were apparently not a common feature in town halls; Tittler 1991, 46. In this case there seems little doubt that the unevenly matched joists would have been plastered from the start, although the ceiling may have been plain.
32. Boys 1792, 789. This has now gone.
33. Tittler 1991, 35–7, 112.
34. For example, 4 Watchbell Street (1556–60) and 31 Mermaid Street (1576) in Rye, Sussex: Martin and Martin 1986, 71; Martin and Martin 1987, 36–8; Martin and Martin 1989, 26–8; and the Staple Inn, High Holborn, London (1586): Hewett 1980, 231–3.
35. EKAC: Sa/AC 4, ff. 194, 204v.
36. Parker 1971, 151, pl. 40A.
37. Vallance 1920, 125–57; Walker 1981, 12–14.
38. EKAC: Sa/AC 6, f. 116v.
39. EKAC: Sa/AC 6, f. 191.
40. No. 13 on Fig. 8.1, where the detail is not easily visible, but see Boys 1792, 316–17 and facing p. 790.
41. EKAC: Sa/AC 9, f. 83; Sa/ZT 14/27.
42. EKAC: Sa/AC 4, f. 161v.
43. EKAC: Sa/ZB3/24; BL: Stowe MS 570, ff. 16–19; Gibson 1993, 347. The term 'houses' was used in one document and 'households' in another; Backhouse 1995, 23–4, discusses which is meant and concludes, as must surely be the case given the reference to seven individuals, that 'households' was the intended term.
44. E.g., CKA: PRC 17/47/2, 17/47/2; EKAC: Sa/AC 6, f. 135.
45. EKAC: Sa/AC 4, f. 243.
46. EKAC: Sa/AC 4, ff. 305v, 114, 313v, 314.
47. EKAC: Sa/AC 4, ff. 296v, 343–344v.
48. EKAC: Sa/AC 4, f. 355v.
49. Andrewes and Zell 2002, 86.
50. EKAC: Sa/AC 5, f. 116.
51. EKAC: Sa/AC 5, f. 165. When the money was repaid the house was occupied by Thomas Tyssar who may, of course, have sub-let; EKAC: Sa/ZB4/12.
52. EKAC: Sa/AC 5, ff. 241v, 245; Sa/AC 6, ff. 29–29v; CKA: PRC 17/46/386.
53. CKS: PRC 17/47/362.
54. EKAC: Sa/AC 5, ff. 53–54v, 83–85v. For a discussion of the lists and of immigrant households and families, see Backhouse 1995, 15–32.
55. Backhouse 1991, 220–21.
56. Jeremy Pynnock the elder died in 1571 leaving his Love Lane properties to his wife. He had a son, John; CKS: PRC 17/42/337, 10/5/274v. His cousin, also Jeremy Pynnock, died in 1572; CKS: PRC 10/6/187v.
57. E.g., Bernard van Lent, CKS: PRC 17/45/273v; Jose de Toor: CKS: PRC 17/51/133.
58. Andrewes and Zell 2002.
59. For similar difficulties in precisely dating houses at this time in Totnes, Devon, see Laithwaite 1984, 70.
60. CKS: PRC 17/46/99.
61. Arnold *et al.* 2001b, 2001c.
62. EKAC: Sa/AC 4, f. 355v. In 1561 he owned the 80 tun bark the *Mary James*, which he had shared with his brother-in-law, the merchant Richard Colyar, who bequeathed his part to Gilbert when he died that year; EKAC: Sa/ZB3/68; CKS: PRC 32/29/59. He also owned a lighter in 1567; EKAC: Sa/AC 4, f. 342v.
63. EKAC: Sa/AC 5, f. 108; CKS: PRC 17/50/195.
64. Ayres 2003, 45–6.
65. Gravett 1981, 23, pls 101–7; Quiney 1993, fig. 26.
66. The same motif was used for the first-floor plaster ceiling of a tiny house at 40 High Street. Despite lack of positive evidence for doorways, this might have been the wing to a range to one side that descended into separate ownership and has been rebuilt. Our thanks to Claire Gapper for her opinion on the date of this motif.
67. The house was not visited for this project and how much decoration remains *in situ* is unclear. It was illustrated by Nathaniel Lloyd in 1931 (Lloyd 1975, 77, 79, figs 688, 738, 774–5).
68. CKS: PRC 10/16/264, 17/47/2v.
69. Ollerenshaw 1990, 118–19.
70. Only the southern half of 24 Fisher Street, the George and Dragon Public House, dates from the sixteenth century; it has now been joined to the house to the north, built in the seventeenth century.
71. A number of relatively narrow medieval open-hall houses that were not fully rebuilt also had rear stacks inserted, e.g., 8 (House 7) and 9 (House 8) Cattle Market (both 4.2m); 5 (House 75) and 42 (House 87) Strand Street (both 4.00m).
72. Parkin 1984, 214.
73. O'Neill 1953. The roofs of Sandwich are not identical to the early seventeenth-century ones in Great Yarmouth. Similar single-cell plans occurred at King's Lynn, where they were also dated to the early seventeenth century; Parker 1971, 100–01, and fig. 25.
74. Martin and Martin 2009, 120–45.
75. Priestley and Corfield 1982, 94–7.
76. CKS: PRC 10/19/113.
77. CKS: PRC 10/16/350, 10/19/46v.

[78] Joyce Buskyn: CKS: PRC 17/43/254, 10/10/207v; John Buskyn: CKS: PRC 17/14/95, 10/15/180.
[79] CKS: PRC 10/25/289.
[80] CKS: PRC 10/24/513.
[81] E.g., Priestley and Corfield 1982, 99.
[82] Priestley and Corfield 1982, 99–100.
[83] CKS: PRC 10/22/463, 10/23/438.
[84] Richardson 1999, 277.
[85] For a discussion of the muster in Kent, and particularly the Cinque Ports, see Hyde and Harrington 2000, viii–xxxi.
[86] Four of the galleries are in inventories dating to the 1570s, five in the 1580s and two in the 1590s.
[87] The years 1550–69: Coventry 24.8 per cent, Derby 27.6 per cent; 1570–89: Coventry 12.7 per cent, Derby 14.3 per cent; 1590–1609: Coventry 10.2 per cent, Derby 12.8 per cent (Dyer 1981, 212).
[88] Richardson 1999, 39–40.
[89] Leech 2000; in 1598 Stow reported fifty open halls surviving in London, almost all in courtyard houses (Schofield 1987, 18), and therefore of higher social status than those found in Sandwich.
[90] Schofield 1994, 113–15.
[91] CKS: PRC 10/16/350, 10/8/158.
[92] EKAC: Sa/AC 4, f. 261v. This is much later than in some other towns. In London, roofs of reed, rushes or straw had been forbidden from as early as 1212 (Riley 1859–62, vol. 2, Lib. Cust. I 86–8), and in the fourteenth century ordinances stated that chimneys were no longer to be of wood but of stone, tiles or plaster (Salzman 1952, 99). In Coventry, thatched roofs were prohibited in 1474 and construction of wooden chimneys in 1493 (VCH Warwickshire 1969, 147).
[93] EKAC: Sa/AC 5, f. 192v.
[94] The percentage of all houses with kitchens was 59.9 per cent, which compares well with Norwich, where it was 'just under 60%'; Priestley and Corfield 1982, 106.
[95] Dyer 1981, 208.
[96] CKS: PRC 10/2/168v.
[97] CKS: PRC 10/24/125, 10/15/160.
[98] CKS: PRC 10/5/84, 10/16/264.
[99] Gryffyn Amoore, William Wollet, Martin Barrel and John Streaton; CKS: PRC 10/8/36v, 10/20/496, 10/23/84, 10/26/58.
[100] E.g., CKS: PRC 10/22/534 and 10/22/432, which have parlour chambers but no parlour.
[101] Dyer 1981, 208; Priestley and Corfield 1982, 99.
[102] The Sign of the White Hart, along with a bowling alley and a quay next to Jesus Quay, was left to Gull, who was already the occupier, by his kinsman Thomas Pache, gent., in 1553; CKS: PRC 32/25/33. In the 1550s Gull was a tippler and had three beds in his house, which seems to have been badly burnt in 1569 and had to be at least partly rebuilt; EKAC: Sa/AC 3, ff. 232–3, 250; Sa/AC 5, f. 18. When Gull died in 1572 the house had three parlours, one of which was new, and five chambers; CKS: PRC 10/7/33. He willed that it should be let for a while, the money to be divided between his children, before passing to his only son; CKS: PRC 17/41/345. For whatever reason, the house, still with three parlours and five chambers, remained let, and was leased by Iden in 1586; CKS: PRC 17/47/2v, 10/16/264.
[103] Richard Marback, former beer brewer (CKS: PRC 10/15/275), and Thomas Yeoman and William Skynner, both once tipplers (CKS: PRC 10/22/432, 10/4/163). In his inventory Yeoman owed £2 15s. for barrels of beer.
[104] There were also parlours next to the street in some Southampton houses; Roberts 2003, 183.
[105] Griffyn Amoore, John Iden and William Crispe; CKS: PRC 10/8/36v, 10/16/264, 10/28/76.
[106] CKS: PRC 10/2/168v.
[107] Janet Pennington, personal communication. The apparel of Griffyn Amoore, vintner and tippler, was listed in the 'chamber next the street parlour'; CKS: PRC 10/8/36v.
[108] CKS: PRC 10/19/113.
[109] For the details of household objects in the Sandwich inventories, see Richardson 1999, 273–83.
[110] Harrington, Pearson and Rose 2000, lxxi.
[111] CKS: PRC 10/11/309, 10/15/253.
[112] Richardson 1999, 63.
[113] CKS: PRC 17/51/299.
[114] CKS: PRC 10/24/80.
[115] CKS: PRC 10/17/299, 10/18/199, 28/3/210.
[116] CKS: PRC 32/37/261, 28/3/199.
[117] CKS: PRC 17/47/362v.
[118] CKS: PRC 17/41/244v, 17/42/161, 17/47/362v, 17/47/272.
[119] Dyer 1981; Priestley and Corfield 1982.
[120] Richardson 1999, 2003.
[121] Richardson 2003, 443–5.
[122] Richardson 1999, 277–9; Richardson 2003, 446–7.
[123] Chris King, lecture at the University of Kent, 2005, and personal communication.
[124] Laithwaite 1984, 68–9.

Chapter 17

[1] Dyer 2000, 752, 768–70; Hinton 2000, 243.
[2] Smith 1970, 61, 72–4; Clarke and Carter 1977, 436.
[3] RCHM 1972; RCHM 1980; Moran 2003.
[4] Population calculated from those who paid the lay subsidy in 1524–5; Dyer 2000, 761–4. In Salisbury houses of early sixteenth-century date or earlier calculated from RCHM 1980, excluding those simply called '16th century'. In Shrewsbury, the numbers are taken from Moran 2003, 135–72.
[5] Portman 1966; Platt and Coleman Smith 1975; Brown 1999.
[6] Parker 1971.
[7] E.g., Clark 2000.
[8] Alston 2004.
[9] For similar dates in London and Canterbury, see Schofield and Vince 1994, 63–9.
[10] Keene 1985, 180–82.
[11] Archaeological assessment document, KHTS 2005, or http://ads.ahds.ac.uk/catalogue/projArch/EUS.
[12] Gould 2008 or www.helm.org.uk.
[13] Milne 2004, 230.
[14] See, for example, Clark 2001.
[15] Gould 2008, particularly as exemplified in the case studies.
[16] Sandwich Survey Report 3.
[17] Sarfatij 2007, 72–3.

References

Abbreviations

BAR	British Archaeological Reports	KAS	Kent Archaeological Society
BL	The British Library	KHTS	Kent Historic Towns Survey
CADW	Welsh Historic Monuments	LP	Lambeth Palace Library
CAT	Canterbury Archaeological Trust	PPG	Planning Policy Guidance
CBA	Council for British Archaeology	RCHM,	
CCA	Canterbury Cathedral Archives	RCHME	Royal Commission on the Historical Monuments of England
CKS	Centre for Kentish Studies		
DAG	Dover Archaeological Group	SAG	Sandwich Archaeological Group
EKAC	East Kent Archive Centre	SLHS	Sandwich Local History Society
EUS	Extensive Urban Survey	TNA	The National Archives, Kew
HLS	Harvard Law School Library	TTA	Trust for Thanet Archaeology
HMSO	Her Majesty's Stationery Office		

Published primary sources

Ammianus   Rolfe, J. C., ed. (1950). *Ammianus Marcellinus*. London: Heinemann, and Cambridge, MA: Harvard University Press.

APC   *Acts of the Privy Council*.

AS Charters   Robertson, A. J., ed. (1956). *Anglo-Saxon Charters*. Cambridge: Cambridge University Press.

ASC   Whitelock, D., ed. (1961). *Anglo-Saxon Chronicle*. London: Eyre and Spottiswood.

Britannia   Copley, G. J., ed. (1977). *Camden's Britannia: Kent*. London: Hutchinson

CChartR   *Calendar of Charter Rolls*

CCR   *Calendar of Close Rolls*.

CFR   *Calendar of Fine Rolls*.

Chronica   Hearn, T., ed. (1729). *Thomae Sprotti Chronica*. Oxford.

Chronicon   Stevenson, J., ed. (1858). *Chronicon Monasterii de Abingdon*, II. Rolls Series, London.

CInqMisc   *Calendar of Inquisitions Miscellaneous*.

CLR   *Calendar of Liberate Rolls*.

CMem Rolls   *Calendar of Memorandum Rolls*.

Coram Rege Roll   Sayles G. O., ed. (1936). *Select Cases in the Court of King's Bench under Edward I*. Selden Society 35, London.

CPR   *Calendar of Patent Rolls*.

CSPDom   *Calendar of State Papers Domestic*.

CSPV   *Calendar of State Papers Venetian*.

DB Kent   *Domesday Book*. London: Alecto Historical Editions.

DM   Douglas, D. C. (1944). *The Domesday Monachorum of Christ Church, Canterbury*. London: Royal Historical Society.

Early Charters   Napier, A. S. and Stevenson, W. H., eds (1895). *The Crawford Collection of Early Charters and Documents now in the Bodleian Library*. Oxford: Clarendon Press.

EHD I   Whitelock, D., ed. (1979). *English Historical Documents, I, c.500–1042*. 2nd edn, London: Eyre Methuen.

Encomium   Campbell, A., ed. (1949). *Encomium Emmae Reginae*. Camden Society, 3rd series, 72.

Gesta Henrici Quinti   Taylor, F. and Roskell, J. S., eds (1975) *Gesta Henrici Quinti*. Oxford: Clarendon Press.

Hall's Chronicle   Ellis, H., ed. (1809). *Hall's Chronicle of the History of England during the Reign of Henry the Fourth and the Succeeding Monarchs*. London.

HE   Colgrave, B. and Mynors, R. A. B., eds (1969). *Bede's Ecclesiastical History of the English People*. Oxford: Clarendon Press.

Itinerary   Chandler J., ed. (1993). *John Leland's Itinerary: travels in Tudor England*. Stroud: Alan Sutton.

Jehan de Waurin   Hardy, W., ed. (1868). *Jehan de Waurin: Receuil des Chroniques d'Engleterre*. Rolls Series 39, London.

L&P   *Letters and Papers Henry VIII*.

Laws   Van Caenegem, R. C., ed. (1990). *English Lawsuits from William I to Richard I*. Selden Society 106: I.

Life of Wilfrid   Colgrave, B., ed. (1927). *The Life of Bishop Wilfrid by Eddius Stephanus*. Cambridge: Cambridge University Press.

Michael of Rhodes   Long, P. O., McGee, D. and Stahl, A. M. (2008). *The Book of Michael of Rhodes: a fifteenth-century maritime manuscript*, 3 vols. Cambridge, MA: MIT Press.

Perambulation   Church, R., ed. (1970). *Perambulation of Kent by William Lambarde*. Bath: Adam and Dart.

Regesta   Bates, D., ed. (1998). *Regesta Regum Anglo-Normannorum: the Acta of William I (1066–1087)*. Oxford: Clarendon Press.

Symeon   Arnold, T., ed. (1898). *Symeonis Monachi Opera Omnia*, II. Rolls Series. London.

Thorne   Davis, A. H., ed. (1934). *William Thorne's Chronicle of St Augustine's Abbey, Canterbury*. Oxford: Basil Blackwell.

Secondary sources

Addyman, P. V. and Black, V. E., eds (1984). *Archaeological Papers from York Presented to M. W. Barley*. York: York Archaeological Trust.

Alston, L. (2004). 'Late medieval workshops in East Anglia'. In Barnwell, Palmer and Airs, eds, 38–59.

Ambrosiani, B. and Clarke, H. (1994). *Developments around the Baltic and the North Sea in the Viking Age*, Birka Studies 3. Stockholm.

Andrewes, J. (1991). 'Land, family and community in Wingham and its environs: an economic and social history of rural society in east Kent from c.1450–1640'. Unpublished Ph.D. thesis, University of Kent.

Andrewes, J. (2000). 'Industries in Kent, c.1500–1640'. In Zell, ed., 105–39.

Andrewes J. and Zell, M. (2002). 'The population of Sandwich from the accession of Elizabeth I to the Civil War'. *Archaeologia Cantiana* 122, 79–99.

Andrews, D. and Stenning, D. (1989). 'Wealden houses and urban topography at the lower end of Maldon High Street'. *Essex Archaeology and History* 20, 103–9.

Andrews, P., Birbeck, V. and Stoodley, N. (2005). 'Concluding discussion'. In Birbeck *et al.*, eds, 190–204.

Archer, I. (2000). 'Politics and Government'. In Clark, ed., 235–88.

Arnold, A. J. *et al.* (2001a). 'Tree-ring analysis of timbers from 39 Strand Street, Sandwich, Kent'. Unpublished, English Heritage, Centre for Archaeology, Report 97/2001.

Arnold, A. J. *et al.* (2001b). 'Tree-ring analysis of timbers from 62 Strand Street, Sandwich, Kent'. Unpublished, English Heritage, Centre for Archaeology, Report 56/2001.

Arnold, A. J. *et al.* (2001c). 'Tree-ring date lists'. *Vernacular Architecture* 32, 94–5.

Arnold, A. J., Howard, R. E. and Litton, C. D. (2003). 'Tree-ring date lists'. *Vernacular Architecture* 34, 106–7.

Arnold, A. J., Laxton, R. R. and Litton, C. D. (2002). 'Tree-ring analysis of timbers from 33 Strand Street, Sandwich, Kent'. Unpublished, English Heritage, Centre for Archaeology, Report 86/2002.

Arnold, C. J. (1982). 'Excavations at Eastry Court Farm, Eastry'. *Archaeologia Cantiana* 98, 121–35.

Astill, G. (2000). 'General survey 600–1300'. In Palliser, ed., 27–49.

Astill, G. (2006). 'Community, identity and the later Anglo-Saxon town: the case of southern England'. In Davies, Halsall and Reynolds, eds, 233–54.

Aston, M. (1990). 'Segregation in church'. *Studies in Church History* 27, 237–94.

Aston, M. and Bond, J. (1976). *The Landscape of Towns*. London: Dent.

Aston, T. H., ed. (1987). *Landlords, Peasants and Politics in Medieval England*. Cambridge: Cambridge University Press.

Austin, R. and Sweetinburgh, S. (2007). '3 Millwall Place, Sandwich'. *Canterbury's Archaeology, 2005–2006*, 61–5.

Ayers, B. (2003). *Norwich: 'A Fine City'*. Stroud: Tempus.

Ayers, B. (2004a). 'The infrastructure of Norwich from the 12th to the 17th centuries'. In Gläser, ed., 31–49.

Ayers, B. (2004b). 'The urban landscape'. In Rawcliffe and Wilson, eds, 1–28.

Ayers, T. and Tatton-Brown, T., eds (2006). *Medieval Art and Architecture in Rochester*. British Archaeological Association Conference Transactions 28.

Ayres, J. (2003). *Domestic Interiors: the British tradition, 1500–1850*. New Haven and London: Yale University Press.

Backhouse, M. (1991). 'The Strangers at work in Sandwich: native envy of an industrious minority, 1576–1603'. *Immigrants and Minorities* 10, 70–99.

Backhouse, M. (1995). *The Flemish and Walloon Communities at Sandwich during the Reign of Elizabeth (1561–1603)*. Brussels: Verhandelingen van Koninklijke Academie voor Wetenschappen, Letteren en Schone Kunsten van België.

Badham, S. (1990). 'London standardisation and provincial idiosyncrasy: the organisation and working practices of brass-engraving workshops in pre-Reformation England'. *Church Monuments* 5, 3–25.

Baker, N. and Holt, R. (1998). 'The origins of urban parish boundaries'. In Slater and Rosser, eds, 209–35.

Baker, N. and Holt, R. (2004). *Urban Growth and the Medieval Church: Gloucester and Worcester*. Aldershot: Ashgate.

Barley, M. W. (1976). 'Town defences in England and Wales after 1066'. In Barley, ed., 57–71.

Barley, M. W., ed. (1976). *The Plans and Topography of Medieval Towns in England*. CBA Research Report 14.

Barnwell, P. S. (2004). 'The laity, the clergy and the divine presence: the use of space in smaller churches of the eleventh and twelfth centuries'. *Journal of the British Archaeological Association* 157, 41–60.

Barnwell, P. S. (2005). '"Four hundred masses on the four Fridays after my decease": the care of souls in fifteenth-century All Saints', North Street, York'. In Barnwell, Cross and Rycraft, eds, 57–87.

Barnwell, P. S. (2006). 'Houses, hearths and historical inquiry'. In Barnwell and Airs, eds, 177–83.

Barnwell, P. S. and Adams A. T. (1994). *The House Within: interpreting medieval houses in Kent*. London: RCHME/HMSO.

Barnwell, P. S. and Airs, M., eds (2006). *Houses and the Hearth Tax: the later Stuart house and society*. CBA Research Report 150.

Barnwell, P. S., Cross, C. and Rycraft, A., eds (2005). *Mass and Parish in Late Medieval England: the Use of York*. Reading: Spire Books.

Barnwell, P. S., Palmer, M. and Airs, M., eds (2004). *The Vernacular Workshop: from craft to industry, 1400–1900*. CBA Research Report 140.

Barron, C. (1981). 'London and the Crown 1451–61'. In Highfield and Jeffs, eds, 88–109.

Barrow, J. (1992). 'Urban cemetery location in the high Middle Ages'. In Bassett, ed., 78–100.

Barrow, J. (2000). 'Churches, education and literacy in towns, 600–1300'. In Palliser, ed., 127–52.

Bassett, S., ed. (1992). *Death in Towns: urban responses to the dying and the dead*. Leicester: Leicester University Press.

Battely, J. (1745). *Antiquitates Rutupiae*. Oxford.

Baxter, S. (2007). *The Earls of Mercia: lordship and power in late Anglo-Saxon England*. Oxford: Oxford University Press.

Beattie, C., Maslakovic, A. and Rees-Jones, S., eds (2003). *The Medieval Household in Christian Europe, c.850–c.1550*. Turnhout: Brepols.

Beer, B. L. (1982). *Rebellion and Riot: Popular Disorder in England during the Reign of Edward VI*. Kent, OH: Kent State University Press.

Bellamy, P. S. and Milne, G. (2003). 'An archaeological evaluation of the medieval shipyard facilities at Small Hythe'. *Archaeologia Cantiana* 123, 353–83.

Bennett, J. (1986). 'The village ale-wife: women and brewing in fourteenth century England'. In Hanawalt, ed., 20–36.

Bennett, J. (1996). *Ale, Beer and Brewsters in England: Women's work in a changing world, 1300–1600*. New York: Oxford University Press.

Bennett, P. (1978). 'Some minor excavations undertaken by the Canterbury Archaeological Trust in 1977–1978: a Roman building, near Sandwich'. *Archaeologia Cantiana* 94, 191–4.

Bennett, P., Blockley, P. and Tatton-Brown, T. (1983). 'Canterbury Archaeological Trust 1983 interim report, Sandwich Castle'. *Archaeologia Cantiana* 99, 243–7.

Bennett, P. and Houliston, M. (1989). 'St George's Gate'. *CAT Annual Report* 12, 17–23.

Bennett, P. and Tatton-Brown, T. (1992). 'St Martin-le-Grand, Dover'. *Canterbury's Archaeology, 1991–1992*, 28–30.

Bentwich, H. (1971). *History of Sandwich*. Deal: T. F. Pain and Sons.

BGS (1988). *Geology of the Country around Ramsgate and Dover*. London: HMSO.

Bindoff, S. T. (1982a). *The House of Commons, 1509–1558*, I. London: HMSO.

Bindoff, S. T. (1982b). *The House of Commons, 1509–1558*, II. London: HMSO.

Binski, P. (1996). *Medieval Death and Ritual Representation*. London: British Museum Press.

Birbeck, V. et al., eds (2005). *The Origins of Mid-Saxon Southampton*. Salisbury: Wessex Archaeology.

Blackman, D. J., ed. (1973). *Marine Archaeology*. Proceedings of the 23rd Symposium of Colston Research Society, Bristol.

Blair, C., Goodall, J. and Lankester, P. (2000). 'The Winchelsea tombs reconsidered'. *Church Monuments* 15, 5–30.

Blair, J. (1991). 'Purbeck marble'. In Blair and Ramsay, eds, 41–56.

Blair, J. (1993). 'Hall and chamber: English domestic planning, 1000–1250'. In Meirion-Jones and Jones, eds, 1–21.

Blair, J. (2005). *The Church in Anglo-Saxon Society*. Oxford: Oxford University Press.

Blair, J., ed. (1988). *Minsters and Parish Churches: The local church in transition, 950–1200*. Oxford University Committee for Archaeology Monograph 17.

Blair, J., ed. (2007). *Waterways and Canal-building in Medieval England*. Oxford: Oxford University Press.

Blair, J. and Ramsay, N., eds (1991). *English Medieval Industries*. London: Hambledon Press.

Blake, P. (1987). 'The Sandwich font'. *Archaeologia Cantiana*, 104, 384–6.

Blockley, K. et al., eds (1995). *Excavations in the Marlowe Car Park and Surrounding Areas, Part I: The Excavated Sites*, The Archaeology of Canterbury, V. Maidstone: CAT and KAS.

Bloxham, M. H. (1855). *On the Charnel Vault at Rothwell, Northants and on Charnel Vaults Elsewhere*. Association of Architectural Societies of Northants, Lincolnshire, Cambridgeshire and Leicestershire.

Bower, J. (2000). 'Kent towns, 1540–1640'. In Zell, ed., 141–76.

Bowler, E. (1983). 'For the better defence of low and marshy grounds: a survey of the work of the Sewer Commissions for North and East Kent, 1531–1930'. In Detsicas and Yates, eds, 28–48.

Boys, W. (1792). *Collections for an History of Sandwich in Kent*. Canterbury.

Britnell, R. H. (1986). *Growth and Decline in Colchester, 1300–1525*. Cambridge: Cambridge University Press.

Britnell, R. (1993). *The Commercialisation of English Society*. Cambridge: Cambridge University Press.

Britnell, R. (1997). *The Closing of the Middle Ages? England, 1471–1529*. Oxford: Blackwell.

Britnell, R. (2006). 'Tax-collecting in Colchester, 1489–1502'. *Historical Research* 79, 477–87.

Brooke, C. and Keir, G. (1975). *London, 800–1216: the shaping of a city*. London: Secker and Warburg.

Brookes, S. (2007). 'Boat-rivets in graves in pre-Viking Kent: reassessing Anglo-Saxon boat-burial traditions'. *Medieval Archaeology* 51, 1–18.

Brooks, F. W. (1928). 'The king's ships and galleys mainly under John and Henry III'. *Mariner's Mirror* 14: 1, 15–48.

Brooks, N. (1984). *The Early History of the Church of Canterbury*. Leicester: Leicester University Press.

Brooks, N. (1994). 'Rochester bridge, AD 43–1381'. In Yates and Gibson, eds, 1–40.

Brooks, N. (2006). 'Rochester, AD 400–1066'. In Ayers and Tatton-Brown, eds, 6–21.

Brooks, N. and Kelly, S., eds (forthcoming). *The Anglo-Saxon Charters of Christ Church, Canterbury*. London: British Academy.

Brown, A., ed. (1999). *The Rows of Chester: the Chester Rows research project*. English Heritage, Archaeological Report 16, London.

Bryan, P. and Wise, N. (2002). 'A reconstruction of the medieval Cambridge market place', *Proceedings of the Cambridge Antiquarian Society* 91, 73–87.

Bulmer-Thomas, I. (1959). 'St Mary's, Sandwich, in the Middle Ages'. *Transactions of the Ancient Monuments Society* NS 7, 33–56.

Bulmer-Thomas, I. (1960). 'St Mary's, Sandwich, after the Reformation'. *Transactions of the Ancient Monuments Society* NS 8, 21–42.

Bulmer-Thomas, I. (1962). 'St Mary's, Sandwich, in later times'. *Transactions of the Ancient Monuments Society* NS 10, 43–56.

Burwash, D. (1947). *English Merchant Shipping, 1460–1540*. Toronto: University of Toronto Press.

Bushe-Fox, J. P. (1926). *First Report on the Excavation of the Roman Fort at Richborough, Kent*. Society of Antiquaries of London Research Report 6, London.

Bushe-Fox, J. P. (1928). *Second Report on the Excavation of the Roman Fort at Richborough, Kent.* Society of Antiquaries of London Research Report 7, London.

Bushe-Fox, J. P. (1949). *Fourth Report on the Excavation of the Roman Fort at Richborough, Kent.* Society of Antiquaries of London Research Report 16, London.

Butcher, A. F. (1977). 'Sandwich in the thirteenth century'. *Archaeologia Cantiana* 93, 25–31.

Butcher, A. (1979). 'Rent and the urban economy: Oxford and Canterbury in the later Middle Ages'. *Southern History* 1, 11–43.

Butcher, A. F. (1980). 'The hospital of St Stephen and St Thomas, New Romney: the documentary evidence'. *Archaeologia Cantiana* 96, 17–26.

Butcher, A. F. (1987). 'English urban society and the revolt of 1381'. In Hilton and Aston, eds, 84–111.

Butler, L. A. S. (1984). 'The houses of the mendicant orders in Britain: recent archaeological work'. In Addyman and Black, eds, 123–36.

Butler, L. A. S. (1990). *Denbigh Castle and Town Walls.* Cardiff: CADW Welsh Historic Monuments.

Butler, L. A. S. and Morris, R. K., eds (1986). *The Anglo-Saxon Church.* CBA Research Report 60.

Campbell, B. M. S., ed. (1991). *Before the Black Death: studies in the 'Crisis' of the early fourteenth century.* Manchester: Manchester University Press.

Campbell, B. M. S. *et al.* (1993). *A Medieval Capital and its Grain Supply.* Historical Geography Research Series 30.

Campbell, J. (1975). *Norwich.* London: Historic Towns Trust.

Campbell, J. (2000). 'Power and authority, 600–1300'. In Palliser, ed., 5–78.

Cannon, H. L. (1912). 'The battle of Sandwich and Eustace the monk'. *English Historical Review* 27, 649–70.

Carpenter, D. A. (1990). *The Minority of Henry III.* London: Methuen.

Carus-Wilson, E. M., ed. (1954). *Essays in Economic History,* I. London: Arnold.

Carus-Wilson, E. and Coleman, O. (1963). *England's Export Trade, 1275–1547.* Oxford: Oxford University Press.

Catney, S. and Start, D., eds (2003). *Time and Tide: the archaeology of the Witham Valley.* Sleaford: Witham Valley Archaeology Research Group.

Cavell, J. and Kennett, B. (1963). *A History of Sir Roger Manwood's Free School, Sandwich, 1563–1963.* London: Cory, Adams and Mackay.

Charles, F. W. B. (1978–9). 'Timber-framed houses in Spon Street, Coventry', *Transactions of Birmingham and Warwickshire Archaeological Society* 89, 91–122.

Chartres, J. A. and Hey, D., eds (1990). *English Rural Society, 1500–1800.* Cambridge: Cambridge University Press.

Chichester, A. M. (1887). 'Notes on the churches of St Clement and St Mary, Sandwich'. *Journal of the British Archaeological Association* 43, 340–43.

Childs, W. R. (1978). *Anglo-Castilian Trade in the Later Middle Ages.* Manchester: Manchester University Press.

Chinnery, V. (1990). *Oak Furniture: the British Tradition.* Woodbridge: Antique Collector's Club.

Clapham, A. W. (1930). 'Sandwich'. *Archaeological Journal* 86, 289–90.

Clark, D. (2000). 'The shop within: an analysis of the architectural evidence for medieval shops', *Architectural History* 43, 58–87.

Clark, K. (2001). 'The role of understanding in building conservation'. In Pearson and Meeson, eds, 41–52.

Clark, P. (1977). *English Provincial Society from the Reformation to the Revolution: religion, politics and society in Kent, 1500–1640.* Hassocks, Sussex: Harvester Press.

Clark, P. (1979). 'Reformation and radicalism in Kentish Towns, c.1500–1553'. In Mommsen, Alter and Scribner, eds, 107–27.

Clark, P., ed. (1984). *The Transformation of English Provincial Towns.* London: Hutchinson.

Clark, P., ed. (2000). *The Cambridge Urban History of Britain, vol. 2: 1540–1840.* Cambridge: Cambridge University Press.

Clarke, H. (1973). 'King's Lynn and east coast trade in the middle ages'. In Blackman, ed., 277–91.

Clarke, H. (1981). 'King's Lynn'. In Milne and Hobley, eds, 132–6.

Clarke, H. (1987). 'Milttelalterliche Häfen an der Nordsee zwischen 1000 und 1500'. In Dolgner and Roch, eds, 197–202.

Clarke, H. (2005a). 'Sandwich before the Cinque Ports: initial findings of the Sandwich Project'. *Kent Archaeological Society Newsletter* 65, 13–15.

Clarke, H. (2005b). 'Introducing the Sandwich Project'. *Society for Medieval Archaeology Newsletter* 33, 7–9.

Clarke, H. (forthcoming). 'The Liberty of Sandwich, Kent, c.1300, and its implications for earlier topography'. In Reynolds and Webster, eds.

Clarke, H. and Ambrosiani, B. (1991). *Towns in the Viking Age.* Leicester: Leicester University Press.

Clarke, H. and Carter, A. (1977). *Excavations in King's Lynn, 1963–1977.* Society for Medieval Archaeology Monograph Series 7.

Coates, R. (1999). 'New light from old wicks: the progeny of Latin vicus'. *Nomina* 22, 75–116.

Coldstream, N. and Draper, P., eds (1982). *Medieval Art and Architecture at Canterbury Cathedral before 1220.* British Archaeological Association Conference Transactions, 5.

Coleman, O. (1963–4). 'Trade and prosperity in the fifteenth century: aspects of the trade of Southampton'. *Economic History Review,* 2nd Series 16, 9–22.

Colvin, H. M., ed. (1963). *The History of the King's Works, I: the Middle Ages.* London: HMSO

Conzen, M. R. G. (1968). 'The use of town plans in the study of urban history'. In Dyos, ed., 113–30.

Cook, G. H. (1954). *The English Mediaeval Parish Church.* London: Dent

Cooper, W. D. (1868). 'John Cade's followers in Kent', *Archaeologica Cantiana* 7, 233–71.

Corke, B. (1995). 'Loop Street Sandwich'. *Canterbury's Archaeology, 1993–1994,* 34–5.

Coupland, S. (2003). 'Trading places: Quentovic and Dorestad reassessed'. *Early Medieval Europe* 11: 3, 209–32.

Cox, J. C. (1916). *Bench Ends in English Churches.* London and New York: Oxford University Press.

Crawford, B. (2006). 'The cult of St Clement in Denmark'. *Jysk Selskab for Historie* 2, 235–82.

Crawford, B. (2008). *The Churches Dedicated to St Clement in Medieval England: a hagio-geography of the seafarer's saint in 11th century north Europe*. Scripta Ecclesiastica, 1. St Petersburg: Axioma.

Creighton, O. H. (2002). *Castles and Landscapes: power, community and fortification in Medieval England*. London and Oakville: Equinox.

Creighton, O. and Higham, R. (2005). *Medieval Town Walls: an archaeology and social history of urban defence*. Stroud: Tempus.

Croft, J. P. (1997a). 'An assault on the royal justices at Ash and the making of the Sandwich custumal'. *Archaeologia Cantiana* 117, 13–36.

Croft, J. P. (1997b). 'The Custumals of the Cinque Ports, c.1290–1500: studies in the cultural production of the urban record'. Unpublished Ph.D. thesis, University of Kent.

Cross, C. and Barnwell, P. S. (2005). 'The Mass in its urban setting'. In Barnwell, Cross and Rycraft, eds, 13–26.

Crumlin-Pedersen, O. (1983). *From Viking Ships to Hanseatic Cogs*. National Maritime Museum Occasional Lecture 4, London.

Cunliffe, B. W. (1968). 'The development of Richborough'. In Cunliffe, ed., 231–51.

Cunliffe, B. W., ed. (1968). *Fifth Report on the Excavations of the Roman Fort at Richborough, Kent*. Society of Antiquaries Research Report 23, London.

Daniels, R. (1986). 'The medieval defences of Hartlepool, Cleveland: the results of excavation and survey'. *Durham Archaeological Journal* 2, 63–72.

Darby, H. C. and Campbell, E. M. J. (1962). *The Domesday Geography of South-East England*. Cambridge: Cambridge University Press.

Davidson, C. F. (1998). 'Written in stone: architecture, liturgy and the laity in English parish churches, c.1125–c.1250'. Unpublished Ph.D. thesis, University of London.

Davidson, C. F. (1999). 'Change and change back; the development of English parish church chancels'. In Swanson, ed., 65–77.

Davidson Cragoe, C. (2005). 'Belief and patronage in the English parish before 1300: some evidence from roods'. *Architectural History* 48, 21–48.

Davies, J. G. (1968). *The Secular Use of Church Buildings*. London: SCM Press.

Davies, W., Halsall, G. and Reynolds, A., eds (2006). *People and Space in the Middle Ages*. Turnhout: Brepols.

Deighton, E. (1994). 'The Carmelite friary at Sandwich'. *Archaeologia Cantiana* 114, 317–27.

Denton, J. H. (1993). 'The valuation of the ecclesiastical benefices of England and Wales in 1291–2'. *Historical Research* 66, 231–50.

Denton, J. H. (2005). *Taxatio Ecclesiastica Angliae et Walliae Auctoritate Papae Nicholai IV*. http://www.hrionline.ac.uk/taxatio.

Detsicas, A. and Yates, N., eds (1983). *Studies in Modern Kentish History*. Maidstone: KAS.

Dimmock, S. (2001). 'English small towns and the emergence of capitalist relations, c.1450–1550'. *Urban History* 28, 5–24.

Dolgner, D. and Roch, I., eds (1987). *Stadtbaukunst im Mittelalter*. Berlin: Verlag für Bauwesen.

Dorman, T. (1886). 'Visits of two queens to Sandwich'. *Archaeologia Cantiana* 16, 58–63.

Dowker, G. (1884). 'Richborough', *Journal of the British Archaeological Association* 40: 3, 260–74.

Dowker, G. (1900). 'Deal and its environs', *Archaeologia Cantiana* 24, 108–21.

Draper, G. (2007). 'Educational provision and piety in Kent, c.1400–1640'. In Lutton and Salter, eds, 75–91.

Draper, G. and Meddens, F. (2009). *The Sea and the Marsh: the medieval Cinque Port of New Romney revealed through archaeological excavations and historical research*. London: Pre-Construct Archaeology Monograph 10.

Draper, P. (2006). *The Formation of English Gothic: architecture and identity*. New Haven and London: Yale University Press.

Drew, C. (1954). *Early Parochial Organisation in England: the origins of the office of churchwarden*. London: St Anthony's Hall Publications 7.

Duffy, E. (1992). *The Stripping of the Altars: traditional religion in England, 1400–1580*. New Haven and London: Yale University Press.

Dunning, G. C. (1941). 'Polychrome pottery from Stonar'. *Archaeologia Cantiana* 54, 56–60.

Dyer, A. (1981). 'Urban housing: a documentary study of four Midland towns, 1530–1700'. *Post-Medieval Archaeology* 15, 207–18.

Dyer, A. (1991). *Decline and Growth in English Towns, 1400–1640*. Cambridge: Cambridge University Press.

Dyer, A. (2000). 'Ranking lists of English medieval towns'. In Palliser, ed., 747–70.

Dyer, C. (1985). 'Towns and cottages in eleventh-century England'. In Mayr-Harting and Moore, eds, 91–106.

Dyer, C. (2002). *Making a Living in the Middle Ages: the people of Britain, 850–1520*. New Haven and London: Yale University Press.

Dyer, C. (2005). *An Age of Transition? Economy and Society in England in the Later Middle Ages*. Oxford: Clarendon Press.

Dyos, H. J., ed. (1968). *The Study of Urban History*. London: Arnold.

Dyson, A. G. (1981). 'The terms "quay" and "wharf" and the early medieval London waterfront'. In Milne and Hobley, eds, 37–8.

Eales, J. (2000). 'The rise of ideological politics in Kent, 1560–1600'. In Zell, ed., 279–313.

Eales, R. (1992). 'Introduction' to *The Kent Domesday*. London: Alecto Historical Editions.

Eddison, J. (2002). 'The purpose, construction and operation of a 13th-century watercourse: The Rhee, Romney Marsh'. In Long, Hipkin and Clarke, eds, 127–39.

Es, W. A. van and Verwers, W. J. H. (1980). *Excavations at Dorestad I: The Harbour, Hoogstraat 1*. Nederlandse Oudheden 9, Amersfoort.

Es, W. A. van and Verwers, W. J. H. (2009). *Excavations at Dorestad 3: Hoogstraat 0, II–IV*. Nederlandse Oudheden 16, Amersfoort.

Everitt, A. (1986). *Continuity and Colonization: the evolution of Kentish settlement*. Leicester: Leicester University Press.

Everson, P. and Stocker, D. (2003). 'Coming from Bardney ... the landscape context of the causeways and finds groups of the Witham valley'. In Catney and Start, eds, 6–15.

Farnhill, K. (2001). *Guilds and the Parish Community in Late Medieval East Anglia, c.1470–1550.* York: York Medieval Press.

Faulkner, P. A. (1975). 'Surviving medieval buildings'. In Platt and Coleman-Smith, 56–124.

Fenwick, V. (1978). 'The site at Graveney and its possible use as a landing place'. In Fenwick, ed., 179–92.

Fenwick, V., ed. (1978). *The Graveney Boat.* BAR British Series 53, Oxford.

Fernie, E. (1983). *The Architecture of the Anglo-Saxons.* London: Batsford.

Fernie, E. (2000). *The Architecture of Norman England.* Oxford: Oxford University Press.

Fisher, F. J. (1954). 'The development of the London food market, 1540–1640'. In Carus-Wilson, ed., 135–51.

Ford, J. (1997). 'Marginality and the assimilation of foreigners in the lay parish community: the case of Sandwich'. In French, Gibbs and Kümin, eds, 203–16.

Fordham, S. J. and Green, R. D. (1973). *Soils in Kent II. Sheet TR35 (Deal).* Soil Survey Record 15.

Freeman, A. (1985). *The Moneyer and the Mint in the Reign of Edward the Confessor.* BAR British Series 145. Oxford: Archaeopress.

French, K. L. (2000). *The People of the Parish: community life in a late-medieval English Diocese.* Philadelphia: University of Pennsylvania Press.

French, K. L., Gibbs, G. G. and Kümin, B., eds (1997). *The Parish in English Life, 1400–1600.* Manchester: Manchester University Press.

Frere, S., Stow, S. and Bennett, P., eds (1982). *Excavations on the Roman and Medieval Defences of Canterbury.* The Archaeology of Canterbury, II. Maidstone: CAT and KAS.

Friel, I. (1995). *The Good Ship.* London: British Museum Press.

Gairdner, J. and Delmar Morgan, E. (1889). 'Sailing directions for the circumnavigation of England. *The Hakluyt Society* 79, 10–37.

Gardiner, D. (1954). *Historic Haven, the Story of Sandwich.* Derby: Pilgrim Press.

Gatch, M. McC. (1993). 'Miracles in architectural settings: Christ Church, Canterbury, and St Clement's, Sandwich in the Old English *Vision of Leofric*'. *Anglo-Saxon England* 22, 227–52.

Gatty, C. T. (1883). *Catalogue of Medieval and Later Antiquities Contained in the Mayer Museum.* Liverpool: Free Public Museum.

Gem, R., ed. (1997). *English Heritage Book of St Augustine's Abbey, Canterbury.* London: Batsford.

Gem, R. (2004). *Studies in Pre-Romanesque and Romanesque Architecture,* 2 vols. London: Pindar Press.

Gibson, A. (1973). 'A "half-wealden" house in Bishop's Stortford'. *Hertfordshire Archaeology* 3, 127–30.

Gibson, A. (1998). 'Two small wealden houses of urban type in Hertfordshire'. *Hertfordshire Archaeology* 13, 93–8.

Gibson, J. (1993). 'The 1566 survey of the Kent coast'. *Archaeologia Cantiana* 112, 341–53.

Gibson, J. (2002). *Records of Early English Drama: Kent: Diocese of Canterbury, vol. 2.* Toronto: British Library and University of Toronto.

Gibson, M. and Wright, S. M. (1988). *Joseph Mayer of Liverpool, 1803–1886.* Society of Antiquaries Occasional Papers, NS 11.

Gibson, M., Heslop, T. A. and Pfaff, R. W. (1992). *The Eadwine Psalter: text, image and monastic culture in twelfth-century Canterbury.* London and University Park: The Modern Humanities Research Association / Pennsylvania State University Press.

Gifford, E. and Gifford, J. (1996). 'The sailing performance of Anglo-Saxon ships derived from the building and trials of half-scale models of the Sutton Hoo and Graveney finds'. *Mariner's Mirror* 82: 2, 131–53.

Gilchrist, R. (1995). *Contemplation and Action: the other monasticism.* Leicester: Leicester University Press.

Gilchrist, R. and Sloane, B. (2005). *Requiem: the medieval monastic cemetery in Britain.* London: Museum of London Archaeology Service.

Giles, K. and Dyer, C., eds (2005). *Town and Country in the Middle Ages: contrasts, contacts and interconnections, 1100–1500.* Society for Medieval Archaeology Monograph 22.

Gläser, M., ed. (2004). *Lübecker Kolloquium zur Stadtarchäologie in Hanseraum IV: Die Infrastruktur.* Lübeck: Schmidt-Römhild.

Godfrey, W. (1929). 'Some medieval hospitals of east Kent'. *Archaeological Journal* 86, 99–110.

Goldberg, J. (2004). *Medieval England: a social history, 1250–1550.* London: Arnold.

Gould, S. (2008). 'Understanding historic buildings: policy and guidance for local planning authorities', *Historic Environment Local Management.* London: English Heritage.

Gransden, A. (1974). *Historical Writing in England,* I, c.550–1307. London and New York: Routledge.

Granshaw, L. and Porter, R., eds (1989). *The Hospital in History.* London: Routledge.

Grant, L., ed. (1990). *Medieval Art, Architecture and Archaeology in London.* British Archaeological Association Conference Transactions 10.

Gras, N. S. B. (1918). *The Early English Customs System.* Cambridge, MA: Harvard University Press.

Gravett, K. (1981). *Timber and Brick Building in Kent.* 2nd edn, London and Chichester: Phillimore.

Green, A. S. (1894). *Town Life in the Fifteenth Century.* London: Macmillan

Greenhill, B. (1995). *The Archaeology of Boats and Ships: an introduction.* London: Conway Maritime Press.

Grenville, J. (1997). *Medieval Housing.* London and Washington, DC: Leicester University Press.

Haines, C. R. (1930). *Dover Priory: a history of the priory of St Mary the Virgin, and St Martin of the New Work.* Cambridge: Cambridge University Press.

Hall, L. (2005). *Period Fixtures and Fittings, 1300–1900.* Newbury: Countryside Books.

Halliwell, G. (1981). 'Flint artefacts from the Sandwich–Deal marshes', *Kent Archaeological Review* 65, 113–16.

Halliwell, G. and Parfitt, K. (1985). 'The prehistoric land surface in the Lydden Valley: an initial report', *Kent Archaeological Review* 82, 39–43.

Hanawalt, B. A., ed. (1986). *Women and Work in Pre-Industrial Europe*. Bloomington: Indiana University Press.

Harding, V. (2002). *The Dead and the Living in Paris and London, 1500–1670*. Cambridge: Cambridge University Press.

Hardman, F. W. and Stebbing, W. P. D. (1940). 'Stonar and the Wantsum Channel, I: physiographical'. *Archaeologia Cantiana* 53, 62–80.

Hardman, F. W. and Stebbing, W. P. D. (1941). 'Stonar and the Wantsum Channel, II: historical'. *Archaeologia Cantiana* 54, 41–55.

Hardman, F. W. and Stebbing, W. P. D. (1942). 'Stonar and the Wantsum Channel, III: the site of the town of Stonar'. *Archaeologia Cantiana* 55, 37–52.

Harrington, D., Pearson, S. and Rose, S., eds (2000). *Kent Hearth Tax Assessment, Lady Day 1664*. British Record Society, Hearth Tax Series 2.

Harris, R. B. (1994). 'The origins and development of medieval townhouses operating commercially on two storeys'. Unpublished D.Phil. thesis, University of Oxford.

Harrison, K. (1967–8). 'Vitruvius and acoustic jars in England during the Middle Ages'. *Ancient Monuments Society Transactions* 15, 49–58.

Harriss, G. (2005). *Shaping the Nation: England, 1360–1461*. Oxford: Clarendon Press.

Harvey, I. M. W. (1991). *Jack Cade's Rebellion of 1450*. Oxford: Clarendon Press.

Haslam, J., ed. (1984). *Anglo-Saxon Towns in Southern England*. Chichester: Phillimore.

Hasler, P. W. (1981). *The House of Commons, 1558–1603*. London: HMSO.

Hasted, E. (1797–1801). *The History and Topographical Survey of the County of Kent*, 12 vols. 2nd edn reprinted 1972.

Hatcher, J. (1986). 'Mortality in the fifteenth century: some new evidence', *Economic History Review* 2nd series, 39, 19–38.

Hatcher, J. (1996). 'The great slump of the mid-fifteenth century'. In Hatcher and Britnell, eds, 237–72.

Hatcher, J. and Britnell R., eds (1996). *Progress and Problems in Medieval England*. Cambridge: Cambridge University Press.

Hattendorf, J. B. *et al.*, eds (1993). 'British Naval Documents, 1204–1960'. *Navy Records Society* 131.

Hawkes, S. C. (1979). 'Eastry in Anglo-Saxon Kent: its importance and a newly found grave'. In Hawkes, Brown and Campbell, eds, 81–113.

Hawkes, S. C. (1982). 'Anglo-Saxon Kent, *c*.425–725'. In Leach, ed., 64–83.

Hawkes, S. C., Brown, D. and Campbell, J., eds (1979). *Anglo-Saxon Studies in Archaeology and History*, I. BAR British Series 72, Oxford.

Hearne, C. M., Perkins, D. R. J. and Andrews, P. (1995). 'The Sandwich Bay underwater treatment scheme archaeological project'. *Archaeologia Cantiana* 115, 239–354.

Herdman, M. (1996). 'Moat Sole, Sandwich'. *Canterbury's Archaeology, 1994–1995*, 35.

Heslop, T. A. (1982). 'The conventual seals of Canterbury Cathedral, 1066–1232'. In Coldstream and Draper, eds, 94–100.

Hewett, C. A. (1980). *English Historic Carpentry*. London and Chichester: Phillimore.

Hewitt, H. J. (1966). *The Organization of War under Edward III*. Manchester: Manchester University Press.

Hicks, A. J. (1998). 'Excavations at Each End, Ash, 1992'. *Archaeologia Cantiana* 118, 91–172.

Highfield, J. R. L. and Jeffs, R., eds (1981). *The Crown and Local Communities in England and France in the Fifteenth Century*. Gloucester: Alan Sutton.

Hill, D. *et al.* (1990). 'Quentovic defined'. *Antiquity* 64, 52–6.

Hill, D. and Cowie, R., eds (2001). *Wics: the early medieval trading centres of Northern Europe*. Sheffield Archaeological Monographs 14.

Hilton, R. H. and Aston, T. H., eds (1987). *The English Rising of 1381*. Cambridge: Cambridge University Press.

Hinton, D. A. (2000). 'The large towns, 600–1300'. In Palliser, ed., 217–43

Hipkin, S. (2008). 'The structure, development, and politics of the Kent grain trade, 1552–1647', *Economic History Review*, 61 S1, 99–139

Hodges, R. (1982). *Dark Age Economics: the origins of towns and trade, AD 600–1000*. London: Duckworth.

Hodges, R. (1988). 'The rebirth of towns in the early Middle Ages'. In Hodges and Hobley, eds, 1–7.

Hodges, R. and Hobley, B., eds (1988). *The Rebirth of Towns in the West, AD 700–1050*. CBA Research Report 68.

Hoey, L. (1995). 'Style, patronage and artistic creativity in Kent parish church architecture, *c*.1180–*c*.1260'. *Archaeologia Cantiana* 115, 45–70.

Hoey, L. R. and Thurlby, M. (2004). 'A survey of Romanesque vaulting in Great Britain and Ireland'. *Antiquaries Journal* 84, 117–84.

Holinshed, R. (1586–7). *Chronicles of England, Scotland and Ireland*. London.

Hollis, S. (1998). 'The Minster-in-Thanet foundation story'. *Anglo-Saxon England* 27, 41–64.

Holman, D. (1989). 'The Late Saxon mints of Kent, I', *Kent Archaeological Review* 98, 181–6.

Holman, D. (1990). 'The Late Saxon mints of Kent, II', *Kent Archaeological Review* 99, 193–8.

Holman, D. (1999). 'Roman cremation burials found at Sandwich, 1846', *Kent Archaeological Review* 138, 170–74.

Holman, D. (2001). 'Sandwich, Kent'. In Hill and Cowie, eds, 101–2.

Holman, D. (2005). 'Iron Age coinage and settlement in east Kent'. *Britannia* 36, 1–54.

Holt, J. C., ed. (1987). *Domesday Studies*. Woodbridge: Boydell.

Holt, R. (2000). 'Society and population, 600–1300'. In Palliser, ed., 79–104.

Hooke, D., ed. (1988). *Anglo-Saxon Settlements*. Oxford: Basil Blackwell.

Horrox, R. (1978). *The Changing Plan of Hull, 1290–1650*. Kingston-upon-Hull City Council.

Horrox, R. (1983). *Selected Rentals and Accounts of Medieval Hull, 1293–1528*. Yorkshire Archaeological Society Record Series, 141.

Horrox, R. and Ormrod, W. M., eds (2006). *A Social*

History of England, 1200–1500. Cambridge: Cambridge University Press.
Houliston, M. (1996). 'No. 14 Knightrider Street, Sandwich'. *Canterbury's Archaeology, 1994–1995,* 36.
Hunter, J. (2002). 'English inns, taverns, alehouses and brandy shops: the legislative framework'. In Kümin and Tlusty, eds, 65–82.
Hussey, A. (1907). *Testamenta Cantiana: East Kent.* KAS Extra Volume.
Hussey, A. (1936). *Kent Chantries.* Kent Records, 12. KAS.
Hutcheson, A. (1995). 'Loop Street, Sandwich'. *Canterbury's Archaeology, 1993–1994,* 33.
Hutchinson, G. (1994). *Medieval Ships and Shipping.* London: Leicester University Press.
Hutchinson, G. (1995). 'Two English side rudders'. In Olsen et al., eds, 97–102.
Hyde, P. (1996). *Thomas Arden in Faversham: the man behind the myth.* Faversham: Faversham Society.
Hyde, P. and Harrington, D. (2000). *Faversham Tudor and Stuart Muster Rolls.* Faversham Hundred Records 3, privately published.
James, M. K. (1971). *Studies in the Medieval Wine Trade.* Oxford: Oxford University Press.
Jarnut, J. and Johanek, P., eds (1998). *Die Frühgeschichte der europäischen Stadt im 11 Jahrhundert.* Cologne: Böhlau.
Jeake, S. (1728). *Charters of the Cinque Ports, Two Ancient Towns, and their Members.* London.
Jenkins, R. C. (1878). 'St Mary's Minster-in-Thanet, and St Mildred'. *Archaeologia Cantiana* 12, 177–96.
Jessiman, I. McD. (1957–8). 'The piscina in the English medieval church', *Journal of the British Archaeological Association* 3rd series, 20–21, 53–71.
Jones, K. (2001). 'Gender and crime in the local courts in Kent, 1460–1560'. Unpublished Ph.D. thesis, University of Greenwich.
Jones, M. J., Stocker, D. and Vince, A. (2003). *The City by the Pool: assessing the archaeology of the city of Lincoln.* Oxford: Oxbow / English Heritage.
Jones, S. et al. (1996). *The Survey of Ancient Houses in Lincoln, IV: Houses in the Bail.* Lincoln Civic Trust.
Jope, E. M., ed. (1961). *Studies in Building History: essays in recognition of the work of B. H. St J. O'Neill.* London: Odhams Press.
Kahn, D. (1991). *Canterbury Cathedral and its Romanesque Sculpture.* London: Harvey Miller.
Karras, R. (1996). *Common Women: prostitution and sexuality in medieval England.* Oxford: Oxford University Press.
KARU (1978). 'The Sandown Gate at Sandwich'. *Kent Archaeological Review* 52, 29.
Keene, D. (1985). *Survey of Medieval Winchester.* Winchester Studies, 2. Oxford: Clarendon Press.
Keene, D. (1989). 'The property market in English towns, AD 100–1600'. In Vigueur, ed., 200–26.
Keene, D. (1990). 'Shops and shopping in medieval London'. In Grant, ed., 29–46.
Keene, D. (2001). 'Issues of water in medieval London'. *Urban History* 28: 2, 157–79.
Keene, D. and Harding, V. (1987). *Historical Gazetteer of London Before the Great Fire: Cheapside.* Centre for Metropolitan History, http://www.british-history.ac.uk.

Keller, P. (1987). 'Investigations on the site of the Tannery, Loop Street, Sandwich, 1987'. *Kent Archaeological Review* 90, 237–8.
Kelly, S. E., ed. (1995). *Charters of St Augustine's Abbey and Minster in Thanet.* Anglo-Saxon Charters 4, London: British Academy / Oxford University Press.
Kilburne, R. (1659). *A Topographie and Survey of the County of Kent.* London.
Kirby, D. P. (1983). 'Bede, Eddius and the "Life of Wilfrid"'. *English Historical Review* 98, 101–14.
Klein, W. G. (1928). 'Roman temple at Worth, Kent', *Antiquaries Journal* 8, 76–86.
Knowles, D. and Hadcock, R. N. (1971). *Medieval Religious Houses in England and Wales.* 2nd edn, London: Longman.
Kowaleski, M. (2000). 'Port towns in England and Wales, 1300–1540'. In Palliser, ed., 467–94.
Kümin, B. and Tlusty, B., eds (2002). *The World of the Tavern: public houses in early modern Europe.* Aldershot: Ashgate.
Laithwaite, M. (1984). 'Totnes houses, 1500–1800'. In Clark, ed., 62–98.
Laker, J. (1917). *History of Deal.* Deal: Pain and Sons.
Leach, P. E., ed. (1982). *Archaeology in Kent to AD 1500.* CBA Research Report 48.
Leech, R. (2000). 'The symbolic hall: historical context and merchant culture in the early modern city', *Vernacular Architecture* 31, 1–10.
Lewcock, R. (1980). 'Acoustics, 1: rooms, 8, medieval times'. In Sadie, ed., 54–8.
Lewis, A. (1939). 'Roger Leyburn and the pacification of England, 1265–7'. *English Historical Review* 54, 193–214.
Lewis, J. (1736). *The History and Antiquities as well Ecclesiastical as Civil of the Isle of Tenet, in Kent.* London.
Lewis, J. (1744). 'A short dissertation on the antiquities of the two ancient ports of Richborough and Sandwich, by the Isle of Tanet in Kent'. *Archaeologia* I, 79–83.
Lewis, T. (2004). '"For the poor to drink and the rich to dress their meat": the first London water conduit'. *London and Middlesex Archaeological Society* 55, 39–68.
Lloyd, N. (1975). *History of the English House.* London: Architectural Press.
Lloyd, T. H. (1977). *The English Wool Trade in the Middle Ages.* Cambridge: Cambridge University Press.
Long, A., Hipkin, S. and Clarke, H., eds (2002). *Romney Marsh: coastal and landscape change through the ages.* Oxford University School of Archaeology Monograph 56.
Lutton, R. and Salter, E. (2007). *Pieties in Transition: religious practices and experiences, c.1400–1640.* Aldershot: Ashgate.
LVRG (2006). 'The geology, archaeology and history of Lydden Valley and Sandwich Bay'. Unpublished Lydden Valley Research Group Report.
Macpherson-Grant, N. (1991). 'Excavations at Stonar, near Sandwich'. *Canterbury's Archaeology, 1989–1990,* 46–8.
Maddicott, J. R. (1987). 'The English peasantry and the demands of the Crown, 1294–1341'. In Aston, ed., 285–359.
Margary, I. D. (1955). *Roman Roads in Britain,* I. London: Phoenix House.

Marks, R. (2004). *Image and Devotion in Late Medieval England*. Stroud: Sutton.

Martin, D. and Martin, B. (1986). *Historic Buildings in Eastern Sussex*, 2. Rape of Hastings Architectural Survey, Robertsbridge.

Martin, D. and Martin, B. (1987). *Historic Buildings in Eastern Sussex*, 4. Rape of Hastings Architectural Survey, Robertsbridge.

Martin, D. and Martin, B. (1989). *Historic Buildings in Eastern Sussex*, 5. Rape of Hastings Architectural Survey, Robertsbridge.

Martin, D. and Martin, B. (2004). *New Winchelsea, Sussex: a Medieval Port Town*. Field Archaeology Unit Monograph 2, Institute of Archaeology, University College London.

Martin, D. and Martin, B. (2009). *Rye Rebuilt*. Romney Marsh Research Trust, Domton Publishers.

Martin, E. (1974). *Sandwich Almshouses, 1190–1975*. Sandwich: SLHS

Martin, E. (1979). *Sandwich Guildhall, 1579–1979*, Sandwich: SLHS

Martin, E. (1980). *Occupations of the People of Sandwich*. Sandwich: SLHS

Mason, M. (1976). 'The role of the English parishioner 1100–1500'. *Journal of Ecclesiastical History* 27, 17–29.

Mate, M. (1982). 'The impact of war on the economy of Canterbury Cathedral Priory, 1294–1340', *Speculum* 57, 761–78.

Mate, M. (1991). 'The agrarian economy of south-east England before the Black Death: depressed or buoyant?' In Campbell, ed., 79–109.

Mate, M. (2006a). *Trade and Economic Developments, 1450–1550: the experience of Kent, Surrey and Sussex*. Woodbridge: Boydell Press.

Mate, M. (2006b). 'Work and leisure'. In Horrox and Ormrod, eds, 276–92.

Matson, C. (1961). 'William Rolfe: a noted local antiquarian', *Archaeologia Cantiana* 76, 180–85.

Mayhew, G. (1987). *Tudor Rye*. Falmer: University of Sussex.

Mayr-Harting, H. and Moore, R. I., eds (1985). *Studies in Medieval History Presented to R. H. C. Davis*. London: Hambledon Press.

McIntosh, M. K. (1998). *Controlling Misbehaviour in England, 1370–1600*. Cambridge: Cambridge University Press.

McIntosh, M. K. (2005). *Working Women in English Society, 1300–1620*. Cambridge: Cambridge University Press.

Meirion-Jones, M. and Jones, M., eds (1993). *Manorial Domestic Buildings in England and Northern France*. Society of Antiquaries Occasional Papers 15.

Menuge, A. (2006). *Understanding Historic Buildings: a guide to good recording practice*. Swindon: English Heritage.

Mercer, E. (1975). *English Vernacular Houses: a study in traditional farmhouses and cottages*. London: RCHM/HMSO

Metcalf, D. M. (1998). *An Atlas of Anglo-Saxon and Norman Coin Finds*. Royal Numismatic Society Special Publication 2.

Miles, D. (1997). 'The interpretation, presentation and use of tree-ring dates'. *Vernacular Architecture* 28, 40–56.

Mills, M. and Scroggs, E. (n.d.). 'The history of the Cinque Port of Sandwich'. Typescript, copy held in Dover Museum and Bronze Age Boat Gallery.

Milne, G. (1992). *Timber Building Techniques in London, c.900–1400*. London and Middlesex Archaeological Society, Special Paper 15.

Milne, G. (2003). *The Port of Medieval London*. Stroud: Tempus.

Milne, G. (2004). 'The fourteenth-century merchant ship from Sandwich: a study in maritime archaeology'. *Archaeologia Cantiana* 124, 227–63.

Milne, G. and Hobley, B., eds (1981). *Waterfront Archaeology in Britain and Northern Europe*. CBA Research Report 41.

Mommsen, W. J., Alter, P. and Scribner, R. W., eds (1979). *Stadtbürgertum und Adel in der Reformation: The Urban Classes, The Nobility and the Reformation*. Stuttgart: Klett-Cotta, and London: Publications of the German Historical Institute University of London, 5.

Moran, M. (2003). *Vernacular Buildings of Shropshire*. Logaston: Logaston Press.

Morillo, S. (1994). *Warfare under the Anglo-Norman Kings*. Woodbridge: Boydell Press.

Morris, C. (1989). *The Papal Monarchy: The Western Church from 1050–1250*. Oxford: Clarendon Press.

Munby, J., Sparks, M. and Tatton-Brown, T. (1983). 'Crownpost and king-strut roofs in south-east England'. *Medieval Archaeology* 27, 123–34.

Murray, K. M. E. (1935). *The Constitutional History of the Cinque Ports*. Manchester: Manchester University Press.

Napier, A. S. (1908). 'An Old English vision of Leofric, earl of Mercia'. *Transactions of the Philological Society* 26: 2, 180–88.

Newman, J. (1980). *West Kent and the Weald*. The Buildings of England, 2nd edn. Harmondsworth: Penguin.

Newman, J. (1987). *North East and East Kent*. The Buildings of England, 3rd edn. Harmondsworth: Penguin.

Niblett, R. and Thompson, I. (2005). *Alban's Buried Towns: an assessment of St Alban's archaeology up to AD 1600*. Oxford: Oxbow Books / English Heritage.

Norris, M. (1977). *Monumental Brasses: the memorials I*. London: Phillips and Page.

Ogilvie, J. D. (1960). 'Mary-le-bone Hill, Sandwich'. *Archaeologia Cantiana* 74, 141–50.

Ogilvie, J. D. (1983). 'A mesolithic adze from Sandwich', *Kent Archaeological Review* 71, 14–15.

Ollerenshaw, Z. L. (1990). 'The civic elite in Sandwich, Kent, 1568–1640'. Unpublished M.Phil. thesis, University of Kent.

Olsen, O., Madsen, J. S. and Rieck, F., eds (1995). *Shipshape: essays for Ole Crumlin-Pedersen on the occasion of his 60th anniversary*. Roskilde (Denmark): Viking Ship Museum.

O'Neill, B. H. St J. (1953). 'Some seventeenth-century houses in Great Yarmouth', *Archaeologia*, 95, 141–80.

Orme, N. and Webster M. (1995). *The English Hospital, 1070–1570*. New Haven and London: Yale University Press.

Ormrod, W. M. (1991). 'The crown and the English economy, 1290–1348'. In Campbell, ed., 149–83.

Oxford Dictionary of National Biography (2004). Oxford: Oxford University Press.

Oxford English Dictionary. Oxford: Oxford University Press.

Palliser, D. M., ed. (2000). *The Cambridge Urban History of Britain,* I: *600–c.1540*. Cambridge: Cambridge University Press.

Palliser, D. M. (2006). 'The English parish in perspective'. In *Towns and Local Communities in Medieval and Early Modern England*. Variorum III, Aldershot: Ashgate, 1–24.

Palliser, D. M., Slater, T. R. and Dennison, E. P. (2000). 'The topography of towns, 600–1300'. In Palliser, ed., 153–86.

Pantin, W. A. (1961). 'Medieval inns'. In Jope, ed., 166–91.

Pantin, W. A. (1962–3). 'Medieval English town-house plans'. *Medieval Archaeology* 6–7, 202–39.

Parfitt, K. (1980). 'A probable Roman villa on the Sandwich by-pass'. *Kent Archaeological Review* 60, 232–48.

Parfitt, K. (1982). 'A Roman occupation site near Sandwich'. *Kent Archaeological Review* 67, 150–59.

Parfitt, K. (1993). 'Excavations at the Carmelite friary, Sandwich, 1971 and 1993'. *Kent Archaeological Review* 113, 59–63.

Parfitt, K. (1999). 'Anglo-Saxon Eastry: some recent discoveries and excavations'. *Archaeologia Cantiana* 118, 45–53.

Parfitt, K. (2001). 'An early excavation plan of Stonar church, near Sandwich'. *Kent Archaeological Rev*iew 145, 95–9.

Parfitt, K. (2003). 'The Old Customs House Sandwich'. *Canterbury's Archaeology, 2001–2002,* 33–4.

Parfitt, K. (in preparation). *Excavations at the Rear of 10 Market Street, Sandwich.*

Parfitt, K., Corke, B. C. and Cotter, J. (2006). *Townwall Street, Dover: Excavations, 1996. The Archaeology of Canterbury* NS 3, CAT.

Parfitt, K. and Sweetinburgh, S. (2009). 'Further investigations of Anglo-Saxon and medieval Eastry'. *Archaeological Cantiana* 129, 313–32.

Parker, V. (1971). *The Making of Kings Lynn*. London and Chichester: Phillimore.

Parkin, E. W. (1984). 'The ancient Cinque Port of Sandwich'. *Archaeologia Cantiana* 100, 189–216.

Parsons, D. (1986). '*Sacrarium*: ablution drains in early medieval churches'. In Butler and Morris, eds, 105–20.

Parsons, D., ed. (1990). *Stone: Quarrying and Building in England*. London: Phillimore / Royal Archaeological Institute.

Parsons, D. (1994). 'Sandwich: the oldest Scandinavian rune-stone in England?'. In Ambrosiani and Clarke, eds, 310–20.

Pearson, S. (1994). *The Medieval Houses of Kent: an historical analysis*. London: RCHME / HMSO.

Pearson, S. (2001a). 'The chronological distribution of tree-ring dates, 1980–2001: an update'. *Vernacular Architecture* 36, 68–9.

Pearson, S. (2001b). 'The archbishop's palace at Charing in the Middle Ages'. *Archaeologia Cantiana*, 121, 315–49.

Pearson, S. (2003). 'Houses, shops and storage: building evidence from two Kentish ports'. In Beattie, Maslakovic and Rees-Jones, eds, 409–31.

Pearson, S. (2005). 'Rural and urban houses, 1100–1500: "urban adaptation" reconsidered'. In Giles and Dyer, eds, 43–63.

Pearson, S., Barnwell, P. S. and Adams A. T.(1994). *A Gazetteer of Medieval houses in Kent*. London: RCHME / HMSO

Pearson, S., and Meeson B., eds (2001). *Vernacular Buildings in a Changing World: understanding, recording, conservation.* CBA Research Report 126.

Peate, I. C., ed. (1930). *Studies in Regional Consciousness and Environment*. Oxford: Oxford University Press.

Pelham, R. A. (1930). 'The foreign trade of the Cinque Ports during the year 1307–8'. In Peate, ed., 129–45

Pelham, R. A. (1932). 'Some aspects of the east Kent wool trade in the thirteenth century'. *Archaeologia Cantiana* 44, 218–28.

Pestell, T. and Ulmschneider, K., eds (2003). *Markets in Early Medieval Europe: trading and 'productive' sites, 650–850*. Macclesfield: Windgather Press.

Pfaff, R. W. (1970). *New Liturgical Feasts in Later Medieval England*. Oxford: Oxford University Press.

Philp, B. (2002). *Archaeology in the Front Line*. Dover: Kent Archaeological Rescue Unit.

Platt, C. and Coleman-Smith, R. (1975). *Excavations in Medieval Southampton, 1953–1969, vol. 1: the excavation reports*. Leicester: Leicester University Press.

Portman, D. (1966). *Exeter Houses, 1400–1700*. Exeter: University of Exeter Press.

Prestwich, M. (1972). *War, Politics and Finance under Edward I*. London: Faber.

Priestley, U. and Corfield, P. J. (1982). 'Rooms and room use in Norwich housing, 1580–1730'. *Post-Medieval Archaeology* 16, 93–123.

Pullen-Appleby, J. (2005). *English Sea Power, c.871–1100*. Hockwold-cum-Wilton: Anglo-Saxon Books.

Pye, A. and Woodward, F. (1996). *The Historic Defences of Plymouth*. Truro: Cornwall County Council.

Quiney, A. (1993). *Kent Houses*. Woodbridge: Antique Collectors' Club.

Quiney, A. (1999). 'Hall or chamber? That is the question: the use of rooms in post-Conquest houses'. *Architectural History* 42, 24–46.

Quiney, A. (2003). *Town Houses of Medieval Britain*. London and New Haven: Yale University Press.

Rawcliffe, C. and Wilson, R., eds (2004). *Medieval Norwich*. London: Hambledon and London.

RCHM (1972). *An Inventory of the Historical Monuments in the City of York, I: The Defences*. London: HMSO.

RCHM (1980). *Ancient and Historical Monuments in the City of Salisbury, I*. London: HMSO

RCHM (1981). *An Inventory of the Historical Monuments in the City of York, V: The Central Area*. London: HMSO.

Reynolds, A. and Webster, L., eds (forthcoming). *Early Medieval Art and Archaeology in the Northern World*. Leiden: Brill Academic Publishing.

Reynolds, S. (1977). *An Introduction to the History of English Medieval Towns*. Oxford: Clarendon Press.

Reynolds, S. (1984). *Kingdoms and Communities in Western Europe, 900–1300*. Oxford: Clarendon Press.

Reynolds, S. (1987). 'Towns in Domesday Book'. In Holt, ed., 295–309.

Reynolds, S. (1998). 'English towns in a European context'. In Jarnut and Johanek, eds, 207–18.

Rhodes, E. (2007). 'Identifying human modification of river channels'. In Blair, ed., 133–52.

Richardson, A. (2005). *The Anglo-Saxon Cemeteries of Kent*. BAR British Series 391, Oxford.

Richardson, C. (1999). 'The meanings of space in society and drama: perceptions of domestic life and domestic tragedy, *c*.1550–1660'. Unpublished Ph.D. thesis, University of Kent.

Richardson, C. (2003). 'Household objects and domestic ties'. In Beattie, Maslakovic and Rees-Jones, eds, 433–47.

Richardson, T. L. (2004). *Medieval Sandwich*. Sandwich: SLHS.

Richmond, C. F. (1970). 'Fauconberg's Kentish rising of May 1471'. *English Historical Review* 137, 673–92.

Rickman, J. (1840). 'On the antiquity of Abury [*sic*] and Stonehenge'. *Archaeologia*, 399–418.

Rigby, S. H. (1995). *English Society in the Later Middle Ages: class, status, gender*. London: Macmillan.

Rigold, S. E. (1965). 'Two Carmelite houses: Aylesford and Sandwich'. *Archaeologia Cantiana* 80, 1–28.

Rigold, S. E. (1968a). 'The Post-Roman coins'. In Cunliffe, ed., 217–23.

Rigold, S. E. (1968b). 'Two types of court hall'. *Archaeologia Cantiana* 83, 1–22.

Riley, H. T., ed. (1859–62). *Munimenta Gildhallae Londoniensis*, 3 vols. London: Guildhall Library, Longman and Roberts.

Rippon, S. (2002). 'Romney marsh: evolution of the historic landscape and its wider significance'. In Long, Hipkin and Clarke, eds, 84–100.

Roach Smith, C. (1882). 'Retrospective observations respecting a hoard of Roman coins found in the sand hills, near Deal'. *Archaeologia Cantiana* 14, 368–9.

Roberts, E. (2003). *Hampshire Houses, 1250–1750*. Hampshire County Council.

Robertson, W. A. Scott (1886). 'St Mary's Church, Sandwich'. *Archaeologia Cantiana* 16, lv–lx.

Robinson, A. H. W. and Cloet, R. L. (1953). 'Coastal evolution in Sandwich Bay'. *Proceedings of the Geologists' Association* 64, 69–82.

Rodger, N. A. M. (1996). 'The naval service of the Cinque Ports'. *English Historical Review* 111, 636–51.

Rogers, A. (1972). 'Parish boundaries and urban history: two case studies'. *Journal of the British Archaeological Association* 35, 46–64.

Rolfe, H. W. (1852). *The Publications of the Antiquarian Etching Club* 3.

Rolfe, H. W. (1853). *The Publications of the Antiquarian Etching Club* 4.

Rollason, D. W. (1979). 'The date of the parish boundary of Minster-in-Thanet'. *Archaeologia Cantiana* 95, 7–17.

Rollason, D. W. (1982). *The Mildrith Legend*. Leicester: Leicester University Press.

Rose, S. (2002). *Medieval Naval Warfare, 1000–1500*. London and New York: Routledge.

Roskell, J. S., Clarke, L. and Rawcliffe, C., eds (1992). *The History of Parliament: the House of Commons, 1386–1421*. Stroud: Alan Sutton.

Ross, C. (1974). *Edward IV*. London: Eyre Methuen.

Rosser, G. (1988a). 'The Anglo-Saxon gilds'. In Blair, ed., 31–4.

Rosser, G. (1988b). 'Communities of parish and guild in the late Middle Ages'. In Wright, ed., 29–55.

Rosser, G. (1997). 'Crafts and guilds and the negotiation of work in the medieval town'. *Past and Present* 154, 3–31.

Rosseter, J. B. (1986). 'The font at the church of St Clement, Sandwich and the Hallam-Berney problem'. *Archaeologia Cantiana* 103, 127–40.

Rubin, M. (1989). 'Development and change in English hospitals, 1100–1500'. In Granshaw and Porter, eds, 41–59.

Ruddock, A. A. (1951). *Italian Merchant Shipping in Southampton, 1270–1600*. Southampton: University College.

Rumble, A. (2001). 'Notes on the linguistic and onomastic characteristics of Old English *wīc*'. In Hill and Cowie, eds, 1–2.

Sacks, D. H. and Lynch, M. (2000). 'Ports, 1540–1700'. In Clark, ed., 377–424.

Sadie, S., ed. (1980). *The New Grove Dictionary of Music and Musicians*, vol. 1. London: Macmillan.

Salemke, G. (1967). 'Das Krantor zu Danzig'. *Das Logbuch* 3: 3, 5–6.

Salzman, L. F. (1952). *Building in England down to 1540*. Oxford: Clarendon Press.

Sartfatij, H. (2007). *Archeologie van een Deltastad: opgravingen in de binnenstad van Dordrecht*. Utrecht: Stichting Matrijs.

Sawyer, P. H. (1968). *Anglo-Saxon Charters*. London: Royal Historical Society.

Schofield, J. (1987). *The London Surveys of Ralph Treswell*. London: London Topographical Society, 135.

Schofield, J. (1994). *Medieval London Houses*. New Haven and London: Yale University Press.

Schofield, J. (1997). 'Medieval parish churches in the City of London: the archaeological evidence'. In French, Gibbs and Kümin, eds, 35–55.

Schofield, J. and Vince, A. (1994). *Medieval Towns*. Leicester: Leicester University Press.

Schütte, L. (1976). *Wik: eine Siedlungsbezeichnung in historischen und sprachlichen Bezügen*. Cologne and Vienna: Böhlan.

Scofield, C. L. (1923). *The Life and Reign of Edward IV*. London: Longmans, Green.

Seaborne, M. (1971). *The English School: its architecture and organization, 1370–1870*. London: Routledge and Kegan Paul.

Seymour, C. (1776). *A New Topographical, Historical and Commercial Survey of the Cities, Towns and Villages of Kent*. Canterbury.

Shelby, L. R. (1967). *John Rogers: Tudor Military Engineer*. Oxford: Clarendon Press.

Shephard-Thorn, E. R. (1988). *Geology of the Country around Ramsgate and Dover*. Memorandum of the Geological Survey, London: HMSO.

Short, P. (1980). 'The fourteenth-century rows of York'. *Archaeological Journal* 137, 86–136.

Skelton, R. A. and Harvey, P. D. A., eds (1986). *Local Maps and Plans from Medieval England*. Oxford: Clarendon Press.

Slater, T. R. and Rosser, G., eds (1998). *The Church in the Medieval Town*. Aldershot: Ashgate.

Smith, J. T. (1992). *English Houses, 1200–1800: the Hertfordshire evidence*. London: RCHME / HMSO.

Smith, J. T. (2000). 'From post-hole to timber framing'. *Journal of the British Archaeological Association* 153, 156–62.

Smith, R. A. L. (1943). *Canterbury Cathedral Priory: a study in monastic administration*. Cambridge: Cambridge University Press.

Smith, T. P. (1970). 'The medieval town defences of King's Lynn'. *Journal of the British Archaeological Association* 3rd series 33, 57–88.

Smith, T. P. (1985). *The Medieval Brickmaking Industry in England, 1400–1450*. BAR British Series 138, Oxford.

Smith, T. P. (1990). 'The Roper Gateway, St Dunstan's Street, Canterbury'. *Archaeologia Cantiana* 108, 163–82.

So, C. L. (1963). 'Some aspects of the form and origin of the coastal features of north-east Kent', Unpublished Ph.D. thesis, University of London.

Southam, A. G. (1980). 'The medieval water-front of Sandwich'. *Bygone Kent* 1: 5, 304–10.

Spufford, M. (1990). 'The limitations of the probate inventory'. In Chartres and Hey, 139–74.

Spurr, G. (2005). 'Former Brown and Mason Yard, Ramsgate Road, Sandwich: a geoarchaeological assessment report'. Unpublished report, Museum of London Archaeology Service.

Stafford, P. (1997). *Queen Emma and Queen Edith: queenship and women's power in eleventh-century England*. Oxford: Blackwell.

Stebbing, W. P. D. (1936). 'The house of the White Friars, Sandwich, AD 1272'. *Archaeologia Cantiana* 48, 225–7.

Stewart, I. J. (1999). 'The Kings Arms, Sandwich', *Canterbury's Archaeology, 1996–1997,* 26.

Stewart, I. J. (2000). 'Archaeological investigations at Sandwich castle'. *Archaeologia Cantiana* 120, 51–75.

Streeten, A. D. F. (1976). 'Excavations at Lansdowne Road, Tonbridge'. *Archaeologia Cantiana* 92, 105–18.

Summerson, J. (1969). *Architecture in Britain, 1530–1830*. 5th edn, Harmondsworth: Penguin.

Sutton, A. (1999). 'Some aspects of the linen trade, c.1130–1500, and the part played by the mercers of London'. *Textile History* 30, 155–75.

Swanson, H. (1988). 'The illusion of economic structure: craft guilds in late medieval English towns'. *Past and Present* 121, 29–48.

Swanson, H. (1989). *Medieval Artisans: an urban class in Late Medieval England*. Oxford: Blackwell.

Swanson, R. N., ed. (1999). *Continuity and Change in Christian Worship*. Studies in Church History, 35, Woodbridge: Boydell and Brewer.

Sweetinburgh, S. (2002). 'Discord in the public arena: a time of conflict in early sixteenth-century Sandwich'. Unpublished paper presented to Staff/postgraduate History Seminar, University of Kent.

Sweetinburgh, S. (2004a). *The Role of the Hospital in Medieval England*. Dublin: Four Courts Press.

Sweetinburgh, S. (2004b). 'Wax, stone and iron: Dover's town defences in the late middle ages'. *Archaeologia Cantiana* 124, 183–207.

Sweetinburgh, S. (2006). 'Mayor-making and other ceremonies: shared uses of sacred space among the Kentish Cinque Ports'. In Trio and de Smet, eds, 165–87.

Sylvester, D. (2004). 'The development of Winchelsea and its maritime economy'. In Martin and Martin, 7–19.

Tait, J. (1936). *The Medieval English Borough*. Manchester: Manchester University Press.

Tatton-Brown, T. (1978). 'The Sandown Gate, Sandwich'. *Archaeologia Cantiana* 94, 153–6.

Tatton-Brown, T. (1980). 'The use of Quarr stone in London and east Kent'. *Medieval Archaeology* 24, 213–15.

Tatton-Brown, T. (1984). 'The towns of Kent'. In Haslam, ed., 1–36.

Tatton-Brown, T. (1988a). 'The Anglo-Saxon towns of Kent'. In Hooke, ed., 213–32.

Tatton-Brown, T. (1988b). 'The churches of Canterbury diocese in the 11th century'. In Blair, ed., 105–18.

Tatton-Brown, T. (1989). 'Documentary evidence'. In Bennett and Houliston, 20–23.

Tatton-Brown, T. (1990). 'Building stone in Canterbury, 1070–1525'. In Parsons, ed., 70–82.

Tatton-Brown, T. (1993). 'Sandwich St Clement'. Unpublished report, Canterbury Diocese Historical and Archaeological Survey.

Tatton-Brown, T. (2006a). 'The topography and buildings of medieval Rochester'. In Ayers and Tatton-Brown, eds, 22–37.

Tatton-Brown, T. (2006b). 'The two mid twelfth-century cloister arcades at Canterbury Cathedral Priory'. *Journal of the British Archaeological Association* 159, 91–104.

Tatton-Brown, T. et al. (1982). 'The West Gate'. In Frere, Stow and Bennett, eds, 107–19.

Taylor, H. M. and Taylor, J. (1965). *Anglo-Saxon Architecture*, 2 vols. Cambridge: Cambridge University Press.

Tester, P. J. (1979). 'The plan and description of remains at Davington Priory'. *Archaeologia Cantiana* 95, 205–12.

Thick, A. E. (1997). *The Fifteenth-century Stewards' Books of Southampton*. Unpublished PhD thesis, University of Winchester.

Tinniswood, J. T. (1949). 'English galleys, 1272–1377', *Mariner's Mirror* 35, 276–315.

Tipping, C. (1994). 'Cargo handling and the medieval cog'. *Mariner's Mirror* 80: 1, 3–15.

Tittler, R. (1991). *Architecture and Power: the town hall and the English urban community, c.1500–1640*. Oxford: Clarendon Press.

Tricker, R. (2002). *St Peter's Church, Sandwich, Kent*. London: The Churches Conservation Trust.

Trio, P. and de Smet, M., eds (2006). *The Use and Abuse of Sacred Places in Late Medieval Towns*. Leuven: Leuven University Press.

Trussler, R. (1974). 'Recovery of ship's timbers at Sandwich, Kent'. *Kent Archaeological Review* 36, 166–9.

Turner, H. L. (1970). *Town Defences in England and Wales*. London: Baker.

Tweddle, D., Biddle, M. and Kjølby-Biddle, B. (1995). *Corpus*

of Anglo-Saxon Stone Sculpture, IV: *South-East*. London: British Academy.
Ulmschneider, K. and Pestell, T. (2003). 'Introduction: early medieval markets and 'productive sites'. In Pestell and Ulmschneider, eds, 1–10.
Unger, R. W. (1978). 'The Netherlands herring fishing in the Late Middle Ages: the false legend of William Beukels of Biervliet'. *Viator* 9, 335–56.
Unger, R. W. (1980). *The Ship in the Medieval Economy*. London: Croom Helm.
Unger, R. W. (1981). 'Warships and cargo ships in medieval Europe'. *Technology and Culture* 22, 233–52.
Urry, W. (1967). *Canterbury under the Angevin Kings*. London: Athlone Press.
Urry, W. (1986). 'Canterbury, Kent, *c*.1153x1161'. In Skelton and Harvey, eds, 3–58.
Vallance, A. (1920). *Old Crosses and Lychgates*. London: Batsford.
VCH Warwickshire (1969). *A History of the County of Warwickshire*, VIII. Oxford: Oxford University Press
VCH Kent (1974a). *Victoria History of the County of Kent*, II. Reprint, London: Dawsons.
VCH Kent (1974b). *Victoria History of the County of Kent*, III. Reprint, London: Dawsons.
Verhulst, A. (1999). *The Rise of Cities in North-West Europe*. Cambridge: Cambridge University Press.
Verwers, W. J. H. (1988). 'Dorestad: a Carolingian town?' In Hodges and Hobley, eds, 52–6.
Vigueur, J.-C. M., ed. (1989). *D'une ville a l'autre: structures matérielles et organisation de l'espace dans les villes Européenes, XIIIe–XVIe siècles*. Rome: Ecole Française de Rome.
Walker, G. P. (1927). 'The lost Wantsum Channel: its importance to Richborough Channel'. *Archaeologia Cantiana* 39, 91–111.
Walker, W. (1981). *Essex Markets and Fairs*. Chelmsford: Essex Record Office, 83.
Wallace, K. J. (1974). 'The overseas trade of Sandwich, 1400–1520'. Unpublished M.Phil. thesis, University of London.
Wallenberg, J. K. (1931). *Kentish Place-Names*. Uppsala: Uppsala Universitets Årsskrift.
Wanostrocht, C. (1993). *Sandwich in Old Photographs*. Stroud: Sutton.
Wanostrocht, C. (n.d.). *Saint Bartholomew's Hospital, Sandwich, Kent*. Sandwich United Charities.
Ward, G. (1933). 'The lists of Saxon churches in the Domesday Monachorum, and White Book of St Augustine'. *Archaeologia Cantiana* 45, 60–89.
Ward, G. (1943). 'The Saxon history of the Wantsum'. *Archaeologia Cantiana* 56, 23–7.
Webster, L. and Cherry, J. (1980). 'Medieval Britain in 1979'. *Medieval Archaeology* 24, 218–64.
Wedgwood, J. C. (1936). *History of Parliament: biographies of the Members of the Commons House, 1439–1509*. London: HMSO
Wijntjes, W. (1982). 'The water supply of the medieval town'. In *Rotterdam Papers*, IV, 189–203.
Williams, A. (1997). 'The Anglo-Norman Abbey'. In Gem, ed., 50–66.
Willson, J. (2005). 'The Butchery, Sandwich'. *Canterbury's Archaeology, 2003–2004*, 22.
Witney, K. P. (1990). 'The woodland economy of Kent, 1066–1348'. *Agricultural History Review* 38, 20–39.
Wood-Legh, K. L., ed. (1984). *Kentish Visitations of Archbishop William Warham and his Deputies, 1511–12*. Kent Records 24, KAS.
Woodfield, C. (2005). *The Church of Our Lady of Mount Carmel and some Conventual Buildings at the Whitefriars, Coventry*. BAR British Series 389, Oxford.
Woodman, F. (1992). 'The waterworks drawings of the Eadwine Psalter'. In Gibson, Heslop and Pfaff, eds, 168–77.
Wragg, E., Jarrett, C. and Haslam, J. (2005). 'The development of medieval Tonbridge reviewed in the light of recent excavations at Lyons, East Street'. *Archaeologia Cantiana* 125, 119–49.
Wright, S. J., ed. (1988). *Parish, Church and People: local studies in lay religion, 1350–1750*. London: Hutchinson.
Wrigley, E. A. and Schofield, J. S. (1981). *The Population History of England, 1541–1871: a reconstruction*. London: Edward Arnold.
Yates, N. and Gibson, J. M., eds (1994). *Traffic and Politics: the construction and management of Rochester Bridge, AD 43–1993*. Woodbridge: Boydell Press / Rochester Bridge Trust.
Youngs, S. M. and Clark, J. (1981). 'Medieval Britain in 1980'. *Medieval Archaeology* 25, 209.
Zell, M., ed. (2000). *Early Modern Kent*. Woodbridge: Boydell Press / Kent County Council.

Sandwich Survey Reports, CAT
Report 1 (2004). 'Sandwich Area Contour Survey, 2004: Notes'.
Report 2 (2004). 'Early Settlement at Sandwich, Part 1: The Prehistoric Background, *c*.8000 BC–AD 43'.
Report 3 (2004). 'Early Settlement at Sandwich, Part 2: The Roman Period, AD 43–*c*.425 (with Appendix on Anglo-Saxon Discoveries)'.
Report 4 (2005). 'Notes on the Geology and Soils of the Sandwich Region'.
Report 5 (2005). 'Database of investigated archaeological sites in Sandwich'.
Report 6 (2005). 'Sandwich Town Wall, Part 1: Description of the Landward (Earthen) Defences'.
Report 7a (2005). 'Sandwich Town Wall, Part 2a: Description of the River-side Masonry Defences (Central and Eastern Sectors), the Town Gates and Towers'.
Report 7b (2006). Sandwich Town Wall, Part 2b: Description of the River-side Masonry Defences (Western Sector)'.
Report 8 (2006). 'A History of Archaeological Investigations in and around Sandwich'.
Report 9 (2006). 'Report on an Archaeological Survey of Mary-le-Bone Hill, Sandwich, 2006'.
Report 10 (2006). 'Report on Test-Pitting across the Sandowns Area, 2005–2006'.

Index

NB: bold type indicates the location of Figures (mentions in text take precedence); italic type indicates medieval street names

administration *see* Sandwich, governance of
agriculture 66, 118, 140, 238, 269 *see also* grazing land
alehouses 141, 232, 237 *see also* inns; taverns
aliens *see also* Flemings; Strangers
    involvement in trade 64, 66, 124–5, 130, 230
    occupations 140, 144, 231
    settling in Sandwich 66, 125–6, 144, 231
almshouses *see* hospitals
apprentices 137, 143, 236, 238
archaeological evidence
    Anglo-Saxon 9, 17–19, 22, 270
    artefacts 10, 18, 270
    coins 17, 18, 19, 22, 29
    excavated ship 55, 69, 73, 268
    metalwork 17
    occupation deposits 11, 15, 21, 22, 36, 49, 68
    pottery 10, 19, 22, 35, 49, 50, 52, 53, 150, 269, 293
    prehistoric 10, 13, 15, 22, 269
    Roman 9, 10, 11, 13, 15, 17, 18, 22, 23, 26, 269
    structures
        hearths/ovens 50, 93, 94
        timber 50–51, 53, 67, 102
        stone 53, 93, 94
archaeological excavations **3**, 4, **5**, 9–10, 18, 19, 93–4, 101, 102, **115**, 149–50, 155, 265, 268, 269, 270, 271, 273–6, 287
archaeological interventions *see* archaeological excavations
architectural decoration
    churches 44, 45, 46–7, 48, 49, 81, 84, 88, 91, 199, 201
        blind arcading 46, **47**
        capitals 42, **43**, 44, 46, 76, 79, 199
        mouldings 44, 46, 77, 91, 199
        string courses 26, 42, 44, 46, 80
        tympanum 44, 46, **47**
    secular buildings **95**, 135, **157**, **158**, 159–60, **161**, 174, 176, 180, 181, 182, 183–4, 185, **190**, 195, **244**, **251**, **252**, 255
        brickwork 135, 154, 157, 216, 250
        mouldings 164, 165, 177, 180–86, **192**, 195, 242, 243, 248, 250, 252, 255
        painting 185, 248, **249**, 261
        panelling 250, 261
        plasterwork 177, 221, **249**, 250, 251, 261, 297, 300
architectural features
    of churches
        arcades 42, **43**, 46, 46, 77, 199, 286

        arches 26, 27, 44, 46, 77, 79, 80, 91
        corbels 42, 80
        doorways 26, 42, 46, **47**, 76, 81, 199
        pier bases **32**, 44, 76, 79, 80
        piers 42, 76, 79, 199, 202, 286
        porches 81, 203
        roofs 27, 44, 46, 76, 77, 79, 80, 84, 87, 199, **200**
        stair turrets 46, **47**, 79, 85
        windows 76, 77, 79, 80, 81, 87, 157, 199, 203, **210**
    of secular buildings 157
        doorways 96, 97, 98, **99**, 101, 108, 114, 169, **174**, 176, 183, 189, 243
        jetties 102, 104, 107, 165, 191, 192, 253, 254
        stairs 98, 104, 108, 172, 176, 215, 242, 243, 244, 247–8, 250, 253
        windows 96, 98, **100**, 101, 108, 172, **173**, **174**, 183, 188, 242, 243, 244, 248, 250
architectural styles 26, 27, 44, 46, 48, 79
arsenal, the 155
attics 104, 193, 194, 242, 243, 244, 247, 250, 252, 254, 256, 261 *see also* garrets; lofts

bakehouses 143, 219, 238
bakers 59, 63, 68, 142–3, 219, 224, 232, 236, 238, 262, 292
Baly, William 166, 181, 218
barbers 63, 143
Barbican, the 135, 155, 156, 157, **158**, 215 *see also* Davis Gate
barns 225, 227, 262
Barnsend 225 *see also* Mill Wall Place
Bay (baize) hall 244
boat builders 63 *see also* shipwrights
Bolle, Henry 132, 140, 191, 207, 209, 221, 290
boom tower 160, **161** *see also* Round House, the
Boston 65, 66, 124, **125**, 139, 155
Boteler family, the 139, 140, 143, 190, 209, 240
Bowling Street (*Serles Lane*) 141, 222, 277
    Nos 6/8 (House 1) 252–3, 256, 258, 261, 277
    No. 7 (Richborough House) (House 2) 250, 259, 261, 277, 288, 292
Boys family, the 140
    John 140, 235
brewers 63, 133, 140–41, 144, 145, 232, 236–7, 238, 292
    other interests of 130, 141, 142, 143, 145, 212, 218, 222
brew-houses 140, 224, 236
brewing 63, 133, 140, 236, 237, 260
brickmakers 135
brickworks 134, 135, 186
bridges 36, 118, 123, 225–6

Bristol 167, 186, 231, 266
brothel, the 134, 135, 225, 291
building materials
    brick 108, 148, 150, 154, 160, 186, 248, 250, 277
        nogging or infill 108, **109**, 248, 288
    combinations of 95, 102, 108, 248
    flint 96, 108, 157, 160
        knapped 81, 96, 108, 114
    importation of 108, 110
    reuse of 109, 159, 247, 250
    stone 148, 155, 158, 159, 226, 277, 287, 288 *see also* masonry
        Caen 42, 44, 45, 47, 48, 96, 108, 114, 159, 203
        Hythe 76, 286
        Marquise 26, **27**
        Purbeck 76, 286
        Quarr 32, 33
        ragstone 108, 151, 156, 158, 160, 203, 293
        sandstone 94, 108, 156
        scarcity of 11, 108
        use of in ecclesiastical buildings 23, 26, 32, 47, 49–50, 55, 112, 209, 211, 213
        use of in secular buildings 49, 50, 53, 55, 68, 93, 94–102, 108–10, 111, 114, 115, 116, 140, 150, 154, 157, 159, 160, 162, 166, 183, 187, 219, 250, 266, 277–80
    thatch 259, 301
    tile 134, 138, 154, 167, 216, 220, 226, 288, 293, 301
    timber 50, 65, 95, 98, 100, 108, 110, 125, 154, 199, 211, 214–15, 217, 226, 243, 248, 277–80 *see also* timber-framed buildings
burials 137, 206, 208
    siting of 88, 200, 201, 203, 204, 207, 296
butchers 63, 114, 133, 142–3, 188, 214, 219, 221, 236, 238, 262, 292, 294
Butchery, The 35, 50, 114, 142, 188, 219, 222, 227, 262, 277
    No. 1 (House 3) 101, 174, 188, 196, 277, 294
    No. 3 (House 4) 101, 277
butteries 181, 195, 196, 224, 242, 257, 259 *see also* services
Butts and Salts, the 136, 142

Calais 124, 126, 128, 130, 138, 139, 144, 147–8, 162
Canterbury 11, **14**, 17, 108, **125**, 138, 195, 263, 283, 284, 293, 297
Canterbury Gate 72, 150, 151, **152–3**, 155, 214, 226, 268, 275, 293, 298
Capel Street 225
carpenters 63, 69, 143, 162, 186, 236, 238
Castle, Sandwich 67–8, 148, 227, 235, 268, 271
    as administrative centre 68, 146, 162
    as assembly point for troops 55, 66, 68, 162
    Castelmead 67, 162, 268
    control of 69, 162, 225
    excavation evidence for 67, 70, 162, 274
    garrison 235
    relationship with town 71, 112, 162
    tower **67**, 68, 162
    waterfront facilities of 55, 115, 117
castles 68, 162, 235
    Canterbury 68
    Dover 68
Cattle Market (*Cornmarket*) **220**, 277
    Nos 2/4 (House 6) 250, 252, 277
    No. 6 118, 273

    No. 8 (House 7) 172, 174, **175**, **188**, 221, 277, 300
    No. 9 (House 8) 170, 190, 221, 277, 300
cellars 95, 141, 165, 218, 257, 259, 287 *see also* undercrofts
    storage in 97, 101, 105, 110, 192
cemeteries 33, 34, 52, 86, 88, 138, 204 *see also* churchyards
    Roman and Anglo-Saxon 9, 17, 18, 20, 270
chamber blocks 49, 166
chambers and solars 110, 179–81, 186, 195, 224, 242, 256–8, 259, 260–61
    first-floor 98, 102, 108, 165, 174, 176, 177, 180–81, 185, 189–91, 195, 196–7, 212, 242, 248, 254, 258–61, 263
    heating of 242, 248, 250, 261, 263
    raised 49, 222
Champneys, Adam 59, 62, 87
chandlers 63, 143, 232, 238, 262, 292
changing coastline 1, 15, 119, 265 *see also* Deal Spit
chantries 62, 81, 201–2, 208, 213, 286, 290
    dissolution of 199, 209, 240
    Thomas Elys' 86, 204, 205, 213, 240
chapels
    St James 52, 204, 206, 207, 222
charity 88, 138, 208–9
Cheldesworth, Robert 124, 224
chimneys 49, 172, 185, 186, 196, 253, 258, 259, 296
    brick 180, 183, 185, 186, 196, 248, 250, 254, 258, 259
    positions of 176, **185**, 242, 248, 250, 252–3, 254, 255, 300
    thatch 259
    timber 185, 186, 196, 254, 259, 294, 301
    stone 185
Christ Church Priory, Canterbury 23, 37, 97, 112, 123, 127, 214, 222
    buildings of in Sandwich 49, 53, 55, 94–5, 112, 208, 240
    excavation at 21
    exchange of rights with king 59, 65, 139
    portreeve of 58, 59, 62
    property of in Sandwich 38–9, 55, 65, 112–14, 208, 248
    records of 8
    relations with town 59
    rights of in Sandwich 29, 40, 41, 49, 53, 55, 64
churches *see also* architectural features; individual entries
    acoustic jars **202**, 203
    advowson 31, 81
    altars 44, 81, 84, 200, 202, 203, 204, 205, 213, 296
        dedications 203, 205, 296
    Anglo-Saxon 26, 46
    bells 46, 200, 203
    benefactors of 55, 81, 88
    bequests to 199, 200, 202, 203, 205, 206, 207–8, 213
    chapels in 44, 79, 81, 84, 85, 86, 200–202, 203, 204, 205, 295
        dedications of 200–201, 203, 204, 205
    charnel houses 33, 57, 86, 204, 207, 286
    decoration *see* architectural decoration
    dedications of 28
    devotional images 80, 81, 200, 201, 202, 205, 286
    effects of liturgical practice on 48, 55, 76
    elements of
        aisles 42, 44–5, 48, 76, 77, 79, 80–81, 84, 87, 199, 204
        chancels 26, 42, 44, 76, 79
        clerestories 42, 44, 79, 199
        crossing 28, 32, 42, 45
        crypts 84–6
        east ends 44, 45, 76–9, 87

naves 26, 32, 42, 44, 48, 199
porticus 26, 32, 46
transepts 26, 32, 46, 47, 79
west ends 35, 42, 44, 79, 80
enlargement of 42, 50, 76–81
fixtures and fittings 76, 77, 79, 84, 85, 87, 200, 201–3, 204, 213
furnishings 81, 201–2, 203, 204, 205
patronage 31, 48, 81
seating 204
secular use of 55, 59, 86–7, 92, 204
size of 48
tombs in 81, 87–8, 205, 207 *see also* burials
towers 26–7, 32, 42, 44–5, 46–7, 199–200, 203, 213, 284
collapse of 76, 79, 80, 283
as landmarks 25, 28, 38, 123, 200
Church Street St Clement 35, 277
No. 10 (House 12) 170, 277
Church Street St Mary 36, 52, 114, 277
Nos 19/21 (House 13) 254, 277
No. 22 (House 14) 222, 277
No. 27 (House 15) 255, 277
Nos 28/30/32 255
churchwardens 80
churchyards 32, 33–4, 206–7, 222
expansion of 56, 61, 86, 219
size of 86
Cinque Ports 8, 40–41, 52, 55–6, 61, 65, 292
courts of 61, 86–7 *see also* courts, Shepway; courts, Brodhull
limbs of 40–41, 56, 61, 284
Sandwich's role in 41
clergy 48, 63, 76, 81, 87, 180–81, 200, 204, 208, 209, 233, 238, 241
cloth industry 74, 124, 144, 228, 231, 232, 236, 266 *see also* weavers
cloth makers 63, 236 *see also* weavers
Cnut 25, 28, 29, 40
Cobb, Alexander 196, 235, 256
cobblers 63, 144, 232
Cok Lane 35, 50, 102, 114, 218, 220, 279 *see also* Potter Street
communications **2**, 12, 36, 265
causeways 12, 21, 24, 35–6, 118, 151, 225
footpaths 34, 35
roads 12–13, 19, 24, 34–6, 50, 57, 71, 91, 118, 149, 235, 225, 226, 235, 268, 271
maintenance of 60, 138
Roman 1, 10, 11, 12, 271, 281
trackways 11, 22
water 1, 11, 12 *see also* watercourses
Condy family, the 62, 81
John 62, 66
coopers 63, 143, 221, 234, 236, 237, 238, 262, 292
cordwainers 63, 143
Cornmarket 134, 170, 179, 189, 190, 220–21, 224, 225, 227, 242, 271, 277 *see also* Cattle Market; marketplaces
cottages 191, 197, 219, 222, 224, 225, 255
court halls 136, 240, **243**
building and repair of 242
in the Cornmarket 242–4
furnishings of
mayor's chair 242, 244
by St Peter's churchyard 87, 131, 204, 219–20, 242, 297
courts 59
bailiff's 59

Brodhull 61, 87, 131
hundred 55, 59, 86
Shepway 59, 61, 86
town 59, 61, 86
Coventry 90, 143, 177, 242, 258, 266, 301
crown, the 38, 40, 55, 128
relations with town 58, 59, 132, 144–5
rights of in Sandwich 59, 132, 139

Davis Gate 70, 117, 123, 135, 155, 156, 157–9, 214–15, 216, 226, 234, 293 *see also* Barbican, the
Davis Quay 60, 117, 135, 157, 158, 234 *see also* town quay
Deal 61, 284
Deal Spit 15, **16**, 35, 117, 121, 123, 265
Shell Ness (*Pepperness*) **14**, 15, 29, 41
Delf, the 24, 36–8, 50, 72, 128, 134, 153, 155, 176, 190, 216, 225–6, 269
Delf Street 52, 114, 277
No. 17 (House 16) 172, 196, 277
dendrochronology *see* tree-ring dating
disease 126, 136, 137, 147, 231, 232, 233
Black Death, the 53, 56, 58, 61 66, 86, 118
disorder 147 *see also* Sandwich, discord in
Cade's rebellion 146–7
Domesday Book 23, 30–31, 38
Domesday Monachorum 31
Dover 11, 31, 69, 86–7, **125**, 130
St Mary in Castro 27–8
Dover Road
No. 2 St Bartholomew's (House 17) 211–12, 277
drainage
lack of 19, 35, 36, 52
of land 11–15, 21, 24, 37, 50, 70, 88, 112, 118, 121, 127
urban 60, 159, 283
Draper family, the 62
Walter 81, 114
drapers 63, 130, 138, 139, 143, 238, 292
Dreggers Lane 222
Drury, John 147, 218

East Anglia 188, 191, 206, 213, 231, 267
Eastry 13, 25, 29, 37, 81, 110, 139, 204
hundred 62, 64
as royal site 19–20, 22, 68
economic distress 137, 233
economy 23, 121, 124, 136, 144, 266 *see also* trade
decline of 111, 130, 137, 138, 146, 272
development of 41
inflation 137
prices 137, 233
recession 126, 222
regulation of 60
revival of 228, 240, 272
Edward I 61, 67
Edward III 68, 73
Edward the Confessor 23, 25, 27, 30
Elizabeth I 228–9, 233, 241, 294, 299
Elys family, the 88, 138
Thomas 138, 165, 196, 203, 209, 219, 222
Thomas the elder 218
Engeham, Vincent 140, 141, 204, 209, 219, 226, 290
entertainment 136, 142

fairs 55, 60–61, 133, 284
    St Clements 50, 60, 61, 133, 224, 290
Faversham 62, 81, 126, 164, 170, 192, 231, 267
ferry 13, 29, 34, 41, 117, 123, 157
fireplaces 104, 180, **181**, 182, 184–6, 244, 251, **252**, 253, 258, 261
    first-floor 180, 186, 196, 248, 261
    fuel 186, 259
    furniture of 186, 259
Fisher Gate 116, 135, 155, 157, **161**, 214, 216, 217, 234, 275
fishermen 224, 227
Fisher Street 176, 179, 196, 224, 277
    No. 3 (House 19) 183, 277
    No. 7 (House 20) 177, **178**, 184, 278
    No. 13 (House 22) 255, 278
    No. 24 (House 23) 255, 278
fishing 23, 63, 230
fishing boats 129
Fishmarket 50–52, 53, 57, 93, 94, 101, 118, 170, 179, 190, 218–19, 221, 224, 227, 267, 279 *see also* Market Street; marketplaces
fishmongers 50, 64, 114, 133
Flanders 62, 64, 65, 74, 122, 127, 128, 141, 231
Flemings 9, 127, 133, 231, 232, 235, 244, 245, 246, 247, 256 *see also* aliens; Strangers
flood plains 11, 127
Fordwich **14**, 30, 61, 66, 86, 284
France
    war with 41, 55, 124, 130, 146
    trade with 108, 121, 130, 230
freemen 8, 41, 58, 59, 87, 138, 139, 143, 233
friary (Carmelite) 55, 70, 76, 88–90, 112, 134, 205, 287
    benefactors of 89, 205, 208
    burial at 205, 207
    church of 89–90, 205, 287
    dissolution of 199, 205, 208
    excavation at 9, 88, 89–90, 205
    founder of 88
    location of 12, 88
    precinct of **89**, 90
    property of 90
fullers 143, 292

Galliard Street 38, 225
gardens 118, 221, 225, 234, 262, 269
Garrard, William 207, 221, 224
garrets 190, 195, 197, 218, 261 *see also* attics; lofts
gentry, the 139, 145, 222, 238 *see also* urban elite, the
geology **15**
    Alluvium 3, 4, **5**, 11–12, 70, 118, 270
    effect on town's development of **5**, 6, 11–12, 24, 35, 50, 114, 115–16, 118
    Marine Sand 3, 11–12
    Peat 114
    Thanet Beds 3, 4, **5**, 11–12, 34–5, 50, 57, 116, 118, 270
Gerard, John 131, 142
Gilbert, John 233, 245, 246–7, 248
glovers 63, 143, 231, 237, 292
goldsmiths 63, 144, 232
grazing land 65, 118, 124, 136, 141, 142, 225, 227
Great Yarmouth 61, 63, 123, **125**, 155, **159**, 235, 256, 265, 286, 300
grocers 127, 236, 238, 238, 262

Guestling, the 37, 72, 134, 216, 226
    North Stream 37, 72, 123
    Pinnock Wall 37, 72, 134
    Roaring Gutter 37, 134
    South Stream 37
Guildhall 41, 50, 114, 243 *see also* court hall
Guildhall Street (*Yeldehallestrete*) 50, 81, 114, 224, 278 *see also* High Street
guilds 41, 203, 204, 283
    religious (brotherhoods, fraternities) 81, 205–6, 209, 213
    trade 133–4, 214, 230, 234, 236
Gunsales, Francis 142, 231

haberdashers 141, 238, 262
hackneymen 238
halls 110, 168, 170, 184, 195, 247, 248, 251, 252, 257–9 *see also* houses
    aisled 102, 111, 169, 219, 294
    ceiled 167, 180, 184, 185, 258, 263
    cooking in 195, 196, 257–8
    galleries in 107–8, **170**, 171–2, 176, 185, 195, 196, 221, 257, 258, 301
    heating of 102, 167–8, 179, 184, 195, 258
    lighting of 172, 258
    open 95, 102, 104, 107, 111, 164, 165, 167–72, 174, 177, 180, 185, 186, 189, 194–5, 198, 218, 221, 255, 258, 301
    position of 102, 110, 166, 167, 168–71, 176, 177, 185, 194, 196
    progression from open to ceiled 172, 180, 184, 185, 186, 258
    size of 177, 178–9, 189
    upper 167, 176
    with vaulted undercroft (first-floor) 49
Harnet Street 52, 108, 110, 114, 224, 227, 278
    No. 11 (House 26) 256, 275, 278
    No. 29 (House 28) 96, 114, 138, 139, 165, **166**, 181, 192, 195, 196, 222, 278
    garden wall of (House 27) **96**, 278
    No. 30 (House 30) 114, 278
    No. 31 (House 29) 165, 278
    No. 32 (House 30) 114, 273, 278
    No. 34 (House 30) 174, 278
    excavations at The New Inn, Harnet Street 114, 273
Haven, the **14**, 15, 34, 55, 72, **129**, **215**, 234 *see also* waterfront, the
    Admiralty inquisition on 128
    assembly of royal and military fleets 23, 25, 66–7, 68–9, 73, 75, 117, 124, 146
    attempts to improve 121, 123–4, 127, 128, 138, 228–9
    Crown involvement in 124, 228–9
    designated anchorages in 117
    deterioration of 58, 119, 121, 123–4, 126, 127–8, 163, 226, 228–9
    proposals for new harbour 128
    regulation of use of 128, 229
    size of 73, 234
head ports 41, 56, 61, 124, **125**, 230, 231
hearths, open 102, 167–8, 180, 195, 258 *see also* halls, heating of
Henry I 40
Henry II 40, 58
Henry VII 124, 133
Henry VIII 132, 144, 162, 205
Henry de Sandwich 62, 90, 285
High Street (*Guildhall Street*) 35, 114, 134, 157, 227, 278 *see also* marketplaces

Nos 11/13 (House 33) 183, 278
Nos 17/19 (House 34) 254, 278
No. 18 (House 35) **95**, 278
No. 20 (House 36) 95–6, 110, 114, 278
No. 22 **95**
No. 25 (House 37) 194, 278
No. 34 (House 38) 172, 176, 194, 196, 255, 278
No. 57 (House 40) 254, 278
hinterland of Sandwich 3, 5–6, 9–10, 35, 265, 270, 271
   agriculture in 65, 118
   archaeological sites 9–10
   communications with 35, 36, 134, 149
   relations with town 63
   source of trade goods 65, 118, 220
   town dwellers' property in 64, 130, 139, 145
Holy Ghost Alley 169
hospitals 76, 120, 199, 208, 267
   foundation of 55, 88
   functions of 88, 92
   domestic arrangements in 296
   St Anthony's 88
   St Bartholomew's 62, 81, 88, 90–91, 118, 141, 209, 211–12, 219, 225, 227, 268, 287
      buildings of 211–12
      chapels 81, 90–91, **92**
      domestic arrangements in 211–13
      foundation of 90, 287
      functions of 91–2, 287
   St John's 62, 88, 92, 112, 118, 209, 219
   St Thomas's 209, 211, 234, 253
      buildings of 209, **210**, 211
      domestic arrangements in 209, 211
householders 134, 143, 144, 197
household objects 195–7, 257–61, 262, 301
households 61, 112, 136, 137, 144, 197, 231, 245, 246–7, 266, 291
house plots 51–2, **97**, 98, 100, 110–11, 167, 168, 176, 267
   reorganisation of 53, 101
   shape of 51, 110, 111, 112, 115, 167, 168, 174, 176, 177, 255, 267
   size of 51–2, 110, 111, 170, 177, 255
   subdivision of 52, 100, 110, 111, 114, 255, 267
houses 95, 217 *see also* architectural features
   abandoned 138, 222, 240, 244, 244, 245
   alignment in relation to street 95, 96, 110, 165, 168, 169–70, 175, 176–7, 180, 195, 198, 248, 250, 260, 267, 271
   building of new 57, 93, 111, 119, 164, 183, 197–8, 240, 245, 247, 248
   chronological change 108, 164, 165, 180, 197, 247, 250, 258, 259, 261, 262–3
   courtyard houses 98, 104, 165–7, 181, 192, 301
   cross wings 96, 169, 194, 219
   dating 7–8, 96, 101, 103, 111, 164, 169, 197, 240, 248, 255–6, 258, 267
   demolition of 119, 138, 174, 180, 227
   distribution of **94**, 111, 168, 170, 176, 179, 198, 214, 219, 221, 222, **223**, 227, **246**, 252, 270, 288
   dual function of 98, 104–5, 110, 111, 167, 172, 176, 187, 192, 197, 266, 295
   and economic prosperity 165, 197, 267
   end jetties 177, 212
   entry/cross passages 169, 171, 177, 179, 195, 242
   extension of 254

fully floored 180–83, 184, 197, 198
functions of rooms 110–11, 194–5, 197, 262–3 *see also* individual entries for rooms
heating of 180, 247, 248, 254 *see also* chimneys
height of 49, 98, 102, 111, 168, **168**, 169, 170, 178–80, 221, 227, 247, 253, 254, 258, 267
interpretation of structures 96, 105, 111, 177, 180, 194, 196, 237, 240, 254, 256, 266
lighting of 104, 174, 175, 192, 250, 256, 263
number within Sandwich 30, 109, 197
patterns of access within 98, 104–5, 107, 171, 263
rear ranges 104, 110, 165, 174, 176, 196, 248, 250, 255
rebuilding of 102, 104, 110, 138, 176, 180, 181–2, 183, 192, 240, 254–5, 263, 267
size of 178–9, 192, 194–5, 219, 224, 227, 240, 247, 248, 252–6, 263, 267, 288, 300
social status of 55, 93, 95, 96, 100, 177, 179–82, 186, 192, 219, 224, 227, 245, 262
storage in 98, 104, 105, 108, 110, 111, 167, 192, 196–7, 247, 261, 295
street-front ranges 102, 104, 107, 165, 167, 168, 248, 250, 255
survival of 1, 2, 55, 93, 95, 102, 119, 164, 169, 180, 197, 199, 213, 240, 261, 263, 266–7
wealdens 177, **178**, 184, 189, 196, 222, 224, 255
housing density 33, 38, 86, 110, 114, 143, 168, 170, 227, 267
husbandmen 143, 225
Hull 65, 66, 115, **117**, **125**, 135, 155, **161**, 231, 265–6
Hythe 30, 47, **125**, 286

inheritance
   female 139, 222
   partible 64, 238
innkeepers 141, 236
inns 100, 136, 141, 186–7, 217, 224, 227, 256, 260 *see also* alehouses; taverns
   Bell, the 136, 141, 186, 219, 237, 245, 291
   Bull Inn, the 100, 136, 140, 141, 142, 186, 190, 218
   Hart and Swan, the 141
   Star, the 141, 221, 237, **247**, 258, 277
   White Hart, the 142, 222, 251, 259, 260, 261, 292, 297
Ives Gate 214

Jesus Quay 234, 269, 292, 295
John de Ho 92, 113
joiners 63, 231, 232, 262

King John 58
King's Lynn 41, 68, 104, 115, **117**, 118, 124, 131, 148, 155, 192, 244, 265, 266, 286, 300
King Street (*Luckboat*) 141, 278, 297
   Nos 1/3 (Houses 41, 42) 191, 221, 278
   No. 4 (House 43) 195, 221, 278
   No. 6 (House 44) 193, 221, 278
   No. 21 (House 45) **182**, 183, 193, 254, 256, 278
     outbuilding (House 46) 193, 278
   No. 24 (House 47) 185, 221, 278
   Nos 27/29 (House 48) (St Peter's rectory) 180–81, 195, 221, 261, 278
   No. 38 (House 49) **171**, 172, 176, 185, 186, 194, 195, 221, 278
   No. 52 (House 51) 221, 250–51, 276, 278

kitchens 181, 186, 195, 196, 242, 248, 257, 258, 259, 301
    detached 49, 175, 183, 194, 196, 259, 262
        hearths in 196
    integral 176, 196, 247, 259
Knightrider Street (*Knythenstrete*) 35, 225, 275
Kyng, John 135, 140, 224

labourers 143, 144, 221, 222, 238, 239
laity, role of in churches 48, 49, 55, 80–81, 199, 205–6, 213, 267, 284
landowners 44, 123, 130, 139, 140, 227
    absentee 128
land reclamation 97, 115, 118, 121, 123, 127–8, 156, 215, 265–6, 268, 269
law and order 60, 142, 220, 228
    gaol 68, 136, 220, 291, 297
    gibbet 136
    pillory 136, 221, 297
    stocks 136, 221
livestock 60, 68, 124, 134, 140, 220, 225, 233, 236, 262
lodgings 141–2, 186, 187, 256
lofts 196, 261 *see also* attics; garrets
London 11, 19, 37, 55, 58, 121, 122, **125**, 148, 155, 197, 228, 265, 266, 283, 284, 286
    buildings in 97, 102, 167, 176, 186, 191, 196, 258–9, 266, 301
    and trade 64, 65–6, 74–5, 118, 122, 124, 126–7, 130, 140, 208, 230–31, 288, 289
Loop Street 36, 274, 275
Love Lane 35, 52, 93, 100, 108, 114, 139, 140, 141, 186, 219–20, 227, 245, 246, 279, 297 *see also* St Peter's Street
    excavations at 35, 50–52, 53, 93, 219
Loveryk family, the 81, 286
    Richard 62, 66
Low Countries
    immigrants from 119, 126, 133, 144, 228, 232 *see also* aliens; Strangers
    trade with or via 19, 121, 125, 127, 128, 130, 135, 140, 230
Luckboat 35, 50, 52, 170, 176, 221, 224, 227, 245, 246, 248, 262, 278, 297 *see also* King Street
Lydden Valley 3, 37, 72, 134, 225

Mærcesfleot see Northmouth
Maidstone 130, 263
malthouses 141, 221, 224
maltsters 63, 145, 237, 238, 252
Manwood family, the 139, 233, 235, 246
    John 224, 235, 245
    Roger 130, 132, 139, 207, 208, 209, 233, 235, 238, 240–41, 248, 256, 263, 296, 299
mariners 143, 144, 196, 208, 224, 227, 230, 236, 238, 252
market cross 221, 231, 244
marketplaces 35, 112, 114
    Cornmarket 50, 114, 118, 136, 209, 219, 220–21
    Fishmarket 35, 36, 50, 114, 136, 190, 219, 221, 224
        shambles 50, 64, 136, 219, 288
        weigh beam 136, 219, 296
    High Street 23, 35, 50, 114, 134, 224
markets 41, 133, 284, 298
Market Street (*Fishmarket*) 35, 114, 188, 279
    No. 4 (House 53) **173**, 278
    No. 6 (House 55) **173**, 186, 278
    No. 7 (House 56) 172, **173**, 174, 278

No. 8 (House 57) **173**, 175, 176, 274, 279
No. 10 (House 58) 50, 51–2, 93, 170, **171**, **173**, 274, 279
No. 13 (House 59) 101, 279
Nos 14/16 (House 60) 175–6, 196, 279
Mary-le-Bone Hill 4, 10, 269
    archaeological evidence from 21
masonry 10, 12, 23, 32, 47, 63, 69, 93, 95–6, 108, 114, 148, 154–6, 159, 283, 293 *see also* building materials, stone
    fragmentary remains of 101–2, 114, 197, 222, 266
masons 148, 150, 158, 162, 162, 292
Master, John 130, 140, 204
members of parliament 138, 139, 140, 145, 235, 291
mercers 127, 232, 289
merchants 52, 62, 63, 88, 119, 130, 138, 139, 145, 198, 208, 238, 252, 262 *see also* urban elite, the
    Flemish 64, 231
    Gascon 66, 285
    Genoese 65, 121–2, 124–5, 127
    Hanseatic 121, 125
    from the Low Countries 121, 125
    ownership of property by 49, 52, 62, 93, 96, 100, 110, 111, 113, 116, 130, 136, 138, 139–40, 143, 187, 214, 216–17, 221, 247, 248
    Venetian 122, 123, 125, 126, 289
messuages 62, 81, 113, 114, 186, 190, 191, 218, 221
Mill Wall Place (*Barnsend*) 35, 225, 279
    No. 3 (House 61) 190, 276, 279
Minster Abbey 21, 41
mints 23, 29
Moat Sole 36, 52, 209, 211
Monkenquay (*Monkenkey*) 55, 60, 65, 112, 115, 117, 156, 216, 234, 269
    crane 55, 115, 128, 216, 234, 244
    storehouses 55, 115, 234
Monkenquay Gate 214
murage grants 69, 72, 123, 148, 149, 155, 162

navigation
    charts 122–3, **129**
    pilots 63, 122
    portolans 122–3, 200
    rutters 123
Newcastle 129, 208, 230, 231
New Gate 38, 71, 149, 150, 151, 153, 176, 179, 225–6, 268
New Street (*Newgate*) 38, 176, 196, 224, 279
    No. 14 (House 62) 209, 224, 279
    Nos 16/18 (House 63) 209, 253, 258, 279
    Nos 70/72 (Houses 64, 65) 177, **178**, 180, 224, 225, 279
No Name Street 189, 279
    No Name Shop (House 66) 188–9, 191, 221, 279
Norwich 37, **125**, 131, 231, 256, 263, 266, 283, 284, 301
Northmouth (*Mærcesfleot*) 14, 18, 29, 41, 229, 282

occupations 62–4, 114, 138–44, 214, 232, 236–7, 238 *see also* individual entries
orchards 118, 225
outhouses 175, 237, 259, 262

Painters Lane 222
Paradise Row (House 67) 49, 101, 114, 279
parishes of Sandwich 3, 90, 114, 136, 137, 139, 140, 142, 143, 144, 188, 206, 207–9, 220, 222, 225, 227, 233, 237, 246, 247, 262, 283

boundaries of 32, **33**, 36, 38, 50, 115, 283
formation of 32–3
St Clement's 29, 37, 38, 95, 135, 205, 224
St Mary's 49, 62, 96, 136, 203, 214, 217, 244, 245, 248, 267, 269
St Peter's 86, 97, 115, 118, 141, 186, 218, 222, 260
size of 32
Parker, Edward 141, 218
Parker, John 225, 294
Parker, Thomas 236, 245, 248
parlours 176, 186, 195, 196, 224, 242, 247, 248, 251, 252, 257, 260, 301
Paston, John 124, 131, 142, 147
paving 134, 158, 215, 217, 220, 233, 235
Peake family, the 235
Edward 234, 235
Nicholas 130, 224
Roger 245
Peny family, the 62, 285
John 62, 65
Pillory Gate 70, 214
piracy 75, 126, 130, 230
place names 19
poor, the 138, 141, 144, 179–80, 191, 197, 205, 208–9, 233, 237
poor relief 208, 232, 233 *see also* charity
population 53, 61–2, 112, 136–7, 144, 198, 301
decline of 56, 58, 111, 118, 119, 136, 137–8, 228, 232, 267
density 86, 138
depopulation 52, 126
growth of 48, 53, 228
size of 23, 30, 41, 56, 136, 231, 266, 291
Potter Street (*Cok Lane*) 50, 102, 114, 279
No. 7 (House 68) 35, 174, **175**, 176, **184**, 279, 294
probate inventories 185–6, 194–6, 212, 236, 237–9, 252, 256, 261, 299
property
bequests of 140, 141, 143, 177, 188, 190, 191, 206, 218, 221, 222, **223**, 225, 233, 248, 296, 301
as investment 130, 141, 198, 219, 238, 240, 245
transactions 8, 62, 138, 143, 147, 224, 245
property ownership 55, 112, 113, 140, 143, 145, 198, 208, 218–19, 221–2, 224, 238, 245, 246, 251–2
by ecclesiastical bodies 41, 114, 118, 191, 208, 225
by the town 58, 118, 134, 135–6, 141, 186, 189, 208, 214, 218, 219, 220–21, 224, 225, 226
by women 219, 233, 236, 256, 262
public hygiene 134, 284 *see also* water supplies
dunghills 134, 221
privies and cesspits 134, 159, 175, 214
public works 60

Quay Lane 101, 157, 217
quays, private 55, 116, 117, 155, 214, 217, 234

Reculver 14, 61, 159, 284
religion 137
Dissolution of the Monasteries, the 120, 199
Jesus Mass 191, 203–4, 206, 295
Protestant Reformation, the 52, 119, 199, 208–9, 213
religious refugees *see* Strangers
rented property 55, 97, 138–40, 167, 188, 191, 198, 218–19, 221, 225, 227, 238, 239, 240, 245, 247, 248, 256

rents 65, 81, 94, 112, 135, 136, 189, 205, 208, 218, 219, 221, 222, 224, 225, 297
difficulty paying 126, 137, 138, 219, 222, 224
research methods 1–7, 270–71
archaeological 4 *see also* archaeological interventions
restrictions on 93
contour surveys 4–6, 19, 21, 50, 270
architectural 7, 10
buildings survey 7–8
documentary 8–9
urban morphology 6–7
Richborough 9, 11, **14**, 15–16, 159
Anglo-Saxon and later evidence from 17–18
Roman occupation in 17
Ringeley, Sir Edward 132, 140, 204, 209, 248, 292, 296
river Stour 11, 12–13, 14, 15–16, 29, 30, 34, 40, 60, 69, 121, 124, 127, 155, 226, 229, 265, 270, 271, 281
river Wantsum 11, 12, 13–14, 16, 29, 121, 229, 265
Rochester 28, 29, 30, 61, **125**, 263
Romney, 30, 31
New 45, 61, 81, 86, 87, 92, 122, **125**, 146, 292
Old 28
Romney Marsh 37, 231
roofs **107**, **109**, 111, 164, 186, 256, 300
clasped side-purlin 244, 248, 250, 254
collar purlin 103, 193
collar-rafter 96, 169
crown-post 104, 107, 165, 176, 177, 180, 183, 191, 193, 194, 199, 215, 248
dropped tie beam 251, 253
hipped 192
king-strut 103, 104
queen-strut 192, 244
sling-brace 248, 250, 253, 254
smoke-blackened 108, 168, 185, 189, 254, 294
vaulting 44, 84, 85, 86, 95, 96, 97, 141, 218, 266, 288
wind braces 248, 250, 254
Round House, the 160, **161** *see also* boom tower
Rye 64, 69, **125**, 130, 146, 164, 170, 180, 184, 197, 229, 230, 256, 267, 294

St Augustine's Abbey, Canterbury 29, 81, 123
property 31, 32, 41, 208
relations with Christ Church Priory 29, 30, 40, 41
relations with Sandwich 48
St Clement's church 10, 25–8, 33, 38, 45–7, 48, 59, **77**, 84, 199–203, 271 *see also* churches
courts in 86
location of 12, 25, 28
plans of **26**, **45**, **77**, **79**, **83**, **201**
remodelling of 76, 79–80, 199, 206
St Jacob's Lane 222
St Mary's church 10, 31–3, 42–5, 48, 52, 79, 81, **82**, 191, 203–4 *see also* churches
date of 32, 44
excavation at 10, 21
location of 12
plans of **42**, **82**
remodelling of 80
St Mary's Gate 214
St Mary's Lane 222
St Peter's church 10, 31–3, 47–8, 50, 77, **78**, 179, 204–5, 206, **218**, 219, **220**, 271 *see also* churches

        courts in 55, 59, 86, 87, 204
        date of 32
        extension of 35, 53
        location of 12
        plans of **31**, **47**, **78**, **85**
        remodelling of 76, 79, 84–5, 87
St Peter's Street (*Love Lane*) 35, 50, 52, 93, 114, 186, 219–20, 227, 279
        No. 3 220
        No. 5 220
        No. 11 136, 220
        No. 16 (House 69) 255, 279
        Nos 18/20 (House 70) 169–70, **184**, 279
        No. 30 (House 72) 176, 219, 279
        No. 50 (House 73) 98, 166, 219, 279
        excavations on 168
Salisbury 167, 176, 198, 266, 301
Sandown Gate 35, 149, 150–51, 235, 268, 274
Sandown Road 35, 154
Sandowns, the 3, 4, 20, 21–2, 268, 269
        archaeological evidence from 22
Sandown Street 225
Sandwich
        bailiwick of 62, 124, 132
        custumal 8, 9, 29, 50, 55, 59, 62
        decline of 119, 197, 213, 226
        defence of 57, 66–7, 69, 146, 147, 148–57, 163, 234–5 *see also* town defences
        discord in 132, 146 *see also* disorder
                the Ringeley affair 132, 140
        dues, local 126
                to archbishop 30–31
                to crown 30, 40, 60
        earliest occupation 6, 18–22, 53
        early history of 11, 18, 22, 24, 270
        as an early medieval ecclesiastical site 21, 22
        governance of 55, 58, 119, 131–2, 144, 145 *see also* urban elite, the
                assembly of townsmen 52, 58
                bailiff 62, 66, 67–8, 86, 132
                common council 123, 131–2, 136, 142, 143, 147, 231, 232–3, 238
                elections 8, 41, 59, 86, 131, 132, 148, 202, 233, 295
                jurats 55, 58, 60, 131–6, 142, 143, 147, 232–3, 235, 238, 299
                mayor 41, 55, 58, 59, 60, 131–6, 139, 140, 147, 220, 232–3, 242, 291
                other officials of 59–60, 87, 209
        hundred of 3, 29 *see also* courts
        importance of location 11, 23, 38, 265
        Liberty of 3, 29, 60, **72**
        lordship of 30
        maintenance of public facilities 114, 134, 158–9, 215, 227, 235
        marketplaces *see* separate entry
        place name (meaning of) 18–19, 20
        plans of **24**, **25**, **51**, **56**, **113**, **120**
        port *see* Haven, the
        precursors to 17, 21–2
        prosperity of 30–31, 42, 48–9, 53, 58, 119, 120, 197, 267, 271
        regulations of 60, 131, 133, 141–2, 228, 232
        revenues of 133, 138

        rights of 31, 40, 58
        status of 55, 58, 64, 120, 144, 163, 198, 226, 256–8, 260, 265, 271
        street pattern 6, 7, 32, 34–6, 38, 40, 50, 52, 53, 113, 118, 214
                alterations to 7, 35, 40, 50, 52, 57, 113–14, 222, 269, 271
                expansion of 52, 118, 214, 252
        town books 8, 87, 119
        urban ranking 30, 40, 56
        wards 131, 132–3, 137, 246
Sarre **14**, 16, 40–41, 53, 61, 284
schools
        church school 204, 240, 295–6
        Manwood School 49, 208, 240–42, 279
                building of 240, 241–2
                excavations at 49
Serles Lane 141, 222, 277 *see also* Bowling Street
servants 63, 137, 144, 261, 292
services 102, 104, 186, 195, 247, 259 *see also* butteries; kitchens
Shelving family, the 62, 287
        Thomas 62, 65, 92, 285
shipbuilding and repair 55, 69, 115, 162, 234, 268, 286
ship fittings 69, 74
shipmasters 62, 63, 144, 230, 236, 238
ship names 73, 74, 75, 162, 224, 230, 231, 300
shipowners 62, 236
ship service 23, 31, 38, 56, 61, 65
ship size 73, 121, 122, 128, 162, 230, 290, 300
ship types 119
        argosies 128
        balingers 122, 126
        barges 122, 126
        barks 224, 230, 300
        batellae 74
        carracks 74, 121–2, 124, 127, 128
        coasters 121, 122, 128, 230, 235
        cogs 74, 121
        colliers 129
        crayers 122, 124, 126, 128, 230
        galleys 74, 122, 124, 128
        haynes 128
        hoys 128, 230
        hulks 73
        ketches 128
        lighters 129, 230
        pinks 128
shipwrecks 123, 127, 298
shipwrights 69, 143, 236, 292 *see also* boat builders
shoemakers 63, 232, 236, 237, 238, 262, 292
shops 108, 110, 114, 136, 143, 167, 172, 176, 186, 187–91, 195, 196, 198, 217–18, 224, 257, 261–2, 266
        with accommodation 166, 176, 188, 190, 221
        with storage 190, 191, 192, 221
Shrewsbury 143, 266, 301
skinners 63, 142, 292
smiths 63, 143–4, 189, 190, 221, 292
smoke bays 172, 186, 190, 294 *see also* chimneys
social structure 143, 191, 198, 208, 209, 238–9, 263, 267, 271
social zoning 179, 214, 225, 227
Southampton 19, 22, 65, 95, 108, 122, 123, **125**, 231, 265, 266, 288, 289, 294
speculative building 143, 191

Index

stacks *see* chimneys
standards of living 144, 198, 232
Stonar 10, **14**, 41, 61, 159
　waterfront at 41
Stonar Bank 13–14, 15
storehouses 193–4, 221, 227, 234, 262
Strand Street 50, 97, 100, 108, 110, 114, 115, **116**, 166, **167**, 170, 179, 186, 190, 217–18, 222, 227, 248, 279, 289
　No. 3 (House 74) 102, **171**, 172, **174**, 185, 192, **193**, 195, 224, 279
　No. 7 (House 76) 102, 279
　No. 11 (Houses 77, 78) 98, **99**, **100**, 102, 110, 166, **167**, 186–7, 279 *see also* Three Kings Yard
　No. 13 (House 79) 102, 110, 166, **167**, 187, 190, 279
　No. 15 (House 79) 110–11, 166, **167**, 187, 190, 279
　Nos 19/21 (House 80) 110, 166, **167**, 186, 192, 279
　No. 23 (House 81) 108, 110, 166, **167**, 181, 187, **188**, 192, 218, 279
　No. 27 (House 82) 96–7, 218, 259, 279
　No. 33 (House 83) 102–4, 108, **109**, 111, 218, 279, 281
　No. 34 (House 84) 217, 279
　No. 39 (House 85) 100, 102, 104, **105–6**, 110, 172, 176, 184, 186, 194, 195, 218, 258, 259, 279, 281, 288
　No. 40 (custom house) 139, 216
　No. 41 (House 86) 102, 104, **105**, 107–8, 110, 171, 218, 275, 279
　No. 42 (House 87) 217, 279, 300
　No. 46 (King's Lodging) (House 88) 222, 248, 251, **252**, 256, 261, 279, 292
　No. 62 (The Long House) (House 90) 248, **249**, 256, 261, 279, 281, 287
　Nos 63/65 (King's Arms) (House 91) 250, **251**, 275, 279
　No. 71 (House 92) **171**, 222, 279
　No. 84 151
　Nos 91/93 (House 93) *see* schools, Manwood School
　excavations on 155–6
Strangers 133, 233, 244, 245 *see also* aliens; Flemings; Walloons
　conflict with 228, 232
　housing of 228, 232, 244–7
　introduction of 228, 272
　occupations of 231–2, 236
　regulations concerning 228, 231–2
Stromble, Oliver 130, 141, 213
surgeons 134, 143, 232, 245

tailors 60, 63, 143, 222, 232, 238, 292
tanners 63, 238, 262
taverners 141
taverns 97–8, 141, 217 *see also* alehouses; inns
　Black Tavern, the 97, 136, 141, 218
taxation 56, 62, 64, 65, 66, 81, 235, 285
　local 66, 136, 230, 291
　national 8
tenants 61, 64, 137, 144, 180, 191, 219, 221, 222, 224, 227, 234
tenements 38, 51–2, 100, 109, 138, 143, 177, 180, 200, 216–19, 221–2, 224–5, 245, 248
Three Kings Yard 98, **99**, **100**, 186 *see also* Strand Street, No. 11
tilers 63, 143, 222, 237
timber-framed buildings 90, 93, 96, 101, 102–8, 104, 109, 111, 164–77, 180–84, 187, 193, 219, 222, 247–56, 266, 277–80, 288, 294
　development of 102, 109–10, 253, 255–6

tipplers 141, 142, 236–7, 238, 259, 260, 292, 301 *see also* victuallers
　licensing 141, 142, 236–7, 260
　other occupations of 142
topography
　of hinterland 1, 4, 6, 11
　urban 6, 34–5, 112–18, 198, 214–27, 265
town defences
　artillery 69, 154, 155, 158, 162, 217, 234, 235, 293
　Bulwark, the 147, 149, 154–5, 162, 217, 235, 268–9, 293
　Butts, The 67, 70, 118, 149, 226
　chronology of 69, 70, 119, 149, 150, 151, 155
　earth ramparts 57, 67, 69, 70, 72, 136, 148, 149, 154, 225, 265, 268
　excavations of 149–50, 155–6
　gates 69–70, 134, 148, 149, 150, 234
　methods of construction 149, 150, 156, 157
　Mill Wall 35, 57, 67, 70–71, 118, **149**, 150, 225, 268, 271, 274
　　effects on town plan of 57, 71, 114, 118, 148, 162, 225
　Rope Walk, The 67, 70, 88, 118, 149, 150
　stone walls on waterfront 67, 69, 70, 148, 149, 155–7, 216–17, 234–5, 265, 269
town quay 34, 129, 134–5, 149, 155, 214, 215, 234, 269 *see also* quays, private
　town crane 122, 127, 128, 129, 131, 135, 136, 158, 159, 161, 215–16, 234, 290
　comparisons **159**, **161**, 271, 290
trade 55, 60, 64–6, 124–30, 238 *see also* economy
　change in nature of 119, 121, 126, 130
　customs 62, 64, 66, 122, 124, **125**, 127, 130, 230, 231, 285
　decline of 119, 126, 198, 228, 230
　disruption of 64, 65, 66, 126, 130, 147
　export 62, 64, 65, 66, 126, 130, 138, 228, 230, 271
　　beer 130, 230
　　cloth 64, 124, 126, 130, 231, 232
　　grain 65, 66, 122, 124, 126–7, 130, 220, 230, 231, 233, 271, 298
　　hides 62, 64, 65, 130
　　malt 66, 124, 130, 230, 231
　　wool 62, 64–5, 74–5, 124, 126, 285
　fees
　　anchorage 64, 66
　　growth of 23, 65, 121
　　import 66, 124–5, 127, 130, 139, 290
　　　of cloth 66, 130, 139
　　　of luxury goods 64, 65–6, 74–5, 122, 124–5, 127
　　　of wine 64, 65–6, 124, 127, 128, 192
　　licences 62, 64
　local 64, 66, 119, 121, 122, 125, 133, 232
　origins of 64, 74, 119, 121
　regulation of 62, 131, 133
　revival of 124, 126, 127, 228
　taxes and tolls 23, 29, 38, 64, 65, 66, 126, 129, 139, 147
　transhipment 64, 66, 73, 74, 121–2
tree-ring dating 7, 101, 102, 103–4, 164, 165, 180, 248, 294

undercrofts 84–6, 96–8, 101, 114, 166, 187, 266 *see also* cellars
Upper Strand Street 35, 115–16, 176, 179, 227, 280
　No. 15 (House 94) 182, 280, 287
　No. 17 (House 94) 101, 182, **184**, 224, 280, 287
　Nos 19/21 (House 95) 177, 196, 275, 280, 288

Nos 22/24 (House 96) 177, 196, 280
Nos 32/34 (House 98) **182**, 183, 195, 196, 259, 280
urban characteristics 23, 29
urban elite, the 62, 111, 138–40, 145, 228, 235, 245
   connections between 138–40
   marriage patterns of 138, 139, 140
   property ownership by 62, 138, 139, 140, 191, 218–19, 227
   role in town 55, 62, 138–9

Vicarage Lane 222, 280
   No. 3 (House 99) **101**, 280
victuallers 63, 133, 144, 236–7 *see also* tipplers
victualling 66, 124, 237
vintners 62, 63, 138, 259

wages 65, 137, 144, 233
Walloons 9, 231, 245, 246–7 *see also* Strangers
Wantsum Channel 12, 13–15, 16, 23, 25, 55, 60, 72, 229
   decay of 1, 58, 121, 123
warehouses 66, 192, 194, 234, 266, 288
warfare 55, 56, 62, 65, 66, 281
   Baron's War 58
   Battle of Sandwich (1217) 90
   effect on economy of 58, 65, 66, 119, 124, 130, 146
   Fauconberg's Rebellion 148, 162
   French attack on Sandwich (1457) 126, 146, 147, 162
   Hundred Years War 66, 68, 69, 121, 124, 146, 150, 155, 162
   Wars of the Roses 147
watercourses *see also* Delf, the; Guestling, the; river Stour; river Wantsum; Wantsum Channel
   changes in courses of 6, 14, 15, 37, 69
   diversions of 37, 72, 134, 283
   navigability of 12, 16, 121, 229, 265
waterfront, the 50, 112, 115, 155, 158, 192, 214, **215**, 234, 265, 271
   at other ports 34, 115, 265
   custom house 139, 216
   development of 29, 34, 97, 111, 214, 217

   installations 41, 135, 271
      buildings on 115
      cranes 112, 122, 127, 129, 134, 135, 214, 215–16, 234
      docks 128
      groynes 55, 128, 128, 217, 228–9
      jetties 34, 217, 248
      quays 34, 49, 55, 97, 112, 115–17, 128, 134–5, 155, 216–17, 288–9 *see also* individual entries
      weigh beams 214, 216
      wharfs 29–30, 34, 55, 115, 214, 215, 217
   movement north 38, 115
   property on 49, 52, 55, 97, 110, 111, 112, 115, 192, 214, 217, 221, 222
watermills 128, 136, 226, 290
water supplies 24, 37, 114, 134, 153, 159, 190, 226, 298
   conduits 134, 136, 141, 153, 156, 159, 226, 235, 283, 287
water table 49, 50
weavers 143, 236, 238, 256 *see also* cloth industry; cloth makers
weights and measures 59, 60
Winchelsea 62, 64, 65, 68, 69, 73, 95, 97, 108, **125**, 266, 292
Winchester 11, 41, 97, 108, **125**, 176, 179–80, 212, 265, 288, 295, 296, 297
windmills 136
Wingham hundred 62, 138
Winterland family, the 62, 113
women *see also* property ownership
   occupations of 144, 236, 237, 299
   role of in economy 63, 144, 299
   widows 66, 142, 196, 222, 225, 238, 256
Woodnesborough 30, 36, 38, 62, 90, 153, 159, 226, 283, 287
   Road 36, 52, 118
Woodnesborough Gate 150, 151, 153, **154**, 226, 235, 268, 298
workshops 172, 189, 190, 219, 257, 266
Worth 13, 139
Wyberd family, the 62, 66

yeomen 219, 237, 248, 259
York 11, 18, 19, 41, 135, 143, 160, 167, 180, 266

Key

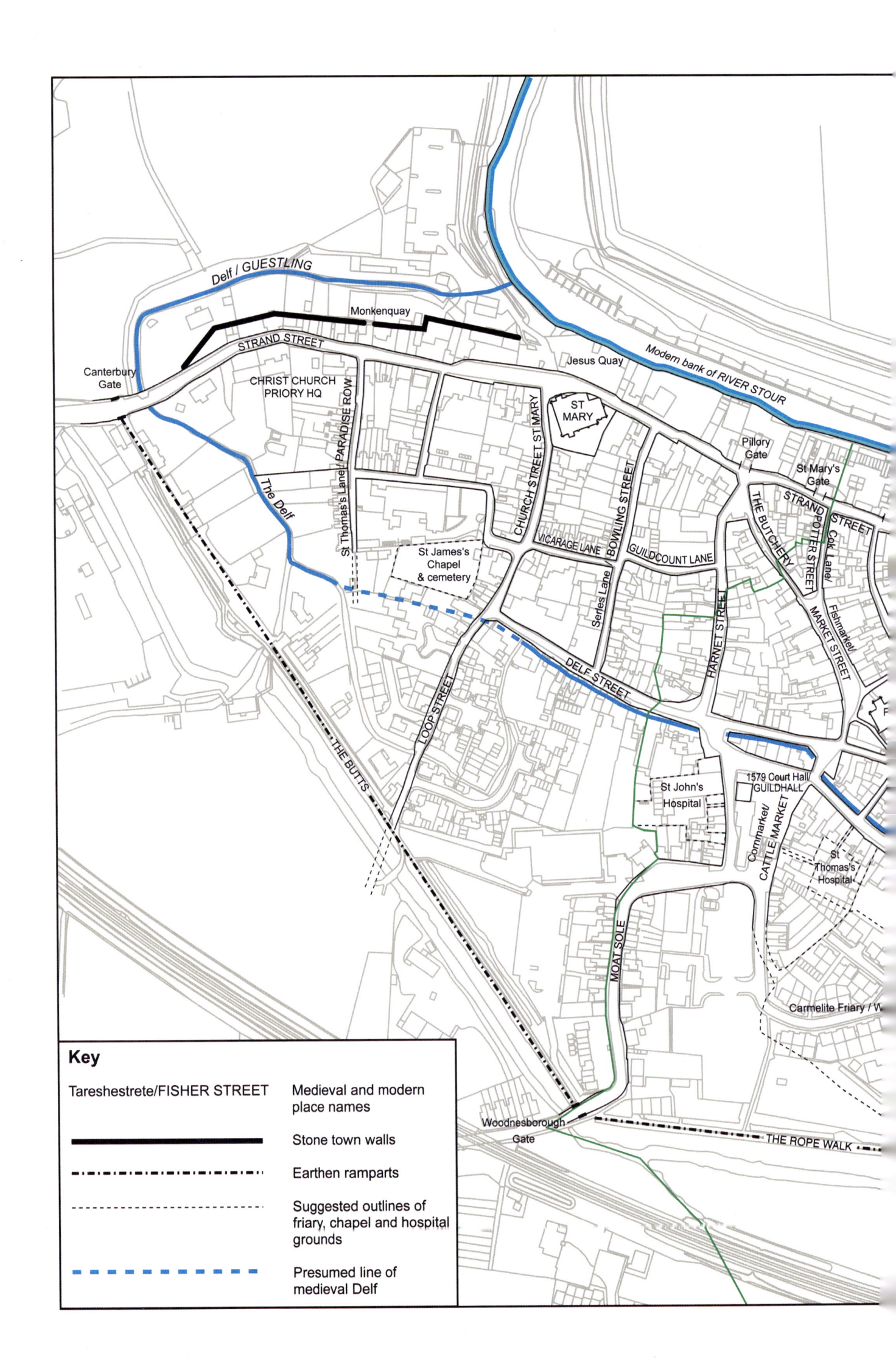

Tareshestrete/FISHER STREET — Medieval and modern place names

▬▬▬▬▬ Stone town walls

▬·▬·▬·▬ Earthen ramparts

---------- Suggested outlines of friary, chapel and hospital grounds

▬ ▬ ▬ ▬ Presumed line of medieval Delf

Labelled features

- Delf / GUESTLING
- Monkenquay
- Canterbury Gate
- STRAND STREET
- CHRIST CHURCH PRIORY HQ
- Jesus Quay
- Modern bank of RIVER STOUR
- St Thomas's Lane / PARADISE ROW
- The Delf
- CHURCH STREET ST MARY
- ST MARY
- Pillory Gate
- St Mary's Gate
- St James's Chapel & cemetery
- VICARAGE LANE
- BOWLING STREET
- Serles Lane
- GUILDCOUNT LANE
- THE BUTCHERY
- Cok Lane / STRAND / POTTER STREET
- Fishmarket / MARKET STREET
- LOOP STREET
- DELF STREET
- HARNET STREET
- THE BUTTS
- St John's Hospital
- 1579 Court Hall / GUILDHALL
- Cornmarket / CATTLE MARKET
- St Thomas's Hospital
- MOAT SOLE
- Carmelite Friary / W
- Woodnesborough Gate
- THE ROPE WALK